The Swiss Guards, who have been in the service of the Pope since 1506, form the armed corps of the Vatican State. They wear a distinctive and picturesque uniform, consisting of pantaloons gathered below the knee and a full-sleeved jacket, both in broad yellow, red and blue stripes, said to have been designed by Michelangelo. They are armed with a halberd and sword.

Those interested in... should visit

Ancient Rome:
- Roman Forum and the Palatine
- Colosseum and Constantine's Arch
- Castel Sant'Angelo
- Pantheon
- Imperial Fora
- Old Appian Way
- Baths of Caracalla
- Hadrian's Villa at Tivoli
- Ostia
- Masterpieces of Classical art in the museums:
  Palazzo dei Conservatori
  Capitolino
  National Roman
  Vatican
  Villa Giulia

Early Christian Rome:
- Santa Maria Maggiore
- Lateran District
- Caelian Hill churches
- Church of St Paul Without the Walls
- Catacombs
- Christian mosaics in churches:
  Santa Maria Maggiore
  Santa Costanza
  St Cosmas and St Damian
  Santa Maria in Dominica
  Santa Maria in Trastevere
  St Clement's Basilica

Renaissance Rome:
- Architectural masterpieces in:
  Piazza del Campidoglio
  Palazzo Farnese
  Palazzo della Cancelleria
  Villa d'Este, Tivoli
- Interior decor:
  Sistine Chapel
  Raphael's Rooms
  Borgia Apartment
  Nicholas V's Chapel
  Villa Farnesina
- Sculptural masterpieces:
  Michelangelo's *Pietà*
  Michelangelo's *Moses*
- Museum church:
  Santa Maria del Popolo

Baroque Rome:
- Bernini's work:
  St Peter's Square
  St Peter's Chair and Baldaquin
  Ecstasy of St Teresa in Santa Maria della Vittoria
  Sculpture in the Borghese Museum
  Sant' Andrea al Quirinale
  Fiumi Fountain
- Borromini's work:
  San Carlo alle Quattro Fontane
  St Ivo's Church
- Trevi Fountain
- Caravaggio's work:
  Santa Maria del Popolo
  San Luigi dei Francesi
  Borghese Museum
  Vatican Picture Galleries
  St Augustine's Church
- Brother Andrea Pozzo's work:
  Ceiling frescores in St Ignatius's Church
  St Ignatius' Chapel in the Gesù Church

Panoramic viewpoints:
- Janiculum Hill
- Pincian Hill
- Dome of St Peter's Basilica
- Castel Sant'Angelo terrace

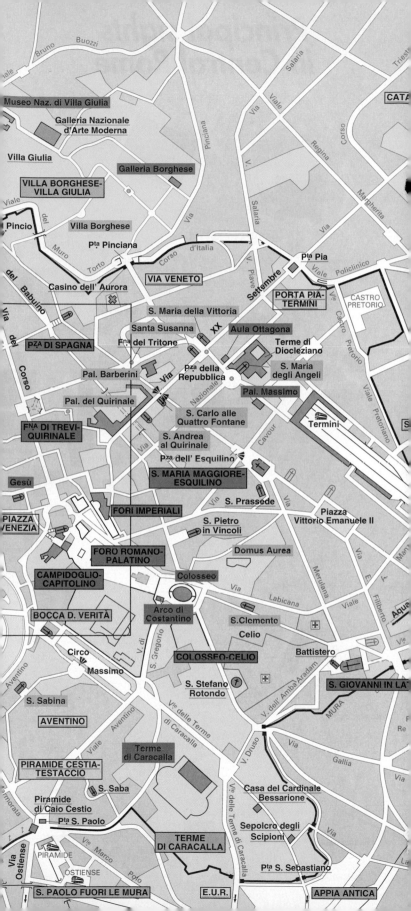

Principal sights in Central Rome

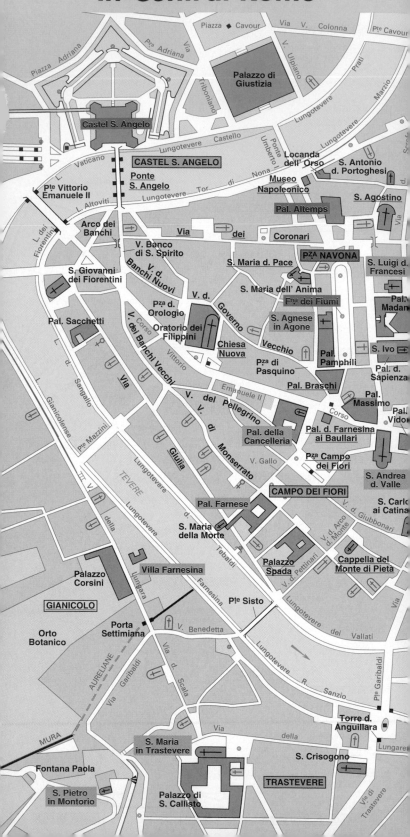

Palazzo di Giustizia

Piazza ◆ Cavour · Via · V. Colonna · Pte Cavour

Castel S. Angelo

CASTEL S. ANGELO

Ponte S. Angelo

Locanda dell' Orso

Museo Napoleonico

S. Antonio d. Portoghesi

S. Agostino

Pte Vittorio Emanuele II

Pal. Altemps

Arco dei Banchi

Via · dei · Coronari

Pza NAVONA

S. Maria d. Pace

S. Luigi d. Francesi

V. Banco di S. Spirito

S. Giovanni dei Fiorentini

V. d. Banchi Nuovi

S. Maria dell' Anima

F.na dei Fiumi

Pal. Madam

Pza d. Orologio

S. Agnese in Agone

Oratorio dei Filippini

Pal. Sacchetti

Chiesa Nuova

Vecchio

S. Ivo

Pal. Pamphili

Pal. d. Sapienza

Pza di Pasquino

Pal. Massimo

Pal. Braschi

Pal. Vido

V. del Pellegrino

V. d. Monserrato

Pal. della Cancelleria

Pal. d. Farnesina ai Baullari

S. Andrea d. Valle

Giulia

V. Gallo

Pza Campo dei Fiori

CAMPO DEI FIORI

S. Carlo ai Catina

Pal. Farnese

S. Maria della Morte

Palazzo Spada

Cappella del Monte di Pieta

Palazzo Corsini

Villa Farnesina

GIANICOLO

Pte Sisto

Orto Botanico

Porta Settimiana

V. Benedetta

Torre d. Anguillara

Fontana Paola

S. Pietro in Montorio

S. Maria in Trastevere

Palazzo di S. Callisto

S. Crisogono

TRASTEVERE

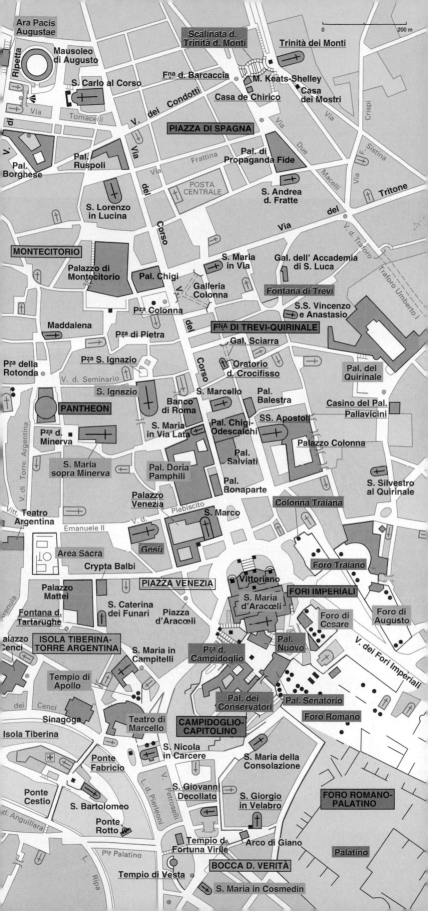

Entrance stairway, Vatican Museums

Practical Points

Planning your Trip

Useful Addresses

INTERNET

The Internet is a useful source of information, enabling visitors to contact tourist offices, consult programmes and brochures and make bookings on line. The following websites provide information on Roman history and art, as well as giving practical suggestions for making the most of your time in the eternal city.

Art and culture in Rome: consult the official site of the Comune di Roma, which lists details of events and exhibitions taking place in the city: www.comune.roma.it/cultura/

Practical information: the Comune di Roma's central database lists regularly updated addresses, as well as details on transport, events, shows, sport and a range of other topics: www.romaturismo.it

The Imperial Fora: this interesting website contains reconstructions of Ancient Rome and virtual visits around the Fora via two web-cams installed on the site. It also provides information on daily life in Ancient Rome and on the excavation work taking place in the fora: www.capitolium.org/

Information for tourists and locals: the www.romainweb.com (in Italian only) and www.roma.vivacity.it websites list information on cultural events, museums, monuments, guided tours, cinemas and theatres, children's activities, bars and nightclubs, shops and much more!

Cinecittà: this site provides information on the history of the Cinecittà studios and the films that have been produced there, as well as virtual reconstructions of famous sets, details of cinema events and festivals taking place around the world, and an introduction to digital technology and other facilities available at the studios: www.cinecitta.it

Friends of Via Giulia: photos, history, tours and a wide range of information relating to Via Giulia and its surroundings (in Italian only):

I Gatti del Foro: information on exhibitions, monuments and museums (in Italian only): www.gattidelforo.it

Castelli Romani: the art, history and monuments of the Castelli Romani region (in Italian only): www.hurricane.it/castelliromani/

ITALIAN STATE TOURIST BOARD ABROAD

The **Ente Nazionale Italiano per il Turismo** (ENIT) has offices abroad and in Italy – for local tourist information services see below:

UK – 1 Princes Street, London W1B 2AY; ☎ (020) 7399 3567; 09065 508 925 (24hr brochure line, calls charged at £1/min); Fax (020) 7493 6695; italy@italiantouristboard.co.uk; www.enit.it *(Office open Mon-Fri, 9am-5pm)*.

USA – Suite 1565, 630 Fifth Avenue, New York NY 10111; ☎ (212) 245 5618; (212) 245 4822 (brochure line). For Los Angeles, ☎ (310) 820 1898; (310) 820 0098 (brochure line).

Canada – Italian Government Tourist Board, 175 Bloor St E, Suite 907 – South Tower, Toronto, Ontario M4W 3R8; ☎ (416) 925 4882; Fax (416) 925 4799; enit.canada@on.aibn.com

TOURIST OFFICES IN ROME

The **APT** (Azienda di Promozione Turistica) has its main office at Via Parigi 11 (☎ 06 48 89 91 or ☎ 06 48 89 92 38), as well as an information office at Fiumicino Airport (☎ 06 65 95 60 74). Both offices give free brochures and maps of the city.

The **Comune di Roma** has set up information kiosks in the city centre which give details on tourist and cultural events taking place in the capital. Open 9am-6pm, they also provide updated leaflets for tourists printed in both English and Italian. The list below gives the location of these kiosks:

– Termini Railway Station, Platform 2 ☎ 06 48 90 63 00
– Termini Railway Station, Piazza dei Cinquecento ☎ 06 47 82 51 94
– Castel Sant'Angelo, Piazza Pia ☎ 06 68 80 97 07
– Fori Imperiali, Piazza Tempio della Pace ☎ 06 69 92 43 07
– Piazza di Spagna, Largo Goldoni ☎ 06 68 13 60 61
– Piazza Navona, Piazza Cinque Lune ☎ 06 68 80 92 40
– Via Nazionale, opposite the Palazzo delle Esposizioni ☎ 06 47 82 45 25
– Trastevere, Piazza Sonnino ☎ 06 58 33 34 57
– San Giovanni, Piazza San Giovanni in Laterano ☎ 06 77 20 35 35.

For further information, consult the Comune di Roma's website *(address given above)* or call 06 36 00 43 99, 9am-7pm.

ITALIAN EMBASSIES AND CONSULATES

To obtain further information, contact the nearest Italian embassy or consulate:

14 Three Kings' Yard, London
W1Y 2EH; ☎ (020) 7312 2200;
Fax (020) 7312 2230;
emblondon@embitaly.org.uk;
www.embitaly.org.uk
3000 Whitehaven St, NW Washington,
DC 20008; ☎ (202) 616 4400;
Fax (202) 518 2154; www.italyemb.org
275 Slater Street, 21st floor, Ottawa,
Ontario K1P 5H9;
☎ (613) 232 2401/2/3;
Fax (613) 233 1484;
ambital@italyincanada.com;
www.italyincanada.com

CONSULATES

38 Eaton Place, London SW1X 8AN;
☎ (020) 7235 9371;
Fax (020) 7823 1609.
Rodwell Tower, 111 Piccadilly,
Manchester M1 2HY;
☎ (0161) 236 9024; Fax (0161) 236
5574;
passaporti@italconsulman.demon.co.uk
32 Melville Street, Edinburgh
EH3 7HA; ☎ (0131) 226 3631;
Fax (0131) 226 6260;
consedimb@consedimb.demon.co.uk
690 Park Avenue, New York NY 10021;
☎ (212) 737 9100; Fax (212) 249 4945;
info@italconsulnyc.org;
www.italconsulnyc.org
3489 Drummond Street, Montreal,
Quebec H3G 1X6; ☎ (514) 849 9544;
Fax (514) 499 9471;
cgi@italconsul.montreal.qc.ca
136 Beverley Street, Toronto, Ontario
M5T 1Y5; ☎ (416) 977 1566;
(416) 977 1119;
consolato.it@toronto.italconsulate.org;
www.toronto.italconsulate.org

Formalities

DOCUMENTS

Passports – British visitors travelling
to Italy must be in possession of a
valid national passport. Citizens of
other European Union countries only
need a national identity card. In case
of loss or theft report to the embassy
or consulate and the local police.

Visas – Entry visas are required by
Australian, New Zealand, Canadian
and US citizens (if their intended stay
exceeds three months). Apply to the
Italian Consulate (visa issued same
day; delay if submitted by mail). US
citizens may find the booklet **Your
Trip Abroad** useful for information
on visa requirements, customs
regulations, medical care etc when
travelling in Europe – available from
the Superintendent of Documents,
PO Box 371954, Pittsburgh, PA 15250-
7954, ☎ (202) 512 1800;
Fax (202) 512 2250;
www.access.gpo.gov

Driving Licence – Nationals of the
European Union require a valid
national driving licence. Nationals
of non-EU countries should obtain an
international driving licence,
obtainable in the US from the
American Automobile Association,
US$18 for members and US$20 for non-
members. The AAA can be contacted
at AAA National Headquarters,
1000 AAA Drive, Heathrow FL 32746-
5080, ☎ (407) 444 7000. Other
documents required include the
vehicle's current **log book** and a
green card for insurance.

HEALTH

As the UK is a member of the
European Union, British subjects
should obtain **medical form E111**
from the Ministry of Social Security,
Newcastle-upon-Tyne, or from main
post offices, before leaving home.
Separate travel and medical insurance
is highly recommended – check with
your local travel agent before
departure.

CUSTOMS REGULATIONS

As of 30 June 1999, those travelling
between countries within the
European Union can no longer
purchase "duty-free" goods. For further
information, there is a free leaflet,
Duty Paid, available from
HM Customs and Excise, Finchley
Excise Advice Centre, Berkeley House,
304 Regents Park Road, London
N3 2JY, ☎ 0845 010 9000;
www.hmce.gov.uk The US Customs
Service offers a free publication **Know
Before You Go** for US citizens,
www.customs.gov

A typical Roman façade (detail)

B. Morandi/MICHELIN

Seasons

CLIMATE

Located 28km/17mi from the coast,
Rome enjoys a mild Mediterranean
climate: bright and crisp in winter,
hot in summer. The most temperate

months are May, September and October, and sometimes June, if the hot Roman summer is late arriving. During the months of July and August the temperature rarely dips below 30°C/86°F and the high humidity makes the heat hard to bear. September and October are splendid, with sunny skies and mild temperatures (although it can sometimes rain heavily in October). November is the wettest month of the year, often the result of heavy downpours, and the temperature falls, signalling the first signs of winter. It can be cold in December, January and February, but it rarely snows (every 20 years or so!). The mild weather returns again in March and April, occasionally accompanied by more rainfall.

BEST TIME

If climate is your main concern, then undoubtedly the best time to visit Rome is in April, May, September or October. Not surprisingly, however, these are also the months when the city receives the most visitors (especially over Easter). If you are not travelling with children or older visitors and you can cope with high temperatures, then July and August have the advantage of being quieter with less traffic. During these months the city empties, as many Romans head to their second homes on the coast. Winter is also an interesting time to visit the capital, as the air is fresh, the light sharp and the sky often a clear blue. Although the winter can be cold, you may not even need to wear a coat in December and with Christmas just around the corner, there are often crib exhibitions in the churches, some of which are particularly impressive. Piazza Navona is especially charming in December, with stalls selling Christmas gifts, along with sweets and toys traditionally given to children at Epiphany.

PUBLIC HOLIDAYS

In addition to the usual Italian public and religious holidays listed below, Rome celebrates 21 April (the birth of Rome) and 29 June, the feast day of St Peter and St Paul, the patron saints of the city.

A working day is *un giorno feriale; giorni festivi* include Saturdays, Sundays and the following public holidays:

January: 1 (New Year) and 6 (Epiphany)
Easter: Sunday and Monday *(lunedì dell'Angelo)*
April: 25 (St Mark's Day and liberation in 1945)
May: 1 *(Festa dei Lavoratori)*
June: 29 (the Feast of St Peter and St Paul, patron saints of Rome)

August: 15 (The Assumption – *Ferragosto)*
November: 1 *(All Saints – Tutti i Santi)*
December: 8 (Immaculate Conception), 25 and 26 (Christmas and St Steven's Day).

TIME DIFFERENCE

The time in Italy is usually the same as the rest of mainland Europe (one hour ahead of the United Kingdom) and changes during the last weekend in March and October between summer time *(ora legale)* and winter time *(ora solare).*

Budget

Compared with other European capitals such as Paris and London, Rome is not an expensive city, although it is not always easy to find value for money, especially when looking for accommodation. For suggestions on how to make your money go further, especially when buying airline or train tickets, see **Concessions** below.

If you are on a **tight budget** it is possible to manage in Rome on a daily allowance of €70. This sum includes accommodation in a double room in a **Budget** category hotel (options in this category also include youth hostels, *pensioni*, bed and breakfast accommodation and campsites; if staying in the latter, your daily budget could come down to around €45), a slice of pizza, pastry or roll (around €5) or a meal in a pizzeria (approx. €13) at lunchtime, and an evening meal in a trattoria or wine-bar (€25). The **Moderate** category is for those on an **average budget**. Allow around €105/130 per day including a room in a comfortable hotel, lunch in a pizzeria and dinner in a medium-priced restaurant (for around €42). If you choose to spend more (over €150 daily) you can select a hotel from the **Expensive** category and enjoy dining in gourmet restaurants. This daily budget excludes any additional costs, such as transport, which is not expensive in Rome *(see Transport below)*, as well as entrances to museums and monuments, which vary from €4 to €8.

Special Needs

Many Roman historic monuments do not have modern lifts or wheelchair facilities. For detailed information prior to departure contact **RADAR** (Royal Association for Disability and Rehabilitation), 12 City Forum, 250 City Road, London EC1V 8AF ☏ (020) 7250 3222; Fax (020) 7250 0212; www.radar.org.uk

For information in Italy on which monuments are accessible to disabled travellers, contact **CO.IN** (Consorzio Cooperative Integrate), Via Enrico Giglioli 54/a; ☎ 06 71 29 011; Fax 06 71 29 01 40. Offices are open Mon-Fri, 9am-6pm. CO.IN also produces **Roma Accessibile** (in Italian only), published by the Officina della Carta, a complete guide to sites and facilties accessible to disabled travellers. Information in English on hotels, restaurants, museums and monuments with facilities for the disabled is available at www.coinsociale.it/turismo Sights in the guide marked with the symbols ♿ or (♿) have full or partial access for wheelchairs.

Two bus services have facilities for wheelchair access. Line **590** runs from Metro line A (inaccessible) on Viale Giulio Cesare to Piazza Cinecittà and line **157** links Via A. Mitelli (Tor Bella Monaca) to Termini Railway Station. Tickets cost €0.98 for 75min, €2.43 for 1 day, €4.13 for 2 days, €5.89 for 3 days, €9.30 for a week and €16.17 for a month.

All the stations on Metro line B, with the exception of Circo Massimo, Colosseo and Cavour have lifts. Many of the city buses now have lower platforms and so are suitable for wheelchair users.

Transport

Airlines and rail companies offer special rates outlined in *Concessions* (p 37).

Getting there

FLIGHTS
Many airline companies fly direct to Rome. The following is a brief selection:

Alitalia
4 Portman Square, Marble Arch, London W1H 9PS; ☎ (020) 7486 8432; Fax (020) 7486 8431. Reservations can also be made on ☎ 08705 448 259; www.alitalia.co.uk
4-5 Dawson Street, Dublin 2; ☎ (01) 677 5171; Fax (01) 677 3373.
666 Fifth Avenue, New York, NY 10103; ☎ (212) 903 3300; Fax (212) 903 3350.
Viale Marchetti 111, 00148 Rome, ☎ 06 65 621.

British Airways
156 Regent Street, London W1B 5LB; ☎ 0845 77 999 77 (enquiries); 0845 77 333 77 (reservations); Fax (020) 7434 4640 (reservations); www.britishairways.com
USA – ☎ (1-800) AIRWAYS.
Via Bissolati 54, 00187 Rome; ☎ 199 712 266 (from Italy only).

For information on low-cost airlines that operate flights to Italy, see *Concessions* on p 37.

Some of the major US airlines which fly to Rome include:
American Airlines – www.aa.com
Continental Airlines – www.continental.com
Delta Airlines – www.delta.com
Northwest Airlines – www.nwa.com
United Airlines – www.ual.com
USAirways – www.usairways.com

Tour operators offering flight-only or package holidays include:
Citalia – ☎ (020) 8686 0677; www.citalia.com
Italy Sky Shuttle – ☎ (020) 8241 5145
The Magic of Italy – ☎ (020) 8939 5453; ☎ 08700 270 480; www.magictravelgroup.co.uk
Page and Moy Ltd – ☎ 08700 106 400; www.page-moy.co.uk

BY AIR
Rome is served by two airports: Leonardo da Vinci Airport at Fiumicino *(26km/16mi SW of Rome)* and Ciampino Airport *(15km/10mi SE of Rome)*.

Fiumicino handles domestic and international scheduled flights. It is linked to the centre of Rome by train: services to **Roma-Termini** (€8.78) depart every 30min, between 7.40am-10.30pm from the airport, between 7am-10pm from Roma-Termini; journey time 32min.

FM1 **Fiumicino-Fara Sabina** services run trains every 15min to Trastevere, Ostiense, Tuscolana and Tiburtina (€4.65); journey time to Tiburtina 41min; services operate from the airport at 5.57am, between 6.27am-9.27pm and then every 30min until 11.27pm; services operate from Tiburtina at 5.06am, between 5.36am-10.36pm, and then every 30min until 10.36pm.

There is also a **night-bus service** from Tiburtina Station (at 0.30am, 1.15am, 2.30am and 3.45am) to the airport, stopping at Termini Station, and vice versa (at 1.15am, 2.15am, 3.30am and 5am); journey time 45min. Cost of ticket: €3.62.

Ciampino handles charter flights (details from travel agencies) and is linked by bus to the Metro line A station Anagnina.

**Useful numbers – Leonardo
da Vinci-Fiumicino Airport**,
☎ 06 65 951; **Ciampino Airport**,
☎ 06 79 49 41.
Domestic Flight Reservations:
☎ 06 65 641; **International Flight
Reservations**: ☎ 06 65 642; **Flight
Information**: ☎ 06 65 95 36 40/40 01;
Passenger Information:
☎ 06 65 95 36 40 or 06 65 95 44 55.

Parking – In addition to a multi-storey
car park, Fiumicino Airport also has a
long-stay car park with a capacity for
3 000 vehicles. The car park is situated
to the east of the airport, and is
directly linked to the Rome-Fiumicino
motorway. A free shuttle bus operates
between the car park and the
domestic and international terminals
every 10min during the day (from
7am-midnight) and every 20min at
night. The cost of parking ranges from
€8.78 per day for the first four days,
€5.16 for the next four days and €3.10
from the ninth day onwards.

By RAIL
The mainline national and
international trains arrive at **Stazione
Termini** or **Tiburtina**. Termini is on
both Metro lines (A – Ottaviano-
Anagnina and B – Laurentina-
Rebibbia) and the bus station in the
forecourt serves almost all the bus
routes in Rome. Several towns just
outside Rome such as Viterbo,
Pantano and Ostia are accessible on
routes from the city: the Rome-Viterbo
line leaves from Piazzale Flaminio
Station; Rome-Pantano from Roma
Laziali Station; the Rome-Lido line
leaves from Porta San Paolo Station
and makes three stops before Ostia
Lido, one of which is at the
archaeological site at Ostia Antica.
Timetables are available at the Italian
Tourist Office in London and from
news-stands in Italy.

**Useful numbers – Italian State
Railways** (Ferrovie dello Stato),
☎ 848-88088 (information in Italy),
information office at Termini Station
☎ 06 147 888 088; information for
disabled travellers ☎ 06 48 81 726;
www.fs-on-line.com
Ultima Travel, 424 Chester Road,
Little Sutton, South Wirral CH66 3RB
☎ 0151 339 6171; fax 0151 339 9199.

By COACH
Coach services from Victoria Coach
Station in London are operated by
Eurolines, 4 Cardiff Road, Luton,
Bedfordshire L41 1PP; ☎ 08705 143
219 (calls charged at standard rate);
Fax 01582 400 694;
welcome@eurolinesuk.com;
www.eurolines.co.uk Alternatively,
contact National Express, 75 Davies
Street, London W1K 5HT, ☎ 0870 901
3190; 08705 80 80 80;
www.gobycoach.com

By CAR
*The Michelin companion maps and
plans for this guide are listed after the
main contents page at the beginning
of the guide.*
On the outer edge of the city is the
Grande Raccordo Anulare (GRA), a
multi-lane ring road from which all
the motorways (A1 to Florence and
Bologna to the north, to Naples in the
south; A12 to Fiumicino, Civitavecchia
and the west coast; A24 east to Aquila
and the Adriatic) and main roads
(strada statale) radiate.
The **Tangenziale Est** links the Stadio
Olimpico to the Piazza San Giovanni
in Laterano via such eastern quarters
as Nomentano, Tiburtino, Prenestino.
If you are approaching Rome from the
north along the A1, and heading to the
north (Cassia, Flaminia or Salaria
districts) or the west (Aurelia) of the
city, leave the motorway at Roma
Nord and follow the Grande Raccordo
Anulare (GRA). For the eastern and
southern districts of Rome, stay on the
motorway, follow signs to Roma Est-
Napoli and take the GRA at the Roma
Est exit.
If you are heading into the city from
the south along the A2 (Naples-Rome),
follow the GRA at the Roma Sud exit in
order to get to the southern (Pontina,
Appia, Tuscolana and Casilina) and
western (Aurelia) districts. For districts
to the east and the north, follow signs
for Roma Est-Firenze and take the
GRA at Roma Est.
From the A16 and A24 motorways, the
GRA is clearly signposted.

Getting about

Visitors are best advised to explore
Rome by foot and on public transport
as heavy traffic and the difficult of
finding somewhere to park make
driving in the capital an unpleasant
experience.
For information on hiring a bicycle or
moped, see *Other Ways of Exploring the
City* on p 47.

By BUS, TRAM AND UNDERGROUND
Public transport services are organised
by **ATAC** (Azienda Tramvie e Autobus
del Comune di Roma, ☎ 800 43 17 84,
open Mon-Fri, 8am-6pm or
☎ 06 46 951; www.atac.roma.it). City
route plans are on sale in bookshops
and kiosks; the plan *Rete dei Trasporti
Urbani di Roma*, published by ATAC, is
sold at the information kiosk in Piazza
dei Cinquecento.
Tickcts should bc purchased before the
beginning of the journey and punched
in the machine in the bus and on the
underground to be validated.
Different types of ticket *(biglietto)* are
sold at newspaper kiosks or in
tobacconists' shops: those bearing the

name **Metrebus** may be used on all means of transport – bus, tram, metro and overground FS *(Ferrovie Statali)* trains in second class except on services Roma Termini – Fiumicino Aeroporto and Ponte Galliera – Fiumicino Aeroporto. Individual tickets may also be acquired from machines at metro stations and end-of-line bus stops.

Tickets available include:
– a BIT ticket costing €0.77, is valid for a journey up to 1hr 15min on various lines from the time it is stamped;
– a BIG ticket, costing €6.10, is valid until midnight of the day of purchase;
– a CIS pass, costing €12.39, is valid for one week.

A monthly pass is also available for €25.82.

Bus and trams stops are indicated by a sign *fermata*; request stop = *fermata richiesta*. The entrance door *(salita)* is at the back of the bus and the exit *(uscita)* in the middle.

Le Floc'h/EXPLORER

Buses operate from 5.30am-midnight. The following established routes are amongst the most useful:
– **64** and **40** from Termini Station to the Vatican, stopping at Via Nazionale, Piazza Venezia, near the Gesù Church, Largo di Torre Argentina and Corso Vittorio Emanuele II. However, beware of pickpockets, notably at rush hour;
– **218** Piazza San Giovanni in Laterano south to Via Ardeatina (passing the north end of the Old Appian Way);
– **310** from Termini Station to Piazza Vescovio;
– **116** and **117** (weekdays only) run through the historic centre using electric minibuses. The former runs from Via Veneto and from Via Giulia, and the latter from Piazza San Giovanni in Laterano and from Piazza del Popolo;
– **85** Colosseum, Imperial Fora, Piazza Venezia, Via del Corso.

Trams operate from 5am-9pm. There are six lines; the following routes are amongst the most useful to tourists:

– **3** Trastevere, Colosseum, San Giovanni in Laterano, Piazza Thorwaldsen (Villa Giulia and the Galleria Nazionale d'Arte Moderna);
– **14** and **516** from the east side of the city (Via Prenestina) to Termini Station, Via Piazzale di Porta Maggiore and Piazza Vittorio Emanuele II;
– **19** from Piazza dei Gerani to the Olympic Village, stopping at Piazza dei Gerani, Piazzale del Verano, Viale Regina Margherita, Piazza Thorwaldsen, Via Flaminia and Viale Tiziano;
– **30b** from Piazzale Ostiense (Piramide de G Cestius) to Piazza Thorwaldsen, passing near the Galleria Nazionale d'Arte Moderna and Villa Borghese and through the city centre past the Colosseum, San Giovanni in Laterano and Piazza Porta Maggiore.
– **8** from Trastevere Station stopping at Viale Trastevere, Via Arenula and Via di Torre Argentina.

Metro (underground) trains operate from 5.30am-11.30pm; the section Termini-Rebibbia runs until 9pm weekdays and 11pm weekends and holidays. There are two lines.
Line A runs from Battistini to Via Anagnina. The most useful stops include Flaminio (Piazza del Popolo, Spagna (Piazza di Spagna), Barberini (Piazza Barberini), Termini (Termini Station), San Giovanni (St John Lateran) and Cinecittà.
Line B runs from Rebibbia to Laurentina via EUR. The most useful stops include Termini (Termini Station), Cavour (Piazza Cavour), Colosseo (Colosseum), Circo Massimo (near the Circus Maximus and the Baths of Caracalla), Piramide (Mausoleum of Caius Cestius), San Paolo (basilica of St Paul Without the Walls) and EUR Fermi (EUR district).

BY TAXI
To call a taxi dial ☎ 06 35 70, ☎ 06 49 94, ☎ 06 88 177, ☎ 06 41 57, ☎ 06 55 51, or ☎ 06 66 45. Fixed starting charge: €2.32 rising €0.10 every 50 seconds. Extra charges apply for luggage (€1.03), night service (between 10pm-7am; €2.58) and Sundays and holidays (€1.03). There is an airport charge of €7.23 from Rome to Fiumicino, €5.94 from Fiumicino to Rome, and €5.16 from Rome to Ciampino.

BY CAR
Driving in Rome is not advised as access to the city centre is very difficult and parking severely restricted; many streets are reserved for pedestrians, taxis, buses and local residents. The historic centre is delineated as blue zone *(fascia blu)* from which private cars are excluded between 6.30am-7.30pm Mon-Fri and 2-6pm Sat.

HIGHWAY CODE

Traffic drives on the right and the **minimum driving age** in Italy is 18 years.

Seat belts must be worn at the front and back of the vehicle. Drivers must wear **shoes**, carry spare lights and a **red triangle** to be displayed in case of a breakdown or accident.

A valid driving licence must be carried at all times.

Motorways (*autostrade* – subject to tolls) and dual carriageways (*superstrade*) are indicated by green signs; ordinary roads by blue signs; tourist sights by yellow signs.

Italian **motorway tolls** can be paid with money or with the **Viacard**, a magnetic card which is sold in Italy at the entrances and exits of the motorways, in Autogrill restaurants and in the offices of ACI (Automobile Club Italiano), Via Marsala 8, 00185 Rome, ☎ 06 99 81.

The following **speed restrictions** operate:

50kph in built-up areas;

90-110kph on open country roads;

90 (600cc)-130kph (excess of 1 000cc) on motorways depending on engine capacity.

PARKING

There are two large underground **car parks** in central Rome: Villa Borghese, near the Porta Pinciana and Parking Ludovisi, Via Ludovisi 60. Other ACI car parks are scattered at random around town. The largest car parks are marked on the map on the inside back cover of the guide.

PETROL/GAS

Fuel is sold as *super* (4-star), *senza piombo* (unleaded 95 octane), *super plus* or *Euro plus* (unleaded 98 octane) or *gazolio* (diesel).

Petrol (US: gas) stations are usually open between 7am-7pm. Many close at lunchtime (12.30pm-3pm), Sundays and public holidays and some refuse payment by credit card. As well as the service stations on the ring road (Raccordo Anulare), petrol can be bought 24hr a day from automatic petrol pumps or petrol stations throughout the city, including those at Corso Francia on the corner of Via di V. Stelluti, Via Salaria on the corner of Viale Somalia, Lungotevere Ripa, Piazzale della Radio, Via Prenestina 187 and Via Tuscolana 1530.

MAPS AND PLANS

A list of Michelin maps that would be useful for getting to Rome and finding your way around the city is given at the beginning of the guide *(see Maps and Plans)*.

ROAD RESCUE SERVICES

ACI (Automobile Club Italiano): ☎ 803 116

CAR HIRE

All the main car hire agencies have offices at Fiumicino Airport and Ciampino Airport and at Termini Railway Station. Call the following numbers for further information (numbers accessible from within Italy only):

Avis: ☎ 199 100 133; www.avis.co.uk

Hertz: ☎ 199 112 211 – if calling from a mobile, dial ☎ 0248 233 662; www.hertz.co.uk

Europcar: ☎ 800 014 410; www.europcar.co.uk

Maggiore: ☎ 848 867 067; www.maggiore.it

Where to Stay

From modest *pensioni* to luxury hotels, Rome has a wide range of accommodation options to suit all budgets and tastes, although finding value for money can sometimes prove difficult. As the capital is very popular with tourists and pilgrims throughout the year, visitors are advised to book well in advance in order to be sure of securing accommodation and avoiding any unpleasant surprises. Generally speaking, the low season includes January, the first half of February, the last two weeks of July, the months of August and November and the first two weeks of December. During these periods many hotels offer reasonable rates and special weekend deals or short breaks.

Visitors are advised to choose a hotel with air-conditioning during the summer, as it is particularly hot during this period (hotels with air-conditioning are indicated in the list given below).

SELECTING A DISTRICT

A good selection of *pensioni* and hotels can be found in the **historic centre**, where the atmosphere and high concentration of tourist sights and shops make it particularly popular with visitors. However, many of these establishments have limited capacity and as a result are often full. The attractive village-like quarter of **Trastevere**, with its lively nightlife, would also be a pleasant area in which to stay, although accommodation options here are somewhat limited.

The **Vatican** and **Prati** districts are close to the centre and are quieter and more reasonably priced than the historic centre and Trastevere (especially the Prati district, which has a good choice of hotels). The choice of accommodation around **Via Cavour** (near the Rione Monti district), between Termini Station and the Fori Imperiali, is also good, especially for mid-range hotels.

Many of the cheaper *pensioni* and smaller hotels are concentrated in the area around **Termini Station**, slightly away from the city centre and somewhat lacking in character, but well served by public buses and the metro system.

The majority of the city's luxury hotels can be found on the **Via Veneto** and in the area around **Villa Borghese**.

Driving in Rome is not advisable as parking in the city can be a major problem (visitors should note that most of the hotels in the city centre do not have private garages or parking). The few private car parks that do exist are extremely expensive and access to the city centre by car is severely restricted (a special permit is required).

TYPES OF ACCOMMODATION
HOTELS AND PENSIONI

It is not always easy to distinguish between a hotel and a *pensione*. Generally, the word *pensione* is used to describe a small family-run hotel, which is sometimes situated within a residential building and which offers simple, basic rooms, often without a private bathroom.

Whatever type of accommodation you choose, it is advisable to check prices before booking, as rates can vary depending on the time of year and availability of rooms. Given the shortage of rooms in Rome, hoteliers usually request confirmation of booking by fax, as well as a credit card number. Breakfast is usually included in the price of the room, although this may not be the case in smaller hotels.

HOSTELS AND BUDGET ACCOMMODATION

Hostel accommodation is only available to members of the Youth Hostel Association. It is possible to join the organisation at any of the YHA hostels; membership then provides access to the many YHA hostels located around the world. There is no age limit for membership, which must be renewed annually. The **Associazione Italiana Alberghi per la Gioventù** (AIG) is situated at Via Cavour 44 ☎ 06 48 71 152. The main office of the Comitato Regionale Lazio is at Viale delle Olimpiadi 61. Those wishing to arrange hostel accommodation in advance can contact the **Youth Hostels Association**, Trevelyan House, Dimple Road, Matlock, Derbyshire DE4 3YH, ☎ (0870) 870 8808; Fax 01629 592 702; www.yha.org.uk or **Hostelling International-American Youth Hostels**, 733 15th Street, NW, Ste. 840, Washington DC 20005, ☎ (202) 783 6161; www.hiayh.org More general information on hostels in the US can be obtained by visiting www.hostels.com

Other organisations offering budget accommodation, such as the YWCA and the Hotel Sandy (listed below), cater mainly for young people and offer dormitories or shared rooms at reasonable rates.

BED AND BREAKFAST

The bed and breakfast formula has gained in popularity in Italy in recent years, offering visitors the chance to stay in private homes. The house or apartment is also often lived in by the hosts, who let out a few of their rooms (usually between one and three) to guests at reasonable prices. However, guests are usually required to stay for a minimum period and credit cards are rarely accepted. For a list of over 200 bed and breakfast addresses, contact the B and B reservation offices from 8am-9pm ☎ 06 67 89 222. There is no charge for reservations. Information is also available on the Italian Bed and Breakfast website at www.bbitalia.it

CONVENTS AND MONASTERIES

As well as providing accommodation for pilgrims, convents and monasteries are also a good option for those on a limited budget. Rooms are reasonably priced, although visitors are usually expected to be in by a specified hour (usually 10.30pm).

Occasionally men and women are required to sleep in separate rooms.

For further information, contact the **Peregrinatio ad Petri Sedem**, *Piazza Pio XII 4 (Vaticano-San Pietro district)*, ☎ *06 69 88 48 96; Fax 06 69 88 56 17.*

CAMP SITES

Although the few campsites that exist in Rome are situated a fair distance from the city centre, they have the advantage of offering cheap accommodation in attractive green surroundings. Shade provided by the trees is particularly welcome in the hot summer months, when the humidity in the city centre becomes almost unbearable. Campsite addresses are given below.

HOTEL RESERVATIONS

Visitors can book hotel rooms through the **Hotel Reservation Service**, ☎ 06 69 91 000, open 7am-10pm. This service is free of charge and offers a choice of 350 hotels in the capital. Visitors booking any of these hotels may also take advantage of a shuttle service from Fiumicino Airport, at a cost of €9.55 per person. Reservations can be made by phone or from the airport desk (in the International, European and National arrival halls), from Termini Railway Station (opposite platform 20), at Ciampino Airport and at the Tevere-Ovest service station on the A1 Milan-Rome motorway. The same service is also available on the Internet at www.hotelreservation.it

FOR ALL BUDGETS

The hotels listed below are grouped according to the districts described in the guide and are subdivided into three categories, each based on the price of a single room. Hotels included in the **Budget** section are usually small and basic, but are fairly comfortable and situated in a particularly good location; expect to pay less than €70 for a single room. This category includes youth hostels and modest *pensioni*, some of which offer rooms without private facilities; visitors are advised to call the hotel for further information before making a reservation.

Those with a larger budget will find hotels offering greater comfort and charm in our **Moderate** category, where prices range from €70 to €130. A selection of luxury and atmospheric hotels offering a wide range of facilities and guaranteeing a memorable stay is given in the **Expensive** section.

Prices are given for single and double rooms in high season, including taxes and service. The hotels listed have been chosen for their value for money, level of comfort and character. Although every hotel has been carefully inspected, it is possible that things have changed since our last visit. We would be grateful for any comments or suggestions from readers.

AND DON'T FORGET THE RED GUIDE
THE RED GUIDE ITALIA

For a more exhaustive list of hotels consult *The Red Guide Italia*, which provides a whole host of details on Rome's hotels and restaurants.

AVENTINO/PIRAMIDE CESTIA – TESTACCIO
• *Moderate*

Hotel Santa Prisca – *Largo M. Gelsomini 25, Aventino district* – ☎ *06 57 41 917 – Fax 06 57 46 658 –* 🅿 ▤ *– 50 rooms.* €*94.00/115.69* 🍽 *– Restaurant €15.* This recently restored hotel is located at the foot of the Aventine hill. It has a restaurant offering guests reasonably priced fixed menus for both lunch and dinner.

Sant'Anselmo – *Piazza Sant'Anselmo 2, Aventino district* – ☎ *06 57 48 119 – Fax 06 57 83 604 – 44 rooms.* €*118.79/180.76* 🍽. This hotel, situated away from the traffic of the city amid the greenery of the Aventine hill, offers rooms with antique furniture in three residential villas. The hotel is surrounded by delightful gardens and graced with a beautiful verandah on which breakfast is served. A wonderful way to experience Rome.

CATACOMBE DI PRISCILLA (VIA NOMENTANA, VIA SALARIA)
• *Moderate*

Hotel Santa Costanza – *Viale 21 Aprile 4, Via Nomentana district* – ☎ *06 86 00 602 – Fax 06 86 02 786 –* ▤ ♿ *– 68 rooms.* €*108.46/144.61* 🍽. Comfortable, colourful armchairs furnish the lobby of this hotel, which has good transport connections to the city centre. The breakfast room, with its attractive floral designs, has large windows looking out on to an internal garden. Comfortable, well-appointed rooms.

COLOSSEO – CELIO/FORI IMPERIALI/ PIAZZA VENEZIA/RIONE MONTI
• *Budget*

Hotel Sandy – *Via Cavour 136, (5th floor, no lift), Fori Imperiali district* – ☎ *06 48 84 585 – gi.costantini@agora.stm.it –* ✉ *– 24 beds.* €*15.49.* This hostel is very popular with foreigners and is particularly suitable for young people looking for budget accommodation. Spacious, colourful rooms are shared by three to five people, with a communal bathroom. Breakfast not available.

Hotel San Paolo – *Via Panisperna 95, (1st floor, no lift), Rione Monti district* – ☎ *06 47 45 213 – Fax 06 46 45 218 – hsanpaolo@tin.it – 24 rooms.* €*38.73/77.47 –* 🍽 €*5.16.* This simple hotel is situated in the Rione Monti district, which still retains a flavour of old Rome. The rooms are small but colourfully decorated and the staff very friendly.

Hotel Perugia – *Via del Colosseo 7, Colosseo district* – ☎ *06 67 97 200 – Fax 06 67 84 635 – htlperugia@isl.it – 13 rooms.* €*56.81/90.38* 🍽. Given its excellent location close to the Colosseum, this small hotel is very reasonably priced. One of the rooms on the fourth floor has a small balcony with views of the amphitheatre, but no private bathroom.

• *Moderate*

Hotel Solis Invictus – *Via Cavour 311, Fori Imperiali district* – ☎ *06 69 92 05 87 – Fax 06 69 92 33 95 –* ▤ *– 16 rooms.*

€123.95/139.44 ⬜. This small, comfortable hotel is family run and is situated on the first floor of a building a few steps away from the Colosseum. The large rooms are the most modern.

• **Expensive**

Hotel Celio – *Via dei Santi Quattro 35/c, Colosseo district* – ☎ 06 70 49 53 33 – Fax 06 70 96 377 – ▤ – 18 rooms. From €196.25 ⬜. Splendid fragments of frescoes add a touch of originality to the rooms in this elegant family hotel. The hotel also has a suite with a view of the Colosseum. Breakfast is served in the rooms.

Fontana di Trevi – Quirinale

• **Expensive**

Hotel Fontana – *Piazza di Trevi 96, Fontana di Trevi district* – ☎ 06 67 86 113 – Fax 06 67 90 024 – 25 rooms. From €180.76 ⬜. One way of admiring the Trevi Fountain without having to fight through the crowds is to stay at this charming hotel situated in Piazza di Trevi, where the charming rooms will satisfy the most romantic of travellers.

Isola Tiberina – Torre Argentina

• **Moderate**

Pensione Barrett – *Largo Torre Argentina 47, Torre Argentina district* – ☎ 06 68 68 481 – Fax 06 68 92 971 – ▱ ▤ – 20 rooms. €77.47/92.96 – ⬜ €5.16. Simple, but well looked after and in an excellent location. The rooms have thoughtful and unusual touches, such as a small footbath and tea- and coffee-making facilities. Visitors in search of peace and quiet should avoid the rooms overlooking the busy square.

Hotel Arenula – *Via Santa Maria de' Calderari 47, (1st floor, no lift), Torre Argentina district* – ☎ 06 68 79 454 – Fax 06 68 96 188 – hotel.arenula@flashnet.it – 50 rooms. €87.80/113.62 ⬜. This charming hotel is situated in a 20C *palazzo* in the Jewish quarter. The light rooms, brightened by colourful curtains, are decorated in grey and white.

Monte Mario

• **Budget**

Ostello Foro Italico A. F. Pessina – *Viale delle Olimpiadi 61, Monte Mario district* – From Termini Station, Metro A to Ottaviano, then bus 32 (7 stops) – ☎ 06 32 36 267 – Fax 06 32 42 613 – ▱ – 400 beds €14.46 ⬜ – Meal €8. This modern building surrounded by gardens is the only official hostel in Rome and has a self-service restaurant and a bar. The hostel offers dormitory accommodation only, with 6-bedded rooms for men and 10-bedded rooms for women. Rooms are cleaned between 10am and 2pm, when they must be vacated by guests. Closed between midnight and 7am.

Pantheon/Montecitorio

• **Budget**

Hotel Mimosa – *Via Santa Chiara 61, (2nd floor, no lift), Pantheon district* – ☎ 06 68 80 17 53 – Fax 06 68 33 557 – hotelmimosa@tin.it – ▱ ⬶ – 11 rooms.

€61.97/98.13 ⬜. The main attraction of this modest *pensione* is its excellent location in an old building behind the Pantheon, close to Santa Maria sopra Minerva. The rooms are basic, but clean and quiet.

• **Moderate**

Hotel Coronet – *Piazza Grazioli 5, Pantheon district* – ☎ 06 67 92 341 – Fax 06 69 92 27 05 – hotelcoronet@tiscalinet.it – 13 rooms. €77.47/144.61 ⬜. Located in the Palazzo Doria Pamphili, this small hotel is well maintained and offers spacious, comfortable rooms. A romantic atmosphere and good service.

Hotel Portoghesi – *Via dei Portoghesi 1, Montecitorio district* – ☎ 06 68 64 231 – Fax 06 68 76 976 – 27 rooms. €129.11/170.43 ⬜. Situated opposite the legendary "Torre della Scimmia" (Monkey Tower), this hotel has pleasant rooms decorated with antique furniture. The glass conservatory, used as the breakfast room, and the terrace, with its views of the rooftops of Rome, are particularly delightful.

Piazza Navona/Campo dei Fiori/ Castel Sant'Angelo

• **Moderate**

Hotel Navona – *Via dei Sediari 8, (1st floor, no lift), Piazza Navona district* – ☎ 06 68 21 13 92 – Fax 06 68 80 38 02 – info@hotelnavona.com – ▱ – 30 rooms. €72.30/103.29 ⬜. This delightful hotel has cool, attractive rooms decorated in English style, as a result of the owner's long period of residence in Australia. The hotel is located in a 16C *palazzo* which was built on top of much older foundations. Breakfast is served at a long table.

Campo dei Fiori market, with a statue of Giordano Bruno in the background

Hotel Due Torri – *Vicolo del Leonetto 23, Piazza Navona district* – ☎ 06 68 76 983 – Fax 06 68 65 442 – ▤ – 26 rooms. €98.13/165.27 ⬜. Once the residence of high prelates, this delightful centrally located hotel is situated in a quiet, attractive street. Each room has its own unique decor and is furnished with a parquet floor and high quality furniture, including some genuine antiques. One of our favourite addresses in Rome.

Hotel Campo dei Fiori – *Via del Biscione 6, Campo dei Fiori district* – ☎ 06 68 80 68 65 – Fax 06 68 76 003 – *campofiori@inwind.it* – 27 rooms. €113.62/139.44 ⌑. This hotel is situated at the top of a narrow flight of steps and has small but comfortable rooms, some of which have a shared bathroom. The top floor has a beautiful terrace with deckchairs where guests can relax and enjoy the views of Piazza Campo dei Fiori.

• *Expensive*

Hotel Teatro di Pompeo – *Largo del Pallaro 8, Campo dei Fiori district*– ☎ 06 68 30 01 70 – Fax 06 68 80 55 31 – ▤ – 13 rooms. From €139.44 ⌑. The unusual dining room of this delightful hotel still retains the original vaults of Pompey's Theatre. The hotel rooms are spacious and simply furnished, with coffered ceilings and tiled floors.

PIAZZA DEL POPOLO/PIAZZA DI SPAGNA
• *Budget*

Pensione Panda – *Via della Croce 35, Piazza di Spagna district* – ☎ 06 67 80 179 – Fax 06 69 94 21 51 – *www.hotelpandaparadise.com* – 20 rooms. €36.15/61.97. This well-kept *pensione* in a 17C *palazzo* not far from the Spanish Steps has quiet, simply furnished rooms, some with shared bathroom. Although lacking in overall charm, the hotel is recommended for its excellent location and reasonable rates.

• *Moderate*

Hotel Pensione Suisse – *Via Gregoriana 54, (3rd floor, lift), Piazza di Spagna district* – ☎ 06 67 83 649 – Fax 06 67 81 258 – *suisse.hotel@tiscalinet.it* – 12 rooms. €85.22/129.11 ⌑. In an elegant mansion near the Casa dei Mostri, this hotel is run by a friendly multilingual family and has well-appointed rooms arranged around an internal courtyard. Guests are requested to return to the hotel no later than 2am. Breakfast is served in the rooms.

Hotel Margutta – *Via Laurina 34, Piazza di Spagna district* – ☎ 06 32 23 674 – Fax 06 32 00 395 – 24 rooms. €87.80/98.13 ⌑. This simple hotel is situated in a side street off the busy Via del Corso – an ideal location for shoppers! The hotel has only double rooms, which are very clean and quiet.

Hotel Parlamento – *Via delle Convertite 5, Piazza di Spagna district* – ☎ /Fax 06 69 92 10 00 – 23 rooms. €98.13/123.95 ⌑. High ceilings and rooms decorated with plants provide this hotel with a pleasant, relaxing atmosphere. The rooms are simple and decorated with antique-style furniture. In summer, breakfast is served on an attractive terrace facing Piazza San Silvestro.

• *Expensive*

Hotel d'Inghilterra – *Via Bocca di Leone 14, Piazza di Spagna district* – ☎ 06 69 98 11 – Fax 06 67 98 601 – ▤ – 88 rooms. From €250.48 – ⌑ €22.72 – Restaurant €49/65. Housed in the old guest-quarters of Palazzo Torlonia, this hotel has retained the elegance and charm of a 15C residence. Furnishings of the period, valuable paintings and precious carpets recall its prestigious past.

PORTA PIA – TERMINI
• *Budget*

Hotel Pensione Tizi – *Via Collina 48, (1st floor, lift), Porta Pia district* – ☎ 06 48 20 128 – Fax 06 47 43 266 – ▱ – 25 rooms. €36.15/56.81 – ⌑ €5.16. The lobby of this small *pensione* is similar to the entrance in houses belonging to a typical Roman family. The hotel is named after the owner's daughter, Tiziana, who is usually at reception to welcome guests. Quiet, attractive rooms, both with and without bathrooms. Good value for money.

Hotel Domus Mea – *Via Calatafimi 31, (5th floor, lift), Stazione Termini district* – ☎ 06 48 81 74 – Fax 06 48 64 96 – 24 rooms. €41.32/98.13 ⌑. This hotel is situated near Termini Station and is run by a friendly Sicilian family. Some of the rooms on the top floor have a small balcony and the hotel also has a pleasant terrace bar. Breakfast is served on the terrace in summer.

• *Moderate*

Hotel Canada – *Via Vicenza 58, Stazione Termini district* – ☎ 06 44 57 770 – Fax 06 44 50 749 – ▤ – 70 rooms. €98.13/134.28 ⌑. This hotel is housed in a beautiful building and is surprisingly quiet, given its proximity to the railway station.

Hotel Venezia – *Via Varese 18, Stazione Termini district* – ☎ 06 44 57 101 – Fax 06 49 57 687 – ▤ – 61 rooms. €103.29/139.44 ⌑. A comfortable, well-kept hotel, with good facilities. The public rooms of the hotel are particularly attractive, with wrought-iron candelabras, beautifully made rustic furniture and delicate fabrics. Recommended.

SANTA MARIA MAGGIORE/ SAN GIOVANNI IN LATERANO
• *Budget*

YWCA – *Via Cesare Balbo 4, Santa Maria Maggiore district* – ☎ 06 48 80 460 – Fax 06 48 71 028 – ▱ ✸ – 70 beds €36.15/72.30 ⌑ – Meal €10. Accommodation available to women, couples and groups (not to single men) in simple, clean rooms. Many of the rooms, both with and without private bathrooms, are rented out by the year to students, giving the hostel the feel of a university residence. Closed from midnight to 7am.

• *Moderate*

Hotel Piccadilly – *Via Magna Grecia 122, San Giovanni in Laterano district* – ☎ 06 77 20 70 17 – Fax 06 70 47 66 86 – ▤ ✸ – 55 rooms. €92.96/142.03 ⌑. This modern hotel extends over eight floors, with the upper floor used as a panoramic breakfast room. The hotel is situated near the basilica of St John Lateran and the market at Via Sannio, which specialises in second-hand clothes.

TRASTEVERE
• *Moderate*

Hotel Trastevere Manara – *Via Luciano Manara 24/a-25, Trastevere district* – ☎ 06 58 14 713 – Fax 06 58 81 016 – *hoteltrastevere@tiscalinet.it* – 9 rooms.

€77.47/98.13 ☺. An excellent location, just a stone's throw from the attractive Piazza Santa Maria in Trastevere. The hotel rooms, all furnished in modern style, include individual safety deposit boxes.

Hotel Cisterna in Trastevere – *Via della Cisterna 7/8/9, Trastevere district* – ☎ 06 58 17 212 – *Fax 06 58 10 091* – ▤ – *19 rooms.* €98.13/118.79 ☺. This hotel, housed within a small 18C *palazzo*, is located in a narrow street named after an unusual fountain, known as the "cisterna". Some of the rooms have dormer windows and wooden beams, and one on the top floor even has a small balcony.

VATICANO – SAN PIETRO
• *Budget*

Pensione Ottaviano – *Via Ottaviano 6, (2nd floor, lift), Vatican district* – ☎ 06 39 73 81 38 – *gi.costantini@agora.stm.it* – ✉ – *25 rooms.* €15.49/46.48. Particularly popular with young foreign visitors, this cheerful *pensione* is decorated with paintings and posters left by previous guests. After 8.30pm guests can check their e-mail free of charge. Breakfast not available.

Bed & Breakfast Maximum – *Via Fabio Massimo 72, (1st floor), Vatican district* – ☎ 06 32 42 037 – *Fax 06 32 42* – *156 bbmaximum@tiscalinet.it* – *www.bbmaximum.com* – ✉ – *4 rooms.* €36.15/72.30 ☺. This B&B situated close to St Peter's offers colourful rooms fitted with ceiling fans. The rooms and bathrooms, one of which has a hydromassage tub, are arranged along an elegant, arched corridor. Breakfast is served in the rooms. Special offers available in low season.

Hotel Casa Tra Noi – *Via Monte del Gallo 113, Vatican district* – ☎ 06 39 38 73 55 – *Fax 06 39 38 74 46* – *tranoi@tiscalinet.it* – *110 rooms.* €55.78/98.13 ☺. This hotel, popular with groups, is housed in a large, modern building at the top of a quiet street from where the dome of St Peter's is visible. The rooms are simple, with basic facilities. Both half-board and full-board available

• *Moderate*

Hotel Alimandi – *Via Tunisi 8, Vatican district* – ☎ 06 39 72 39 48 – *Fax 06 39 72 39 43* – *alimandi@tin.it* – *Closed for 10 days in Jan.* – ▣ – *35 rooms.* €90.38/139.44 ☺. The rooms in this hotel in the immediate vicinity of the Vatican Museums are well appointed and comfortable (safety deposit boxes available). The hotel has a terrace on the first floor and a roof garden for summer barbecues. Medieval decor in the hotel bar. Free shuttle service to the airport.

Hotel Gerber – *Via degli Scipioni 241, Vatican district* – ☎ 06 32 16 485 – *Fax 06 32 17 048* – *27 rooms.* €98.13/123.95 ☺. This hotel has a pleasant semicircular lobby with comfortable sofas and cushions. The simple rooms are functional, with light wood furnishings. In summer, the buffet breakfast is served in the small internal garden.

• *Expensive*

Hotel Atlante Star – *Via Vitelleschi 34, Vatican district* – ☎ 06 68 73 233 – *Fax 06 68 72 300* – ▤ – *70 rooms. From* €263.39 ☺. This elegant hotel close to St Peter's has a lovely roof garden with a magnificent view of the basilica. The hotel restaurant, **Les Étoiles**, makes the most of this splendid location in summer.

VIA VENETO
• *Moderate*

Hotel Pensione Merano – *Via Vittorio Veneto 155, (4th floor, lift), Via Veneto district* – ☎ 06 48 21 796 – *Fax 06 48 21 810* – *hotel.merano@tiscalinet.it* – *30 rooms.* €74.89/103.29 ☺. This quiet, charming *pensione* is situated in one of the smartest streets in the capital. The wooden chairs and floral designs in the attractive breakfast room give the hotel a typically English ambiance.

Hotel Invictus – *Via Quintino Sella 15, Via Veneto district* – ☎ 06 42 01 14 33 – *Fax 06 42 01 15 61* – ▤ – *13 rooms.* €113.62/154.94 ☺. The rooms in this well-maintained hotel are pleasant and comfortable with good quality furnishings. A good location for those wishing to experience the "Dolce Vita" ambiance of the nearby Via Veneto.

VILLA BORGHESE – VILLA GIULIA
• *Expensive*

Hotel Lord Byron – *Via de Notaris 5, Villa Giulia district* – ☎ 06 32 20 404 – *Fax 06 32 20 405* – ▤ – *32 rooms. From* €229.82 ☺. This small, elegant hotel overlooks the Villa Borghese gardens and has an attractive 1920s atmosphere. The hotel restaurant, the **Relais Le Jardin**, serves fine cuisine.

Aldrovandi Palace Hotel – *Via Aldrovandi 15, Villa Borghese district* – ☎ 06 32 23 993 – *Fax 06 32 21 435* – ▤ ✳ – *125 rooms. From* €361.52 – ☺ €18.08. This prestigious hotel just a few steps from the Villa Borghese has fine lounges furnished with antique items and magnificent chandeliers, and elegant bedrooms, tastefully decorated in pink and green tones. In summer, the hotel's excellent restaurant, **Relais La Piscine**, sets out its tables alongside the swimming pool.

Eden – *Via Ludovisi 49, Villa Borghese district* – ☎ 06 47 81 21 – *Fax 06 48 21 584* – ▤ – *107 rooms. From* €433.82 – ☺ €36.93. This luxury hotel is located in a 19C *palazzo* and has spacious, elegant rooms with marble bathrooms. It is home to the renowned **La Terrazza** restaurant which, as its name suggests, is situated on the roof garden of the hotel, from where there is a magnificent view of the Villa Medici and the rooftops of Rome.

CAMPSITES
• *Budget*

Happy Camping – *Via Prato della Corte 1915 – 10km/6mi from the centre. From Termini Station, take Metro line A to Piazzale Flaminio, then the train to Prima Porta and a shuttle bus which operates between 8.30am-noon and 5-10.30pm.* – ☎ 06 33 62 64 01 – *Fax 06 33 61 38 00* – *info@happy camping.net* – *Open Mar to mid-Sep* –

150 pitches €19.63. This pleasant campsite in the northwest of the city has a restaurant, bar, supermarket, children's playground and a swimming pool.

Village Flaminio Camping – *Via Flaminia Nuova 821 – 8km/5mi from the centre. From Termini Station, take bus n° 910 to Piazza Mancini and then bus n° 200 – ☎ 06 33 32 604 – Fax 06 33 30 653 –*

info@villageflaminio.com – Closed mid-Nov to mid-Dec and Feb to mid-Mar – 300 pitches €24.27. Shaded by acacia trees, this campsite has a restaurant, grocery store, an open-air swimming pool, and a residential area for chalets. In high season, entertainment staff organise games and dance lessons.

Where to Eat

Visitors are spoilt for choice in Rome, with a wide selection of places to eat, ranging from pizzerias and simple trattorias to elegant restaurants serving fine cuisine.

DIFFERENT TYPES OF RESTAURANTS
RESTAURANTS, TRATTORIAS AND OSTERIAS

Although the distinction between these different types of restaurants is not as obvious as it once was, in general, a **ristorante** offers elegant cuisine and service, whereas a **trattoria or osteria** is more likely to be a family-run establishment serving home-made dishes in a more relaxed, informal atmosphere. Prices are usually lower in the latter and house wine (of varying quality) is served by the carafe. In typical trattorias, the waiter will often tell you what dishes of the day are on offer. If ordering these, make sure that you know how much you are paying ahead of time to avoid any unpleasant shocks when the bills arrives! (A list is usually available; if in doubt ask to see it.) Be wary of choosing the tourist menu, which usually has very limited choice. In Rome, lunch is usually served from 12.30-3pm and dinner from 8-11pm; restaurants generally close around midnight. Most places will close for one day a week, which varies from restaurant to restaurant, but is not usually at weekends. Many restaurants, especially trattorias, close for two to three weeks in August.

WINE BARS

Wine bars *(enoteche)* have become increasingly popular in Italy in recent years, offering customers the chance to sample a selection of fine wines accompanied by various hors d'oeuvres and delicate snacks, without having to order a full meal.

PIZZERIAS

Pizzerias are usually only open in the evening and are good meeting places for those who want to eat out at reasonable prices. As a result, they tend to be very popular and visitors are advised to book in advance where possible to avoid the inevitable queue outside. The addresses below include a number of pizzerias which specialise in the Neapolitan-style pizza, which is becoming more and more popular. Neapolitan-style pizzas have a rim and are thicker than the

Roman variety. The Romans tend to prefer their pizza thin, crispy and drenched in olive oil. They are also unlikely to forego the traditional *entrée* of **bruschetta** (toasted bread rubbed with raw garlic, sprinkled with salt, drizzled with olive oil and in some cases topped with freshly chopped tomatoes, basil or capers) or *fritto misto alla romana. Fritto misto* comprises a number of different seasonal delicacies, such as courgette flowers stuffed with mozzarella and anchovies, fillets of salted cod, stuffed giant green Ascoli olives, and potato croquettes dipped in batter and deep fried. Those not wishing to order pizza may like to try a **crostino** instead: this toasted bread is similar to *bruschetta*, but is covered with melted cheese and Parma ham, or perhaps with *porcini* (cep) mushrooms.

FOREIGN RESTAURANTS

As Italians tend to be very attached to their own culinary traditions, non-Italian restaurants are rather thin on the ground in Rome, with the exception of a few recently opened places serving international, Japanese or Indian cuisine. The list below includes details of some of these restaurants.

SNACKS

For those not wishing to sit down for a large meal at lunchtime, or who are on a limited budget, there are a number of self-service restaurants and places offering slices of pizza *(pizzeria al taglio)* in the city. These small stalls, which are usually only open during the day, often have a bar area with stools for customers to sit and enjoy their pizza.
In addition to the numerous *pizzerie al taglio* in the city, slices of pizza can also occasionally be bought at bakeries, some of which are particularly well known for their plain or tomato-topped pizza. Visitors should be aware that these bakeries keep shop opening hours and will not therefore be open at lunchtime.

PASTRY SHOPS AND ICE-CREAM PARLOURS

Pastry shops *(Pasticcerie)* – In addition to the larger *pasticcerie*, which offer a range of mouth-watering delicacies, Rome has a wide choice of smaller establishments which fiercely maintain the oldest traditions of confectionery. Typical Roman cakes and pastries worth trying include **panpepato**, made from flour mixed with almonds, crystallised fruit, honey, orange rind and spices, **pangiallo**, prepared with maize flour, almonds, walnuts, pine nuts and raisins, **torta di ricotta e visciole** (ricotta and sour cherry tart) of Jewish origin, **zuppa inglese** and **bignè di San Giuseppe**, puff pastry filled with cream.

Ice-cream parlours (Gelaterie) – If you ask a Roman where you can buy the best ice cream in the city, he will nearly always give you the address of a gelateria in his own neighbourhood. Good ice cream is not difficult to find in Rome and many producers have their own specialities. What better way to cool down on a hot summer's day or evening in the capital than with an ice-cream cone or a granita or grattachecca in your favourite flavour.

The grattachecca is the Roman version of the crushed ice drink known as granita elsewhere in Italy. It's sold in kiosks on street corners in the summer months. The pieces of ice, which are scraped off large blocks with a spatula, are placed in paper cups and covered with sweet, colourful syrups. Pieces of fresh fruit are then put on top.

Addresses for where to buy snacks, such as pizza by the slice, ice-cream parlours and pastry shops are given in the central section of the guide (see Selected Sights), within the district where they are located.

Relaxing in Piazza Navona

B. Pérousse/MICHELIN

FOR ALL BUDGETS

The list below gives details of restaurants, trattorias, pizzerias and wine bars to suit all tastes and budgets, divided up according to the districts described in the guide. Once again, addresses are grouped into three categories according to price, starting with the least expensive. The prices given (in euros) are based on the average cost of a meal per person, excluding drinks.

The **Budget** category includes typical trattorias, pizzerias or wine bars where the cost of a meal is under €22.

Restaurants with a more refined atmosphere serving fine cuisine for between €22 and €42 are given in the **Moderate** category and are suitable for visitors on a larger budget.

The **Expensive** category includes some of the best and most elegant restaurants in the city – with prices to match!

The prices given for each restaurant and trattoria indicate the minimum and maximum cost of a meal including a starter, a main course and a dessert, excluding drinks. An average price is indicated for wine bars, where full meals are not served. Prices are not given for each individual pizzeria; in general, expect to pay around €13 per person, including drinks, in a pizzeria, and €2.50 for a slice of pizza from a stall.

Service is usually included, although it is customary to leave a small tip on top of this if the service has been good. In those rare cases when service is not included, this is indicated on the menu; as a guideline, expect to leave about a 10% tip.

Cover charge (coperto) – According to law, the old cover charge should now be included in the price of the meals, but in some trattorias and pizzerias it is still listed separately.

Visitors should be aware that credit cards are rarely accepted in small restaurants or family-run trattorias.

Booking – It is advisable to book in advance on Fridays and Saturdays, although some small trattorias and pizzerias do not accept reservations, in which case be prepared to queue or choose another restaurant!

AND DON'T FORGET THE RED GUIDE

THE RED GUIDE ITALIA

For a more exhaustive list of places to eat consult The Red Guide Italia, which gives details on a huge range of restaurants in the capital and lists the minimum and maximum cost of a meal.

Typical Roman Cuisine

Roman cuisine is often referred to as cucina povera – peasant cooking – and is typified by its simplicity and reliance on fresh produce. A meal in a traditional Roman trattoria may start with an antipasto (hors d'œuvre) of vegetables or mixed cold meats. The primo (first) course could be any one of a number of pasta dishes – the famous **fettuccine** egg pasta, **bucatini all'amatriciana** (a sauce made with olive oil, pecorino cheese, tomatoes, onions and streaky bacon), **spaghetti alla gricia** (a type of amatriciana, but without tomato), **tonnarelli con cacio e pepe** (a cheese and pepper sauce), **gnocchi alla romana** (dumplings made from bran dough) or potato gnocchi (traditionally prepared on Thursdays), as well as the well-known **carbonara** dish. The most typical secondi – main course – include **saltimbocca** (veal escalope rolled around a slice of ham and sage), **abbacchio** – suckling lamb cooked in a chasseur sauce (alla cacciatora) or grilled on a spit (alla scottadito in the Roman dialect), **trippa** (tripe cooked with tomatoes and herbs), **coda alla vaccinara** (oxtail cooked with bacon fat, garlic, green vegetables, salt, pepper, herbs, spices and white wine), **pajata** (lamb offal) and **baccalà** (dried cod), usually fried. Typical *contorni* (side dishes) include **puntarelle** (salad flavoured with garlic and anchovies), **agretti** (another kind of very delicate salad vegetable served with vinegar), **carciofi alla giudìa** (artichoke hearts fried in olive oil with garlic and parsley), and **rughetta** (rocket, known as *rucola* in northern Italy). Cheese, especially pecorino, is often accompanied by broad beans. In the more simple *trattorias* the choice of desserts is usually limited to *tiramisù, panna cotta, crème caramel* or ice cream, but in more expensive restaurants visitors may be able to sample a home-made **torta di ricotta** or **zuppa inglese** which, despite its name, has typically Roman origins. And what better accompaniment to your meal than a carafe of white Frascati wine from the Castelli Romani region.

AVENTINO/PIRAMIDE CESTIA – TESTACCIO
• *Budget*

Pizzeria Addò Mastro 2 – *Via G. Bove 43, Piramide Cestia-Testaccio district* – ☎ 06 57 46 372 – *Closed Mon* – ✄. Deep, soft pizzas for those who enjoy the traditional Neapolitan pizza. Despite the spacious dining room and tables outside in the summer, there is never an empty table.

Tuttifrutti – *Via Luca della Robbia 5, Testaccio district* – ☎ 06 57 57 902 – *Closed Aug, Mon and school holidays – Booking recommended* – €14/26. This restaurant is run by a cultural association which gives work to young artists. The cuisine is simple, yet original, and includes appetizing *antipasti*. The white wine and chocolate are produced by Trappist monks. Pleasant atmosphere.

• *Moderate*

Lo Scopettaro – *Lungotevere Testaccio 7, Testaccio district* – ☎ 06 57 42 408 – ▤ – €23/34. This family-run *trattoria*, with its rustic decor and welcoming atmosphere, offers a range of traditional, home-made Roman dishes.

Checchino dal 1887 – *Via Monte Testaccio 30, Testaccio district* – ☎ 06 57 46 318 – *Closed 24 Dec-2 Jan, Aug, Sun and Mon – Booking recommended* – €34/62. A good address for quality Roman cuisine, accompanied by the best Italian wines. Specialities include *rigatoni alla pajata*, sweetbreads in a white wine sauce and oxtail. Cheaper meals of cheese and vegetables available at lunchtime.

CATACOMBE DI PRISCILLA (VIA NOMENTANA, VIA SALARIA)
• *Budget*

La Mora – *Piazza Crati 13, Catacombe di Priscilla district* – ☎ 06 86 20 66 13 – *lamora@lamora.it – Closed Aug and Mon* – €19/39. This friendly, informal restaurant serves typical Tuscan cuisine and crispy pizzas baked in a wood oven. Other dishes on the menu include *focaccia* with *provola* cheese and pork sausage, and, for steak-lovers, a delicious *bistecca alla fiorentina* from cattle raised in the Chiana Valley.

• *Moderate*

Dai Toscani – *Via Forlì 41, Via Nomentana district* – ☎ 06 44 23 13 02 – *Closed Aug and Sun* – ▤ – €26/41 + 10% *service*. As the name suggests, this restaurant specialises in Tuscan cuisine, including *crostini*, cooked meats, *ribollita* stew and *bistecca alla fiorentina*. Finish off your meal with traditional *cantucci* biscuits served with *Vin Santo*, a Tuscan dessert wine.

COLOSSEO – CELIO/FORI IMPERIALI/ PIAZZA VENEZIA/RIONE MONTI
• *Budget*

La Base – *Via Cavour 274/276, Fori Imperiali district* – ✄. This pizzeria-restaurant attracts a young crowd and is one of the few places in Rome where you can order a roll, a salad, a plate of spaghetti or a pizza until 5am. Famous Italian actors can often be seen here late at night.

Enoteca Al Vino al Vino – *Via dei Serpenti 19, Rione Monti district* – ☎ 06 48 58 03 – *Closed the last three weeks in Aug – Booking recommended* – €13/26. This charming wine bar has an excellent selection of wine, colourful ceramic tables and a lively atmosphere. Try the selection of cooked meats and cheeses (the saltiest of which are served with honey) and delicious Sicilian specialities. Friendly service.

• *Moderate*

Hasekura – *Via dei Serpenti 27, Rione Monti district* – ☎ 06 48 36 48 – *hasekura@tiscalinet.it – Closed Aug, for four days at Christmas and Sun* – €31. In a city with a limited choice of international cuisine, this simply furnished Japanese restaurant is noted for its fresh ingredients and excellent sushi. A trendy address which tends to offer better value for money at lunchtime.

EUR
• *Moderate*

Shangri Là-Corsetti – *Viale Algeria 141, EUR district* – ☎ 06 59 18 861 – *Closed 10-26 Aug* – ▤ – €31/52. This restaurant in the hotel of the same name is surrounded by greenery and has spacious dining rooms furnished in contemporary style. In summer, tables are also laid out around the pool. House specialities include an *antipasti* buffet and fish dishes. Attentive service.

FONTANA DI TREVI – QUIRINALE
• *Budget*

Pizzeria Est Est Est – *Via Genova 32, Quirinale district* – ☎ 06 48 81 107 – *Closed Mon and Aug* – ✄. One of the oldest pizzerias in Rome, it is known for its interior decor dating from the beginning of the 20C, and for the small cherub shown pouring the so-called "mayor's water". The white wine which gives its name to the restaurant is highly recommended.

L'Archetto – *Via dell'Archetto 26, Fontana di Trevi district* – ☎ 06 67 89 064 – ✄ – €13/26. A choice of 60 different types of pasta, all served in generous portions, including the popular three-pasta selection. Home-made mousse and tiramisù.

• **Moderate**

Maharajah – *Via dei Serpenti 124, Quirinale district* – ☎ *06 47 47 144* – ▤ – *€31/34*. An excellent address for fans of genuine Indian food, where soft lighting, exotic scents, paintings and carpets give this restaurant its decidedly Eastern flavour. The lunch menu is particularly good value for money. Warm, friendly service.

Isola Tiberina – Torre Argentina

• **Budget**

Enoteca La Bottega del Vino da Anacleto Bleve – *Via S. Maria del Pianto 9/a, Largo Argentina district* – ☎ *06 68 65 970 – Closed evenings and public holidays – Booking recommended – €10/26*. This wine bar is situated in the heart of the Jewish quarter. Before sitting down, choose from the delicate soufflés, roulades, salads and cheeses displayed at the bar. Delicious lemon or coffee ice cream. Family run with attentive service.

Quelli della Taverna – *Via dei Barbieri 25, Torre Argentina district* – ☎ *06 68 69 660 – Closed Aug, 24-26 Dec and Mon – Booking recommended – €13/21*. The Quelli della Taverna serves drinks and pasta in traditional terracotta crockery, as in days gone by. Try the *antipasti* of grilled vegetables, cooked meats and cheeses, accompanied by delicious *focaccia* served on a wooden board. Friendly atmosphere.

• **Moderate**

Al Pompiere – *Via S. Maria de' Calderari 38, Torre Argentina district* – ☎ *06 68 68 377 – Closed Sun and 15 Jul-30 Aug – €26/39*. A range of Roman-Jewish traditional dishes served in the spacious rooms of an old *palazzo*. The *crostata di ricotta e visciole* (ricotta and sour cherry tart) is highly recommended.

Sora Lella – *Via di Ponte Quattro Capi 16, Isola Tiberina district* – ☎ *06 68 61 601 – Closed Sun, 1 Jan, Easter, Aug and 24-26 Dec.* – ▤ – *€34/67*. This famous restaurant was once run by Lella Fabrizi, the sister of the actor Aldo. It is now managed by her son, who has extended the traditional range of family recipes to include new specialities. Don't miss the *formaggi alle marmellate* (cheese with sweet fruit jelly) and the home-made desserts.

Monte Mario

• **Budget**

Osteria dell'Angelo – *Via G. Bettolo 24, Monte Mario district* – ☎ *06 37 29 470 – Closed Sun and public holidays, lunchtime (except Tue and Fri) and for 10 days in Aug –* ⊄ – *€15/21*. This lively trattoria, decorated with rugby shirts, serves a selection of traditional Roman dishes, including *tonnarelli cacio e pepe*, *rigatoni con pajata*, *coda alla vaccinara* and *trippa alla romana* (see *Typical Roman Cuisine*). The fixed-price dinner menu is particularly good value for money.

Pantheon/Montecitorio

• **Budget**

Eau Vive – *Via Monterone 85, Pantheon district* – ☎ *06 68 80 10 95 – Closed Sun and Aug –* ▤ *≒ – Booking recommended – €8/26*. This restaurant is run by missionary nuns of different nationalities and is located inside the 16C Palazzo Lante, near the Pantheon. French specialities can be sampled in the large, frescoed dining room on the first floor.

Trattoria dal Cavalier Gino – *Vicolo Rosini 4, Montecitorio district* – ☎ *06 68 73 434 – Closed Sun and Aug –* ⊄ – *€18/23*. A friendly atmosphere and good food at affordable prices make this trattoria a popular choice with office workers from the surrounding neighbourhood. For this reason, and because of the restaurant's limited capacity, it can be difficult to get a table here at lunchtime.

Vecchia Locanda – *Vicolo Simibaldi 2, Pantheon district* – ☎ *06 68 80 28 31 – Closed Sun and 22 Dec-22 Jan – Booking recommended – €18/34*. Situated in a typical narrow street between Largo Argentina and the Pantheon, this small, elegant restaurant is known for its fresh home-made pasta and beef. The atmosphere is that of a traditional Roman inn, with tables outside in the summer months.

• **Moderate**

Osteria dell'Ingegno – *Piazza di Pietra 45, Montecitorio district* – ☎ *06 67 80 662 – www.osteriadellingegno.it   Closed Sun and Aug – Booking recommended – €24/36*. This charming bistro is always crowded at lunchtime. The menu includes elaborate dishes flavoured with herbs and a wide selection of charcuterie and cheeses, as well as a good choice of wine. Friendly, attentive service.

Campana – *Vicolo della Campana 18, Montecitorio district* – ☎ *06 68 67 820 – Closed Mon and Aug –* ▤ – *€26/39*. Long popular with locals, this typical Roman trattoria has now been discovered by tourists and business people, who are attracted here by the excellent food and reasonable prices. A selection of appetizing *antipasti* is laid out on the old bar.

• **Expensive**

La Rosetta – *Via della Rosetta 9, Pantheon district* – ☎ *06 68 61 002 – Closed Sat lunchtime, Sun and 8-22 Aug* ▤ – *Booking recommended – €70/108*. This restaurant is well known throughout Rome because of the high quality of its fish and seafood specialities. Don't miss the delicious Mediterranean sashimi (raw fish).

Piazza Navona/Campo dei Fiori/ Castel San Angelo

• **Budget**

Pizzeria Da Baffetto – *Via del Governo Vecchio 114, Piazza Navona district* – ☎ *06 68 61 617 –* ⊄. Excellent crispy pizza served in a traditional pizzeria which has been popular with students since the 1960s. Expect to queue, but once you're seated the service is remarkably swift.

Pizzeria La Montecarlo – *Via dei Savelli 12, Piazza Navona district* – ☎ *06 68 61 877 – Closed Mon –* ⊄. Close to the famous Pizzeria Da Baffetto, this restaurant is known for its crispy pizzas and lightly fried dishes. The home-made desserts are also excellent.

Osteria Ar Galletto – *Piazza Farnese 102, Vicolo del Gallo 1, Campo dei Fiori district –* ☎ *06 68 61 714 – Closed Sun, 14-21 Aug and 23 Dec-mid-Jan –* €9/31. This restaurant located in Piazza Farnese, not far from Campo dei Fiori, was founded in 1484 and was once known as the Osteria dei Borgia. Ham is still cut by hand in front of customers and there is a wide choice of sauces for pasta. A friendly, lively atmosphere with tables outside in summer.

Tonino – *Via del Governo Vecchio 18, Piazza Navona district –* 🖅 *–* €10/15. The size of this small *trattoria*, which has no sign outside, means that customers often have to share a table with strangers in a very friendly atmosphere. Delicious pasta and meat sauces, mopped up with home-made bread.

Enoteca Cul de Sac – *Piazza Pasquino 73, Piazza Navona district –* ☎ *06 68 80 10 94 – enoteca.culdesac@tiscalinet.it –* €13/26. Situated opposite the famous statue of Pasquino, the name of Rome's first wine bar comes from its long, narrow shape. The bar has a good selection of both Italian and foreign wines and a wide choice of hot and cold dishes.

Enoteca L'Angolo Divino – *Via dei Balestrari 12, Campo dei Fiori district –* ☎ *06 68 64 413 – Closed Sun lunchtime and Mon evening –* €15/26. This old wine and oil store has been converted into a rustic, simply furnished wine bar, lined with bottle-filled shelves. The snacks on offer include tarts and roulades. Wine tastings are regularly organised by the bar.

Da Francesco – *Piazza del Fico 29, Piazza Navona district –* ☎ *06 68 64 009 – Closed Tue lunchtime –* 🖅 *– Booking recommended –* €15/31. The attractive Piazza del Fico is home to this lively trattoria which serves typical Roman dishes, including pizzas, an excellent focaccia with dry-cured ham and various types of pasta. A cheerful atmosphere, with a mixed clientele of tourists and well-known faces.

• *Moderate*

Ditirambo – *Piazza della Cancelleria 74, Piazza Navona district –* ☎ *06 68 71 626 – Closed Mon lunchtime and Aug –* 🍽 *– Booking recommended –* €23/39. Situated directly behind Campo dei Fiori, this friendly restaurant has two small, well-furnished rooms where a range of sophisticated dishes are served. The different types of bread, the pasta and the desserts are home-made. A popular choice.

Enoteca Al Bric – *Via del Pellegrino 51, Campo dei Fiori district –* ☎ *06 68 79 533 – Closed Mon and for two weeks in Aug – Booking recommended –* €23/41. This popular bistro offers a wide choice of wines, cheeses and charcuterie from several countries, with an emphasis on French cuisine.

Costanza – *Piazza del Paradiso 63/65, Campo dei Fiori district –* ☎ *06 68 61 717 – Closed Sun and Aug –* €28/44. Traditional Italian meat and fish dishes are served in this

atmospheric restaurant-cum-museum, housed in the ruins of Pompey's theatre. Parts of the vaulting and walls date from the 1C BC.

Enoteca Il Simposio di Pietro Costantini – *Piazza Cavour 16, Castel San Angelo district –* ☎ *06 32 11 502 – Closed Sat lunchtime, Sun and public holidays –* €28/44. This spacious, well-stocked wine bar serves fine cuisine, accompanied by excellent wines at reasonable prices for the quality offered. There is a restaurant area and a bar for wine tasting.

Il Drappo – *Vicolo del Malpasso 9, Piazza Navona district –* ☎ *06 68 77 365 – Closed Sun, lunchtimes and Aug* 🍽 *– Booking recommended –* €31/36. Traditional Sardinian specialities are the order of the day in this quiet, friendly restaurant, which is decorated with draped curtains, mirrors, candles and tables set close together.

• *Expensive*

Il Convivio – *Vicolo dei Soldati 31, Piazza Navona district –* ☎ *06 68 69 432 – Closed Sun, Mon lunchtime and 9-15 Aug –* 🍽 *– Booking recommended –* €52/83. This quiet, elegant restaurant is known for its innovative cuisine based on traditional Mediterranean dishes. Discreet background music.

Camponeschi – *Piazza Farnese 50, Campo dei Fiori district –* ☎ *06 68 74 927 – Closed Sun, lunchtimes and 13-22 Aug –* 🍽 ✖ *– Booking recommended –* €59/90. The Camponeschi's menu includes several fish dishes, as well as a choice of typical Roman and international specialities. The service is professional, and the surroundings elegant, particularly in summer, when food is served at tables outside in the charming Piazza Farnese.

Piazza del Popolo/Piazza di Spagna

• *Moderate*

Margutta Vegetariano-RistorArte – *Via Margutta 118, Piazza del Popolo district –* ☎ *06 32 65 05 77 –* 🍽 *–* €26/46. This tastefully decorated restaurant, nestling amid the art galleries of Via Margutta, is known for its fine vegetarian cuisine. The two spacious rooms are also used to house exhibitions of contemporary art.

La Penna d'Oca – *Via della Penna 53, Piazza del Popolo district –* ☎ *06 32 02 898 – Closed Sun, Sat lunchtime, for 10 days in Jan and 20 days in Aug – Booking recommended –* €26/62. Not far from Piazza del Popolo, this charming restaurant serves traditional cuisine, innovative fish and seafood dishes (try the conch pie served with red onion) and home-made bread. Meals are served on a pleasant veranda in summer.

• *Expensive*

La Terrazza – *Via Ludovisi 49, Piazza di Spagna district –* ☎ *06 47 81 21 –* 🍽 *– Booking recommended –* €80/120. The roof garden of the Hotel Eden is home to this elegant restaurant, which offers stunning views of the city and is popular with famous personalities. The creative cuisine served here is mainly based on fish and seafood recipes. Prices for Sunday brunch are more affordable.

Porta Pia – Termini

• Budget

Pizzeria Al Forno della Soffitta – *Via dei Villini 1e/1f, Porta Pia district* – ☎ *06 44 04 642* – ✄. Genuine Neapolitan pizza is the speciality of this restaurant, where all the ingredients used come from the Campania region. Neapolitan-style pizzas have a rim and are thicker than the Roman variety. They are served on a round, wooden board, then cut into segments, each covered with the different ingredients chosen.

Trimani il Wine Bar – *Via Cernaia 37/b, Porta Pia district* – ☎ *06 44 69 630 – Closed Sun and public holidays and for two weeks in Aug.* – €*15/52*. This wine bar, run by one of the oldest families in the Roman wine business, offers an impressive selection of good wines and fine cuisine. Pleasant outdoor terrace for summer dining.

San Lorenzo fuori le Mura

• Budget

Pizzeria Il Ministero della Pizza – *Via die Campani 65, San Lorenzo Fuori le Mura district* – ✄. Situated in the student district, this pizzeria offers a number of first courses and specialities from Calabria, as well as pizzas. The owner is welcoming and friendly and always happy to advise customers.

Il Pulcino Ballerino – *Via degli Equi 66/68, San Lorenzo Fuori le Mura district* – ☎ *06 49 41 255 – Closed Sun and public holidays* – ✄ – €*13/26*. This pleasant and informal restaurant has hit on an original formula for Rome: customers cook their own vegetables, meat or cheese on a stone placed in the middle of their table.

Da Marcello – *Via dei Campani 12, San Lorenzo Fuori le Mura district* – ☎ *06 44 63 311 – Closed Sat evening and Sun* – ✄ – €*15/21*. This attractive *trattoria*, very popular with students, offers its customers typical Roman cuisine, including dishes such as the traditional *tonnarelli cacio e pepe, spaghetti alla gricia and spaghetti all'amatriciana.* Reasonably priced, with a good wine list.

• Moderate

Pommidoro – *Piazza dei Sanniti 44, San Lorenzo Fuori le Mura district* – ☎ *06 44 52 692 – Closed Sun* – €*26/31*. A genuine Roman *trattoria* specialising in game dishes and grilled meat and fish. Frequented by politicians, artists and journalists.

Il Dito e la Luna – *Via dei Sabelli 51, San Lorenzo Fuori le Mura district* – ☎ *06 49 40 726 – Closed lunchtime* – ✄ ▦ – *Booking recommended* – €*30/40*. This restaurant in the middle of the student district has a pleasant bistro atmosphere. Theme evenings are occasionally held here, when Sicilian recipes, such as fish *cuscus* and *caponata* (Mediterranean vegetables served cold in a sweet-sour sauce), and fine wines are often served.

Santa Maria Maggiore/ San Giovanni in Laterano

• Budget

Pizzeria La Gallina Bianca – *Via A. Rosmini 9, Santa Maria Maggiore district* –

☎ *06 47 43 777* – ✄. This popular, rustic-style pizzeria also serves excellent *fritti* (deep-fried specialities) and a wide range of vegetables. Make sure you leave space for the home-made desserts, including a tiramisù with strawberries.

• Moderate

Charly's Saucière – *Via di San Giovanni in Laterano 270, San Giovanni in Laterano district* – ☎ *06 70 49 56 66 – Closed Sat and Mon lunchtimes, Sun and 5-20 Aug* – ▦ – *Booking recommended* – €*28/36*. Renowned as one of the genuinely French restaurants in the city, Charly's Saucière has an old-fashioned, welcoming ambiance. Traditional French meat and fish dishes predominate, in addition to Swiss specialities, in honour of the chef's country of origin. Excellent desserts!

• Expensive

Agata e Romeo – *Via Carlo Alberto 45, Santa Maria Maggiore district* – ☎ *06 44 66 115 – Closed Sat-Sun, 6-12 Jan and 4-19 Aug* – ▦ – *Booking recommended* – €*52/93*. This restaurant offers excellent traditional cuisine and a range of imaginative dishes. It also has an impressive, well-researched selection of wines. Don't miss the excellent desserts, which include the well-known millefeuille.

Trastevere

• Budget

Pizzeria Panattoni – *Viale Trastevere 53, Trastevere district* – ☎ *06 58 00 919 – Closed Wed* – ✄. Locals have nicknamed Panattoni the "mortuary" because of its long, marble-topped tables. The waiters provide an efficient and courteous service.

An old façade in Trastevere

Pizzeria Dar Poeta – *Vicolo del Bologna 45, Trastevere district* – ☎ *06 58 80 516 – www.darpoeta.it* – ✄. This warm and lively pizzeria serves pizzas made from a special dough. Also on offer is a wide selection of *bruschette* and even a Ricotta and nutella calzone for those with a sweet tooth.

Augusto – *Piazza de' Renzi 15, Trastevere district* – ☎ *06 58 03 798 – Closed Sat evening and Sun* – ✄ – €*13/17*. During the summer this family-run restaurant has large wooden tables outside, overlooking one of the most typical squares in this district. The food here is simple and the atmosphere warm and informal. Expect to wait for a table.

Da Lucia – *Vicolo del Mattonato 2, Trastevere district – ☎ 06 58 03 601 – Closed Mon, for two weeks in Aug and one week at Christmas – ✂ – Booking recommended – €13/26.* This simple restaurant, founded in 1938, serves traditional Roman cuisine. Enjoy the typical atmosphere of Trastevere in summer, when you can eat outdoors in the quiet narrow street. Dishes include the local *spaghetti cacio e pepe*, *spaghetti alla gricia*, *gnocchi* on Thursday and *baccalà* on Friday (*see Typical Roman Cuisine*).

• *Moderate*

Paris – *Piazza San Callisto 7/a, Trastevere district – ☎ 06 58 15 378 – Closed Sun evening, Mon and Aug – ▤ – €28/52.* This restaurant is situated in the heart of Trastevere and offers mainly Roman-Jewish cuisine, served in an attractive Baroque-style room. Dishes include *tagliolini al sugo di pesce* (thin noodles in a fish sauce), *carciofi alla giudìa* (artichoke hearts fried in olive oil with garlic and parsley), fried vegetables, and to end your meal, delicious ricotta cheese.

Asinocotto – *Via dei Vascellari 48, Trastevere district – ☎ 06 58 98 985 – Closed Mon, lunchtimes and 15-31 Jan – Booking recommended – €31/44.* A warm, welcoming atmosphere awaits you in this simply furnished restaurant with plain white walls and a wooden ceiling. The traditional dishes served here are beautifully presented and offer excellent value for money.

Checco er Carettiere – *Via Benedetta 10, Trastevere district – ☎ 06 58 17 018 – Closed Sun evening – ▤ – €31/57.* This well-known restaurant has been serving fresh, high-quality and reasonably priced food for over 50 years. In addition to the usual Roman specialities, the menu also includes a number of fish dishes. The ice cream and desserts are home-made.

Fantasie di Trastevere – *Via S. Dorotea 6, Trastevere district – ☎ 06 58 81 671 – fantasieditrastevere@tin.it – Closed 1 Jan, Easter and 25 Dec – Booking recommended – €41/77.* A successful combination of gastronomy and culture, where diners can enjoy a folk show every evening (starting at 9.15pm).

Vaticano – San Pietro
• *Budget*

Al Limone – *Viale Angelico 64/66, Vaticano district – ☎ 06 37 22 003 – info@al limone.com – Closed Sat lunchtime and Sun – ✂ – €15/36.* Lemon is the focal point for this restaurant, including the decor and the cuisine. Innovative regional cuisine, barbecued dishes and home-made bread.

• *Moderate*

Taverna Angelica – *Piazza delle Vaschette 14/a, Vaticano district – ☎ 06 68 74 514 – Closed Sun, Mon lunchtime, 10-30 Aug and 23 Dec-3 Jan – ▤ – Booking recommended – €31/49.* This pleasant restaurant serves specialities from all over Italy. Dishes include *maltagliati ai calamari freschi* (fresh squid), *orecchiette con ricotta* (pasta with ricotta cheese) and fillet of sea bass with potato soufflé. A delightful dining experience by candlelight, with excellent service.

• *Expensive*

La Pergola – *Via Cadlolo 101, Vaticano district – ☎ 06 35 091 – Closed Sun, Mon, lunchtimes and Jan – ▤ – Booking recommended – €62/110.* Located in the roof garden of the Cavalieri Hilton Hotel, this elegant restaurant offers modern, innovative cuisine with attention to detail and impeccable service. The magnificent panorama of Rome is one of the most evocative views in Italy.

Via Veneto
• *Expensive*

Sans Souci – *Via Sicilia 20/24, Via Veneto district – ☎ 06 42 01 45 10 – Closed lunchtimes and 10-20 Aug – ▤ – Booking recommended – €59/83.* A well-established restaurant offering traditional and regional cuisine with an innovative flavour. The decor recalls the golden age of the *Dolce Vita* period.

Villa Borghese – Villa Giulia
• *Budget*

Ditta Marcello Testa il Wine Bar – *Via Metauro 31, Villa Borghese district – ☎ 06 85 30 06 92 – www.testafoodandwine.it – Closed Sun – €15/21.* This traditional English-style restaurant has recently opened its own wine bar. Prices are lower than in the restaurant and a range of interesting snacks are served to accompany the 300 wines available.

• *Moderate*

Al Ceppo – *Via Panama 2, Villa Borghese district – ☎ 06 85 51 379 – Closed Mon and 8-24 Aug – Booking recommended – €34/54.* Situated in the smart Parioli district, this restaurant has a rustic, yet elegant feel. The innovative cuisine uses seasonal produce and is based on traditional recipes. Desserts include chestnut ice cream with hot chocolate.

Services

Concessions

Visitors trying to keep costs down will find information on budget accommodation in the **Where to Stay** section which includes bed and breakfasts, *pensioni*, youth hostels, camp sites and convents and monasteries.

Discounts

BY TRAIN

The **Carta Prima** (€67.14, valid for a year) gives card-holders a 20% discount on first-class travel throughout Italy. This card is valid for the card-holder only and is non-transferable.

The **Carta Amicotreno** (€51.13, valid for a year) gives a 50% discount on some local trains and a 20% discount on many medium- and long-distance trains, and is ideal for travellers spending an extended period in Italy, doing most of their travelling by rail. Certain restrictions apply to days of travel. Concessions also apply to a companion travelling with the card-holder.

BY AIR

Several airlines offer budget fares to Rome and other destinations in Italy, although prices vary according to how far in advance the booking is made. Weekend rates and further advantages are also available for those booking on line:
Go: www.go-fly.com; Virgin Express:www.virgin-express.com; BMI (British Midland): www.flybmi.com; Ryan Air: www.ryanair.com
Alitalia has various special offers for passengers buying their ticket one, two or three weeks before departure. The airline also offers special weekend rates for travellers departing on a Saturday and returning on a Sunday of the same weekend (*tipo corto*) and for the same type of ticket, but valid for a month (*tipo lungo*).

Discounts for young people

BY TRAIN

The **Carta Verde** (€25.82, valid for a year) gives young people a 20% discount in both first and second class, on all trains within Italy, including fast Eurocity trains and Eurostar. This card is valid for the card-holder only and is non-transferable.

BY AIR

Discounted rates exist for young people aged between 12 and 26 (under 26 on the day of departure).

Discounts for senior citizens

BY TRAIN

For travellers over 60 years of age, the **Carta d'Argento** (€25.82, valid for a year) offers a 20% discount in first and second class on the Italian section of all routes, including fast Eurocity trains and Eurostar. This card is valid for the card-holder only and is non-transferable.

BY AIR

Senior citizens are also eligible for discounts on some airlines.

Discounts for families and small groups

BY TRAIN

Families and groups of at least three people and no more than five are entitled to a 20% discount in both first and second class if they are travelling together. Children aged between four and 12 travel at half-price of the discounted fare and children under four travel free. This discount is available on all trains, including the Italian sections of Eurocity trains and on Eurostar, although it is not valid in July and August, or during the Easter and Christmas holiday periods.

BY AIR

Families qualify for discounted tickets on certain airlines, if they fulfil the following conditions: the family must travel together and must comprise at least four people, with a maximum of two adults and a minimum of two children (between the ages of two and 11). At least one of the adults must be a parent of the children; the second adult does not necessarily need to be related to the family.

Practical Information

Electricity

The voltage is 220V, 50 cycles per second; the sockets are for two-pin plugs. It is therefore advisable to take an adaptor for hairdryers, shavers, computers, etc.

Emergency numbers

General Emergency Services – ☎ 113
Central Police Headquarters,
Via S. Vitale 15 – ☎ 06 46 86
Foreign Residents' Bureau,
Via S. Vitale – ☎ 06 86 21 02
ACI Emergency Breakdown Service
– ☎ 803 116
Police (emergencies) – ☎ 06 67 691
Fire Brigade – ☎ 115
Carabinieri (emergencies) – ☎ 112
Lost Property, Via N. Bettoni 1 –
☎ 06 58 16 040

Emergency Health Services – ☎ 118
Ambulance – Red Cross –
☎ 06 55 10
Permanent Medical Service –
☎ 06 58 20 10 30
San Camillo Hospital,
Circonvallazione Gianicolense 87 –
☎ 06 58 701
Policlinico A Gemelli (hospital),
Largo Gemelli 8 – ☎ 06 30 151
Umberto I Hospital, Viale del
Policlinico 155 – ☎ 06 49 971/06 49 97
09 00

FOREIGN EMBASSIES AND CONSULATES IN ROME

Australia – Via Alessandria 215, 00198
Rome; ☎ 06 85 27 21;
www.australian-embassy.it
Canada – Via GB de Rossi 27, 00161
Rome; ☎ 06 44 59 81;
rome@dfait-maeci.gc.ca
Ireland – Piazza di Campitelli 3, 00186
Rome; ☎ 06 69 79 121;
Fax 06 67 92 354
UK – Via XX Settembre 80a, Rome;
☎ 06 42 20 00 01; Fax 06 48 73 324
USA – Via Veneto 119a, 00187 Rome;
☎ 06 46 741; Fax 06 48 82 672;
www.usembassy.it

MONEY

The unit of currency is the **euro**
which is issued in notes (€5, €10, €20,
€50, €100, €200 and €500) and in
coins (1 cent, 2 cents, 5 cents, 10
cents, 20 cents, 50 cents, €1 and €2).

BANKS

Banks are usually open Monday to
Friday, 8.30am-1.30pm and 2.30pm-
4pm. Some branches open in the city
centre and shopping centres on
Saturday mornings, almost most are
closed on Saturdays, Sundays and
public holidays. Most hotels will
change travellers' cheques. Money
can be changed in post offices (except
travellers' cheques), money-changing
bureaux and at railway stations and
airports. Commission is always
charged.

CREDIT CARDS

Payment by credit card is widespread
in shops, hotels and restaurants and
also some petrol stations. *The Red
Guide Italia* and *The Red Guide Europe*
indicate which credit cards are
accepted at hotels and restaurants.
Money may also be withdrawn from a
bank but may incur interest pending
repayment.

NEWSPAPERS

The main Roman newspapers
(available throughout Italy) are *La
Repubblica, Il Messaggero* and *Il Giorno*.
The *Osservatore Romano* is the official
newspaper of the Vatican City.
Foreign newspapers are widely
available throughout the city.

PHARMACIES

These are identified by a red and
white cross. When closed each will
advertise the names of the pharmacy
on duty and a list of doctors on call.
Some of the most central 24hr
pharmacies include those at: Piazza
dei Cinquecento 49/50/51 (Termini
Station), Via Cola di Rienzo 213/215,
Corso Vittorio Emanuele 343/343A,
Corso Rinascimento 44/50, Piazza
Barberini 49, Via Arenula 73, Piazza
della Repubblica 67 and Via
Nazionale 228.

POSTAL SERVICES

In Italy post offices are open from
8.30am-1.50pm (Sat 11.50am). In the
city centre some post offices also open
in the afternoon on weekdays until
6pm and Sat until 2pm. The main post
office is at Piazza San Silvestro, and is
open day and night; letters sent **poste
restante** *(fermo posta)* can be collected
from this post office.
To phone or send a telegram abroad,
go either to the main post office or to
Telecom in Via Santa Maria in Via
(offices open until 10pm). Stamps are
sold in post offices and tobacconists.

TELECOMMUNICATIONS

The telephone service is organised by
TELECOM ITALIA (formerly SIP).
Each office has public booths where
the customer pays for units used
(scatti) at the counter after the call.
Reduced rates operate after 6.30pm
and even less between 10pm-8am.

PHONE CARDS

Phone cards *(schede telefoniche)* are
sold in denominations of €1, €2.50, €5
and €8 and are supplied by CIT offices
and post offices as well as tobacconists
(sign bearing a white T on a black
background).

PUBLIC PHONES

Telephone boxes may be operated
by telephone cards (sold in post
offices and tobacconists) and by
telephone credit cards. To make a call:
lift the receiver, insert payment, await
dialling signal, punch in the required
number and wait for a response.

TELEPHONING

It is now mandatory to dial the area
code (06 for Rome) for all telephone
numbers, even when making a local
call.
For international calls dial 00 plus the
following country codes:
61 for Australia
1 for Canada
64 for New Zealand
44 for the UK
1 for the USA
If calling from outside the country, the
international code for Italy is 39 and
the code for Rome is 06. Dial the full
area code, even when making an
international call; for example, when

Conversion Tables

Weights and measures

| 1 kilogram (kg) | 2.2 pounds (lb) | 2.2 pounds |
| 1 metric ton (tn) | 1.1 tons | 1.1 tons |

to convert kilograms to pounds, multiply by 2.2

| 1 litre (l) | 2.1 pints (pt) | 1.8 pints |
| 1 litre | 0.3 gallon (gal) | 0.2 gallon |

to convert litres to gallons, multiply by 0.26 (US) or 0.22 (UK)

| 1 hectare (ha) | 2.5 acres | 2.5 acres |
| 1 square kilometre (km²) | 0.4 square miles (sq mi) | 0.4 square miles |

to convert hectares to acres, multiply by 2.4

1 centimetre (cm)	0.4 inches (in)	0.4 inches
1 metre (m)	3.3 feet (ft) - 39.4 inches - 1.1 yards (yd)	
1 kilometre (km)	0.6 miles (mi)	0.6 miles

to convert metres to feet, multiply by 3.28, kilometres to miles, multiply by 0.6

Clothing

Women	EU	US	UK		EU	US	UK	Men
	35	4	2½		40	7½	7	
	36	5	3½		41	8½	8	
	37	6	4½		42	9½	9	
Shoes	38	7	5½		43	10½	10	**Shoes**
	39	8	6½		44	11½	11	
	40	9	7½		45	12½	12	
	41	10	8½		46	13½	13	
	36	6	8		46	36	36	
	38	8	10		48	38	38	
Dresses &	40	10	12		50	40	40	**Suits**
suits	42	12	14		52	42	42	
	44	14	16		54	44	44	
	46	16	18		56	46	48	
	36	30	8		37	14½	14½	
	38	32	10		38	15	15	
Blouses &	40	34	12		39	15½	15½	**Shirts**
sweaters	42	36	14		40	15¾	15¾	
	44	38	16		41	16	16	
	46	40	18		42	16½	16½	

Sizes often vary depending on the designer. These equivalents are given for guidance only.

Speed

kph	10	30	50	70	80	90	100	110	120	130
mph	6	19	31	43	50	56	62	68	75	81

Temperature

Celsius (°C)	0°	5°	10°	15°	20°	25°	30°	40°	60°	80°	100°
Fahrenheit (°F)	32°	41°	50°	59°	68°	77°	86°	104°	140°	176°	212°

To convert Celsius into Fahrenheit, multiply °C by 9, divide by 5, and add 32.
To convert Fahrenheit into Celsius, subtract 32 from °F, multiply by 5, and divide by 9.

calling Rome from the UK,
dial 00 39 06, followed by the
correspondent's number.

Useful numbers – Directory
Enquiries: ☎ 12; Directory Enquiries
(addresses): ☎ 14 12; International
Enquiries: ☎ 176; Urgent Calls:
☎ 197; TIM Customer Service: ☎ 119;
OMNITEL Customer Care: ☎ 190;
Traffic Information: ☎ 155.

TOBACCONISTS

Besides cigarettes and tobacco,
tabacchi sell postcards and stamps,
confectionery, phone cards, public
transport tickets, lottery tickets and
such like. Those at Via del Corso 11
and Viale Trastevere 275 stay open all
night.

Sightseeing

Information on admission times and
charges for museums and monuments
is given in the Selected Sights section
of the guide.
Admission times and charges are
liable to alteration without prior
notice. Because of fluctuations in the
cost of living and the constant change
in opening times, the information
given in this guide should merely
serve as a guideline. Visitors are
advised to phone ahead to confirm
opening times.
The admission prices indicated are
for single adults benefiting from no
special concession; reductions for
children, students, the over-60s and
parties should be requested on site
and be endorsed with proof of ID.
Special conditions often exist for
groups but arrangements should be
made in advance. For nationals of
European Union member countries,
State-run or City of Rome-run
museums provide free admission to
visitors under 18 and over 65 with
proof of identification, and a 50%
reduction for visitors under 25 years
of age.
During National Heritage Week, which
takes place at a different time each
year, access to a large number of
sights is free of charge. Contact the
tourist offices for more detailed
information.
When visits to museums, churches
or other sites are accompanied by
a custodian, it is customary to leave
a donation.

MUSEUMS, ARCHAEOLOGICAL SITES AND GARDENS

Museums are closed all day Mondays;
on other days ticket offices usually
shut 30min or 1hr before closing time.
Ancient monuments, archaeological
sites and public parks (Roman Forum,
Colosseum etc) close about one hour
before dusk according to the following
timetable:
9am-3pm, 1 Nov-mid Jan
9am-3.30pm, mid Jan-mid Feb
9am-4pm, mid Feb-mid Mar
9am-4.30pm, mid Mar-last day of
winter time
9am-5.30pm, first day of summer
time-mid Apr
9am-6pm, mid Apr-1 Sep
9am-5.30pm, 2 Sep-last day of summer
time
9am-4.30pm, first day of winter time-
30 Sep
9am-4pm, 1–31 Oct
Many museums require visitors to
leave bags and backpacks in a luggage
deposit area at the museum entrance.
Taking photos with a flash is usually
forbidden.

CHURCHES

The major basilicas (St Peter's, St John
Lateran, St Paul Without the Walls,
St Mary Major) are open from 7am-
6pm but most churches close at noon
and reopen in the afternoon from
4-8pm; exceptions are marked in
the Selected Sights section.
Visitors should be appropriately
dressed: long trousers for men; no
bare shoulders or very short skirts for
women. Those who do not observe
this convention may be refused entry
by the Verger or others in authority.
Churches are closed during services
and so tourists should avoid visiting at
that time. Visitors are advised to visit
churches in the morning, when the
natural light provides better
illumination of the works of art; also
churches are occasionally forced to
close in the afternoons because of lack
of staff.
As many of the works of art are
positioned high up, it is a good idea
to take binoculars. Small change is
needed for the light switches.

GUIDED TOURS

Travel agents and the ATAC offices in
Piazza del Cinquecento provide details
of organised guided tours in foreign
languages. For independent group
visits contact the Sindacato Nazionale
CISL, Centro Guide Turistiche,
Via S. Maria alle Fornaci, 8
☎ 06 63 90 409.

Ideas for your Visit

The aim of the suggestions outlined below is to help you plan your visit to Rome. These include day itineraries for those on a short break, as well as ideas for those on a longer visit to the capital. The Themed Visits section highlights aspects of the city for those with special interests.

Walks described in the Selected Sights section will give visitors with more time available interesting insights into Italy's capital.

Weekend Breaks

A SNAPSHOT OF ROME

Day 1 – One of the highlights of Rome is, of course, the **Colosseum**. Start your sightseeing at this famous monument and then continue to the **Imperial Fora**, with the imposing **monument to Victor Emmanuel II** in the background.

Once you've climbed the staircase leading to **Piazza del Campidoglio**, retrace your steps and make your way to the **Pantheon** and the attractive Piazza della Rotonda, strolling from here to Piazza Navona. Take a rest at the **Antico Caffè della Pace**, where you can sit back, watch the world go by and admire this lovely square. If you are still in the neighbourhood at nightfall, make sure you return to the square to see the fountains illuminated – a truly romantic sight. In the evening, after dinner, why not take a walk to the magnificent **Trevi Fountain?** This famous monument is one of the best-known sights in Rome and, as a result, its tiny piazza is always crowded, but the view is well worth it.

Day 2 – Visitors interested in churches and museums should spend the morning visiting **St Peter's** and the **Vatican** (even the briefest of visits requires at least half a day); those more interested in ancient civilisations may like to explore the **Roman Forum**.

In the afternoon, make your way to **Piazza di Spagna** to admire the Spanish Steps and then enjoy a stroll along the elegant **Via dei Condotti** and Rome's main shopping street, the **Via del Corso**.

The **district of Trastevere** is the perfect choice for the evening, where you can combine a walk through one of the most typical areas of medieval Rome with an enjoyable dinner at one of its many local trattorias.

ANCIENT ROME

Rome is first and foremost the city of the Ancient Romans. Much of the ancient city is still visible, although imagination is required to visualise the original splendour of the ancient monuments from the ruins and fragments that you see today.

Day 1 – The **Colosseum** is the best starting point for your walk. This grandiose amphitheatre was once the venue for shows and games, and its imposing size still recalls its former days of glory. Spend time admiring the **Arch of Constantine** which stands behind the Colosseum and which is still almost completely intact. A stroll through the **Roman Forum** will take you past remains of columns, arches and other ruins; a visit to the excavations on the **Palatine Hill** is also highly recommended, although it's a good idea to avoid both these sites in the middle of the day. If it is particularly hot, make plans to return in the cool of the morning. You may like to finish your walk with a stroll to the attractive Piazza della Rotonda to admire the **Pantheon**, followed by a well-earned rest in one of the many pleasant cafés in this district.

Day 2 – If you visited the Roman Forum on Day 1, then today you may like to visit the **Imperial Fora** and **Trajan's Market**, followed by **Caracalla's Baths**. A long walk along the **Appian Way** and a visit to one of the catacombs will complete this day of sightseeing exploring the very spirit of Ancient Rome.

BAROQUE ROME

Few cities are able to equal Rome in terms of Baroque splendour. Many of the greatest 17C artists lived and worked in Rome, including famous names such as Bernini, Borromini, Caravaggio and Pietro da Cortona.

Day 1 – Piazza Navona is the obvious starting point for today's sightseeing, with its magnificent Baroque masterpieces by Bernini (the Fountain of the Four Rivers) and Borromini (the Church of Sant'Agnese in Agone). Also worth seeing to the east of the piazza is the small church of **Sant'Ivo alla Sapienza**; from here, a short walk takes you to **Sant'Andrea della Valle**, one of the most elegant of the Baroque churches, and then on to the opulent interior of the **Chiesa del Gesù**.

The afternoon could be spent visiting the **Galleria Doria Pamphili**, whose masterpieces include the famous *Rest after the Flight into Egypt* by Caravaggio. From here it is a short walk to the delightful **Piazza Sant'Ignazio**, a small square designed in imitation of a theatre set.

Day 2 – Begin your visit with the lively **Piazza di Spagna**, and the nearby Baroque churches of **Sant'Andrea al Quirinale** and **San Carlo alle Quattro Fontane**. Not far away is the beautiful palazzo which was once home to Cardinal Barberini and his family, and which now houses a rich collection of 17C paintings. Cross the Tiber to admire the memorable **St Peter's Basilica**, then return to the **Villa Borghese,** where you can admire sculptures by Bernini and rest on one of the benches in the villa's attractive gardens. A wonderful way of ending the day is to make your way to the famous **Trevi Fountain**, best seen when illuminated at night. Throw a coin in the fountain and, according to popular legend, you are assured that you will return one day to Rome.

St Peter's Basilica at night

G. Biadzin/MICHELIN

Longer Breaks

The one-day itineraries listed below are designed specifically for visitors who are spending a few days in the capital and who wish to see as much as possible in a relatively short space of time.

Visitors interested in monuments dating from a particular historical and artistic period should consult the list on the right of the map of Principal Sights at the beginning of the guide, as well as the suggestions for Ancient Rome and Baroque Rome given above. Maps of the various sights can be found at the beginning of the guide and within the chapters in the Selected Sights section *(see index at the end of the guide).*

OPTION 1

Spend the first part of the day in the fora, starting in the **Imperial Fora**, and then continuing to the **Roman Forum** and the **Palatine Hill,** concentrating on the most important monuments (marked with stars in the main text) in all sites. You may also wish to visit the **Domus Aurea** (Nero's Golden House), not far from the Colosseum.

Continue with a visit to the **Colosseum** itself, pausing to admire the **Arch of Constantine** on the way, then make your way to the **Basilica of St John Lateran**. En route to the basilica, make a brief stop at **San Clemente** to admire its magnificent mosaics.

OPTION 2

Start at the busy **Piazza Venezia**, dominated by the imposing bulk of the **monument to Victor Emmanuel II** and continue towards the **Santa Maria d'Aracoeli** steps. After pausing to admire the Renaissance elegance of **Piazza del Campidoglio**, spend some time in the **Capitoline Museums**, concentrating on the museum's most important exhibits. The **Chiesa del Gesù**, with its magnificent interior, is just a short walk away. From here the walk continues to the **Pantheon**, an exceptional domed building dating from the 1C BC, and then on to **Piazza Navona**. The nearby church of **San Luigi dei Francesi** houses masterpieces by Caravaggio. Other churches well worth a visit nearby include **Santa Maria della Pace**, the hidden gem of **Sant'Ivo alla Sapienza**, and **Sant'Andrea della Valle**.

OPTION 3

Begin at the colourful market in **Piazza Campo dei Fiori**. Having soaked up the atmosphere of this picturesque little square, continue to the quieter **Piazza Farnese**, overlooked by the beautiful *palazzo* of the same name.

A stroll along Via di Monserrato and the elegant **Via Giulia** will bring you to **Castel Sant'Angelo**. It is a short walk from this papal fortress to the centre of religious Rome: Via della Conciliazione leads directly to **St Peter's**, the heart of the Roman Catholic Church. After admiring the famous square and enjoying a short tour inside the basilica, make your way to the magnificent **Vatican Museums**, where you can visit the Sistine Chapel – the highlight of any trip to Rome.

OPTION 4

After visiting **Santa Maria Maggiore**, a long walk will take you towards **Piazza di Spagna**. En route it is worth stopping at **San Carlo alle Quattro Fontane** and **Sant'Andrea al Quirinale**, as well as making a short detour via **Piazza del Quirinale** to the **Trevi Fountain**. Explore the district

You can't leave Rome without taking a photo of the Trevi Fountain!

between **Piazza di Spagna** and **Piazza del Popolo**, strolling along some of the most elegant streets in Rome (**Via del Corso** and **Via dei Condotti** for the lastest fashions and gold, **Via Margutta** for arts and crafts and **Via del Babuino** for antiques). At sunset, climb the Pincian Hill to admire the breathtaking view of the city from the gardens.

Themed Visits

FRESCOES IN ROME

Frescoes that should not be missed include those in the **Sistine Chapel** and **Raphael Rooms** in the **Vatican Museums**; also worthy of note here is the **chapel of Nicholas V**, painted in the 15C by Fra' Angelico and Benozzo Gozzoli, and the Chiaroscuri Rooms, adorned with unusual monochrome frescoes painted by pupils of Raphael. Staying on the same side of the Tiber, you may wish to visit the magnficent **Villa Farnesina**, beautifully decorated with 16C frescoes by Raphael, Giulio Romano, Giovanni da Udine, Baldassarre Peruzzi and Sodoma. From here, a walk up the Janiculum Hill takes you to the church of **San Pietro in Montorio** which houses the fresco of the **Flagellation** by Sebastiano del Piombo. In Trastevere, discover a masterpiece of medieval painting, the fresco of the **Last Judgement** by Pietro Cavallini, in the church of **Santa Cecilia**. Crossing the Tiber by the Ponte Garibaldi, continue to the **Chiesa del Gesù** to admire the **frescoes** by Baciccia on the ceiling, and then climb the steps of **Santa Maria d'Aracoeli** to see the **frescoes** by **Pinturicchio** in the chapel of San Bernardino da Siena. A diversion through the centre of the historic city will take you to the Caelian Hill and the basilica of **San Clemente**, which houses 15C **frescoes** by Masolino da Panicale in the chapel of Santa Caterina.

Returning to Piazza Venezia and then heading towards the Pantheon, pause in the splendid Baroque church of **Sant'Ignazio** to admire the **fresco on the ceiling** with its unusual trompe-l'œil effect. The Carafa chapel in the church of **Santa Maria sopra Minerva** is adorned with delicate 15C **frescoes** by Filippino Lippi. The church of **San Luigi dei Francesi** towards the Piazza Navona district is decorated with **17C frescoes** by Il Domenichino, illustrating the legend of St Cecilia in the chapel of the same name. Cross Corso Vittorio Emanuele to reach the 16C **Palazzo della Cancelleria**, whose Sala dei Cento Giorni is adorned with a historical fresco, painted by Vasari in 100 days. On the other side of the city, the church of **Santa Maria del Popolo** houses the **fresco** of the Adoration of the Child by Pinturicchio in the Della Rovere chapel; the **salon** of **Palazzo Barberini**, overlooking the square of the same name, contains a Baroque fresco by Pietro da Cortona, celebrating the glory of the Barberini family.

MUSEUMS IN ROME

Of major importance in the city – how could it be otherwise? – are the museums dedicated to Ancient Rome. The collections of the **Museo Nazionale Romano** are housed in a number of different locations, the most important of which are the **Palazzo Massimo alle Terme**, the **Aula Ottagona** and **Palazzo Altemps**. Further exhibits can also be seen in the **Sezione Epigrafica e Protostorica** (at Diocletian's Baths) and at the **Crypta Balbi**. The **Capitoline Museums**, dedicated mainly to Roman art, are also of major importance. Unusual for its layout and location in an old power station is the **Centrale Montemartini**, situated slightly outside the historic centre. Visitors interested in seeing for themselves how Ancient Rome once looked should make their way to the **Museo della Civiltà Romana**, where they can admire a large model of Rome during the period of Constantine, as well as models of the low reliefs adorning Trajan's Column.

Etruscan art has pride of place in the **Museo Nazionale di Villa Giulia**, which houses some of the most beautiful and interesting works of art from this period.

Visitors with a particular interest in Renaissance and Baroque art are spoilt for choice in Rome. The most important galleries include the **Galleria Borghese**, which exhibits both Renaissance masterpieces (Raphael) and works by Baroque masters such as Bernini and Caravaggio, to name two of the most famous; the **Galleria Doria Pamphili**, with paintings by Carracci, Caravaggio, Velázquez and Titian; and the **Galleria d'Arte Antica** in **Palazzo Barberini**, whose most important exhibits include paintings by Sodoma and Raphael.

Art from outside Europe can be admired in the **Museo Preistorico Etnografico L Pigorini** situated in the EUR district. The interesting **Museo delle Arti e Tradizioni Popolari Italiane** is also located in the same area.

Lastly, the best-known and most important museum in Rome, the **Vatican Museums**, is actually a group of museums housing a vast collection of paintings, sculptures and other exhibits from both ancient and modern civilisations.

ART AND GARDENS

The following suggestions combine visits to art galleries and museums with leisurely strolls through quiet parks and gardens (known as *ville* in Italian), which provide welcome respite from the incessant noise of the city's traffic. The most famous of Rome's public gardens is without a doubt the **Villa Borghese,** started in the 17C by the cardinal of the same name and now busy on Sundays with locals walking, jogging and enjoying the fresh air. After strolling past its lakes and statues, spend some time in the magnificent **Galleria Borghese**, home to splendid works by Raphael, Bernini and Caravaggio. If visiting the **Vatican Museums** has left you exhausted, what better way to relax than exploring the Vatican City and its beautiful **gardens** (reservation necessary). The walk suggested in the GIANICOLO chapter is ideal for those wishing to combine gardens, museums, shaded avenues and Renaissance residences: walk from **Villa Farnesina** to the **Orto Botanico**, visit **San Pietro in Montorio**, and finish with the panoramic **Janiculum walk**. Conclude your visit to the **Capitoline Museums** on Capitol Hill in the heart of Ancient Rome with a stroll through the elegant, shaded gardens behind the Palazzo dei Conservatori, on the site of the legendary Tarpeian Rock. After admiring the magnificent **mosaics in the church of San Clemente** or after a tiring walk among the ruins of the **Forum** and the **Colosseum**, why not take a relaxing stroll in the delightful **Villa Celimontana park**. Another green oasis dotted with old churches is the Aventine Hill: enjoy the view from the panoramic **Giardino degli Aranci** (Parco Savello) next to **Santa Sabina**, an impressive palaeo-Christian church founded in the 5C, or combine a visit to **Santa Prisca** with a walk through the rose gardens, the **Roseto**

Comunale. Nor should you miss the **Casina delle Civette,** nestling in the elegant Villa Torlonia gardens on Via Nomentana, with its interesting collection of **Liberty stained-glass windows**.

UNUSUAL SIGHTS

The following suggestions include a number of unusual sights or views in the city. Perhaps the most famous is the view of St Peter's visible through the **keyhole** of n° 3, Piazza dei Cavalieri di Malta, on the Aventine Hill. Further south in the city stands the **Cestius Pyramid**, the unusual mausoleum of a Roman magistrate who lived during the time of Augustus. The **Centrale Montemartini**, where a collection of ancient sculptures from the Capitoline Museums provide an interesting contrast to the turbines and engines of the old power station, is also of modern architectural interest. If you happen to be in this part of the city in the evening, make sure you visit the nearby **Testaccio district** with its myriad bars and restaurants, and the **Testaccio Village** (*see Going Out for the Evening*), the setting for concerts and shows in summer.

Back in the historic centre, why not explore the many crypts and reliquaries of the city? The crypt of **Santa Maria della Concezione**, in Via Veneto, contains the bones of around 4 000 Capuchin monks, some of which are incorporated into its macabre decoration. According to legend, the head of St John the Baptist, who was beheaded at the request of Salome, has been housed in the church of **San Silvestro in Capite** in the square of the same name for almost 1 000 years. In Via Giulia, the **oratory of Santa Maria della Morte** is known for its highly unusual decor: the skulls inserted into the walls recall the fact that the order that once lived here was responsible for the organisation of Christian funerals for the poor (*the oratory is only open for mass on Sunday evening at 6pm and is closed during August*).

The eclectic architectural style of the small *palazzi* around **Piazza Mincio** in the **Coppedè district** dates from the beginning of the 20C. To the north of the city, not far from Porta Pia, the nearby **Villini district** is of the same period; the unusual **Villino Ximenes** is worthy of particular note here. Although Rome is the very heart of the Roman Catholic Church, it is also home to a modern **mosque** built in bold architectural style on the slopes of Monte Antenne, as well as to a **synagogue,** constructed in the heart of the old Jewish district, and an interesting **Museum of Jewish Art**. Lastly, the sporting complex of the

Foro Italico, built during the Fascist period and renovated for the 1960 Olympic Games, is also worthy of note. The complex includes a swimming pool, the Marble Stadium, the Olympic Stadium and, on the opposite bank of the Tiber, the Palazzetto dello Sport.

FOUNTAINS

Rome's many fountains are part of its charm and include grandiose Baroque creations, as well as more modest, traditional sculptures. Only the most famous or most unusual are mentioned below, although you are sure to come across many other delightful examples as you explore the city. Visitors wishing to learn more of the history of these fountains should refer to the index, or log onto the www.romaturismo.it website. Without a doubt, the best known of the city's fountains and one of the most famous images of Rome is the **Trevi Fountain**, which dominates the small piazza of the same name. Of equal renown are the three **fountains in Piazza Navona**, in particular the Fountain of the Four Rivers, a magnificent sculpture by Bernini. After window shopping along the elegant Via Condotti, you will come to the busy Spanish Steps, popular with tourists and locals alike, where you can admire the unusual **Fontana della Barcaccia (boat fountain)**. Legend states that the Via del Babuino (Baboon Street) took its name from the silenus on the **fountain close to the church of Sant'Atanasio**, given the statue's resemblance to a monkey. The **Fontana della Botticella**, located close to Augustus's Mausoleum and built by boatmen from Ripetta, is also of interest. The area between Via Veneto and Via XX Settembre is dotted with fountains: the **Fontana del Tritone** (Triton fountain) and the **Fontana delle Api (bee fountain)**, the symbol of the Barberini family, both by Bernini; the **four 16C fountains** adorning the crossroads of Via delle Quattro Fontane and Via XX Settembre, constructed by private citizens during the urban renovation promised by Sixtus V; and the **Fontana dell'Acqua Felice,** crowned with a monumental statue of Moses. When exploring the area around the Pantheon, you may like to cool down at the 16C **fountain in Piazza della Rotonda** which, like so many others in Rome, was sculpted by Giacomo della Porta; in the same district is the typical **Fontana del Facchino,** the subject of a local legend *(see PANTHEON)*. The Campo dei Fiori district is full of fountains: the **fountain in Piazza Sant'Andrea della Valle**, the **fountains in Piazza Farnese**, the **Fontana del Mascherone**

in Via Giulia, and the **Fontana della Terrina** which once adorned the Piazza di Campo dei Fiori and was moved to Piazza della Chiesa Nuova at the beginning of the last century. Other fountains worthy of note include the delightful **Fontana delle Tartarughe** (turtle fountain) near Largo Argentina which, according to legend, was built in a single night; the 16C **fountain in Piazza d'Aracoeli** at the foot of Capitol Hill; the unusual **Fontana della Navicella**, opposite the church of Santa Maria in Domnica; and the monumental **Fontana Paola** on the Janiculum ... the list is endless!

Trevi Fountain (detail)

BRIDGES AND BANKS OF THE TIBER

The Tiber, which cuts the city in two, provides some fascinating views of the city *(for information on boat trips, see Other Ways of Exploring the City)*. The following suggestions offer a number of interesting views of the river, following it either on foot or by bike (short sections of the river bank have proper cycle tracks). Although major roads run alongside the river, often carrying heavy traffic, the footpaths, shaded by lovely plane trees, still provide a pleasant walk, perhaps because the sight of the water below has a relaxing and soothing effect. The most attractive section of the river bank for walkers is without a doubt the stretch from the Ara Pacis Augustae to Piazza Bocca della Verità, near the site of the Ancient Romans' trading and military ports. The peaceful **Isola Tiberina**, still home to the Hospital of the Brothers of St John of God, has a charm of its own, and the bridges which connect the island to the two banks of the river are particularly evocative: **Ponte Cestio** leads to Trastevere and the Janiculum, and **Ponte Fabricio**, which has survived intact since it was built in the 1C BC, leads to the synagogue and the old Jewish quarter on the opposite bank. Nearby is **Ponte Sisto**, built in the 15C by Pope Sixtus IV, which crosses the Tiber near Piazza Trilussa, a delightful corner of Trastevere; from the bridge there is a good view of the tiled rooftops of the Janiculum district. Another unforgettable view is to be had from **Ponte Sant'Angelo**, the arches of which date from the time of the Emperor Hadrian, but which was embellished with its beautiful angels, the work of Bernini, in the 17C. You may wish to continue as far as **Ponte Milvio**, the site of the famous battle which took place in AD 312 between Constantine and Maxentius; the bridge which stands today is the result of restoration work carried out in the 15C and 19C.

BIRD'S-EYE VIEWS

The best time to enjoy a view of the tiled rooftops and marble domes of the capital is undoubtedly at sunset, when the sky is streaked with pale red in winter and blazing scarlet in summer. Don't miss the magnificent **view from the Janiculum**: for this, make your way to the small square opposite San Pietro in Montorio or the piazza in front of the Bambin Gesù Hospital, where you will be rewarded by one of the most romantic views of the city from almost any point on the Janiculum Walk. Equally impressive is the wide panorama from Piazzale Napoleone I in the **gardens on the Pincian Hill**, or the splendid view from the **dome of St Peter's**. Views of the city can also be enjoyed from **Piazza del Campidoglio**. For the best views, however, take a seat at the **Caffè Capitolino**, in Palazzo Caffarelli, or pause in the **Galleria del Palazzo Senatorio** during your visit to the Capitoline Museums. For an excellent view of the Roman Forum, walk along Via del Campidoglio to behind the Palazzo Senatorio, or climb the Palatine Hill, where the views from the **Orti Farnesiani** extend from the temples in the forum to the Basilica of Maxentius, the bell-tower of San Francesca Romana, and the Colosseum. Enjoy another fine view

of Rome from the **terrace of Castel Sant'Angelo:** this panorama sweeps across the city, from the Borghese Gardens, to the unmistakable dome of the Pantheon, the monument to Victor Emmanuel II, and the impressive dome of St Peter's. Two final suggestions are the view from the **portico of the monument to Victor Emmanuel II** and the delightful view from the peaceful **Giardino degli Aranci** (Parco Savello) near Santa Sabina on the Aventine Hill.

Gardens

Rome has a number of lovely parks and gardens where visitors can escape the hustle and bustle of the city and where locals meet for the traditional first picnic of summer, or simply for a stroll in the shade of the magnificent pine trees. Most of these gardens, known as *ville* (villas) because they once belonged to families of the nobility, are open from dawn to dusk.

Villa Borghese – In this large, popular park, decorated with statues and fountains, it is still possible to find quiet areas, such as the Giardino del Lago, an English-style garden with magnolias, aloe and yucca, or the Italian-style Parco dei Daini. For those interested in aerobics, free classes are held every weekend near the Casina dell'Orologio. A visit to the Bioparco, with its mammals, reptiles and birds, is a must for children.

Roseto di Roma – This rose garden on the Aventine Hill is open exclusively when the roses are in bloom (end of April to end of June). Prizes are awarded annually to new varieties and the prize-giving ceremony draws great crowds.

Villa Sciarra – Situated in the Monteverde Vecchio district, this park is full of statues, fountains and antiquities. It rediscovered its Baroque charm at the beginning of the century and is renowned for its collection of plants. The park also accommodates the library of the Italian Institute for Germanic Studies.

Villa Celimontana – *COLOSSEO-CELIO*
This is one of the few parks in Rome with a skating rink. It provides a popular backdrop for wedding photos and in summer hosts jazz concerts.

Villa Ada Savoia – *CATACOMBE DI PRISCILLA*
This park has recently undergone a programme of major restoration during which it acquired a cycle track, a network of signed trails and nature paths, and a recently-restored small temple. The park is also home to the Egyptian Embassy, one of the WWF's

A fountain in the Pincio gardens

G. Bludzin/MICHELIN

offices, riding stables and carousels for children. Bicycles can be hired from near the main lake, where free aerobic classes are held every weekend. A number of concerts are held in the park in summer as part of the *Estate Romana* festival.

Villa Torlonia – *CATACOMBE DI PRISCILLA*
A rare species of palm tree, known as the Californian palm, grows in this park, the former residence of the Mussolini family. The **Casina delle Civette** *(see Selected Sights)*, with its collection of Liberty-style stained glass, designs and other articles, is open to the public.

Villa Glori – *PARIOLI district*
This spacious garden with its many olive trees has pony rides and traditional donkey rides for children.

Villa Doria Pamphili – *GIANICOLO district*
This park is considered to be the lungs of the western part of the city and is very popular late in the evening with athletes and kite flyers. It houses a number of buildings (Palazzina Algardi, arches from the Paolo acquaduct, the Casino del Bel Respiro and Villa Vecchia), greenhouses, and a 18C lake, as well as many rare plants, including the camphor tree.

Parco dell'Appia Antica – This park has finally rediscovered its original appearance after major restoration work. Guided tours are organised here on Sundays, led by specialists who provide information on the monuments and villas of the past, along a route which can also be followed by bicycle.

Orto Botanico di Villa Corsini – Not far from Trastevere, these gardens have a wonderful variety of cacti, orchids and tropical plants. A small garden of flowers and plants with particularly strong scents has been planted for the benefit of the visually-impaired. Trees grown here include a species known to have existed more than 300 million years ago.

Riserva Naturale di Monte Mario – This aim of this nature reserve is to protect vegetation and animal species, but it is also interesting from an archaeological and historical point of view. It contains a number of ruins dating from the Prehistoric, Ancient Roman and Renaissance periods. Botanical circuits with explanatory panels enable visitors to add to their knowledge of flora and fauna.

Riserva Naturale del Litorale Romano – This reserve is characterised by its typical Mediterranean vegetation and spacious open areas of dunes and holm oak woods. It also contains archaeological Roman ruins from sites such as Ostia Antica, Trajan's Ports, ruins from the ancient Via Severiana and Pliny's villa, with its wealth of mosaics.

Other Ways of Exploring the City

With the Children

Unless they have studied some Roman history, young children are unlikely to want to spend hours trailing around ruins, museums and churches. However, Rome does have a number of sights that will interest youngsters, especially in its large parks. The most popular of these is **Villa Borghese**, with its wide selection of activities, including carousels, pony rides (a familiar sight in many of the public parks in Rome), and a zoo, now known as the Bioparco, with over 1 000 animals. A walk around the **Janiculum** is also suitable for children, with puppet shows every afternoon, pony rides, and the daily firing of a cannon at noon. Other attractive public gardens include the vast **Villa Doria Pamphili**, whose small lake is now home to the gentle coypu, a type of aquatic rodent similar in appearance to a small beaver; the delightful **Villa Sciarra** in old Monteverde; and **Villa Celimontana**, not far from the Colosseum. The **Orto Botanico**, behind Palazzo Corsini, is one of the most important botanical gardens in Italy and contains a varied collection of rare plants.

The **Museo delle Paste Alimentari** (the National Pasta Museum), near the Trevi Fountain, is both informative and entertaining and is likely to be popular with children. The EUR district is also worth exploring as a family: visit the interesting Museo delle Arti e Tradizioni Popolari (Folk Museum), enjoy the rides at the funfair (Luna Park), which although not as large as some of the more modern amusement parks in Italy is still worth a visit, or walk around the small lake, stopping for an ice cream at the popular Giolitti *gelateria*. The perfect time to visit Rome with children is over the Christmas period, when the churches are decorated with delightful nativity scenes and Piazza Navona is crowded with colourful market stalls selling a wide range of sweets and toys.

On Two Wheels

Rome is not an ideal city to explore by bike or moped because of its dense, chaotic traffic, heavy pollution and the uneven surface of some of its roads. However, keen cyclists may like to follow the route along the Tiber or explore the city's public parks. The only sections of dedicated cycle track run from Ponte Risorgimento to Villa Borghese and then from Villa Borghese to Villa Ada, and from Ponte Sublicio, in the south of the city, to Ponte della Magliana and on to Ponte di Mezzocammino.

Bicycle hire – Bicycles can be hired at several places in the city centre: Piazza di Spagna, near the entrance to the metro; Piazza del Popolo, on the corner of the street containing Café Rosati *(open in summer, 6am-1am, in winter Sun mornings only)*; Piazza San Lorenzo in Lucina, in Via del Corso *(open Mar-Oct, 10am-6pm [2am in summer])*; Villa Borghese underground car park, sector III.

On Sundays and public holidays bikes can be taken on Metro line B and the train to Lido di Ostia, for those interested in cycling outside the city or along the coast (in the first train carriage only). Tickets cost €0.77 per person + €0.77 per bicycle. Authorisation must be obtained by calling ☎ 06 57 48 087 (for the metro) and ☎ 06 57 54 913 (for the train) at least 24hr in advance.

BY SCOOTER

Scooters and mopeds *(motorino)* ply the streets of all Italian cities and are a typical feature of Italian life. If you feel brave enough to join the crowd, then scooters may be hired from the third level of the underground parking at Villa Borghese (between 9am-7pm); from Via di Porta Castello, a stone's throw from St Peter's; from Via Filippo Turati, near Termini Station; and from Via della Purificazione, by Piazza Barberini.

By Horse-drawn Carriage

A more romantic view of Rome is to be had from an open horse-drawn carriage (*carozzella* or *botticella* in Roman dialect), which can be hailed

from St Peter's Square, the Colosseum, Piazza Venezia, Piazza di Spagna, Piazza Navona , near the Trevi Fountain, Via Veneto and Villa Borghese. ☎ 06 57 901.

By Bus

Public services have implemented a number of new routes that allow visitors to discover the historical centre from the comfort of a bus:
– **110** departs from Termini (Piazza dei Cinquecento) from 9am-8pm (summer) and from 10am-6pm (winter), with departures every 30min. There are two types of ticket available: – a **non-stop** ticket costs €7.75 (€8.26 if bought on board the bus);
– a **stop and go** ticket allows passengers to get off the bus at one of 10 stops and to take another bus later in the day. This ticket costs €12.91 (€13.94 if bought on board).
The ATAC ticket office is situated in zone C of Piazza dei Cinquecento.
The Basilica line leaves Termini (Piazza dei Cinquecento) at 10.30am and 3pm and costs €7.75.
For further information or to make a booking, call ☎ 06 46 95 22 52 or 06 46 95 22 56 (open 9am-7pm).

On the Water

For an unusual view of the city, why not take a **boat trip on the River Tiber** operated every weekend by a private company, Conoscere il Tevere, from Ponte Marconi (on the corner of Lungotevere Dante) to the Molo di Ripa, near Isola Tiberina (cost €10.33). On Sundays, the company also offers a one-way boat trip to Ostia Antica (cost €18.59), with a guided tour of the excavations (return trip by metro). A guide from the WWF provides information on the flora and fauna that can be seen during the boat trip. For information and bookings, contact ☎ 06 56 64 982 or 0347 62 45 246 (mobile); Fax 06 50 18 523.
Tourvisa also organises **boat trips** on the Tiber, from Ponte Umberto I to Ponte Duca d'Aosta, from May-Oct, at 10.30am and 12.45pm. The trip lasts approximately 1hr 30min and costs €10.33 per person. ☎ 06 44 63 481.

By Plane

For a bird's-eye view of the city in a Cessna 182 or Highlander, contact the dell'Urbe Airport at Via Salaria 825. 20min flights available. Advanced reservation necessary. Cost €61.97 per person; minimum of two people required. For information contact City Fly, ☎ 06 88 333, www.cityfly.com

Going out for the Evening

Nightclubs

For those who enjoy music and dancing, Rome has a wide selection of venues ranging from the best-known nightclubs to disco bars and bars with live bands. Nightlife is mainly concentrated in three areas, each offering different kinds of entertainment and attracting a different crowd. The district between **Piazza Campo dei Fiori** and **Piazza Navona** has a wide choice of pubs and bars, drawing a mix of young students, foreign tourists and the theatre crowd (especially in the elegant bars around Piazza Navona). On the streets of **Trastevere**, the bars and restaurants are generally typically Roman in character and host shows with live music. The majority of the city's most popular night-clubs are concentrated in the **Testaccio** district, particularly in Via di Monte Testaccio, and more recently, in the nearby Via di Libetta. A list of suggestions for bars, pubs and nightclubs is given below. Further information can be found in the Selected Sights section of the guide.

THE ESTATE ROMANA FESTIVAL

During the summer months most of the nightclubs in Rome move out to their cooler, temporary premises along the exclusive Fregene Beach. A number of open-air concerts are held in the various "villages" within the capital, where books, records, home-made products and clothes, as well as sandwiches and drinks can be bought before dancing the night away or sitting at a table to enjoy the music. The most famous of these include **Testaccio Village**, which welcomes a number of international artists every year, the **Foro Italico**, where annual cabaret shows are held, **Parco di Villa Celimontana**, for jazz concerts featuring musicians from around the world, **Parco di Villa Ada Savoia**, for new sounds, and a new venue dedicated to Latin-American music, the **Fiesta**. For information on concerts, consult any of the magazines recommended in the section Shows *(below)*.

Akab-Cave – *Via di Monte Testaccio 69, Piramide Cestia-Testaccio district* – ✆ 06 57 82 390 – *Open Mon-Sat, 10pm–4am.* A large number of new venues have opened in this district in the last few years. Akab has a cellar and an upper floor, which is used for concerts and theme evenings.

Alexanderplatz – *Via Ostia 9, Vaticano-San Pietro district* – ✆ 06 39 74 21 71 – *grubei@tin.it* – *Open Mon-Sat, 9pm-2am.* An excellent address for jazz lovers. Some of the greatest jazz musicians in the world have played here in the past 12 years. Concerts start at 10.30pm.

Alpheus – *Via del Commercio 36, Piramide Cestia-Testaccio district* – ✆ 06 57 47 826 – *9pm-3.30am, closed in Aug.* One of the many nightclubs in this district, located in one of the market's old warehouses. The club has three dancefloors and occasionally hosts concerts and cabaret shows.

Big Mama – *Vicolo S. Francesco a Ripa 18, Trastevere district* – ✆ 06 58 12 551 – *Open Tue-Sun, 9pm-1.30am.* For more than 10 years, this nightclub has been a venue for some of the world's best blues and jazz musicians.

Centro Sociale Brancaleone – *Via Levanna 11, NE of the Catacombe di Priscillia district* – ✆ 06 82 00 09 59 – *Open 8pm-2am (dawn on Fri and Sat).* Housed in a renovated social centre, this popular, trendy venue is known for bringing in famous DJs from Italy and abroad, who specialise mainly in electronic music.

Dome Rock Café – *Via Domenico Fontana 18, San Giovanni in Laterano district* – ✆ 06 70 45 24 36 – *Open 8am-2am (3am Fri and Sat).* A decor of glass, candelabras and wrought-iron chairs adds to the medieval atmosphere of this bar, which plays different types of music each evening, including drum and bossa, electronic pop, soul and jungle. The work of young artists is often on display in the café.

Gilda – *Via Mario dei Fiori 97, Piazza di Spagna district* – ✆ 06 67 84 838 – *info@ gildabar.it* – *Open Tue-Fri, 11pm-4am; Sat-Sun, 4-8pm.* The most frequently mentioned nightclub in the society columns is still popular with the theatre crowd, who organise parties and shows in its elegant piano bar.

Goa – *Via di Libetta 13, Piramide Cestia-Testaccio district* – ✆ 06 57 48 277 – *Open Tue-Sat, 11pm-3am.* This large loft, in a street lined with bars and clubs, is now one of the most popular nightclubs in the area, largely the result of the well-known DJs who perform here. The long drapes give the club a distinctly Oriental flavour.

Il Locale – *Vicolo del Fico 3, Piazza Navona district* – ✆ 06 68 79 075 – *Open Tue-Sun, 10pm-3am.* This old garage is divided into a number of simply furnished rooms. The bar regularly books new Italian rock groups.

Jonathan's Angels – *Via della Fossa 16, Piazza Navona district* – ✆ 06 68 93 426 – *Open 5pm-4am.* It's often difficult to find a seat in this popular piano bar, which is deliberately kitsch in style and decorated with paintings by the owner, an enigmatic figure who dominates from behind the till. It's worth a visit to the toilets to admire the decor.

Piper – *Via Tagliamento 9, Catacombe di Priscilla district* – ✆ 06 85 55 398 – *info@piperclub.it* – *Open 10.30pm-4am; Sat, 4-8pm. Closed Mon-Wed.* Opened in 1965, this famous nightclub now organises theme evenings, including rock, underground, and 1970s music.

A NIGHT-TIME SNACK

After a long night out in the city's clubs and bars, or wandering through the streets of Rome, one of the most enduring of Roman traditions is, without a doubt, the early-morning croissant. Some bakeries in the city (where the dough is made for the bars in the district) open their doors to night owls. These bakeries can be difficult to find as they have no sign outside. Some of the best known are in **Trastevere** and **Testaccio** (see TRASTEVERE and PIRAMIDE-TESTACCIO in the Selected Sights section). For those with access to the Internet, the website at www.freeweb.org/freeweb/guac/cornetterie.html provides detailed information in Italian on places selling croissants in Rome.

Shows

A wide range of drama and entertainment to satisfy all tastes is available at the city's theatres, assuming that you can get by in Italian. Venues range from traditional theatres, usually located in the old centre of Rome, to modern venues staging more contemporary and experimental shows.

Tickets for plays, concerts and sporting events can be purchased from a number of agencies in Rome. The most central include **Orbis** (Piazza Esquilino 37, Santa Maria Maggiore district, ☎ 06 47 44 776, www.cdflash.com), **Gesman 92 Primafila** (Via A. Emo 65, ☎ 06 39 74 07 89) and **Interclub Service** (Piazza I. Nievo 3/5, ☎ 06 58 94 54 31, www.interclubservice.com). The **Box Office di Ricordi** (Via del Corso 506, Piazza del Popolo district, ☎ 06 36 12 68; Viale Giulio Cesare 88, Vaticano district, ☎ 06 37 20 216; and Via Cesare Battisti 120, Fontana di Trevi district, ☎ 06 67 98 022) offers a comprehensive ticketing service. **AMIT** (☎ 06 80 88 352, www.chartnet.it) takes telephone and Internet bookings (by credit card) for concerts in the Santa Cecilia auditorium and performances in Rome's major theatres. A whole range of musical events can be also booked through **Il Sogno – Gente e Paesi** (Via Adda 111, ☎ 06 85 30 17 55). Information on films, plays, concerts and exhibitions is listed in the **Roma c'è** magazine, published every Friday and on sale for €1.03, and in **Trovaroma**, a supplement of the La Repubblica daily newspaper which comes out on Thursdays. These two publications also include bar and restaurant listings, as well as activities taking place outside Rome, and provide a summary of the week's events in English; both also have a section on children's activities. Cultural events are also detailed in the monthly magazine **Time Out Rome** (€2.07), which publishes articles and interviews on the latest trends and events in the capital.

Theatre by bus – Bus n° 116t serves the various theatres within the city centre, departing from Via Veneto and Via Giulia. Buses run Mon-Fri, 8pm-1.30am, with departures every 15min.

THEATRES AND CLASSICAL MUSIC CONCERTS

Teatro dell'Opera – Piazza Beniamino Gigli 1, Santa Maria Maggiore district – ☎ 06 48 16 02 55 – www.opera.roma.it – Ticket office open Tue and Sat, 9am-5pm; Sun, 9am-1.30pm. Tickets can also be purchased 1hr prior to shows.
Recommended for fans of classical music, opera and ballet, this large theatre provides subtitles for shows in foreign languages. In summer, open-air performances are organised in the romantic setting of Caracalla's Baths.

Teatro Olimpico – Piazza Gentile da Fabriano 17, Monte Mario district – ☎ 06 32 65 991 – Ticket office open 11am-1pm and 3-7pm, and 8-9pm on the day of performance. This theatre on the banks of the Tiber is the headquarters of the Accademia Filarmonica Romana. Musical shows, ballet and some comic opera are staged here.

Teatro Sistina – Via Sistina 129, Piazza di Spagna district – ☎ 06 42 00 711 – il.sistina@flashnet.it – Ticket office open 10am-1pm and 3.30-7pm. Renowned for its excellent acoustics, this theatre hosts famous musicals from around the world, as well as concerts by acclaimed international performers.

Auditorium dell'Accademia Nazionale di Santa Cecilia – Via della Conciliazione 4, Vaticano district – ☎ 06 68 80 10 44. This prestigious concert hall is the setting for concerts by some of the best-known orchestras and conductors from across the globe.

Teatro Argentina – Largo Argentina 52 – ☎ 06 68 80 46 01 /2 – info@teatrodiroma.net – Ticket office open Tue-Sat, 10am-2pm, 3-7pm and 8-10pm. Built at the beginning of the 18C, this large theatre staged the first performance of the Barber of Seville in 1816. The theatre enjoys an excellent location opposite the Roman ruins of Largo Argentina, and offers a programme of mainly traditional drama.

Teatro Quirino – Via Marco Minghetti 1, Fontana di Treve district – ☎ 06 67 94 585 – Ticket office open Tue-Sun, 10am-2pm, 3-

7pm and 8-10pm. Like the Teatro Argentina and Teatro Valle, this theatre is run by the Italian Theatre Assocation (Ente Teatrale Italiano-ETI). The theatre is known for its emphasis on traditional drama, although experimental plays are occasionally also performed here.

Teatro Valle – *Via del Teatro Valle 21, Piazza Navona district* – ☎ *06 68 80 37 94* – *teatrovalle@libero.it* – *Ticket office open Tue-Sun, 10am-7pm.* This magnificent 18C building, situated near Piazza S. Eustachio, hosts performances of many of the Italian classics.

Teatro Eliseo – *Via Nazionale 183, Quirinale district* – ☎ *06 48 82 114* – *www.teatroeliseo.it* – *Ticket office open Tue, Thu, Fri and Sat, 8.30am-2.30pm, 3.30-7pm and 8-8.40pm; Wed and Sun, 9.30am-7pm.* In addition to the best-known drama from around the world, this theatre hosts works by the greatest 20C Italian writers, such as Aldo Palazzeschi and Eduardo de Filippo. Dance performances are also occasionally held here.

Colosseo – *Via Capo d'Africa 5/a, Colosseo-Celio district* – ☎ *06 70 04 932* – *Ticket office open Tue-Sat, 7-10.30pm; Sun, 4-8pm.* Avant-garde drama performed by young aspiring actors can be seen in the two auditoriums of this theatre.

Teatro dell'Orologio – *Via dei Filippini 17/a, Castel Sant'Angelo district* – ☎ *06 68 30 83 30* – *www.teatroorologio.it* – *Ticket office open Tue-Sat, 5-9pm; Sun, 4-5pm.* This small theatre club has four auditoriums and offers a programme of varied modern drama.

Teatro Parioli – *Via Giosue' Borsi 20, Parioli district* – ☎ *06 80 83 523* – *Ticket office open Tue-Sat, 10am-1.30pm and 2.30-7pm; Sun, 10-1.30pm and 3-5pm.* Tickets bought for the shows performed in this theatre (usually comedies) also include entrance to the live recording of the popular Italian television programme, the *Maurizio Costanzo Show*. Spectators are provided with binoculars.

Alfellini – *Via Francesco Carletti 5, Piramide Cestia district* – ☎ *06 57 57 570.* The Alfellini is a popular comedy venue that hosts a range of cabaret and variety shows

CINEMA

Rome has a number of multiscreen cinema complexes showing recent releases, as well as smaller alternative cinemas and associations which screen different films daily. The latter show a mix of old films, cult movies and foreign-language films.

OPEN-AIR CINEMAS

A number of cinemas close during July and August. During these months the open-air "villages" set up during the *Estate Romana* festival offer cinema-lovers the chance to see a number of films. Among the long-standing venues taking part in this festival, **Cineporto** screens the most successful films of the previous season every year under the pine trees near the Ministero degli Affari Esteri (in the Monte Mario district), **Sotto le Stelle di San Lorenzo** provides visitors with the opportunity to watch films in their original language in the beautiful Villa Mercede gardens, and the most recent **Notti di Cinema a Piazza Vittorio** has both successful and lesser-known films on its programme. Unfortunately, **Massenzio**, housed in the delightful surroundings of the Parco del Celio in 1997 and 1998, has not yet found a permanent home, and the **Isola del Cinema** has been forced to move from Isola Tiberina as a result of the restoration work which took place for the Jubilee in the year 2000.

Azzurro Scipioni – *Via degli Scipioni 82, Vaticano district* – ☎ *06 39 73 71 61.* This cinema screens a varied selection of films by well-known directors from Italy and abroad. The programme varies depending on the day and time of the screening and admission is free on the first day of the month.

Cineclub Detour – *Via Urbana 47/a, Santa Maria Maggiore district* – ☎ *06 48 72 368.* A few days a week are dedicated to film reviews in this cinema, which also organises theme evenings. Subtitled foreign films are shown on Thursdays.

Nuovo Sacher – *Largo Ascianghi 1, Trastevere district* – ☎ *06 58 18 116.* Owned by the director and actor Nanni Moretti, this cinema shows Italian and foreign films not usually screened in the larger cinema complexes of the city. Open-air cinema in summer.

Pasquino Multiscreen – *Piazza di S. Egidio 9, Trastevere district* – ☎ *06 58 33 33 10.* Situated in one of the most delightful squares in Trastevere, this is the only cinema to show films in their original language (mainly in English) without subtitles every day of the week.

Quirinetta – *Via Marco Minghetti 4, Fontana di Trevi district* – ☎ *06 67 90 012.* This cinema, located in the heart of the historic centre, a stone's throw from the famous Trevi Fountain, also shows a number of foreign-language films.

Warner Village Cinemas Moderno – *Viale Parco dei Medici, Porta Pia district* – ☎ *06 65 85 51.* This recently opened complex is one of the most modern cinemas in the capital. One of the screens shows only subtitled foreign films. Late-night screenings take place on Friday and Saturday.

Shopping

Unlike other capital cities in Europe, Rome does not have many large department stores, preferring a wide range of small shops and boutiques to suit all tastes and budgets. Visitors will have no difficult in buying antiques, craft products and high-quality food produce throughout the city, especially in the historic centre, as well as an excellent selection of the latest fashions. The following section gives information on where to shop in Rome, with descriptions of the different areas of the city which specialise in certain products. Each category gives a list of shops, which are described in detail in the Selected Sights section of the guide *(see the appropriate chapter)*.

In general, clothes stores are closed on Monday morning; food shops close on Thursday afternoon. With the exception of the historic centre, where shops tend to stay open all day, shops are open from 10am-1pm and from 4-7.30pm (winter) or 5-8pm (summer). Credit cards are accepted in most stores, with the exception of small food shops.

If you're looking for an unusual souvenir, why not have your portrait painted in Piazza Navona?

FASHION

Many luxury stores are located in **Via Veneto**, and some of the best-known names in the Italian fashion world can be found in the area between **Via del Corso** and **Piazza di Spagna**, especially in Via Frattina, Via Borgognona (Laura Biagiotti, Versace, Fendi etc) and Via Bocca di Leone (Versace). Particularly worthy of mention in this district is **Bulgari**, one of the original goldsmiths in Rome, which is situated at the beginning of **Via dei Condotti**. In the same street, **Raggi** is very popular with young people for its reasonably priced and striking jewellery. Other famous names in this district include Armani, Gucci, Prada and Valentino.

Via del Corso, which is packed with young people on a Saturday afternoon, is home to a variety of shops selling all kinds of goods at reasonable prices, as are Via Nazionale, Via del Tritone and Via Cola di Rienzo.

The following shops have been selected for their reasonable prices and original goods.

Bomba *see PIAZZA DEL POPOLO*
Claudio Sanò *see SAN LORENZO FUORI LE MURA*
David Saddler *see PIAZZA DEL POPOLO*
De Clercq & De Clercq *see PIAZZA DI SPAGNA*
Il Discount dell'Alta Moda *see PIAZZA DEL POPOLO and SANTA MARIA MAGGIORE – ESQUILINO*
Franco Borini *see CAMPO DEI FIORI*
Fratelli Viganò *see FONTANA DI TREVI-QUIRINALE*
Galleria di Orditi e Trame *see PIAZZA NAVONA*
Sergio di Cori Gloves *see PIAZZA DI SPAGNA*

ANTIQUES

Antique collectors will enjoy a stroll in the Piazza di Spagna district along **Via del Babuino**, home to the city's most prestigious antique dealers, and **Via Margutta**, with its many art galleries and craft shops, which still specialise in the restoration of marble and silver objects. The most lively antiques area, especially during antique fairs, is **Via dei Coronari**, not far from Piazza Navona. Wandering through the narrow alleyways around **Piazza Campo dei Fiori** and **Piazza Farnese**, don't be surprised to see second-hand dealers and craftsmen busy at work out in the sunshine.

Particularly worthy of note are some of the long-established shops, which have practised their trade with skill and enthusiasm for many years, and smaller shops with a real flavour of the past, but which are located far from the city's most famous streets.

Antica Erboristeria Romana *see ISOLA TIBERINA-TORRE ARGENTINA*
Antonella Marani *see PIAZZA NAVONA*
Le Bambole *see PIRAMIDE CESTIA-TESTACCIO*
Comics Bazar *see CAMPO DEI FIORI*
Ditta G Poggi *see PANTHEON*
Farmacia Pesci *see FONTANA DI TREVI-QUIRINALE*
Fratelli Alinari *see PIAZZA DI SPAGNA*
Hausmann & C *see PIAZZA DI SPAGNA*
Italia Garipoli *see VATICANO-SAN PIETRO*
Lattonieri *see TRASTEVERE*
Libreria Antiquaria Rappaport *see PANTHEON*
Maria Favilli *see MONTECITORIO*
Orsantico *see PIAZZA NAVONA*
Set *see PIAZZA NAVONA*
Siragusa *see PIAZZA DI SPAGNA*

FOOD AND DRINK

Biscottificio Artigiano Innocenti *see TRASTEVERE*

La Bottega del Cioccolato *see FORI IMPERIALI*

Cooperativa Agricola Stella *see CATACOMBE DI PRISCILLA*

Fattoria la Parrina *see PIAZZA DEL POPOLO*

Gatti e Antonelli *see CATACOMBE DI PRISCILLA*

Latteria Ugolini *see TRASTEVERE*

Latticini Micocci *see PORTA PIA*

BOOKS

The most famous bookshops tend to be located in spacious premises in the centre of Rome, often on a number of floors. They offer a wide selection of books of all kinds, and also sell videos, CD-ROMs and stationery. **Feltrinelli** has opened three bookshops at stategic locations throughout the city, such as Via del Babuino 39, ☎ 06 36 00 18 42, Via Orlando 78/81 (near Piazza della Repubblica), where the whole shop is dedicated to foreign books, and Largo Argentina 5A/6, ☎ 06 68 80 32 48. **Rizzoli** has stores at Via Tomacelli 156 (in the Montecitorio district) and in Largo Chigi (near Galleria Colonna in the Fontana di Trevi district); **Mondadori** has branches at Via Cola di Rienzo 51 (Vatican district) and Via Appia Nuova 51 (San Giovanni in Laterano district). Other bookshops include **Mel Book Store** (Via Nazionale 254/255) and **Rinascita** (Via delle Botteghe Oscure 1).

The smaller bookshops mentioned below either contain interesting and original features or offer visitors a chance to purchase rare literary works.

Al Tempo Ritrovato *see TRASTEVERE*

All American Comics *see SAN GIOVANNI IN LATERANO*

Bibli *see TRASTEVERE*

Farenheit 451 *see CAMPO DEI FIORI*

Invito alla Lettura *see CASTEL SAN ANGELO*

Libreria del Viaggiatore *see CAMPO DEI FIORI*

Mel Bookstore *see FONTANA DI TREVI-QUIRINALE*

La Procure *see PANTHEON*

The Lion Bookshop *see PIAZZA DI SPAGNA*

MUSIC

Archivio Fonografico *see AVENTINO*

Art & Music *see PIRAMIDE CESTIA-TESTACCIO*

Città 2000 *see CATACOMBE DI PRISCILLA*

Disfunzioni Musicali – Disfunzioni Musicali Usato e Rarità *see SAN LORENZO FUORI LE MURA*

Metropoli Rock *see SANTA MARIA MAGGIORE-ESQUILINO*

Tendenza *see PIRAMIDE CESTIA-TESTACCIO*

OTHER SHOPS

Arredamento Liturgico *see ISOLA TIBERINA-TORRE ARGENTINA*

Barbiconi *see PANTHEON*

Becker & Musicò *see FONTANA DI TREVI-QUIRINALE*

Boutique Jaguar Collection *see VILLA BORGHESE-VILLA GIULIA*

Jaracandà *see PIAZZA NAVONA*

Myricae *see PIAZZA DI SPAGNA*

Savelli *see VATICANO-SAN PIETRO*

DEPARTMENT STORES

The most exclusive department stores include **La Rinascente** (Via del Corso 189, on the corner of Largo Chigi, ☎ 06 67 97 691, Montecitorio district, and Via Aniene 1, on the corner of Piazza Fiume, Porta Pia district; also open Sun, 10.30am-8pm), and **Coin** (Piazzale Appio 7, ☎ 06 70 80 020, San Giovanni in Laterano district, and Via Cola di Rienzo 177, Vatican district; open 9.30am-8pm), whose larger outlets also have a household articles and furnishings department.

MAS – *Via dello Statuto 11, Santa Maria Maggiore district – ☎ 06 44 68 078 – Open Mon-Sat, 9am-1pm and 4-7.30pm (open Sun from 10am)*. This store, located a stone's throw from Piazza Vittorio, is divided into several sections selling different items of clothing, in which customers can rummage through the shelves looking for the perfect dress, jumper, trousers, shoes or even a leather jacket, all of which are sold at reasonable prices.

Ricordi Mediastore – *Via del Corso 506, Piazza del Popolo district – ☎ 06 36 12 370 www.ricordimediastores.it – Open Mon-Sat, 9.30am-8pm; Sun, 10am-1pm and 3-8pm*. With five shops in the most central districts of Rome, Ricordi is one of the largest music stores in the city. Other branches are

Off shopping in Rome

at: Via Orlando 73 (Piazza Repubblica district), Via C. Battisti 120/c (Piazza Venezia district), Viale G.Cesare 88 (east of the Vaticano – San Pietro district) and Galleria Stazione Termini.

LATE-NIGHT SHOPPING

Shops in Rome close at around 7.30pm in winter and 8pm in summer, although some may stay open later.

Newspapers can now be bought late at night or early in the morning almost as soon as they are printed from a number of **newsstands**. Some of the most centrally located can be found at Via Veneto, Viale Trastevere and Piazza Sonnino, Piazza dei Cinquecento, Piazza Colonna, Piazza Cola di Rienzo, Viale Manzoni and Via Magna Grecia.

For those visitors who require more than just an early morning croissant after a long night in the capital, the **Museum Drugstore** (Via Portuense 313) offers a wide range of groceries and other items, and is open 24hr a day; the store also has a bar and an archaeological area with graves dating from the 2C AD. Other 24hr outlets include **Rosati Due** (Piazzale Clodio, ☎ 06 03 97 41 138, Monte Mario district), which has a supermarket and a fast-food counter, and **Tiburtina Station** which has a pizzeria, pastry shop and gift store.

Inveterate smokers have been able to buy cigarettes from automatic machines for some years now and will also find a few **bar-tabacchi** (tobacconists) that stay open late. These include those at Piazza d'Ara Coeli, Piazza Venezia (open all night), Via del Tritone 144, Piazza del Popolo 16, Viale Trastevere 354, Tiburtina Station and Via Cesare Battisti 135.

To buy **fresh flowers** at any time of the day or night, head for the flower stalls at Lungotevere Milvio, Piazzale degli Eroi and Via Latina on the corner of Piazza Galeria, Piazzale del Parco della Rimembranza and Via Portuense on the corner of Via Rolli.

MARKETS

The local fruit and vegetable markets held in the different districts of the city offer a panoply of bright colours and fresh smells, where the lively conversation of the locals, punctuated by the cries of the stallholders, provide a genuine flavour of everyday Rome.

"Er Cicala"

G. Bludzin/MICHELIN

It is also pleasant to wander through the many antique and flea markets, where you might just pick up an unusual souvenir or original item of clothing.

Borgo Parioli – *Via Tirso 14, Catacombe di Priscilla district – Open Sat-Sun, 9am-8pm.* This antique market is held in a large garage and has a selection of paintings, prints, frames, clocks, embroidery, lace, books and magazines. Unusual culinary specialities may also be sampled here.

Garage Sale. Rigattieri per Hobby – *Piazza della Marina, Borghetto Flaminio 32, Villa Giulia district –* ☎ *06 47 82 42 71 – Open Sun, 10am-7pm.* Stalls can be rented for the sale of clothes and other items at this market, which specialises in chic second-hand goods, antiques and general bric-a-brac.

La Soffitta sotto i Portici – *Piazza Augusto Imperatore, Piazza di Spagna district – 3rd Sun in the month, 10am-dusk.* Frequented by collectors of paintings, prints, frames, small items of furniture, ceramics and lace.

Mercatino Biologico – *Via Cardinale Merry del Val, Trastevere district – 2nd Sun in the month, 9am-7pm.* This market sells environmentally friendly produce, including organic food, recycled paper, plant-based soaps and wooden toys.

Mercatino di Ponte Milvio – *Lungotevere Capoprati, Monte Mario district – 1st weekend in the month, Sat, 3-7pm; Sun, 8am-7pm.* This market is held under Milvio Bridge and sells furniture, craftwork, art and other articles.

Mercato dell'Antiquariato di Fontanella Borghese – *Piazza Borghese, Piazza di Spagna district – Open Mon-Sat, 7am-1pm.* An excellent market for those interested in old books and prints.

Mercato dell'Antiquariato di Piazza Verdi – *Piazza Verdi, Villa Borghese district – 4th Sun in the month, 9am-8pm.* As well as antiques and arts and crafts, this market also sells amphorae, old friezes and coats of arms. Entertainment and a wide selection of books for children.

Mercato di Campo dei Fiori – *Campo dei Fiori – Open mornings, daily.* Once the largest in Rome, this is now a small local market with a limited number of stalls set up around the square. Typical Roman vegetables, such as *crescione* (watercress) and magnificent flower stalls which stay open in the afternoon.

Mercato di Piazza Alessandria – *Piazza Alessandria, Porta Pia district – Open mornings, Mon-Sat.* A food market situated inside a Liberty-style building.

Mercato di Piazza S. Cosimato – *Piazza San Cosimato, Trastevere district – Open mornings, Mon-Sat.* This market is one of the busiest in central Rome, and is divided into two sections: the *fruttaroli*, who buy their produce every morning from the wholesale market, and the *vignaroli*, who sell produce grown in their own garden.

Mercato di Piazza Vittorio Emanuele – *Piazza Vittorio Emanuele, Santa Maria*

Maggiore district – Mornings, all week.
This is one of the cheapest markets in Rome.
Renowned for its fresh fish at reasonable
prices, its excellent selection of cheeses and
horse meat, and its choice of Oriental spices.
Mercato di Testaccio – *Piazza di Testaccio* –
Mon-Sat, all morning. Nicknamed *"er core de
Roma"*, the heart of Rome, this market has a
wide selection of high-quality goods. A large
number of stalls selling shoes at factory
prices.
Mercato di Via Sannio – *Via Sannio, San
Giovanni in Laterano district* – *Mon-Sat,
10am-1pm.* A wide choice of reasonably
priced new and second-hand clothes,
as well as shoes sold at factory prices.
Mercato di Viale Parioli – *Viale Parioli,
Catacombe di Priscilla district* – *Sat-Sun,
10am-7pm.* This market starts in Viale Parioli
with stalls selling costume jewellery,
household goods and clothing, and
continues into Via Locchi, where the
main food stalls are located.
Porta Portese – *Trastevere district* – *Sun,
from dawn-2pm.* This market sells a bit of
everything and is often referred to as the
flea market. It opened officially during the
Second World War, formed by stalls from
other local markets, and is held along Via
Portuense. Articles on sale include general
bric-a-brac, new and second-hand clothes,
photographic equipment, books and records.

Suk – *Via Portuense 851 – Sun-Fri,
3-7pm; Sat, 11am-7pm.* This ethnic
market is held in a supermarket car
park. Ethnic goods, antiques and a
wide selection of unusual items.
Underground – *Via Crispi, Parcheggio
Ludovisi 96, Piazza di Spagna district – ☎ 06
99 40 40 – 1st weekend of the month, Sat,
3-8pm; Sun, 10.30am-7.30pm.* This
5 000m/54 000sq ft exhibition area, situated
in the old centre of Rome, has a wide variety
of antiques, collectors' items, modern
articles, jewels and costume jewellery.

J.P. Lescourret/PIX

*Porta Portese market offers something
for everyone*

Books

Rome has long been a favourite
subject with writers of all nationalities.
The selection below includes
recommendations of guide books,
fiction and historical works on the city.

ART AND ARCHITECTURE
Roman Building Jean Pierre Adam
(Routledge 1999)
Roman Art and Architecture Sir
Mortimer Wheeler (Thames & Hudson
1964)
*A Handbook of Roman Art: A Survey
of the Visual Arts of the Roman World*
Martin Henig (Phaidon 1995)
Roman Imperial Architecture JB Ward
Perkings (Penguin 1981)
Lives of the Artists G Vasari (Penguin
Classics 1965, 1987 [2 vols])
The Italian Painters of the Renaissance
B Berenson (Ursus Press 1999)

COMMENTARIES AND FICTION
Pictures from Italy Charles Dickens
(1846, Penguin Books 1998)
Italian Journey Wolfgang Goethe
(1788, Penguin Books 1970)
Italian Hours Henry James
(1909, Penguin Books 1995)
Daisy Miller Henry James
(1878, Penguin Books 1986)
The Child of Pleasure Gabriele
d'Annunzio (1889, Dedalus Ltd 1990)

HISTORY
A History of Italy Stuart Woolf
(Routledge 1979, 1991)
A Traveller's History of Italy Valerio
Lintner (The Windrush Press 1989,
1993)
Roman Society D Dudley (Penguin
1991)
*The Romans: An Introduction to their
History and Civilization* K Christ
(University of Chicago Press 1985
[translated from German])
Rome: Its People, Life and Customs
UE Paoli (Bristol Classical Press 1990
[translated from Italian])
Renaissance Rome: 1500-59 P Partner
(University of Chicago Press 1980)
The Counter Reformation AG Dickens
(Thames & Hudson 1969)
*The Risorgimento and the Unification
of Italy* D Beales (Addison Wesley
Longman Higher Education 1982)
Italy in the Age of the Risorgimento
H Hearder (Addison Wesley Longman
Higher Education 1983)
The Pope and the Duce PC Kent
(Macmillan Press Ltd 1981)

JUBILEE
The Holy Year in Rome: Past and Present
EM Jung-Inglessis (International
Scholars Publications 1998)

Pilgrims at Prayer (Cassell 1999)
Pilgrims in Rome (Cassell 1999)
Pilgrims at Prayer: The Official Vatican Prayerbook for the Jubilee Year 2000 (Continuum Publishing Company 1999)

PEOPLE
Stories of Rome Livy, translated by R Nicholls (1982)
The Caesars Allan Massie (Sceptre 1994)
The Italians Luigi Barzini (Penguin 1964, 1991)

Romans, their Lives and Times Michael Sheridan (Phoenix Paperbacks 1995)
Rome, the Biography of a City Christopher Hibbert (Penguin 1995)
The New Italians Charles Richards (Penguin 1995)

USEFUL GUIDES
Guide to the Vatican Museums; Guide to the Vatican City (Monumenti, Musei e Gallerie Pontificie)
The Companion Guide to Rome Georgina Masson (Companion Guides 1998)

Cinema

Rome was a favourite venue for directors of Italian neo-realist films during the late 1940s and the city continues to be a popular backdrop for Italian cinema today. Below is a list of well-known movies that have been shot in the capital.

Roma, città aperta by R Rossellini, 1945. A portrayal of the Italian Resistance in Nazi-occupied Rome. This film represents a landmark in the history of Italian cinema, with a memorable performance by Anna Magnani.

Ladri di biciclette by V de Sica, 1948. This film depicts the working-class districts of Rome in the post-war period, when a bicycle represented survival. Another masterpiece of neo-realism.

Domenica d'agosto by L Emmer, 1949. Episodes from daily life taking place at the same time on a Sunday in August on the road leading from Rome to the beach in Ostia.

Roman Holiday by W Wyler, 1953. This brilliant comedy tells the story of a princess discovering Rome on the back of a Vespa, in the company of a journalist. A delightful performance by Audrey Hepburn.

Le notti di Cabiria, by F Fellini, 1957. Giulietta Masina stars in this extraordinary tale of a prostitute who dreams of true love, surrounded by exploiters and cynics.

Poveri ma belli by D Risi, 1958. This entertaining film features cars, beautiful women, parties and music from the 1950s, as well as Marisa Allasio, a famous actress of the time.

I soliti ignoti by M Monicelli, 1958. A group of unemployed, penniless youths organise the robbery of a security firm in this realistic portrayal of poverty in the 1950s.

Fantasmi a Roma by A Pietrangeli, 1960. This clever surrealist comedy recounts the story of four ghosts who succeed in saving an old *palazzo* from demolition.

La dolce vita by F Fellini, 1960. Delightful shots of Rome serve as a backdrop to the portrayal of an empty-headed generation with little interest in anything other than forgetting the past and enjoying themselves.

Satyricon by F Fellini, 1969. A satyrical portrayal of the decadence of the Roman Empire, based on the work by Petronius.

Roma by F Fellini, 1971. An autobiographical journey of the great Fellini shot in the city that served as a backdrop to his earliest films.

C'eravamo tanto amati by E Scola, 1974. Three friends who were in the Resistance together meet up again in Rome years later and bitterly compare their loss of hope and illusions.

In nome del papa re by L Magni, 1977. This splendid film portrays corruption and violence in the Papal Court during the final years of the Papal States, with a magnificent performance by Nino Manfredi.

Un borghese piccolo piccolo by M Monicelli, 1977. Alberto Sordi in one of his few dramatic performances in this film about a father who takes justice into his own hands after his son is killed in an armed robbery.

Una giornata particolare by E Scola, 1977. This film tells the story of an intense relationship between a resigned housewife (Sophia Loren) and a homosexual anti-fascist (Marcello Mastroianni) on the day in May 1938 when Hitler visited Rome and was welcomed by Mussolini.

Un sacco bello by C Verdone, 1979. One of the first comedies in Roman cinema. The three episodes of this film paint a portrait of an average man from Rome, with all his faults and qualities.

Bianca by N Moretti, 1983. Nanni Moretti brings a hint of subtle irony to his portrayal of a high school teacher in search of himself, as he attempts to reconcile his ideals with reality.

Caro Diario by N Moretti, 1994. One of the three episodes that make up this film is a wonderful autobiographical trip through Rome by scooter. Entertaining and full of irony.

La parola amore esiste by M Calopresti, 1998. A story of loneliness, love and psychological hardship, made by one of the up-and-coming directors in Italian cinema.

Events and Festivals

A detailed calendar of events can be obtained from the Vatican Information Office (Ufficio Informazioni Pellegrini e Turisti) and from local tourist offices (APT). *See map on the inside back cover of the guide.*

6 JANUARY
Festival of the *Befana*: the last of the Twelve Days of Christmas; market stalls in Piazza Navona overflow with presents and sweets (*cenone* or candy coal), to the great delight of the children.

21 JANUARY
In the Church of Sant'Agnese Fuori le Mura, the saint's feast day is celebrated with the benediction of two lambs before being presented to the Benedictines of Santa Cecilia who use the wool to weave the *palium* which each new archbishop receives from the Pope.

9 MARCH
The blessing of automobiles near the Church of Santa Francesca Romana, patron saint of drivers.

19 MARCH
In the Trionvale district on the Feast of St Joseph stalls sell typical *bignè*, a sort of doughnut, and *frittelle*, a sort of choux pastry, made specially for the occasion.

GOOD FRIDAY
Stations of the Cross by night between the Colosseum and the Palatine Hill.

EASTER
At noon in St Peter's Square the Pope gives his *Urbi et Orbi* blessing.

APRIL
To mark the arrival of spring the steps of Trinità dei Monti are decked with blooming azaleas, a dazzling sight.

21 APRIL
Solemn ceremony on the Capitoline Hill to commemorate the anniversary of the founding of the Eternal City (753 BC).

MAY
Open-air art exhibition in Via Margutta.
Antique Fair in Via dei Coronari.
Roses in bloom in the municipal rose gardens of the Roseto di Roma (Via di Valle Murcia).

JUNE
Industrial and Commercial Fair, Via Cristoforo Colombo.

23-24 JUNE
On the Feast of St John, in the district bearing his name, there is great rejoicing: popular games and spectacles; snails in broth and roast pork.

29 JUNE
Service in St Peter's Basilica on the Feast of St Peter and St Paul, the most solemn of the religious festivals in Rome.

JUNE-JULY
Tevere-Expo: exhibition of Italian and international crafts on the banks of the Tiber.

15-30 JULY
Fiesta de Noantri: popular festival in the streets of Trastevere.

JULY-AUGUST
Estate Romana (Roman Summer): musical concerts and various spectacles are held throughout the City (especially in Caracalla's Baths).

5 AUGUST
Commemoration in the basilica of Santa Maria Maggiore of the miraculous fall of snow which led to the construction of the church: a shower of white flower petals is released in the Pauline Chapel.

8 DECEMBER
Celebration of the doctrine of the Immaculate Conception in Piazza di Spagna in the presence of the Pope.

DECEMBER
In Via Giulia every year there is an exhibition of over 50 nativity scenes, with beautiful cribs in the following churches: Santi Cosma e Damiano, Santa Maria in Via, Sant'Alessio, Basilica dei Santi Apostoli, San Marcello, the Gesù Church, Santa Maria d'Aracoeli, Santa Maria del Popolo and Santa Maria Maggiore (13C crib).
Midnight mass is celebrated with particular solemnity in Santa Maria Maggiore and in Santa Maria d'Aracoeli. In St Peter's Square the Pope's blessing, *Urbi et Orbi,* is bestowed.
Throughout the Christmas period red carpets are laid in the streets and in front of the shops.

Sports Fixtures

MAY
International Equestrian Competition in Piazza di Siena

FIRST TWO WEEKS IN MAY
International Tennis Championship

END OF MAY-BEGINNING OF JUNE
Sette Colli International Swimming Competition

JUNE
Golden Gala Athletics Event

Notes and Coins

The euro banknotes were designed by Robert Kalinan, an Austrian artist. His designs were inspired by the theme "Ages and styles of European Architecture". Windows and gateways feature on the front of the banknotes, bridges feature on the reverse, symbolising the European spirit of openness and co-operation.

The images are stylised representations of the typical architectural style of each period, rather than specific structures.

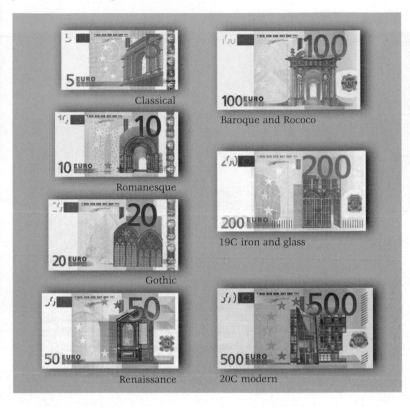

Classical

Baroque and Rococo

Romanesque

19C iron and glass

Gothic

Renaissance   20C modern

Euro coins have one face common to all 12 countries in the European single currency area or "Eurozone" (currently Austria, Belgium, Finland, France, Germany, Greece, Ireland, Italy, Luxembourg, The Netherlands, Portugal and Spain) and a reverse side specific to each country, created by their own national artists.

Euro banknotes look the same throughout the Eurozone. All Euro banknotes and coins can be used anywhere in this area.

An unusual view of the baldaquin in St Peter's

G. Simeone/PHOTONONSTOP

Insights and Images

The City of the Seven Hills

For centuries, travellers have been captivated by the charms of the Eternal City. Fascinated by the exuberant beauty of Italy's capital, visitors return time and time again to admire its opulent architecture, bathed in the unforgettable golden light of sunset. Few remain indifferent to this striking city, which is characterised by the history of its ancient ruins, yet is also full of life and firmly in the 21C. For Rome is a city of contrasts: dusty and unkempt in places, yet also graced with stately monuments and majestic avenues, and quiet, sleepy piazzas and narrow alleyways just a stone's throw from its noisy main thoroughfares. The city's many charms ensure that once seen, Rome is never forgotten.

B. Morandi/MICHELIN

On the streets of Rome

From the belvedere on the Janiculum Hill there is a wide view over the roofs of the city. Above them rise countless domes of all shapes and sizes, such as the elegant Sant'Ivo alla Sapienza, the Pantheon, and the majestic dome of St Peter's, designed by Michelangelo. In the streets, statues of the Virgin adorned with little cherubs watch over the life of every narrow alley. Rome is the **city of churches**: there are said to be about 300 in all, a fitting number for the home of the Roman Catholic Church. Since the 7C Christians from all over the world have been making pilgrimages to the tombs of St Peter and St Paul and the catacombs, and, more recently, to the Vatican State. Rome is also a **city of fountains and obelisks**. The cooling sound of water can be heard throughout the city, whose fountains include simple structures on street corners, the Baroque splendour of the Trevi Fountain, the delicate

Renaissance tracery of the Turtle Fountain, and a number of elaborate sculptures by Bernini. The water pours forth from the depths of a basin, from the mouth of an Egyptian lion, from a dolphin, a monster, or Triton's shell. As for obelisks – Egyptian, Imperial and Papal – they seem to grow in Rome like trees: curiously perched on an elephant's back, contrasting starkly with the façade of the Pantheon, boldly mounted on the Fountain of the Four Rivers, or even acting as the pointer for a gigantic sundial in Piazza Montecitorio.

It is impossible to talk about Rome without mentioning its ancient **ruins**, which form an integral part of the city; these are scattered around the city and are nowadays often hemmed in by modern buildings. Considering the numerous times the city was plundered and attacked during the Middle Ages, and the way that ancient columns and capitals were used to build new palaces during the Renaissance period, it is a miracle that the Roman Forum and the ruins at Largo Argentina can still be admired today. Churches and monuments in Rome often have several layers, each of which dates back to a different historical period. The best example of this is the basilica of San Clemente sul Celio, built for the first time in the 4C on the foundations of structures dating from the Republican era, then rebuilt in the 12C, and modified in the 18C.

Another important characteristic of Rome is its old villas, built by noble families in the past and now part of the city's heritage. The gardens of the Villa Borghese, Villa Doria and Villa Ada provide an attractive and essential splash of greenery in the heart of the city.

Although Rome still operates under the emblem of the wolf and uses the old Republican formula SPQR (Senatus Populusque Romanus), not much remains of the marble capital left by Augustus and the emperors. The Renaissance and Baroque periods have both left their mark, mainly as a consequence of the architectural ambition of many of the Popes, and the modern city has had to adapt to modern life.

To fulfil its modern role as capital of a united Italy since 1870, the city has had to double in size, to use concrete, metal and glass to house its new population, to construct administrative buildings and to improve its public transport and traffic flow. A city with more than 2 500 years of heritage is bound to contain contrasting elements, which make it all the more fascinating and "eternal".

One of the elegant nymphs of the Fontana delle Naiadi

History
and Legend

According to legend, the heroic founder of Rome, Aeneas, was the son of Venus. Such divine origins helped to give credence to the city's grandiose destiny and its position as the "capital of the world". The decadence of the Empire led to the rise and fall of Rome, and despite becoming the cornerstone of the Christian world, the city was repeatedly sacked by barbarian tribes during the early Middle Ages. Restored to its former splendour during the era of the Papal States, Rome was finally declared the capital of a united Italy in 1870.

The Origins of Rome and the Monarchy (753-509 BC)

Ancient sources refer to old fortifications surrounding a small territory, known as *Roma quadrata* (square Rome) because of the shape of the walled city. Evidence of the influence of the **Etruscan** civilisation on the old city of Rome can be seen in the religion *(haruspicy)*, the political structure (the Etruscan Tarquin family was the most important in the city of Rome), culture (according to Livy, young men received an "Etruscan" education until the 4C) and vocabulary (the word *persona* comes from the Etruscan *pershu* = mask). The Sabine influence was also considerable, as shown by the tradition of legends (King Titus Tatius and Romulus) and historical criticism (the noble Claudian family was of Sabine origin). This mix of peoples is illustrated by the old division of the inhabitants of Rome into three tribes: the *Titienses* (Sabines), the *Ramnes* (Etruscans) and the *Luceres* (Latins). According to tradition there were seven kings; the existence of the first four of these at the very least is confused with legend. The most important kings in relation to the development of the city were Romulus, the founder, **Numa Pompilius**, who organised the religious rites and the calendar, and **Servius Tullius**, who reformed the citizens' assemblies (the *comitia centuriata*, probably established in the 4C BC). The lower Tiber Valley was occupied by the Etruscans on the right bank and by the Latins and Sabines to the southeast and northeast (on the left bank). The hills on the left bank, shaped by erosion of the volcanic lava-flows from the Alban Hills (Monti Albani), made excellent defensive positions: particularly the Palatine, its steep sides rising from the surrounding marshy ground and its twin peaks giving a clear view of the Tiber. This site was, moreover, an ideal staging post on the salt road **(Via Salaria)** between the salt pans at the mouth of the Tiber and the Sabine country. These favourable features no doubt led to the development of Sabine and Latin settlements around the Palatine.

sans légende

- **753** – Legendary foundation of Rome by **Romulus** on the Palatine Hill.
- **715-616** – Reigns of three Sabine kings – Numa Pompilius, Tullus Hostilius, Ancus Martius.
- **616-509** – Etruscan hegemony – Tarquin the Elder, who laid out the Forum, Servius Tullius and Tarquin the Proud. With the fall of the monarchy, the Etruscan yoke is thrown off by Rome.

B. Morand/MICHELIN

THE LEGENDARY ORIGINS OF ROME

According to Livy in his *Roman History* and the Greek historian Dionysius of Halicarnassus in his *Early Roman History*, Aeneas, son of the goddess Venus and the mortal Anchises, fled from Troy when it was captured, landed at the mouth of the Tiber and married Lavinia, the king of Latium's daughter. He defeated Turnus, with the aid of Evander, chief of a settlement on the Palatine, and founded Lavinium (now Pratica di Mare). On Aeneas's death, his son Ascanius (or Iulus) left Lavinium to found Alba Longa *(see Index)*. The last king of this Alban dynasty was Amulius, who deposed his brother Numitor and forced the latter's daughter, Rhea Silvia, to enter the sacerdotal order of the Vestals. Her union with the god Mars gave birth to the twins **Romulus** and **Remus** whom Amulius tried to eliminate by abandoning on the Tiber. The basket carrying the twins came to rest at the foot of the Palatine where they were nursed by a wolf and brought up by a couple of shepherds, Faustulus and Larentia. When they reached adolescence they reinstated their grandfather Numitor on the throne and then left to found a new town in the place where they had spent their childhood. There they consulted the birds to discover the omens and Romulus marked a furrow around the sacred area on which the new city was to be built. Jesting, Remus stepped over the line; Romulus killed him for violating the sacred precinct *(pomoerium)*. The date given for the foundation of Rome by the Roman scholar Varro Marcus Terentius is 753 BC. According to a malicious Greek source (Dionysius of Halicarnassus), Romulus populated his village with outlaws who settled on the Capitol and whom he provided with Sabine wives *(see CAMPIDOGLIO – CAPITOLINO)*. An alliance grew between the two peoples who were ruled by a succession of kings, alternately Sabine and Latin, until the Etruscans arrived.

These events are legend rather than history. They contain a number of mythical elements found in many legends of ancient peoples, such as the abandonment of a favourite of the gods in a basket on the river (Moses and Sargon); fratricide or the struggle between two brothers for supremacy (Cain and Abel, Jacob and Esau); the migration of the young in the so-called "holy spring" *(ver sacrum)* in order to build a new city; the Indo-European custom of drawing the sacred limits of a city; and the devotion to the wolf, the totemic animal par excellence of the Italic peoples.

Museo Nazionale Romano

The Lupercalia (Altar to Mars and Venus), Palazzo Massimo alle Terme

The Republic (510-27 BC)

According to tradition, the Republic was proclaimed in 510 BC with the expulsion of the powerful Etruscan family, the Tarquins, and the granting of executive and military power to two consuls who were elected annually. The **Senate**, the assembly formed by the old patrician leaders of the *gentes* and founded according to tradition by Romulus, had a purely advisory role; its members were appointed for life and, from the 4C, were also drawn from the plebeian class. Judiciary power was invested in the **praetors**, and administrative and financial tasks carried out by the **aediles** and **quaestors**; all of these officials were appointed for one year.

The city was divided into two *ordines:* the **patricians** (the aristocrats "able to trace their ancestors") and the **plebeians**, who were forbidden to assume political or priestly office (the role of pontifex, flamen or augur could therefore only be assumed by patricians), or to marry into the patrician class.

The first Republican era is marked by the struggle between the patricians and the plebeians. The patricians saw their privileges gradually reduced over the years and a new patrician-plebeian ruling class, known as the *nobilitas,* was formed at the end of the 4C, with the eventual lifting of the regulations restricting plebs from acting as magistrates or priests. The last prohibitions to fall were those relating to censorship and the priestly offices of pontifex and flamen (a type of tutelary priest for cults of the major divinities).

The patricians controlled a substantial number of slaves, who formed the most wretched section of society, but who could be freed by their owners to become *liberti.* The *clientela* became important in Roman society during this period. This term referred to the personal relationship between an influential *patronus* and a succession of *clientes.* The latter provided reciprocal support during elections and tribunals, as well as protecting the interests of the *patronus,* who, in return provided his *clientes* with financial assistance or assistance in kind. This period saw Roman expansion within the Italian peninsula and across the Mediterranean. The increasing importance of the army resulted in the appearance of powerful characters who gained considerable political influence and wealth during periods of war. The late Republican period was characterised by conflict between various factions headed by the army generals.

The provinces conquered by the Roman legions were administered by **propraetors** and **proconsuls**. During the Empire, the powers exercised by the consuls were united in the person of the **Emperor**, who was responsible for appointing senators and, as head of the army and principal pontefix, for declaring peace or war. At this time some provinces came under direct control of the Emperor and were governed by magistrates of equestrian status (**prefects** and **procurators**).

● **494 –** Clash between Rome and the 30 cities of the Latin League; in 493 the pact imposed by Spurius Cassius confers hegemony upon Rome, which leaves the League. First secession of the plebeians, who obtain a magistrature to defend their rights (tribunate of the plebeians).

● **451-449 –** A commission of 10 magistrates *(decemviri)* codified civil and penal laws in the **Twelve Tables**, described by Cicero as "the very height and pinnacle of the law".

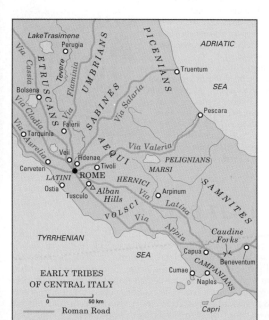

EARLY TRIBES
OF CENTRAL ITALY

0   50 km

—— Roman Road

● **396 –** The Etruscan capital, Veia, which controlled the River Tiber, is captured by the Romans after a 10-year siege.

● **390 –** Invasions by the Gauls and Roman defeat on the River Allia. Sacking and burning of Rome *(see CAMPIDOGLIO-CAPITOLINO).*

● **367 –** Passing of Licinio-Sextian laws by the tribunes of the same name. Plebeians granted access to consulship, reform of magistrature of censorship, and proposal for the distribution of territorial areas to citizens *(ager publicus).*

● **343-341 –** Rome forms alliances with Greek cities of the Campania region, provoking a reaction from the Samnites from the southern Apennines. This leads to the **First Samnite War**.

B. Kaufmann/MICHELIN

One of the two Dioscuri which grace Piazza del Campidoglio

• **326-304 – Second Samnite War**. Rome suffers the famous defeat of the **Claudine Forks**. A tactical reform of the legions (organised into groups of 60 men known as *maniples*, with lighter armour resulting in better mobility) guarantees Rome a partial victory.

• **312** – Appius Claudius Caecus, writer and orator, becomes censor. Construction of the first section of the Appian Way (the road was extended to Brindisi during the late-Republican period).

• **298-290 – Third Samnite War**, resulting in the victory of Rome; the combined armies of the Samnites, Etruscans, Gauls and Umbrians are defeated at the battle of Sentinum, in the present-day Marche region. The victory brings central Italy under Roman control.

• **282-272** – War against Tarentum, the last powerful Greek *polis* on the Italian peninsula. Tarentum calls upon Pyrrhus, king of Epiros, an experienced strategist who had married into the family of Alexander the Great, to come to its aid. Despite assistance from the Ptolemy of Egypt and diversionary tactics in Sicily, Pyrrhus is beaten at Maleventum (now Benevento). The capture of Tarentum brings the Romans into contact with the Hellenic culture (the Latin writer Livius Andronicus, author of the *Odusia*, a version of the Greek *Odysseus*, came from Tarentum).

• **264-241 – First Punic War** between Rome and **Carthage** over the possession of Sicily. After fierce fighting on land and at sea, Rome captures Sicily, with its prosperous cities, and the island becomes the first province controlled by Rome and governed by a propraetor. A few years after the end of the war, Rome conquers Sardinia.

• **218-201 – Second Punic War** and march by Hannibal from Spain to Italy. **Hannibal** defeats the Romans in Ticinus and Trebia in 218 and at Lake Trasimene in 217. The Roman legions are also crushed at Cannae, not far from Venosa. The Roman counter-offensive chases the Carthaginians out of Spain and prevents supplies from reaching Hannibal's army. **Scipio Africanus** (a young general from the noble Cornelii Scipiones family who had already distinguished himself in Ticinus) settles in Sicily; from here he extends the fighting to Africa. Hannibal, summoned home, is defeated by the army of Scipio Africanus at Naraggara-Zama. The peace treaty gives the Romans control over the western section of the Mediterranean basin. The destructive war has far-reaching consequences in Italy, such as an influx of slaves, the destruction of small peasant farms, and an increase in the population of the city of Rome, which received a substantial proportion of food provisions.

• **c 201** – The first comedies of Plautus.

• **197-168** – War in the east against the Hellenistic states of Macedonia, the Seleucids in Asia Minor and the Syrian-Mesopotamian region. Hellenistic influence on Roman culture. The victorious consul Emilius Paulus transports the Greek library from the Macedonian capital back to Rome.

- **179** – Construction of a wooden theatre. The first theatre in stone was built by Pompey in 55.
- **148-146** – **Third Punic War** against Carthage. Capture and destruction of Carthage.
- **133-121** – The brothers **Tiberius** and **Caius Gracchus** (The Gracchi), both tribunes of the plebeians, promulgate social and economic reforms. Tiberius insists on the distribution of the *ager publicus* to those without property and Caius attempts to confront the more general problem of the urban *plebs*, the founding of colonies, and concession of Roman citizenship granted to the Italic people. The discontented Senate orders the assassination of the brothers: Tiberius in 133 and Caius in 121.
- **111-105** – War against Jugurtha of Numidia. The continuous wars and probable corruption of the Roman senators had the effect of weakening the Roman republic. Two famous generals are victorious: **Caius Marius**, consul for the first time in 107, and **Lucius Sulla**.
- **91-88** – War between Rome and its Italian allies, who were demanding Roman citizenship. After much violent fighting the toughest rebels are defeated, although citizenship is awarded to all Italian peoples. Most of the inhabitants of the Po Plain were granted citizenship by Caesar in 49.
- **88** – **First Civil War** between the Senate (nobility) and people (*populares*). Lucius Sulla, supporter of the Senate and the *nobilitas,* is deprived of supreme command of the war against Mithridates in favour of **Marius**, a supporter of the *populares*. After marching on Rome in order to silence the opposition of the *populares*, Sulla is given overall command of the war.
- **87** – After the departure of Sulla, Caius Marius and Cornelius Cinna set up the rule of the *populares*.
- **84** – Return of Sulla to Italy and defeat of Cinna (Marius was killed in 86). The following year Sulla assumes dictatorial powers: a list of proscriptions against enemies is published, exiles have no recourse to law, and anyone killing an exile is able to claim part or all of the assassinated person's property.
- **82-79** – Sulla assumes the role of dictator and reforms the Republic. The Senate is strengthened and the powers of the plebeian tribunes reduced. Sulla retires from public life and dies the following year. He was described by one of his biographers as a frustrated monarch: unlike Augustus, he did not actually abolish the Republican political system.
- **73-70** – **Licinius Crassus**, a rich businessman, is elected consul in 70 with **Pompey**, an official of Sulla, after putting down the slave revolt led by Spartacus (6 000 prisoners crucified). Pompey is away from Rome fighting Mithridates and pirates until 62.
- **63** – **Catiline Conspiracy**, secretly supported by Caesar. The conspiracy is put down by the consul, Cicero, the champion of the agreement drawn up between senators and *equites* (which included businessmen and speculators). Catiline is killed in battle near Pistoia.
- **60** – **First triumvirate**, a private agreement between Crassus, Pompey and Caesar is signed at Lucca. The following year Casear was elected consul.
- **58-52** – Caesar's campaign against the **Gauls**, followed by his conquest of Britain and fighting against Germanic tribes. Troubles in Asia Minor, where in 54 Crassus is defeated and killed by the Parthians near Carrhae in Upper Mesopotamia.
- **49-45** – Civil war between Caesar and Pompey.
- **49** – Caesar as dictator.
- **48** – Assassination of Pompey, who had taken refuge at the court of the Ptolemy in Egypt.
- **44** – Assassination of Caesar on the **Ides of March** (15 March).
- **43** – **Second triumvirate** (no longer a private agreement, but a recognised magistrature) composed of the young **Octavian** (Caesar's great-nephew, who was adopted by him and took the name Gaius Julius Caesar Octavian), **Mark Antony** (Caesar's fellow consul) and **Lepidus** (Caesar's *magister equitum*). Antony is assigned the east, Octavian the west and Lepidus Africa. Assassination of Cicero, who had attacked Antony in public debates.

Caesar

AVE CAESAR!

Gaius Julius Caesar (101-44 BC), soldier and statesman, orator and writer (*The Gallic Wars* and *The Civil
War*), was instrumental in the establishment of the
Roman Empire. A supporter of the *populares*, he
proved his outstanding political abilities while he was still
very young. According to a speech he made from the Rostra on the occasion of his Aunt Julia's funeral in 68, he and his
family claimed descent from Venus.

While consul in 59 he reduced the second consul Bibulus to silence; this was so marked that "certain
facetious people ... wrote ... not of the consulate of Caesar and Bibulus – but – of the consulate
of Julius and Caesar" (Suetonius).

In 58 Caesar became Governor of Cisalpine Gaul and of Provincia (now Provence); by 51 he had
conquered the whole of Gaul, at the cost of perhaps a million lives. In January 49 he crossed the
Rubicon (the limit at that time of the *pomoerium*) and marched on Rome against the official
powers; Pompey, who had been sole consul since 52, and the Senate fled. Civil war followed.
Pompey's army was defeated at Pharsalus in Thessaly, Pompey himself was murdered in Alexandria
and other supporters of Pompey were defeated in Africa and Spain.

Early in 44 Caesar was appointed consul and dictator for life; he gave his name to the month of
his birth (July), pardoned his enemies and weakened the power of the senators by reducing their
number to 900. On 15 March 44 BC (the Ides of March), while planning a campaign against the
Parthians, he was stabbed to death by a group of senators in the *Curia Pompeia*.

● **31** – Battle of **Actium** (not far from Patras) between the troops of Octavian and
those of Mark Antony (who was married to Cleopatra, Queen of Egypt). The
Roman authorities resist the growing eastern influence advocated by Antony.
Antony and Cleopatra commit suicide; Octavian annexes Egypt to Rome and proclaims himself successor to the Ptolemy dynasty.

The Splendour
and Decadence
of the Roman Empire

The Julio-Claudian Dynasty (27 BC-AD 69)

● **27** – The Senate grants Octavian the title
Augustus (from the Latin *augere*, meaning to grow),
which had sacred and religious connotations.

Augustus

AUGUSTUS AND HIS POLITICAL ACHIEVEMENTS

Augustus instigated a complete reform of the administration of the provinces. Certain provinces
were assigned magistrates of senatorial rank; the more restless provinces, requiring a military presence, were administered by officials of equestrian rank (Egypt, whose cereal production was
important for Rome, was governed by a prefect and senators required Augustus's permission to
live there). The city of Rome was divided into 14 *regiones* each administered by a *vicimagister*.
Government of the city was entrusted to the *praefectus urbis*, of senatorial rank, a move considered illegal by many contemporary commentators. Nine cohorts of praetoria, seven urban
cohorts and various cohorts of *vigiles* (a type of military firemen) gave the city a garrison of around
15 000 men, which proved to be a determining factor in political life from this time. Augustus promoted an ambitious building programme and attempted to address moral issues of public life,
especially for the city-dwelling aristocracy, encouraging marriage and giving a boost to traditional
religious and Roman cults (on 12 August he was declared **Pontifex Maximus**, the High Priest).

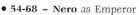
Museo Capitolino, Roma/S. Chirol

Nero

THE MAD EMPEROR

Nero became *princeps* after Claudius was assassinated by his wife Agrippina, mother of Nero, whom Claudius had adopted in 50. Nero's tutor was Seneca, who succeeded in controlling the young Emperor's behaviour for the first five years he was in power, tempering his more absolute tendencies. The repression of a senatorial conspiracy led to the suicide of Seneca and to violent and authoritarian behaviour by the Emperor. His diplomatic successes (the annexing of Armenia to the Roman Empire) did nothing to dispel the general level of discontent. Violent persecution of the Christians took place in 64, followed by the famous fire. The German legions rebelled and imposed Sulpicius Galba as the new Emperor. Nero committed suicide.

● **14 BC** – Augustus dies at Nola having witnessed the premature death of many family members who were expected to succeed him. He is succeeded by **Tiberius**, the son of his wife Livia, who distinguished himself through his military achievements in Germany and Pannonia. He was an introvert who was proud of his family tradition (he belonged to the noble Claudian family); towards the end of his life (AD 27) he retired to the island of Capri. The historian Tacitus was one of his most fierce detractors.

● **AD 30 – Jesus of Nazareth**, known as Christ, is condemned to death.

● **37-41 – Caligula** as *princeps* (head of State). He suffers from bouts of madness, but is determined to wield absolute power as Emperor, moving away from the compromise with Republican ideals achieved by Augustus. He falls victim to a conspiracy and is assassinated.

● **41-54 – Claudius**, Caligula's uncle and a scholar of the Etruscan civilisation, becomes *princeps*. Britain annexed to the Empire. Administrative reforms instigated, and some of Claudius's freed slaves, very loyal to him, are appointed in official posts. The reaction of the Senate is violent. **Seneca** is one of the victims of repression and is exiled to the island of Corsica.

Musée du Louvre, Paris/Nimatallah/ARTEPHOT

Tiberius

● **54-68 – Nero** as Emperor

● **69** – Succession disputed. Galba is followed by the prefect of Lusitania, Otho, who is in turn defeated and forced to commit suicide by Vitellius. Vitellius is challenged by Flavius Vespasian and **civil war** breaks out in the city of Rome. One of the most serious acts committed during this time was the fire in the Campidoglio, which damaged the Temple of Jupiter and was considered a highly sacrilegious act.

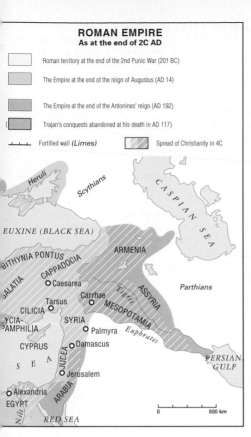

ROMAN EMPIRE
As at the end of 2C AD

Roman territory at the end of the 2nd Punic War (201 BC)

The Empire at the end of the reign of Augustus (AD 14)

The Empire at the end of the Antonines' reign (AD 192)

Trajan's conquests abandoned at his death in AD 117

Fortified wall *(Limes)*   Spread of Christianity in 4C

Heruli
Scythians
CASPIAN SEA
EUXINE (BLACK SEA)
ARMENIA
BITHYNIA PONTUS
CAPPADOCIA
GALATIA   O Caesarea
Tarsus   Carrhae   Parthians
CILICIA   O   MESOPOTAMIA   ASSYRIA
LYCIA-   SYRIA   Tigris
PAMPHILIA   O Palmyra   Euphrates
CYPRUS   O Damascus
S E A   JUDEA   PERSIAN GULF
O Jerusalem
O Alexandria   ARABIA
EGYPT
Nile   RED SEA
0   500 km

THE BEST OF EMPERORS

Marcus Ulpius Trajan was a Spaniard of Italian descent, and was the first Emperor to come from the provinces. Intelligent and energetic, he was described as the best of Emperors (*optimus princeps*). He carried out great public works such as building a forum with markets and two libraries (one Greek and one Latin), enlarging the ports of Ostia and Ancona, and constructing a bridge in Alcantara and an aqueduct in Segovia, both in Spain. In Italy, he instituted the *alimenta* for children, the first major example of social spending. His conquests in Dacia brought gold and slaves to Rome and helped to improve the economy of the Empire. He also led campaigns against the Parthians and penetrated as far as the Persian Gulf to enable the Empire to profit from the trade between the Far East and the Mediterranean. Other campaigns included those against the Nabataean kingdom and the capture of the capital Petra, an important commercial centre on the caravan route. In 117 he died of exhaustion while returning to Rome.

Flavian Emperors (AD 70-96)

● **69-79** – After much destruction and a year of civil war, **Flavius Vespasian**, from Rieti, head of a troop responsible for putting down the Jewish revolt, is proclaimed Emperor. He is a skilful administrator who restores the finances of the state and promulgates the *Lex de imperio* which sets out the powers of the *prin ceps* (head of State) for the first time. He promotes the construction of public works, such as the huge Flavian Amphitheatre, now known as the **Colosseum**.

● **79-81** – **Titus**, Vespasian's eldest son, becomes Emperor. In 79, Vesuvius erupts, destroying Herculaneum, Stabia and Pompeii. **Pliny the Elder** is killed while valiantly attempting to rescue the victims.

● **81-96** – Titus's brother, **Domitian**, becomes Emperor. He advocates anti-Senate policies, carries out military offensives in the Germanic regions and in Dacia with little success, and instigates the persecution of the Christians in 93. A conspiracy leads to his assassination.

Museo Capitolino, Roma-S. Chirol

Antonine Emperors and adopted heirs

● **96-98** – **Nerva**, a former senator, becomes Emperor. He inaugurates the procedure of Emperors nominating their successor.

● **98-117** – **Marcus Ulpius Trajan** is elected Emperor.

Marcus Aurelius

● **117-38** – **Hadrian** becomes Emperor. He promotes peace, abandoning Mesopotamia and building fortifications to defend the boundaries *(limes)* of the Empire. He was a cultured and passionate Hellenist who travelled widely throughout the Empire: he spent time in Africa in 128 and in Asia Minor from 128-134. His reign was blighted by a serious Jewish revolt in Palestine, Egypt and Cyrene (131-35).

● **138-61** – A long period of peace under the reign of **Antoninus Pius**. During this period Rome had a population of around one million, a figure exceeded only by imperial Peking.

Museo Capitolino, Roma/S. Chirol

Vespasian

- **161-80** – Reign of **Marcus Aurelius**, a Stoic philosopher and statesman who wrote a philosophical work in Greek entitled *Meditations*. After a campaign against the Parthians, he faced the dangerous threat of the German tribes (Quadi and Marcomanni) in the Upper Danube region.

- **180-92** – Reign of **Commodus**, son of Marcus Aurelius. Commodus was immature and not very capable; he was killed by a conspiracy of the Senate.

Severan Emperors and military anarchy (3C)

- **193-211** – The African general **Septimius-Severus** becomes Emperor after the civil war between Albino and Nigro. He disbands the Praetorian Guard which had become too powerful, and starts the offensive against the Parthians and the Scots. Government assumes the form of a military autocracy.

- **211-17** – Rule of Aurelius Antoninus, known as **Caracalla**, a fierce and unstable character. In 212 he publishes the *Constitutio Antoniniana de civitate* which granted Roman citizenship to all free men in the Empire, probably for tax purposes. High inflation, which was to continue until the beginning of the 4C.

- **218-22** – Reign of **Elagabalus**, high priest of the sun god, El-Gabal, from the city of Emesa in Syria. His outrageous behaviour leads to his assassination.

- **222-35** – **Severus Alexander** attempts to work with the Senate to prevent the invasions by German tribes. He is killed by Maximinus from Thracia, an uncouth professional soldier. A period of military **anarchy** follows, during which the Empire comes under increasing threat from invasions by German tribes and the Persians.

- **256-60** – Persecution of Christians under **Valerian**. The Emperor and his army are defeated by the Persians and Valerian is held prisoner in Persia. He is succeeded by his son **Gallienus**, protector of the famous philosopher **Plotinus**, who opened a school in Rome.

- **270-75** – **Aurelian**, a skilful general, takes Palmyra, the capital of a state in Syria which had been liberated from Rome by Zenobia. Preoccupied by the invasion of Germanic tribes on Italian soil, Aurelian has a new wall built around Rome, later reinforced by Honorius. The wall had 16 gates and 383 towers.

Imperial autocracy (4C-5C)

The Empire was reorganised under Diocletian and Constantine. During this time Italy and Rome lost some of their importance, Imperial power became autocratic, and administrative and fiscal reforms replaced the old Augustinian laws. Christianity became the religion of the Emperor and his family, and the seat of Imperial power gradually moved to the east, with the founding of Constantinople in 331.

- **284-305** – **Diocletian**, a high-ranking official, becomes Emperor. He attempts to harness inflation with the publication of a fixed price *(Edictum de pretis)* and devises a system that splits the Empire administratively, at the same time guaranteeing a peaceful succession. The **tetrarchy**, or rule by four, creates two leaders under the title of Augustus, assisted by two Caesars (who were also heirs). In 286 **Maximian** becomes Augustus in Milan; Galerius is given the title of Caesar and control of the east in Mitrovizza, assisting Diocletian, and **Constantius-Chlorus** assists Maximian as his Caesar and settles in Trier, governing Gaul and Britain. Rome is no longer the capital, but assumes a symbolic value as the original home of the Empire.

- **303** – Systematic and ruthless persecution of Christians by Diocletian.

- **311** – Freedom of worship granted to Christians in the east by Galerius.

- **306-37** – Chlorus's son, **Constantine**, takes advantage of the dissolution of the tetrarchy and proclaims himself Augustus. He goes on to rout all his enemies, including the pagan, Maxentius, who lived in Rome and was supported by the Senate, at the battle of Milvian Bridge.

- **337-60** – The Empire is divided among Constantine's three sons who soon enter into conflict with each other. **Constantinus II**, supporter of the Arian faith, emerges victorious. He makes a rare visit to Rome.

- **360-63** – **Julian** as Emperor. He was a cousin of Constantius II, and a very cultured man. He embraces paganism and attempts to reinstate this ancient religion. Christian teachers are refused work, although there are no real acts of hostility towards the Church. He leads a successful campaign against the Persians, but dies in battle near Ctesiphon, in Mesopotamia.

- **378** – Disastrous Roman defeat at **Adrianopolis** (Thracia) at the hands of the **Goths**. The Emperor Valentian is killed and the Goths establish themselves in the Balkans, often acting as mercenaries for the Roman army.

Constantine

CONSTANTINE AND
CHRISTIAN ROME

Constantine ruled as sole Emperor. In 313 he issued an **edict** in Milan, along with Licinius, stating that henceforth all religions would be tolerated, except Manicheism. Christianity was therefore officially recognised for the first time and Constantine himself converted to the religion. In 325 the Emperor headed the **First Ecumenical Council** of Christianity, which was held in Nicaea (Asia Minor), during which the Arian heresy was outlawed. Constantine was responsible for the construction of basilicas in Jerusalem (Holy Sepulchre) and Rome (St Peter's and St John Lateran, which remained the Papal seat for centuries). The conversion of Constantine confirmed the birth of a Christian empire.

The Church of Rome assumed superiority over the other Bishoprics and the other four Patriarchates of Christianity because Peter and Paul were said to have preached and been martyred in Rome. Tertullian states that Paul was beheaded in 67 and in 2C AD the Gaulish writer Irenaeus recorded the *principalitas* of the Church of Rome. Other writers recounted Paul's martyrdom and Peter's crucifixion during the reign of Nero. Eusebius of Caesarea (4C AD) recalls the words of Gaius about the trophies of the Apostles: "I can point out the trophies of the apostles. For if you are willing to go to the Vatican or the Ostian Way, you will find the trophies of those who founded this Church". Gaius's trophy can be identified in the crypt of St Paul Without the Walls – and archaeological evidence would appear to agree with this interpretation; a more recent tradition suggests that the tomb of the first Pope is located in the catacombs of **St Peter's.** Christian preaching, according to Suetonius and Tacitus, would appear to have taken place near the Jewish community which was established in Trastevere as early as the end of the 1C BC (this community is therefore the oldest in Rome), and was soon to interest the Gentiles. The aristocrat Acilius Glabrio was martyred in 91 and **Flavius Clemens,** Domitian's cousin, was killed because he was Christian. It is believed that it was his wife Domitilla who donated the land for use as a Christian cemetery. A number of churches were built over the martyrs' tombs or near the homes of the rich protectors of the Christian community *(tituli).*

● **382** – Pope **Leo the Great** proclaims the Pope Head of the Church and the fount of episcopal authority, reinforcing the supremacy of the Roman Church over that of Constantinople. During this period, Gratian, a pupil of Ambrose, renounces the traditional and pagan title of *Pontifex Maximus,* once the prerogative of all Emperors after Augustus.

● **379-95** – **Theodosius I** becomes Emperor. He resolves the problem of the Goths and reigns as sole Emperor (the last in Roman history). In 380 Nicean Christianity is proclaimed the state religion by the Emperor in Thessalonica. In 392, at the suggestion of **Ambrose** of Milan, paganism is outlawed. Following Theodosius's death, the Empire is divided between his sons: **Arcadius** in the east and **Honorius,** whose guardian was the Vandal general Stilicho, in the west.

● **403** – Following the invasion of the Po Plain by the Visigoth, **Alaric** (later defeated by Stilicho), Honorius leaves Milan and settles in Ravenna, a city defended by the marshland surrounding it. Stilicho is murdered by a conspiracy in 407.

● **410** – Rome sacked by Alaric for three days. A huge outcry follows. The writers Jerome and Augustine write pages on the desecration of the city. The previous year, various Germanic tribes had invaded Gaul. The west is on the verge of collapse.

● **430** – **Aurelius Augustine**, a Christian writer and philospher, dies at Ippona (in present-day Algeria), attacked by Vandals. He wrote the *Confessions* and a major work on the civilisation and decadence of Rome, *De Civitate Dei.*

● **455** – **Genseric**, king of the Vandals, sacks Rome from his African territory with extreme ferocity. Just four years earlier the Roman general Ezio had stopped the Huns in Gaul, and in 452 **Attila** had turned back at the Po Plain, either as a result of the intervention of the Pope, or from fear of an outbreak of plague in Italy.

● **476** – The last Emperor of the west, **Romulus Augustus**, deposed by the barbarian **Odoacer**. The Emperor of the east is now universally recognised as the legitimate Emperor.

ROME
DURING THE EMPIRE

from 1C to 4C AD

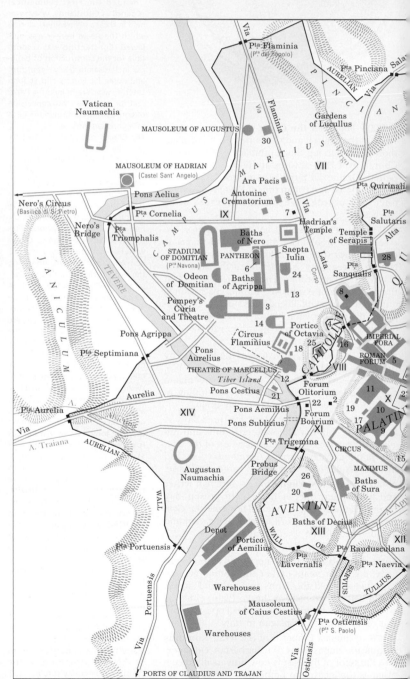

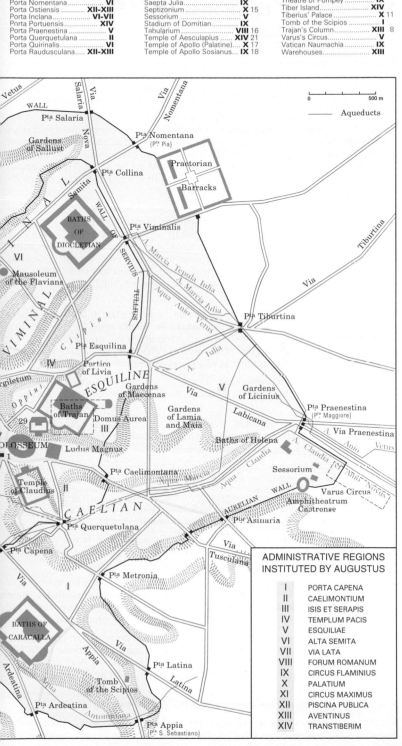

ADMINISTRATIVE REGIONS INSTITUTED BY AUGUSTUS

I	PORTA CAPENA
II	CAELIMONTIUM
III	ISIS ET SERAPIS
IV	TEMPLUM PACIS
V	ESQUILIAE
VI	ALTA SEMITA
VII	VIA LATA
VIII	FORUM ROMANUM
IX	CIRCUS FLAMINIUS
X	PALATIUM
XI	CIRCUS MAXIMUS
XII	PISCINA PUBLICA
XIII	AVENTINUS
XIV	TRANSTIBERIM

The Power of the Popes (6C-15C)

- **493** – The Arian **Ostrogoths** settle in Italy. Their educated king, **Theodoric**, initiates a period of collaboration with the Romans.

- **527-65** – **Justinian** becomes Emperor of Byzantium. In 540 he orders his general Belisarius to invade Sicily. This leads to the disastrous Gothic War which devastated parts of Italy and effectively marked the end of Italy's ancient era. Rome is captured and then lost by Belisarius. In 552 Italy is annexed to the eastern Empire.

- **568** – Invasion by the **Lombards**, a Germanic people who were more barbarian and uncultured in nature than the Visigoths. Rome at this time is officially part of the Byzantine Empire, but is, in fact, defended and sustained by the Pope. The Byzantine exarch has his residence in Ravenna and not in Rome. The disappearance of the Senate and the destruction of the city signals the beginning of Rome's decay.

- **590-604** – Papacy of **Gregory the Great**, known as *Consul Dei* because of his political ability. A writer and theologian, he was responsible for the evangelisation of Britain. Under his Papacy, the Bishop of Rome becomes a moral and political force of European importance. In spite of this, records of the time (many of which are pilgrims' accounts of their time in the city published at the end of the 7C) show Rome to be a small city, with a population of less than 20 000. The influx of monks from the east and the Greek language would have a marked effect on the city for two centuries.

- **752** – Rome is threatened by the Lombards. Pope Stephen II appeals for help from the king of the Franks, **Pepin the Short** (the Franks were Catholics, unlike the other Germanic tribes, who were Arian), marking the beginning of the alliance between the French and the Pope. The latter had little faith in distant Byzantium, which was involved in the conflict over iconoclasm, rejected by Rome.

- **758** – Donation of Querzy-sur-Oise. The Pope acquires Sutri and other territories, leading to the birth of the *Patrimonium Petri*, otherwise known as the **Papal States**.

- **800** – **Charlemagne**, who had conquered the Lombards in 776, is crowned Emperor by Pope Leo III, despite the opposition of Byzantium, reviving the Roman Empire of the west. Rome is the seat of this *Respublica Christiana*.

- **824** – Ludovic the Pius, son and successor to Charlemagne, passes his *Constitutio* stating that no Pope could be elected without first swearing allegiance to the Emperor.

- **846** – The Moors, landing at Ostia, sack the basilica of St Peter's. As a result, the Leonine Walls are built around the Vatican basilica in 852.

- **9C-10C** – Unsettled period for the Papacy. The aristocratic families of Rome (the Theophylacti, **Crescenzi** and later the Tuscolani) all push for the election of their family members, who are often weak and dissolute.

- **962** – John XII calls **Otho I**, king of Germany, to Rome and crowns him Emperor. Otho imposes major reforms on the Papacy, establishing that a Pope could not be elected without the consent of the Emperor. In 963 Pope John XII is deposed and Leo VIII, a German prelate loyal to the Emperor, elected.

- **996** – **Otho III** resides in Rome, on the Aventine, and dreams of restoring Rome to its ancient grandeur. The Pope at this time is the scholar **Sylvester II**. In 998 the Emperor issues a *Privilegium* attesting the pre-eminence of Rome above all other cities in the Empire. The city's renaissance is cut short by the death of Otho in 1002.

- **1057** – Stephen IX elected Pope without the Emperor's approval.

- **1075** – **Gregory VII**, a strong advocate of absolute theocracy, confirms the superiority of the Papacy over the Empire and declares that laymen cannot make ecclesiastical appointments (the **Investiture Controversy**). He also denounces the sale and acquisition of Church goods and the marriage of priests. In his *Dictatus Papae* the Pope sets out the holy and political power of the Papacy, which exceeds that of all bishops and other Christians, including the Emperor. The Emperor Henry IV, angered by this statement, captures Rome. He is then expelled by the Norman army of Robert Guiscard, called upon by Gregory VII. Rome is violently sacked and its population massacred; many of those inhabitants not killed are sold as slaves.

● **1122 – Concordat of Worms**. The Pope and the Emperor reach a compromise to end the Investiture Controversy. Accepting the suggestion of the canonist, Yves (Ivo) of Chartres, the Pope will from now on invest future bishops spiritually with a ring and pastoral staff; the Emperor will concede temporal power with a sceptre.

● **1130-55 –** Arnaldo da Brescia, a monk who was a pupil of the philosopher Abelard, attempts to reform the Papacy and institute a republic in Rome, divided into *Comune*.

● **1153 –** Pope protected by **Frederick Barbarossa** under the Treaty of Constance. Arnaldo da Brescia captured and hanged. New conflict between the Pope and the Emperor. Rome fortified with towers *(Roma turrita)* built by powerful aristocratic families, some supporters of the Pope and some of the Emperor.

● **1198-1216 –** Papacy of **Innocent III**. This period represents the culmination of medieval Papal theocracy.

● **1309-77 – Avignon captivity**. As a result of the influence of the French monarchy, the Popes (most of whom were French) move to Avignon. The Pope returns to Rome following the protests and prayers of Catherine of Siena, Bridget of Sweden and the poet Petrarch.

● **1347 –** Rome dominated by **Cola di Rienzo**, a notary of the city and ardent admirer of the ancient history of Rome, who is eager to return the city to its former glory. His attempt fails miserably because of the hostility of the aristocratic families of Rome and after only three years he is forced to flee the city. He returns, having been given the support of the Pope, but is soon forced to flee once more and is tragically slaughtered. Information on his life is recounted in the anonymous work, *The Life of Cola di Rienzo*, written in the vulgar Roman dialect.

● **1357 –** Cardinal Egidio di Albornoz publishes his *Constitutiones Aegidianae*, laws with which the Papal States were ruled until the 19C.

● **1378-1417 – Great Schism of the West**. Two Popes reign simultaneously, one in Rome and one in Avignon. In 1409 there was a third in Pisa. The Roman Pope **Martin V** brings the seat of the Papacy back to Rome and rules as sole Pope.

● **1447-55 –** Nicholas V founds the **Vatican Library**, which today has around 500 000 books and 60 000 manuscripts. Rome becomes a centre of the European Humanist movement.

● **1453 –** Constantinople captured by the Turks, signalling the end of the eastern Empire. The Humanist Pope Pius II (Enea Silvio Piccolomini) issues a protest over the apathy of western sovereigns.

Rome in the Modern Era

● **1494 –** The French king, **Charles VIII**, en route for Naples, enters Rome. This marks the beginning of foreign intervention in central and northern Italy.

● **1508-12 –** After a period of fighting to subjugate the aristocratic families to the power of the Church, **Julius II** goes to war to retain Romagna, to weaken the Venetian Republic and to expel the French king, Louis XII, from Italy.

● **1517 – Luther**, who had visited Rome and been shocked by the immorality of the Curia, nails his *95 Theses* on the church door at Wittenberg. The Medici Pope Leo X underestimates the danger of Luther's gesture.

● **6 May 1527 –** The **sack of Rome** by the Protestant Swiss and Spanish troops under Emperor Charles V, who holds Rome for seven months. By November only

32 000 of the 55 000 inhabitants of Rome remain. The later influx of people from central Italy had the effect of distancing the Roman dialect from other dialects of the south. In November Clement VII surrenders to the imperial troops, promising a council to reorganise Catholicism.

- **1543-63 – Council of Trent** and birth of the Counter-Reformation.

- **1585-90 –** Pontificate of **Sixtus V**, during which crime and brigandry are rife. The Church and State are divided into 15 congregations at this time, each administered by a cardinal. The presence of prelates and Italian officials was absolute and would remain like this until the end of the 17C. Sixtus V was responsible for a number of building projects. With the help of Domenico Fontana he erected the obelisks of Piazza dell'Esquilino, Piazza del Popolo, Piazza San Pietro and Piazza San Giovanni in Laterano. He constructed the Via Sistina, partially linked the main churches and numerous districts of Rome with wide roads, rebuilt the Lateran and constructed the Scala Santa, replaced the statue of the Emperor on Trajan's Column with that of St Peter and had a chapel built to house his own tomb in the basilica of Santa Maria Maggiore.

- **1600 –** The philospher **Giordano Bruno** is burnt at the stake in Campo dei Fiori.

- **1631 – Urban VIII** obtains the duchy of Urbino. The Papal States reach their greatest territorial extent.

- **1791 –** Renunciation by the Papacy of Avignon and the Comtat-Venaissin, which are annexed to France.

- **1798 –** Rome occupied by the French troops of **Napoleon**; the Jacobin Roman Republic proclaimed. Pius VI is driven from Rome and dies in exile in Valence.

- **1800 –** The new Pope, Pius VII, is elected in Venice and returns to Rome, where the Republic is defeated. The following year the Pope signs a concordat with Napoleon.

- **1808 –** Rome occupied by the French. Following political disagreements (Pius VII refused to apply the continental blockade aimed at isolating Britain), the Papal States are invaded by Napoleonic troops and the Pope banished to Savona, then Fontainebleau. Pius VII returns to Rome in 1814.

- **1820-61 –** Struggle for the unification of the Italian States.

- **1848 – Pius IX** sends troops to fight the Austrians, during the First War of Independence. The Pope's conservative stance leads to the proclamation of the Roman Republic, defended by **Garibaldi** against the French troops, who take the city to ensure the return of the Pope.

Rome, Capital of Italy

- **1870 –** Rome captured by the Italian army, ending the temporal authority of the Pope. Pius IX retires to the Vatican. The Law of Guarantees, whose aim was to safeguard the Pope's liberty, is proposed by the State but refused by the Pope. Rome is declared the capital of the Italian kingdom.

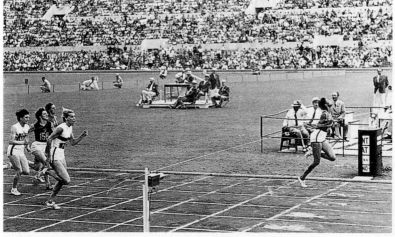

Wilma Rudolph's victory in the 200m sprint at the 1960 Olympic Games

- **28-29 October 1922** – Fascist march on Rome. **Mussolini** named Prime Minister.
- **1929** – Mussolini and Cardinal Gasparri sign the **Lateran Treaty** (renewed in 1984). Foundation of the Vatican City State.
- **1937** – Creation of Cinecittà and the Istituto Luce.
- **1943 (19 July)** – Bombardment of the San Lorenzo district; Pope Pius XII attempts to console the population.
- **4 June 1944** – Rome liberated by British and American forces.
- **1946 – Proclamation of the Republic**. Italy divided into regions for administrative purposes. Rome becomes the administrative centre of the Lazio region.
- **1957** – Treaty of Rome setting up the Common Market (now the European Union). Rome also becomes the headquarters of the Food and Agriculture Organisation (FAO), a United Nations organisation.
- **1960** – Olympic Games held in Rome.
- **1963-65 – Second Vatican Council**, called by John XXIII (1958-63) and completed by Paul VI (1963-78). The Church promotes a dialogue with non-believers and ecumenism in an attempt to enter the modern world. At the same time liturgical reform abolishes the use of Latin in church services.
- **1968** – Clashes between students and police near Villa Giulia in one of the first episodes of student protests.
- **1975** – Holy Year celebrated by Paul VI.
- **1978** – Aldo Moro kidnapped and killed by the Red Brigades. Paul VI dies and is succeeded by John Paul I, who was Pope for only 33 days. The Archbishop of Cracow, Karol Wojtila, is elected Pope and takes the name **John Paul II**.
- **1983** – Exceptional Holy Year declared by John Paul II.
- **1984** – Renewal of the Lateran Pact between the Holy See and the Italian Government.
- **1990** – Football World Cup held in Rome.
- **November 1998 – Jubilee** of the year 2000 announced by the Pope.
- **2000** – Celebration of the **Jubilee**.

THE GRAND TOUR

A continental tour of one or two years, culminating in a visit to Rome, was a peculiarly British custom which lasted 300 years, reaching its height in the 18C when the Grand Tour formed part of a gentleman's education. A young man would set out with a tutor, known as a "bear leader", who would superintend his studies, protect him from bad company and show him the sights. On arriving in Rome, preferably at Easter time, these early tourists would set out "equipped with all things needful to measure the dimensions of the antiquities they would be shown". It was important to engage a good guide such as Winckelmann, a German archaeologist, who was superintendent of antiquities in Rome, or Gavin Hamilton, who became well known as a dealer and antiquary. The tour had great influence at home on manners, architectural style and the formation of art collections. **Lord Burlington**, the arbiter of good taste in the early 18C, made two tours, which led to his patronage of **William Kent** and the introduction of the **Palladian** style into England.

Many English artists studied in Rome: **Richard Wilson** (1752-56); and **Sir Joshua Reynolds** (1750-52); and **Sir George Romney** (1773-75), whose portraits show the influence of the Classical style in their backgrounds and draperies; **John Flaxman**, the sculptor (1787-94), nicknamed the "English Michelangelo", who encouraged **John Gibson** to become a pupil of Canova. **Benjamin West** (1760-63) and *John Copley* (1774) from America visited Rome before settling in London.

In the 19C, instead of the established tour of the most famous cities, works of art and monuments, with its accent on antiquities, visitors preferred to settle in less well-known towns, taking an interest in Italian life and customs and even in the nationalist movement. **Charles Dickens** visited Rome in 1845 while writing a travel book, *Pictures of Italy*.

Rome provided poetic inspiration: in May 1817 **Byron** toured the ruins gathering material for the Fourth Canto of Childe Harold; **Shelley** composed *Prometheus Unbound* and *The Cenci* while lodging in the Corso in 1819; in 1860 **Robert** and **Elizabeth Barrett Browning** made a visit to Rome which inspired his greatest work, *The Ring and the Book*, a poem based on a 17C Roman murder trial. Rome still attracted many artists: **Eastlake** made invaluable purchases of early Italian art for the National Gallery in London; **Turner** visited Rome twice (1819, 1828) and used quotations from *Childe Harold* as titles for his paintings. From America came **William Page** (1849-60), who painted portraits of Robert and Elizabeth Browning; he had trained under **Samuel Morse**, an artist who studied in Europe in 1832 and invented the electric telegraph.

Many American writers visited Rome: **Washington Irving** (1804-06), **Fenimore Cooper** (1820-27), **Longfellow** (1828), **Herman Melville** (1856-57), **Nathaniel Hawthorne** (1858-59) and **Mark Twain** (1867), while collecting material for *Innocents Abroad*. Most famous of all was **Henry James**, who first visited Italy in 1869; his first important novel was set in Rome.

Influential Families in the History of Rome

Barberini

This Roman family, originally from Tuscany, produced Pope **Urban VIII** (1623-44). He commissioned the Barberini Palace on the Quirinal on which both the young **Bernini** and Borromini worked: it contains a magnificent picture gallery. He commissioned the Triton Fountain and the Fountain of the Bees in Piazza Barberini. He was a friend of Galileo and the first to employ Bernini, from whom he commissioned a bust of himself and the baldaquin above the high altar in St Peter's Basilica.

Borghese

This noble family from Siena settled in Rome when one of its members was elected Pope **Paul V** (1605-21). The family has left its mark in the Palazzo Borghese, in the city centre, and in the Villa Borghese to the north of Rome. During his Papacy the Villa became a museum and houses many important works of art collected over the years by generations of the family. Paul V also commissioned the Pauline Fountain (Fontana Paolina) on the Janiculum. He is buried in the Pauline Chapel in the church of Santa Maria Maggiore.

Borgia

Originally from Spain, this family produced two Popes: **Calixtus III** (1455-58) and **Alexander VI** (1492-1503). It was during Alexander's reign that America was discovered. He used gold from Peru to decorate the ceiling of Santa Maria Maggiore; his coat of arms is shown there. He was also responsible for the decoration of the Borgia Apartments in the Vatican. His son, **Cesare**, is remembered for his uncontrollable lust for power which inspired Machiavelli to write *The Prince*; his daughter, **Lucrezia**, was the victim of political intrigue between her father and her brother.

Chigi

This family of Roman bankers originally came from Siena. They became more important from the 15C through **Agostino Chigi**, who commissioned the young Raphael to decorate his residence, the Villa Farnesina. The Chigi Palace, official residence of the president of the Council of Ministers, owes its name to **Alexander VII** (1655-67), a member of the illustrious family who acquired it in the 17C. The Pope commissioned Bernini to build the colonnades of St Peter's. The Chigi coat of arms also appears on the fountain in Piazza d'Aracoeli.

Colonna

This ancient noble Roman family was very powerful in Rome from the 13C to the 17C. The election of one of its members, **Martin V** (1417-31), as Pope during the Council of Constance ended the Great Schism of the West. When the papacy returned to Rome, Martin concentrated totally, right up to his death, on reinstating the primacy of the Vatican.

Della Rovere

Two great Popes were born into this family from Savona: Sixtus IV and Julius II. **Sixtus IV** (1471-84), whose secular name was Francesco della Rovere, was a scholarly and industrious man. He wrote a thesis on the blood of Christ and a study on the Immaculate Conception. He was also responsible for major works which contributed to the architectural heritage of Rome, such as the rebuilding of Sante Maria del Popolo and the construction of Santa Maria della Pace and the Sistine Chapel. Sixtus IV called upon some of the greatest artists of the day, including Botticelli, Ghirlandaio and Perugino, to decorate the chapel. Having appointed his nephews Gerolamo and Pietro Riario as Bishop and Archbishop of Imola, he came into conflict with Lorenzo de' Medici and was involved in the Pazzi conspiracy, which led to the assassination of Giuliano de' Medici (Lorenzo's brother) in Florence Cathedral, and to the massacre of the conspirators by the mob. Like his nephew Giuliano della Rovere (the future Pope Julius II), Sixtus IV was a warrior Pope; he fought against other Italian states and was victorious against Muhammad II, who had landed at Otranto and massacred many of the local inhabitants. **Julius II** (1503-13) was blessed with great gifts both as a politician and as a generous patron: the implementation of Bramante's design for St Peter's, the painting of the Vatican Rooms by Raphael, the designing of his mausoleum, which remained unfinished, by Michelangelo (in the church of San Pietro in Vincoli), and the collection of antique sculptures in the Vatican. He was also responsible for the building of Via Giulia, a long, straight thoroughfare between the bend in the Tiber and the island downstream.

Farnese

This aristocratic family from Umbria, which was already famous by the 12C, came to Rome through **Paul III** (1534-49), the Pope who convened the **Council of Trent** (1545-63). He was the driving force behind major projects and, while still a cardinal, commissioned Sangallo to build the Farnese Palace which was finished by Michelangelo. When he became Pope, he turned once again to the Florentine master for the *Last Judgement* in the Sistine Chapel and put him in charge of work on St Peter's Basilica. The family also held dukedoms in Parma and Piacenza from 1545-1731.

Medici

This Florentine merchant and banking family ruled Florence and the whole of Tuscany from the 15C to the 18C. It produced several Popes: **Leo X** (1513-21), son of Lorenzo the Magnificent, a man of letters and patron of the arts, who put Raphael and Giulio Romano in charge of the Loggias in the Vatican; **Clement VII** (1523-34), an ally of François I, who was not able to prevent the sack of Rome or the Lutheran reforms which erupted during his Papacy; **Pius IV** (1559-65) who presided over the closure of the Council of Trent (1545-63); and **Leo XI**, who died a few days after he was elected in 1605, but who, while still a cardinal, had acquired the Villa Medici, which later became the French Academy in Rome.

Pamphili

Originally from Umbria, the family settled in Rome during the 15C. In 1461 its members were honoured with the title of Counts of the Holy Roman Empire. In the 16C Giovanni Battista became Pope **Innocent X** (1644-55). He was responsible for many changes in Piazza Navona: the rebuilding of the Pamphili Palace, the transformation into a family chapel of the church of Sant'Agnese in Agore, for which the façade and dome were built by Borromini; and the building of the Fountain of the Four Rivers (Fontana dei Quattro Fiumi) which he commissioned from Bernini. He turned, however, to Borromini, a rival of Bernini, for the Palace for the Propagation of the Faith and the rebuilding of St John Lateran. The Villa Doria Pamphili was built for the Pope's nephew, Camillo Pamphili, whose wife inherited the palace known as the Palazzo Doria Pamphili.

Life and Art in Ancient Rome

During the Republican period, art was valued for its practical and social significance rather than for its aesthetic value, as is seen in the major architectural works of the time. Priorities were to change, however, under the Roman Empire, when art celebrated the power of the Empire and demonstrated the prestige of the capital, which was to attract a huge foreign population eager to live close to the corridors of power. The decadence of the Empire and the recognition of Christianity as the state religion saw the development of the first large basilicas, which have often been restored or rebuilt and which still welcome thousands of visitors and pilgrims today.

Baths of Caracalla

Roman Art

Architecture

The remains of only a few public works have survived from the period of the kings and the early Republic, such as the channel of the **Cloaca Maxima** (a sewer dug in the 6C BC), the **town wall** built by **Servius Tullius** (578-534 BC), the **Appian Way** and the **Aqua Appia**, both the work of **Appius Claudius Caecus**, censor in 312 BC. The major artistic influences on the Romans came from the Etruscans, whose works they pillaged, and from the East, whence their victorious generals returned, dazzled by the splendours they had seen and accompanied by the artists they had engaged in cities such as Athens or Alexandria.

Materials and techniques – In the early days Rome was built of very simple materials: **tufa**, a soft brownish stone, volcanic or calcareous in origin; and **peperine**, also of volcanic origin, which owes its name to its greyish hue and its granular texture, suggestive of grains of pepper (*pepe* in Italian). **Travertine**, a whitish limestone, mostly quarried near Tivoli, is a superior material to the earlier ones and was used only sparingly in the early centuries. **Marble** made rare appearances as a decorative material from the 2C BC but became very popular under the Empire. **Brick** was first used in the 1C BC; it is usually seen today stripped of its marble facing. The principles of Classical Roman architecture were undoubtedly modelled upon those used in Ancient Greece. The mastery of three distinctive feats of civil engineering, however, heralded new building practices in Rome.

Firstly, as distinct from their Greek counterparts, the Romans discovered how to make and use concrete, allowing them to build more quickly and therefore more prolifically.

Secondly they learnt how to apply marble (and any other finely finished stone like granite, porphyry and alabaster) as surface decoration rather than having to use large (and expensive) quantities as building blocks: hence the reason for Roman ruins surviving today as sad reddish or greying husks of brick or concrete, stripped of their marble facing and friezes, which have long been removed.

Thirdly, the Romans learnt from their campaigns in the eastern Mediterranean (modern-day Turkey and Syria) the use of the arch, vaulting, squinches and, consequently, the art of constructing domes. At last they were able to break the linearity of the Hellenistic style with round arcs.

Concrete was usually poured between simple brick parapets to make a solid wall or over a brick layer to anchor the voussoirs of an archway, vault or dome: indeed, the Romans seem to have avoided using wooden coffering because of its expense. One particular feature of Roman concrete is its ability to harden with time through the centuries: the honeycomb appearance of ruins that survive is largely caused by the erosion of the brickwork, leaving a lattice of now bare mortar.

Several distinctive bricklaying techniques were adopted through time: square bricks or tiles could be split diagonally and laid with the right angle facing inwards to provide a broader area wedged in the concrete; cubes of terracotta were laid obliquely making a decorative trellis pattern; in some instances different methods are used in the same wall.

In their constructions the Romans used the **semicircular arch**. The one built over the Cloaca Maxima in about the 2C BC is a true masterpiece. Circular rooms were covered by hemispherical domes, niches set in walls were covered by half-domes and the lintel over an opening was surmounted by a rounded arch. There are some impressive examples of vaulting in the Domus Augustana on the Palatine, in the Pantheon, in Hadrian's Villa at Tivoli, in the Baths of Caracalla and in the Colosseum.

The Romans were masters of the technique of building theatres on level ground rather than set into a hillside as was the Greek practice. This involved the construction of vaults to support the terraces, as in the Theatre of Marcellus.

Classical orders – *See p 88.* They used the Greek architectural **orders** with modifications: in the Tuscan or Roman Doric order the column rests on a base rather than directly on the ground; the Ionic order was seldom used in Rome; the Corinthian order, however, was very popular – the Romans sometimes replaced the curling acanthus leaves on the capital with smooth overhanging leaves and for the flower in the centre of the curved side they substituted various motifs: animals, gods, human figures.

To the three Classical orders they added a fourth, called Composite, which was distinguished by a capital in which the four scrolls of the Ionic order surmounted the acanthus leaves. The entablature (comprising the architrave, frieze and cornice) was very ornate, richly decorated with pearls, ovoli and ornamental foliage.

The names of two architects have survived: Rabirius, active under Domitian (AD81-95), and Apollodorus of **Damascus** who worked for Trajan (AD98-117) and Hadrian (AD117-138).

Public buildings and monuments

Theatres – The first permanent theatre was built by Pompey (Teatro di Pompeo). Previously, mobile wooden stages had been used. Theatres were designed for the staging of comedies and tragedies; they were also used for political, literary and musical events as well as for competitions and lotteries and the distribution of bread or money.

Unlike the Greeks, the Romans built a certain number of theatres on flat sites, using vaults to support the rows of seats which often ended in a colonnade. The space in front of the stage (orchestra) was reserved for actors and later people of rank, who came to watch the play. The leading actors came on the stage, which was raised above the orchestra, through three doors in the wall at the back of the stage. Animals and chariots came in from the sides.

The rear wall, the most beautiful part of the theatre, was decorated with many columns, statues set in recesses, and facings of marble and mosaic. Behind the rear wall of the stage were the dressing rooms, storerooms and a portico overlooking a garden.

The stage hands were responsible for special effects: smoke, lights, thunder, apparitions and grand finales, gods and heroes who descended from heaven or disappeared into the clouds. The actors wore masks to enable the audience to identify the different characters. The acoustics were influenced by the canvas awning slanting down over the stage, which concentrated the sound so it penetrated to the top row of the terraces and also, perhaps, by resonant vessels strategically placed to act as loud speakers. It has been suggested that when the actors sang, they stood in front of the rear wall of the stage so the doors acted as sounding boards.

Amphitheatres – Amphitheatres, such as the magnificent Colosseum, were invented by the Romans for holding displays of gymnastics and horse-drawn chariot races. Their main use, however, was for combats between gladiators, who were mostly slaves or prisoners and faced death if they lost, or between wild beasts, which were specially kept for the major spectacles held either in Rome or in the provinces and which were attended by the Emperor.

These bloody spectacles, which were offered to the people, were considered so important by the Romans that candidates for public office treated them as an element of entertainment in their electoral campaigns.

During the spectacle, slaves burned or sprayed perfume to neutralise the smell of the animals, covered the sand in the arena with red dust to hide the bloodstains and used lead-weighted whips to coerce human contestants or animals into the fray. Loud music played throughout the spectacle.

Amphitheatres were more or less oval in shape. The outer wall consisted of three storeys of arcades, surmounted by a wall in which were fixed the poles which supported the huge awnings shading the spectators from the sun. The many doors under the arcades, the three circular galleries which formed the balconies for spectators and the stairs and corridors *(vomitoria)* where the spectators congregated, allowed access to the seats without any intermixing of the classes and without the danger of people being crushed. The most important spectators sat on a podium, protected by a balustrade; it was raised above the arena and positioned in the centre of one of the longer sides at the foot of the terraced area *(cavea)* which surrounded the arena on all sides.

Baths – Going to the baths occupied an important place in the Roman day, particularly during the Empire. These were free public clubs providing thermal baths, gymnasia and places to stroll, read or converse. These were built on a large scale and decorated with columns, capitals, mosaics, coloured marbles, statues and frescoes (Baths of Caracalla).

Basilicas – Originally, basilicas were built to accommodate law courts and stall-holders. Located in the forum, the basilica was where people might congregate out of the sun or rain; it had no religious function as such. The term, which literally means "royal portico", referred to it being a covered area; the roof was supported by rows of free-standing columns, dividing the internal rectangular space into a "nave" flanked by two side aisles. The first basilica to be built in Rome was the Basilica Porcia; this was erected at the foot of the Capitolino in 185 BC. Unfortunately nothing of the building remains. The use of basilicas for religious functions was assumed with the rise of the early Christian Church.

Triumphal arches – These arches were built to commemorate the triumph of a victorious general or to raise the statue of a prominent person into prominent view. Some had only one arched opening (Arch of Titus); others had three arched openings (Arch of Septimus Severus, Arch of Constantine). It is thought that the original designs of these monuments were linked to the belief that a defeated army lost its powers of destruction on passing under the arch.

Circuses – The huge oblong arenas were built to host popular chariot races; these include the Circus Maximus and Maxentius's Circus off the Old Appian Way. The layout of the arena can be likened to a quadrangle with rounded corners: at one end was the **oppidum** which opened out on to the concourse; the internal perimeter would have been lined with rows of steps for the spectators. In the centre of the concourse was the **spina**, a long divided track around which the chariots ran.

Stadiums – These, too, were oblong in shape but were used rather for athletic competitions. The site of Domitian's Stadium (Stadio di Domiziano) is now occupied by Piazza Navona.

Aqueducts – The impressive engineering of these great constructions has probably contributed more than anything else to the Roman reputation for building. The Aqua Appia, the oldest aqueduct, was originally more than 16km/10mi in length and was built in 312 BC by Appius Claudius the Blind. Approximately 100m/328ft of the aqueduct is still standing.

Roads – In some places, considerable stretches of the original paving are still intact. The word *civus* alludes to a street going up or down hill; a *vicus* is a side street.

Temples and worship

Temples *(see illustration, p 88)* were places devoted to the worship of the gods and of the Emperor, who, since the time of Caesar, had risen to the status of a god. Their design was inspired by Etruscan and Greek models and varied from the elemental simplicity of the Temple of Fortuna Virilis to the more complex design of the Temple of Venus and Rome. Each temple had a place **(cella)** reserved for the statue of the divinity to whom the temple was dedicated.

In front of the cella was a **pronaos** set behind a colonnade. The whole structure stood on a podium.

As far as religion was concerned, Rome drew on all mythological sources for her deities; the 12 main gods and goddesses were the same in number, if not always in name, as their Greek counterparts on Mount Olympus. Public worship was held in the temples but people also worshipped the various household gods *(lares et penates)* in their own homes. Many houses had a sort of shrine **(lararium)** where offerings were made to the souls of ancestors.

THE ROMAN GODS

Jupiter *(Zeus in Greek)*, senior god and ruler of the heavens, the elements and light, is often shown with an eagle, holding a thunderbolt and wearing a crown.

Juno *(Hera)*, his wife, protectress of womanhood and marriage, is shown with a peacock and a pomegranate.

Minerva *(Athena)*, goddess of wisdom, is represented by an owl. She is the third member of the Capitoline Triad together with Juno and Jupiter, her father, from whose head she sprang fully armed, and is often shown with a shield and a helmet.

Apollo, god of beauty, the sun and the arts, sings to a lyre accompaniment and carries a bow like his sister **Diana** *(Artemis)*, goddess of hunting, chastity and the moon (she wears a crescent moon on her head). The animal representing Diana is the doe.

Mercury *(Hermes)*, protector of commerce and travel, wears winged sandals and carries a staff (caduceus) in his hand.

Vulcan *(Hephaistos)*, god of fire, works in a forge with an anvil and hammer.

Vesta, goddess of the hearth, carries a simple flame as a symbol of fire in the home.

Mars *(Aries)*, god of war, is identified by his weapons and his helmet.

Venus *(Aphrodite)*, goddess of love and goodness, is represented by a dove. Born out of the foam of the sea, she is often represented standing in a shell or surrounded by sea deities such as **Neptune** *(Poseidon)*, god of the sea who is armed with a trident.

Ceres *(Demeter)*, protectress of the earth, tillage, corn and fecundity, is represented with a sheaf of corn and a scythe.

Cult of the Dead

Burial sites in Rome were located outside the city walls; the roads leading into the city were often lined with **tombs**.

Romans practised both burial and cremation. The oldest inhumations were, in the case of burial, in a **pit tomb** *(fossa)* dug to accommodate a full-length sarcophagus possibly carved from a tree trunk and, in the case of cremation, in a **shaft tomb** *(pozzo)*, a small hole in the ground in which the amphora or urn containing the ashes was placed; the container was often in the shape of a small house. Etruscan influence brought about an increase in the practice of burial: during the Republic tombs with several chambers were built where the sarcophagi were placed. The most common and elementary way of indicating a tomb was to erect a **memorial tablet** *(cippus)*, a simple block of stone bearing an inscription. More elaborately worked memorials with a greater level of decoration, made of stone or marble, were called **steles** *(steli)*.

Much later, large underground communal chambers **(colombarium)** became the popular form of burial for the poor and for slaves. The walls were lined with small recesses in which the urns were placed. The dead person was often "accompanied" on his journey to the other world with clothing, weapons, tools, jewellery (for a woman) and playthings (for a child) to be used in the new existence.

Housing

Depending on their social and financial status, the Ancient Romans lived in a multi-storey building **(insula)** containing several dwellings *(see OSTIA ANTICA in the Excursions from Rome section)*, a small middle-class house, or a large-scale patrician house **(domus)**. Although in the luxury bracket, these patrician houses were modest. The walls were simple and and had no windows.

These early houses contained a large rectangular room *(atrium)* with an open roof in the centre which allowed rainwater *(pluvial)* to be collected in a basin *(impluvium)*. This atrium contained the room where the head of the family worked and received visitors, as well as other smaller rooms. Top-ranking officials, wealthy farmers and prosperous merchants had a second house, built in a more elegant Greek style, which was reserved for the family. It was used only at certain times of the year and consisted of rooms built round various atria and a colonnaded courtyard *(peristylium)*, with a garden or sometimes a fishpond in the centre. In the dining room *(triclinium)*, guests sat in a semi-reclining position on couches arranged around the table.

Sculpture

It was in this discipline that the Romans were most imitative of Greek art. Such was the enthusiasm for statues that they were erected all over Rome. They were mass produced: bodies were supplied (dressed in togas) ready to receive suitable heads. There were workshops in Rome employing Greeks and local artists but figures were also imported from Greece: a ship loaded with statues, which was wrecked in about the 1C BC and found near Madhia in Tunisia, was probably on its way to Rome. The Romans liked white and coloured marble, dark red spotted porphyry and alabaster. They also worked in bronze (Marcus Aurelius's statue).

The originality of Roman sculpture is to be found in the **portraits**. The taste for likenesses was fostered by the practice in aristocratic families of preserving death masks made of wax. Caesar's portraits always show a calm, reflective and energetic character whereas Augustus, with his prominent ears, displays serenity and coldness. There is malice in Vespasian's face set on his thick neck. Trajan must in reality have had a very broad face and his hairstyle curiously accentuates this peculiarity. The equestrian statue of Marcus Aurelius *(see Index)* is the sole survivor of a tradition established by Julius Caesar which portrays the Emperor as an all-powerful conqueror.

The Romans also excelled in **historical low-relief sculptures**. The scenes on a sarcophagus or on Trajan's column are models of composition and precision.

Low relief on the Arch of Constantine (detail)

Decorative sculpture, which was exceptionally rare in the Republican era as the sarcophagus of Scipio Barbatus *(see Museo Pio-Clementino, p 319)* shows, reached its apogee in the Augustan era with the **Ara Pacis** *(see Index)*. One type of sculpture gave expression to **popular taste**, depicting various crafts and scenes from everyday life on the tombstones of working people.

Decadence in sculpture became apparent in the 3C AD: the folds of garments were scored too deep making the figures rigid, the expressions became fixed because of excessive hollowing out of the pupil of the eye and the hair was carelessly treated.

Painting

A study of the frescoes in Pompeii has identified four periods in Roman painting. The "first style" consists of simple panels imitating marble facing. The "second style" is marked by architectural features in *trompe l'oeil* to which small illustrated panels were added in the "third style". With the "fourth style" the *trompe l'œil* became excessive and the decoration overloaded. Examples of Roman painting can be seen in Livia's House and the Griffin House on the Palatine and in the National Roman Museum (housed in the Palazzo Massimo alle Terme).

Mosaic

This technique developed from an attempt to strengthen the floor surface, which was made of a mixture of broken tiles and chalk, by inserting pebbles and then small pieces of marble which could be cut to a uniform size and arranged to form a design.

The simplest method, which was used for floors, consisted of inserting small cubes of marble all cut to the same size into a bed of cement. Larger surfaces (baths) were covered with black figures on a white ground.

Sometimes the cubes were cut in different sizes to form curved lines; very small cubes could produce the effect of light and shade. This method was less durable and was reserved for wall panels or for the centrepiece of a floor.

Roman workshops also copied the **opus sectile** technique which originated in the East. A stencil of a decorative motif was cut out and applied to a marble base. The outline was traced on to the marble which was then hollowed out within the outline. The hollow itself was filled with small pieces of coloured marble. Examples of this technique can be seen on display at the entrance to the Picture Gallery in the Conservators' Palace *(see Index)* and in the Ostia Museum *(see OSTIA ANTICA in the Excursions from Rome section)*.

Christian Art

The pagan cult of idols and the commandment in the Bible against "graven images" inhibited the spontaneous development of a new style of art among the early Christian communities.

At first Christian art borrowed from the pagan repertoire those subjects which could be used as symbols of Christianity: the vine, the dove, the anchor etc.

The earliest Christian **paintings** appeared on the walls of the catacombs as a result of people following the pagan tradition and decorating the tombs of their relatives. The oldest date from the 2C AD.

The evolution of Roman **sculpture**, both in the round and in relief, can be traced in the Christian Museum in the Vatican from the use of symbols to the representation of Christ, the Apostles (St Peter, St Paul) and scenes from the Bible.

The chief Christian building was the **basilica** (not to be confused with the pagan basilicas which had nothing to do with religion). The first buildings of this type were erected by Constantine over the tombs of Peter and Paul the Apostles (St Peter's in the Vatican; St Paul Without the Walls) and next to the Imperial Palace (St John Lateran).

Three new files created for Medieval and Renaissance, Baroque, and Classical art in line with the Italian files.

Architecture

Ancient Art

Peripteral temple

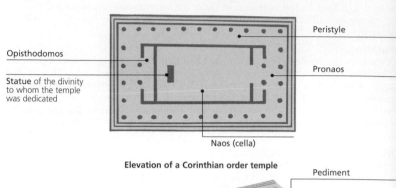

Opisthodomos

Statue of the divinity to whom the temple was dedicated

Peristyle

Pronaos

Naos (cella)

Elevation of a Corinthian order temple

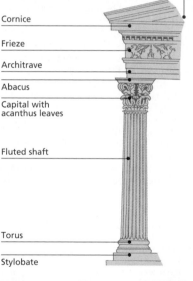

Pediment

The section comprising the architrave, frieze and cornice is known as the **entablature**

Cornice

Frieze

Architrave

Abacus

Capital with acanthus leaves

Fluted shaft

Torus

Stylobate

Doric   Tuscan   Ionic   Corinthian   Composite

Baths of Caracalla (3C AD)

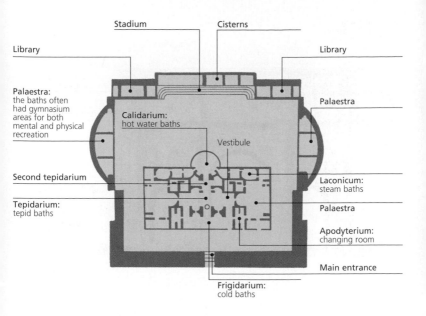

Stadium

Cisterns

Library

Library

Palaestra:
the baths often
had gymnasium
areas for both
mental and physical
recreation

Palaestra

Calidarium:
hot water baths

Vestibule

Second tepidarium

Laconicum:
steam baths

Tepidarium:
tepid baths

Palaestra

Apodyterium:
changing room

Main entrance

Frigidarium:
cold baths

Colosseum (1C AD)

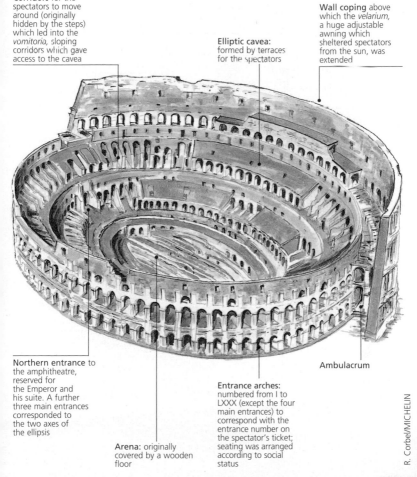

Corridors for the
spectators to move
around (originally
hidden by the steps)
which led into the
vomitoria, sloping
corridors which gave
access to the cavea

Elliptic cavea:
formed by terraces
for the spectators

Wall coping above
which the *velarium,*
a huge adjustable
awning which
sheltered spectators
from the sun, was
extended

Northern entrance to
the amphitheatre,
reserved for
the Emperor and
his suite. A further
three main entrances
corresponded to
the two axes
of the ellipsis

Ambulacrum

Arena: originally
covered by a wooden
floor

Entrance arches:
numbered from I to
LXXX (except the four
main entrances) to
correspond with the
entrance number on
the spectator's ticket;
seating was arranged
according to social
status

Arch of Constantine (4C AD)

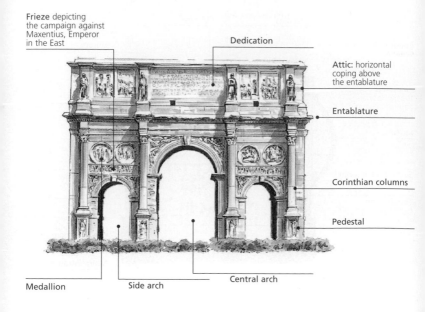

Frieze depicting the campaign against Maxentius, Emperor in the East

Dedication

Attic: horizontal coping above the entablature

Entablature

Corinthian columns

Pedestal

Medallion

Side arch

Central arch

Castel Sant'Angelo: from mausoleum to fortress

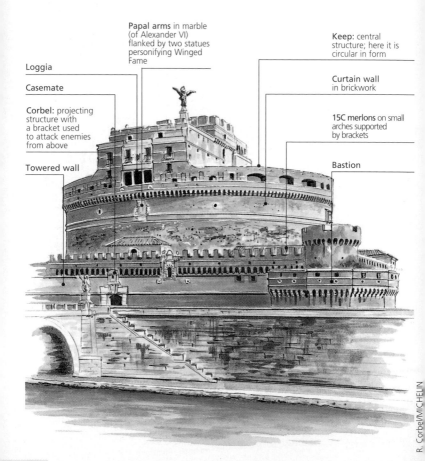

Papal arms in marble (of Alexander VI) flanked by two statues personifying Winged Fame

Keep: central structure; here it is circular in form

Curtain wall in brickwork

15C merlons on small arches supported by brackets

Bastion

Loggia

Casemate

Corbel: projecting structure with a bracket used to attack enemies from above

Towered wall

Religious architecture

Sant'Andrea della Valle (1591-1623)

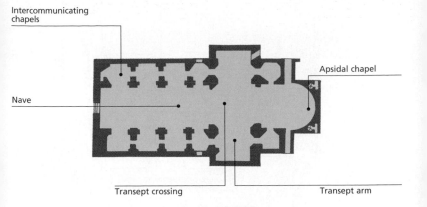

Intercommunicating chapels

Apsidal chapel

Nave

Transept crossing

Transept arm

Gesù Church, façade (1575)

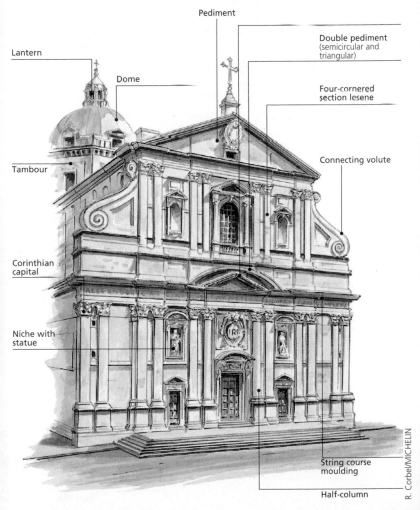

Pediment

Double pediment (semicircular and triangular)

Lantern

Four-cornered section lesene

Dome

Connecting volute

Tambour

Corinthian capital

Niche with statue

String course moulding

Half-column

R. Corbel/MICHELIN

San Giovanni in Laterano, interior (4C-17C)

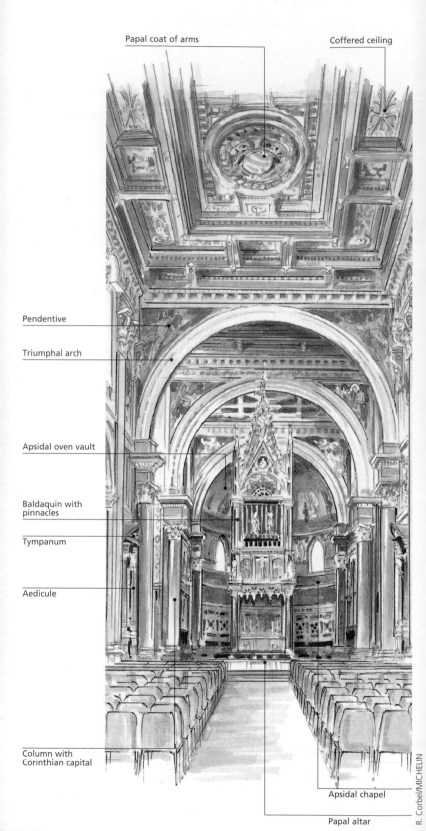

Papal coat of arms

Coffered ceiling

Pendentive

Triumphal arch

Apsidal oven vault

Baldaquin with pinnacles

Tympanum

Aedicule

Column with Corinthian capital

Apsidal chapel

Papal altar

R. Corbel/MICHELIN

Civil architecture

Palazzo Senatorio (16C)

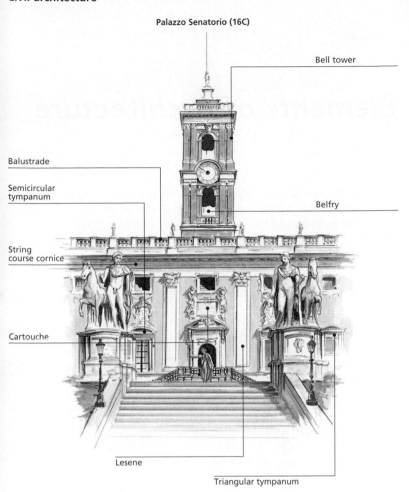

Bell tower

Balustrade

Semicircular tympanum

Belfry

String course cornice

Cartouche

Lesene

Triangular tympanum

Villa Borghese (17C)

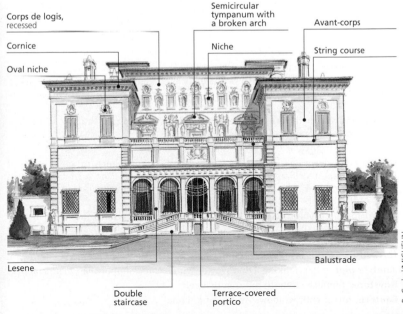

Corps de logis, recessed

Semicircular tympanum with a broken arch

Avant-corps

Cornice

Niche

String course

Oval niche

Lesene

Balustrade

Double staircase

Terrace-covered portico

Elements of Architecture

Some of the terms given below are further explained by the illustrations on the previous pages.

(Words in italics are Italian.)

Altarpiece (or **ancona**): a large painting or sculpture adorning an altar.

Ambulatory: extension of the aisles around the chancel for processional purposes.

Antependium: a covering hung over the front of an altar.

Apse: semicircular or polygonal end of a church behind the altar; the outer section is known as the chevet.

Apsidal chapel: small chapel off the ambulatory of a Romanesque or Gothic church.

Archivolt: arch moulding over an arcade or upper section of a doorway.

Atlantes (or **Telamones**): male figures used as supporting columns.

Atrium (or **four-sided portico**): a court enclosed by colonnades in front of the entrance to a palaeo-Christian or Romanesque church.

Avant-corps: part of a building which projects out from the main façade.

Bastion: in military architecture, a polygonal defensive structure projecting from the ramparts.

Bay: the area between two supporting columns or pillars.

Buttress: external support of a wall, which counterbalances the thrust of the vaults and arches.

Caisson (or **lacunar**): decorative square panel sunk into a flat roof or vaulted stonework.

Caryatid: female figure used as a supporting column.

Cathedra: high-backed throne in Gothic style.

Chancel: the part of the church behind the altar, with carved wooden stalls for the choir.

Ciborium: a canopy (baldaquin) over an altar.

Coffer or panel: small square ornamental panel, painted or sculpted in various materials.

Console: projecting stone or wooden bracket which supports cornices or beams.

Corbel (or **truss**): triangular bracket, usually made of wood, supporting a roof.

Counter-façade: internal wall of church façade.

Cross (church plan): churches are usually built either in the plan of a **Greek cross**, with four arms of equal length, or a **Latin cross**, with one arm longer than the other three.

Exedra: section in the back of Roman basilicas containing seats; by extension, curved niche or semicircular recess outside.

Ghimberga: a triangular Gothic pediment adorning a portal.

Grotesque: a decorative style popular during the Renaissance in which parts of human, animal and plant forms are distorted and mixed. The term comes from the old Italian word *grotte*, the name given in the Renaissance period to the Roman ruins of the Domus Aurea.

High relief: sculpture or carved work projecting more than one half of its true proportions from the background (halfway between low relief and in-the-round figures).

Intrados: inner surface of an arch or vault.

Jamb or **pier**: pillar flanking a doorway or window and supporting the arch above.

Keystone: topmost stone in an arch or vault.

Lantern: turret with windows on top of a dome.

Lesene (or **Lombard strips**): decorative band of pilasters joined at the top by an arched frieze.

Matroneo: the gallery reserved for women in palaeo-Christian and Romanesque churches.

Modillion: small bracket supporting a cornice.

Moulding: an ornamental shaped band which projects from the wall.

Narthex: interior vestibule of a church.

Overhang: overhanging or corbelled upper storey.

Ovolo: egg-shaped decoration.

Pala d'altare: Italian term for altarpiece.

Pediment: ornament in Classical architecture (usually triangular or semicircular) above a door or window.

Pendentive: connecting piece positioned at a corner of a square space to support an octagonal or circular dome.

Pilaster strip: structural column partially set into a wall.

Pluteus: decorated balustrade made from various materials, separating the chancel from the rest of the church.

Polyptych: a painting or relief consisting of several folding leaves or panels.

Portico: an open gallery facing the nave in palaeo-Christian churches; it later became a decorative feature of the external part of the church.

Predella: base of an altarpiece, divided into small panels.

Presbiterio: the chancel or sanctuary of a church, reserved for the clergy.

Pronaos: the space in front of the *cella* or *naos* in Greek temples; later the columned portico in front of the entrance to a church or palace.

Protiro: small porch on columns in front of the portal in Romanesque churches.

Pulpit: an elevated dais from which sermons were preached in the nave of a church.

Pyx: cylindrical box made of ivory or glazed copper for jewels or the Eucharistic host.

Retable: large and ornate altarpiece divided into several painted or carved panels, especially common in Spain after the 14C.

Rib: a projecting moulding or band on the underside of a dome or vault, which may be structural or ornamental.

Rustication: deliberately rough texture of dressed and uniformly cut stone which projects from the outer wall of a building and has deeply chiselled markings. In fashion during the Renaissance.

Splay: a surface of a wall that forms an oblique angle to the main surface of a doorway or window opening.

String course: projecting ornamental band or continuous moulding that separates one floor from another.

Tambour: a circular or polygonal structure supporting a dome.

Triforium: an open gallery above the arcade of the nave, comprised mainly of three-light windows.

Vault: arched structure forming a roof or ceiling; **barrel vault**: produced by a continuous rounded arch; **cross vault**: formed by the intersection of two barrel vaults; **oven vault**: semicircular in shape, usually over apsidal chapels, the termination of a barrel-vaulted nave.

Vaulting cell: one of the four segments of a cross vault.

Volute: architectural ornament in the form of a spiral scroll.

Window cross: a stone or wooden post which divides the opening of a window or door. The vertical posts are known as **mullions**.

The Dark Ages and the Renaissance

B. Kaufmann/MICHELIN

Mosaic in the apse
of Santa Maria in Trastevere

Only a few rare but splendid examples of art from the Middle Ages have survived in Rome. However, after almost 10 centuries of invasions and plundering, the Popes brought new life and renewed prosperity to the capital of the Roman Catholic Church, thanks to the contribution of talented artists such as Michelangelo, Bramante and Raphael. This new explosion of art attracted wealthy patrons to the city, and this period saw the construction of a number of fine Renaissance palazzi. After the Council of Trent, the canons of religious architecture were influenced mainly by the religious orders, who created an austere, yet grandiose style; in painting, the first hints of the bold new art of the 17C could be seen.

Medieval Period

Supplanted by Constantinople as the capital of the Empire and invaded by barbarians, by the 6C Rome was a ruined city with barely 20 000 inhabitants. In the 10C it became the battleground in the struggle between the Pope and the German Emperor. Until the 15C only simple constructions were built.

Architecture

Civil architecture consisted mainly of fortresses built by the noble families on strategic sites (Crescenzi House, Militia Tower).

Churches were constructed of material taken from ancient monuments which provided a great choice of capitals, friezes and columns such as can be seen in Santa Maria Maggiore, Santa Sabina etc. As such material grew scarcer, items from different sources were combined in one church (columns in San Giorgio in Velabro, Santa Maria in Cosmedin etc).

The **basilical plan** of the early churches was retained during the medieval period *(see plans of Santa Maria d'Aracoeli, p 129; Santa Maria in Cosmedin, p 126; San Clemente, p 162)*. It consisted of a rectangular building divided down its length into a nave flanked by two or four aisles separated by rows of columns; one of the shorter sides contained the entrance, the other the apse (with quarter-sphere vault). Between the apse and the nave and at right angles to them ran the transept. The nave extended above the side aisles and was lit by clerestories. It was covered by a pitched roof, left open or masked by a flat ceiling in the interior. The main entrance was sometimes preceded by a square court surrounded by a portico *(quadriporticus)* or by a simple portico supported on columns which served as a narthex (the area reserved for those who had not yet been baptised).

The façade was often flanked by a bell tower *(campanile)*. In Rome these towers are decorated with horizontal cornices dividing them into several storeys, with white mini columns standing out against the brickwork and ceramic insets in brilliant colours.

By the 6C a rail had been introduced separating the congregation from the clergy and creating the chancel **(presbyterium)** on either side of the bishop's throne **(cathedra)** which stood in the apse. In front were the choristers in the **schola cantorum**. Churches also often housed a **martyrium**, where the martyrdom of the patron saint of the church was believed to have taken place; the relics of the saint are often still kept here. The high altar was covered by a baldaquin or canopy **(ciborium)**.

Sculpture, painting and mosaic

The architect and sculptor **Arnolfo di Cambio** (c 1235-c 1302) moved to Rome from Florence in about 1276. He created the baldaquins in St Paul Without the Walls and in Santa Cecilia, and the statue of Charles of Anjou in the Museo del Palazzo dei Conservatori.

Frescoes and mosaics were the chief forms of medieval decoration. The Romans had a taste for anecdotes and bright colours.

The period from the 12C to the 14C is dominated by the **Cosmati**, who were descended from one Cosma and formed a guild of marble workers to which the Vasselletto family was related. The Cosmati workshops used fragments of ancient materials to create beautiful floors with decorative motifs of multicoloured marble and the furniture of a medieval church: episcopal throne, *ambones* (lecterns), paschal candlesticks. The early works, composed entirely of white marble, are very simple. Later they added porphyry and serpentine marble (green) cut in geometric shapes (roundels, lozenges etc); they produced very lively effects with incrustations of enamels – blue, red and gold – on the friezes and wreathed columns of cloisters. In the latter half of the 5C but particularly in the 6C the influence of Byzantine mosaics was introduced to Rome by the entourage of Justinian's general, Narses, who occupied Rome in 552, and also by Eastern monks who took refuge in Rome in the 7C (St Sabas). The mosaics of this period show figures with enigmatic expressions, often richly dressed, in conventional poses, which express the mysticism of the Eastern Church through symbolism.

Through the good relations enjoyed by the Papacy with Pepin the Short and then Charlemagne, Carolingian art brought a less rigid style to Roman mosaics, eg works dating from the reign of Paschal I (817-24) (Santa Prassede; Santa Maria in Domnica). From the 11C to 13C the Roman workshops produced sumptuous work (the apse in San Clemente). **Pietro Cavallini**, the greatest artist in this period, must have worked in Rome at the end of the 13C and early in the 14C. He was both painter and mosaicist and a master of the different influences; his very pure art is best known through the mosaic of the life of the Virgin in Santa Maria in Trastevere and by the fresco of the Last Judgement in Santa Cecilia. **Jacopo Torriti** and **Rusuti** were disciples of his.

Renaissance Art

The Renaissance made less impact on Rome than on Florence. At the beginning of the 15C Rome was exhausted by the struggles of the Middle Ages and had nothing to show of artistic merit. By the end of the century the city was an important archaeological centre and was famous for its abundant artistic activity commissioned by Popes and prelates. It was **Martin V** (1417-31), the first Pope after the Great Schism, who inaugurated this brilliant period. It came to an end in 1527 when Rome was sacked by the troops of Charles V.

Architecture

The inspiration for Roman Renaissance buildings is to be found in Classical monuments: in the Colosseum – its superimposed orders and engaged columns are imitated in the court of the Farnese Palace; in Maxentius's Basilica – the vaulting inspired the dome of St Peter's in the Vatican; and in the Pantheon – the curved and triangular pediments in the interior have been reproduced many times.

The churches are austere in appearance. The nave is covered by rib vaulting and flanked by apsidal side chapels; the arms of the transept end in rounded chapels. The first domes began to appear (Santa Maria del Popolo, Sant'Agostino). The screen-like façade is composed of two stages one above the other linked by scrolls. Broad flat surfaces predominate; shallow pilasters are preferred to columns. The first hints of the Counter-Reformation and the Baroque can be seen in the use of broken lines, of recesses and columns progressively more and more accentuated. **Sixtus IV** (1471-84) was responsible for the majority of the Renaissance churches: Sant'Agostino, Santa Maria del Popolo and San Pietro in Montorio were built in his reign. He founded Santa Maria della Pace and made great alterations to the Church of the Holy Apostles.

The *palazzi* were large private houses built in the district between Via del Corso and the Tiber, in the streets which were used by the pilgrims and by the Papal processions which proceeded on feast days from the Vatican to the Lateran: Via del Governo Vecchio, Via dei Banchi Nuovi, Via dei Banchi Vecchi, Via di Monserrato, Via Giulia etc. They supplanted the medieval fortresses; the Palazzo Venezia which was begun in 1452 has retained its crenellations. From the outside the *palazzi* are gaunt and austere (barred windows on the ground floor). The inside was designed to accommodate an elegant and cultivated life-style, associated with men of letters and artists in a setting of ancient sculptures and paintings.

Sculpture and painting

The personalities of Michelangelo and Raphael predominated. After working in Rome from 1496-1501 **Michelangelo** returned in 1505 to design a tomb for Julius II. He designed a magnificent monument, but was confronted by a sudden lack of interest from the Pope, who was fully occupied with the construction of the new church of St Peter's. In 1508 the Pope summoned Michelangelo back to Rome and commissioned him to decorate the Sistine Chapel. The painter revolutionised the concept of religious decor and produced a huge architectural structure, dominated by powerful figures (the Prophets, Sybils and *Ignudi* or naked figures) and panels illustrating episodes from Genesis. In both his painting and sculptures Michelangelo emphasises the human body and radically changed the way man was represented. He portrays man as both grandiose and dramatically aware of his own existence, and creates physically powerful, muscular and tormented figures.

The other artist of major importance in the Renaissance period was **Raphael**. He, too, attempted to portray pure beauty, firstly in his gentle and balanced portraits, then by using the *sfumato* technique perfected by **Leonardo da Vinci**, and finally

The Annunciation *by Filippino Lippi – Cappella Carafa*

by acquiring the anatomical mastery of Michelangelo. The artist had lived in Urbino, his home town, Perugia and Florence before coming to Rome in 1508; he was presented to Julius II by Bramante.

In **decorative sculpture** delicate ornamental foliage and floral motifs are often picked out in gold (door frames, balustrades etc). Funeral art flourished under **Andrea Bregno** and **Andrea Sansovino**, who combined a taste for decoration with a taste for ancient architecture.

Mino da Fiesole, who was usually based in Tuscany, made several visits to Rome. He became famous for his very simple representations of the Virgin and Child in low-relief sculpture.

An artistic melting-pot

The Renaissance style reached Rome after being developed elsewhere and all the artists came from outside the city: the Umbrians were known for their gentle touch, the Tuscans for their elegant and intellectual art and the Lombards for their rich decoration.

– **Gentile da Fabriano** and **Pisanello** were summoned to Rome in 1427 by Martin V and Eugenius IV to decorate the nave of St John Lateran (destroyed 17C-18C).

– **Masolino da Panicale,** who came from Florence, painted St Catherine's Chapel in St Clement's Basilica between 1428 and 1430.

– From 1447-1451 **Fra Angelico**, also from Florence, decorated Nicholas V's Chapel in the Vatican.

– For the painting of the Sistine Chapel walls Sixtus IV called on **Pinturicchio**, **Perugino** and **Signorelli** from Umbria and on **Botticelli**, **Ghirlandaio**, **Cosimo Rosselli** and his son **Piero di Cosimo** from Florence. He also commissioned **Melozzo da Forli** to paint the Ascension in the apse of the Church of the Holy Apostles (fine fragments in the Vatican Picture Gallery and in the Quirinal Palace).

– In about 1485 **Pinturicchio** painted the life of St Bernard in Santa d'Aracoeli and a Nativity in Santa Maria del Popolo. Between 1492 and 1494 he decorated the Borgia Apartment in the Vatican for Alexander VI.

– From 1489-1493 **Filippino Lippi** was at work on the Carafa Chapel in Santa Maria Sopra Minerva.

– **Bramante**, who arrived in 1499, designed the *tempietto* beside San Pietro in Montorio (1502), built the cloisters at Santa Maria della Pace (1504) and extended the choir of Santa Maria del Popolo (1505-09).

– From 1508-12 **Michelangelo** was at work painting the ceiling of the Sistine Chapel for Julius II. In 1513 he began the Pope's tomb. The *Last Judgement* was painted between 1535 and 1541 and he worked on the dome of St Peter's from 1547 until his death in 1564. His last work was the Porta Pia (1561-64).

– From 1508-11 **Baldassarre Peruzzi** built the Villa Farnesina for Agostino Chigi.

– In 1508 **Raphael** began to paint the *Stanze* in the Vatican. In 1510 he designed the plan for the Chigi Chapel in Santa Maria del Popolo. From 1511 he worked on the decoration of the Villa Farnesina for Agostino Chigi. In 1512 he painted Isaiah in Sant'Agostino and the Sibyls in Santa Maria della Pace in 1514.

– **Sodoma** arrived in Rome from Milan in 1508 to paint the ceiling of the Signature Room in the Vatican for Julius II. He worked on the Farnesina in about 1509.

– Early in the 16C **Jacopo Sansovino** built San Giovanni dei Fiorentini for Leo X.

– In 1515 **Antonio da Sangallo the Younger** began to build the Farnese Palace; Michelangelo took over in 1546.

Counter-Reformation

The Counter-Reformation, which covered the period from the reign of Paul III (1534-49) to the reign of Urban VIII (1623-44), was marked by the sack of Rome in 1527 and by the rise of Protestantism. The Counter-Reformation movement sought to put down the heretics, restore the primacy of Rome and to rally the faithful to the Church. The Society of Jesus, which was formed in 1540, proved to be a most efficacious instrument in the struggle. Henceforward the influential power of art was put at the service of the Faith.

The initial period of struggle was followed by several successes – the battle of Lepanto (1571), the conversion of Henri IV of France (1593) and the Jubilee (1600) – all expressed in an artistic style which presaged the Baroque.

Architecture

The style used for **churches** is sometimes called **"Jesuit"** because of the comprehensive contribution made by the Society of Jesus. The architecture combines an austere solemnity with a rich marble decor: churches were to appear majestic and powerful. Since they were designed to assemble the faithful together, the churches of the Counter-Reformation are vast. The Gesù Church is a typical example. The nave is broad and uncluttered so that every member of the congregation could see the altar and hear the preaching. On the façade, the plain surfaces of the Renaissance are replaced with recesses and projections and engaged columns are gradually substituted for the flat pilasters.

The most flourishing period for **civil architecture** was the early years of the Counter-Reformation during the reigns of Paul III, Julius III, Paul IV and Pius IV, who continued to live like Renaissance princes.

The Borghese family illustrates the era of the Church triumphant: Paul V acquired the Borghese Palace and built the Pauline Fountain; his nephew, Cardinal Scipione Borghese, led a cultivated life, evident from the splendours of the Palazzo Pallavicini and the "Palazzina" Borghese, which now houses the Borghese Gallery.

Sculpture and painting

In the spirit of the Counter-Reformation painting had to exalt the themes rejected by the Protestants: the Virgin, the primacy of St Peter, the doctrine of the Eucharist, the cult of the saints and their intercession for the souls in purgatory. The work of the Counter-Reformation artists followed in the wake of Michelangelo and Raphael and continued to be in the attenuated "manner" of these two giants – hence the term **Mannerist**, which is applied to 16C sculpture and painting.

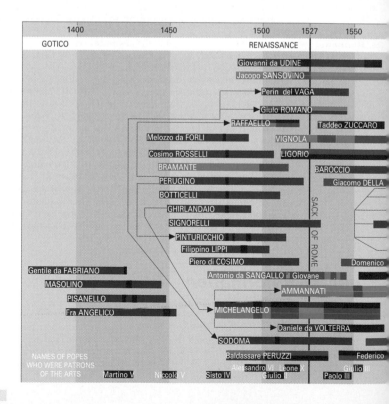

In sculpture there is the work of two of Michelangelo's close followers: **Ammanati** (1511-92) and **Guglielmo della Porta** (?1500-77). The end of the period is marked by the presence in Rome of **Pietro Bernini** (1562-1629), the father of Gian Lorenzo Bernini.

Among the painters are **Daniele da Volterra**, who worked with Michelangelo, **Giovanni da Udine**, **Sermoneta**, **Francesco Penni** and **Giulio Romano**, who formed part of the "Roman School" around Raphael. The style of the next generation – **Federico** and **Taddeo Zuccari**, **Pomarancio**, **Cesare Nebbia**, **Cavaliere d'Arpino** etc – is a direct development of Raphael's art. **Barocci**, whose soft and emotional style never lapsed into affectation, deserves a special place.

In their attempts to imitate, the Mannerist painters were often guilty of excess. Their colours are pallid as if faded by the light; fresco paintings are framed with stucco and gilding or elaborate combinations of marble; large areas are often divided into smaller panels which are easier to paint.

Reaction

Reaction to Mannerism was introduced by Caravaggio, who heralded the first signs of the Baroque, and the **Bologna group**, led by the **Carracci** who ran an academy in Bologna from 1585-95: Ludovico (1555-1619), founder of the academy, and his cousins Agostino (1557-1602) and **Annibale** (1560-1609), who were brothers. Guido **Reni** (1575-1642), **Domenichino** (1581-1641) and **Guercino** (1591-1666) tried to achieve more verity of expression without abandoning idealism.

Michelangelo Merisi (1573-1610), known as **Caravaggio** after the name of his home village near Bergamo, began to work in Rome with Cavaliere d'Arpino in 1588 but he was quarrelsome and had to flee from the city in 1605. His painting was quite unconventional: his powerful figures are illuminated by a harsh light which causes contrasting heavy shadow. His influence had repercussions throughout Europe and many artists were said to paint in the style of Caravaggio.

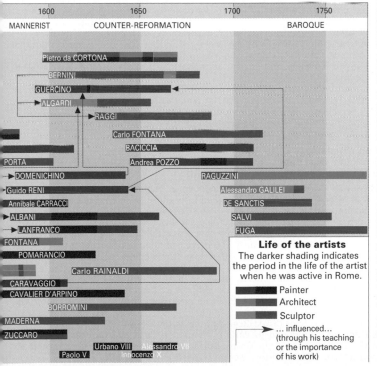

ARTISTS WHO WORKED IN ROME FROM THE 15C TO 18C

1600	1650	1700	1750
MANNERIST	COUNTER-REFORMATION		BAROQUE

Pietro da CORTONA
BERNINI
GUERCINO
ALGARDI
RAGGI
Carlo FONTANA
BACICCIA
PORTA
Andrea POZZO
DOMENICHINO
RAGUZZINI
Guido RENI
Alessandro GALILEI
Annibale CARRACCI
DE SANCTIS
ALBANI
SALVI
LANFRANCO
FUGA
FONTANA
POMARANCIO
Carlo RAINALDI
CARAVAGGIO
CAVALIER D'ARPINO
BORROMINI
MADERNA
ZUCCARO

Urbano VIII   Alessandro VII
Paolo V   Innocenzo X

Life of the artists
The darker shading indicates the period in the life of the artist when he was active in Rome.

■ Painter
■ Architect
■ Sculpter

⟶ … influenced…
(through his teaching or the importance of his work)

Roman Baroque

B. Kaufmann/MICHELIN

The Baroque style is characterised by its theatrical architecture, comprising a riot of concave and convex curves and twisted columns, sculptures which capture a moment of action, and are embellished by putti statues and golden rays, and trompe l'oeil ceilings which suggest non-existent domes. The overriding feature of the Baroque style is movement, and it is often difficult to know where to rest the eye as it is pulled from façade to fountain to piazza, each sight as stunning as the last. This rich, dramatic artistic style found the perfect home in the Italian capital, evolving over the years to create its own specific characteristics, now known as Roman Baroque.

The Baroque style evolved in the 17C and 18C *(see also previous chapter).* Several theories expound the origin of the term Baroque: in Portuguese *barroco* alludes to an uneven or irregular pearl (from which the French derived the term *baroque* meaning bizarre, eccentric, profusely decorative). In both cases, however, the attributed meaning tends to be pejorative, deriding the intentions of Baroque artists to create their own values rather than follow the established Classical rules and canons of harmony and beauty. It was a long time before the style was re-evaluated and appreciated.

Baroque, meanwhile, enjoyed a great vogue in the Papal city during the reign of Urban VIII (1623-44), becoming synonymous with the triumph of the Roman Church over heresy. The Church, with its newly acquired strength and spiritual power, and the Popes, with their desire to glorify God through new works of art, attracted the most illustrious artists to the city.

Leading artists

The two most important artists in the world of Roman Baroque art were **Gian Lorenzo Bernini** and **Francesco Borromini**.

Gian Lorenzo Bernini (1598-1680) was born in Naples. From the very first his talent was recognised by Cardinal Scipione Borghese, who commissioned him to do the sculptures for his villa (now in the Borghese Gallery). At the age of 17, Bernini produced his first work, *Jupiter and the Goat Amalthea,* which was followed by the magnificent sculptural groups of the *Rape of Proserpina* and *Apollo and Daphne.* On the election of Urban VIII, he was appointed official artist to the Papal court and to the Barberini family. After Maderno's death in 1629, the Pope put him in charge of the rebuilding of St Peter's Basilica.

During the reign of Innocent X (1644-55) Bernini sculpted his extraordinary *Ecstasy of St Theresa* and the *Fountain of the Four Rivers (see PIAZZA NAVONA).* In the reign of Alexander VII (1655-67) he built the church of St Andrew on the Quirinal, the colonnade enclosing St Peter's Square, redesigned St Peter's Chair and built the Royal Stair (Scala Regia) in the Vatican Palace.

In 1665 he was summoned to Paris by Louis XIV and his minister, Colbert, to design the façade of the Cour Carrée in the Louvre, but as the King turned his attention to Versailles, Bernini's design was never carried out.

Ceiling by Andrea Pozzo in Sant'Ignazio

Bernini was not only an architect and sculptor but also a theatrical scene designer, poet and painter. He probably painted some hundred pictures of which only a few have survived. He produced a great deal of work, rose rapidly and was very successful.

His genius was recognised in his lifetime and he received many decorations; his contemporaries saw in him another Michelangelo. He was welcome in the most brilliant circles; he put on plays for his friends, designing the stage sets, writing the words and playing a role. He was fleetingly eclipsed by Borromini when Innocent X succeeded Urban VIII but soon returned to favour with his Fountain of the Four Rivers.

Francesco Borromini (1599-1667) was the son of Giovanni Domenico Castelli, an architect to the Visconti family in Milan. He trained as a stonemason and acquired great technical experience. In 1621 he was in Rome, where he worked as Carlo Maderno's assistant on St Peter's, Sant'Andrea della Valle and the Barberini Palace. In 1625 he received the title of *maestro* and in 1628 took his mother's name of Borromini. He based his art on rigour and sobriety excluding marble decorations and paintings. In Borromini's art the Baroque style is expressed by the lines of the architecture which he cut and curved with a sure hand. As an architect, he was critical of Bernini's style, which he considered to be over-dramatic and excessive. Perhaps not surprisingly, the two artists were supported by different patrons: Bernini's work was mostly commissioned by the papal court; Borromini's style found favour mainly with the religious orders, such as the Trinitarians and the followers of St Philip Neri.

San Carlo alle Quattro Fontane, which was Borromini's first full-scale work (1638, although the façade was designed much later, in the year in which he died), probably shows his genius at its best. At the same period he designed the façade of the Oratory of St Philip Neri which is typical of his original and balanced style. Around 1643 he built the small church of Sant'Ivo alla Sapienza, with its convex and concave curves culminating in a multi-lobed cupola. These projects earned him the protection of Fra Spada, who became Innocent X's adviser. The Pope raised him to the first rank and appointed him to renovate St John Lateran for the Jubilee of 1650.

Borromini, an introvert who shunned the world, lived in constant anxiety and never knew the fame enjoyed by his rival. One night in a fit of anguish and anger against his servant he took his own life.

There were other architects working in Rome at that period. **Carlo Maderno**, the designer of the façades of St Peter's and Santa Susanna, and **Giacomo della Porta**, probably the most active architect around 1580, were both great admirers of Michelangelo and are often included among the Mannerists. **Flaminio Ponzio** worked for the Borghese (façade of the Borghese Palace, Pauline Fountain). **Giovanni Battista Soria** designed the façades of Santa Maria della Vittoria and St Gregory the Great. The well-proportioned architecture of **Pietro da Cortona** is most attractive (St Luke and St Martina, the façade of Santa Maria in Via Lata, the dome of San Carlo al Corso); in contrast with the dramatic architecture of Bernini and Borromini, this artist took his inspiration from the 16C models of Bramante and Palladio and paid particular attention to the position of his work in an urban context (eg the façade of Santa Maria della Pace). The name of **Carlo Rainaldi** deserves to be remembered for his work in Santa Maria in Campitelli (1655-65) and for his arrangement of the "twin" churches in the Piazza del Popolo, which frame the entrance to Via del Corso.

Baroque art

An inherent quality of Baroque art is its restlessness, its sense of movement and contrast. Water, with its undulations and powers of reflection, was an essential element. Dazzling effects were created with expensive materials such as marble and precious stones. Stucco (chalk, plaster and marble dust mixed with water) was often used for its plastic qualities. Allegories were taken from Cesare Ripa's dictionary which appeared in 1594 and explained how to express an abstract idea.

In architecture, even the plan of the buildings was contrived to express movement (San Carlo alle Quattro Fontane, Sant'Andrea al Quirinale). Façades are embellished with disengaged columns, bold projections, curved contours and recesses.

Sculpture is dominated by flowing garments and figures expressing abstract qualities. The altarpieces are decorated with pictures of sculpted marble and wreathed columns; the latter, a feature of ancient Roman art, were very popular with Bernini (baldaquin in St Peter's). Church interiors are full of cherubs perched on pediments and cornices.

In addition to the sculptors associated as pupils with Bernini (Antonio Raggi, Ercole Ferrata, Francesco Mochi etc) mention must be made of **Alessandro Algardi** (1592-1654), who was inspired by Classical art; he produced some remarkable portraits and marble pictures, including the funerary monument of Leo XI in St Peter's.

B. Kaufmann/MICHELIN

Sant'Ivo alla Sapienza

Bernini – Ecstasy of St Theresa (Santa Maria della Vittoria)

Baroque **painters** sought to achieve effects of perspective and *trompe l'oeil* with spiralling or diagonal compositions. They included **Pietro da Cortona**, an architect as well as an interior designer, whose masterpiece is the fresco depicting the triumph of the Barberini family in the palace of the same name. Also worthy of note is Giovanni Battista Gaulli, who was known as **Baciccia** and was a protégé of Bernini; he painted the magnificent fresco on the ceiling of the Chiesa del Gesù. The artist **Giovanni Lanfranco** (1582-1647), from Parma, painted the dome of Sant'Andrea della Valle with great technical skill. **Andrea Pozzo,** a Jesuit, who was a painter, studied the theory of architecture and had a passion for *trompe l'oeil,* the best expression of which is without a doubt his fresco on the ceiling of the church of Sant'Ignazio: it is hard to believe that the cupola figured here is only an illusion. His book *Prospettiva de' pittori e architetti* appeared in 1693 and circulated throughout Europe.

Rome attracted artists of all nationalities. Nicolas Poussin died there in 1665, Claude Lorrain in 1682. Rubens made several visits; he admired Michelangelo, the Carracci and Caravaggio and completed the paintings in the apse of the New Church. During his long stay in Rome, Velázquez painted a fine portrait of Innocent X *(now in the Galleria Doria Pamphili).*

From Classicism to the Present Day

G. Bludzin/MICHELIN

It is difficult to recognise present-day Rome in the 18C etchings by Piranesi. After 1870, in an attempt to fulfil its role as the capital city of the newly united Italy, the city changed beyond all recognition with the creation of vast new residential districts. However, it was during the Fascist period that the city's layout was completely overhauled. Buildings such as the Law Courts ("palazzaccio"), the monument to Victor Emmanuel II (the "wedding-cake" or "typewriter"), and the Palazzo delle Civiltà del Lavoro ("square colosseum") may initially have been unpopular with locals, but they now form a familiar and integral part of the city.

Neo-Classicism – This trend developed from the middle of the 18C until the early 19C and was marked by a return to Greek and Roman architecture which had recently been discovered during the excavations of Herculaneum, Pompeii and Paestum. Following Baroque exuberance, neo-Classicism was characterised by simplicity and symmetry, even a touch of frigidity. This was the period when Winckelmann, who was Librarian at the Vatican and in charge of Roman antiquities, published his works on Classical art, when Francesco Milizia launched his violent criticism of the Baroque style and superfluous decoration, and praised the simplicity and nobility of ancient monuments.

Piranesi (1720-78), engraver and architect, took up permanent residence in Rome in 1754. He produced some 2 000 engravings, including the series "Views of Rome", which was published in 1750 and constitutes an incomparable collection full of charm and melancholy. It was he who designed the attractive Piazza dei Cavalieri di Malta.

Antonio Canova (1757-1821) was the dominant talent at this time and Napoleon's favourite sculptor. The calm regularity of his work enchanted his contemporaries. In architecture mention should be made of **Giuseppe Valadier**, who laid out Piazza del Popolo (1816-20). In painting it is the non-Italians, such as the German Mengs and the French at the Villa Medici who stand out *(see PIAZZA DI SPAGNA)*. David in particular came to Rome twice.

The end of the 19C saw artists such as Cesare Maccari (frescoes in the Palazzo Madama) and Guilio Aristide Sartorio (frieze in the chamber of the Parliament building) working in Rome.

Modern artists and contemporary art movements – An exponent of Roman Futurism, Giacomo Balla (1861-1958) moved to Rome in 1895; with Fortunato Depero he signed the 1915 manifesto of the "Futurist Reconstruction of the Universe"; after 1930 his painting reverted to pre-Futurist themes. Other important artists were Mario Mafai (1902-65) and Gino Bonichi (also known as Scipione) (1904-33), members of the Roman School which Renato Guttuso joined in 1931. The major developments in both painting and sculpture can be seen in the National Gallery of Modern Art *(see p 348)*.

Architecture and town planning – For its first 20 years as the capital of Italy Rome was a building site. The town plans of 1871 and 1883 provided for the construction of housing for the new civil servants around Piazza Vittorio Emanuele, Piazza dell'Independenza, at Castro Pretorio and in the Prati; for the demolition of the slum districts of the inner city; for the construction of administrative buildings;

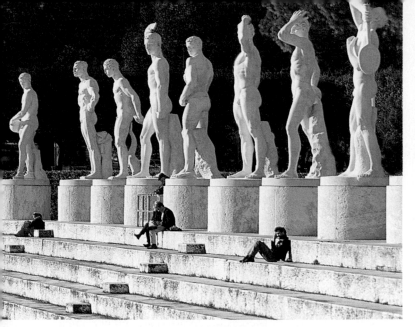

Gigantic statues of athletes in the Stadio dei Marmi, Foro Italico

for the establishment of banks and newspapers; and for the provision of arterial roads. Via del Corso and Via Nazionale, which were opened soon after the inclusion of Rome in the kingdom of Italy, were followed by Corso Vittorio Emanuele II and Via XX Settembre.

First Quarter of the 20C – More public works were undertaken. In 1902 the Humbert I tunnel was built linking the Quirinal and the business centre. Extensive parks, formerly the private property of the great families, were opened to the public or, like the Villa Ludovisi, sold as building lots for residential development. The Tiber embankment was constructed and the Campidoglio was cut away to make room for the monument to Victor Emmanuel II. The International Exhibition in 1911 was responsible for the development of the district around Piazza Mazzini and a huge museum of modern art in a garden setting was bestowed on the capital. The year 1920 brought the beginning of the garden suburbs: near to Monte Sacro in the north and at Garbatella in the south.

Mussolini's Rome – The arrival of Mussolini in 1922 ushered in a policy of grandiose town planning linked to the Fascist ideology which favoured a return to Ancient grandeur.

Three new streets – Corso del Rinascimento, Via della Botteghe Oscure and Via del Teatro di Marcello – were opened up to allow traffic to penetrate the Campus Martius. Via dei Fori Imperiali was opened in 1932 to give a clear view of the Colosseum from Piazza Venezia. The reconciliation of the Church and State, sealed in the Lateran Treaty in 1929, was marked by the opening of Via della Conciliazione (1936) to the detriment of the medieval district of the Borgo. As it had been decided that Rome should expand towards the sea, construction began on the new district known as EUR.

From the Second World War to the present day – The Holy Year in 1950, when masses of pilgrims were expected, saw the completion of both Via Cristoforo Colombo and the railway station (Stazione Termini). The Flaminia Stadium, the small Sports Palace in Via Flaminia and the Sports Palace in EUR were built for the 1960 Olympic Games. The Olympic Village in Via Flaminia was built on a site cleared of old run-down housing. Corso di Francia, a wide elevated highway, is also a daring piece of architectural design. In the west, Via Olimpica connects the Foro Italico to EUR. In 1961 the international airport at Fiumicino (Leonardo da Vinci) was built to complement the existing one at Ciampino. In 1970 the main orbital road round the city (Grande Raccordo Anulare – 70km/44mi) was finished. Among Rome's modern buildings, mention should be made of the RAI block *(see MONTE MARIO)*, the British Embassy *(see PORTA PIA)*, some of the buildings in EUR, the Chamber for Papal Audiences built by Pier Luigi Nervi in 1971 and the Gregorian Profane and Christian Museums which date from 1970 (both in the Vatican), and some large hotels, including The Jolly, with its glass walls, which reflect the trees in the park of the Villa Borghese, and the Hilton, which stands on Monte Mario and caused great controversy when it was built.

Literature

Rome has long been a popular subject for foreign writers and has been described in detail by travellers such as Mark Twain, Stendhal and Goethe. However, perhaps the best portraits of this fascinating and contrasting city can be found in the satirical works of the Roman author Bellini, or more recently in the complex novels of the 20C author Moravia.

Rome's contribution to the history of Italian literature is an important one. Over a period spanning at least seven centuries (from the 3C BC to the famous sack of Rome in AD 410), Latin literature flourished. The different literary genres included epics, by writers such as **Ennius** (239-169 BC), **Virgil** (70-19 BC), **Lucan** (39-65) and **Statius** (40-96); comic dramas by **Plautus** (?250-184 BC) and **Terence** (?184-?159 BC; satirical works by **Lucilius** (?168-102 BC), **Horace** (65-8 BC) and **Juvenal** (2C AD); didactic poetry by **Lucretius** (?98-?55 BC); love poetry by **Catullus** (87-?55 BC), **Propertius** (97-16 BC), **Tibullus** (55-19 BC) and **Ovid** (43 BC-AD 17); rhetorical and philosphical prose by **Cicero** (106-43 BC) and **Seneca** (?4 BC-AD 65); and romances by **Petronius** (2C AD) and **Apuleius** (AD 125-180). Historians have left fascinating accounts of the city and its Empire. **Caesar** (100-44 BC) wrote about his own military campaigns in *The Gallic Wars* and *The Civil War*. Two monographs by **Sallust** (86-35 BC) have survived, the *Bellum Lugurthinum* (an account of the war in Numidia from 105-11 BC) and the *Bellum Catilinae*, on the Catiline conspiracy of 63 BC, which was also the subject of four famous orations by **Cicero** (known as the *Catilinarie*). These works, along with others by the same author (such as the *Pro Murena* and *Pro Milone*), paint an illuminating picture of the political climate during this period of the Republic.

Other annalistic works include the *Libri Ab Urbe Condita* by **Livy** (59 BC-AD 17), containing vivid desciptions of events that took place between the founding of the city and the 9C BC (of which about 30 books have survived intact), and the *Annales* (a history of the period from the death of Augustus to that of Nero) and *Historiae* (the period from Galba to Domitian) by **Tacitus** (55-117).

These official histories are complemented by the *Lives of the Caesars* (from Julius Caesar to Domitian) by **Suetonius** (?70-?125) – a kind of biography – and the 10 books of the *Epistulae* by **Pliny the Younger** (61-113), letters on a range of themes written to characters of the time, including the Emperor Trajan, which are fascinating for their portrait of high society during the Imperial era. In contrast, **Petronius** paints a grotesque and parodistic portrait of this society in his *Satiricon* (brilliantly adapted for cinema by the director Fellini).

From the Middle Ages Rome gradually lost her supremacy in the literary arts to other cities in Italy (especially Florence) and it was not until the founding of the Roman Academy by **Pomponio Leto** (1428-97) that the city once again assumed an important role as a literary centre. This role was consolidated by the establishment of the **Arcadia Society** in 1690 by **Giambattista Felice Zappi** (1667-1719) and his wife **Faustina Maratti** (1680-1745). This society, situated at the time on the Janiculum Hill, championed a style reminiscent of the *Canzoniere* by Petrarch, as opposed to the Baroque "bad taste" of the 17C. Among the main exponents of this style were **Paolo Rolli** (1687-1785) and **Pietro Metastasio** (1698-1782). The latter was appointed official poet at the Imperial court in Vienna and his melodramas, such as *Catone in Utica* and *Dido Abandoned*, met with notable success both in Italy and abroad.

The city played a marginal role in cultural debate during the Enlightenment, a movement which influenced Milan and Naples more than Rome. Those scholars who visited Rome seemed to appreciate the unique nature of the city, which set her apart from other cultural centres in Europe and gave rise to extremes of high praise or fierce condemnation. Thus, although **Goethe** hurled abuse at the noise in Via del Corso during the Carnival, he confessed that he felt as if he had been reborn the day he arrived in Rome *(Italianische Reise – Italian Journey)*. **Mark**

Alberto Moravia

Twain did not look favourably on the Papacy or its superstitious trappings, and said that walking through the streets of Rome it was difficult to believe in the city's magnificent past *(The Innocents Abroad)*. **Leopardi** had a deeply disturbing impression of the city at the beginning of the 19C; he saw it as somehow shut in, lacking in imagination, and full of "quite repulsive" women.

Giuseppe Gioacchino Belli (1791-1863) wrote in dialect, using popular themes similar to those of the Romantic movement. Belli wrote over 2 000 sonnets *(sonetti)* which portray the life of the common people, using the language and vocabulary of the lower social classes. He succeeds in painting a clear picture of Roman society, divided between the aristocracy and clerics on the one hand, and the "plebs" on the other, interspersed with occasional references to folklore. Another author who wrote in the Roman dialect was Carlo Alberto Salustri, better known as **Trilussa** (1873-1950), whose colourful and witty works describe popular dissatisfaction with the Fascist regime of the time.

A superb evocation of Rome is found in *Il Piacere* (1889) by **Gabriele D'Annunzio**: 16C courts and sumptuously decorated Baroque palaces are described in great detail, providing the backdrop for the elegant receptions and grand banquets held by high society, and appearing as symbols of the various characters, so that the city almost becomes one of the main characters of the novel.

Two other leading lights of the city were **Vincenzo Cardarelli** (1887-1959) and **Antonio Baldini** (1889-1962) who produced the magazine *La Ronda* between 1919 and 1923.

Among contemporary writers, **Alberto Moravia** (1907-90) described the apathy and inadequacy of Rome's bourgeoisie in *Gli Indifferenti* and *La Noia*, and put forward a clear portrayal of the lower echelons of Italian society in *La Romana*, *Raconti romani* and *La Ciociara* (successfully adapted for the cinema by De Sica). Born and educated in Milan, **Carlo Emilio Gadda** (1893-1973) owed some of his fame to a novel based in Rome, entitled *Quer pasticciaccio brutto de via Merulana* (1946). The title translates literally as "That Awful Mess on Via Merulana", and the novel is an effective portrayal of Rome during the Fascist period, set around events taking place in 1927 and depicting all strata of society, from the bourgeoisie to the working class. Much of the novel's success lies in its use of the Roman dialect, for which Gadda consulted with friends who were experts on the subject, resulting in a new, bold and original mix of language.

An important figure in the cultural world of the 1960s and 1970s was **Pier Paolo Pasolini** (1922-75), also not orginally from Rome. This widely debated figure was a poet, novelist, critic, film director and dramatist; he portrayed a sadly realistic picture of the Roman underclass in *Ragazzi di vita* and *Una vita violenta*.

Cinema

Much of the history of Italian cinema is bound up with the film studios at Cinecittà, on the outskirts of Rome, where films by famous Italian producers, such as Fellini, as well as exciting new American features, were produced. Rome has always provided the perfect backdrop for the big screen and for a few decades it was also home to the most important film studios in Europe.

Cinema in Rome is synonymous with Cinecittà. The studios in Via Tuscolano *(see CASTELLI ROMANI)* were built in 1937 by Mussolini, whose aim was to create the largest film studios in Europe, and were used to produce the many films extolling the virtues of the Fascist regime. When they opened, the studios covered an area of 600 000m/6 456 000sq ft and housed 16 film sets, offices, restaurants, a huge pool for shooting water scenes and all the latest technology and gadgetry. These state-of-the-art facilities contributed to an increase in domestic film production, which was now completely autonomous, and which flourished even at the beginning of the war; in the first six years of the studios' existence, some 300 films were produced here, not all of which were works of propaganda. It was in Cinecittà that neo-realism was born. Although films of this type are usually shot out of doors, far from any studio, famous film-makers, like **Vittorio de Sica** and **Roberto Rossellini**, did make some of their earliest films in the studios. To bridge the gap between life and its imaginary portrayal on the screen, a development of the Fascist period, these directors tried to return to realism, to the detailed observation of daily life; the main theme of the neo-realists was the war and all its tragic consequences. In *Roma città aperta* (1945), *Paisà* (1946) and *Germania anno zero* (1948) Rossellini portrayed Nazi-Fascist oppression. De Sica, in *Sciuscià* (1946) and *Ladri di Biciclette* (1948),

Cahiers du Cinéma

Lara Pessina/MICHELIN

drew a portrait of Italy after the war with its unemployment and misery. In *Riso amaro* (1949) and *Pasqua di Sangue* (1950) **De Santis** described a working class divided between submission to the dominant ideology and revolutionary aspirations.

At the beginning of the 1950s neo-realism faded out: it no longer met the need of a people keen to forget the hardship of that time. It was during those years that the big-budget American films were shot at Cinecittà. The Hollywood Italian-made films which have earned a place in the history of cinema are *Quo vadis* (1950), *War and Peace* (1956), *Ben Hur* (1959) and *Cleopatra* (1963).

For Italian cinema, the 1960s were a golden age. Supported by the powerful industrial infrastructure of the studios, very many films were made – more than 200 a year – and of the best quality. The major directors included Fellini and Visconti; of the two, it was **Federico Fellini** who made most use of the studios and who consolidated their repu-

Sophia Loren and Marcello Mastroianni in Una giornata particolare *by Ettore Scola (1977)*

tation. *La Strada* (1957), with Giulietta Masina, was followed in 1960 by *La Dolce Vita*, a mirror of those infamous nights in Rome. Fellini included some fantastic, dream-like shots in some of his films which included *Otto e mezzo* (1963) *Amarcord* (1974), *La Città delle donne* (1980), *E la nave va* (1984) and *Ginger e Fred* (1986). **Luchino Visconti**'s early work focused mainly on themes relating to social injustice; his later films examined the decadence and disenchantment of the middle classes. Among Visconti's masterpieces were *Notti bianche* (1957) and *Ludwig* (1972).

The 1960s also brought a new generation of directors keen to record their political and social commitment, such as **Pasolini**, **Rosi** and **Bertolucci**. During the same period, the work of **Sergio Leone**, who produced a vast quantity of "spaghetti westerns", not always of the highest quality, also kept the studios at Cinecittà in the limelight. Since the end of the 1970s, however, hit by competition from television and a declining market, the cinema has been going through a period of crisis both in terms of production and creativity, which only a very few *films d'auteur* have managed to resist. Among the most recent are *La Famiglia* (1987) by **Ettore Scola**, *Caro DIARIO* (1994) and *La Stanza del Figlio* (2001) by **Nanni Moretti,** none of which were produced at Cinecittà. Nowadays, despite the latest in sophisticated technical equipment and its 22 studios, Cinecittà is used almost exclusively for the production of television films and commercials.

Piazza del Popolo from the Pincian Hill

Selected Sights

Appia Antica★★

The Old Appian Way is a narrow, paved road flanked by rows of graceful pine trees and studded with ruins and ancient tombs. The road runs through an attractive landscape, a semi-rural oasis which has fortunately been spared the prolific construction seen elsewhere in the city. With its catacombs and the Quo Vadis Church, the Old Appian Way is also an important part of Christian Rome.

Location

Michelin map 38 or Michelin spiral atlas of Rome: pp 86-87 U 15 to W 15-16. Metro line A: S. Giovanni; buses for the catacombs of St Callistus, St Sebastian and Domitilla depart from Piazza di Porta S. Giovanni (consult a local transport directory for further information). From the tomb of Cecilia Metella to Casal Rotondo the Old Appian Way is only accessible by car.

Tour: half a day (3hr for the catacombs of St Callistus, St Sebastian and Domitilla). On Thu, Fri and Sat all the monuments and catacombs are open. Visitors are shown round in guided parties. The speed of the tours, dictated by the large numbers of visitors, and the gloom in the passages mean that visitors must follow the guide closely. The part of the Old Appian Way (Via Appia Antica) which holds most interest for the tourist is the stretch which passes the catacombs and the nearby Ancient monuments (Romulus's Tomb, Maxentius's Circus and the tomb of Cecilia Metella). The catacombs of St Callistus, St Sebastian and Domitilla are particularly worthy of note.

The itinerary can be combined with an excursion to the CASTELLI ROMANI by turning left into Via Casal Rotondo and taking Appia Nuova (n° 7) in the direction of the Grande Raccordo Anulare (GRA) – Albano.

Background

The Via Appia is named after Appius Claudius Caecus, under whose magistracy the road was opened in 312 BC. Before the construction of the Aurelian Wall in the 3C, the Via Appia left Rome through the Porta Capena *(see TERME DI CARACALLA)*, and more or less followed the line of Via delle Terme di Caracalla and Via di Porta San Sebastiano and then continued to Capua, Beneventum and Brindisi. In the early stages it was lined by tombs, owing to a law which was already in force in the 5C BC, forbidding burials within the city. In the Middle Ages the Appian Way became unsafe; members of the Caetani family converted the tomb of Cecilia Metella into a fortress and plundered passing travellers. This led to the opening of the New Appian Way. Late in the 17C the Old and New Appian Ways were linked by the Via Appia Pignatelli.

Special features

CATACOMBS★★★

In medieval Rome the Latin expression *ad catacumbas* referred to St Sebastian's Cemetery which lay in a hollow beside the Appian Way. When other similar cemeteries were discovered in the 16C they were referred to by the same name. **Catacomb** now means an underground Christian cemetery composed of several storeys of galleries which generally extended downwards. When there was no more room in an upper gallery, excavation began on a lower one, so that the galleries nearest to the surface are usually the oldest.

> **DOMINE, QUO VADIS?**
>
> The "Domine, quo vadis?" Church recalls a famous legend. While fleeing from persecution in Rome, **Peter** is supposed to have met Christ on the road and asked him "Domine, quo vadis? (Lord, whither goest thou?)". "To Rome, to be crucified a second time", replied Christ and disappeared, leaving his footprints in the road. Ashamed of his weakness, Peter returned to Rome and met his death.

Catacombs have been found not only elsewhere on the outskirts of Rome but also around Naples, and in Sicily, North Africa and Asia Minor.

Christians in the catacombs – Until the middle of the 2C there were no formal Christian cemeteries. Very often a private burial ground belonging to a family, some of whom were pro-Christian, would be made available to Christians of their acquaintance for burying their dead. The situation changed early in the 3C when Pope Zephyrinus put Callistus in charge of the cemetery on the Appian Way. This was the first step in formalising Christian burials and creating cemeteries for Christians only on land belonging to the Church.

For a long time the catacombs were simply graveyards where Christians came to pray at the tomb of a loved one. Visits became more frequent in the 3C when the persecutions (by Septimius Severus in 202, Decius in 250, Valerian in 257 and Diocletian in 295) created many martyrs; the Popes strongly urged the faithful to pray at the martyrs' tombs. The catacombs, however, were never a place of refuge where Christians lived in hiding; they were known to the Imperial authorities who closed them at the height of a persecution. It was only rarely, when they had broken the closure rule, that Christians were killed in the catacombs.

After a period of great popularity in the 4C, when Christianity experienced a great expansion, the catacombs were abandoned (except for St Sebastian's which was always a place of pilgrimage). In the 5C and 6C the Roman countryside was ravaged by barbarians; gradually the martyrs' relics were transferred to the town where churches were built to house them. It was not until the 16C, when an underground cemetery was discovered in Via Salaria by Antonio Bosio, an Italian archaeologist, that interest in the catacombs started up again. Their systematic investigation is primarily due to another archaeologist Giovanni Battista de Rossi (1822-94).

Special terms used – A **hypogeum** is an underground tomb belonging to a noble Roman family. From the *hypogeum* a network of galleries developed; each gallery was about 1m/3ft wide and 2-3m/7-10ft high. Opening off the galleries were small rooms, **cubicula**, where the sarcophagi were placed; sometimes there was a **lucernarium**, an opening in the roof through which air and light could enter.

When lack of space became acute, recesses **(loculi)** were hollowed out one above another in the gallery walls; the corpse was wrapped in a shroud and laid in the recess, which was sealed off with a marble slab or a row of terracotta tiles inscribed with the name of the dead person and a sign to show their religion. An **arcosolium** consists of a boxed tomb, closed with a marble slab, set into an arched opening which is often frescoed.

As the cult of the martyrs developed so did the custom, borrowed from the pagans, of holding a funeral feast, called **refrigerium** by the Christians. The faithful would gather round a martyr's tomb to ask him to intercede on their behalf and to share a meal.

Near to the catacombs there is often a **columbarium**; this is a communal burial chamber, containing niches where the urns holding the ashes were placed, usually reserved for pagans of modest means.

DECORATIVE MOTIFS

Originally, Christians decorated their tombs with motifs found on pagan tombs (garlands of flowers, birds and cherubs). Then other motifs began to appear, illustrating the metaphors of the Holy Scriptures, depicting scenes from the Bible and symbolising manifestations of spiritual life. The meaning of the paintings and symbols found in the catacombs is still a subject of much controversy

The **dove** holding a twig in its beak is a symbol of reconciliation between God and man. The **anchor** signifies hope; sometimes the horizontal bar is stressed to form a cross. The **fish** is a symbol for Christ: the Greek word for fish is composed of the initial letter of each word in the Greek phrase meaning "Jesus Christ, God's son, Saviour".

The **dolphin** which comes to the rescue of shipwrecked sailors indicates Jesus the Saviour.

The **fisherman** means a preacher because of Jesus's words to his disciples "I will make you to become fishers of men".

Jonah and the whale foretells the Resurrection.

The **Good Shepherd** or Jesus searching for the lost sheep was one of the most popular ways of representing Christ among early Christians.

Other favourite scenes were the miracle of the feeding of the 5 000, the healing of the man suffering with the palsy and the baptism of Jesus, or the institution of baptism.

Catacombe di San Callisto★★★ (St Calixtus Catacombs)

Guided tours only in various languages (45min), daily (except Wed), 8.30am-12.30pm and 2.30-5.30pm (5pm in winter). Closed 1 Jan, Feb, Easter and Christmas. €5; no charge the last Sun in Sep. Lucina's precinct open to specialists only. ☎ 06 44 65 610 or 06 44 67 601; Fax 06 44 67 625; arc.sacra@flashnet.it

The catacombs extend over an area bounded by the Appian Way, Via Ardeatina and Via delle Sette Chiese. This cemetery, where almost all the 3C Popes, were buried is also famous for its exceptional collection of paintings. In GB de Rossi's opinion, the Christian cemetery could have grown out of the family tomb of the Caecilii who were patricians. By the 2C the property belonged to the Church and was developed as a huge burial ground for Christians. The remains of about 500 000 people have been interred here.

It was probably **Calixtus** who was chiefly responsible for the Church becoming the legal owner of the cemeteries. This change in circumstances occurred at the very end of the 2C during the reign of the Emperor Commodus (180-92), which was a peaceful period for Christians: it was said that Commodus's concubine, Marcia, was a Christian.

The Good Shepherd – *Domitilla Catacombs*

Calixtus, who may have been a native of Trastevere, was a slave whose Christian master entrusted him with his money matters. Financial failure caused Calixtus to flee. He was caught, denounced as a Christian by some Jews and sentenced to hard labour in the Sardinian quarries. He was released under an amnesty but excluded from Rome by the Pope, Victor I, who regarded him as an adventurer. Calixtus returned to favour under Zephyrinus, Victor's successor. He was made a deacon and appointed administrator of the cemetery which bears his name. In 217 he succeeded Zephyrinus as Pope: five years later he died. He was not, however, buried in his cemetery on the Appian Way but in Calepodius's Cemetery on the Aurelian Way, near the Janiculum, where his tomb was found in 1962.

Cripta dei papi (Papal Crypt) – Calixtus decided that his cemetery should be the Popes' official burial place and the remains of the 3C Popes were placed in the *loculi* hollowed out of the walls of this chamber. Among them was Sixtus II, who was put to death on 6 August 258 together with four of his deacons; they had been surprised while holding a meeting in the cemetery, an act which contravened an edict issued by the Emperor Valerian forbidding Christian assemblies and closing the catacombs. The marble plaques sealing the *loculi* bear the names and titles of the dead Popes. The Greek letters M T P, which are the main consonants (M T R in the Roman alphabet) in the Greek word "martyr", meaning witness, have been added to the names of Pontianus and Fabian; the former was deported to Sardinia where he died in 235; the latter was a victim of the Emperor Decius who organised one of the worst persecutions ever suffered by the Christians.

The wreathed columns and the *lucernarium* date from the 4C.

The inscription – a few verses to the glory of all the saints who lie buried in this place – also dates from the 4C, put up by Pope Damasus.

Cripta di Santa Cecilia (St Cecilia's Crypt) – This chamber was already being venerated by pilgrims as St Cecilia's tomb in the 7C. Her sarcophagus was found by Paschal I in the 9C in the *loculus,* which now contains a copy of the statue of the saint sculpted by Maderno *(see TRASTEVERE: Santa Cecilia).*

Sala dei Sacramenti (Sacraments' Crypt) – This group of chambers contains an extraordinary collection of paintings dating from the late 2C or early 3C. The majority of the subjects generally found elsewhere in the catacombs appear here. There are no purely decorative motifs, except in a simple band framing the scenes. Calixtus's cemetery also contains the crypt in which Pope **Eusebius** (309-10) is buried (he was deported to Sicily where he died but his body was recovered by his successor); the crypt where Pope **Caius** (283-96) is buried; and the crypt where, in the opinion of GB de Rossi, Pope **Melchiades** (also Miltiades) (311-14) was buried.

Lucina's Precinct, which is named after a noble Roman lady, and the Papal Crypt are the oldest part of the cemetery; Lucina is thought to have recovered the remains of Pope Cornelius (251-53) and to have buried them in a chamber decorated with paintings showing Cornelius with his friend Cyprian, Bishop of Carthage. In another chamber in Lucina's precinct, also decorated with paintings, are two very faint illustrations of the mystery of the Eucharist: two fish with two baskets of bread and glasses of wine. These paintings, which are on the left wall of the chamber, date from the 2C.

Near the entrance to the underground is a **chapel with three apses**, probably built in the 4C, which may have contained the remains of Pope Zephyrinus.

Catacombe di Domitilla★★★ (Domitilla Catacombs)

Entrance at Via delle Sette Chiese 282. Guided tours only in various languages (45min), daily (except Tue), 8.30am-12.30pm and 2.30-5pm. Closed 1 Jan, Easter and Christmas. €5; no charge the last Sun in Sep. ☎ 06 44 65 610 or 06 44 67 601; Fax 06 44 67 625; arc.sacra@flashnet.it

This extensive network of galleries began in the private cemetery of Domitilla, whose uncle, the Emperor Domitian (81-96), belonged to the rich Flavian family. In 95 Domitilla's husband, **Flavius Clemens**, was denounced as a Christian and executed on Domitian's orders. Domitilla was exiled to the Isle of Pandataria (now called Ventotene).

Domitilla's Catacombs became famous in the 4C when a basilica was built over the graves of St Nereus and St Achilleus. According to legend they were two of Domitilla's servants who, like their mistress, converted to Christianity. In fact they were two soldiers martyred under Diocletian (284-305). Not far from their tomb lay St Petronilla, whose sarcophagus was transferred to the Vatican in the 8C.

Domitilla's cemetery was discovered in the 16C by Antonio Bosio; in the 19C it was excavated by GB de Rossi and then by the Papal Commission for Sacred Archaeology.

Basilica dei Santi Nereo e Achilleo – The **basilica of St Nereus and St Achilleus**, which consisted of a nave and two side aisles preceded by a narthex, was built between 390 and 395 to the detriment of the upper galleries, which belonged to one of the oldest parts of the cemetery. The sarcophagi of the two saints must have been placed in the apse near St Petronilla's. Pieces of the original structure, in particular of the *schola cantorum* which separated the chancel from the rest of the church, have been put back in place. In front of the chancel on the right one of the small columns which supported the canopy now bears a sculpture of Achilleus the martyr.

In this basilica in the late 6C Gregory the Great preached one of his homilies deploring the misery being suffered by Rome under the barbarian menace. By the end of the 8C the basilica was deserted; in future the saints were venerated within the city walls in the new church dedicated to Nereus and Achilleus *(see TERME DI CARACALLA: Santi Nereo e Achilleo)*, which was built by Leo III.

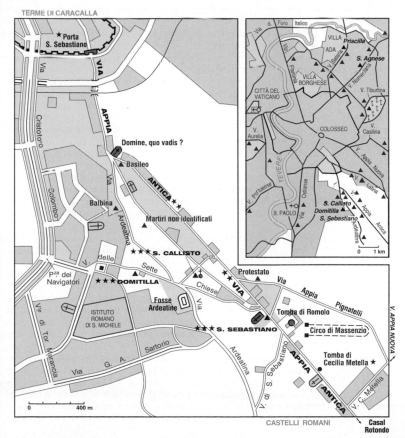

Cubicolo di Veneranda – This chamber behind the apse testifies to the popular enthusiasm for the cemetery in the 4C. The faithful were keen to be buried near to the tomb of a saint, hence Veneranda's wish to be buried next to St Petronilla. A painting on the *arcosolium* shows them both entering Paradise.

"Vestibolo dei Flavi" – This is the name given to the *hypogeum (see p 115)* on the right of the basilica. It is one of the oldest parts of the cemetery and dates from the 2C. It consists of a long wide gallery decorated with vine tendrils, birds and cupids. Branching off it are *cubicula* to contain the sarcophagi; when there was no more room, *loculi* were created. Late in the 3C a room for the funeral meal was created on the right of the entrance. Linked to it is a *cubiculum* named after Love and Psyche because of its decorations, which date from the 3C but have been partially damaged by the creation of *loculi*.

Ipogeo dei Flavi Aureli – To the left of the basilica is another *hypogeum* containing the names of the freed men employed by the Flavians and the Aurelians. It is contemporary with the Flavian Vestibule. There are examples of the simple symbols such as the anchor or a monogram used by the early Christians.

Domitilla's Catacombs contain a multitude of galleries and *cubicula* such as the *cubiculum* of Diogenes and the *cubiculum* of Ampliatus.

Catacombe di San Sebastiano*** (St Sebastian Catacombs)

Guided tours only in various languages (45min), daily (except Sun), 8.30am-12.30pm and 2.30-5.30pm (5pm in winter). Closed mid-Nov to mid-Dec, 1 Jan, Easter and Christmas. €5; no charge the last Sun in Sep. ☎ 06 44 65 610 or 06 44 67 601; Fax 06 44 67 625; arc.sacra@flashnet.it

Near the catacombs, the Appian Way passes through a valley. On its slopes houses and columbarii were built. In the valley bottom three mausoleums were erected, which probably marked the beginning of the cemetery.

When the Church became the owner of the site in the 3C the mausoleums were covered by a platform arranged as a covered courtyard called a *triclia (see below)*. In the 4C a basilica with a nave and two aisles was built above the earlier structures and surrounded by mausoleums (those round the apse and on the south side have been preserved). It was here, near where the Apostles Peter and Paul were venerated, that St Sebastian was buried; he was a soldier martyred during the persecution in Diocletian's reign (284-305). His cult became so popular that in the 5C a crypt was excavated around his tomb. The basilica was altered in the 13C and then rebuilt in the 17C for Cardinal Scipio Borghese; the new church was built above the nave of the previous building.

The tour of St Sebastian's Catacombs includes a colombarium. Other graves, similar to the one on display, also exist.

Mausoleums – These three structures with their brick façades, pediments and travertine door frames probably date from the early 1C. At first they were used by pagans and then by Christians. The left-hand and central mausoleums have some beautiful stucco decorations. From these and the inscriptions found within, it seems that the structures belonged to religious sects which developed alongside Christianity; the central mausoleum contains the Greek symbol for the Son of God, the Christian Saviour. The right-hand mausoleum is decorated with paintings and bears the name of its owner, Clodius Hermes.

"Triclia" – This section of the catacombs has proved the most controversial among archaeologists. The graffiti on the walls invoking the Apostles Peter and Paul suggest that from 258 onwards Christians used to meet here to celebrate their memory; they may have met here because the relics of the two saints had been lodged here temporarily while the basilicas of St Peter in the Vatican and St Paul Without the Walls were being built. The participants sat on the stone benches for the meal *(refrigerium)*.

Catacombe e cripta di San Sebastiano – The network of galleries (catacombs and crypts) which began to develop in the 4C round St Sebastian's tomb was badly damaged in the Middle Ages by a ceaseless procession of pilgrims who came to invoke the martyr's name against the plague, since the searing pain of bubonic boils was thought to equal the agony of his multiple arrow wounds.

Mausoleo di Quirino e Domus Petri – These two chambers are supposed to have housed the relics of Peter and Paul. One contains the graffito *Domus Petri* (Peter's House), which may indicate that Peter's remains once rested there. The other, built in the 5C, was the **mausoleum of St Quirinus** who was martyred in Pannonia (western Hungary).

Present basilica – The atmosphere in the single nave with its white walls and beautiful 17C painted wooden ceiling is fairly solemn and chill. In the relics chapel *(right)* is exhibited the stone in which Christ is said to have left his footprints. It may, in fact, be an old votive offering. St Sebastian's Chapel *(left)*, which was built in the 17C over his tomb, contains a statue of the saint by one of Bernini's pupils (17C).

In the sacristy *(right of St Sebastian's Chapel)* there is a beautiful 14C wooden crucifix.

Worth a Visit

Circo di Massenzio e Tomba di Romolo (Maxentius's Circus and Romulus's Tomb)

Open daily (except Mon) Apr-Sep, 9am-7pm; rest of the year, daily (except Mon), 9am-5pm (last admission 30min before closing time). Closed 1 Jan, 1 May and Christmas. €2.58. ☎ 06 78 01 324; Fax 06 68 92 115.

Emperor Maxentius (306-312) built his Imperial residence beside the Appian Way. He had a handsome tomb erected nearby when his young son died in 309 and also a hippodrome for chariot races. The oblong shape of the circus is well preserved, as are the stables and the remains of the two towers which stood at the western end flanking the stalls, and the magistrates' box where the starting signal was given.

Tomba di Romolo – The **tomb of Romulus**, which is surrounded by a wall punctuated by a quadriporticus, is a domed rotunda preceded by a *pronaos* in a style reminiscent of the Pantheon on a smaller scale. It is partly hidden by a house built onto the front.

Fosse Ardeatine (&) *Open daily, 8.15am-5pm. Closed 1 Jan, Easter, 1 May, 15 Aug and Christmas. No charge. ☎/Fax 06 51 36 742.*

These tombs commemorate a particularly painful episode during the Second World War. Here on 24 March 1944 the Nazis killed 335 Italians as a reprisal for an attack by the Resistance in Rome in Via Rasella, in which 32 German soldiers were killed. The tombs *(fosse)* of the victims are sheltered by a sanctuary; a museum gives information on the period.

Tomba di Cecilia Metella★

(&) Open daily (except Mon), 9am-1hr before dusk (last admission 1hr before closing time). €2. ☎ 06 48 89 91; Fax 06 48 19 316.

This handsome tomb dates from the late Republic. The crenellations were added in the 14C when the Caetani family turned it into a keep and incorporated it into the adjacent 11C fortress which extended across the road. Its bulky silhouette is one of the best known in the Roman countryside. The cylindrical mausoleum standing on a square base was the tomb of the wife of Crassus, son of the Crassus who was a member of the first triumvirate with Caesar and Pompey in 60 BC. The decorative frieze of ox heads has caused the locality to be known as "Capo di Bove". Fragments of tombs from the Appian Way can be seen within the ruins of the medieval fortress *(right of the entrance).*

On the left of the entrance is the way into the conical funeral chamber of the original tomb.

Tour

FROM TOMBA DI CECILIA METELLA TO CASAL ROTONDO

5km/3mi. 800m/875yd beyond Cecilia Metella's tomb the Old Appian Way becomes a one-way road.

Although the road surface is poor, this stretch of the Old Appian Way provides a pleasant view of the Roman countryside where the reddish tones of the tombs and the ruined aqueducts blend with the dark green of the cypresses and umbrella pines. The tombs on the Appian Way were some of the finest in Rome. Shaped like pyramids or tumuli and topped by a mound covered in undergrowth, sometimes only an inscription or a few carvings remain.

The tomb on the right just after the junction with via Erode Attico was long thought to be the **tomb of one of the Curiatii**, who took part in the famous combat with the Horatii.

The **Quintilian Villa** (Villa dei Quintili) was a huge property going back to the time of Hadrian (117-38); part of it was turned into a fortress in the 15C. & *Open daily (except Mon), in summer, 9am-1hr before dusk; rest of the year, 9am-5.30pm (last admission 1hr before closing time). Closed 1 Jan and Christmas. Tours with archaeologist available by prior appointment. €4; €20 for a "Roma archeologica" card, valid for nine archaeological sites. ☎ 06 39 96 08 071; Fax 06 39 75 09 50; pierreci@pierreci.it*

Sepulchre on the Via Appia

Aventino*

From Ancient Roman times through to the Fascist era, the Aventine has played an important role in the history of Italy and its capital city. Today it is a pleasant residential district, dotted with magnificent villas and opulent religious houses, which acts as a peaceful oasis in the heart of the city. The area is also home to a number of palaeo-Christian churches which are well worth a visit. A superb view of Rome can be enjoyed from the attractive Giardino degli Aranci, also known as the Parco Savello.

Location

Michelin map 38 or Michelin spiral atlas of Rome: pp 70-71 P 11-12. Metro line B: Circo Massimo. Tour 1hr 30min. The **Aventine** is the southernmost of the seven hills of Rome (about 40m/131ft high); it has two peaks separated by a gully down which runs Viale Aventino. The tour described below winds its way over the western-most side of the hill, overlooking the Tiber, which is separated from the Palatine Hill by the wide oblong space of the Circus Maximus.
Neighbouring sights are described in the following chapters: BOCCA DELLA VERITÀ; PIRAMIDE CESTIA-TESTACCIO.

Background

Throughout the Ancient Roman Republican period it was a popular district, in-habited particularly by merchants who traded among the quays and warehouses on the banks of the Tiber. Many religious shrines were built; among the oldest are the Temples to Diana, Ceres and Minerva, situated between Via di S. Melania and Via di S. Domenico.

During the Empire the Aventine became a residential area. Trajan lived there before becoming Emperor and his friend Licinius Sura built his own private baths there *(northwest of the church of Santa Prisca);* Decius also built a bathhouse there in 242. So much luxury aroused the envy of the Visigoths. In 410, under their leader Alaric, they sacked Rome for three days, leaving the Aventine utterly devastated. Nowadays it is a residential district, quiet and green, with many religious houses.

A plebeian stronghold – After the expulsion of the last king (509 BC) the insti-tution of the Republic was marked by a struggle between the patricians and the plebeians. In the 5C BC the plebeians, weary of fighting, which brought them only misery, withdrew to the Aventine as a protest. Menenius Agrippa, who was sent to reason with them, told them the parable of the human body and its limbs: since their effort benefited only the body, the limbs decided to stop work; the result was the death of the whole body including the limbs. As a result of the crisis two trib-unes were elected from among the plebeians to protect them against the consuls.

Death of a tribune – The plebeian tribune Caius Gracchus and his brother Tiberius **(the Gracchi)** were among the group of Roman citizens who shaped the history of the Republic. Continuing the work begun by Tiberius (assassinated in 133 BC), Caius pro-posed reforms in the ownership of land confiscated by Rome from neighbour-ing peoples, which was administered by the Senate and exploited by the wealthiest. He took refuge from sol-diers recruited by one of the consuls on the Aventine, until forced to flee over the Sublician Bridge to the foot of the Janiculum, where he was finally mur-dered in 121 BC.

WHERE TO EAT
See "Where to Eat" in the Practical Points section at the beginning of the guide.

SHOPPING
Archivio Fonografico – *Viale Aventino 59 –* ☎ *06 57 42 93 – Open Mon-Fri, noon-7pm; Sat, 10.30am-1pm and 3.30-7pm; Sun, 10.30am-1pm.* The only outward signs of this shop are a small sign and a bell. Appearances can be deceptive, however, as the Archivio Fonografico sells a wide selection of records and CDs, ranging from old songs to classical music. As an added bonus, visitors can listen to their prospective purchases from the comfort of one of the armchairs in the "living room".

Walking About

From the Piazzale Ugo la Malfa there is a fine **view★** of the ruins of the semicir-cular façade of the Domus Augustana on the Palatine Hill.
In the square stands a **Monument to Giuseppe Mazzini** (1805-72), a writer and politician. In 1849 he proclaimed the Republic of Rome but Papal power was restored by the French under General Oudinot.

"Circus Maximus"

The Great Circus, laid out in the Murcia Valley between the Palatine and the Aventine and now transformed into a long esplanade, was the largest in Rome. It was used exclusively for two-, three- and four-horse chariot (*biga*, *triga* or *quadriga*) races which drew larger crowds than any other spectacle.

The track (over 500m/550yd long) was bordered by banks of seats; the stand at the northwest end was reserved for the magistrates in charge of the spectacle; beneath it were the stalls; at the southeast end stood an archway.

From the 4C BC the arena was divided down its length by a central reservation, called the *spina*, which linked the two conical turning-posts *(metae)* around which the chariots raced.

In the Augustan era the Circus Maximus became truly grandiose. In 10 BC an obelisk (now in the Piazza del Popolo) more than 23m/75ft high was erected on the *spina* and a splendid stand was built below Flavian's Palace for the Emperor and his family. The Circus Maximus could accommodate 150 000 spectators.

The Emperors continued to make improvements. Claudius (41-54) replaced the wooden turning-posts with new ones in gilded bronze and substituted marble for tufa in the stables. After the fire in 64 his successor Nero extended the circus to 600m/656yd long and 200m/219yd wide. Domitian (81-96) and Trajan (98-117) increased the number of stands and the capacity of the circus grew to 300 000 places.

The major events took place during the September games which originated in the 6C BC. In the Imperial era the games became pure entertainment, offered by the Emperor to the people, and a passion for racing often led the Emperors to the worst excesses: Vitellius (68-69) who championed the "Blues" (there were four stables each distinguished by a different colour) quite simply had his favourite charioteer's rivals put to death; Caracalla (211-17) dealt out the same fate to the "Greens".

The circus was still in use in the 4C and Constantinus II set up a second obelisk (now in the Piazza di San Giovanni in Laterano).

The few remains which can be seen near the Porta Capena belong to Trajan's period. The little tower at this end dates from the Middle Ages; it was part of a fortress built by the noble Frangipani family.

Take Via di Valle Murcia on the right of the Mazzini monument.

The road is bordered by the **Rome Rose Garden** (Roseto di Roma) *(in flower in May)*

Turn left into Clivo dei Publicii.

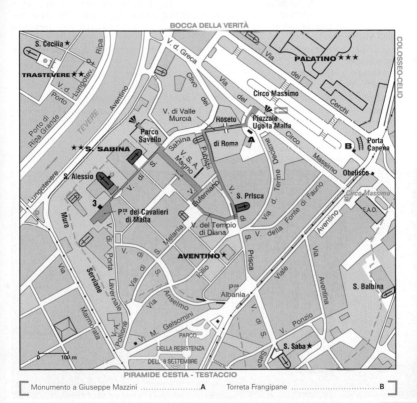

| Monumento a Giuseppe Mazzini ....A | Torreta Frangipane ....B |

Santa Prisca

The church was reconstructed in the 17C and 18C but its origin goes back to the 2C; it is one of the very first places of Christian worship in Rome.

Various touching legends are connected with the name of the holy woman venerated here. Prisca is said to be the first woman to have suffered martyrdom in Rome: she was baptised by Peter himself but denounced to the Imperial authorities and martyred by execution on the road to Ostia. In the 13C a Classical capital was set up as a font *(south aisle)* and inscribed with the "fact" that Peter had used it.

According to another legend Prisca was the wife of Aquila, whose memory is recalled by St Paul in his Epistle to the Romans: "Greet Prisca and Aquila, my helpers in Christ Jesus, who have for my life laid down their own necks ..."

Excavations have uncovered a late 2C **Mithraeum** *(access from the south aisle of the church)*. Contemporary with it is a neighbouring twin-nave building which may have been an earlier place of Christian worship on which the present church was built. *Open 2nd and 4th Sun of the month, 4pm. €5. For information and reservations, contact the Centro Servizi per l'Archeologia, Mon to Fri, 9am-6pm, ☎ 06 68 33 759; Fax 06 68 97 091.*

Traces of even older buildings, dating from the late 1C and early 2C have been found nearby; they may belong to Trajan's residence (98-117) or to the house of his friend, Licinius Sura, next to the baths he had built (Terme di Sura).

Take Via del Tempio di Diana, Via Eufemiano and then Via SA Magno.

Parco Savello

Better known as the **Giardino degli Aranci**, this park hugs the apse of Santa Sabina. In the 10C fortifications were built to defend the hill; in the 13C they became the stronghold of the Savelli family. From the northwest side high up above the river there is a pleasant **view★** of Rome: from the Janiculum, St Peter's dome and the Monte Mario with its TV mast round to the monument to Victor Emmanuel II and the Militia Tower.

Santa Sabina★★

Open 7am-noon and 3.30-7pm (6pm in winter). Cloisters and gardens open by appointment only ☎ 06 57 94 01.

The church was built in the 5C by Bishop Peter of Illyria who had officiated as priest to a *titulus* on this site. From the first it was dedicated to Sabina; the legend about this saint, which arose in the 6C, does not say clearly whether she lived and died on the Aventine or whether her remains were brought back here after her martyrdom in Umbria under Hadrian (117-138). The building has undergone many alterations: a campanile was added in the 10C; the crenellations were removed in the 17C. In the 13C Pope Honorius III, a member of the Savelli family, gave the church to St Dominic, who built the cloisters and convent to house the members of his order.

In the 16C the enterprising Sixtus V (1585-90) and his architect Domenico Fontana transformed the interior into a typical example of the Counter-Reformation style; this together with subsequent Baroque additions completely effaced the medieval character of the church.

Extensive restoration work has revived its earlier appearance in all its glory.

Exterior – In the 15C a portico was added to the door in the side wall. The narthex on the west front was one side of a four-sided portico surrounding an atrium which disappeared in the 13C when the convent was built.

The light, spacious interior of Santa Sabina

Opening into the nave is a very beautiful **door★★** made of cypress wood; it belonged to the original church and dates from the 5C. The two leaves are divided into panels, 18 of which are decorated with the original low-relief carvings illustrating scenes from the Old and New Testaments. High up on the left is a representation of the Crucifixion, the oldest example of a representation of this scene in a public place.

Interior★★ – The well-proportioned interior with light streaming through the clerestory windows reflects the vigorous expansion of the flourishing early Christian Church.

The basilical plan (the two side chapels added in the 16C and 17C have been retained) consists of a nave and two aisles separated by two rows of columns with Corinthian capitals directly supporting a very light arcade (no architrave). The overhead windows have been restored to their original appearance.

The mosaic above the entrance, the only one left of many which extended along both sides of the nave between the arches and the windows, bears an inscription in gold lettering commemorating the construction of the church by Peter of Illyria during the reign of Pope Celestine I (422-32); the female figures on either side are allegories of the church of the Jews ("Ecclesia ex circumcisione") converted by St Peter and the church of the Gentiles ("Ecclesia ex gentibus") converted by St Paul.

Nave: the frieze of tessellated marble above and between the arches dates from the 5C; the mosaic tomb on the floor in front of the *schola cantorum* (the space reserved for the choristers in front of the chancel) belongs to a Master General of the Dominican Order who died in 1300.

Chancel: the rich marble decor *(schola cantorum, presbyterium, ambones)* dating from the 9C and destroyed by Sixtus V has been reconstructed from fragments of the original; the ambones (Early Christian pulpits) and the Paschal candlestick are reconstructions. The Mannerist mosaic in the apse by Taddeo Zuccari (retouched in the 19C and 20C) replaced the original 16C mosaic which depicted the saints who were venerated in the church.

South aisle: the upper part of a Classical column, discovered during excavations underneath the church, may have belonged to the 3C-4C house, the *titulus* of the early church.

At the east end of the aisle is a chapel dedicated to the Virgin in the 15C by Cardinal Poggio del Monte di Auxia; his attractive tomb recalls the funeral art of Lombardy at the time of the Renaissance, introduced to Rome by Andrea Bregno.

North aisle: the 17C Baroque chapel dedicated to St Catherine of Siena has been preserved; its multicoloured marbles, frescoes and painted dome clash with the serenity of the rest of the church.

In the monks' garden, perfumed by roses and geraniums and shaded by clementine and lemon trees, is a sculpture of the *Last Supper* (1974) by Gismondi. *(For access, apply to the sacristan.)*

Sant'Alessio (St Alexis)

This is a church for those who are interested in legends. On the left, immediately inside the door, is St Alexis's staircase: the son of a patrician family, St Alexis set out for the Holy Land as a mendicant, returning to Rome to die, but his family did not recognise him and he spent his last days beneath the staircase of his father's house. The legend of the "beggar beneath the stairs" was one of the main subjects of mystery plays in the 15C.

Continue along the road to Piazza dei Cavalieri di Malta.

This charming **square** was designed by Piranesi in the 18C.

> **AN UNEXPECTED VIEW**
> The door into the Priory of the **Knights of Malta** (Villa del Priorato di Malta, n° 3 Piazza dei Cavalieri di Malta) is famous for the view through the keyhole, which reveals the dome of St Peter's at the end of a well-clipped avenue of trees.

Bocca della Verità★★

The Piazza della Bocca della Verità takes its name from the carved face in the portico of the church of Santa Maria in Cosmedin: legend says that the open "mouth of truth" would close on the hand of anyone found telling a lie. The piazza lies in a pleasant district not far from the river, close to Ancient temples and palaeo-Christian and Renaissance churches.

Location

Michelin map 38 or Michelin spiral atlas of Rome: pp 56-57 N 11-12. Metro line B: Circo Massimo (800m/880yd from Piazza della Bocca della Verità). Tour: 1hr 30min. The small piazza lies on an area of flat land alongside the Tiber, wedged between the Capitoline and Palatine Hills, with the Aventine Hill to the south. The marshy Velabro Valley occupied this area in Ancient times.

Neighbouring sights are described in the following chapters: AVENTINO; CAMPIDOGLIO-CAPITOLINO; ISOLA TIBERINA-TORRE ARGENTINA; TRASTEVERE.

Background

To visualise the unity of this part of the town, hemmed in by the Capitoline, the Palatine and the Tiber, one must go back 2 500 years to the time of the Etruscan kings and the Republic. As early as 6C BC crowds thronged the vegetable market (Forum Holitorium) at the foot of the Capitoline and the cattle market (Forum Boarium) at the foot of the Palatine. This area was also a religious centre, containing several temples, some of which were thought to have been founded by King Servius Tullius (578-34 BC).

At the end of the Republican period Caesar began the construction of the magnificent Theatre of Marcellus. Nearby was the Circus Flaminius, a vast oblong arena, built in 221 BC, where chariot races, hunting events and processions took place.

When Rome declined, these buildings fell into ruins. In the Middle Ages the area was heavily populated, particularly by artisans. Small businesses abounded, owned in particular by Jews who congregated there from the 13C. The removal of the Ghetto in 1888, the clearances undertaken in 1926 to reveal the Ancient monuments and the opening of new roads, have all destroyed a proportion of the narrow lanes and old houses.

Forum Holitorium and Forum Boarium – From the earliest days, not far from the Roman Forum, the administrative and political centre, there were other fora devoted to trade.

One of them, the vegetable market **(Forum Holitorium),** extended from the Porticus of Octavia along the riverbank to Vicus Jugarius. Another, the cattle market **(Forum Boarium)**, extended further south to the foot of the Aventine and reached as far east as the Arch of Janus (Arco di Giano) and the Arch of the Moneychangers (Arco degli Argentari). These two markets were next to the Port of Rome; the boats sailed up the Tiber, which was then navigable, and moored by the left bank level with the Pons Aemilius (Ponte Rotto).

From the beginning this district had contained altars for the worship of the gods. Hercules, who was thought to have driven Geryon's cattle through the Forum Boarium, was honoured near to Santa Maria in Cosmedin, in recognition of his victory over Cacus *(see Scala di Caco, p 201),* the blind cattle thief. Parallel to the Temple of Apollo, traces have been found of another temple attributed to the Roman goddess of war, Bellona. Three temples stood side by side on the site of the church of San Nicola in Carcere. Not far from the church of St Omobono, beside the Vicus Jugarius, a group of sanctuaries has been uncovered; further south stands the Temple of Fortune which Servius Tullius, the slave who became king, dedicated to the god who changes man's destiny. Naturally Portumnus, the protector of harbours, had a place of worship near the port; this has sometimes been identified as the very old sanctuary known as the Temple of Fortuna Virilis *(see p 127).*

Upstream from the Forum Boarium and its quays must have been the military port, known as Navalia inferiora (later on another port, Navalia superiora, was built on the Campus Martius). In 338 BC, when Rome embarked on the conquest of the Mediterranean, her citizens came to the port to admire the ships captured at Antium; the prows were displayed on the Rostra in the Forum. It was here, too, that Cato of Utica disembarked in 58 BC laden with treasures from King Ptolemy Auletes, after an expedition to Cyprus.

Walking About

Piazza della Bocca della Verità★

This open space more or less covers the site of the Forum Boarium. The combination of Ancient, medieval and Baroque buildings, framed by umbrella pines and pink and white oleanders, makes a typical Roman scene.

Opposite the medieval façade of Santa Maria in Cosmedin stands an 18C fountain supported by two tritons.

Santa Maria in Cosmedin★★

Crypt: open 9am-6pm. ☎ *06 67 81 419.* €2.

The slender bell-tower of Santa Maria in Cosmedin contrasts sharply with the church's wide façade

The church's soaring **bell-tower★** with its bold arcading was built early in the 12C and is one of the most elegant in Rome.

Foundation – In the 6C the district between the Aventine and the Tiber was inhabited by Greeks, who like other foreign colonies in Rome, formed themselves into a fighting force *(schola)* to protect Rome from the threat of the Lombards. In order to feed these soldiers, the Church was obliged to form **deaconries** *(diaconiae)*, composed of religious and lay people who inherited the duties performed by similar bodies under the Roman Empire. Their duty was to fix the price of wheat and to distribute the grain, sometimes free of charge. The Imperial organisation was administered by the *praefectus annonae* from the *Statio Annonae.* It was on the site of this building that the Church set up one of its deaconries, with an oratory in one of the storerooms. It was enlarged in the 8C by Pope Hadrian I and became the Greek church, called Santa Maria in Schola Greca. It later became Santa Maria in Cosmedin after the name of a district of Constantinople.

Early in the 12C the church was restored; the porch and campanile were added by Pope Gelasius II and Pope Callistus II. The church was restored to its medieval appearance in the 19C.

Interior – In the north aisle, on either side of the entrance door and in the sacristy, now incorporated into the construction of the church, are the huge Corinthian columns which belonged to the *Statio Annonae* which extended from left to right across the back half of the church.

The three parallel apses, inspired by the plan of Oriental churches, date from the period of Pope Hadrian I (8C); the columns dividing the nave and aisles come from Ancient monuments. The beautiful floor and marble furnishings (ambones, Paschal candlesticks, canopy above the high altar and the episcopal throne) are all Cosmati work. The *schola cantorum* **(1)** for the

> **BOCCA DELLA VERITÀ**
> In the porch is the marble disc known as the **Bocca della Verità** (Mouth of Truth). According to popular legend the mouth would snap shut on the hand of anyone with a guilty conscience. The name was also attributed to the fact that the mouth had never spoken. The face is that of a marine divinity, perhaps the Ocean, with two bulls' horns symbolising the surging power of the sea. The plaque is, in fact, a drain cover, possibly from the nearby Temple of Hercules.

choristers and the presbytery **(2)** for the priests are 19C reconstructions. The presbytery has been screened off by a *pergula*, a colonnade hung with curtains which are drawn at certain moments in the Eastern liturgy.

The 8C crypt, with its nave and aisles separated by small columns, is an original design for this period, when it was usual to follow the semicircular plan designed by Gregory the Great (590-604) for the *confessio* in St Peter's in the Vatican.

The beautiful 8C mosaic **(3)** in the sacristy comes from St Peter's Basilica.

From Piazza Bocca della Verità go east into Via del Velabro.

Piazza della Bocca della Verità
● Columns of the "Statio Annonae"

The valley of the **Velabro** (Velabrum), between the Palatine and the Capitoline Hills, used to be a very marshy place.

Arco di Giano (Arch of Janus)

This massive 4C construction with four faces, each one pierced by an arch, was a *janus*, ie a public gateway spanning a busy crossroads. It marked the northern edge of the Forum Boarium. The name reflects the power of the god Janus to protect road junctions.

Arco degli Argentari (Arch of the Moneychangers)

This construction is more like a monumental gate against the west wall of San Giorgio in Velabro. It was built in 204 by the Guild of Moneychangers in honour of the Emperor Septimius Severus and his wife, Giulia Domna, who both appear on the arch *(inside right panel)* making an offering before a tripod. The sharp relief and the abundance of decoration are characteristic of 3C art.

San Giorgio in Velabro★

Founded originally as a deaconry *(see above)* in the 7C, the church was rebuilt and enlarged by Pope Gregory IV (827-44). Since its restoration in 1926 San Giorgio in Velabro has recaptured the charm of the Roman churches of the Middle Ages. The façade, the porch and the bell tower date from the 12C. The interior has a monumental simplicity. In the Middle Ages Rome was poor: builders used existing foundations resulting in asymmetrical designs; columns and capitals were re-employed in a random manner.

The apsidal fresco of Christ flanked by the Virgin and St George, St Peter and St Sebastian is attributed to **Pietro Cavallini** (1295).

At the west end of Via del Velabro turn right into Via di S Giovanni Decollato.

Oratorio di San Giovanni Decollato★

Guided tour by prior arrangement only (apply to Governatore della Circonfraternità della Misericordia, Via San Giovanni Decollato 22, 00186 Roma). For further information, contact ☎ 06 67 91 890.

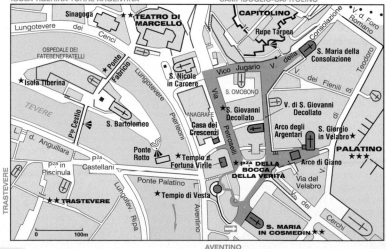

The Oratory of the Confraternity of St John the Beheaded was built at the end of the 15C to assist people who had been condemned to death; those who died in a state of grace were buried beneath the cloisters.

The oratory was used for the meetings of the members of the brotherhood. The decoration is by a group of Mannerist artists drawing inspiration from Michelangelo and Raphael without, however, following the style of the two masters too slavishly.

Starting from the right-hand wall, near the altar, are:

The Angel Gabriel appears to Zacharias (Jacopino del Conte); on the left of the painting is a portrait of Michelangelo, who was himself a member of the brotherhood; *The Visitation* (Salviati); *Birth of St John the Baptist* (Salviati); above the entrance: *St John the Baptist preaching* (Jacopino del Conte); *Baptism of Christ* (Jacopino del Conte);

On the left-hand wall, near the entrance: *Arrest of St John the Baptist* (Battista Franco); *Dance of Salome* (Pirro Ligorio); *Beheading of St John the Baptist;*

On either side of the altar: *St Andrew and St Bartholomew* (Salviati);

Above the altar: *Deposition* (Jacopino del Conte).

The church adjacent to the oratory is decorated with stuccoes and paintings (late 16C) *(open 24 Jun)*.

Continue north and east into Via della Consolazione.

Santa Maria della Consolazione

Before the broad white façade of the church, at the top of the steps, is a good place to pause. A 14C chronicler recounts how a prisoner condemned to death asked for an image of the Virgin to be placed near the place of execution on the Capitol. As she brought comfort to poor wretches about to die, she was called the Virgin of Consolation.

The first church was built in 1470. In the 16C a hospital was added; it was constructed between 1583 and 1600 according to plans by Martino Longhi the Elder. He also began the façade of the church, which was eventually completed in the 19C in a style inspired by the Counter-Reformation.

Take Vico Jugario and Via Petroselli to return to Piazza Bocca della Verità.

Casa dei Crescenzi

This curious building is one of the rare remains of "Roma Turrita" when Rome was bristling with fortresses. It was built in the 12C to defend the bridge (Ponte Rotto) on which the **Crescenzi** family had the right to collect tolls. The random use of antique elements (in the cornices and in the arch over the main door) shows how insensitively the Roman monuments were despoiled in the Middle Ages.

Tempio della Fortuna Virilis★

The attribution of this temple to human fortune is without foundation. Some archaeologists think it is a sanctuary dedicated to Portunnus, the god of rivers and harbours. It dates from the late 2C BC and is one of the best preserved temples in Rome. It has an air of austere solemnity typical of the rigour of the Republican era. At this period the Romans were still greatly influenced by the Etruscans and built rectangular temples, set on a high podium. The temple was used as a church probably from the 9C and dedicated to St Mary the Egyptian in the 15C.

Tempio di Vesta★

This temple has acquired its name solely because of its circular shape; in fact there was only one temple dedicated to Vesta, the one in the Roman Forum. It is thought that the Tempio di Vesta was dedicated to Hercules, shown by the base of the statue of the god found nearby.

With its well-proportioned fluted columns and Corinthian capitals it is an elegant building which dates from the reign of Augustus. A church was established in the *cella* in the Middle Ages. In the 16C it was dedicated to St Mary of the Sun, after an image of the Virgin found in the Tiber was placed there: when the coffer containing the image was opened a ray of light shone out.

Campidoglio-Capitolino★★★

This section of the city takes its name from one of the smallest but most famous hills in Rome, the Capitoline (Campidoglio in Italian). This district has always been associated with the centre of power in the city and is today is the seat of the local authority which administers the capital. The stepped ramp known as the Cordonata leads to the magnificent square designed by Michelangelo and to the oldest public museum in the world, the Musei Capitolini; from the recently restored Tabularium there is a breathtaking view of the Roman Forum. The foot of the hill is graced with impressive remains from the past; here the noise of the city's traffic can be overwhelming, but a short walk leads to the quiet, picturesque alleyways around Piazza Margana.

Location

Michelin map 38 or Michelin spiral atlas of Rome: pp 56-57 M 11-12. Tour: 1hr 30min. The hill has two summits: the **Capitolino** and the **Arx** (the Citadel), upon which the church of Santa Maria d'Aracoeli is situated. The dip between them is now occupied by the Piazza del Campidoglio. The tour starts at the monumental Aracœli staircase.

Neighbouring sights are described in the following chapters: BOCCA DELLA VERITÀ; FORO ROMANO-PALATINO; ISOLA TIBERINA-TORRE ARGENTINA; PIAZZA VENEZIA.

Directory

TAKING A BREAK

Caffè Capitolino – *Piazzale Caffarelli 4 –* ☏ *06 67 10 20 71 – Open Mon-Sat, 9.30am-9pm.* Situated on the terrace of Palazzo Caffarelli, the Capitoline Museum bar provides a stunning panorama of the surrounding area. Sandwiches and hot and cold drinks, including a range of cocktails, are served here. The view is particularly impressive at sunset.

La Dolce Roma – *Via Portico d'Ottavia 20/b –* ☏ *06 68 92 196 – Open Tue-Sat, 8.30am-1.30pm and 3.30-8pm; closed Sun, 10am-1pm.* Although situated in the Jewish quarter, this *pasticceria* offers a range of cakes and pastries which have a decidedly Austrian (apple strudel or sachertorte) and American (apple pie, carrot cake and peanut butter cookies) influence.

Background

It was in 1764, as Edward Gibbon later wrote, "on the fifteenth of October in the gloom of the evening, as I sat musing on the Capitol, while the barefoot fryars were chanting their litanies in the temple of Jupiter, that I conceived the first thought of my history... the decline and fall of the Roman Empire."

In the days of Ancient Rome, this area was both the religious and political centre of the city, providing access to the Forum and dominated by the Temple of **Jupiter Capitolinus** on the Capitoline and that of **Juno Moneta** (Counsellor) perched on the Citadel. The impressive Tabularium, the depositary of the Roman state archives, was built in the late-Republican period; Palazzo Senatorio was subsequently built on top of this structure. On the southwest edge of the Capitoline Hill, just by the Temple of Jupiter, above Via della Consolazione, is the bluff where, it is said, the legendary **Tarpeian Rock** was situated. From here traitors were hurled to their death during the Republic.

THE RAPE OF THE SABINES AND TARPEIA

The origins of this legend are lost in the mists of time with those of Rome's foundation. With his brother dead and the new city established, Romulus was anxious to increase Rome's populus quickly. Having declared the Campidoglio a safe haven for outlaws seeking refuge, the area soon became crowded with a band of men. To counter this imbalance of the sexes Romulus decided to draw the young Sabine women from a neighbouring tribe and organise a series of games for the occasion: these involved the rape of all the young girls of marriageable age.

Outraged, Titus Tatius, king of the Sabines, set out to rescue his womenfolk and marched on Rome. According to legend as soon as Tarpeia, the daughter of the keeper of the Roman Citadel, set eyes upon the Sabine king she fell hopelessly in love with him; she offered him and his men access to the Citadel in exchange for his love. Tatius quickly accepted, but once he was through the city gates the poor girl was crushed by his soldiers.

The inevitable bloody confrontation of Sabine against Roman that may have ensued, it is said, was prevented by the Sabine women, who threw themselves between their fathers and new husbands. Thus a new alliance was formed between Romulus and Titus Tatius.

Jupiter Capitolinus

By 6C BC the Etruscan king, Tarquin the Proud, had already built a temple on the Capitol to Jupiter, the Best and Greatest. This was considered second only to the heavens as the god's abode. During triumphal ceremonies the generals, dressed in gold and purple, made their way to the temple bearing an ivory sceptre surmounted by an eagle, the symbol of Jupiter.

The temple was built on the Etruscan plan and divided into three sanctuaries, the central one dedicated to Jupiter and those on either side to Juno and Minerva. These three deities comprised the Capitoline Triad. The city treasure was kept beneath Jupiter's statue. In the sanctuary dedicated to Juno, the Romans placed a silver goose in memory of the **"geese of the Capitol"**, as it was the cries of these geese which alerted the Romans, entrenched in their Citadel, when the Gauls attacked Rome (390-388 BC).

Having been destroyed by fire, the temple was rebuilt twice, first by Augustus and then by Domitian.

Walking About

Scalinata d'Aracoeli (Aracoeli Steps)

In 1348 the plague ravaged Italy; Rome miraculously was spared and built the steps as an offering of thanks. The first person to climb them was **Cola di Rienzo.** At this time the Pope was in Avignon; Rome was in a state of anarchy at the hands of the noble families. Cola gave himself the task of restoring the grandeur of Rome. He stood at the top of the steps dressed like an Emperor and roused the people with his speeches. **Petrarch** himself had begged the Pope to restore the capital to its former splendour. In 1354 he set out to lend his support to Cola di Rienzo, but before reaching the Capitol he learned that the "tribune of Rome" had been killed in a riot by a servant of the Colonna family.

From the top of the steps there is a fine view of the dome of St Peter's in the background, of the Synagogue *(left)* and of Sant'Andrea della Valle and the Gesù Church.

> **THE ORIGIN OF THE WORD "MONEY"**
> The word "money" comes from the Italian "moneta", the name of the goddess Juno, whose temple once stood here. This derivation is explained by the fact that the building was also used as the Roman mint.

Santa Maria d'Aracoeli★★

From the earliest days of the city's existence the Citadel *(arx)* stood here to defend the northern flank of the Palatine, which was naturally protected to the west by the Tiber. During the Republic a temple was built here to Juno Moneta (Counsellor). According to legend it was here that the Virgin and Child appeared to the Emperor **Augustus** after he had asked the Tiburtine Sibyl whether there would one day be a greater man than himself.

Following the arrival in 552 of General Narses from Greece, several Greek monasteries were established in Rome. One of them occupied an oratory which was turned into the church of Santa Maria d'Aracoeli in 1250 by Franciscan monks. The name comes from an altar *(ara)* dedicated to the goddess of the sky or from the Citadel *(arx)* (see above).

The severity of the brick façade is relieved by the Renaissance doorway and two Gothic rose windows. The shallow concave band at the top was originally covered with mosaic.

Interior – The interior is built on the basilical plan and contains several works of art. The side chapels and the aisle ceilings were added in the 16C and 17C when the chancel and the upper part of the nave were remodelled according to contemporary taste. The **wood-coffered ceiling** was an ex-voto offering by **Marcantonio Colonna**, who fought with the troops of the Holy League at Lepanto in Greece on 7 October 1571 when the Christians scored a victory against the Turks. The **floor** is one of the best preserved examples of the work of the Cosmati, Romans who worked in marble from the 12C to the 14C *(see The Arts in Rome: Medieval Period, p 96)*.

Cardinal d'Albret's tomb (1) is one of **Andrea Bregno**'s best works. The fine working of motifs, particularly on the sarcophagus, and the use of architectural elements (pilasters, arcades) are characteristic of his style. Next to it, **Giovanni**

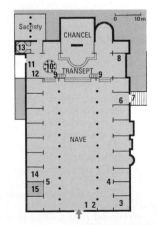

Crivelli's tombstone (2) is attributed to **Donatello**, whose signature used to be legible, it is said, but was worn away when the stone lay on the ground.

The decorative **frescoes★** in the **Cappella di San Bernardino da Siena (3)** were painted by **Pinturicchio** in about 1485 and illustrate the life and death of Bernardino. The funeral scene *(left wall)* shows some well-composed portraits against an accomplished landscape. The huge statue of Gregory XIII **(4)** complements that of Paul III **(5)**; both are Counter-Reformation works.

In the passage leading to the side door there is a tomb **(6)** designed by Michelangelo of a young man, Cecchino Bracci.

Step outside to admire the doorway.

The **mosaic of the Virgin and Child (7)** can be seen over the side door on the outside of the church. It comes from the Cosmati workshop and reveals the influence of **Pietro Cavallini**, the greatest Roman artist in the Middle Ages; his style is characterised by balanced composition, rich in Byzantine influence and knowledge of Classical art.

Although Piazza del Campidoglio can be reached from the side door of the church (down the steps), it is best approached up the "Cordonata" from the bottom of the hill to appreciate the full effect of the architecture.

Go back into the church.

The **tomb of Luca Cavelli (8)** contains an ancient sarcophagus reused for the burial of Luca Savelli. The mosaic decoration and the tiny *Virgin and Child* are the work of Arnolfo di Cambio (14C).

Like the floor, the **ambones (9)** are Cosmati work. They are signed by Lorenzo di Cosma and his son Giacomo and belong to the very elaborate Cosmati work typical of the late 12C. Earlier Cosmati work usually comprises only white marble.

The **Cappella di Sant'Elena (10)** is an elegant 17C domed construction. Beneath the porphyry urn is a 12C altar decorated with Romanesque sculptures and mosaic insets commemorating the appearance of the Virgin to Augustus.

Cardinal Matteo d'Acquasparta's Monument (11) is a typical Italian Gothic tomb (vertical composition with angels drawing curtains round the deathbed). The painting of the Virgin and Child is related to the art of Pietro Cavallini. Cardinal d'Acquasparta, Vicar General of the Franciscans, who died in 1302, is mentioned by Dante in his *Divine Comedy* as a man who relaxed the severity of the rule.

In the left transept is an enormous statue **(12)** of Leo X (16C).

The **Cappella del Santo Bambino** (the chapel of the Holy Child) **(13)** took its name from a statuette which, according to legend, had miraculous curative powers; many letters were addressed to it from all over the world. Unfortunately it was stolen on 1 February 1994, and has never been recovered.

The **third side chapel in the north aisle (14)** was decorated in the 15C with frescoes by Benozzo Gozzoli, Fra Angelico's assistant; only St Antony of Padua remains above the altar.

In the pre-Christmas period young children gather in the adjoining **chapel (15)** to recite or improvise verses *(sermoni)* before the Santo Bambino.

Go down the Aracoeli Steps and turn left into the "Cordonata".

La "Cordonata"

Michelangelo's design for this ramp was not faithfully executed. The two lions guarding the entrance are Egyptian (restored in 1955); they were found on the Campus Martius and placed here in 1582. In 1588 **Giacomo della Porta** converted them into fountains, which at one time on feast days flowed with red and white wine. A **statue** of Cola di Rienzo was put up in the 19C on the spot where he was killed.

Piazza del Campidoglio★★★

The visitor who is only passing through Rome should pause a moment in **Capitol Square**, a haven of peace where charm and majesty mingle in harmony. To see it as it was in Antiquity one must envisage the monuments and temples facing the Forum.

In the Middle Ages Capitol Square was known simply as "Monte Caprino" (Goat Hill); goats grazed among the ruins. Change came in the 16C. On the occasion of Charles V's visit in 1536, Pope Paul III decided that Rome, which had been sacked nine years earlier by the same Charles V, should be restored to its former elegance and he commissioned **Michelangelo** to draw up plans for the Capitol. The design was executed over the next 100 years or so and altered in certain respects. The square is lined by three buildings (Palazzo Senatorio, Palazzo dei Conservatori and Palazzo Nuovo) and is shaped like a trapezium to accommodate the position of the Palazzo dei Conservatori (Conservators' Palace) which had already been built. Michelangelo turned the square round to face the modern city rather than the ancient Forum. The balustrade with its overlarge statues was not part of Michelangelo's design.

At the centre of a beautiful geometric design, conceived by Michelangelo but executed only recently, is a copy of the equestrian statue of Marcus Aurelius. The statue which graced the square for many years and has undergone extensive restoration is on display in the Palazzo Nuovo.

BOCCA DELLA VERITÀ

Statua di Cola di Rienzo .... A   Statue dei Dioscuri .... B

On Saturdays the square is particularly busy; after the wedding ceremonies in the register office of the Palazzo dei Conservatori, dozens of newlyweds pose for photographs in front of the statue of the Tiber and the wolf's head or on the Cordonata Steps.

Statue dei Dioscuri★ – The two knights are shown standing beside their horses (*see Tempio di Castore e Polluce, p 192*). The statues are Roman and date from the late Empire; they were found in the 16C on the Campus Martius and restored (the head of one of them is modern).

"Trofei di Mario" – **Marius's Trophies** is the name given to the sculptures (1C BC) which commemorate Domitian's conquest of the German people. Until the 16C they adorned a fountain in Piazza Vittorio Emanuele II.

The Roman custom of piling up the arms of the vanquished goes back to earliest times when at the end of a battle they would stack up breastplates, helmets and shields against a tree.

Milestones – *Next to the statues of Constantine and Constantine II.* One was the first and the other the seventh milestone on the Appian Way.

Palazzo Senatorio★★★ (Senate House)

Closed to the public; occupied by the offices of the local authority. The Tabularium is described as part of the Musei Capitolini (see "Worth a Visit"). In 1143, under the influence of **Arnold of Brescia**, who inveighed against the corruption of the clergy in his speeches, the Roman people deprived the Pope of his temporal power and set up the Roman Commune. Senators were created to lead the government; the palace was constructed like a castle on the ruins of the Tabularium (built in the 1C BC and used to store the bronze *tabulae* on which laws and official documents were inscribed) to house the meetings of the magistrates.

Michelangelo kept the walls of this old building but designed a new façade. His plans were carried out from 1582-1605 by Giacomo della Porta and then by Girolamo Rainaldi.

The municipal tower was built by Martino Longhi the Elder from 1578-82.

The double staircase is the only part of the building to be completed during Michelangelo's lifetime. The fountain which was added in 1588 on Sixtus V's initiative was not part of the original design. The goddess of Rome, in porphyry and marble, seems lost in her recess, perched on a pedestal which is disproportionately high. The flanking statues come from Constantine's baths on the Quirinal

The Dioscuri, with the Palazzo Senatorio in the background

and represent the Nile and the Tiber. The latter statue *(right)* originally represented the Tigris, but the tiger's head was replaced with a wolf's head to indicate the Tiber.

Some blocks of stone from the old **Arx Capitolina** (Citadel) can be seen in a little garden on the left of the Senate House.

Palazzo dei Conservatori and Palazzo Nuovo★★★

The **Conservators' Palace**, which was built in the 15C to house the meetings of the Conservators, magistrates who governed the town with the Senators, was altered in 1568 by Giacomo della Porta according to Michelangelo's designs.

Although not built until 1654, the New Palace, which was the work of Girolamo and Carlo Rainaldi, was identical to the Conservators' Palace as Michelangelo had intended. At this time Via delle Tre Pile was opened and the development of the Capitol was complete. The two palaces house the collections of the Musei Capitolini *(see "Worth a Visit")*; with their porticos at ground level and façades decorated with a single order of flat pilasters, they form an elegant ensemble.

From Piazza del Campidoglio take Via del Campidoglio on the right of Palazzo Senatorio.

From the corner of the palace one has a beautiful **view★★** of the Roman Forum and in particular the Tabularium, the Portico of the Dei Consentes, the Temple of Vespasian and the Temple of Concord.

Return to Piazza del Campidoglio and take the steps on the left of the Palazzo dei Conservatori and then Via del Tempio di Giove.

Below Via del Tempio di Giove there are several stone blocks which formed a corner of the Temple of Jupiter *(see above)*. Beyond is a pleasant garden overlooking the area identified as the Tarpeian Rock *(see below)* which gives a good **view** of the Roman Forum, the Palatine, and the Caelian and Aventine Hills.

Take Via di Monte Caprino and go down to the left to Piazza della Consolazione.

Rupe Tarpea

Via della Consolazione, an extension of Vico Jugario, is dominated on the left by the southern slope of the Capitol, where, after some considerable hesitation, scholars have sited the **Tarpeian Rock**. In Antiquity it was the rock face which took its name from the traitress Tarpeia *(see Introduction to the Tour)*.

In Ancient times the Vicus Jugarius (now called Vico Jugario) was lined with the shops of craftsmen making yokes. It wound along under the Capitol and connected the Forum Holitorium to the Roman Forum. At the entrance to the street, on the left, can be seen vestiges of porticos built at the base of the Capitol during the Republican era.

Cross Via del Teatro di Marcello.

San Nicola in Carcere and the Temples of the Forum Holitorium

Open daily, 9am-noon and 4-7pm. Closed Aug and Christmas. ☎ 06 68 69 972.

The little church was built in the 11C on the ruins of three Republican temples which stood side by side overlooking the **Forum Holitorium** *(see BOCCA DELLA VERITÀ)*.

The church has been restored several times: the façade was designed by Giacomo della Porta in 1599. The nave is built on the site of the *cella* and *pronaos* of the middle temple and is flanked by aisles so that the side walls of the church incorporate columns belonging to the side walls of the two outer temples. The left-hand temple was the oldest; it was built in the Doric style in the 2C BC and probably dedicated to Janus. The right-hand temple was in the Ionic style – two columns from its right-hand side stand on their own to the right of the church – it was probably dedicated to Hope and has been dated to the 1C BC. The middle temple is the most recent and was probably dedicated to Juno. The tower, originally defensive, dates from the 12C when the district belonged to the Perleoni family. The words *in carcere* in the title refer to a Byzantine prison which occupied the left-hand temple in the 7C and 8C.

The **crypt** contains the foundations of ancient temples; fragments of a frieze are visible from the roof of the church.

Teatro di Marcello★★

The **Theatre of Marcellus** was begun by Caesar and completed between 13-11 BC by Augustus, who dedicated it to Marcellus, his sister Octavia's son.

The two tiers of arches which remain were probably topped by a third row of Corinthian pilasters. They form the semicircular part of the building which contained the tiers of seats; the stage, of which nothing is left, backed onto the riverbank. It was the second largest theatre in Rome after Pompey's Theatre in the Campus Martius; it could hold about 15 000 spectators. Its severe and sober style, with the three architectural orders – Doric, Ionic and Corinthian – one above the other, served as a model for the Colosseum which was built of the same stone, travertine from the Tivoli quarry. On the day of the inauguration Augustus suffered a slight mishap which Suetonius recorded: "the official chair *(sella curulis)* gave way beneath him and he fell backwards".

The theatre was damaged in the fire in AD 64 and during the struggle between Vespasian and Vitellius and was finally abandoned early in the 4C. It was soon being used as a quarry; some of the stone went to repair the Ponte Cestio in the 4C. Houses were built against the walls and in 1150 it was transformed into a fortress and saved from further depredations.

In the 16C the noble family of Savelli turned it into a palace. It is the remains of this house, which was built by Baldassarre Peruzzi, which are visible today above the old arches. The palace later passed to the Orsini. The Ancient theatre was cleared of its accretions and excavated from 1926-29.

Tempio di Apollo Sosiano★★

The Greek god Apollo was venerated by the Romans chiefly for his power to ward off disease (Apollo medicus). The first temple dedicated to him was raised on this site in the 5C BC. In 34 BC Caius Sosius, governor of Cilicia and Syria, rebuilt the sanctuary in marble and it became known as the **Temple of Apollo Sosianus**. The three elegant fluted **columns★★** with Corinthian capitals belonged to the porch *(pronaos)* of the temple and were re-erected in 1940.

B. Kaufmann/MICHELIN

The Theatre of Marcellus and the Temple of Apollo Sosianus

Turn left into Piazza di Campitelli.

Santa Maria in Campitelli

When Rome was struck by the plague in 1656 the Romans prayed ceaselessly in front of an image of the Virgin in the church of Santa Maria in Portico; now demolished, this church stood on the site of the present Anagrafe on the riverbank. When the epidemic ceased it was decided to build a new sanctuary to house the holy image. The first stone of Santa Maria in Campitelli was laid in September 1661. The building was entrusted to **Carlo Rainaldi** (1611-91) who drew up his own design and executed it himself.

The exterior, like the interior, is a forest of columns. Those on the façade are clearly detached and form a pleasant harmony. Variety and movement are provided by the broken and curved pediments, the jutting cornices and multiple recessing.

The **interior★** space is defined by the columns. The variation on the Greek cross plan which is extended and constricted towards the apse, the grandiose elevation of the vault and the dome and the alternating projections and recesses create a bold effect of perspective.

The church contains a few fine 17C paintings including a canvas of *St Anne, St Joachim and Mary (second chapel on the right)* by Luca Giordano (1632-1705), whose picture frame is supported by two kneeling angels. Another Baroque painting *(left of the choir)* is by Giovanni Battista Gaulli (1639-1709), who was called **Baciccia**. He painted the vault of the Gesù Church. Above the high altar is a Baroque glory surrounding the 11C enamel of the Virgin which came from the church of Santa Maria in Portico.

Turn right into Via dei Delfini which leads to Piazza Margana.

Piazza Margana is a charming and peaceful small square criss-crossed by narrow medieval streets and seemingly far removed from the noise and chaos of modern Rome. The **Margana Tower** *(part of Via Margana 40)* was constructed on the remains of a Roman portico; a column with an Ionic capital is still extant.

Fountain in Piazza d'Aracoeli

This fountain is a modest work by Giacomo della Porta (1589), the great designer of the fountains of Rome; at least he produced the design. In the 17C the arms of the Chigi family were added and 100 years later the base with two flights of steps designed by Della Porta was replaced by the present circular basin.

Worth a Visit

MUSEI CAPITOLINI★★★

Allow at least 2hr. Open daily (except Mon), 9.30am-8pm (ticket office closes 7pm). Closed 1 Jan, 1 May and Christmas. €6.20. ☎ 06 67 10 32 38; Fax 06 67 10 31 18.

The collections of Classical art on display in the Capitoline Museums were started by Sixtus IV in 1471, enlarged by Pius V in 1566 and opened to the public in 1734 by Clement XII. This excellent 18C collection has changed little since it was established and ranks as one of the most important in Rome.

Palazzo Nuovo

The fountain in the courtyard is dominated by the recumbent statue of a god of Antiquity christened **"Marforio"**. The huge peaceful figure seems a little bored watching

The Colossus of Constantine in the courtyard of the Palazzo dei Conservatori

the water in the basin. In the Middle Ages the statue was one of the group of "talking statues" and received satirical comments directed against the people in power.

For a long time Marforio was to be found next to the church of St Luke and St Martina and the cost of moving him (1595) was so great that the government raised the price of wine. Marforio thereupon "wrote" to Pasquino, another talking statue, that the Romans were having to do without wine so that he could preside over a fountain.

On the right is the famous **equestrian statue of Marcus Aurelius★★** which was transferred from the square outside St John Lateran to Piazza del Campidoglio by Michelangelo in 1538.

RESTORATION WORK

Temporary exhibitions are held in the **Palazzo Clementino-Caffarelli**, which was built in the 16C alongside the Palazzo dei Conservatori. Once restoration work is completed here, the palace will house the Medagliere Capitolino; it is also intended to leave the foundations of the Temple of Jupiter Capitolinus visible to the public.

Part of the Capitoline Museum's collection, such as Roman works discovered in excavations around the city, is housed in the **Centrale Montemartini** at Viale Ostiense 106 *(see PIRAMIDE CESTIA-TESTACCIO)*.

He greatly admired the statue and restored it himself. Cast in bronze and once gilded, it is a fine example of late 2C Roman Realism. It has survived intact because it was thought to represent Constantine. Had they known the facts, the medieval Christians would never have tolerated the survival of an effigy of the Emperor who persecuted St Blandina, St Pothinus and St Justin.

The three small rooms on the ground floor *(right of the entrance)* display **inscriptions**, **busts** and a fine **sarcophagus** decorated with low reliefs of the life of Achilles; the latter is surmounted by figures portraying the dead husband and wife (2C AD). *Take the stairs to the first floor.*

Gallery – The rooms in the museum are connected by a gallery. The layout of the statues, reliefs and inscriptions exhibited here has hardly changed since the 18C; the collection is not arranged according to any particular historical or artistic criteria.

Sala delle Colombe (I) – The Dove Room takes its name from the finely crafted **mosaic★★** which decorated the floor of a room in Hadrian's villa at Tivoli. It is probably a 2C AD copy of a 2C BC Greek mosaic from Pergamum. The interesting **mosaic of the masks** (2C AD) is also on display in this room.

The statue of a young girl holding a dove in her arms and warding off a serpent is a Roman copy of a 2C BC Hellenistic sculpture. During restoration the serpent was substituted for the original animal (a dog or a cat).

Gabinetto della Venere (II) – This charming room was built at the beginning of the 19C to house the famous **Capitoline Venus★★★**. The Greek original which inspired this statue (1C BC) depicted the goddess leaving her bath, protecting herself with a double gesture of modesty.

Sala degli Imperatori (III) – This room houses an exceptional collection of some 70 portraits of famous people and provides an insight into the development of portraiture and Roman fashion. In the male portraits, note the evolution from short to long beards, favoured by philosophers; in women's fashion, hairstyles show the evolution from tall layers of curls to the later penchant for ringlets. Every Emperor is represented here. Particularly noteworthy are two portraits of Octavian **Augustus**: one shows him at the time of the Battle of Actium *(upper row)*, the other *(facing the window)* depicts him as an older man, crowned with myrtle.

Sala dei Filosofi (IV) – The Philosopher's Room contains over 80 busts of poets, philosophers and rhetoricians. There are many portraits of Homer, whose blindness makes him easily identifiable.

Salone – Built in the 18C to house the sculptures on display here, this room is the most typical of the museum. Note the two contrasting statues of **centaurs★★**: the young centaur is happy and laughing; the older one appears sad and tired. These are Roman works from Hadrian's reign (117-138), reproductions in sombre marble of Hellenistic originals in bronze. Other works exhibited in the room include the elegant Apollo with cithara – a 2C BC copy of an original by Praxiteles – and the **wounded Amazon★**, a fine Roman copy of a statue sculpted by Polyclitus.

Sala del Fauno (V) – The Faun Room houses the famous *Drunken Faun★★* made from precious red marble and dating from Hadrian's reign,. Note the two strange growths on the faun's neck which seem to emphasise the creature's bestial characteristics.

Also worthy of note is the statue of a child wringing a goose's neck, a 2C Roman sculpture which was inspired by a bronze by the Greek Boethos.

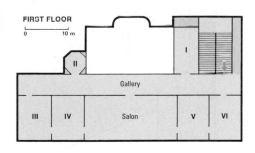

Sala del Gladiatore (VI) – The Gladiator Room is so-called because the magnificent sculpture in the middle of the room was long thought to be a gladiator. It is, in fact, the *Dying Gaul★★★*, a Roman imitation of a work in bronze or perhaps even an original work from the Pergamum School (late 3C, early 2C BC). It was probably part of a group of sculptures commemorating the victory of Attalus I, king of Pergamum, against the invading Gauls. All the nobility and suffering of the body in its agony are sensitively expressed in this work, which ranks among the most beautiful pieces of art from Antiquity.

Return to the ground floor and continue down to the Tabularium (basement).

Palazzo Senatorio-Tabularium

A staircase to the left of the underground connecting gallery, excavated in 1930 below the Palazzo Senatorio to link the Palazzo Nuovo to the Palazzo dei Conservatori, leads to the rooms of the Tabularium, used to house the Roman archives in the 1C BC, and later transformed into a storehouse and prison *(see FORO ROMANO-PALATINO)*. A headless statue of Veiovis, discovered in the temple dedicated to this little-known god, stands to the left. A corridor on the right leads to the remains of the temple, built in the 2C BC and later incorporated in the Tabularium. The gallery overlooks the Roman Forum and offers a magnificent view of the archaeological ruins, the Colosseum and the Palatine Hill. It houses a display of materials found during the restoration work carried out on the building.

Return to the connecting gallery and take the stairs back to the ground floor of the Palazzo dei Conservatori.

Palazzo dei Conservatori

In the internal courtyard are the Gothic arches of the 15C palace *(right)* and a few pieces of a colossal statue of **Constantine** (4C) which used to be in Constantine's Basilica in the Forum. The statue of a seated figure (10m/33ft high) was probably an acrolith statue, where only the parts of the body uncovered by clothing were made of stone and the rest was of wood covered in bronze.

Take the stairs to the upper floor.

On the first landing are some **high-relief sculptures** taken from monuments built in honour of Marcus Aurelius and Hadrian: these depict a sacrifice, the triumph and clemency of Marcus Aurelius and the entry of Hadrian into the city. The high relief of Marcus Aurelius at the sacrificial ceremony is remarkable for containing a reproduction of the Temple of Jupiter Capitolinus *(back left)*, of which almost nothing remains.

The rooms of the Appartamento dei Conservatori, decorated from the 16C onwards, recall the grandeur and magnificence of Ancient Rome. The frescoes in these rooms depict the birth of the Republican era and show various episodes from this period.

Sala degli Orazi e dei Curiazi (Horatii and Curatii Room) **(I)** – The marble statue of **Urban VIII** was sculpted by **Bernini** and his pupils; that of **Innocent X**, in bronze, is a masterly piece by Algardi dating from the mid-17C. Other works on temporary display in the room include parts of the bronze statue of Constantine and a statue of Hercules in gilded bronze.

The wall frescoes which give the room its name were painted by **Cavaliere d'Arpino** at the end of the 16C *(see p 99)*. Treated like tapestries and framed by fake drapes and marble friezes, they depict episodes from the foundation of Rome and the reigns of the early kings, including the *Discovery of the She-Wolf*, the *Battle*

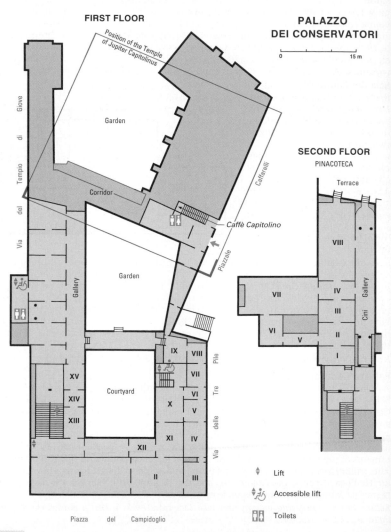

FIRST FLOOR

PALAZZO DEI CONSERVATORI

SECOND FLOOR
PINACOTECA

between the Horatii and Curatii, the *Rape of the Sabine Women* and *Romulus tracing the outline of the city.*

Sala dei Capitani (II) – The Captains' Room is named after the 16C-17C statues of Papal generals Marcantonio Colonna and Alessandro Farnese, which are displayed there. The **coffered ceiling★** with historical scenes painted in the panels comes from a 16C palace, now demolished.

The late-16C pictures hanging on the walls illustrate legendary episodes in the history of Republican Rome: *Brutus condemning his sons to death*; *The Battle of Lake Regillus*; *Horatius Cocles defending the bridge*; *Mucius Scaevola and Porsenna.*

Sala dei Trionfi (Triumph Room) **(III)** – The painted frieze on the walls dates from the 16C and illustrates the triumph of Emilius Paulus over Perseus, king of Macedon in 168 BC. This room houses the famous *"Spinario"*★★, an original Greek work or a very good 1C BC copy. The charming pose of this boy who is removing a thorn from his foot and the studied treatment of his hair and face make this an admirable work.

B. Kaufmann/MICHELIN

The Spinario *– Palazzo dei Conservatori*

The bust of *Junius Brutus*★★ is a magnificent bronze portrait (3C BC) of the first consul, whose legendary severity and integrity seemed to find expression in this head. Also note the *camillus*, a work of art from the Augustan era (1C): *camillus* was the name given to the young servers who assisted the priests in the religious ceremonies.

Sala della Lupa (IV) – Here is the famous bronze statue of the *She-Wolf*★★★, the *"Mater Romanorum"* and emblem of the city. It is said that in Antiquity the wolf stood on the Capitol and was struck by lightening in 65 BC, as the marks on the rear paws of the statue would seem to testify. The statue dates from the 6C or 5C BC and could be the work of a Greek or Etruscan artist. The anatomical accuracy is treated in a remarkably stylised manner. The twins were added during the Renaissance.

Sala delle Oche (V) – Two small bronze geese give this room its name. Mounted in a beautiful stucco frame, the geese recall a famous incident in Roman history, when the Capitoline Rock was said to have been saved from the Gauls by the gaggling of geese. Also on display here are the head of Medusa by Bernini and a bust of Michelangelo.

Room VI leads into Room X.

Sala degli Arazzi (Tapestry Room) **(X)** – The huge tapestries were woven in a Roman workshop in the 18C; they depict works exhibited in the museum (*The She-Wolf and the Twins* by Rubens) and themes relating to Ancient Rome. Note the fine coffered ceiling dating from the 16C.

Sala di Annibale (Hannibal's Room) **(XI)** – This room is the only one in the museum to have retained its original 16C frescoes, which depict episodes from the Punic Wars. The wooden ceiling is the oldest in the palace and dates from 1516-19. The 16C **chapel (XII)** to the right is dedicated to the Virgin Mary, to St Peter and St Paul.

Exit through the Sala degli Orazi e Curiazi.

At the end of the corridor are the three **Sale dei Fasti Moderni (XIII-XV)**, which house the Marsia – an important Roman reproduction (2-1C BC) of a Greek original – and a few Egyptian works.

Take the stairs to the second floor.

Pinacoteca

The paintings in the **picture gallery** are grouped according to their school, genre and artist and are exhibited in chronological order.

On the entrance landing are two fine panels of marble intarsia work depicting tigresses attacking cattle; these are 4C Roman and were produced using the technique known as *opus sectile* (see p 87), developed mainly in Egypt.

Central Italy from the Middle Ages to the 16C (I) – Most of the paintings on display in this room are religious in nature.

The 16C in Ferrara (II) – The paintings from Ferrara exhibited here combine the bold colouring so typical of the Venetian School with the spatial solidity that is characteristic of the Central Italian School.

The 16C in Venice (III) – Venice, with Florence and Rome, was one of the most important centres of Italian painting during the Renaissance period. Characteristic features of the Venetian School were the rich use of colour in painting and the attention paid to colour rather than form. Among the works exhibited here, note the *Baptism of Christ*, an early work by Titian, which shows an exquisite balance between the use of colour and composition, and the delightful *Rape of Europa* by Veronese.

Return to Room II and turn right.

The 16C in Emilia (V) – In addition to paintings from the Emilian School, this room contains two works by Cavalier d'Arpino, who worked in Rome (Caravaggio worked in his studio) in the 16C and 17C.

Painting in Bologna from the Carracci to Guido Reni (VI) – The works exhibited in this room were painted in the 16C and 17C and demonstrate the new religious sensitivity characterised by the Carracci, and the elegant Classicism of Guido Reni *(St Sebastian)*.

Sala di Santa Petronilla (VII) – This room is dominated by the large **painting★** by Guercino in honour of St Petronella, which is particularly noteworthy for its harmony of blue and brown hues and its tortuous vertical lines presaging the Baroque style in art. Also on display are a number of masterpieces from the early 17C Roman School. The *Gypsy Fortune-teller★★* is an early work by Caravaggio, in which the characters are emphasised by clever lighting; note also the subtle psychological play between the arrogant youth and the gypsy girl who is carefully stealing his ring. In *St John the Baptist★★*, Caravaggio pays tribute to Michelangelo's nudes in the Sistine Chapel and portrays the saint as a young ephebe, which contrasts sharply with traditional religious iconography. Other paintings in the room worthy of note include *Romulus and Remus* by Rubens.

The 17C in Rome (IV) – This room houses paintings by both Italian and foreign artists.

Sala di Pietro da Cortona (VIII) – Pietro da Cortona was the first major painter of the Baroque period; his work is characterised by the fluid, asymmetrical lines of his *Rape of the Sabine Women★★* (1627-29).

Galleria Cini (Cini Gallery) – This rooms contains 18C porcelain from Meissen, Capodimonte and Cin; several tapestries; a series of views of Rome by Vanvitelli; portraits from the 15C-17C (including a self-portrait by Velázquez and two double portraits by Van Dyck); and examples of 18C painting.

Campo dei Fiori★★

The area around Campo dei Fiori is one of the liveliest districts in Rome, with narrow streets full of fashionable shops, craft boutiques, cafés and restaurants. The early morning bustle of the market in the square is replaced in the evening by crowds of tourists and locals sitting on café terraces and strolling along the busy streets, many of whose names recall the old trades once practised in the neighbourhood. In the small squares of this district, it is not uncommon to see a graceful patrician *palazzo* standing alongside older, shabbier properties, providing one of the contrasting images that are so typical of the city.

Location

Michelin map 38 or Michelin spiral atlas of Rome: p 96 L 10-11, M 10-11. Tour: 2hr. The walk follows the narrow streets of the district lying between the Tiber, Corso Vittorio Emanuele II and the Capitol.

Neighbouring sights are described in the following chapters: CASTEL SANT'ANGELO; GIANICOLO; ISOLA TIBERINA-TORRE ARGENTINA; PANTHEON; PIAZZA NAVONA.

Background

In Antiquity the district was just to the south of the Campus Martius and was chosen by **Pompey** for the construction of several important buildings in 55 BC: a huge theatre, the first in Rome to be built of stone, a temple to Venus and a curia to house occasional meetings of the Senate. It was in **Pompey's curia** (Curia di Pompeo) that a decisive event in Roman history occurred: on the Ides of March 44 BC **Julius Caesar** was assassinated at the foot of Pompey's statue. Almost nothing remains of this building.

The first Christian sanctuary in the district was San Lorenzo in Damaso, founded in 380 in the reign of Pope Damasus. In the Middle Ages churches and castles grew in number. The churches were quite simple buildings serving the needs of the tradesmen, who, in their various guilds, gave a certain character to the district: many leather curriers *(vaccinari)*, boiler-makers *(calderari)*, and rope-makers *(funari)* prospered along the streets, which were used by pilgrims heading to St Peter's. Their trades are recalled in many of the street names of the district. After Charles V's troops had sacked Rome in 1527, civil architecture revived. Cardinal Riario spent the money he had won at the gaming tables building the Palazzo della Cancelleria, thus countering the scruples of his relative, Sixtus IV. Cardinal Farnese, later Pope Paul III, built the Farnese Palace in line with the status of his family, which he led to the heights of glory.

Directory

WHERE TO EAT
See "Where to Eat" in the Practical Points section at the beginning of the guide.

TAKING A BREAK
Forno di Campo de' Fiori di Bartocci e Roscioli – *Piazza Campo dei Fiori 22 – ☎ 06 68 80 66 62 – Closed Sun – ⌨*. This bakery, visible from the street and therefore easily identifiable, is literally besieged by locals for its excellent pizza and bread.

Pica – *Via della Seggiola 12 ☎ 06 68 68 405 – Open 8.30am midnight; closed Sun morning*. This excellent gelateria is renowned for its rice and ricotta flavour ice creams. No surcharge for the tables outside.

BARS
Bookowsky – *Via Pomponio Leto 1 – ☎ 06 68 33 844 – Open Tue-Sun, noon-3pm and 8.30pm-2am*. This small bar has adopted the idea of literary cafés from other European capitals. Browse among the many different types of books while enjoying a glass of wine, accompanied by canapés, *bruschetta* and other hot and cold snacks.

Vineria Reggio – *Piazza Campo dei Fiori 15 – ☎ 06 68 80 32 68 – Open 9am-2am*. Situated opposite the statue of Giordano Bruno, this typical wine bar, with its wooden benches in front of the long bar and its outdoor terrace, is a favourite pre- and post-dinner meeting place for locals.

SHOPPING
Comics Bazar – *Via dei Banchi Vecchi 127/128 – ☎ 06 68 80 29 23 – Open Mon-Sat, 9.30am-7.30pm*. Entering this shop, the visitor is struck by the furniture and various bits and pieces piled on top of one another. Interesting items can be found here, especially furniture produced by Thonet.

Farenheit 451 – *Piazza Campo dei Fiori 44 – ☎ 06 68 75 930 – libreriafahrenheit @tiscalinet.it – Open Tue-Sat, 10am-12.30pm and 4pm-midnight; Mon, 4pm-midnight; Sun, 9.30am-1.30pm and 6pm-midnight*. Although this bookshop on Campo dei Fiori looks tiny from the outside, inside it is a maze of small rooms and nooks and crannies that are perfect for browsing.

Libreria del Viaggiatore – *Via del Pellegrino 78 – ☎ 06 68 80 10 48 – Open Tue-Sat, 10am-2pm and 4-8pm*. As its name suggests, this small shop specialises in travel literature, including books on Italian cities and regions by famous authors.

Franco Borini – *Via dei Pettinari 86/87*. If you have original taste and are looking for square-toed shoes, extremely high heels or bright colours, this is the place for you.

Walking About

Piazza Campo dei Fiori★
The origin of the name (which means Square of the Field of Flowers) probably goes back to the Middle Ages when the area was one vast meadow dominated by the fortress of the powerful Orsini family, who were lords of the manor. By the 16C the area had become the centre of Rome, a meeting place for people of all ranks, crowded with inns. The **"Hostaria della Vacca"** belonged to **Vanozza Caetani** (1442-1518), famous for her liaison with Rodrigo **Borgia**, who became Pope **Alexander VI**. She bore him several children including Cesare and Lucrezia. The façade of her hostelry still bears an escutcheon showing the Borgia arms alongside those of Vanozza and those of one of her husbands.

CAMPO DEI FIORI MARKET
Campo dei Fiori market *(see "What to Buy Locally" in the Practical Points section at the beginning of the guide)* is one of the busiest and most lively in Rome. Cheese and cream, cured meats, seasonal fruit and vegetables, meat and poultry, colourful arrays of flowers, accented voices trading local gossip and exchanging ills for miraculous cures, the square bustles with action under the tacit eye of the astronomer and philosopher Giordano Bruno. A regular visitor amongst the housewives is the knife-sharpener with his pedal-powered grindstone.

In the streets around, bric-a-brac, Sicilian ex-votos, furniture and elaborate copies of old masters are all traded ...

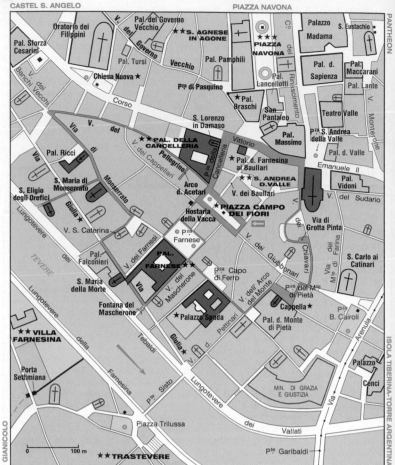

The Campo was the site of all sorts of festivals as well as a place of execution. At the centre stands a statue of Giordano Bruno, a monk who was burned for heresy on 17 February 1600 during the Counter-Reformation. Every morning the Campo dei Fiori is filled with the bustle of an extensive food market.

Palazzo della Cancelleria★★

Open Thu and Sat, 4-8pm. Closed on Vatican holidays. €3. Visits by prior appointment to Signora Meli, ☎ 06 69 88 48 16.

The **Chancery Palace** was built by an unidentified architect between 1483 and 1513 for Cardinal Raffaele Riario, upon whom "honours and riches were heaped" by his great-uncle Pope Sixtus IV. The inscription above the balcony states that the building housed the "Imperial Court", the law courts during the Napoleonic occupation (1809-14). Strengthened and restored between 1937 and 1945, the palace is now occupied by the Papal Chancery, which is responsible for drafting pontifical acts,

> ### MICHELANGELO'S "FAKE" CUPID
> Cardinal Riario's well-known taste for antiquities gave Michelangelo the idea of sculpting a magnificent Cupid, skilfully applying an artificial patina of age and selling it to the Cardinal for 200 ducats as a genuine antique. The collector got wind of the deceit and decided to recover his money and return the statue to the artist, but Michelangelo never saw his Cupid again. It was transferred to France and disappeared.

and therefore enjoys the privilege of extra-territoriality granted to Vatican property under the terms of the Lateran Treaty *(see "Background" in VATICANO-SAN PIETRO).*

Façade and courtyard – These two features make the building the most elegant product of the Renaissance in Rome. The broad smooth surfaces, the straight lines and the shallow pilasters of the travertine façade give it a majestic quality. A light and delicate touch is added by the roses of Riario, which decorate the second-floor windows.

The central doorway was added in 1589 by Cardinal Alessandro Peretti, great-nephew of Sixtus V.

The granite columns which support the two storeys of the arcading surrounding the courtyard – a harmonious composition attributed to Bramante – come from the building of the church of San Lorenzo in Damaso.

Interior – On the main floor of the palace are the Aula Magna (the Great Hall) and the so-called *Sala dei "Cento Giorni"* (Room of the Hundred Days). The latter is decorated with a fresco painted by Giorgio Vasari which depicts the meeting of Paul III, Charles V and François I in 1538 in Nice (now in France). The name of the room may derive from the fact that the fresco was completed in 100 days.

San Lorenzo in Damaso

Within Palazzo della Cancelleria.

The church, which was founded by Pope Damasus in the 4C, was later rebuilt as part of the palace. It was used as a stable during the Napoleonic occupation and restored at various times during the 19C. The ceiling, which was damaged by fire in 1939, has been entirely renewed.

The church consists of a nave and side aisles preceded by a vestibule. The first chapel on the right contains a 14C wooden crucifix; the last chapel on the left in the nave contains a 12C painting of the Virgin inspired by Byzantine icons.

Turn right into Corso Vittorio Emanuele II.

Palazzo della Farnesina ai Baullari★

This little Renaissance building was begun in 1523 for Thomas le Roy, a French diplomat accredited to the Holy See. Raised to the peerage by François I of France, he added the lily of France to the ermine of Brittany, his country of origin. The lily was mistaken for the iris of the Farnese and the building was called the "Piccola Farnesina". As it overlooks **Via dei Baullari** (luggage-makers: *baule* means trunk), it acquired the name of Farnesina ai Baullari. The façade giving onto Corso Vittorio Emanuele II was erected from 1898-1904; the original Renaissance style of the palace can be admired by walking around the building.

The interior, which was radically restored in the 19C, houses the collection of Antique sculpture left by Baron Giovanni Barracco *(see "Worth a Visit" below)*.

Continue along Corso Vittorio Emanuele II.

Sant'Andrea della Valle★★

Piazza Sant'Andrea della Valle is graced with a fountain attributed to Carlo Maderno: it bears the eagle and dragon of the Borghese family and was probably put up for Pope Paul V.

Construction of the **church** began in 1591 under the direction of **Giacomo della Porta**: it was completed between 1608 and 1623 by **Carlo Maderno**. The **façade★★** (1661-67), one of the most elegant of the Baroque style, was built by **Carlo Rainaldi**. The two-storey elevation ripples with columns and projections; the original scrolls intended to unite the two levels have been replaced by angels with a spread wing – although only the left-hand statue was executed.

Interior – The Latin-cross plan with a single nave flanked by intercommunicating side chapels, as in the Gesù Church, is typical of the Counter-Reformation. The

Dome of Sant'Andrea della Valle

severity of the art of this period is to be found in the extremely sober architecture of the second chapel on the right and the altar in the right transept. Conversely, the nave vaulting and left transept were decorated early in the 20C.

The dome★★, built by Carlo Maderno, is one of the loveliest in the city and second only to St Peter's in size. It was painted between 1624 and 1627 by **Lanfranco**, the first artist to implement the technique of painting a curved surface successfully. The *Glory of Paradise*, with its rich colouring, is an imitation of the fresco painted by Correggio on the dome of Parma Cathedral. The Evangelists on the pendentives were painted by Domenichino. The vigour and expressiveness of the painting are reminiscent of Michelangelo's art.

The upper section of the **apse★**, which was frescoed by **Domenichino** (1624-28), is in late Renaissance style: *St Andrew is led to his death (right); the Calling of St Andrew and St Peter (centre); the Flagellation of St Andrew (left); St Andrew being received into heaven (above); St Peter and St Andrew are shown the Saviour by St John the Baptist (arcade centre).*

The large painted panels (1650-51) round the main altar depicting the death of St Andrew are by Mattia Preti, inspired by Caravaggio and Lanfranco.

The Piccolomini Popes' tombs can be admired above the last bay in the nave before the transept. The monuments to Pius II *(left)* and Pius III *(right)* are typical of late-15C funeral art.

Take Via dei Chiavari beside the church.

Via dei Giubbonari runs very close to the site of Pompey's great theatre (Teatro di Pompeo) of which nothing remains except the semicircular line followed by the houses in Via di Grotta Pinta. By tradition it is the street where doublet-makers (*giubbone* = doublet), silk merchants and garment repairers were to be found. It has remained very commercial. Behind the theatre the great crowned portico of Pompey's Curia is where Julius Caesar was fatally stabbed in 44 BC. The remains of the Curia can be seen in the Largo Argentina Sacred Precinct *(see Area Sacra del Largo Argentina, p 212).*

Turn right into Via dei Giubbonari and left into a side street leading into Piazza del Monte di Pietà, where the Cappella del Monte di Pietà can be seen (see "Worth a Visit" below). Take Via dell'Arco del Monte; turn right into Piazza Capo di Ferro.

Palazzo Spada★

This palace was built in about 1540 for Cardinal Gerolamo Capo di Ferro, probably by an architect in Sangallo's circle. In 1632 it was acquired by Cardinal Bernardino Spada (who had a number of alterations carried out, including the addition of a wing to the palace), and in 1927 it became the property of the Italian Government for the Council of State.

Althought it was built only a few years after the Farnese Palace, the Spada Palace is quite different in conception. The noble austerity of Renaissance architecture has been replaced by fantastic decorations in the Mannerist style. The **façade** is almost smothered in statues, stucco garlands, medallions and scrolls bearing Latin inscriptions about the famous Classical figures which appear in the niches on the first floor. On the second floor, which is dominated by the Spada coat of arms, the decoration becomes overwhelming.

The delicate execution of the friezes in the **courtyard★★** is quite admirable. On the wall facing the entrance is the French coat of arms flanked by the arms of Julius III, a souvenir of Cardinal Capodiferro who was Papal legate to France and a friend of Julius III.

Borromini "Perspective" – *On the ground floor, behind the library and visible from the courtyard. For access ask the museum staff (see "Worth a Visit" below for a description of the collection).* This long corridor built by Borromini is known as the Borromini "Perspective" because of an optical illusion: the columns, which decrease in size, and the cleverly placed arches make this passageway appear longer than its 9m/29ft.

Continue to Piazza Farnese.

Palazzo Farnese★★

Not open to the public. At either end of this quiet and elegant piazza are two huge granite basins found in the Baths of Caracalla and converted into fountains in 1626. On the far side stands one of the most beautiful of Roman palaces, which bears the name of the family for whom it was built. The fame of the Farnese began when Cardinal Alessandro was elected Pope in 1534, taking the name of **Paul III**. As the first Pope of the Counter-Reformation he set up the Council of Trent, yet conducted his reign like a Renaissance monarch: he had four children whose mother has not been identified, made three of them legitimate and loaded them with riches. He was a patron of the arts, continuing the work on St Peter's and the Sistine Chapel and building the Farnese Palace. He and his descendants amassed a magnificent collection of works of art. One of his grandchildren, Ranuccio (1530-65), commissioned Salviati to celebrate the glory of the Farnese in a series of frescoes. Another, Odoardo (1573-1626), invited the Carracci to paint the gallery on the first floor. The last of the Farnese was Elizabeth (1692-1766), who married Philip V of Spain. Their son, Don Carlos of Bourbon, who became king of Naples in 1735, inherited the Farnese family riches; almost all the works of art from the Farnese Palace are now in the Naples Archaeological Museum or in the Royal Palace at Capodimonte.

The palace was purchased by the French Government in 1911 and bought back by the Italian Government in 1936. It was then leased to France for 99 years in exchange for the La Rochefoucauld-Doudeauville Palace, the building occupied by the Italian Embassy in Paris.

Façade – The absence of pilasters and the clear horizontal lines contribute to a masterpiece of balance and proportion. Construction began in 1515 on Cardinal Alessandro Farnese's orders, to the designs of his favourite architect, Antonio da Sangallo the Younger. When Sangallo died in 1546, Michelangelo took over. He retained the first-floor windows, framed by columns with alternate pediments, curved or triangular like the recesses in the Pantheon. He added the impressive upper cornice and over the central balcony he carved the irises of the Farnese coat of arms (not to be confused with the French lily). Recent restoration work has brought to light a delicate decorative design in pinkish tones.

The **courtyard** *(not open to the public)* is a model of Renaissance elegance. It was designed by three great architects: Sangallo, Vignola and Michelangelo. The **rear façade** overlooking Via Giulia *(see below)* is the best example of the building's elegant architecture.

The palace treasures include remarkable **frescoes** (1595-1603) painted by Annibale Carracci (in the Farnese Gallery) with the assistance of his brother Agostino and his pupils Domenichino and Lanfranco.

To admire the rear façade of the palace, take Via del Mascherone and turn right into Via Giulia (for a description of Via Giulia, see CASTEL SANT'ANGELO).

At the intersection of Via del Mascherone and Via Giulia stands the **Fontana del Mascherone**, built in 1626. The marble mask and huge granite basin probably come from an Ancient building.

Via Giulia then runs past the Farnese Palace's **rear façade**. This was designed by Vignola who took over from Michelangelo as architect. In 1573 he was succeeded by Giacomo della Porta, who built the loggia. Last to be built in 1603 was the *"Passetto Farnese"*, the bridge over Via Giulia, linking the palace to the convent of Santa Maria della Morte and to several rooms where the Farnese kept their collection of Antiquities.

On the left stands the church of **Santa Maria della Morte**, whose Baroque-influenced façade is by Ferdinando Fuga (18C).

Further on turn right into Via di S Caterina and left into Via de Monserrato.

Under the kindly eye of its many beautiful madonnas, **Via di Monserrato** is lined by craft and antique shops, by palaces where the many Spanish prelates, who came to Rome in the suite of the Borgia Popes (Calixtus III and Alexander VI), used to live. Many of the courtyards are worth a glance: the beauties of the Renaissance have not all disappeared. The church of **Santa Maria di Monserrato** is the Spanish national church.

Turn left into Via della Barchetta.

Sant'Eligio degli Orefici

Open 10am-1pm. Closed 28 July-3 Sept and 22-31 Dec. To visit, press the intercom at Via S. Eligio 9 (custodian) or Via S. Eligio 7 (office). Donations welcome. For information contact ☎/Fax 06 68 68 260.

This small church takes its name from the goldsmiths to whom it once belonged, many of whom owned shops in this area ("orafo" is the Italian word for goldsmith). The church, built in the shape of a Greek cross, was designed by Raphael; the interior is covered by an elegant Renaissance **cupola** at the intersection of the two arms. The high altar frescoes are by Matteo da Lecce (16C); above the altar, in the right arm of the cross, the 17C *Adoration of the Magi* by Francesco Romanelli is worthy of note.

Return to Via di Monserrato.

The elegant **Palazzo Ricci**, tucked in at the back of its attractive little Renaissance square, has great charm; the façade bears traces of decorations by Polidoro da Caravaggio and Maturino da Firenze *(see Index)*.

Via del Pellegrino, created by Sixtus IV in 1483 to provide pilgrims with easier access to St Peter's, was once home to a number of bookshops and printing houses. Where it merges with Via di Monserrato the corner house, which otherwise follows the line of the streets, has been cut back to open up the crossroads; this was an innovation in town planning for those days. The façade of Palazzo della Cancelleria facing Via del Pellegrino is decorated with fine corner balconies and has retained the arcades of the ground-floor shops that were once rented out by the Chapter of the church of San Lorenzo in Damaso.

The small and picturesque **Via Arco degli Acetari**, a

Houses in the picturesque Via dell'Arco degli Acetari

popular photo spot, heads away from Via del Pellegrino directly in front of the palazzo.

Worth a Visit

Museo Barracco (Barracco Museum)

Closed for restoration at the time of going to press. ☎/*Fax 06 68 80 68 48.*

The collections range over Egyptian, Assyrian, Greek and Roman sculpture from their origins to the end of Antiquity. The museum also houses a number of original Greek statues.

The elegant internal courtyard stairs lead up to the first floor, where the arch is decorated with admirable 17C frescoes. The **Egyptian sculptures** exhibited date from the third millennium and include the head hewn in black granite of the young Pharaoh Ramses II, and two low-relief sculptures dating from the Old Kingdom, IV Dynasty *(Room I)*. Among the **Assyrian exhibits** *(Room II)*, note the low relief showing a group of women in a palm grove (late 8C BC); on display in the same room are a very beautiful woman's funeral mask in gilded pasteboard from the period of Ptolemy, an interesting head in painted stucco of a mummy from Ermopoli, and Egyptian art from the Roman period (2C). Rooms III and IV house a group of **Etruscan and Cypriot works**: Etruscan *antefixae* and memorial stones; a woman's head (2C BC) found near Bolsena; a little statute of the god Bes, a minor Egyptian deity also venerated by other races; interesting Cypriot statues such as the quadriga (6C BC) and the man's head with beard (5C BC).

On the second floor are **Greek, Roman and medieval works of art**. Among the Greek sculptures from the Classical period (5C BC) and the copies from the Roman era, note the head of an ephebe, an original work; a head of Marsyas, a rare copy of the work by Myron who brought together the goddess Athena and the Satyr Marsyas in the same composition; a head of Apollo, a fine copy of a work by Phidias; a head of Diadumenos (victorious athlete), a copy of the original by Polyclitus. The works of Roman and medieval art exhibited *(Room IX; access from the end of the loggia)* include a fine 1C Roman bust of a young boy and a portrait of a youth.

Galleria Spada★

In Palazzo Spada. Open Tue-Sun, 8.30am-7.30pm. Closed Mon, 1 Jan, 1 May and at Christmas. €5. ☎ *06 68 74 896 ; Fax 06 68 61 158.*

The gallery presents the works of art collected by Cardinal Spada in their original setting and is typical of the private collection of a wealthy Roman in the 17C. The cardinal was the patron of Guercino and Guido Reni, whose noble manner pleased him. At the same time he was interested in *bambocciate*, realistic paintings which appeared in Rome in about 1630 in the circle of the painter Pieter Van Laer, a Dutchman nicknamed *Il Bamboccio* (the puppet) because of his physical deformity. The gallery is of interest both for its collection and for the building in which this is housed. In Room I, crowned by an 18C ceiling, note two canvases by **Guido Reni** (1575-1642): *Portrait of Cardinal Bernardino Spada*, a good example of the artist's use of pure delicate line, and the *Slave of Ripa Grande*.

The frieze along the top of the walls in Room II (tempera on canvas) is, in fact, the same design repeated four times. The original frieze can be seen on the wall opposite the window and was produced by Perin del Vaga, possibly as a model for a tapestry to be placed under the *Last Judgement* in the Sistine Chapel, which was never completed. **Room III**, created in the 17C, was the cardinal's original gallery. On the ceiling, a series of panels dating from the end of the 17C portrays allegories of the four continents of the world (the first two panels), the four elements and the four seasons. The decoration of the fascia around the top of the walls is echoed by the *trompe l'oeil* low reliefs in the two middle panels. The console tables in gilded wood are by late 17C Roman craftsmen. Paintings on display include a delightful and masterly *Landscape with Windmills* by Bruegel the Elder (1607) and the allegory of the *Massacre of the Innocents,* a masterpiece by Pietro Testa (first half of the 17C); note how the violent contrast between light and dark accentuates the dramatic aspect of this work. Jesus (escaping in the boat) is depicted embracing the cross, symbol of the Passion.

The two globes in the centre of the room (one of the earth, the second of the heavens) are by the Dutch cartographer and printer, Bleau (Caesius) and date from 1616 and 1622.

Room IV contains works by artists influenced by Caravaggio. Particularly worthy of note is the portrait of an enraptured *Saint Cecilia* (149) by Artemisia Gentileschi.

Cappella del Monte di Pietà★

Open by prior appointment only. Contact the Banca di Roma, Via Marco Minghetti 87, 00186 Roma, at least three weeks in advance. ☎ *06 67 00 83 01 (Signora Amadio).* This small oval **chapel** within the Monte di Pietà Palace is a gem of Baroque art. Originally the work of Maderno, it was then redesigned by the architects Giovanni Antonio de' Rossi (who worked with Bernini) and Carlo Bizzaccheri (a pupil of Carlo Fontana), who took over on his death in 1695 and was responsible for the entrance hall and dome.

The chapel was consecrated in 1641, although decoration was not completed until 1725. The interior retains a number of works whose themes reinforce the aim of the institution: to put down usury.

Castel Sant'Angelo★★

This itinerary centres around the River Tiber, known to the Ancient Romans as the *flavus Tiber* (the fair or yellow Tiber). The walk starts at the imposing, fortress-like building of Castel Sant'Angelo, with its secret passages and splendid Renaissance rooms, and then crosses the Tiber via the magnificent Ponte Sant'Angelo, graced with fine sculptures of angels. This is one of the most famous and romantic districts of Rome, dominated by the old fortress of the Popes, with the dome of St Peter's visible in the distance. The other bank of the river is home to expensive antique shops in streets such as Via Giulia and Via dei Coronari, where the occasional image of the Madonna can be seen gracing buildings in this district, recalling the days when pilgrims used these streets to make their way to St Peter's.

Location

Michelin map 38 or Michelin spiral atlas of Rome: pp 38-39, 55 K 9-10, L 9-10. Tour: 2hr 30min. Castel Sant'Angelo is situated in the northwest section of Rome's historic centre, on a sharp loop of the Tiber. From here, Via della Conciliazione runs straight up to the Vatican City.

Neighbouring sights are described in the following chapters: CAMPO DEI FIORI; PIAZZA NAVONA; VATICANO-SAN PIETRO.

Background

This district, which was densely populated in the Middle Ages, was gradually cleared and redeveloped to become a centre for commerce and business; it was **Sixtus IV** (1471-84) who initiated the transformation. As the district lay on the route of religious processions passing between the Vatican and the basilica of St John Lateran, magnificent mansions were built along the Holy Pontiff's route, lining Via Banco di Santo Spirito and Via dei Banchi Nuovi – which formed the **Papal Way** (Via Papalis) – and Via del Governo Vecchio.

> **WHERE TO EAT**
> See "Where to Eat" in the Practical Points section at the beginning of the guide.
>
> **SHOPPING**
> **Invito alla Lettura** – *Corso Vittorio Emanuele 283* – ☎ *06 68 61 396 – Open Mon, 9am-midnight; Tue-Thu, 9am-1am; Fri-Sat, 9am-2am; Sun, 10am-midnight.* This bookshop organises regular meetings with authors.

Special Features

CASTEL SANT'ANGELO★★★

Open daily (except Mon), 9am-8pm (last admission 7pm). Closed 1 Jan and Christmas. €5, €20 for a "Roma archeologica" card, valid for nine archaeological sites. ☎ *06 39 08 071; Fax 06 39 75 09 50; pierreci@pierreci.it*

Mausoleo di Adriano (Hadrian's Mausoleum) – This fortress-like building was intended as a sepulchre for **Hadrian** and his family. Begun by the Emperor in AD 135, it was finished four years later by his adopted son and successor to the Imperial throne, Antoninus Pius.

The base (84m/276ft square) is surmounted by a drum (20m/66ft high), on which was heaped a small mound of earth *(tumulus)*. It was crowned by a statue of the Emperor and a bronze *quadriga* (four-horse chariot). The mausoleum contained the cinerary urns of all the Emperors from Hadrian to Septimius Severus (AD 211). When Aurelian surrounded the city with a wall in 270 he incorporated the mausoleum within the precinct and turned it into a fortress.

Fortress – During the medieval struggle between the Papacy and the noble Roman families, the building became a fortified stronghold. Nicholas V (1447-55) built a brick storey on top of the original construction and added turrets at the corners.

The octagonal bastions were the work of Alexander VI (1492-1503). In 1527 Clement VII took refuge there from the troops of Charles V and made several rooms habitable. These were

> **THE ANGEL'S CASTLE**
> In 590 Pope **Gregory the Great** led a procession against the plague which was decimating the city. Suddenly there appeared on top of the mausoleum an angel sheathing his sword. The gesture was interpreted as a sign that the plague would abate and in gratitude the Pope had a chapel built on the mausoleum.

later improved by Paul III, who already knew the castle as he had been imprisoned there by Innocent VIII when he was only Cardinal Alexander Farnese. In his autobiography **Benvenuto Cellini**, the sculptor and metalworker, admits that he, too, had been in the castle jail, as had Cagliostro, so it is said. After the unification of Italy the Castel Sant'Angelo became a barracks and military prison but today, surrounded by a public garden, it knows only the assaults of tourists.

A high defensive wall, the **Passetto**, built by Leo IV (847-55) links the castle to the Vatican Palace. Alexander VI created a passage along the top of the wall so that the Pope could reach the fortress from the palace in case of siege.

Tour *1hr*

From the outside the Castel Sant'Angelo presents a somewhat squat structure; its Ancient sections can be recognised from the large blocks of peperine and travertine stone. The statue of the Angel dominates the whole complex.

Entry is through the old entrance to the mausoleum raised higher (some 3m/10ft) than its original position.

Spiral Ramp – *The entrance to the spiral ramp is below on the right, next to the entrance to the Tiber embankment.* When the castle was a mausoleum, the ramp (125m/410ft) led up to the chamber where the funeral urns were kept. The walls were originally covered in marble, the floor was paved with mosaic, of which some traces still remain, and the vault was decorated with stucco. The holes in the vault were air vents with the exception of one (on the left at the back of the entrance hall), which was made to house a lift built in the 18C. At the top of the ramp is a transverse stairway. Originally it led to the Roman cinerary chamber, but Boniface IX had it transformed into a passage leading from one side of the castle to the other following the north-south diameter of the drum. The part of the ramp which goes down towards the drawbridge leads to an area *(right)* where the guardroom has been reconstructed as it would have been in the 16C. At the other end of the ramp is a 19C bridge built above the funeral chamber to link the first section of the ramp to the second, which emerges onto the main courtyard.

Main courtyard – This is also known as the Angel Courtyard from the 16C statue which graced the top of the castle until the 18C. There are piles of cannon balls which were used as ammunition for the catapults, bombards and cannons from the 15C-17C .

On the right is a series of rooms from the medieval period which were reconstructed in the 17C and now make up the lower armoury. The end of the courtyard is closed by a shrine designed by Michelangelo which forms the side wall of the chapel built for Leo X; it probably stands on the site of Gregory the Great's cell *(see above)*.

On the left are the Papal rooms.

Clement VIII's Rooms – *Open for temporary exhibitions.* These rooms in Leo X's apartments were first rearranged by Paul III and later by Clement VIII – their names can be seen above the doors. Note in the first room the fine 17C fireplace.

Sala della Giustizia – *Open for temporary exhibitions.* Located above the Cinerary Chamber and immediately below the great circular room probably intended as Hadrian's Mausoleum (Mausoleo di Adriano), this room was used throughout the 16C and 17C for legal hearings.

Sala dell'Apollo – *Access from Sala della Giustizia or from the main courtyard.* Over the doorways and fireplace is the name of Pope Paul III and the date 1547. The room takes its name from the painted scenes framed with grotesques, attributed to Perin del Vaga. The fine panels decorating the walls and ceiling illustrate figures, grotesques and racemes drawn from Roman mythology. One of the two openings in the floor is the door to the lift *(see above)*. The other leads to a 9m/29ft-deep shaft that opens into a small room. Castel Sant'Angelo has many of these trapdoors and secret passageways, which have given rise to a number of gruesome legends.

Sala di Clemente VII – The wooden ceilings bear the name of Pope Clement VII and 15C and 16C paintings.

From Sala dell'Apollo take the small corridor which leads to the semicircular courtyard.

Cortile di Alessandro VI – In the courtyard is a handsome well dating from the reign of this Pope (1492-1503). The alternative name – Theatre Court – recalls the theatrical performances given here by Leo X and Pius IV, both men of letters.

Bagno di Clemente VII★ – *Access from the corridor separating Cortile di Alessandro VI from Cortile Leone X and the stairs up on the left.* The beautiful decor by Giovanni da Udine, a pupil of Raphael, is evidence of the civilised lifestyle of the Pope in the 16C.

Prigioni (Prisons) – *Access by steps leading down from Alexander VI's Court.* Beatrice Cenci *(see Palazzo Cenci, p 211)*, Giordano Bruno, the heretic monk, and Benvenuto Cellini are supposed to have been imprisoned here.

Oil and grain store – The jars could hold 22 000 litres/4 839gal of oil and the capacity of the five large silos was about 100kg/3 700cwt of grain. It was Alexander VI who made these provisions in case of siege.

Return to Alexander VI's Court and take the steps up from the centre of the semicircle which lead to the loggias of Pius IV, Paul III and Julius II (walking anticlockwise).

Loggia di Pio IV (Pius IV's Loggia) – The rooms which open onto the loggia were used as living quarters for the castle staff, before becoming prisons. The loggia was rebuilt in the 19C to house political prisoners. It was here that for many years the gun was fired to tell Romans that it was noon.

Bear left.

Loggia di Paolo III (Paul III's Loggia) – The Pope commissioned Antonio da Sangallo (the Younger) to design the loggia *(which faces north)* in 1543 and had it decorated with stucco work and grotesques. There is a view of the bastions and the defensive wall.

Continue beyond the restaurant-bar.

On the left is the **upper armoury** *(armeria superiore)*, containing a collection of arms and uniforms belonging to the Italian and Papal armies.

Loggia di Giulio II (Julius II's Loggia) – It faces south with a fine view of St Angelo Bridge (Ponte Sant'Angelo) and the city of Rome. It was probably built by Giuliano da Sangallo for Julius II.

From here steps lead up to the Papal apartment.

Appartamento papale★ (Papal apartment) – After the siege of 1527 when Clement VII was forced to take refuge in Castel Sant'Angelo, Paul III had a suite of rooms constructed on top of the castle and well protected by the succession of ramps and steps.

The Sala del Consiglio (Sala Paolina) was used as a waiting room for visitors to the Pope. Its floor is marble and the frescoes are by a group of artists instructed by Perin del Vaga, a Florentine artist who was a follower of Raphael, from whom the Papal court commissioned a number of important works. The name of the **Camera del Perseo** (Perseus's Room) is derived from the subject of the frieze painted by Perin del Vaga. In the **Camera di Amore e Psiche** (Cupid and Psyche's Room), the frieze beneath the ceiling illustrates the story of the beautiful young woman who was loved by Venus's son.

Return to the Sala del Consiglio and, after the steps, turn into the corridor decorated with frescoes.

Two sets of steps linked by a passage lead up to the **library** and two series of rooms *(one above the other)* named after their decorations: **Hadrian's Mausoleum Room** and the **Festoon Room**, which opens into a smaller apartment where Cagliostro was imprisoned, now comprising the **Dolphin Room** and the **Salamander Room**.

Return to the library.

The **Sala del Tesoro** (Treasure Room), at the centre of the fortress, is a circular chamber, lined with walnut presses containing the Papal records which were transferred here from the Vatican in 1870. The cupboards (probably 14C) originally held the precious objects, relics and silver belonging to Julius II, Leo X and Sixtus V.

Beside the Sala del Tesoro.

Scala Romana (Roman Staircase) – The staircase, part of Hadrian's Mausoleum, leads to the Hall of Flags and Columns (Sala Rotonda) and the terrace.

Terrace – The bronze statue of the angel (repaired in 18C) presides over a **panorama★★★** of Rome, one of the most famous. From left to right: the Prati district and the green patch of the Villa Borghese; close to the castle, the great white mass of the Law Courts, then the Quirinal Palace, the Militia Tower and the shallow dome of the Pantheon; further right, the monument to Victor Emmanuel II and the domes and turrets of the

Lara Pessina/MICHELIN

The Angel of Castel Sant'Angelo

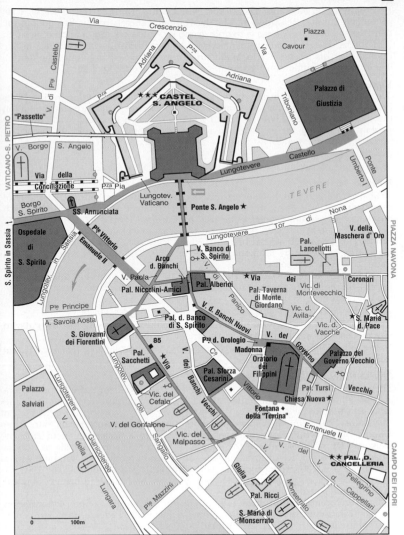

city: the Gesù Church, St Ivo's corkscrew tower, the belfry of Santa Maria dell'Anima with its ceramic tiles, Sant'Andrea delle Valle, San Carlo ai Catinari and the Synagogue. On the extreme right is the Janiculum Hill, San Giovanni dei Fiorentini, Via della Conciliazione, St Peter's and the Vatican Palace linked to Castel Sant'Angelo by the "Passetto", Monte Mario.

It is also possible to take the parapet walk linking the four bastions: St John's, St Matthew's, St Mark's (which gives access to the "Passetto") and St Luke's.

Walking About

Ponte Sant'Angelo★

This is one of the most elegant bridges in Rome. It goes back to the time of Hadrian who built a fine bridge (AD 136) linking the Campus Martius with his mausoleum; its three central arches have survived. The other arches date from the 17C and were altered when the Tiber embankments were built in 1892-94. The statues of St Peter and St Paul *(south bank)* were erected by Clement VII in 1530; the 10 Baroque angels are the work of **Bernini**, commissioned by Clement IX (1667-69).
Cross the Ponte Sant'Angelo and bear right into Via Paola.

San Giovanni dei Fiorentini

It was Pope Leo X, a Medici from Florence, who decided to build a "national" church for his fellow countrymen in Rome. The most famous Renaissance artists were invited to compete for the commission, including Peruzzi, Michelangelo and Raphael. The artist chosen was Jacopo Sansovino. Work began early in the 16C; it was continued by Antonio da Sangallo and Giacomo della Porta and completed in 1614 by Carlo Maderno. The façade, which dates from the 18C, is in the style of the late Counter-Reformation. The decoration of the chancel is Baroque: in the centre is the *Baptism of Jesus*, a marble group by Antonio Raggi, a pupil of Bernini. The tombs on either side were designed by **Borromini**, who is buried in the church near his teacher **Carlo Maderno** (tombs in the paving under the dome). There is no inscription on Borromini's tomb, as he committed suicide.

Via Giulia★

The street gained its notoriety in the 16C. It was named after **Pope Julius II**, its creator, and is one of the few straight streets in Rome. It had a good reputation during the Renaissance but lost favour in the 17C when Innocent X had the state prisons transferred there. Owing to recent restoration work and the arrival of antique shops and modern art galleries, it has regained some of its former standing.
Continue along Via Giulia.

N° **85** is one of the houses where Raphael is said to have lived.

Palazzo Sacchetti

N° 66 Via Giulia. It may have been designed by Sangallo the Younger, architect of the Farnese Palace or by Annibale Lippi, the architect of the Villa Medici; both buildings were commissioned in the 16C by Cardinal Ricci di Montepulciano.
Between the next two side turnings on the right, Vicolo del Cefalo and Via del Gonfalone, are huge blocks of masonry which were the foundations for Julius II's law courts, designed by Bramante but never built. The Romans have christened them "the Via Giulia sofas".
N° 52 is the prison which Innocent X had built in 1655. The inscription on the face of the building speaks of a model institution designed for a more humane type of detention.
Turn left into Vicolo del Malpasso and left again into Via dei Banchi Vecchi.

It was in **Via dei Banchi Vecchi**, the street of bankers in the 15C, that the **Palazzo Sforza Cesarini** was built by Pope Alexander VI, then only a cardinal.
Turn right into Via Sforza Cesarini and cross Corso Vittorio Emanuele II to reach Piazza della Chiesa Nuova.

Chiesa Nuova★ (New Church)

The church was founded in the 12C as Santa Maria in Vallicella; the name is probably an allusion to the little valley *(vallicella)*, the Tarentum, which lay near the Tiber in Antiquity.
The history of the church is linked to the memory of **St Philip Neri**, the Florentine founder of the Oratorians who were promoted into a Congregation in 1575 by Gregory XIII, who also offered the church of Santa Maria in Vallicella to Neri as a base for his order. Reconstruction was set in hand and the new building, which was finished in 1605, was called the New Church. It was restored in the 19C.
The **façade** is decorated with the shallow pilasters and recessed columns typical of the Counter-Reformation.
Philip Neri wanted the **interior** to be plain but during the Counter-Reformation it was given a more elaborate Baroque format inspired by **Pietro da Cortona**. On the coffered stucco ceiling, he painted *St Philip's Vision* (1664-65): during the building of the church, Neri had a vision of the Virgin holding up a piece of the ceiling of the old building which threatened to collapse onto the altar where Mass was being celebrated.
Pietro da Cortona, who had become the acknowledged master among decorative painters, enjoyed equal celebrity in Rome with Bernini. Between 1648 and 1651 he had already painted the dome which depicts Christ presenting the instruments of the Passion to God, thus abolishing punishment for mankind. In the pendentives he placed the Prophets Isaiah, Jeremiah, Ezekiel and Daniel (1659-60). Meanwhile, he began painting an *Assumption* on the vault of the apse.
The chapel *(left of the chancel)* contains the remains of St Philip Neri and is decorated in grandiose style with gold, bronze and marble encrusted with mother-of-pearl. The painting of the saint over the altar is by G Reni.
A number of Mannerist and Baroque paintings can be seen in the church, including three early works by Rubens (1608) in the chancel and the *Presentation in the Temple* by Cavalier d'Arpino *(first chapel on the left).*
The chapel *(left transept)* contains a picture by the Mannerist painter Barocci, in a style very typical of the second half of the 16C. A beautiful *Visitation (fourth chapel on the left)* is by the same painter.
On the altar in the sacristy *(entrance via the chapel in the left transept)* stands a beautiful marble sculpture of St Philip with an angel, executed in 1640 by Alessandro Algardi.

Oratorio dei Filippini

Closed for restoration at time of going to press. For information, call ☎ 06 67 10 81 00; Fax 06 67 70 81 30.
The building adjoining the New Church was built between 1637 and 1662 to house the assemblies of the Congregation of the Oratory, where laity and clergy met under the spiritual direction of St Philip Neri.

Nowadays the oratory is also known as Borromini Hall and is used for conferences and various cultural activities. In addition to the Oratorian priests, the vast palace also houses the Vallicelliana Library, the Roman Library, the archives of the city of Rome, which include a collection of Roman newspapers dating back to the 18C, and various cultural institutes.

The **façade★** overlooking Piazza della Chiesa Nuova is, in fact, the side elevation of the Oratory. It was designed by Borromini to form a unit with the church. It is monumental yet subtle, an interaction of calm and frenzied movement in line and detail so characteristic of this great Baroque architect.

The façade is composed of two orders; the central section undulates with contrasting curves: convex on the lower floor and concave on the upper. The complex design combines recessed windows at ground-floor level and a slightly concave pediment in the upper section.

Fontana della "Terrina"

The **fountain** was transferred here in 1925 after standing in the Campo dei Fiori until 1899. The basin was carved in 1590 but a few years later was covered with a travertine lid bearing the inscription: "Love God, do good and let others talk".

Take Via della Chiesa Nuova beside the church and turn right into Via del Governo Vecchio.

Via del Governo Vecchio

This was one of the main streets of the district, continuing the Papal Way as Via di Parione. It is lined with craft shops, junk shops and antique dealers occupying the ground-floor premises of the Renaissance palaces, some still bearing the coats of arms of the noble families who once lived there.

Palazzo del Governo Vecchio – The building at n° 39 was completed in 1478. In 1624 it became the residence of the Governor of Rome. When the Government was transferred to the Palazzo Madama under Benedict XIV (1740-58), the building became known as the Old Government Palace. It has an attractive doorway decorated with friezes and diaper-work.

Return to Piazza dell'Orologio.

Piazza dell'Orologio

The plain front which the Oratory presents in Via dei Filippini ends unexpectedly on the corner of Via del Governo Vecchio in a graceful clock tower. The wrought-iron scroll work on the bell cage is recognisable as Borromini's work (1647-49). Beneath the clock is a mosaic of the Virgin of Vallicella.

On the corner of the building is a beautiful **Madonna** surrounded by a "glory" of cherubs, in typical Baroque taste.

Take Via dei Banchi Nuovi.

MADONNAS

In Rome images of the Madonna are to be found in almost every street – at intersections, along alleyways, at the corner of a piazza – and may be painted, frescoed or in terracotta bas-relief, brightly coloured or monochrome. They seem to keep a watchful eye over passers-by and many still retain the little lanterns which for many years often provided the only illumination after sunset.

It was not until January 1854 that street lighting by gas was introduced to Rome – in Via del Corso – by James Shepherd, an Englishman, who is buried in the Testaccio Cemetery.

In December the street Madonnas were the object of a particular cult: peasants from the Abruzzi mountains, dressed in sheep skins, would come and give performances on their bagpipes before their favourite shrine in return for a small payment.

E.Baret

Via dei Banchi Nuovi and Via Banco di Santo Spirito

These streets gave the district the air of a commercial centre. By the 15C bankers from Florence, Siena and Genoa had set up in business. Their fortunes were immense. Under the supervision of Cardinal Camerlengo, the Chigi family administered the finances of the Holy See for over 20 years; later the Strozzi, relatives of the Medici, took over. The Papal State also granted the bankers concessions on mining and customs dues. They controlled the Pope's personal finances and those of the great Roman families.

Together with money changing, which was conducted freely in the streets, there was betting: people bet on the election of the Pope, on the sex of unborn babies ... Until 1541 there was a working mint in the **Palazzo del Banco di Santo Spirito**. From the end of Via Banco di Santo Spirito there is a pleasant view of Castel Sant'Angelo and the bridge leading to it.

Early in the 16C the **Palazzo Niccolini-Amici** was built by Jacopo Sansovino for the Strozzi. The **Palazzo Alberini** opposite was rented in 1515 to bankers from Florence.

Via dei Coronari★

This is one of the most attractive streets in Rome, with its antique shops and its palaces glowing in ochre and stone.

In Antiquity it was part of the Via Recta, which led from the Piazza Colonna to the river.

Overall it has retained the form it acquired under Sixtus IV (1471-84). It is named after the vendors of rosaries *(corone)* and other pious objects who set up their shops in the path of the pilgrims, who entered the city by the Porta del Popolo and made their way to the Vatican over the Ponte Sant'Angelo.

Arco dei Banchi

The Bankers' Arch leads to the Chigi bank. On the left under the arch is a stone with a Latin inscription which comes from the nearby church of St Celsus and St Julian: it shows the height reached by the Tiber when it flooded in 1277.

Turn left under Arco dei Banchi.

Ponte Vittorio Emanuele II (Victor Emmanuel II Bridge)

There was a bridge here in AD 60, built by Nero, which collapsed in the 4C. The present construction, which is decorated with allegorical groups and winged Victories, was begun soon after the unification of the Italian State and completed in 1911, thus linking Rome and the Vatican.

Cross the bridge to the right (north) bank and turn right.

On the left is the imposing **Santo Spirito Hospital**, which was founded by Innocent III and rebuilt in the 15C by Sixtus IV. The **Church of the Santissima Annunciata** (Most Holy Annunciation), although small, is graced by an attractive façade full of movement (18C).

Santo Spirito in Sassia

The church was built in the 8C for Anglo-Saxon pilgrims and rebuilt in the 16C after being sacked in 1527. The architect was **Sangallo the Younger** who died before it was finished. The façade, which bears the arms of Sixtus V (1585-90), in whose reign the building was completed, is in the Renaissance style, with flat pilasters and an oculus, according to Sangallo's design.

The interior, beneath a beautiful coffered ceiling, is richly decorated with paintings in the Mannerist style (divided into small panels, overworked). There is a fine 16C organ.

Palazzo di Giustizia

The **Law Courts**, referred to by locals as the "Palazzaccio", were built from 1889-1911 by Guglielmo Calderini and are among the most conspicuous modern buildings in Rome. With a bronze quadriga by Ximenes (1855-1926) and colossal statuary, the Law Courts can claim both Classical and Baroque inspiration.

Catacombe di Priscilla★

The tour described below heads away from the city's best-known monuments and explores the fascinating district around Via Nomentana. Visit the palaeo-Christian churches of Sant'Agnese and Santa Costanza, the catacombs of Priscilla and the mosque, one of the most interesting buildings to have been constructed in the city in the past few decades. Stroll along pleasant residential streets lined with elegant *palazzi* and dotted with the attractive gardens of patrician villas. The walk finishes in the delightful Coppedè quarter, with its eclectic array of early-20C buildings.

Location

Michelin map 38 or Michelin spiral atlas of Rome: pp 10-11 B 14-15, pp 26-27 D 16-G 15-16, p 28 F 17. Tour: 2hr. The sights described below do not follow any particular itinerary. This district is situated outside the old walls to the northeast of the city, and is wedged between the River Aniene to the north, and the intersection of Via Nomentana and Viale Regina Margherita to the south.

Neighbouring sights are described in the following chapters: PORTA PIA-TERMINI; SAN LORENZO FUORI LE MURA.

Background

The district is often referred to as "African" because many of the streets are named after the countries which made up the Italian Empire. It was developed during the Fascist era.

The regular streets, lined with large blocks of comfortable flats built in the 1930s and elegant, ochre-coloured *palazzi*, give way in the **Piazza Mincio** to extravagantly decorated buildings in a mixture of Renaissance, Baroque and Egyptian styles, designed between 1922 and 1926 by the architect Gino Coppede.

The vast **Parco di Villa Ada** contains the site of the Monte Antenne, which is closely connected with the founding of Rome. Here stood the Sabine city of the Antennates who, according to Livy, were conquered by Romulus after attacking the Romans in retaliation for the rape of the Sabine women.

Worth a Visit

Chiesa di Sant'Agnese Fuori le Mura and Mausoleo di Santa Costanza★

The history of these two buildings begins with the death of Agnes, a young girl of 12 who was martyred under Diocletian (284-305).

Legend of St Agnes – Both St Ambrose and Damasus, writing at a period soon after the Diocletian persecution, mention the martyrdom of Agnes. The 6C legend was therefore founded on truth. Agnes refused to marry the son of the Praetor, declaring that she had vowed her soul to God. She was condemned to stand naked in a place of ill repute, possibly below the steps to Domitian's stadium, the church of Sant'Agnese in Agone nearby. Her nakedness was miraculously covered by her

Directory

WHERE TO EAT
See "Where to Eat" in the Practical Points section at the beginning of the guide.

PASTRY SHOPS AND ICE-CREAM PARLOURS

Cavalletti – *Via Nemorense 179/181* – ☎ *06 86 32 48 14* – Open Wed-Mon, 7.30am-1.30pm and 2.30-8pm. Known throughout the city for its light *millefeuilles*, this small *pasticceria* also bakes excellent Neapolitan cakes and pastries, and lemon tarts.

Cds Artigiana Dolciumi – *Via S. Maria Goretti 24* – ☎ *06 86 21 86 22* – Open 9am-2pm and 3-7pm. A small shop specialising in chestnut-based products, such as jams, cakes and delicious *marrons glacés*.

Marinari – *Piazza S. Emerenziana 20/21* – ☎ *06 86 21 93 32* – Open Tue-Sun, 7am-9pm. This *pasticceria* is renowned for its cream and berry tarts, and also offers a range of fruit tarts, exquisite desserts and savoury snacks.

Romoli – *Viale Eritrea 140* – ☎ *06 86 21 62 08* – Open until 2am. This popular bar-*pasticceria* sells a wide selection of filled *fagottini* (stuffed parcels). Try the *dama*, a house speciality, split in half and filled with a choice of cream, confectioner's cream, chocolate or nutella.

Di Lanzallotto Domenico – *Viale Somalia 96* – ☎ *06 86 21 22 57* – Open Wed-Mon, 7am-midnight. This *gelateria* attracts the crowds on summer evenings with its nutella-flavoured ice-cream, which is more like a mousse than an ice cream. Other excellent flavours are also available.

Duse (da Giovanni) – *Via Duse 1/e, zona Parioli* – ☎ *06 80 79 30 00* – Open Mon-Sat, 8am-midnight. Known to one and all as "Da Giovanni", this small *gelateria* is located in one of the most elegant districts of Rome. Recommended for its excellent ice cream with unusual flavours such as date, passion fruit, papaya and mandarin.

CAFÉS

Excape Internet Café – *Viale Somalia 227* – ☎ *06 86 32 94 92* – www.excape.it – Open Mon-Sat, 9.30am-2am, Sun, 5pm-2am. As well as its 30 computers with Internet access, this high-tech café also has a range of original video games. In the summer, customers can surf the Net outdoors.

SHOPPING

Città 2000 – *Via Domenico Cassini 4* – ☎ *06 80 83 000* – music@citta2000.it – Open Mon-Sat, 9am-1.30pm and 3.30-8pm. This shop, situated near Viale Parioli, sells a variety of music, including trip-hop, fusion and jazz, as well as rare items by Japanese groups.

Gatti e Antonelli – *Via Nemorense 211* – ☎ *06 86 21 80 44* – Open Mon-Wed and Fri-Sat, 7am-1.30pm and 4.30-7.30pm. A small shop in the middle of the African district, which some claim makes the best fresh pasta in the city.

Cooperativa Agricola Stella – *Via Garigliano 68* – ☎ *06 85 42 681* – Open Mon-Sat until 8pm. This shop offers cheese-lovers the chance to taste some excellent mozzarella and ricotta made from buffalo's milk.

long hair and a dazzling cloak. She was then condemned to the stake but escaped unscathed, the flames turning on her executioners. Finally she was beheaded with a sword and buried in the cemetery in the Via Nomentana.

Legend of St Constantia – The saint's name is derived from that of Constantia, the Emperor Constantine's daughter or granddaughter. Such great benefactions were attributed to Agnes that Constantia, who was suffering from leprosy, spent a night by the saint's tomb. The young martyr appeared to her in a dream, urging her to convert to Christianity; when Constantia awoke the leprosy had gone.

Early church – After 337 **Constantia** erected a huge basilica near St Agnes's tomb. Traces of the apse still exist, clearly visible from Via Bressanone and Piazza Annibaliano. Subsequently, to the southwest of the basilica, she built a circular construction which was to be her mausoleum and has become the church of Santa Costanza. Constantia's Basilica fell into ruin but a small chapel was built on the site of St Agnes' tomb. This chapel was rebuilt and enlarged by Pope Honorius (625-38). It is now known as St Agnes' Church and has been much restored, particularly in the 19C.

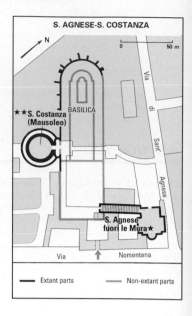

Sant'Agnese Fuori le Mura★

Open 8am-noon and 4-7.30pm. ☎ *06 86 10 840; www.santagnese.net*
The church of St Agnes Without the Walls can be reached from below from Via Sant'Agnese or from above from Via Nomentana through the convent courtyard and down a long flight of steps into the narthex; the steps, which were restored in the 16C, were already part of the 7C construction. The walls are covered with fragments from the catacombs, in particular *(almost at the bottom on the right going down)* a low relief of St Agnes praying, which decorated her tomb, and an inscription to the glory of her martyrdom, which was commissioned by Pope Damasus (366-84).

Despite the addition of 19C painting above the chancel arch, between the clerestories and over the arcades in the nave, the interior still gives some idea of its 7C appearance; it was designed like a basilica with a nave and two aisles and galleries.

The ceiling and baldaquin are 17C. It was during the restoration undertaken by Paul V (1605-21) that the bones of St Agnes were discovered next to another body, probably that of Emerentiana, who continued to pray by St Agnes's body when the other Christians fled from the stones thrown by pagans. Paul V arranged for her bones to be placed in a shrine beneath the altar.

The statue of St Agnes on the altar is a curious work by the French sculptor Nicolas Cordier (1567-1612), who used the torso of an old alabaster statue of Isis. On the left of the altar is a very fine Antique candelabra made of marble.

The **mosaic★** in the apse was part of the 7C building; it shows St Agnes with Pope Symmachus (498-514), who restored the early chapel, and Pope Honorius, who is offering the church he built. The work is typical of Roman art with Byzantine influences: Agnes is dressed like a Byzantine empress; the colours are muted and repetitive (same for all three robes); the vertical lines are very clear, in perfect accord with the lines of the vault.

Catacombs – *Open daily (except Sun and public holiday mornings and Mon afternoons), 9am-noon and 4-6pm. Guided tours only. €5.* ☎ *06 86 10 840.*
A cemetery was already in existence when St Agnes's remains were buried here. The oldest part on the north side of the church dates back to the 2C. After St Agnes's burial the graves spread round behind the apse and down between the church and the mausoleum.

Mausoleo di Santa Costanza★★

Open 9am-noon and 3.30-6pm; Sun and public holidays 3.30-6pm only. Closed Mon afternoon. ☎ *06 86 10 840.* The Emperor Constantine's daughters, Helen and Constantia, were buried in this circular mausoleum which dates from the 4C. It was probably converted into a church in the 13C. The outline of an oval vestibule can still be traced in front of the entrance. The rotunda itself is covered by a dome resting on a drum which is supported on a ring of twinned columns linked by elegant arches. The surrounding barrel-vaulted gallery is still adorned with its original 4C **mosaic★**, an example of the artistic renewal which followed in the wake of Constantine's reign. The vault is divided into panels and covered with a variety

of motifs against a light background: floral and geometric details, portraits in medallions, vine tendrils entwined with harvest scenes. The mosaics in the side recesses have Christian themes: God handing down the Law to Moses (or, according to another interpretation, St Peter receiving the keys) and Christ giving the New Law (the Gospel) to St Peter and St Paul.
In the recess opposite the entrance is a copy of Constantia's sarcophagus.

The ambulatory in Santa Constanza is decorated with vines and scenes from the grape harvest.

B. Kaufmann/MICHELIN

Catacombe di Priscilla★★

Guided tours only (45min; available in several languages), 8.30am-12.30pm and 2.30-5.30pm (5pm in winter). Closed Mon, Easter and Christmas. €5; no charge last Sun in Sept. ☎ 06 44 65 610 or 06 44 67 601; Fax 06 44 67 625; arc.sacra@flashnet.it

The catacombs developed out of a private underground chamber *(hypogeum)* beneath the house of the Acilii, a noble family to which Priscilla belonged. Excavations in this chamber have uncovered inscriptions mentioning Priscilla and a certain Acilius Glabrio, who was mentioned by Suetonius; he was condemned to death in AD 91 by Domitian for the same offence as Domitilla's husband, Flavius Clemens *(see APPIA ANTICA: Catacombe di Domitilla, p 117)*. The family converted to Christianity and allowed the Christian community to create underground galleries in which to bury their dead. During the 3C two storeys of galleries developed round the *hypogeum*. In the 4C St Sylvester's Basilica, in which several Popes are buried, was built by Pope Sylvester (314-35) over the Christian graves.
The **Chapel of the Taking of the Veil** (Cappella della Velata) is named after a scene painted on the far wall and originally interpreted as showing a young virgin taking the veil in the presence of the Virgin Mary. Nowadays it is thought to represent three episodes in the dead woman's life: marriage, worship, motherhood.
The **Chapel of the Virgin and Child★** (Cappella della Vergine col Bambino) contains the earliest representation of the Virgin *(on the ceiling)*, who is holding the

Christ child on her knees while another figure points to a star. The scene is thought to be an illustration of a passage from Isaiah, Chapter 7 ("Behold, a virgin shall conceive, and bear a son ..."). The **Greek Chapel★** (Cappella Greca), in which there are Greek inscriptions, consists of two chambers separated by an arch. Over the arch in the inner room is a painting of a banquet at which one of the figures *(left)* at the table is breaking bread; on the table are a chalice and a plate of fish; at the sides are seven baskets of bread which could be an allusion to the miracle of the feeding of the multitude. The presence of all these items has led to the painting being interpreted as a representation of the Eucharist. Archaeologists date it as 2C because of the hairstyle of one of the women seated at the table, a style made fashionable by Faustina, the wife of the Emperor Antoninus Pius (138-61).

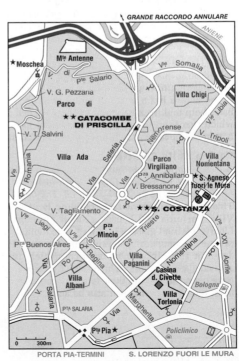

Interior of the mosque

Moschea★

Open Wed and Sat, 9-11.30am. For groups, by appointment only (Fax 06 80 79 515). Closed Aug and during the month of Ramadan. For further information contact ☎ 06 80 82 167.

The **mosque**, set in the green surroundings of Mount Antenne, forms part of the largest group of monuments built in Rome within the last few decades. The mosque is not, in fact, the only building in the new Islamic Centre, having been built next to a library, an auditorium for 300 people, and several rooms for meetings and lectures. The design of Rome's Islamic Centre is the result of the joint efforts of three architects: P Portoghesi, V Gigliotti and S Moussawi. Building began in 1984 and ended in 1992.

To underline the Islamic Centre's links with the city, typical Roman materials have been used in the construction, such as straw-coloured brick and travertine stone. The result is that, despite being Islamic, this building does not seem very different from the city's own traditional architecture. The **interior★** is the real masterpiece of the mosque; the prayer hall (capacity 3 000) is surmounted by a large stepped dome and 16 other small side domes, supported on 32 sunken pillars made of white cement and marble dust. The exterior walls, which constitute the base of the domes, are suspended from and supported by the same sunken pillars. Indeed, the domes do not actually rest on the rectangular base of the building; this allows a band (80cm/2ft 6in) of light to run around the base (170m/555ft), creating an amazing effect. Light is the main feature of the interior. Every "step" of the domes has a series of little openings which, together with the band at the base, help to diffuse light and create a surreal atmosphere. The interlacing arches which rise from the pillars are also very beautiful and suggest an impression of continual movement reminiscent of the sinuous lines of Italian Baroque.

Casina delle Civette

   Open Apr-Sep, 9am-7pm; rest of the year, 9am-5pm. Closed Mon, 1 Jan, 1 May, 15 Aug and Christmas. Guided tours available (1hr). €2.58, no charge on 21 Apr. ☎ 06 44 25 00 72 or 06 44 25 00 88; Fax 06 44 25 01 66; g.scitella@comune.roma.it

This original medieval-style building is hidden amid the green surroundings of **Villa Torlonia** and houses a small museum in which a collection of beautiful Liberty **stained-glass windows★** is exhibited. The building was designed as the private residence of the Prince of Toriona (1908) and was abandoned after his death in 1939. It has now been completely restored, and the multicoloured lead stained-glass windows, which depict scenes from legends and the natural world, have been returned to their former glory. Sketches and models for other windows from the same period can also be seen.

Colosseo-Celio★★★

This walk spans several centuries, focusing on the Colosseum and the Arch of Constantine, built in the time of the Emperors and now crowded with souvenir stalls, horse-drawn carriages and tourist groups. It then heads to the Caelian Hill, one of the greenest of the seven hills of Rome, to explore the many medieval treasures of this tranquil district.

Location

Michelin map 38 or Michelin spiral atlas of Rome: pp 57-58, 72 M 13-14, N 13-14, P 13-14). Metro line B: Colosseo. Tour: 2hr. The Colosseum stands in the heart of Ancient Rome and is built on an area of flat land at the end of the Roman Forum. It is surrounded by the Palatine Hill to the southwest, the Caelian Hill to the southeast and the Esquiline Hill, home to the Domus Aurea, to the north.

Neighbouring sights are described in the following chapters: FORO ROMANO-PALATINO; SAN GIOVANNI IN LATERANO; SANTA MARIA MAGGIORE-ESQUILINO; TERME DI CARACALLA.

Special Features

COLOSSEO★★★ (COLOSSEUM)

(&) *Open summer, 9am-1hr before dusk; winter, 9am-5.30pm (last admission 1hr before closing time). Closed 1 Jan and Christmas. €8 (combined ticket with Palatine Hill); €20 for a "Roma archeologica" card, valid for nine archaeological sites. ☎ 06 39 08 071; Fax 06 39 75 09 50; pierreci@pierreci.it*

Construction – Vespasian, the first of the Flavian Emperors, decided to devote a part of the huge area occupied by Nero's Domus Aurea to public entertainment. It was on the site of the lake in the grounds of Nero's house that Vespasian built the largest Roman amphitheatre in the world as a venue for the great spectacles which acquired a legendary reputation.

The **Flavian amphitheatre**, begun in AD 72, took the name of the Colosseum either because it stood near the huge **statue of Nero**, the *Colosseum*, or because of its own colossal dimensions (527m/1 728ft in circumference and 57m/187ft high). It is one of the most memorable reminders of Roman grandeur of that time. The position of the **statue of Nero** is marked by a few slabs of travertine stone lying on the ground. The Emperor's head was surrounded by rays like a sun. According to Suetonius, the statue was 36m/120ft high.

Circuses – Originally they held a religious significance for the Romans and constituted a rite intended to maintain good relations between the city and the gods. For many years the spectators attended bare-headed, as at a sacrifice. Suetonius, the Emperors' biographer, reproached Tiberius strongly for disliking the spectacle. The Colosseum, though still incomplete, was inaugurated in AD 80 by Titus, Vespasian's son. The spectacle he organised on this occasion lasted 100 days. The racing and the duels between gladiators were followed by bouts between men and wild animals: 5 000 animals died. Even naval engagements were re-enacted in the flooded arena. In 249, to celebrate the millennium of the founding of Rome, 1 000 pairs of gladiators met in combat; 32 elephants, a dozen tigers and over 50 lions, brought from the Imperial provinces, were killed.

The spectacle usually lasted from dawn to dusk. Some were very cruel and caused the arena to be covered in blood. Others, such as the presentation of wild animals, were like modern circus acts. Contrary to popular belief, Christians were never martyred in the Colosseum.

The last days of the Colosseum – Gladiatorial duels were banned in 404 by the Emperor Honorius. Wild animal fights disappeared in the 6C. In the 13C the Frangipani family turned the Colosseum into a fortress, which then passed to the Annibaldi. It was, however, in the 15C that the building suffered its greatest damage: it literally became a quarry and the huge blocks of travertine were taken for the construction of Palazzo Venezia, Palazzo della Cancelleria and St Peter's Basilica. Benedict XIV put an end to the quarrying in the 18C by consecrating the building to the Christian martyrs who were thought to have perished there. The Stations of the Cross were set up round the arena.

According to custom one should stand before the Colosseum, massive in its imperturbability, and in Byron's well-known words quote the prophecy made early in the 8C by the Venerable Bede, an English monk and historian:

"While stands the Colosseum, Rome shall stand;
When falls the Colosseum, Rome shall fall;
And when Rome falls, also the world."

Tour

The whole construction consists of three tiers of arcades supported on engaged columns, Doric on the ground floor, Ionic on the first and Corinthian on the second, surmounted by a wall divided into sections by regularly spaced engaged pilasters which alternate with small recesses. In Domitian's time the flat wall spaces were decorated with bronze shields. The projections supported wooden poles, inserted through holes in the upper cornice; the poles carried a linen awning which could be extended over the amphitheatre to protect the spectators from sun or rain. The job of putting up the awning, which was made more difficult by the wind, was entrusted to the sailors of Misenus's fleet.

The Colosseum

The huge blocks of travertine, which were never covered in marble, were originally held together with metal tenons; these were removed in the Middle Ages, although the sockets are still visible. The blocks of stone were brought from the quarries at Albulae, near Tivoli, along specially built roads, 6m/20ft wide. The spectators entered the amphitheatre through entrances numbered to corres-

pond with the entrance number which appeared on their ticket *(tessera)* and made their way to their seats through vaulted passages and stairways decorated with stuccowork.

Terraces – The construction is a rounded oval (188m/617ft and 156m/512ft on the axes). In the middle of the longer sides were the seats reserved for the Emperor and his suite *(north)* and for the Prefect of Rome and the magistrates *(south)*.

The *cavea,* the terraces for the spectators, began 4m/13ft above the arena. First came the *podium,* a terrace protected by a balustrade and reserved for the marble seats of the important spectators. Then came three series of terraces, separated from one another by passages and divided by sloping corridors *(vomitoria)* down which the multitude poured out after the show. Places were allotted according to social station. The women sat at the top under a colonnade; the slaves stood on the terrace supported by the colonnade. In all there were probably about 45 000 seats and standing space for 5 000.

The gladiators, dressed in purple and gold, entered through doors at either end of the longer axis. Marching in ranks, they toured the arena and then halted before the Emperor. With right arm raised they pronounced the formula: *Ave, Imperator, morituri te salutant* ("Hail, Emperor, those who are about to die salute thee").

During excavations the floor of the arena where the spectacle took place disappeared, revealing the underground warren where the wild animals waited before being brought to the surface by a system of ramps and lifts, for the pleasure of the assembled crowd. "This degraded people clamours with covetous anxiety for only two things in the world, bread and circuses," said Juvenal at the end of the 1C.

ARCO DI TRIONFO DI COSTANTINO★★★ (ARCH OF CONSTANTINE)

At the height of the tourist season it is sometimes difficult to come close to the arch. Such is its fame that anyone merely passing through Rome comes to see it. This magnificent construction, with its three arches, was built in 315 by the Senate and the Roman people three years after Constantine's victory over his rival Maxentius at the Milvian Bridge *(see MONTE MARIO, p 220)*. Like the Colosseum it was incorporated into the medieval fortifications. It was first restored in the 18C and changed to its present state in 1804. The proportions are harmonious. The abundant decoration was not all 4C work. Many of the sculptures were taken from 2C monuments (by Trajan, Hadrian and Marcus Aurelius) and reused.

North face

The statues of four Dacian prisoners on the upper storey belonged to a monument erected in honour of Trajan (98-117). The way in which they are set up on a huge base above the entablature is characteristic of 4C taste. The four low reliefs between the statues date from the 2C (a further three are part of the collection of the Musei Capitolini); they belonged to monuments set up in honour of the Emperor Marcus Aurelius. From left to right they represent: Marcus Aurelius being greeted by a personification of Via Flaminia on his return to Rome in 174 after fighting in Germany; his triumph; distribution of bread and money to the people; interrogation of a royal prisoner.

The four medallions come from a monument to Hadrian (117-138). The subjects are hunting, a sport of Oriental origin to which Hadrian was particularly partial, and sacrifices: *(from left to right)* wild boar hunting and a sacrifice to Apollo; lion hunting and a sacrifice to Hercules, who is wearing a lion skin.

The other sculptures, which date from the 4C, illustrate the reign of Constantine.

South face

The design is identical to that on the north face. At the top are four low reliefs belonging to the same series as those in the Musei Capitolini and on the other side of the arch; on the left, two incidents in the wars of Marcus Aurelius; on the right, the Emperor addresses his army beside a sacrificial ceremony (below are the animals being led to the sacrifice).

The four medallions (which are damaged) show *(from left to right)* the hunt moving off and a sacrifice to Silvanus, god of the forest; bear hunting and a sacrifice to Diana, goddess and huntress par excellence.

"Meta Sudans"

Only the site now remains of this fountain which was built by Titus and repaired by Constantine. It took the form of a cone of porous stone oozing water. What remained of it was demolished in 1936.

Walking About

Go to Via di S. Giovanni on the east side of the Colosseum.

The ruins on the north side of the street may have belonged to the **Ludus Magnus**, a gymnasium built by Domitian for training gladiators.

Proceed north up Via N. Salvi and Via di Terme di Tito. Turn left into Via Eudossiana to reach Piazza San Pietro in Vincoli.

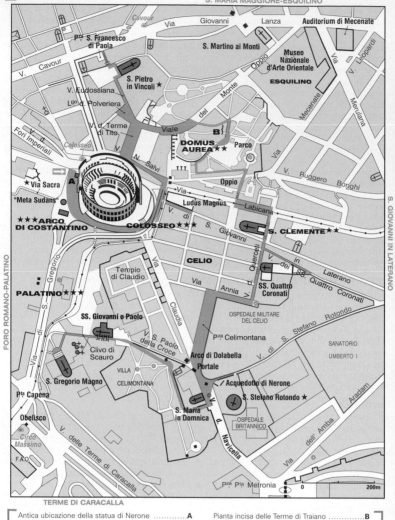

Antica ubicazione della statua di Nerone ....A   Pianta incisa delle Terme di Traiano ....B

San Pietro in Vincoli★ (St Peter in Chains)

The church was consecrated in the 5C by Sixtus III (432-40) although it was probably built on a much older construction. During the Renaissance the cardinals of
the **della Rovere** family were the incumbents: Francesco, who became Pope
Sixtus IV (1471-84), and then Giuliano, who became Julius II (1503-13), had it
restored.

The church is one of the chief tourist attractions in Rome, as it contains the
famous *Moses* by Michelangelo. It also attracts pilgrims who come to venerate the
chains which bound St Peter.

In 1475 Cardinal Giuliano della Rovere added the porch, which would be quite
elegant if an upper storey had not been added in the 16C.

The broad interior is divided into a nave and two aisles by two rows of Doric
marble columns, beautiful in their solemn austerity. The medieval decor was
altered in the 17C and 18C: the nave was vaulted and painted with frescoes.

On the left of the main door is the tomb of Antonio and Piero Pollaiuolo, famous
Renaissance artists from Florence.

Mausoleo di Giulio II (Julius II's Mausoleum) – This monument occasioned the
meeting of two of the most powerful personalities of the Renaissance: **Julius II**
and **Michelangelo**. The Pope, with his unquenchable appetite for grandeur, conceived the idea of a tomb of such splendour that it would reflect the glory of his
Pontificate for ever. In 1505 he summoned Michelangelo from Florence to assist
in the project. The tomb was to be placed in the centre of St Peter's Basilica, three
storeys high, with 40 huge statues, bronze low reliefs, surmounted by the sarcophagus. Michelangelo left for Carrara where he spent eight months choosing the
blocks of marble from which this superhuman work was to be created. While there
he dreamed of sculpting a single gigantic figure out of the mountain of marble. He

returned to Rome to the indifference of the Pope, who now swore only by Bramante. Michelangelo returned to Florence hurt. After Julius II's death in 1513 the project for his tomb declined steadily; Michelangelo sculpted only the *Slaves* (in Florence and Paris) and the *Moses*; he began the statues of the daughters of Laban, Leah and Rachel, but left the mausoleum itself to his pupils.

Moses*** – **Pope Paul III** grew tired of seeing Michelangelo working on the tomb of Julius II and, being anxious for him to start as soon as possible on the *Last Judgement* in the Sistine Chapel, he went one day to see the sculptor at work. There, in front of the *Moses*, one of his cardinals remarked with great diplomacy that the statue was so beautiful that it alone would suffice to honour the Pope's grave.

The authoritative attitude of the huge seated figure is enhanced by the steady gaze of the eyes.

St Peter's Chains – The chains are displayed in the *confessio* beneath the chancel. Originally there were two chains: one which had bound the Apostle in Jerusalem, the other in Rome. The legend of the miraculous joining of the two chains arose in the 13C.

Moses by *Michelangelo*

Crypt – *Not open to the public.* The crypt is visible through the grill in the *confessio* (beneath the high altar). A fine 4C sarcophagus conserves the relics of the Maccabees, seven brothers whose martyrdom is recounted in the Old Testament.

On leaving the church take the covered passage (right) which leads to Piazza San Francesco di Paola.

The steps are dominated by what used to be the Borgia Palace (attractive 16C loggia); it was the residence of Vannozza Caetani, mother of Caesar and Lucrezia Borgia, the children of Pope Alexander VI.

Return via Piazza San Pietro in Vincoli to Via Eudossiana which leads into Viale del Monte Oppio.

Parco del Colle Oppio contains the relics of **Trajan's Baths** (Terme di Traiano). The immense palace built by Nero, known as the **Domus Aurea**, once stood here *(see "Worth a Visit" below).*

Walk south along Via Labicana and then turn right towards San Clemente.

BASILICA DI SAN CLEMENTE**

The church was founded in the 4C in a private house belonging to a Christian *(titulus)* and was immediately dedicated to St Clement, the fourth Pope. It is, therefore, one of the oldest Roman basilicas. It was ruined in 1084 but rebuilt on the same site by Paschal II in 1108.

Upper basilica

The main entrance through an atrium shows the simple austerity of medieval buildings *(usual entrance into south aisle from Via di S. Giovanni in Laterano).*

THE SAD END OF AN ETRUSCAN KING
The modern flight of steps leading up to Piazza San Francesco di Paola covers a site linked with the legendary history of early Rome, when the city was administered by Etruscan kings. King **Servius Tullius's** daughter Tullia was married to **Tarquin**. Devoured by ambition, she incited her husband to unseat her father, who, wounded in a struggle in the old Curia fomented by his son-in-law, died in the street linking Suburra to the Esquiline, which followed the line of the present steps. Seven centuries later Livy tells in his history of Rome how Tullia, led astray by her husband's fury, "drove her chariot over her father's body"; the street was then called Vicus Scelaratus (Crime Street).

MONTE CELIO (Caelian Hill)
The Caelian is the greenest and most pleasant of the seven hills of Rome. It was incorporated into the city in the 7C BC: when the city of Alba broke the peace treaty which had united it with Rome following the combat between the Horatii and Curiatii, King Tullus Hostilius captured the rebellious city and transferred its population to the Caelian Hill. It was continuously inhabited until the 11C, when the Investiture Controversy brought war to Rome. In 1084 the army of Robert Guiscard "liberated" the Papal capital from the German troops but caused terrible devastation. Since then there has been little rebuilding on the Caelian Hill.

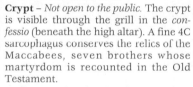

Interior of the Basilica di San Clemente

The interior has preserved its 12C basilica plan with a nave and two aisles divided by Ancient columns taken from a variety of sources. The unity of style, however, has been broken by the addition of Baroque stucco decorations and 18C alterations (ceiling and wall frescoes). The marble furnishings are particularly remarkable: in the *schola cantorum* **(1)** where the choristers sang, the sober *ambones*, where the Epistle and Gospel were read, and the Paschal candlestick are very fine 12C work; the screen separating the *schola cantorum* from the chancel belonged to the early Church and dates from the 6C. The **Cosmati** floor (12C) is one of the best preserved in Rome.

Apse Mosaic★★★ – This composition with its dazzling colours dates from the 12C. The richness of the symbolism is enhanced by the diversity and beauty of the style.

At the top of the apse, against a background of ornamental foliage interspersed with small decorative objects in the manner of the mosaicists of the early centuries, is an illustration of the Crucifixion: on the cross itself are 12 doves symbolising the Apostles, flanked by the Virgin and St John. Above is Paradise, shown in irridescent colours *(fan-shaped)* with the hand of God the Father holding out the crown to his Son. Below the cross are stags coming to quench their thirst (symbolising candidates for baptism), while Humanity gets on with its work.

Lower down in the apse is a frieze of sheep leaving the cities of Jerusalem and Bethlehem, symbols for the Old and New Testaments, and heading towards a distant prospect to adore the Lamb. Above the chancel arch the style is influenced by Byzantine art. The Prophets, Jeremiah and Isaiah (above the two towns), proclaim the triumph of God, shown as Christ surrounded by the symbols of the Evangelists. Between Christ and the Prophets are the martyrs: St Clement with his boat is accompanied by St Peter *(right)*; St Lawrence with his grill is accompanied by St Paul *(left)*.

Cappella di Santa Caterina (St Catherine's Chapel) **(2)** – The decorative **frescoes★** by **Masolino da Panicale** (1383-1447) combine a taste for the attitudes, thin faces and subtle colours of the Primitives with the early Renaissance search for well-defined space: consider the architectural decor in the Annunciation scene above the entrance arcade.

The scene to the left of the arcade shows St Christopher carrying Jesus; in the chapel are scenes from the life of St Catherine of Alexandria *(left wall)*, the Crucifixion *(end wall)* and scenes from the life of St Ambrose *(right wall – damaged)*.

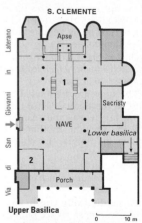

Upper Basilica

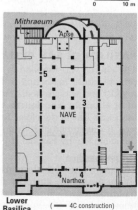

Lower Basilica (▬ 4C construction)

Lower Basilica

Open 9am-12.30pm and 3-6pm, Sun and public holidays, 10am-12.30pm and 3-6pm. Closed Christmas. €3. ☎ 06 70 45 10 18.

From the north aisle steps lead down to the lower basilica (4C).

This basilica consists of a narthex, a nave and two aisles and an apse. The upper basilica is built over the nave and south aisle of the lower one; a wall supporting the upper construction **(3)** divides the lower church into four.

Frescoes★ – Some of these **(4)** date from the 11C and 12C; others are older (9C). Those in the nave **(5)**, which are notable for their good state of preservation and their lively scenes, illustrate the legend of Sisinius, Prefect of Rome: he went to arrest his wife, who was attending a clandestine Mass celebrated by Pope Clement, but was struck blind in the presence of the holy man; above this scene his servants, also blinded, are carrying off a column thinking it to be his wife.

The figures are accompanied by sentences spoken by the people depicted in the frescoes; the language used is occasionally quite colourful. They are, perhaps, the first example in history of the comic strip! Even more important is the fact that this is an extremely rare example in writing of the linguistic transition from Classical to vulgar Latin.

Mithraeum – Beneath the 4C basilica are the remains of two houses built in Republican times. The house beneath the apse was converted in the 3C into a *mithraeum*, a small temple for the cult of the god **Mithras**. Ancient steps lead down to the mithraeum, which is well preserved, with two parallel stone benches where the initiates sat. A statue of the god was placed at the far end; in the centre is the altar showing the god cutting the throat of the bull while the dog, the serpent and the scorpion, symbols of evil, try to prevent the sacrifice which releases life-giving forces.

Take Via dei SS. Quattro Coronati.

SANTI QUATTRO CORONATI

In the Middle Ages the church of the **Four Crowned Saints** was part of a fortress which protected the Papal Lateran Palace against attack, a constant threat, from the strongholds of the noble families on the Palatine and in the Colosseum.

The Early Christian Church (4C) erected by Leo IV (847-55) lasted until 1084, when it was sacked and left in ruins by Robert Guiscard's troops. Paschal II (1099-1118) built a much smaller church, shorter and without side aisles. From the 12C to the 15C it belonged to Benedictine monks, but in the 16C the whole building passed to a community of Augustinian nuns.

Neither archaeologists nor historians have been able to identify the four saints to whom the church is dedicated.

The story of four martyred soldiers is mixed up with the story of five sculptors martyred in Pannonia (western Hungary). According to a list of martyrs drawn up by Leo IV, their remains were all placed in the crypt of this church.

Tour

The door beneath the tower, which served as a belfry in the 9C, leads into an outer courtyard. The wall opposite the entrance was the eastern façade of the early church. In the inner courtyard on the right are the columns which separated the nave and north aisle, now incorporated into a wall.

The **interior** of the church is as Paschal II built it. The space taken up by the nave and aisles corresponds to the width of the nave only in the early church. This makes the apse seem abnormally large. In the walls of the side aisles, as in the inner courtyard, the columns which separated the nave and aisles in the early church are incorporated in Paschal II's building. The wooden ceiling and the women's galleries *(matronea)* date from the 16C. In the 17C the apse was decorated with paintings and stuccoes depicting the history of the two groups of saints venerated in the church with a glory of saints in the vault.

Against the pillar on the left of the chancel arch is a 15C tabernacle, its fine carving picked out in gold. The surrounding paintings were added in the 17C.

The crypt goes back to the time of Leo IV. The sarcophagi of four martyrs were found in it, together with the silver reliquary containing St Sebastian's head.

Chiostro★ – These delightful **cloisters** were added in the 13C by the Benedictines. The Augustinian nuns replaced the simple roof with vaulting. The ornamental basin placed at the centre of the garden dates from the time of Paschal II. The charming simplicity of the small columns is offset by the capitals, which are decorated with waterlily leaves. In the eastern walk is St Barbara's Chapel, with three small apses, added by Leo IV (9C).

Cappella di San Silvestro★ – *Entrance beneath the portico in the inner courtyard. Key available in the convent entrance on the north side of the inner court.* The **chapel of St Sylvester** was built in the 13C and is decorated with a curious collection of frescoes, very naïve in execution. Beneath the figure of Christ, who is flanked by Mary, John the Baptist and the Apostles, is an illustration of the legend of Pope Sylvester (314-35): the leprosy of the Emperor Constantine (lying down and covered in sores), his being cured by the Pope, his baptism, the offering of his power to the Pope and the Pope's entry into Rome preceded by the Emperor.

FROM ARCO DI DOLABELLA TO SAN GREGORIO MAGNO

From Via dei SS. Quattro Coronati, walk south to Piazza Celimontana.

Arco di Dolabella

The **Arch of Dolabella** (1C), which stands at the narrow entrance to Via S. Paolo della Croce, carries the remains of **Nero's Aqueduct**, which supplied water to the Palatine Hill from the Porta Maggiore; further traces of the aqueduct are visible in Via di S. Stefano Rotondo and Via della Navicella, where one of the pillars is still standing.

Next to the Arch of Dolabella is an attractive **doorway**; it was decorated by Roman marble workers in the 13C with a mosaic showing Christ flanked by two figures, one black and one white, representing the Trinitarians, who devoted themselves to ransoming captives. There used to be a Trinitarian hospice next to the church of San Tomaso in Formis.

Santo Stefano Rotondo★

Visits by appointment only, in summer 9am-1pm and 3.30-6pm; rest of the year 9am-1pm and 1.50-4.20pm. Closed Mon mornings, Sun and public holidays. Donation welcome. ☎ 06 42 11 99 ; Fax 06 42 11 91 25.

The plan of this unusual round church was inspired by the church of the Holy Sepulchre in Jerusalem. It was built on the Caelian Hill in the late 4C to early 5C and dedicated to St Stephen (Stefano) by the Pope at the end of the 5C. The church, with its concentric aisle and two naves articulated by columns with Ionic capitals, and its marble and mosaic decoration, was originally one of the most opulent in Rome. By 1450 the church had lost its roof and for conservation purposes the outer aisle was demolished and walls built along the line of columns of the second circle. The diameter of the basilica was thus reduced from 65m/213ft to 40m/131ft. In the 16C Pomarancio (1530-92) painted the walls with 34 frescoes depicting scenes of martyrdom.

Santa Maria in Domnica

The **Navicella Fountain**, in front of the church porch, was created in 1931 out of a 16C sculpture, in imitation of an Ancient boat. This church, a favourite with the Romans for weddings, has retained the charm of a country church. It was founded in the 7C and greatly altered during the Renaissance. The façade and elegant, round-arched porch were restored at the request of Pope Leo X (1513-21) by Andrea Sansovino; the Pope's name is echoed by the lions on the keystones. The interior has retained certain 9C features: the basilica plan with a nave and two aisles, the columns with Antique capitals and the beautiful apsidal **mosaic★**, an example of the artistic renewal which took place in the reign of Paschal I (817-24). The artist has abandoned the Byzantine rigidity for a more lifelike representation: a current of air seems to stir the raiment of the angels, attractively grouped round the Virgin; similarly the Apostles above the arch are shown as men rather than in the symbolic form of lambs joyfully approaching Christ and his two angels. The green meadows of the background are dotted with brightly coloured flowers. Enthroned at the centre of the vault is the Virgin; Pope Paschal kneels at her feet, identified by the square nimbus of the living. The wooden coffered ceiling was commissioned by Ferdinando de Medici and dates from 1566; the patron's coat of arms can be seen in the middle of the ceiling, together with symbols depicting the Litany of the Virgin.

Walk through the Villa Celimontana Park (entrance next to the church) to Piazza dei Santi Giovanni e Paolo.

Basilica dei Santi Giovanni e Paolo

Domus antica (Ancient house) closed for restoration at the time of going to press. ☎ 06 70 05 745.

The quiet square is dominated by the porch and the bold campanile, both dating from the 12C. The campanile rests on the foundations of the **Temple of Claudius** (Tempio di Claudio), which are visible beneath the porch of the convent of the Passionist Fathers. Its history is similar to that of other buildings on the Caelian Hill: in the 4C a certain Pammachius established a church in a private house; it was sacked by Robert Guiscard's Normans in 1084 but rebuilt in the 12C.

The five arches above the porch and the gallery, which comprise the upper stage of the façade, belong to the original building.

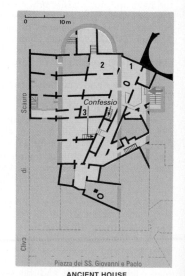

ANCIENT HOUSE
BENEATH THE BASILICA

Roman wall ▪ Excavations ▫
Substructure of the basilica ▪

Two handsome medieval marble lions guard the entrance portal. The **interior** dates almost entirely from the 18C. The main interest lies underground in the rooms of the **Ancient house★** where excavations have revealed traces of beautiful paintings *(access by steps at the west end of the north aisle)*.

At the foot of the stairs is a *nymphaeum* decorated with a marine fresco **(1)** dating from the 2C; its fine state of preservation is due to a coat of whitewash applied to cover up the pagan decor when the house became a Christian place of worship. There follows a suite of parallel rooms beneath the nave and the south aisle; one **(2)** contains traces of sophisticated paintings of adolescents and spirits among garlands of flowers, vine tendrils and birds. The introduction of Christianity is evoked in a vaulted room; one wall **(3)** shows a woman at prayer, her arms extended as if on the cross, surrounded by a decor of scrolls and animals. Two stairways lead to a small chapel, a *confessio*, built by Pammachius's family; the 4C frescoes depict the martyrdom of two Oriental saints whose relics, placed in the *confessio*, had led to the construction of the basilica.

Take Clivo di Scauro on the left of the church.

This tranquil, picturesque little street, built in the 2C BC by the Roman magistrate Scauro, passes under the medieval buttresses of the church. From here the apse of the basilica, the only one of its kind in Rome, can be admired. With its small columns it is reminiscent of Romanesque churches in Lombardy.

At the end of Clivo di Scauro, the road turns to the left and the church of San Gregorio Magno comes into view.

San Gregorio Magno (St Gregory the Great)

Open 9am-5pm. Closed Mon. Chapels: €2.58 ☎ 06 488 10 94; Fax 06 48 90 43 92.

Its imposing 17C façade rises at the top of a steep flight of steps framed by cypresses and umbrella pines. It was begun in 1633 by **GB Soria** for Cardinal Scipione Borghese (the eagle and dragon of his arms appear above the lower arches). Legend tells how in the 6C Gregory converted his house into a church and convent. It was from here that he sent a group of monks to evangelise England; among them were **St Augustine**, the first Archbishop of Canterbury, St Lawrence, St Melitas, St Justus and St Honorius who all succeeded him to the see of Canterbury. In the 12C the church was rebuilt and dedicated to the saintly Pope. The present building was restored in the 17C and 18C. Beyond the façade a four-sided portico at the top of the steps leads into the church.

In the chapel at the head of the south aisle stands Gregory's altar (15C), decorated with low reliefs depicting his legend. To the right of this chapel is a little cell containing an Ancient throne which passes for the one used by the saint.

At the head of the north aisle is a chapel decorated with 17C paintings; it contains a curious Virgin painted on the wall (13C) and, opposite, a 15C tabernacle.

At the top of the steps enter the small square to the left of the church.

In the small square there are three **chapels**, linked by a portico of Antique columns. Two were built in the 17C and the third, which is older, was restored at the same time. In St Sylvia's chapel *(right)*, dedicated to St Gregory's mother, the apse is painted with a concert of angels (1608) by Guido **Reni**. St Andrew's Chapel *(centre)* has the *Flagellation of St Andrew* (1608) painted by **Domenichino** and the saint going to his martyrdom by Guido Reni. The altarpiece is by Pomarancio and portrays the Virgin with St Andrew and St Gregory. St Barbara's Chapel *(left)* was first restored in the 17C. According to legend, the table in the centre was used by St Gregory to offer a meal to the poor; one day an angel came to sit with them, an event recorded in fresco.

Worth a Visit

Domus Aurea★★

Entrance in Viale Domus Aurea, behind the Colle Oppio gardens. The west wing of the building is still undergoing restoration and refurbishment. ⚑ Open 9am-7.45pm (last admission 1hr before closing time). Closed 1 Jan and Christmas. €5 + €1 compulsory booking fee. ☎ 06 39 08 071; Fax 06 39 75 09 50; pierreci@pierreci.it

The **Golden House** is the palace built by **Nero** after the fire in AD 64. The vestibule was on the Velia (where the Arch of Titus stands) and contained the famous statue of Nero; the rooms were on the Oppian Hill. In the hollow between, now occupied by the Colosseum, was a vast lake, and all around were gardens and vineyards, creating a truly rural environment. Inside the house "the dining-room ceilings were composed of movable ivory tiles pierced with holes so that flowers or perfume could be sprinkled on the guests below; the main dining room was circular and turned continually on its axis, day and night, like the world".

Nero committed suicide in AD 68; the Senate condemned him. The lake was drained and the Colosseum was erected on the site. Then the upper part of the house was razed and what remained was used as foundations for the Baths of Titus

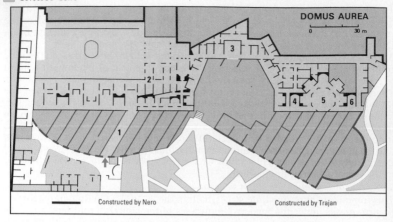

DOMUS AUREA

0   30 m

Constructed by Nero   Constructed by Trajan

and Trajan. The Golden House was not discovered until the Renaissance. Raphael and some of his fellow artists were very enthusiastic about the paintings they found: geometric designs, foliated scrolls, decorations with faces and animals. As the rooms decorated in this way were underground like caves or grottoes, the decorative motifs were called **grotesques**.

Tour – This residence, whose beautiful brick façade belonged to Trajan's Baths, was divided into two wings. The Imperial apartments were located in the left wing; the right wing housed the banqueting halls, galleries and libraries. The visit starts. in one of the side galleries **(1)**, built in front of Nero's house as a basement to Trajan's Baths, and continues through a series of rather dark rooms, one of which houses remains of the buildings destroyed by the fire of 64 **(2)**. The visitor then arrives at the Nymphaeum of Ulysses and Polyphemus and the Room of the Golden Vault **(3)**, both of which were decorated by the painter Fabullus with brilliantly coloured landscapes and mythological scenes. The visit continues along a number of corridors to the cryptoporticus which links the two wings of the palace; signatures of artists who had found their way into the ruins can be seen on the corridor ceiling. Just before the eastern wing of the building, the Room of Achilles **(4)** is decorated with friezes and garlands on the walls. The eastern wing houses the Octagonal Room **(5)**, in which the skilful architectural design of the house may be fully appreciated. The room is well lit by an opening in the ceiling and opens into a nymphaeum and four triclinia. The visit ends in the Room of Hector and Andromache **(6)**, where the Laocoön statue is thought to have been discovered in 1506 (now on display in the Vatican). According to art historians, the decorations of the vault evoke the marriage of Amphitrite and Poseidon.

EUR★

The EUR district (EUR stands for *Esposizione Universale di Roma*) is graced with monumental white marble buildings and wide avenues, and has changed little since its construction during the Fascist period. According to art historian Sylvia Pressouyre, in "a certain light, the district resembles the imaginary cities painted by Giorgio de Chirico", an image conjured up by the myriad examples of modern architecture here. Leisure options in this area include the hiring of pedalos on the lake or a pleasant stroll along the lake shore.

Location

Michelin map 38 or Michelin spiral atlas of Rome: pp 94-95 T 2, T 3, U 2, U 3, U 4, V 2 and V 3. Metro line B: EUR Palasport or EUR Fermi. Tour: about half a day, including visits to the museums. The sights described below do not follow any particular itinerary. This district is situated to the south of Rome, between the Via del Mare leading to Ostia to the west, and Via Laurentina to the east; it is intersected by Via Cristoforo Colombo.

The itinerary can be combined with a visit to OSTIA ANTICA by catching the Acotral train from Magliana Station (Metro line B: EUR-Magliana) or from Ostiense Station (Metro line B: Piramide).

Background

The origins of the district go back to 1937 when the Government conceived a grandiose project for a universal exhibition to be held in 1942 (the district was also called E42). The idea was to develop Rome along the motorway built in 1928 to link the city of Rome and Ostia. The contract was given to the architect Marcello Piacentini. Building began in 1939; on 10 June 1940 Italy entered the war allied to Germany and in 1941 work stopped. Following the bombing of Rome on 19 July 1943 and the fall of the Fascist Government, the scheme was abandoned.

Two events – Holy Year in 1950 and the Olympic Games in 1960 – brought it to the fore once again: in 1950 Via Cristoforo Colombo was opened linking Rome and the EUR. The Metro, which runs from Stazione Termini to the new district in less than a quarter of an hour, stimulated the building of an administrative and cultural centre, a business forum and residential accommodation.

The **Sports Palace**, by Marcello Piacentini and Pier Luigi Nervi, and the cycle racetrack were built for the Olympic Games.

Inspired by an obsession with size, the colossal white buildings of the actual EUR mean that it looks very much like the scheme proposed by the Fascists.

> ### WHERE TO EAT
>
> See "Where to Eat" in the Practical Points section at the beginning of the guide.
>
> ### ICE-CREAM PARLOURS
>
> **Giolitti-La Casina dei Laghi** – *Via Oceania 90* – ☏ *06 59 24 507 – Open 7.30am-midnight.* This famous *gelateria,* surrounded by the greenery of the small lake in the EUR district, serves delicious ice cream at outdoor tables.

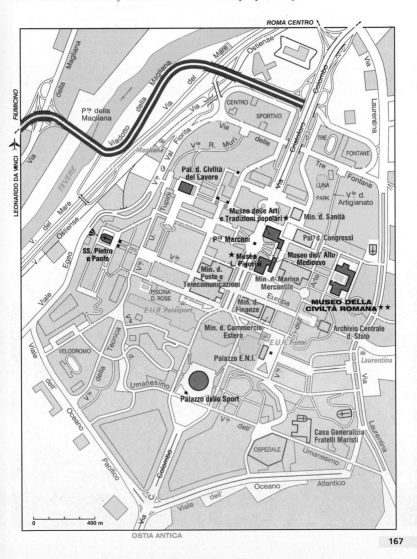

Worth a Visit

Museo della Civiltà Romana★★

⅏ (assisted visits). Open Tue-Sat, 9am-7pm; Sun and public holidays, 9am-2pm (last admission 30min before closing time). Closed Mon, 1 Jan, 1 May and Christmas. €4.13; no charge on 21 Apr. ☏ 06 59 26 135; www.comune.roma.it

The huge **Museum of Roman Civilisation** is housed in two buildings linked by a portico and illustrates, by means of reproductions, the history of Ancient Rome from the origins of the city to the end of the Empire. The many relief models, together with individual monuments, provide visitors with a concrete picture of the overall layout of the city, where only fragments of individual buildings remain today. The main attraction of the museum is the way it traces the development of a peasant people who founded an empire which has influenced the history of the whole world for more than a thousand years.

The exhibition opens with a large **model of Ancient Rome** (5C BC), showing the geographical area controlled by the city. The two hills of the Campidoglio are easily identified within the city walls, with the large Temple of Jupiter and the Arx (the citadel), along with the loop of the River Tiber and the island of Tiberina. At the foot of the two hills lies the area of the Roman Forum, demarcated to the south by the Palatine Hill. The Ponte Sublicio, the first major permanent bridge built during the reign of Ancus Martius (640-616 BC), spans the river.

Subsequent rooms display information relating to major events in the history of Rome, including reconstructions of battles and famous victories, and models which bring to life the well-known monuments of the city, such as the Colosseum, Domitian's Stadium (Stadio di Domiziano), and Hadrian's Villa. From Room XV onwards the exhibits concentrate on all aspects of Roman civilisation, including Christianity, the economy, public works, social life and entertainment.

Of particular interest is the model depicting the spiral of low-relief panels on **Trajan's Column** *(Room LI)*, which record Trajan's wars against the Dacians. Room XLVII displays the reconstruction of a small library.

> **MODEL OF ROME**
> The visit to the museum concludes with a superb 1:250 scale **model★★** of Rome at the time of Constantine (306-37), made by the architect Italo Gismondi in 1937. The model shows the city in all its glory and allows the visitor to identify its many monuments, some of which survive today and others which no longer exist.

Museo delle Arti e Tradizioni Popolari★ (Folk Museum)

Open daily (except Mon), 9am-6pm. Visitors are advised to phone and check opening times before visiting. Closed 1 Jan, 1 May and Christmas. €4. ☏ 06 59 26 797; Fax 06 59 11 848; popolari@arti.beniculturali.it

This beautiful museum introduces visitors to Italian folklore and traditions. Exhibits are grouped by theme and explore various aspects of everyday life, starting on the ground floor with a collection of old vehicles, including some fine Sicilian carriages and a cart for transporting grapes. To the left of the stairs, slightly out of view, is

Detail of the model of Rome

a beautiful Venetian **gondola**, a gift from the Venetian Republic to Queen Margherita of Savoy (1882). The folklore theme is continued in the other rooms, which house exhibits relating to peasant life, bread-making, stock farming, hunting, sailing and fishing. Domestic and social life is portrayed through a collection of betrothal gifts, wedding trousseaux and dowries; the theme of entertainment is represented by a display of musical instruments, puppets and marionettes.

Museo Preistorico Etnografico L. Pigorini★

 ♿ *Open 9am-8pm. €4. ☎ 06 54 95 22 38; Fax 06 54 95 23 10; www.pigorini.arti.beni-culturali.it*

The **Museum of Ethnography and Prehistory** houses one of the largest ethnographical collections in the world. At the entrance to the museum is a wooden pirogue dating from 5500 BC found on Lake Bracciano; information is provided on the history of a typical lakeside Neolithic village. The first floor houses ethnographical collections and temporary exhibitions held in the Salone delle Scienze. In addition to a section dedicated to the Americas, the rich **African Section** brings together more than 60 000 objects including weapons, utensils, costumes and religious articles. The **Oceanic Section** is subdivided according to theme; here visitors can admire various items for worship, masks, sculptures and paintings which depict the life and customs of the different peoples. A huge ceremonial canoe from the Trobriand Islands provides the focal point of the room. The third section of the first floor is soon to house collections from America and Asia.

The second floor is entirely dedicated to Italian prehistory and is divided into different sections examining the evolution of mankind. A large part of the exhibition explores the development of various cities in Europe, especially in Italy, from the Neolithic to the Iron Age, and includes explanations on cultural traditions, including the techniques used for the production of utensils and the use of funeral rites. The last room focuses on the increasing Eastern influence on the peninsula during the early Etruscan era (late-8C to mid-6C BC). The **Praenestina fibula**, which bears one of the oldest inscriptions in Latin, is of particular interest.

Museo dell'Alto Medioevo

 ♿ *Open 9am-2pm (last admission 1.30pm). Closed Mon, 1 Jan, 1 May and Christmas. €2. ☎ 06 54 22 81 99; Fax 06 54 22 81 30.*

The **Medieval Museum** contains exhibits covering the 5C to the 11C, as well as plans of Classical and Christian Rome.

Piazza Marconi

A huge obelisk in marble (sculpture finished in 1950) has been raised to the glory of the Italian physicist Guglielmo Marconi (1874-1937), inventor of wireless telegraphy.

Palazzo della Civiltà del Lavoro

The building, which is one of the most characteristic of the EUR, was designed in 1938 by three architects: Guerrini, La Padula and Romano. Devoid of capital or cornice to delight the eye, its stark mass is accentuated by the rows of superimposed arches.

The ground-floor arcade contains allegorical statues representing the various arts, symbols of the grandeur of Rome. The building houses several organisations connected with the improvement of working conditions.

The Palazzo della Civiltà del Lavoro, also known as the "Square Colosseum"

Santi Pietro e Paolo

This spectacular travertine church, dedicated to **St Peter and St Paul**, was built between 1937 and 1941 on the highest point in the EUR. Set among shrubs and flowers, its white mass dominates the whole district. The principal architect was Arnaldo Foschini. At the top of the steps stand two large statues of St Peter and St Paul. The Greek cross plan is stressed by the clean angles and sober lines. The dome, covered in little tiles overlapping like fish scales, rests on a drum pierced by *oculi*.

The main door, designed by Giovanni Prini (1877-1958), is made of bronze, ornamented with low reliefs illustrating the lives of St Peter and St Paul.

From the surrounding terrace, flanked by two porticos, there is a view of the suburbs of Rome.

Fontana di Trevi-Quirinale★★★

The Trevi Fountain, one of the most famous sights in Rome, has been immortalised in numerous films, including the American-produced *Three Coins in the Fountain* and Federico Fellini's *La Dolce Vita*. Nowadays the piazza around the fountain is crowded with souvenir sellers and tourists, yet the sight of this white marble monument lit up at night still takes the breath away, especially when it comes into view unexpectedly from one of the narrow streets surrounding the square. From the fountain, a short walk uphill leads to the Quirinal Hill, the highest in Rome. The piazza here has one of the best views in the city and is home to the President's palace, as well as to a number of fine palazzi and churches.

Location
Michelin map 38 or Michelin spiral atlas of Rome: pp 40-41 and 56-57 K 12-13, L 12-13. Metro line A: Barberini (500m/550yd from the Fontana di Trevi). Tour: 2hr 30min. This district is situated to the southwest of the Quirinal Hill, the most northerly of Rome's hills, and is bordered by Via del Corso to the west and Via del Tritone to the north.

Neighbouring sights are described in the following chapters: MONTECITORIO; PANTHEON; PIAZZA DI SPAGNA; PIAZZA VENEZIA; VIA VENETO.

Background

The name Quirinal is now synonymous with Italian politics, since the Quirinal Palace is the official residence of the President of the Republic.

The hill was the traditional home of the Sabines and took its name from one of their lesser-known gods, **Quirinus**, who, with Mars and Jupiter, formed the basis of Roman religion. It is thought that the god's name may have derived from the Sabine word *curi*, which meant spear. Although uncertainty surrounds his exact role and attributes, Quirinus is believed to have been a warrior god who, unlike Mars, was responsible for maintaining peace and order in the city. A legend identifies this god with the founder of Rome: during a solar eclipse, Romulus is said to have disappeared and been captured by the gods, who then transformed him into Quirinus. Until the end of the 19C only the fringes of the city reached the Quirinal; the Flavian Mausoleum (Mausoleo dei Flavi) was built there by Domitian (81-96); Caracalla built a temple to Serapis (the ruins survived until the Middle Ages); Constantine built a bathhouse which disappeared in the 17C.

Directory

WHERE TO EAT

See "Where to Eat" in the Practical Points section at the beginning of the guide.

ICE CREAM

Il Gelato di S. Crispino – *Via della Panetteria 42 – ☎ 06 67 93 924 – Open Wed-Mon, 11am-midnight.* The owners of this *gelateria*, considered to be one of the best in Rome, only make flavours they like themselves. Try the ice cream with honey, ginger and cinnamon, cream with Armagnac, liquorice, meringue with hazelnut or chocolate and cream with Pantelleria raisin wine.

SHOPPING

Becker & Musicò – *Via di S. Vincenzo 29 – ☎ 06 67 85 435 – Open 10am-7.30pm.* Becker & Musicò specialises in articles for smokers, and also has a workshop which makes wooden pipes from the white heath tree (*Erica arborea*).

Farmacia Pesci – *Piazza Fontana di Trevi 89 – ☎ 06 67 92 210 – Open Mon-Sat, 8am-7.30pm.* Rome's oldest pharmacy, dating back to the middle of the 16C, retains a number of its old features, including jars, documents and the huge structure which once separated the laboratory from the shop.

Fratelli Viganò – *Via Minghetti 7/8 – ☎ 06 67 95 147 – Open Mon-Sat, 10am-1pm and 5-7.30pm.* This shop is one of the oldest in the city and started as a hat shop. It now sells a wide range of men's clothing, as well as a selection of hats, including the genuine Panama.

Mel Bookstore – *Via Nazionale 254/255 – ☎ 06 48 85 405 – Open Mon-Sat, 9am-8pm; Sun, 10am-1.30pm and 4.30-8pm.* This bookshop is tastefully decorated in early-20C style and offers a wide selection of all kinds of books. There is a café on the top floor.

Piazza di Trevi, with the famous fountain in the foreground

Special Features

Fontana di Trevi★★★

This late Baroque fountain, one of the most famous monuments of Rome, is an impressive sight, made all the more striking by its position in a tiny piazza. The key to the work is given in two high-relief carvings: in 19 BC Agrippa decided to build a long canal (20km/13mi) to bring water to Rome *(left)*; the canal was called Acqua Vergine after a young virgin who revealed the spring to the Roman soldiers *(right)*. Repairs were made under Pope Nicholas V and Urban VIII. It was Clement XII who commissioned Nicolà Salvi (1732) to adorn the end of the canal with a fountain. Salvi's fountain fills the whole width of the façade which forms a backdrop to it and gives the impression of a commemorative arch. The fountain was completed 30 years later during the reign of Clement XIII. Salubrity and Abundance stand in the wings flanking the central figure, the Ocean, which rides in a chariot drawn by two sea horses and two tritons, and provides a photogenic spectacle for the faithful tourists, who continue to visit the piazza in order to throw two coins over their shoulders into the fountain as tradition demands: one coin to return to Rome and the other for the fulfilment of a wish.

Walking About

In front of the fountain, set slightly back from the square, stands the church dedicated to St Vincent and St Anastasius **(Santi Vincenzo e Anastasio)**, built in 1650 by Martino Longhi the Younger for Cardinal Mazarin. Detached columns, pediments, projections and recesses create an interplay of light and shade typical of Baroque art.

Vicolo Modelli to the side of the church leads to Piazza Scanderberg, home to the National Pasta Museum (see "Worth A Visit" below).

South of the church turn left into Via della Dataria which leads to Piazza del Quirinale.

Piazza del Quirinale★★

Lined by handsome palaces, adorned with an obelisk and ancient statues and refreshed by a fountain, the square typifies Roman elegance.

Its embellishment was begun by Sixtus V (1585-90), who transferred the statues of the **Dioscuri** from Contantine's Baths nearby; they are fine Roman copies of original Greek works. Some two centuries later, Pius VI moved them slightly apart to make room for one of the obelisks which had stood at the entrance to Augustus's mausoleum.

Finally Pius VII (1800-23) completed the group with a handsome Antique basin which had served as a water trough when the Forum was known as Campo Vaccino and used for grazing cows.

Palazzo del Quirinale★★

(&) *Open Sun, 8.30am-12.30pm. Closed 7 Jan, Easter, 15 Apr, 22 Jul-2 Sept, 23 and 30 Dec. €5.* ☎ *06 46 99 25 68; Fax 06 46 99 23 58.*

Palazzo del Quirinale

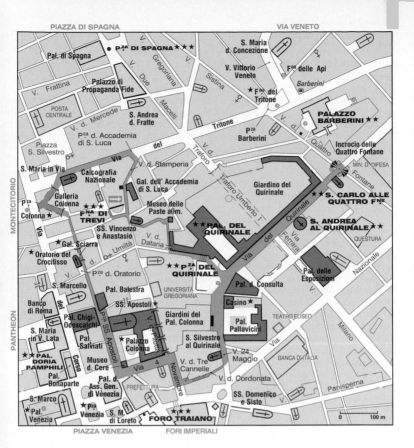

The **Quirinal Palace** is the work of some of the finest architects of the Counter Reformation and the Baroque period. It was commissioned in 1573 by Gregory XIII from Martino Longhi the Elder as a summer residence for the Popes. Sixtus V commissioned Ottaviano Mascherino, Domenico Fontana and Flaminio Ponzio. Under Paul V Carlo **Maderno** added the monumental door with its two half-reclining statues of St Peter and St Paul. **Bernini** was brought in by Alexander VII. The palace was completed by Ferdinando Fuga for Clement XII.

Interior – The courtyard of the presidential palace, guarded by sentries who must be of a certain height (1.82m/6ft 3in), leads to the grand staircase. The fresco of Christ (*above the arch*) by **Melozzo da Forlì** (1438-94) was originally part of the *Ascension* painted on the apse of the church of the Holy Apostles. The tour includes a succession of rooms, all sumptuously decorated, the chapel painted by Guido **Reni** (Annunciation on the altar piece), and the Pauline Chapel, which is decorated with 17C stucco.

Palazzo della Consultà

The **façade★** is by **Ferdinando Fuga** (18C) who often used Baroque motifs. The three doorways, their pediments crowded with statues and sculptures, and the coat of arms of Clement XII, supported by a swarm of cherubs, make a lively contrast with the bare façade of the Quirinal Palace. This is now the seat of the Constitutional Court. *Take Via del Quirinale beside the palace.*

NAPOLEONIC STORM

In 1808 **Napoleon** was declared king of Italy and his brother Joseph king of Naples, but Pius VII, as head of the Papal States, refused to apply an economic blockade or to recognise any king other than Ferdinand IV of Naples. On 2 February General Miollis was ordered to enter Rome with 8 000 French soldiers to bring His Holiness to reason. Pius VII shut himself up in the Quirinal Palace.

In Vienna, on the evening of 17 May 1809, Napoleon wiped the Papal States off the map of Europe. Pius VII issued a Bull of Excommunication: "Let sovereigns learn once and for all that they are subject by the law of Christ to our throne and our commands." At dawn several French soldiers were found dead in the streets of Rome. On 7 July 1809 French troops broke down the door of the palace. The Pope, in cape and stole, awaited them. Despite their great respect for the Pope the soldiers took him away to spend the rest of the Napoleonic era at Fontainebleau. Thus Napoleon rendered "unto Caesar the things that are Caesar's and unto God the things that are God's".

The east wing of the palace, overlooking Via del Quirinale, was built in the 17C and 18C.

Sant'Andrea al Quirinale★★

Usually open Wed-Fri, 8am-noon and 4-7pm; closed Aug. Telephone for details. Donations welcome. ☎ 06 48 90 31 87; Fax 06 48 71 203.

The church of St Andrew on the Quirinal by **Bernini** and the church of St Charles by the Four Fountains (San Carlo alle Quattro Fontane) by Borromini express with unusual clarity the genius of two artists whose styles were diametrically opposed. The façade of the former, which opens into a semicircular atrium, bears a crown showing the arms of Cardinal Camillo Pamphili, Innocent X's nephew, who commissioned the church in 1658. It was completed in 1678.

Interior★★ – The interior, as in San Carlo, is elliptical but oriented on the shorter axis and defined by the entrance and the magnificent choir stalls. To some extent the smaller dimensions of the building are cunningly masked. The deep rectangular side chapels and the impression of depth created by the false portico in front of the high altar give a feeling of spaciousness, which helps to disguise the true proportions of the church. Bernini's skilful use of coloured marble, gilding and stucco figures has created a rich and beautiful decor.

The second chapel on the right contains three paintings by Baciccia (1639-1709); the *Crucifixion of St Andrew* by Jacques Courtois (1621-76), known as the Burgundian, can be admired in the apse. The gilt *Glory* by Raggi over the high altar, which is lit from above, is a reminder that Bernini had a great liking for theatricality. In a chapel to the left **(1)** note the painting by Carlo Maratta (1625-1713) showing the Virgin appearing to St Stanislas.

St Stanislas's Rooms (Camere di San Stanislao) **(2)** *(entered from the fourth chapel on the right; to visit apply to the sacristan)* contain a recumbent statue of the saint in polychrome marble by Pierre Legros (1629-1714).

In the **sacristy (3)** there is a beautiful vault in *trompe l'oeil*.

Continue along Via del Quirinale.

San Carlo alle Quattro Fontane★★

Open 10am-1pm and 3-5pm; Sat, 10am-1pm. Closed Sun and public holidays. No charge. ☎/Fax 06 48 83 261.

The **church of St Charles at the Four Fountains**, which is also known as San Carlino, is probably the best expression of Borromini's creative genius. Commissioned in 1638, it was his first known work. The façade, which was added some 30 years later, was his last; it was unfinished when he committed suicide in 1667. It reveals the torment of a man whose art was full of contradictory statements: every curve is followed by a counter curve (in particular the façade and the cornices). A convex shrine (below the medallion) is set against the central concave section of the upper storey.

The concave surfaces of the belfry and the lantern on the dome also express, in architectural terms, Borromini's contrary spirit.

Interior★★ – The form is that of an ellipse oriented on the longer axis. The movement is supplied by the alternating concave and convex surfaces of the walls themselves. The

The unusual ceiling of San Carlo alle Quattro Fontane

174

confined space – no larger, it is said, than one of the pillars supporting the dome of St Peter's – is perfectly suited to the architect's distinctive style. It is affected and austere, bizarre and elegant and quite out of sympathy with the Baroque taste for sheer size. The intricately designed coffering in the dome is surmounted by a lantern harbouring the Holy Ghost.

Cloisters★ – Borromini's cloisters – two orders of Doric columns and slightly convex canted corners – are perfectly proportioned.

Continue to the crossroads with Via delle Quattro Fontane.

Incrocio delle Quattro Fontane

The **Four Fountains crossroads** was created by Sixtus V (1585-90) whose efforts at town planning introduced more alterations to Rome than the city had known since the end of the Roman Empire. His aim was to link the main basilicas and the main districts by means of broad straight roads. The creation of these four straight streets opened up **views★** of the obelisks in front of the Trinità dei Monti *(west)*, the Porta Pia *(north)*, the west end of Santa Maria Maggiore in Piazza dell'Esquilino *(east)* and in Piazza del Quirinale *(south)*. The corners of the crossroads are canted to make room for four fountains decorated with statues (16C).

To get to the Palazzo delle Esposizioni, return to Via del Quirinale and turn left onto Via Ferrara.

Palazzo delle Esposizioni

Temporary exhibitions, cinema and theatre productions. Entrances at Via Nazionale 194 and Via Milano 9a. Café and restaurant. The **Exhibition Hall**, which was opened in 1883, was designed by the architect Pio Piancentini. The main prospect is neo-Classical and its large central arch and two side entrances are reminiscent of a commemorative arch. It was the first complex in Rome built to house art and other exhibitions.

The palace was restructured by the architect C Dardi who, although not exactly destroying the original design, installed new technical and lighting systems and new facilities: conference room and cinema for 200 people, a 130-seat theatre, cafeteria, bookshop and a restaurant on the top floor. As well as being the venue for the various exhibitions, film shows and plays that are held there, the palace has become a popular meeting place.

Return to Piazza del Quirinale and take Via 24 Maggio.

Palazzo Pallavicini

The courtyard, with its palm trees, laurels, pines and holm oaks, is lined on two sides by the palace built in 1603 by Cardinal Scipio Borghese, Paul V's nephew, more or less on the site of Constantine's Baths.

Just inside the main gates stands the **Casino★** opening onto a terrace. This charming 17C pavilion is famous for the **Aurora fresco** painted on the ceiling by Guido Reni, a pupil of the Carracci. This is a fine example of the academic Classical style. The goddess is shown opening the gates of heaven to the sun's chariot. *Open 9am-noon, by appointment only. Contact Amministrazione Pallavicini, Viale Mazzarino 14, 00184 Roma, at least three weeks in advance. ☎ 06 48 14 344; Fax 06 47 42 615.*

On the right of the street *(Via 24 Maggio)* the impressive doorway approached by a flight of steps is the entrance to the **garden of the Palazzo Colonna** *(see below)*.

San Silvestro al Quirinale

Entrance to the left of the façade. Closed for restoration at the time of going to press. ☎ 06 67 90 240. The façade of the church of **St Sylvester on the Quirinal** is purely decorative; it was constructed in the 19C to disguise the difference in level between the church and the street. The latter had been widened and lowered and the church itself truncated.

The interior decor is surprisingly rich. The coffered ceiling, which dates from the 16C, was restored in the 19C. Among the Mannerist decorations are some paintings in the **first chapel** on the left by Polidoro da Caravaggio and Maturino da Firenze *(see PIAZZA NAVONA: Via della Maschera d'Oro, p 234)*. The floor has been paved with fragments of ceramic floor tiles which used to decorate the Raphael Loggia in the Vatican.

In the left arm of the transept is a beautiful octagonal domed **chapel★**: Domenichino painted the medallions in the pendentives (1628); the stucco statues of Mary Magdalene *(left of the entrance)* and St John *(left of the chancel)* were sculpted at the same time by Alessandro Algardi.

The **chancel** vault is decorated with a late-16C fresco on a beautiful grey base. To the left of the chancel is a door opening onto a quiet terrace where Vittoria Colonna, who had composed poems to the glory of her dead husband, spent many hours in the company of scholars and holy men. Sometimes Michelangelo came to join them. He developed a great affection for this noble and cultivated lady and was present at her death.

Turn right into Via della Cordonata and right again into Via 4 Novembre.

Palazzo Colonna

The palace dates from the 15C but was rebuilt in 1730. It is linked to its gardens by four arches spanning the Via Pilotta. **Pope Martin V** (1417-31), a member of the Colonna family, took up residence here when he returned to Rome after the Great Schism of the West. The **picture gallery**, a suite of richly furnished rooms, contains many 15C-18C paintings *(see "Worth a Visit" below)*.

Take Via 4 Novembre west; turn left into Piazza Santi Apostoli.

In the square at n° 67 is the **Museo delle Cere** (Waxworks Museum). ☼ *Open 9am-8pm (Jul and Aug, 11pm). €5. ☎ 06 67 96 482; Fax 06 67 81 125.*

Basilica dei Santi Dodici Apostoli★ (Basilica of the Twelve Holy Apostles)

Open 7.30am-noon and 4-7pm. ☎ 06 69 95 71 or 06 67 94 085.

The church goes back to the 6C when a basilica on the site was dedicated by Popes Pelagius I and John III to the Apostles Philip and James the Less, whose relics they had received.

The greatest alterations were carried out by Sixtus IV (1471-84), of which only the lower part of the porch remains. The loggia above the porch was closed with rectangular windows in the Baroque era and topped with a balustrade and statues. The upper section is a 19C neo-Classical composition.

In the porch, guarding the entrance, are three lions from the medieval building. On the nave vault Baciccia painted the *Triumph of the Franciscan Order* (1706). A few years earlier this artist had painted his masterpiece on the ceiling of the Gesù Church.

The chancel contains the Renaissance tombs of the two Riario cardinals, Pietro and Raffaele, who helped their uncle, Sixtus IV, to reconstruct the church: **Cardinal Pietro Riario's tomb★** *(left)* is the result of three masters of funerary art working in collaboration: Andrea Bregno, Mino da Fiesole and Giovanni Dalmata; Raffaele's tomb *(right)* is inspired by Michelangelo's favourite designs. On the chancel ceiling Giovanni Odazzi (18C) has achieved a fine *trompe l'oeil* effect with the Fallen Angels.

The **monument to Clement XIV** at the top of the left aisle is the first work executed in Rome by the neo-Classical sculptor Antonio Canova (1787).

Palazzo Chigi-Odescalchi

The palace, which stands in front of the basilica of the Holy Apostles, was redesigned by **Bernini** when the Chigi family acquired it in 1664. The master's involvement in the project laid down rules which were to have a great influence on the architecture of central and northern Europe.

Palazzo Balestra

At the end of the square stands a Baroque palace (now occupied by the Banco di Roma) where the **Stuarts**, the royal family of Scotland and England, lived in exile. Originally known as Palazzo Muti since it was built in 1644 for the Muti-Papazzuri family, it was given by Clement XI to James Stuart, the Old Pretender, in 1719, when he married Maria Clementina Sobieska of Poland. His two sons, Charles Edward, the Young Pretender, and Henry, Cardinal of York, were born in the palace and "Bonnie Prince Charlie" returned to die there in 1788.

Oratorio del Crocifisso★ (Oratory of the Crucifix)

The building's construction was entrusted to Tommaso dei Cavalieri, a young Roman noble, who inspired a warm affection in Michelangelo yet chose as his adviser one of Michelangelo's bitterest enemies, Nanni di Baccio Bigio. The façade was designed by Giacomo della Porta in 1561. It marked the beginning of a brilliant career which led to his being in charge of work on the Capitol and at St Peter's (1573). The façade, which was finished in 1568 and which harmonises so well with the square it overlooks, bears traces of Michelangelo's teaching (the pediments over the recesses flanking the door). The interior is decorated with a series of frescoes by Mannerist artists. On the reverse side of the façade is the history of the Confraternity of the Crucifix of St Marcellus. The wall paintings, which are reminiscent of theatre decor, are by Giovanni de' Vecchi, Pomarancio and Cesare Nebbia and illustrate the story of the Cross.

Take the alley on the right of the oratory.

The **Galleria Sciarra★**, with its metal framework, glass canopy and fine paintings, is a highly original late-19C arcade.

Continue north along Via di Santa Maria in Via.

Galleria Colonna

This arcade was built in 1923 linking Via di Santa Maria in Via with Via del Corso and Piazza Colonna.

Santa Maria in Via

A miracle led to the foundation of St Mary's Church: an image of the Virgin, painted on a tile, fell into a well; the well overflowed and the image reappeared. Many pilgrims still come to drink the water of the famous well and to venerate the

"Madonna of the Well" (*Madonna del Pozzo*). The late-17C Baroque façade is by Francesco da Volterra and Carlo Rainaldi.

Turn right into Via del Tritone.

Via del Tritone

This street is full of shops and is one of the busiest in Rome; it links the city centre with the northeastern suburbs.

From Piazza dell'Accademia di S. Luca, take Via della Stamperia.

Palazzo Carpegna houses the Galleria dell'Accademia di San Luca *(see "Worth a Visit" below).*

The **Calcographia** (*n° 6 Via della Stamperia*) houses over 23 000 engravings, including some by Giovan Battista Piranesi (1720-78), who produced some remarkable views of Rome. The collec-

Paintings of elegant women in the Galleria Sciarra

tion now belongs to the Istituto Nazionale per la Grafica *(also see GIANICOLO)*. Temporary exhibitions and courses on engraving techniques are also held here. Photo engravings are on sale to the general public.

Worth a Visit

Galleria di Palazzo Colonna★

Entrance at n° 17 Via della Pilotta. Time: 30min. Open Sat, 9am-1pm; Mon to Fri and Sun by appointment only. Closed in Aug. €7. ☎ *06 67 84 350 (Dottoressa Piergiovanni); Fax 06 67 94 638.*

In the **Sala della Colonna Bellica** (Column Room), note *Narcissus at the fountain* by Tintoretto (1518-94) and a portrait, which may be of Vittoria Colonna *(see p 176)*. The name of the room is a reference to the red column which was the family emblem.

A cannon ball is lodged in the middle of the half-dozen steps leading down into the salon. It was fired by the French troops who besieged Rome in 1849 in an attempt to re-establish Pius IX on the Papal throne.

The **Salone**★★ (Salon) offers a very handsome perspective, resplendent with gilt, mirrors, crystal chandeliers, yellow marble and paintings. The vault is painted with a 17C fresco depicting the triumph of Marcantonio Colonna who led Pius V's troops at the Battle of Lepanto (1571). The **Sala degli Scrigni** (Casket Room) contains two **caskets**★, small 17C chests: one in ebony decorated with ivory low-relief carvings (in the centre, copy of Michelangelo's *Last Judgement*); the other in sandalwood, inset with precious stones and bronze gilt. In the **Sala dell'apoteosi di Martino V** (Apotheosis of Martin V Room), whose name comes from the subject of the ceiling decoration, note *Fine portrait of a gentleman* (197) by Paul Veronese (1528-88); the famous painting **Peasant eating beans**★ (43), which is attributed to Annibale Carracci (1560-1609), is a fine example of Naturalism. The **Sala del Trono** (Throne Room) was intended for the reception of the Pope.

Galleria dell'Accademia di San Luca (St Luke's Academy Gallery)

Open daily (except Sun and public holidays) 10am-12.30pm. Closed Jul and Aug. No charge. ☎ *06 67 98 850; Fax 06 67 89 243.*

This collection of paintings was assembled from works painted and donated by members of the academy, which was founded in 1577. Among the paintings on display, note the *Portrait of Clement IX* by Baciccia (1639-1709), a fine fragment of a fresco by Raphael, *Judith and Holophernes* by the Venetian Piazzetta (1682-1754) and a *Virgin and Angels* by Sir Anthony van Dyck.

Museo Nazionale delle Paste Alimentari

&. *Open 9.30am-5.30pm. Closed on public holidays. €7.75.* ☎ *06 69 91 119; Fax 06 69 91 109; www.pastainmuseum.com*

Housed in Palazzo Scanderberg, the **National Pasta Museum** charts the history of this staple Italian dish, starting with the raw materials and their nutritious components, and finishing with amusing portrayals of famous people enjoying the end product. Displays are both imaginative and informative.

Fori Imperiali★★★

Although they are nowadays crowded with souvenir stalls and tourists and are undergoing extensive excavation work, the Imperial Fora once evoked the power and splendour of Ancient Rome. Yet, despite their position in the heart of a busy, modern city, monuments such as Trajan's Markets and Trajan's Column, which recall the glorious days of the Roman Empire, continue to inspire awe in visitors to Rome. Moving away from the crowds, it is still possible to find quiet corners in this district where time seems to stand still. Take time to explore the area's medieval past, perhaps passing under the window of the Marquess del Grillo, and to stroll through the narrow alleyways of the once disreputable Suburra district, now lively with craft shops and frequented by groups of university students.

Location

Michelin map 38 or Michelin spiral atlas of Rome: p 57 L 12-13 M 12-13. Metro line B: Colosseo or Cavour (both Metro stations are approximately 400m/440yds from the Foro di Augusto). Tour: 2hr. As a result of extensive excavation work, sections of the Fora are closed to the public. It is impossible to suggest a specific tour of the site, as connecting walkways and passageways are opened and closed as work progresses, although visitors are advised to start their visit with Trajan's Markets. The Imperial Fora extended approximately from the basilica of Maxentius to Piazza Venezia, with each Emperor in succession adding to them by building his own forum in the valley between Capitol Hill to the southwest and the Quirinal and Viminal Hills to the northeast.

Neighbouring sights are described in the following chapters: COLOSSEO-CELIO; FONTANA DI TREVI-QUIRINALE; FORO ROMANO-PALATINO; PIAZZA VENEZIA; SANTA MARIA MAGGIORE-ESQUILINO.

Background

When the old forum, the Roman Forum, became too small to hold the Assemblies of the People, the judicial hearings, the conduct of public affairs and commercial matters, Caesar began the construction of a new forum to the north of the old one; he was followed by Augustus, Vespasian, Nerva and Trajan. The Imperial Fora formed a monumental expression of Imperial prestige with their porticoes, temples, libraries and basilicas. The old forum was not in any way abandoned. Octavius erected a temple there to the divinity of Caesar; as the Emperor Augustus he was himself honoured with a commemorative arch in 19 BC, despite the fact that work on his own forum had been under way for over 10 years. A temple to Vespasian stood at the foot of the Capitol.

The fora were excavated in the 19C and the medieval buildings which had been erected on the site were removed between 1924 and 1932 when the present **Via dei Fori Imperiali** was being constructed.

This road (30m/98ft wide and 85m/279ft long) was opened in 1932 as Via dell'Impero. It passes straight through the middle of the Imperial Fora in a straight line from Piazza Venezia, opening up a clear view of the Colosseum, a solid reminder of Roman grandeur. Pedestrians may now enjoy a pleasant stroll here on Sundays, when the road is closed to traffic until 6pm.

B. Kaufmann/MICHELIN

Special Features

MERCATI DI TRAIANO★★ (TRAJAN'S MARKET)

Entrance in Via Quattro Novembre. Time: 1hr. See map on p 180. (&) Open Apr-Sep, 9am-6pm; rest of the year, 9am-4.30pm. Closed Mon, 1 Jan, 1 May, Christmas and afternoons of public holidays. €6.20. ☎ 06 69 78 05 32 or 06 71 08 303 (Dottoressa Tittoni); Fax 06 67 10 31 18.

*The **Museo dei Fori Imperiali** will shortly open in the old market buildings. The museum will provide information on the surrounding area, as well as exhibiting items discovered during the excavation of the site.*

WHERE TO EAT
See "Where to Eat" in the Practical Points section at the beginning of the guide.

SHOPPING
La Bottega del Cioccolato – *Via Leonina 82 – ☎ 06 48 21 473 – Open 9.30am-7.30pm.* As the name suggests, this shop specialises in items made from chocolate.

There were about 150 shops, arranged in terraces against the Quirinal Hill above the forum. The market was not simply a retail market like the Forum Boarium and the Forum Holitorium, but a centre for the acquisition, division and redistribution of supplies, administered by the Imperial authorities, under the Prefect of Rome and the Prefect of the Annona.

First comes a magnificent vaulted room where the civil servants may have worked. The buttresses which support the pillars on which the vaulting rests are of interest; no equivalent structure has been found among the monuments of Ancient Rome.

Via Biberatica★ serves the upper part of the semicircle which forms the façade of the market and is lined with well-preserved shops and houses. The name of the street is thought to have derived from the Latin verb *bibere* (to drink), suggesting that it was once home to a number of taverns. It is still covered with its original paving and runs in a curve from the Torre del Grillo to the present Via Quattro Novembre.

From Via Biberatica the visitor walks down through the market. The shops on the first floor, which are long and vaulted, were probably used for the sale of wine and oil; they open on to a vaulted arcade.

Semicircular Façade – The façade and the arrangement of the shops in tiers demonstrate the genius of the architect **Apollodorus of Damascus**, who gave a monumental appearance to this utilitarian complex.

The shallow shops on the ground floor opened directly onto the curving street which still has its original paving; they may have sold fruit and flowers; one has been reconstructed.

The elegance of the first-floor arcades is enhanced by the curved and triangular pediments.

FORO TRAIANO★★★

Trajan's Forum consisted of a covered market with a concave façade and the forum itself, which comprised a square, the Basilica Ulpia, Trajan's Column, two libraries and the Temple of Trajan.

The forum was inaugurated by Trajan, the best of the Antonine Emperors, in 113. Its construction had involved work on a huge scale, including the cutting back and levelling of a spur of the Quirinal which extended towards the Capitol. Just as Caesar had financed the construction of his forum with booty taken from the

Trajan's Market

Gauls, so Trajan used the spoils of war won from the Dacians, a redoubtable people who lived in what is now Romania. Even after Trajan's death the prestige of his forum did not fade. It was the setting for official demonstrations: here Hadrian publicly burned the records of debts owed by certain of his citizens; here Marcus Aurelius (161-80) held an auction of his personal treasures to finance his wars against the Marcomanni, a German tribe, who were threatening the Empire.

Trajan's Forum, which extended from Caesar's Forum to beyond the two domed churches of St Mary of Loreto and the Holy Name of Mary, was the largest of the Imperial Fora and certainly the most beautiful, if one is to believe the historian **Ammianus Marcellinus** (c 330-400); he gives an account of a visit made by **Constantinus II** (356), Emperor in the east, to the superseded Imperial capital; already on seeing the old Forum, "the sanctuary of the old power" he had been speechless. "but on arriving in Trajan's Forum ... he was stupefied."

Forum

The entrance to the forum was set in a slightly curved wall facing southeast. The northeast and southwest walls were relieved by two apses, one of which is still visible, running parallel with the concave façade of the market and marked by two columns (one of which is standing). The wall on the far left of the apse is the outer wall of the forum and is composed of huge blocks of peperine and travertine.

Colonna Traiana★★★ (Trajan's Column)

Originally there were rooftop terraces on the libraries which made it easier than it is today to view this extraordinary work. Designed by **Apollodorus of Damascus**, the column stands about 38m/125ft high and consists of 17 marble drums sculpted in a spiral of panels showing episodes in Trajan's wars against the Dacians. If the spiral of panels were laid out in a straight line it would be 200m/656ft long; no other Imperial victories have ever been celebrated with so much talent and genius. The artistic ability of the sculptor and the technical skill required to achieve a perfect fit between two parts of a panel at the junction of two drums are matched by such precision of detail that the column serves as a faithful historical record of the Dacian campaigns and of Roman military technique. The scenes depicted on the column are explained in the Museo della Civiltà Romana *(see EUR)*.

The diameter of the shaft is not uniform from top to bottom; two-thirds of the way up it increases slightly to prevent the illusion of concavity which would otherwise result from the effect of the height. The size of the panels and the figures increases towards the top of the column, which was originally brilliantly coloured.

A bronze statue of Trajan was placed on top of the column, probably after his death. In 1587 Pope Sixtus V had it replaced with the statue of St Peter that one sees today. Although a pagan monument, Trajan's Column was never maltreated

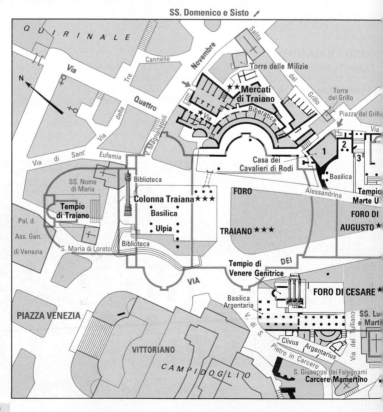

by the Christians, who believed that Trajan's soul had been saved by the prayers of St Gregory. A golden urn containing the Emperor's ashes was placed in a funerary chamber within the column; the urn was stolen in the Middle Ages.

Inside the column is a spiral staircase *(not open)* leading to the top which is lit by windows in the decorative panels; part of the designer's skill lies in the fact that these windows are scarcely visible from the outside.

Trajan's successor, Hadrian, erected a temple to the deified Emperor after his death but nothing remains visible.

Basilica Ulpia and Libraries

The basilica was named after Trajan's family. The ends open into two semicircles, one beneath the building at the corner of Via Magnanapoli. The basilica was opulent with five aisles, a marble floor and two storeys of marble and granite columns (some standing, some marked by their bases).

Beyond the basilica were two public libraries *(biblioteca)*: one contained Greek works, the other Latin works and Trajan's personal records. Between the two libraries was a courtyard; at its centre stood Trajan's Column, a masterpiece of Classical art which is beyond compare.

Piazza del Foro

At the centre of the forum stood an equestrian statue in gilded bronze of the Emperor Trajan (statua equestre di Traiano) which Constantinus II dreamed of imitating. Ammianus Marcellinus recounts that a prince in the Imperial suite made a subtle suggestion: "Begin, Sir, by building a stable in this style ... so that the horse you envisage will be as well housed as this one." Down the sides of the forum were porticoes ornamented with statues of illustrious men, as in Augustus's Forum.

There is an overall view of the ruins from Via Alessandrina.

FORO DI AUGUSTO★★

Augustus's Forum is separated from Trajan's Forum by a building **(1)** constructed by Domitian, which later became home to the Knights of Rhodes *(see below)*; the edifice is embellished with a fine 15C loggia. Octavian, who took the name **Augustus** when he became Emperor, wanted to avenge the murder of his adopted father Caesar. When he finally defeated the murderers, Cassius and Brutus, at Philippi (a town in northern Greece) in 42 BC, he vowed to dedicate a temple to Mars Ultor (the Avenger), to be sited in a new forum. This would be in addition to the two which already existed (the Roman Forum and Caesar's Forum) and would be devoted particularly to the administration of justice. Building began in 31 BC after a considerable amount of demolition work. The site extended from the old forum to the edge of the unsavoury Suburra district; a high wall, forming the back of the new forum, was built to isolate it from the hovels and frequent fires of Suburra; its irregular line reveals the difficulties the builders had to overcome. The two sides facing southeast and northwest bowed out in two semicircles which are still visible. In the recesses in the walls stood bronze statues of the most famous Romans "who had brought Rome from insignificance to greatness" (Suetonius): Aeneas, the kings of Alba, the founding fathers of the Julian family, Romulus, Marius, Sulla and other great generals of the Republican era. Against the centre of the back wall stood the **Temple of Mars Ultor** which was approached by a majestic flight of steps. A few columns to the front and side still stand.

This temple played an important role in public life; it served as a reliquary for Caesar's sword. It was here that members of the Imperial family came for the ceremony of the *toga virilis* which they received on passing from adolescence to manhood (at about 17). It was here, too, that magistrates appointed to the provinces were invested with their authority *(imperium)*.

FORI IMPERIALI

0   100 m

— Extant parts
∙∙∙∙ Non-extant parts
▢ Excavations

Arco dei Pantani
Conti
Torre de' Conti
Argiletum
Tor de'
Basilica
FORO
IMPERIALI
Tempio di Minerva
DI VESPASIANO
Tempio della Pace
FORO
DI
NERVA
Biblioteca
SS. Cosma e Damiano
FORO ROMANO★★★
Curia★★
Via Sacra★
Baccina
Via Madonna dei Monti
Cavour
Via del Colosseo

The basilicas

These were formed by two porticoes, one on each side of the temple, in front of the semicircular recesses. Marble statues stood between the columns.

Two columns have been re-erected in front of a room **(2)** which housed a colossal statue of Mars or Augustus.

Two flights of steps flanking the temple linked Augustus's Forum with Suburra. At the top of the steps near the three re-erected columns is a fine arch, known as Arco dei Pantani. *(There is a better view of it from Via Tor de' Conti.)*

Augustus's successors made further embellishments: **Tiberius** (14-37) erected two commemorative arches **(3)**, one on each side of the temple, in honour of Drusus and Germanicus, who pacified Germany and Pannonia (western Hungary). The Emperor Claudius (41-54) continued to dispense justice there as, according to Suetonius "One day when he was hearing a case in Augustus's Forum he was attracted by the cooking smells coming from the Temple of Mars next door: leaving his court, he went to join the Salian priests at their table."

FORO DI NERVA

Although begun by Domitian, this forum was completed and inaugurated by Nerva in 98. Very little remains of the forum, which was long and narrow in shape and traversed by the Argiletum, a street linking the old Roman Forum with the Suburra district; for this reason it was also known as the Forum Transitorium. Here stood the Temple of Minerva; its fine ruins were still visible early in the 17C until Pope Paul V had them demolished; the columns and cornices were used in the construction of the Pauline Fountain on the Janiculum. Against the east wall stand two beautiful **columns★ (4)** and some fragments of a frieze which adorned the wall enclosing the forum.

The junction of Via dei Fori Imperiali and Via Cavour stands more or less at the point where the Fora of Nerva *(west)* and Vespasian *(east)* met. There are very few remains.

FORO DI VESPASIANO

This forum was built by Vespasian from 71-75. It formed a square adjoining the old Forum and extended approximately from the basilica of Maxentius in the south to the Conti Tower (Torre de' Conti) in the north. In the south corner there was a library which is now occupied by the church of St Cosmas and St Damian. It was also called the Peace Forum. To commemorate his conquest of the Jews in 71, Vespasian erected a Temple of Peace which contained the treasures looted from the Jewish Temple in Jerusalem: the golden seven-branched candlestick, the tablets of the Law of Moses and the silver trumpets.

FORO DI CESARE★★

For his forum Caesar chose a central position at the foot of the Capitol, near the old Roman Forum. In order to clear the site he had to relocate the Curia Hostilia and the Comitium and purchase and demolish the elegant houses already in situ.

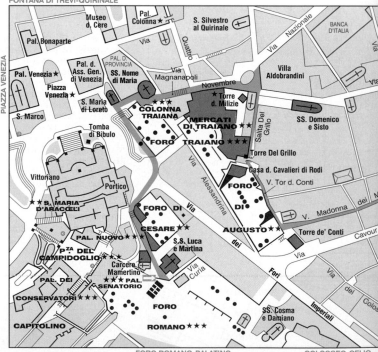

FORO ROMANO-PALATINO   COLOSSEO-CELIO

This exercise cost him the exorbitant sum of 60 million sesterci according to Cicero (then consul and a friend of Caesar's), although Suetonius, the Emperor's biographer, puts the figure at 100 million. Negotiations began in 54 BC when Caesar was rich with the booty gained in the conquest of Gaul (58-51 BC); work began three years later in 51 BC.

Caesar's forum was rectangular and extended from the Curia *(east)* to Via di San Pietro in Carcere *(west)*, the long sides running more or less parallel with the Clivus Argentarius. Domitian undertook restoration work (81-96) following the fire which destroyed part of the Capitol in 80. Trajan completed the work. About two-thirds of Caesar's forum has been uncovered; the rest is beneath Via dei Fori Imperiali.

The ruins

First to catch the eye are three beautiful standing columns, richly sculpted, which belonged to the **Temple of Venus Genitrix** and date from the time of Domitian and Trajan. Caesar claimed that his family (the gens Iulia) were descended from Venus through her son, Aeneas, and Aeneas's son, Iulus. He decided to dedicate a temple to her after his victory at Pharsalus in 48 BC against Pompey, who was killed by Ptolemy, Cleopatra's brother.

This temple, to the north of the forum, was a veritable museum: besides the statue of Venus in the *cella*, there was a golden statue of Cleopatra, some Greek paintings and, in front of the temple, a statue of Caesar's horse: this extraordinary animal had curiously split hooves, which resembled human feet; according to the soothsayers this abnormality was a sign of divine intervention and meant that his master would be ruler of the world.

The edge of the forum was lined with shops, still visible beneath the Clivus Argentarius. During Trajan's reign (2C) a portico was added down the long side nearest the Clivus Argentarius; its two long rows of granite columns still remain. It has been identified as the **Basilica Argentaria** where the money-changers *(argentari)* plied their trade.

Walking About

Santi Luca e Martina (Church of St Luke and St Martina)

On the site of the Senate archive (Secretarium Senatus, an annex of the Curia) a church was built in about the 7C and dedicated to Martina, who had been martyred under Septimius Severus. From 1588 it was also dedicated to St Luke, since in that year Pope Sixtus V gave the church to the members of St Luke's Academy, a guild of painters who recognised the Evangelist as their patron saint; according to a 6C legend he had painted a portrait of the Virgin Mary.

In 1634 a terracotta sarcophagus was found containing the remains of St Martina. Cardinal Francesco Barberini commissioned Pietro da Cortona to build a new

shrine above the old one. Da Cortona designed a beautiful **façade★**. Its shallow convex curve is reminiscent of the style of Borromini; so, too, is the interior, which is designed on the Greek cross plan and decorated all over with pale stuccoes revealing a search for complicated forms.

The **Carcere Mamertino**, the old prison used by the Roman State, stands opposite the church *(see "Worth a Visit" below).*

Follow the Clivus Argentarius and cross Via dei Fori Imperiali. Walk alongside Trajan's Forum as far as Trajan's Column.

Note the symmetry of the domes of **SS. Nome di Maria** and **Santa Maria di Loreto**. The latter was begun by Antonio da Sangallo the Younger in 1507 to a square design and was completed in 1577 by Giacomo del Duca, from Sicily.

Torre delle Milizie★ (Militia Tower)

Entrance from Trajan's Market. Open daily (except Mon) 9am-4.30pm (6pm in summer) by appointment only. Closed 1 Jan, 1 May and Christmas. €6.20, combined ticket with Trajan's Market. This is one of the best-preserved buildings of medieval Rome. It was the keep of a castle built by Pope Gregory IX (1227-41) at a time when the Pope often had to use force to establish the faith in the Empire. The tower leans slightly because of an earthquake in the 14C; it has lost its top storey and crenellations. It has been known as "Nero's Tower": according to the legend it was from the top of this tower that the mad Emperor, dressed in theatrical costume, watched the fire that he himself had caused, "charmed by the beauty of the flames", in Suetonius's account, and strumming his lyre and singing.

From Via Quattro Novembre there is a view of the beautiful trees in the terraced public gardens of the **Villa Aldobrandini** and of the Baroque façade of the **church of San Domenico** e San Sisto (completed in 1655).

Turn right into Salita del Grillo.

This quiet, picturesque street takes its name from the Marquess del Grillo, known for his jokes and jibes. Beside the arcade stands the **tower** of his mansion.

Casa dei Cavalieri di Rodi (House of the Knights of Rhodes)

Open Tue and Thu by prior appointment, 9.30am-1pm. Guided tours only (45min). €2.07. Apply at least two weeks in advance to the Ufficio Monumenti medievali e moderni, Mon-Fri, 9am-1pm. ☎ 06 67 10 32 38; Fax 06 67 10 31 18.

Marco Bembo, Bishop of Vicenza and Cardinal of St Mark's Basilica, was appointed Grand Master of the Order of the Knight Hospitallers of St John by his uncle Pope Paul II (1464-71). He reconstructed this building in the 15C in part of a medieval convent constructed around the remains of the Temple of Mars Ultor. Some of the windows show that Venetian craftsmen were employed. The beautiful 15C loggia overlooking Trajan's Forum is supported on Roman columns, their capitals carved with leaves and rosettes; the walls are decorated with frescoes.

Continue along Via Tor de' Conti.

The Via Tor de' Conti skirts the imposing wall built of large blocks of tufa and travertine which separated Augustus's Forum from the Suburra district. Note the fine arch (Arco dei Pentani) which marked the entrance to the Forum. At the end of the street can be seen the imposing mass of the **Torre de' Conti**. Pope Innocent III had it built around 1238 with material taken from Nerva's Forum. The tower was inhabited until reduced to its present state by an earthquake in 1348.

Turn left into Via Madonna dei Monti and left again into Via del Boschetto to reach Via Panisperna.

The peaceful Via Madonna dei Monti leads to what was the **Suburra** district, the most disreputable in Ancient Rome. This zone, which harboured thieves and hired assassins, bequeathed its name to a nearby square. The narrow alleys, now lively with craft shops, were once frequented by the outrageous Empress Messalina who frequented the local brothels in secret.

Via Panisperna crosses the **Viminale**, one of the seven hills of Rome, which probably takes its name from the very large number of willow trees or from the temple dedicated to Jupiter Vimineus which stood there. The tree-lined courtyard of the **church of San Lorenzo in Panisperna** (St Lawrence in Panisperna) is a tiny oasis from another era separating this place of worship from the chaos of the city. On 10 August, the feast of St Lawrence, the nuns carry on an age-old tradition of offering blessed bread.

VIA PANISPERNA 89

From 1926-37, this building was home to the group of young Italian physicists known as the "boys of Via Panisperna", which included Ettore Majorana, Emilio Segré, Franco Rasetti and Bruno Pontecorvo, brother of the film director Gillo. Under the tutelage of Enrico Fermi, these young scientists set about revolutionising the history and physics of the 20C. The palazzo, which is part of the Viminal complex, now houses the offices of employees of the Polizia di Stato.

Worth a Visit

Carcere Mamertino (Mamertine Prison)

Open daily 9am–noon and 2.30–5pm (6pm in summer). Donations welcome. Guided tour available (10min). ☎ 06 67 92 902.

The Mamertine Prison was the Roman State prison; it consists of two rooms, one above the other, hollowed out of the Capitoline Hill beneath the church of San Giuseppe dei Falegnami (St Joseph of the Carpenters).

On the right of the entrance is a list of names of well-known people who perished here. In 104 BC **Jugurtha** died of starvation while his conqueror Marius led his victory parade through the forum. **Vercingetorix** was beheaded here in 46 BC after Caesar's triumph. However, worthy enemy chiefs often escaped death; Jugurtha and Vercingetorix had not been considered worthy of such clemency. It was here on 5 December 65 BC that Catiline's fellow conspirators were strangled after Cicero had given his fourth Catiline speech.

In the Middle Ages a legend arose that **St Peter** had been imprisoned here; hence the name San Pietro in Carcere (St Peter in Prison). On the left of the entrance is a list of Christian martyrs who died in the prison. At the head of the staircase linking the two rooms is a hollowed-out stone said to bear the imprint of the Apostle's head as he was jostled by his jailers.

The lower chamber *(tullianum)* was built at the end of the 4C BC out of huge blocks of tufa arranged in a vault and was used as a cistern or a tomb.

Foro Romano-Palatino★★★

This site, a complex of columns standing among ruined walls and crumbling foundations, bears traces of the 12 centuries of history which forged the Roman civilisation; as such it is one of the most popular sights in Rome. Once the political and civil heart of the powerful Roman Empire, the Forum is the obvious starting-point for a visit to Italy's capital city.

Overlooking the Forum is the Palatine Hill, an area awash with magnificent pine trees and the impressive ruins of aristocratic houses. It is the most symbolic of Rome's seven hills and a delightful place for a quiet stroll away from the noise of the city.

Location

Michelin map 38 or Michelin spiral atlas of Rome: p 57 M 12-13, N 12-13. Metro line B: Colosseo. Tour: half a day. Certain parts of the ruins may be closed owing to lack of staff or restoration work. The best places for a view of the ruins are the Capitol terrace and the Farnese Gardens on the Palatine Hill.

Neighbouring sights are described in the following chapters: CAMPIDOGLIO-CAPITOLINO; COLOSSEO-CELIO; FORI IMPERIALI; PIAZZA VENEZIA.

FORO ROMANO (ROMAN FORUM)

In about 750 BC the site of the Forum was a marshy valley, subject to flooding by the Tiber and by streams from the seven surrounding hills: the Palatine, the Caelian, the Esquiline, the Velia, which linked the Palatine to the Esquiline, the Viminal, the Quirinal and the Capitoline *(see Map of Rome during the Empire, p 74).* Small villages composed of rough shacks grew up on the hillsides. Their inhabitants, the Latins and the Sabines, were principally engaged in agriculture but would take up arms in defence of their homesteads when threatened with invasion by their neighbours. The valley, which lay roughly at the centre of the circle of hills and which later became the Forum, was used as a burial ground and a meeting place where the leaders made decisions affecting the community. It was also where the people exchanged goods and gathered for worship.

Two centuries later the marshy valley had completely changed in appearance and become a real square at the centre of a town: the cemetery had been abandoned and covered with houses; the west side of the Forum had been paved. The people responsible for this transformation were the **Etruscans**. Originally from the right bank of the Tiber, they extended their dominion as far as Cumae on the borders of Magna Graecia (southern Italy). They settled on the site of Rome, built a citadel on the Capitol, unified the villages and organised the social life of the community. From 616 to 509 BC Rome was governed by kings of Etruscan origin. The city was enclosed by fortifications; the stagnant water in the Forum was drained into the Tiber through a channel which was to become the Great Sewer *(Cloaca maxima).*

The Republican Era

The last Etruscan king, Tarquin the Proud, was thrown out in 509 BC and the Consulate was instituted. The Republican era had begun: from being a rural town Rome began to develop into the capital of an Empire. The Forum, barely 2ha/5 acres in extent, was the focal point of events which ushered in the new era. The Republican period was first and foremost a time of territorial expansion: from early in the 5C BC Rome was at war with her neighbours. Victories were celebrated in the Forum: a temple was built in honour of the Dioscuri *(see Tempio di Castore e Polluce, p 192),* who came to the assistance of the Romans at Lake Regillus. In 260, during the First Punic War, a column was raised to Caius Duilius who gained the first Roman naval victory at Milazzo in Sicily. All victorious generals processed in triumph through the Forum.

Commercial centre – The Roman conquests brought with them immense riches: the contents of confiscated enemy treasuries, indemnities paid by the conquered nations and the tribute paid by the provinces. By the 3C BC Rome was an important financial centre. Money-changing, loans and credit were arranged in the Forum. The shops which had formerly housed small traders were taken over by bankers.

Political centre – The five centuries of the Roman Republic which preceded the Empire were full of activity. The men who decided the destiny of Rome met in the **Comitium**, an area in the northwest corner of the Forum where the popular assemblies *(comices)* were held.

Right in the corner stood the Senate House *(Curia).* It was also called the "Hostilia" because, so it was said, it had been created by Tullius Hostilius, a Sabine king who ruled from 672-640 BC. The **Curia** was the seat of the highest level of Republican government, the **Senate**; 200 senators, appointed for life, decided foreign policy, directed military operations, drew up peace treaties and enacted measures for public safety. Opposite the Curia were the Rostra where the tribunes held forth.

People came to listen to the pitiless logic and measured accents of Tiberius and Gaius Gracchus. Next to it stood the *Graeco-stasis*, a platform where foreign ambassadors waited. In 185 BC the **Basilica Porcia**, the first building of this sort in Rome, was erected on one side of the Comitium by Porcius Cato, thus enabling the citizens to assemble under cover.

Religious centre – In 497 BC the Temple of Saturn was built in the Forum; other religious buildings already existed from the Regal period. Troubled times were approaching and religious belief was waning. The practice of offering the spirits of the dead a combat which ended in the death of one of the participants degenerated into an entertainment: by 264 BC gladiatorial combats were being held in the Forum.

Troubled times – For 100 years the Republican regime tore itself to pieces in civil war. In 52 BC the tribune Clodius was killed by Milo; his body was carried to the Comitium and cremated. The fire spread, destroying the Curia and the Basilica Porcia.

Caesar had already decided that the Forum was too small and intended to enlarge it. In 44 BC he moved the Rostra and rebuilt the Curia in a slightly different position.

Scarcely anything of the Republican Forum survives. The early buildings were of tufa, peperine or wood. The Emperors faced them with marble, then built others larger and more magnificent. Augustus could boast that he had inherited a town built of brick and left a city built of marble.

The Forum during the Empire

On 16 January 27 BC the Senate granted Octavian the title **Augustus** (protected by the gods in every act); a new regime was born under the sign of grandeur. Taking up Caesar's project, Augustus, and then Vespasian, Domitian and Trajan, enlarged the old Forum and built the Imperial Fora. In the Augustan era the original Forum lost some of its uses: the huge popular assemblies and the reviews of the troops were moved to the Campus Martius.

The Forum became the chosen site for erecting monuments: commemorative arches, basilicas and temples dedicated to Emperors deified after their death. Even in the 2C BC confusion reigned according to Plautus, a satirist who died in 184 BC. Every sort of citizen could be found there: "vicious or virtuous, honest or dishonest. If you want to meet a perjurer, go to the Comitium; for a liar and a braggart, try the Temple of Venus Cloacina; for wealthy married wasters, near the Basilica. There, too, you will find well-perfumed prostitutes and men ready to do a deal, while the fish market is frequented by members of the eating clubs. Wealthy and reputable citizens stroll in the lower Forum; the middle Forum near the canal is favoured by the merely showy set ... Behind the Temple of Castor are those whom you would do well not to trust too lightly; in the Tuscan district those who are willing to sell themselves."

In the 3C building came to a halt: not only for lack of space but also because of the spread of a new religion which entailed the worship of one god. At first it was preached by a handful of nobodies and then from AD 60 by a certain Paul of Tarsus. The Emperors resisted but in AD 391 Theodosius finally closed the pagan temples.

The Forum's downfall began in 410 when Alaric the Goth swept in from the Danube with his savage hordes and set fire to the Curia and the Basilica Aemilia. There followed an earthquake in 442, the depredations of Genseric's Vandals in 455, the armies of Theodoric in 500 and of Belisarius in 537, after which the Forum was dead. Rome's prestige no longer lay in grandiose monuments but, as the resting place of St Peter the Apostle, the city was celebrated throughout the Christian world.

From the Middle Ages to the Renaissance

Once the Church became organised, the Bishop of Rome, the Pope, was recognised as the head of Christianity. Gradually the Imperial buildings were converted into places of Christian worship. Some still survive, a curious juxtaposition of traditions; many have disappeared – such as the two oratories in the portico of the Basilica Aemilia or the church of St Sergius and St Bacchus which existed between the Temples of Saturn and Concord until the 16C, or the church of Santa Maria in Cannapara in the Basilica Julia. In the 9C the buildings began to crumble away; the earth built up around them and the ruins were buried.

In the 12C the quarrel between the Pope and the Holy Roman Emperor caused civil war between the noble Roman families. The Ancient structures were turned into fortresses; towers rose between the Temple of Antoninus and Faustina and Caesar's Forum. The old buildings were stripped of their decoration which was used to embellish churches and palaces; the statues and columns were baked in lime kilns to produce chalk.

The deserted Forum became a sewage farm. By the 15C the pillars of the Temple of Vespasian were half underground and the podium of the Temple of the Dioscuri was completely buried; both were surrounded by fields. The Forum had become

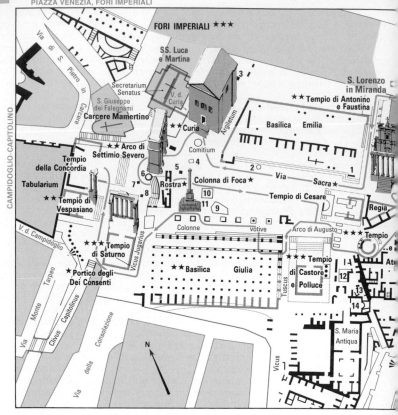

a cows' field *(campo vaccino)*. Near the Temple of the Dioscuri the marble basin of a fountain was being used as a drinking trough for animals; it is now in the Piazza del Quirinale. When Charles V visited Rome in 1536, Pope Paul III laid out a broad avenue from the Arch of Titus to the Arch of Septimius Severus.

Excavations

The names of many famous archaeologists, Italians and non-Italians, are connected with the history of the excavation of the Roman Forum; Carlo Fea, who began investigations in 1803, Antonio Nibby, Bunsen and Canina, Pietro Rosa after 1870, Giuseppe Fiorelli, Rodolfo Lanciani, H Jordan, C Hülsen and particularly Giacomo Boni, who carried out methodical excavations from 1898 onwards, reaching the oldest levels which were essential to an understanding of early Rome.

Tour

Descend into the Forum; immediately on the right are the remains of the Basilica Emilia.
♿ *Open daily 9am-1hr before dusk (5.30pm in winter). Last admission 1hr before closing time. Closed 1 Jan, 1 May and Christmas. No charge.* ☏ *06 39 08 071; Fax 06 39 75 09 50; pierreci@pierreci.it*

Basilica Emilia (Basilica Aemilia)

This was the second basilica to be built in Rome (in 179 BC) after the Basilica Porcia *(see p 186)* had been built not far away in 185 BC. Like all the monuments in the Forum, it was frequently restored and reconstructed. The present remains are those of the 1C rebuilding. It was named after the Aemilia family *(gens Aemilia)* who were responsible for its maintenance. Like all the Ancient basilicas it served no religious purpose. The huge covered hall was used for business transactions and for sheltering from the heat or cold; judges and litigants retreated here to hold their hearings out of the hubbub of the more public places.

Along the south side of the basilica there was a line of shops opening into a portico; the party walls can still be seen (some have been reconstructed). The shops sold jewellery and perfume. Behind the shops was the main hall divided into three by two rows of coloured marble columns with a finely carved entablature of white marble; fragments of the architrave and columns are displayed against the rear wall. In the southeast corner of the Basilica Aemilia stands a Latin **inscription (1)** dedicated to Augustus's adopted grandsons, Caius and Lucius, who died before reaching manhood.

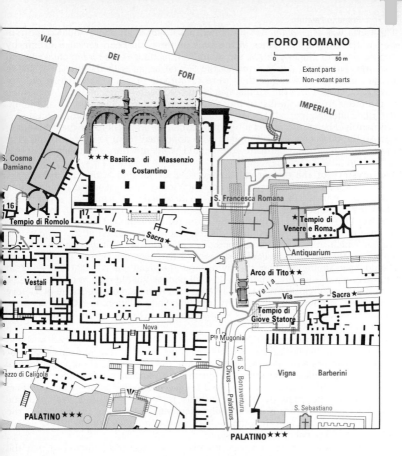

Via Sacra★ (Sacred Way)

This was the most famous street in Ancient Rome. From the earliest days of the Forum, the Temple of Vesta and the Regia flanked the Sacred Way along which victorious generals rode in triumphal procession. Dressed like Jupiter and standing in a four-horse chariot, they proceeded to the Capitoline Hill to give thanks to Jupiter, the Best and Greatest, for his protection during the campaign.

Santuario di Venere Cloacina (Sanctuary of Venus Cloacina) (2)

A travertine circle on the ground marks the site of the sanctuary dedicated to the goddess who protected the main sewer *(cloaca)*; traces of the steps leading down to it are still visible. Here in the 5C BC Verginius, a humble plebeian officer, took his daughter's life to save her from the lust of Appius Claudius, a decemvir. Livy tells how the latter was prepared to abuse his power in his desire to make Virginia his slave; he provoked a riot among the people and the abdication of the decemvirs.

Argiletum

This street, one of the busiest in Rome, separated the Basilica Aemilia from the Curia and led to Suburra, a slum district. There remain some fine sections of travertine paving. During the reign of the kings there was said to be an arch over the Argiletum, flanked by a shrine containing the two-faced statue of the god Janus. Legend tells how during the war against the Sabines Janus had produced a jet of hot water from the ground which stopped the enemy dead in their attack on the Capitol. The shrine was always left open in time of war so that Janus could come to the aid of the Romans.

Curia★★

May close at 1pm for administrative reasons. The brick building visible today is not the one in which the **Senate** met in the Republican period when it was in charge of Roman policy. The first Curia was more or less on the site of the chancel and left transept of St Luke's Church, but facing in a different direction. In the 1C BC Caesar moved it and enlarged it and Diocletian rebuilt it in the 3C.

Diocletian's Curia was restored in 1937 after the removal of St Adrian's Church which had occupied the building since the 7C. It was less austere than it is today: the façade, faced with marble and stucco, was surmounted by a tympanum covered in travertine; the bronze door was removed to St John Lateran by Alexander VII in the 17C.

The Curia was a *templum*, a consecrated place where an augur could communicate to the people the wishes of the gods as they had been revealed to him by certain signs: the flight of birds, the manner of feeding of the sacred chickens and any unusual events. Every sitting of the Senate began with the president taking the auguries to see whether they were favourable or not. The senators did not have fixed seats. Once the agenda had been read each senator in turn – according to the order fixed by the list in the *album* – was called upon to give his opinion. For a considerable period the Senate had immense power but once Imperial government had been introduced it became practically impossible for the senators to oppose the decisions of the Emperor who appointed them to office. At the very most, after an Emperor's death, they could condemn him and thus oppose his deification.

The mystery of the Statue of Victory – At the far end of the Curia there are traces of a pedestal on which the statue of Victory stood: it was a golden statue placed there in 29 BC by Octavian, who defeated the armies of Antony and Cleopatra at Actium in Greece in 31 BC and became the ruler of the Roman Empire. For over three centuries the Emperors worshipped the statue, burning incense on the altar. At their funerals the statue was carried at the head of the cortège which culminated in the apotheosis and deification of the Emperor. In his Epistle to the Romans, St Paul had asserted that the one God of the Christians should have dominion over the living and the dead. In AD 380 the Edict of Thessalonica was issued, stipulating that all people "should rally to the faith transmitted to the Romans by the Apostle Peter ...". From then on the statue of Victory constituted an offence to Christianity, the new State religion; in 382 the Emperor Gratian had the statue removed. Symmachus, Prefect of Rome, protested but the statue never reappeared.

Bassorilievi di Traiano★★ (Trajan's Plutei) – The Curia houses two sculpted panels found in the Forum and probably commissioned by Trajan or his successor Hadrian to decorate the Rostra. On the back of the two panels are represented the three animals which were sacrificed during the purification ceremony: a pig, a sheep and a bull; in Latin: *sus*, *ovis* and *taurus*, hence the name of the sacrifice: *suovetaurilia*. The anatomy of the animals is represented in a very realistic manner; each detail has been carefully executed, particularly the fleeces of the sheep. The sculptures on the other side illustrate Imperial beneficence.

The right-hand panel shows two scenes:

– Trajan, standing on the Rostra with his lictors, has just announced that the interest due on loans made to smallholders will be used to assist poor children. This is the institution of the *Alimenta* which Hadrian continued to implement.

– the Emperor seated receiving a woman and child, symbolising Italy.

The left-hand panel shows:

– the Emperor watching a group of men piling up documents. He is about to give the order for the destruction of these records, which contain details of overdue taxes, thus freeing a number of citizens from their debts.

The sculptor has set these scenes against a local background showing several of the Forum buildings. The edges of the panels are decorated with the sacred fig tree and a statue of Marsyas, his flayed skin about his shoulders.

Behind the Curia is a small brick altar **(3)** with a recess for relics, proving that the place was used for Christian worship in the 7C-8C.

Lapis Niger (Black Stone) (4)

In 1899 Giacomo Boni, who was in charge of the excavation of the Forum, discovered an area paved with black marble slabs (currently protected by a low fence). Beneath the slabs among some piled-up blocks of tufa the archaeologists found a stele bearing an inscription whose meaning is obscure. They concluded that they had uncovered a monument dating from the 6C BC. When Caesar rearranged the Forum he had protected this area because it was sacred; the Romans believed it was the tomb of Romulus, Faustulus (the shepherd who had seen the wolf suckling the twins) or Hostus Hostilius, the father of Tullus Hostilius, the third king after Romulus and Numa Pompilius.

Comitium

See The Republican Era, p 185. It extended from the Curia to the Lapis Niger and contained a fountain with a circular base of which the remains are still visible.

Decennalia Caesarum (5)

In 286 Diocletian decentralised the government of the Empire; he himself took charge of the affairs of the eastern Empire and Maximian of the western. Both were known by the title Augustus. Seven years later Maximian entrusted the administration of Gaul and Britain to Constantius and Diocletian put Galerius in charge of the Balkan peninsula. Constantius and Galerius bore the title of Caesar. The first 10 years' reign *(decennalia)* of the two Caesars and the 20 years of the Augusti were celebrated with the erection of a column of which only the base remains. The carving shows the animals of the *suovetaurilia* and certain events in the religious ceremonies. The quality of the sculpture is inferior to that of Trajan's period *(see above);* the background figures are flattened and simply indicated by a deep line; the costumes are stiff, the fold lines being too deeply chiselled.

Rostra★

After 338 BC the **orators' platform** was always called the Rostra. In that year the Romans had attacked Antium (modern Anzio), then notorious for its pirates, and captured the prows *(rostra)* of the enemy ships, which they fixed to the orators' platform. In the Republican period the Rostra resounded with the speeches of all the great exponents of the oratorical art. In those days the platform stood between the Lapis Niger and the present Curia. The remains which can be seen today are those of the Rostra moved in 44 BC by Julius Caesar. After his assassination, Octavian, **Antony** and Lepidus formed the second triumvirate (late October 43 BC). The period of proscriptions began; **Cicero** was one of the most famous victims. A declared enemy of Antony, whose illegal acts and Imperial ambitions he had denounced in his Philippics, he was sacrificed for reasons of State by Octavian and murdered in his house in Gaeta in December 43 BC by agents of the triumvirate. His hands and head were exposed on the Rostra.

The construction known as the Rostra was a raised platform reached by a curving staircase at the rear (Capitoline side). When the Emperors were all-powerful, the great assemblies of the people, roused by the speeches of their tribunes, had no power of decision. The platform, therefore, was used only for dignified official ceremonies. Before the erection of the two commemorative columns, the crowd could congregate in front of the Rostra. It became very noisy on the days when food was distributed; the numbers of the poor grew incessantly and when Caesar came to power there were about 300 000 citizens on the lists for the distribution of free corn.

Arco di Trionfo di Settimio Severo★★ (Triumphal Arch of Septimius Severus)

The arch was built in 203 and is surmounted by statues of Septimius Severus, his two sons (Caracalla and Geta) and the figure of Victory. The Emperor had just won a series of victories over the Parthians (197-202) and organised a new province, Mesopotamia *(see Insights and Images, Map of Rome during the Empire, p 74)*. The heroes' names appeared in the dedicatory text; Geta's was obliterated after Caracalla had him murdered so he himself would be the sole successor.

In the 3C architecture became more complicated: four detached Corinthian columns stand before the façade, forming a false portico. Decoration is abundant. At the base of the columns are prisoners in chains.

The panels on the façade are divided into horizontal bands by thick ribs. The figures are too small, and although this style of presentation serves well for triumphal columns *(see Colonna Traiana, p 179 and Piazza Colonna, p 213)* here it only causes confusion.

Umbilicus Urbis (6)

The remains of a 3C circular temple which marked the symbolic centre of the city.

Altare di Vulcano (7)

The **Altar of Vulcan**, a venerable hollow in the tufa, goes back to the time of the kings. Under the Republic the day of 23 August was devoted to the Volcanalia Festival: little fishes or other animals symbolising human lives that people wished to preserve were offered to the god of fire.

Colonna miliare d'Oro (8)

The **Golden Milestone** marble column covered with gilded bronze was set up by Augustus to mark the point from which mileages were measured. The distances between the capital and the major cities of the Empire were written on it.

At the foot of the Capitol a group of splendid monuments flanked the **Clivus Capitolinus**, the road used for religious processions and to celebrate military triumphs. It led from the Forum to the Temple of Jupiter on the Capitol.

Retrace your steps to the Temple of Caesar.

Tempio di Cesare (Temple of Caesar)

Almost nothing is left of this building, which started the cult of Emperor worship. On the evening of the Ides of March 44 BC the body of Caesar, who had been stabbed to death in the Curia of Pompey, was carried to the Forum and cremated before the Rostra. A column and altar were set up nearby but were immediately pulled down by Caesar's enemies. They were replaced by a temple consecrated by Octavian in 29 BC to the "god" Julius Caesar.

The podium was extended forward to form a raised terrace containing a semicircular recess at ground level in which stood a round altar (traces visible). In the *cella* stood a statue of Caesar, a star on his head. Suetonius explains why he was always represented in this way: "after his apotheosis, during the first days of the games given in his honour by his successor Augustus, a comet appeared at about the eleventh hour and burned for seven days; it was thought to be Caesar's soul being admitted to heaven ..."

When Octavian defeated the fleets of Antony and Cleopatra at Actium in Greece on 2 September 31 BC, he took the prows *(rostra)* of the enemy ships and fixed them to the terrace of Caesar's Temple; the terrace became known as Caesar's Rostra and later Emperors often spoke from there.

Arco di Trionfo di Augusto (Triumphal Arch of Augustus)

Two commemorative arches were erected by Augustus between the Temples of Caesar and Castor: the first was built in 29 BC after his victory at Actium in Greece; 10 years later, as the first became dilapidated, a second was built to celebrate Augustus's recovery of the Roman standards which had been captured by the Parthians at the Battle of Carrhae in Mesopotamia in 53 BC.

Only the foundations have been discovered (the bases of two pillars are visible).

Vicus Tuscus

This street curved round the foot of the Palatine to join the cattle market near the Tiber *(see BOCCA DELLA VERITÀ: Forum Boarium)*. Many Etruscan merchants had shops there, hence its name (the Romans called the Etruscans *Tusci*).

Tempio di Castore e Polluce★★★ (Temple of Castor and Pollux)

The temple was dedicated to Castor and Pollux, known as the **Dioscuri**. The chief remains are three columns supporting an architrave fragment, which form one of the most famous sights of the Roman Forum. The founding of the temple goes back to the beginning of the 5C BC; it has remained on its original site.

Its whole history is surrounded by legends. Early in the 5C BC, Rome, targeted by the other cities in the Latin League, who were watching the city's growing influence with concern, took the offensive against her poorer, envious neighbours: the conflict came to a head on the shores of Lake Regillus in about 496 BC. During the battle the Romans saw two divine knights fighting on their side; these were Castor and Pollux, sons of Jupiter and Leda. They subsequently made their way to Rome to announce the victory to the people gathered in the Forum; their thirsty horses drank at Juturna's spring. A temple dedicated to Castor and Pollux was built on the site of this apparition by the son of the dictator Postumius, who had directed the battle against the Latins.

The three beautiful columns, which were pulled down in 1811, date from a reconstruction undertaken in the Augustan era and belong to the long left-hand side of the sanctuary. The very high podium which emphasises the height of the tall columns, the magnitude of the Corinthian capitals and the use of very white marble combine to give a majestic effect. The remains of the Temple of Castor and Pollux show what magnificence Augustus sought to bestow on the city to replace the damage caused in the civil war.

It is said that the Emperor **Caligula** (AD 37-41), whose excesses led to his being presumed insane, built a bridge from the Temple of Castor and Pollux (the antechamber to his palace on the Palatine) to the Temple of Jupiter on the Capitol so that he could go and converse with the god whom he considered his equal, or sometimes even take his place.

Basilica Giulia★★ (Basilica Julia)

In 170 BC the Censor Sempronius Gracchus, father of the tribunes Tiberius and Caius, built a basilica on this site which was called "Sempronia". In 55 BC Julius Caesar, who was Consul, replaced it with another basilica, larger and more elegant, which started the trend for gigantic buildings in the Forum: 109m/358ft long, 40m/131ft wide and divided into five aisles, it was paved with precious marble in the centre and white marble in the side aisles. Close observation of some of the paving stones will reveal geometric designs which were marked out by idlers for their games.

There was a portico on the northeast side and shops on the opposite side.

Julius Caesar was murdered in 44 BC before the basilica was finished; it bears his name nonetheless, although it was Augustus who completed it.

In about the 8C the church of Santa Maria in Cannapara was established in the west corner (traces of brick walls).

Colonne votive (Votive columns)

There were seven, probably erected during Diocletian's reign (AD 284-305) to commemorate army generals. Two have been partly reconstructed.

Lago di Curzio (9)

The **Curtian Lake** refers to a circular area paved with stone within a shallow surround, protected by a roof and a railing. During the early Republic it was a cleft full of water that could not be drained away. The Oracle was consulted and pronounced that the opening would close when Rome threw her dearest treasure into it. A valuable young soldier called **Curtius** rode into it fully armed and the abyss closed up, leaving a small pool of water. The adjacent low-relief sculpture illustrating the legend was executed in the 1C BC *(now housed in the Museo del Palazzo dei Conservatori)*; it does not reveal whether this legend should be given more credit than another which says that Curtius was a Sabine soldier who was nearly sucked down into the marshy ground of the Forum during the legendary war between Romulus and Tatius.

Colonna di Foca★ (Phocas's Column)
In AD 608 the eastern Emperor Phocas gave the Pantheon to Pope Boniface IV and it was turned into a church. In gratitude a statue of the donor was set up on a column in the Forum. The column had to be taken from an already existing building because by then there were no artists capable of producing fine sculpture. This was the last monument to be erected on the old public place.

The sacred **fig tree**, symbol of the tree beneath which the cradle of Romulus and Remus had been found, the **vine** and the **olive tree (10)**, symbols of the prosperity which Rome owed to agriculture, have been replanted. Here also stood the very popular statue of Marsyas, brought from Greece in the 2C BC. It represented a Silenus looking, as they all did, like an old satyr, very ugly and often drunk, wearing a skin over his shoulders. He wore a Phrygian cap, symbol of liberty; newly-freed slaves would come and touch the statue.

The large **inscription (11)**, reconstructed in bronze letters, bears the name of Naevius and commemorates the relaying of the paving carried out by this magistrate in 15 BC.

Vicus Jugarius
This important street ran between the Temple of Saturn and the Basilica Julia and led to the vegetable market *(see BOCCA DELLA VERITÀ: Forum Holitorium).*

Tempio di Saturno★★★ (Temple of Saturn)
From 497 onwards a temple dedicated to Saturn stood on this site. This god was supposed to have taught the Romans to cultivate the earth; hence his prestige with this peasant people. The temple was restored several times under the Republic and then rebuilt in the 4C after a fire. The eight columns of the *pronaos* which remain date from this period; the travertine podium goes back to the 1C BC.

Saturnalia
This celebrated festival took place in December in the Temple of Saturn. The general licence which accompanied it was intended to help the sun rise again in the sky. During the Saturnalia all distinctions between masters and slaves were suspended; the latter, in particular, were entitled to free speech.

State Treasury
The treasure was lodged in the temple basement. This place may have been chosen because the cult of Saturn was associated with that of Ops, the goddess of abundance. The Senate administered the treasure, assisted by the censors and the quaestors. Late in 49, during the civil war, Caesar did not hesitate to draw on the funds.

Portico degli Dei Consenti★ (Portico of the Di Consentes)
The best view is from the Capitoline Hill and Via del Foro Romano The 12 columns with Corinthian capitals were reconstructed in 1858. The portico was built by Domitian in honour of the 12 great gods in the Roman pantheon who met in council to assist Jupiter. Their statues stood in the portico, two by two: Jupiter and Juno, Neptune and Minerva, Mars and Venus, Apollo and Diana, Vulcan and Vesta, Mercury and Ceres.

It was restored in 367 by the Prefect of Rome, Vettius Agorius Praetextatus, who had been a friend of **Julian the Apostate** and shared his great sympathy for the pagan religions; it was certainly the last gesture made to paganism in Rome, where 37 Popes had already acceded to the throne of St Peter.

Tabularium
See Musei Capitolini, CAMPIDOGLIO-CAPITOLINO. The podium and a few extant pillars form the base of the Senatorial Palace. The Tabularium filled the depression between the Citadel and the Capitol, the two peaks of the Capitoline Hill. Its façade formed the west side of the Forum. It was built in 78 BC to house the state records, including some bronze tablets on which were inscribed the old Roman laws, hence the name Tabularium. The use of peperine, a very simple building material, and of the Doric order, a plain architectural style, typify the austerity of Republican architecture.

Tempio di Vespasiano★★ (Temple of Vespasian)
Three very elegant columns, excavated by Valadier in 1811, are still standing; they formed a corner of the earlier part of the temple. Above the architrave is a detailed decorative frieze: a cornice with dentil, ovolo and palm leaf moulding above a band decorated with bucranes and sacrificial instruments. The temple was approached by steps from the Clivus Capitolinus.

Vespasian became Emperor in AD 69 following the struggles which arose among the pretenders to Nero's succession. He therefore established the principle of a hereditary monarchy founded on primogeniture. He announced to the Senate that "his sons would succeed him or there would be no successor". His elder son Titus therefore succeeded him and began to build a temple in honour of his father who had been deified on his death. In practice, if an Emperor had ruled well, the Senate would issue a decree raising him to the rank of the gods; all that was needed was a witness who had seen an eagle carry off the dead man's soul during the cremation ceremony.

Titus died before the temple was finished; it was Domitian, his brother and successor as Emperor, who completed the building and dedicated it to Vespasian and Titus. Their two statues stood on a pedestal in the *cella*.

Tempio della Concordia (Temple of Concord)

The Romans always attributed a divine character to the mysterious forces which influenced events; thus they worshipped as gods such abstract ideas as concord, justice, liberty and abundance. Most of these divinities were represented by the statue of a female figure: the attributes of concord were two linked hands and a dove.

There had been a Temple of Concord in the Forum since 367 BC; it commemorated the re-establishment of peace between the patricians and the plebeians who had been at odds since the beginning of the 5C BC. Some two-and-a-half centuries later, when the assassination of the people's tribune, Caius Gracchus, had restored peace at home, concord was again held in honour and the temple rebuilt.

The plan of the building is quite unusual: the *cella* extends laterally beyond the width of the *pronaos*, which was reached by steps from the Clivus Capitolinus. *Retrace your steps and go around the Temple of Castor and Pollux.*

Cinta sacra di Giuturna (Sacred Precinct of Juturna) (12)

Juturna was a nymph who reigned over all the springs in Latium and was made immortal by Jupiter, who loved her. Her shrine contained a spring which played a part in the legend of the Dioscuri. In the basin stands an altar, probably 2C, with low-relief sculptures representing Castor and Pollux and a woman bearing a long torch *(on the front and back)*, and Leda and the swan, and Jupiter *(on the sides)*. The adjacent **aedicule (13)**, partially reconstructed, the round well and the altar were also part of the sacred precinct. The well is inscribed with the name of Barbatius Pollio, who put up a dedication to Juturna, probably in the reign of Augustus; low-relief figures on the altar.

Santa Maria Antiqua

Closed for restoration at the time of going to press. Church open for specialist study only. ☎ 06 39 08 071; Fax 06 39 75 09 50; pierreci@pierreci.it
Paintings dating from the Byzantine period can still be seen in this 6C church.

Oratorio dei Martiri (Oratory of the Forty Martyrs) (14)

The original purpose of the building is unknown; in the 7C it was decorated with paintings and dedicated to the 40 martyrs of Sebastea in Armenia, who were exposed in chains on a frozen pond.

Tempio e Atrio delle Vestali★★★ (Temple and Atrium of the Vestal Virgins)

In the days when fire was still a precious commodity, the village on the Palatine where Romulus lived must have included a round hut, similar to all the other huts, where the communal fire was kept alight. This process was organised around Vesta, the goddess of fire.

The institution of the cult in Rome goes back to Romulus or Numa Pompilius (715-672 BC). A group of priestesses, known as the Vestal Virgins, at first four in number but later increased to six, officiated in the cult of Vesta.

When the first temple was built, probably late in the 6C BC, it conserved the circular form of the earlier hut. It was destroyed by fire and rebuilt several times, always in circular form, until the time of Septimius Severus. Only the central foundation and a few marble fragments survived to be used in the 1930 reconstruction. It was an enclosed shrine, surrounded by a portico supported on 20 fluted Corinthian columns; the frieze showed the instruments of sacrifice in low relief. The *cella* housed an altar where the fire was kept burning constantly. There was also a secret place, where certain objects which were supposed to have made Rome's fortune were jealously guarded; they included the famous Palladium, a statuette in wood or bone of the goddess Pallas, which was able to protect the city which possessed it. It had fallen from the sky on the city of Troy, possibly thrown by Zeus on Olympus. The Romans thought it had come into their possession through Aeneas, who had stolen it from Troy and brought it to Italy.

Next to the temple was the house of the Vestal Virgins, the **Atrium Vestae**. It was a large two-storey building enclosing a rectangular courtyard with a portico, containing two pools of water and a garden.

The Vestal Virgins were chosen from the patrician families. They entered into service at the age of 10 and stayed for at least 30 years: 10 as pupils, 10 performing their duties and 10 teaching. Most of the Vestals spent their whole lives in the house. Discipline was strict: a virgin who let the fire go out, a portent of disaster for Rome, was severely punished and one who broke her vow of chastity was buried alive. From the 3C, statues were erected to the Vestals in recognition of their service. Some of these statues with an inscription on the base have been placed in the courtyard of the house.

Regia

Religious observance in Rome centred on the Regia and the Temple of Vesta. The Regia was held to have been the residence of King Numa Pompilius, who succeeded Romulus and organised the state religion. Later it was the residence of the Pontifex Maximus, the head of the college of priests. During the Regal period it was the Pontifex Maximus who kept the religious records. Under the Republic he took charge of the national religion and became so influential that the Emperors appointed themselves to the position.

The Regia and the House of the Vestals mark the limit of the Forum at the time of the kings and the Republic. The section extending to the Arch of Titus was added later.

> **THE LEGEND OF THE SHIELDS**
> One day King Numa received a shield (*ancile*) from heaven which was thought to foretell victory for the Romans. He entrusted it for safe-keeping to the priests of the cult of Mars, and to prevent it from being stolen he had 11 copies made; all were kept in the Regia. The workman who made the shields asked as his reward to be remembered in the chanting that accompanied the procession of the shields.

Tempio di Antonino e Faustina★★ (Temple of Antoninus and Faustina)

The Emperor Antoninus Pius, who succeeded Hadrian in AD138, belonged to a rich family originally from Nîmes in France. He was well known for his kindness and reigned for 23 years in peace and moderation. On the death of his wife, Faustina, in AD 141, he raised her to the ranks of the goddesses, in spite of her scandalous behaviour. A huge temple to her was erected in the Forum.

When Antoninus himself died, in AD 161, the Senate decided to dedicate the temple to both husband and wife.

The beautiful monolithic columns of the *pronaos* still stand on their high podium. The frieze of griffins and candelabra on the entablature is a masterpiece of fine craftsmanship.

In the 11C the church of San Lorenzo in Miranda was established in the ruins. When Charles V visited Rome in 1536 the façade of the church was set back to reveal the colonnade. In 1602 the church was rebuilt.

Excavations beside the Temple of Antoninus and Faustina have uncovered a **cemetery (15)** dating from the time of Romulus (8C-7C BC).

Tempio di Romolo (Temple of Romulus)

The Romulus to whom the temple is thought to be dedicated was not the founder of Rome but the son of the Emperor Maxentius. Romulus died in 307.

Dating from the early 4C, the construction is circular and flanked by two rooms with apses: it may have been built in honour of Constantine, to celebrate his victory over Maxentius in 312, or in honour of the divine city of Rome. In the 6C, when the room behind the temple became the church of St Cosmas and St Damian, the temple itself became a vestibule to the church.

The doorway between two porphyry columns in the concave façade is closed by the original 4C bronze doors; the lock still works.

On the left of the Temple of Romulus are traces of six small **rooms (16)** on either side of a corridor; they may have belonged to a brothel in the Republican era.

The remains of a medieval arcaded building **(17)** high above the Sacred Way indicate how much the ground level in the Forum had risen by the Middle Ages.

Higher up the slope, quite in harmony with the Ancient monuments below, is the church of Santa Francesca Romana with its Romanesque belfry and three parapet statues.

Basilica di Massenzio e Costantino★★★ (Basilica of Maxentius and Constantine)

This building is well known for its summer symphony concerts. Maxentius was proclaimed Emperor by the people after the abdication of joint rulers, Maximian, his father, and Diocletian, in 305. Almost immediately he began to build a basilica, the last to be erected in Rome. Built of brick beneath a groined vault, it was different from the other two basilicas, Aemilia and Julia. It was rectangular and divided into three by huge pillars flanked by columns; one long side ran parallel to the Sacred Way and the other followed the line of the present Via dei Fori Imperiali; one of the short sides constituted the main façade (facing east towards the Colosseum) and the other projected in an apse.

The Imperial throne, however, was coveted by Constantine, son of the Emperor Constantius, who had reigned jointly with Maximian and Diocletian. He defeated Maxentius at the battle of the Milvian Bridge in 312 and completed the basilica with modifications. He moved the entrance to the façade overlooking the Sacred Way and graced it with a portico of four porphyry columns *(still visible)*; an apse was added to the opposite façade.

This grandiose building housed some colossal statues; fragments of the statue of Constantine, which stood in the west apse, can still be seen in the courtyard of the Palazzo dei Conservatori. The gilded bronze tiles were used in the 7C to roof St Peter's Basilica.

Antiquarium

The exhibits in this museum, which is housed in a former convent attached to the church of Santa Francesca Romana, are mostly connected with the Roman Forum: the earliest traces of Ancient Rome taken from tombs dating from 1 000-600 BC or found in the Forum or on the Palatine (hut-shaped urns and hollow tree trunks used as coffins).

Arco di Trionfo di Tito** (Triumphal Arch of Titus)

The arch stands on the **Velia**, a spur of the Palatine jutting out towards the Esquiline, and appears in all the views of the Forum.

Titus, the eldest son of Vespasian, succeeded his father as Emperor but his reign was brief: from AD 79-81. In 70 he had captured Jerusalem, thus bringing to a successful conclusion a campaign his father had been pursuing since 66. After his death an arch was erected to commemorate his success. The fall of Jerusalem was among the most tragic events in Jewish history. The city was destroyed and the temple, the spiritual bond between Jews of the diaspora, was burned down. In its place Hadrian built a sanctuary to Jupiter and the city was called Aelia Capitolina (Hadrian's family name was Aelius). The single archway of the Arch of Titus was restored by Luigi Valadier in 1821.

At the centre of the panelled vault is a sculpture depicting the apotheosis of Titus: his soul is carried up to heaven by an eagle; this event made him eligible for deification.

The frieze *(above the arch on the side facing the Colosseum)* is indistinct: in a sacrificial procession a recumbent figure represents the Jordan, symbolising the defeat of Palestine.

The two low reliefs under the vault are among the masterpieces of Roman sculpture. On one side, Titus rides in his chariot in triumph, crowned with victory. On the other, the triumphal procession exhibits the booty pillaged from the temple in Jerusalem: the seven-branch candlestick which Moses had made and placed in the Tabernacle as commanded by God on Mount Sinai, the table for the shewbread which was placed in the temple each week in the name of the 12 tribes of Israel, and the silver trumpets which announced the festivals.

It was on the Velia that Nero built the vestibule to his Golden House.

Tempio di Giove Statore (Temple of Jupiter Stator)

On 8 November 63 BC **Cicero** delivered his first Catiline oration here before the Senate. Feelings ran high among his audience, who were impressed by the security measures considered necessary to protect the State.

Bear right up the hill (Clivus Palatinus) to the Palatine.

PALATINO (PALATINE HILL)

Of the seven hills of Rome, it is the Palatine which captures the visitor's imagination. As the cradle of the Eternal City it is a prime archaeological site. Since the Renaissance it has offered pleasant walks among flower beds and shady trees.

Byron wrote of the beauty of the Palatine and its overgrown ruins:

"Cypress and ivy, weed and wallflower grown

Matted and mass'd together, hillocks heap'd

On what were chambers, arch crush'd, column strown

In fragments, choked up vaults, and frescos steep'd

In subterranean damps ..."

Origins

It was inconvenient for political reasons that **Romulus** and **Remus** *(see Insights and Images, p 65)*, twin sons of the Vestal Rhea Silvia and the god Mars, should survive. They were therefore abandoned on the banks of the Tiber but the river was in spate and their cradle came to rest on the Palatine. They survived thanks to a she-wolf which suckled them in the Lupercal cave. The shepherd Faustulus, who witnessed this unusual event, took charge of the twins and brought them up. In the middle of the 8C BC Romulus ploughed a deep furrow around the Palatine lifting his ploughshare in three places. This was the beginning of Rome, a symbolic enclosure with three gateways: the Porta Mugonia, the Porta Romana and the Porta Scalae Caci.

This is obviously a legendary account ... but in 1949 traces of huts thought to date from the 8C and 7C BC were excavated on the legendary site of Romulus's house.

During the Republic the Palatine was a quiet residential area. **Cicero** lived on the hill, as did Antony, the Triumvir, and Agrippa – Octavian's friend before becoming his son-in-law. Foreigners came to visit the shepherd's hut and the wolf's cave in the southwest face of the hill.

In 63 BC "on the ninth day before the Kalends of October, a little before daybreak" Octa-

The nymphaeum in the Domus Flavia, built during the time of Domitian

vian was born. When he became the Emperor Augustus, the Palatine began to alter. He enlarged his house and then rebuilt it after it was destroyed by fire in the 3 BC. Tiberius, who succeeded him, Caligula, Claudius and Nero all lived on the Palatine, but it was **Domitian**, the last Flavian Emperor (AD 81-96), who transformed the hill by turning it into the Imperial Palace and giving it the appearance that has now been revealed by archaeologists. The hollow which divided it into two peaks (Germalus and Palatium) was filled with new buildings, whose ruins now occupy the central section of the plateau: they are the **Domus Flavia** and the **Domus Augustana**; the **Stadium** also dates from this period. In 191 the buildings on the Palatine were seriously damaged by fire. The Emperor Septimius Severus was not content with simply undertaking repairs. He enlarged the Imperial Palace to the south and built a monumental façade, the Septizonium, parallel with the Old Appian Way, so that travellers arriving in Rome by this route would be immediately impressed by the grandeur of the capital. This section of the palace remained standing until Pope Sixtus V demolished it to provide building materials at the end of the 16C.

The Palatine began to go into decline in the 3C when Diocletian, Galerius, Maximian and Constantius deserted Rome and built new Imperial residences in Nicomedia, Sirmium, Milan and Trier respectively. In 330 **Constantine** moved the Imperial capital to Constantinople, formerly Byzantium, and the Palatine was abandoned.

The Christians generally ignored the Palatine plateau and built only on the slopes: in the 4C a sanctuary was dedicated to St Anastasia on the south side; on the north face the church of St Sebastian was established in what had been a temple to the sun; it had been built by the Emperor Elagabalus (218-222), a native of Emesa (modern Homs) in Syria, who dreamed of a religion which would combine the various Oriental cults and appointed himself high priest to the sun god.

In the 11C and 12C Rome became the prize in the struggles between the Pope and the Emperor and was studded with fortresses and towers; hence the description *Roma turrita*. The Frangipani family, who supported the Emperor, fortified the whole of the southeast face of the Palatine. By the time of the Renaissance the buildings on the Palatine (from which the word "palace" is derived) were in ruins. The wealthy Roman families built villas on the site, surrounding them with vineyards and gardens: the Barberini near to St Sebastian, the Farnese on the northwest part of the hill between Tiberius's and Caligula's palaces. In the 16C the Mattei built a villa on the site of the Domus Augustana; three centuries later an Englishman, Charles Mills, converted it into a sort of Romantic Gothic castle. This extraordinary building was demolished at the end of the 19C at the instigation of P Rosa, the archaeologist in charge of the excavations.

Excavations

Investigative digging began in 1724 at the suggestion of Francis I of Parma, who had inherited the Farnese Villa. The Domus Flavia was the first building to see the light of day. About 50 years later a Frenchman, the Abbé Rancoureuil, excavated the Domus Augustana and the buildings overlooking the Circus Maximus. In 1860, under Napoleon III, archaeologists discovered Tiberius's Palace, Livia's House and the Temple of Apollo, which was first attributed to Jupiter. The identification of the buildings on the Palatine has provoked passionate argument between archaeologists and historians. Many of the constructions have never been discovered but excavations on the Palatine continue, particularly in the area of the Temple of Apollo.

Very little of the ruined buildings remains standing and it requires a great effort of the imagination to evoke the splendour of the Ancient palaces on the Palatine.

Tour

& *Open daily 9am-1hr before dusk (5.30pm in winter). Last admission 1hr before closing time. Closed 1 Jan and Christmas. €8, combined ticket with the Colosseum; €20 for a "Roma archeologica" card, valid for nine archaeological sites.* ☎ *06 39 08 071; Fax 06 39 75 09 50; pierreci@pierreci.it*

Clivus Palatinus

This road approximately follows the hollow between the two peaks: the Palatium to the left, the Germalus to the right.

Walk straight up the path (south) leaving on the right the steps which go up to the Farnese Gardens.

The rectangular ditch **(1)** marks the site of Domitian's Arch. The sections of high brick wall facing down the hill belonged to the portico of the Domus Flavia. The path emerges at the top of the hill in the centre of the artificial plateau which was created when Domitian filled in the hollow between the Palatium and the Germalus.

Domus Flavia★

This was the centre of official Imperial activity. Although the buildings have been razed to the ground, it is still possible to envisage them. There were three rooms behind the portico:

– the **Lararium** – the shrine of the household gods, the Lares – was the Emperor's private chapel;

– the **Throne Room** (Sala del Trono) was enormous (over 30m/98ft wide by 40m/131ft long) with huge statues standing in the recesses in the walls;

– the **Basilica**, where the Emperor dispensed justice, had an apse at one end and a row of columns down each of the long sides. Outside the west wall are traces of the west portico of the Domus.

Behind these three rooms is a courtyard **(Peristilium)** originally surrounded by a portico (traces of the columns remain). Suetonius wrote that Domitian was so hated by everyone for his injustice and cruelty that he had the walls of the portico faced with phengite (a very shiny stone) so that he could "see by reflection what was going on behind his back". The octagonal

basin at the centre of the court, which is now planted with flowers, was probably a fountain.

Beyond the peristyle is the **Triclinium**, the dining room, which was certainly the most beautiful room in the palace; part of the coloured marble floor has been preserved. It was supported on little brick pillars to allow the passage of warm air produced by an underground stove to heat the room.

The *triclinium* was flanked to right and left by two small leisure rooms, known in Latin as the *nymphaea*. The one on the right is well preserved.

The extant building in the far corner of the *nymphaeum* dates from the Farnese era (16C).

★★★ FORO

Via

Pta Romana

Palazzo di Caligola

Orti   Farnesiani

Domus

Victoriae

Tiberiana

Clivus

S. Teodoro

G
E
R
M
A
L

T. di Cibele   ★★Casa di Livia   9

Scala
di Caco

Tempi
di Apol

S. Anastasia

Via

PALATINO

0   50 m

—— Extant parts

—— Non-extant parts

dei

CIRCO

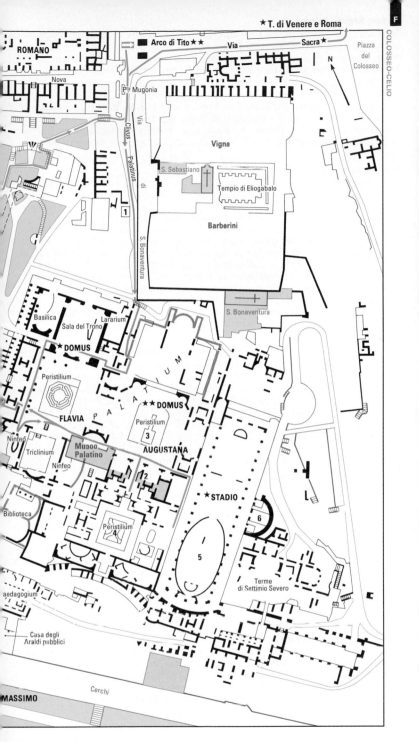

The traces of walls, columns and apses on the terrace behind the *triclinium* may mark the site of the libraries of the Imperial Palace.

Sale sotterranee★ (Underground rooms) – These rooms are all that remained of houses from the Republican era and of Nero's constructions when they were buried under Domitian's building projects.

– Beneath the basilica, a rectangular room: the paintings with which it was decorated are conserved in a room **(2)** east of the Antiquarium; they probably date from the Augustan era and depict the cult of Isis.

– Beneath the lararium, the **Griffin House** (Casa dei Grifi), sometimes also erroneously called "Catilina's house": it was built in the 2C BC (walls composed of irregular-sized stones mixed with mortar), altered in the 1C BC (walls composed of regular stone blocks arranged in a diamond pattern) and then altered again by Nero; many of the paintings have been removed to the Antiquarium for safe keeping; one room contains a stucco relief of two griffins face to face.

– Beneath the peristyle: a circular chamber containing a well which communicates with another room by a passage. The discovery of this complex early this century caused quite a stir among archaeologists who thought they had found the *Mundus*. At the time of the founding of Rome the *Mundus* was a well into which a handful of earth was thrown by each new immigrant who, through this symbolic gesture, became a citizen of the new city. In fact, it is probably only a silo for water or grain.

Museo Palatino

The **Palatine Museum** is housed in a building which once belonged to the Convent of the Visitation, built over the ruins of Domitian's Imperial Palace (structural remains of which can be seen in Rooms 3 and 4), and contains articles and fragments found on the Palatine. The ground floor is dedicated to the period spanning the foundation of Rome (model of 8-7C BC huts built on the Germalus) and the Republican era; the upper floor contains exhibits relating to the Imperial period. Exhibits include remains of "second style" frescoes from Augustus's House, with architectural cornices and columns and suspended festoons of leaves and flowers between them; a collection of portraits of Emperors and famous characters; and two inlaid-marble panels which demonstrate the fine quality of wall decoration during the Nero period (AD 54-68). At the end of Room 9, the statue known as the Borghese Hera, a Roman copy of a Greek work from the end of the 5C BC, towers over the other exhibits.

Domus Augustana★★

This is not Augustus's own private house but the official Imperial residence. The rooms are arranged around two peristyles *(peristilium)*; one is very much lower than the other. At the centre of the upper peristyle **(3)**, marked by an umbrella pine, is the base of a construction which was reached by a bridge from the edge of the surrounding basin. Around the sides are various living rooms.

The rooms on the south side of the upper peristyle overlook the lower peristyle. The central basin **(4)**, which is composed of a pattern of compartments, was designed to collect rain water. The palace itself faces the Circus Maximus from behind a concave façade.

Even in ruins the Domus Augustana gives an impression of grandeur and luxury because of its sophisticated design, its soaring walls and the daring of some of the vaulting.

Stadio★ (Stadium)

This was one of Domitian's projects. It looks like a gigantic trough (some 145m/159yd long) surrounded by a two-storey portico. Some say it was designed to stage private games and spectacles for the Emperor; others say it was a garden or an athletics ground. The small oval track **(5)** at the southern end dates from the 6C and is the work of Theodoric, the Ostrogoth, who occupied the Palatine at that period. The huge recess **(6)** in the centre of the long east side may have been reserved for the Emperor.

On the east side of the Stadium are the ruins of a bathhouse attributed to Septimius Severus but probably built by Maxentius.

Pass the museum and retrace your steps.

Tempio di Apollo (Temple of Apollo)

For many years this temple was thought to be dedicated to Jupiter but it is probably the one mentioned by Suetonius: Augustus built a temple to Apollo "in a corner of his house on the Palatine which had been struck by lightning and which, according to the omens, Apollo was claiming for himself".

The temple is fenced off; the podium and a column of the *pronaos* are recognisable.

Casa di Livia★★ (Livia's House)

This house, which is named after Augustus's wife, was probably where the Emperor himself lived. The diamond pattern on the walls and the style of the decor date the building to the end of the Republic. The wall paintings which had already deteriorated somewhat were detached and erected just in front of the walls to which they belonged; this means they can be appreciated in their original setting. The names given to the various rooms do not necessarily correspond to their use. On either side of the centre room (*tablinum* – study) are two narrow rooms (wings) where wax images of the family ancestors were kept or which, in more modest houses, were used as storerooms.

Left wing – The lower part of the wall is decorated to look like marble; above are panels showing people and griffins face to face.

Tablinum – On the right-hand wall: a central panel, surrounded by architectural motifs, shows Io, Argos's daughter; Zeus fell in love with her and turned her into a heifer to protect her from the fury of his wife, Hera, who was nevertheless suspicious and set Argus, who had 100 eyes, to watch over the animal. The painting shows Hermes, who was sent by Zeus to rescue Io.

On the left-hand wall: lead pipes engraved with the name IVLIAE AV (Julia Augusta). The archaeologists who discovered this inscription in 1869 thought it referred to Augustus's wife, the Empress, and attributed the house to Livia.

The rear wall depicts Galatea fleeing from Polyphemus.

Right wing – The decorations on the left-hand wall, although damaged by the opening of the door, are still fresh: simulated columns flanking beautiful garlands of fruit and leaves from which hang baskets, sticks, horned animal heads, lyres and other representations of nature. Above, on a yellow ground, is a frieze showing people at work in the open air.

Cisterne (Cisterns) (7)
They date from the 6C BC; one is shaped like a beehive and the other is uncovered.

Scala di Caco (Cacus's Steps)
This was one of the three original approaches to the Palatine. The steps are named after a local villain, **Cacus**, who is linked in legend to Hercules. When Hercules was returning to the Argos with the cattle stolen from Geryon, he halted on the banks of the Tiber. Cacus, an evil three-headed monster who breathed fire from his three mouths, took the opportunity to steal three animals. He made them walk backwards to avoid detection but Hercules was not fooled and he killed Cacus.

Capanne del villagio di Romolo (Cabins from Romulus's village) (8)
Together with the Forum cemetery these huts form some of the earliest traces of the city (8C-7C BC). The modern roof which covers them creates a real reliquary. Three huts have been discovered, oval or rectangular and sunk in the ground. The ring of holes held the posts which supported the walls and the roof. The gap in the south side (facing the Tiber) marks the doorway and is flanked by smaller post holes which indicate the possibility of a porch. The ditch surrounding each emplacement was probably to drain off the rain water from the roof.

Tempio di Cibele (Temple of Cybele)
Cybele, the great goddess of Phrygia (also called the Mother of the Gods, the Great Mother or Magna Mater), was the personification of the powers of nature. Her cult was introduced into Rome late in the 3C or early in the 2C BC. In 204 BC, at the height of the Second Punic War, a hail of stones fell on Rome. The priests appealed to the gods and the Senate was obliged to send for the **"black stone"**, symbol of the goddess Cybele, from Pessinus in Asia Minor. The temple on the Palatine was inaugurated in 191 and then rebuilt by Augustus after several fires. Today only the base of the *cella* walls remains in the shade of a group of holm oaks.

Each year from 4-20 April a festival took place in front of the temple. Called the Megalesia, it consisted of theatrical presentations and circus acts and had been founded in 204 in honour of Cybele. Terence's comedy "Andria" was played for the first time during the festival in 168 BC, but on that occasion the audience preferred the tightrope walkers, perhaps because Terence did not have Plautus's biting wit "nor his coarse jokes, his broad humour, his puns, his quips ...".

Domus Tiberiana
The arches facing the Temple of Cybele belonged to the rear façade of Tiberius' Palace. Only a few traces of this huge rectangular building are visible since Cardinal Farnese's gardens cover the greater part of it.

The main façade of the palace faced the Forum. Caligula extended the building as far as Via Nova; Trajan and Hadrian added the ranges overlooking Clivus Victoriae.

Cryptoporticus
This is a network of passages, partially underground, which probably linked the various Imperial buildings which occupied the hill. It dates from Nero's reign, although the arm linking up with Domitian's Domus Flavia must have been added later.

The stuccoes which decorated the vaulting in the section of the passage near Livia's House have been removed to the Antiquarium and replaced by copies.

The oval basin (9) on the left of the steps leading up to the Farnese Gardens was a fish tank in the southeast corner of Tiberius's Palace.

Orti Farnesiani (Farnese Gardens)
The gardens were laid out in the middle of the 16C by Cardinal Alexander Farnese, Paul III's nephew. The entrance, set in a semicircle at the level of the Forum (which was higher then than now), gave access to a series of terraces rising up the north face of the Palatine. On the flat top of the hill, over the ruins of Tiberius's Palace, stretched the Farnese's magnificent botanical garden, one of the richest in the world at that time. The northwest corner of the gardens gives an excellent

view★★ of the Forum, the Tabularium, the Senatorial Palace, the monument to Victor Emmanuel II, the domes of the church of St Luke and St Martina and of the two churches next to Trajan's Column, the Militia Tower etc. In the northeast corner of the gardens are two buildings (reconstructed) which formed a complex comprising two aviaries above a nymphaeum. From the terrace there is a pleasant **view**★★, particularly at sunset, of the basilica of Maxentius, the belfry of Santa Francesca Romana and the upper storeys of the Colosseum.

Below the aviaries there used to be a monumental gate marking the entrance to the gardens. It was begun by Vignola and completed by Girolamo Rainaldi but taken down in 1882. It now stands on the east side of Via di S. Gregorio *(see plan, p 160)*.

Leave the Palatine by Clivus Palatinus, turning right into Via Sacra at the Arch of Titus to visit the other monuments which belong to the Forum.

Tempio di Venere e Roma★ (Temple of Venus and Rome)

The temple was built between AD 121-136 by Hadrian, completed by Antoninus Pius and restored by Maxentius, on the site of the vestibule to Nero's Golden House. It was the largest temple in Rome (110m/361ft by 53m/174ft) and designed in the Greek style with steps on all sides (the majority of Roman temples had only one flight of steps leading up to the *pronaos*). It was surrounded by a colonnade and uniquely comprised two cellae with apses back to back. One was dedicated to the goddess Rome and faced the Forum; the other was dedicated to Venus and faced the Colosseum.

The plans for the temple were drawn up by Hadrian, who was keen on architecture. He also designed two gigantic seated figures to be set in niches which were disproportionately small. Trajan's brilliant architect, Apollodorus of Damascus, commented that "if the figures tried to stand they would bump their heads on the vault". He had already poured scorn on the Emperor's rather peculiar taste for painting pumpkins. It was too much; Hadrian had the architect silenced once and for all.

The part of the temple which faces the Forum has been incorporated into the church of Santa Francesca Romana and the adjoining convent of Olivetan monks. An idea of the temple's appearance is given by a few columns which were re-erected in 1935; the position of the missing parts is marked by bushes of privet, box and oleander.

Santa Francesca Romana

In the 8C an oratory dedicated to St Peter and St Paul was built in the western half of the Temple of Venus and Rome by Pope Paul I. In the following century it replaced the church of Santa Maria Antiqua in the Forum and was called Santa Maria Nova. The church was placed under the patronage of Santa Francesca Romana **(St Frances of Rome)** when she was canonised in 1608.

The 12C Romanesque **bell-tower**★ is one of the most elegant in Rome.

The façade by Carlo Lombardi (1615) is characteristic of the Counter-Reformation. The use of a single order of flat pilasters resting on a high portico lends it a certain solemnity. Inside there is a beautiful 17C coffered ceiling.

Apsidal mosaic – The Virgin and Child are enthroned between St Peter and St Andrew, St James and St John. The mosaic dates from c 1160 at a period when mosaic art was marked by a certain eclecticism: the vivid colours of the Ancient art, together with the rigidity of the figures, is typical of Byzantine art.

Right transept – Two stones are preserved behind a grating; they are supposed to bear the print of St Peter's knees. He prayed at length to God to prevent Simon Magus from flying and Simon crashed to earth near the church. The *Acts of the Apostles* (VIII, 9-25) tell the story of the sorcerer who practised in Samaria and who wanted to acquire spiritual powers from the Apostles for money. He is the source of the word simony.

There is also a monument (16C) to Gregory XI, the last French Pope, who brought the Holy See back to Rome from Avignon in 1377. The central low relief shows St Peter entering Rome; the flanking statues are Faith and Prudence.

Crypt – Opposite the remains of St Frances of Rome is a marble low relief showing the saint and an angel (17C work by one of Bernini's pupils).

Sacristy – Beautiful painting of Santa Maria Nova showing a Virgin and Child which art historians date to the 5C or 8C.

Take Via dei Fori Imperiali.

Santi Cosma e Damiano (Basilica of St Cosmas and St Damian)

The basilica was dedicated in 526 by Pope Felix IV to two saints of Arabian origin, Cosmas and Damian, twin brothers whose help was invoked to cure illness. The church was established in the Temple of Romulus and in an adjacent room which had been the library of Vespasian's Forum; it was the first Christian church to occupy a pagan building in the Roman Forum. When the relics of the two saints were discovered in the 16C the Popes began to alter the original church. In the 17C Clement VIII reduced the width of the nave by creating side chapels which cut off the outer edges of the mosaic on the chancel arch. The floor was raised, a doorway opened in the west wall and a plaster arcade added in front of the apse.

Ceiling★ – Beautiful 17C coffered ceiling showing the triumph of St Cosmas and St Damian *(centre)* and *(at each end)* the coat of arms with the bees of Cardinal Francesco Barberini, who promoted the greater part of the 17C alterations.

Mosaics★ – Those on the chancel arch date from the late 7C and show the Lamb of God surrounded by seven candelabra and four angels. The angels on the left and right, symbolising the Evangelists, St Luke and St John, have survived the 17C alterations. The lamb and the throne were restored in 1936.

The mosaics in the apse date from the 6C. In the centre is the figure of Christ against a sunset sky. At his sides are the Apostles Peter and Paul presenting St Cosmas and St Damian, dressed in brown. On the left is Pope Felix IV offering a model of his church and on the right St Theodore dressed in a handsome chlamys (short mantle), like a Byzantine courtier. Below, partially screened by the Baroque altar (1637), is the Paschal Lamb surrounded by 12 beautiful angels representing the apostles and the Church.

Southeast chapel – *Facing the entrance.* Above the altar is a curious fresco showing the living Christ on the cross, a work in the Byzantine style, repainted in the 17C.

Gianicolo★

The Janiculum, or Gianicolo in Italian, is a favourite Sunday destination for locals, who come to the ridge to take a leisurely stroll, buy an ice cream and savour the magnificent views of their city. This area is particularly popular with tourists, a fact borne out by the numerous horse-drawn carriages here, but there is no better place to take in the beauty of Rome, especially on a summer's evening when the soft light adds to the magical atmosphere of the city. If, however, you choose to come here in the morning, make sure that you stay for the legendary firing of the cannon at noon, a sound that can be heard throughout the city.

Location

Michelin map or Michelin spiral atlas of Rome: pp 54-55 L 9, M 9, N 9. Tour: 2hr. The Janiculum Hill stands on the west bank of the Tiber, within the 17C walls built by Urbano VIII, in which the entrance gate Porta San Pancrazio is built. Beyond the hill to the west lies Villa Doria Pamphili, one of the largest areas of greenery in the city.

Neighbouring sights are described in the following chapters: CASTEL SANT'ANGELO; TRASTEVERE; VATICANO-SAN PIETRO.

Background

One of the oldest legends in Roman mythology maintains that the **Janiculum** Hill (Monte Gianicolo) was the site of the city founded by the god **Janus**, hence its name. Janus had several children, one of whom, Tiber, gave his name to the river. For many years the Janiculum was a country district. It was not until the 17C that Urban VIII constructed a defensive wall with bastions on the line of the present-day Viale delle Mura Aurelie and Viale delle Mura Gianicolensi.

From Mucius Scaevola to Garibaldi – Many of the heroic acts, legendary or true, which have shaped the history of Rome, seem to have taken place on the Janiculum.

The oldest goes back to the 6C BC, when the town had broken free of the Etruscan kings and was being besieged by **Lars Porsenna. Mucius**, a young Roman noble, infiltrated the enemy camp on the Janiculum in order to kill their chief. Unfortunately he made a mistake and killed one of the chief's aides; he was immediately arrested. To prove to Lars Porsenna that life was of little account to a Roman defending his country, Mucius put his right hand on a burning brasier. Porsenna was so struck by this bravery that he let him go. Mucius was henceforth nicknamed Scaevola, left-handed.

In his footsteps came Cloelia, a young woman who, according to Livy, showed courage "without precedent among women". Held hostage in Porsenna's camp, she escaped with her companions and made them swim the Tiber to reach Rome.

In 1849 the Janiculum was the scene of one of the battles in the struggle for Italian unity. **Garibaldi** defended it valiantly in the name of the Roman Republic against the French troops commanded by General Oudinot; on 4 July the Papal Government was re-established after a month of bloody combat, particularly in the Villa Pamphili.

Special Features

Villa Farnesina★★

 ♿ *Open daily (except Sun and public holidays) 9am-1pm; Thu, Sat and the first Sun in the month, also 2.30-6.30pm. €4.50. ☎ 06 68 80 17 67; Fax 06 68 38 831.*

The villa in its garden setting was built between 1508-11 for Agostino Chigi (1465-1520) the great banker. Known as the Magnificent, he entertained his guests, including Pope Leo X, in sumptuous style.

The villa is designed as a suburban house with two projecting wings. For the construction and the decor Chigi commissioned the best Renaissance artists: **Baldassarre Peruzzi**, architect and painter, and Raphael with his usual following of Giulio Romano, Francesco Penni, Giovanni da Udine, Sebastiano del Piombo and Sodoma.

The friendship linking all these men is enshrined in Villa Farnesina: Agostino Chigi was Raphael's most ardent patron and Leo X had a sincere affection for him. None of them saw the sack of the city which brought the Roman Renaissance to an end. Raphael died, aged 37, on Good Friday 1520; a few days later came Chigi's death; the following year Leo X succumbed to a "slight fever".

Later in the 16C the villa was sold to Cardinal Alessandro Farnese and assumed the name of its new owner.

Tour – The collection of paintings to be seen in this house is one of the gems of the Renaissance. On the ceiling of the **gallery** along the garden front is a fresco depicting the legend of Cupid and Psyche (in the centre *The Council of the Gods* and *The Marriage of Cupid and Psyche*), painted by Raphael, assisted by Giulio Romano, Francesco Penni and Giovanni da Udine. Finished in 1520, these paintings contain elements which were to become characteristic of the Mannerist style (a series of scenes, as in a tapestry, framed by garlands).

At the eastern end of the gallery is the **Galatea** room (1511) where Nereus's sea maiden has been painted by **Raphael** riding in a shell drawn by dolphins *(right of the entrance)*. The monstrous Polyphemus, as well as the scenes from Ovid's *Metamorphoses (in the lunettes),* are by **Sebastiano del Piombo**. The Constellations on the ceiling are the work of **Baldassarre Peruzzi**. The young man's head painted in grisaille *(left of the entrance)* is probably by Sebastiano del Piombo, but tradition attributes it to Michelangelo, who wanted to show Raphael that his figures were too small.

On the **first floor** the **salon** is decorated with landscapes in *trompe l'oeil* by Peruzzi and his assistants; views of Rome are revealed between the painted columns.

In the next room, formerly a bedroom, the *Marriage of Roxana and Alexander* is by Sodoma (1477-1549). Dismissed from his work in the Vatican by Julius II in favour of Raphael, Sodoma was commissioned by Agostino Chigi to decorate this

*Council of the Gods (detail of vault fresco),
Galleria della Villa Farnesina*

room, probably in 1509. In a Renaissance setting, Alexander extends the crown to Roxana against a cloud of cherubs. The merit of this pleasant painting lies in the beauty of the figures and the harmony and balance of the composition.

These qualities are lacking in the other scenes: Alexander and Darius's mother, Vulcan and three little angels *(on either side of the chimney piece)*, the battle scene. To the left of the entrance are Alexander and Bucephalus (late 16C).

Gabinetto Nazionale delle Stampe – ♿ *Open 8.30am-1.30pm (also 2.30-4.30pm Tue and Thu, by appointment); Sat (by appointment only). Closed Sun and public holidays, 29 Jun, 10-19 Aug and 27-30 Dec. No charge.* ☎ *06 69 98 03 14; Fax 06 68 80 65 65.* The National Printing Office has been accommodated in Villa Farnesina since 1950. In 1975 it was merged with the **Calcografia Nazionale** to form the Istituto Nazionale per la Grafica, a body which houses a collective archive of prints and drawings from the 15C-19C. Highlights include Baroque works of the Roman and Florentine Schools. The reference section includes photographic material and computer databases which may be consulted by appointment only.

Walking About

Palazzo Corsini

The palace was built in the 15C by the Riario, nephews of Sixtus IV, and passed in the 18C to Cardinal Corsini, nephew of Clement XII, who had it rebuilt by Ferdinando Fuga. It now houses an art gallery and the **Accademia dei Lincei**, a learned society of scholars and men of letters.

On the south side of Palazzo Corsini a street of the same name leads to the Orto Botanico.

Orto Botanico (Botanic Garden)

♿ *Open Tue-Sat, 9.30am-5.30pm (Apr-Oct, 6.30pm). Closed in Aug and on public holidays. Audioguides available.* €2.07. ☎ *06 49 91 71 06; Fax 06 49 91 71 08.* This garden (c 12ha/30 acres) contains over 3 500 cultivated species and eight glasshouses (1 800m²/19 380sq ft); it provides a pleasant place of relaxation among the luxuriant vegetation of the Janiculum.

Porta Settimiana

This was one of the gates in the Aurelian Wall (Mura Aureliane); it was repaired by Alexander VI (1492-1503) and reinforced with merlons.

Turn right into Via Garibaldi; beyond the junction with Via G. Mameli, take the second steps on the right which lead to San Pietro in Montorio.

San Pietro in Montorio★

This church, which has a commanding view of Rome, was built in Sixtus IV's reign at the end of the 15C by Ferdinand II of Spain and dedicated to St-Peter who, according to a 15C legend, was crucified on the site.

The simple façade is typical of the Renaissance, as is the interior, which consists of a nave flanked by apsidal chapels. The chancel was damaged in the siege of 1849 and has been restored.

Several Renaissance works have survived, particularly the *Flagellation★ (first chapel on the right)*, a fresco by Sebastiano del Piombo, clearly influenced by the monumental art of Michelangelo.

The ceiling in the next chapel was painted by **Baldassarre Peruzzi** (1481-1536). The pale fresco of the Virgin, by Pomarancio (1552-1626), and the two transept chapels were added at the Counter-Reformation. In the right-hand chapel the allegorical figures on the tombs and the cherubs on the balustrade are by Bartolomeo Ammanati, a pupil of Michelangelo. Beatrice **Cenci** is buried beneath the high altar.

The fourth chapel on the left, with its multitude of statues, is typical of the Counter-Reformation.

Bernini designed the second chapel on the left in the Baroque period; his pupils were responsible for the sculptures.

Il "tempietto★★

Access from outside the church through the iron gates on the right, from inside the church through the fourth chapel on the right.

This charming miniature temple was one of Bramante's first works on his arrival in Rome in 1499. Despite its small scale, the construction has all the grandeur and rigorous conformity of a Classical building. Perfectly proportioned, it is surrounded by a portico supported on Doric columns and surmounted by a dome. Behind the building in a little chapel is a small cavity said to have held St Peter's cross.

View of Rome★★

From the open space in front of the church.

The view extends from Monte Mario *(left)* and Castel Sant'Angelo right across the city with its various roofs and domes: to the right of the monument to Victor Emmanuel II and the Capitol are the arches of the Basilica of Maxentius in the Forum; further right again, beyond the green expanse of the Palatine, is the façade of St John Lateran spiked with statues.

Return to Via Garibaldi.

On the left is a **monument** set up in 1941 to those who died to ensure that Rome was not excluded when Italy was unified.

Fontana Paola (Pauline Fountain)

This fountain was commissioned by Pope **Paul V**; its shape – a commemorative arch – shows the nascent taste for Baroque pomp.

Either make a detour uphill to Porta San Pancrazio and the road of the same name which leads to the Villa Doria Pamphili (1km/0.5mi – 45min on foot return) or turn right into Passeggiata del Gianicolo.

Villa Doria Pamphili

A vast public park surrounds a 17C-country house *(casino)* which is decorated with statues and low relief sculptures and set among terraces.

PASSEGGIATA DEL GIANICOLO (Janiculum Walk)

This road winds along the crest of the hill beneath the umbrella pines; it is lined by busts of Garibaldi's men and has some of the finest **views★★★** of Rome.

Monumento a Giuseppe Garibaldi (Giuseppe Garibaldi Monument)

In Emilio Gallori's grandiose work (1895) the hero is shown on horseback, gazing towards the Vatican, the object of his revolutionary struggles.

From here there is a **view★★★** of Rome from Villa Medici to St John Lateran; in the distance are the Alban Hills. The cannon is fired daily at noon from below the parapet.

Monumento ad Anita Garibaldi (Anita Garibaldi Monument)

Garibaldi's wife is shown as an Amazon as she appeared at her husband's side. After the 1849 retreat they tried to reach Venice, which was fighting the Austrians, but Anita fell ill and died near Ravenna. This monument was erected in 1932.

Further on near the lighthouse there is a fine **view★★★** over the whole of the city of Rome.

Further on go down the steps on the right which cut off the hairpin bend of the Passeggiata.

The old tree stump is all that remains of the oak tree beneath which Tasso *(see below)* used to sit and reflect on all his misfortunes *(inscription)*.

> ### VIEW OF ROME
> From the square in front of the Ospedale del Bambino Gesù (Hospital of the Infant Jesus) there is a spectacular view★★★ of Rome. To the left is the drum of Castel Sant'Angelo surmounted by its angel and the white mass of the Law Courts; just below the Janiculum, across the river, is the dome of San Giovanni dei Fiorentini; in the background on the edge of the park is the Villa Medici with its two towers and the dome of San Carlo al Corso; slightly to the right are the two belfries of the Trinità dei Monti; then the Quirinal Palace behind the shallow dome of the Pantheon; next, nearer the river, is the high dome of Sant'Andrea delle Valle with the lower dome of the Gesù Church behind it; in the background is the Militia Tower; before it rise the monument to Victor Emmanuel II and the flat façade of Santa Maria d'Aracoeli.

Sant'Onofrio

Open 8.30am-2.30pm; Sat, 9.30am-3.30pm. Closed in Aug. ☎ *06 68 64 498.*

This church has retained the appearance and atmosphere of a hermitage which it received from its founder, a monk of the order of the Hermits of St Jerome, in 1434. It was here that **Tasso** (1544-95) came to die, pursued to the end, even to madness, by his religious doubts; his poem, *The Liberation of Jerusalem*, is a masterpiece of Italian Renaissance poetry. Chateaubriand, too, would have liked to finish his days here; on the outside wall of the church overlooking the river is a long quotation from his *Memories from Beyond the Grave*. On the right of the main door beneath the arcade are frescoes by **Domenichino** illustrating the life of St Jerome (1605). The attractive frescoes in the **apse★** were probably painted by Baldassarre Peruzzi assisted by Pinturicchio.

The graceful cloisters were built in the 15C.

Worth a Visit

Galleria Nazionale d'Arte Antica (National Art Gallery)

In Palazzo Corsini. ♿ *Open daily (except Mon) 8.30am-7pm. Closed 1 Jan, 1 May and Christmas. Guided tours available.* €4. ☎ *06 68 80 23 23; Fax 06 68 21 45 63.*

This gallery houses a collection of mainly 17C and 18C paintings by Italian and non-Italian artists, with special emphasis on the Venetian, Emilian and Neapolitan Schools. Particularly worthy of note are the *Portrait of Philip II* by Titian, in which the stiff posture and death-like complexion are striking; *St John the Baptist* by Caravaggio; and, in the room devoted to Tuscan Primitive paintings, an admirable *Triptych* by **Fra Angelico** showing the *Last Judgement*, the *Ascension and Pentecost*. This painter, who experienced the silence of the cloister, expressed his deep faith by painting serene and saintly faces (central panel of the *Last Judgement*) and a Christ who inspires adoration (right panel of the *Ascension*).

The best examples of works by 17C artists, who tried to recreate the rich colours of Venetian painters a century earlier, include the *Triumph of Ovid* by Nicolas Poussin and the *Portrait of a Gentleman* by Andrea Sacchi.

Isola Tiberina-Torre Argentina★★

The peace of Isola Tiberina (Tiber Island) provides a striking contrast to the hustle and bustle of the old Jewish district, which extends along Via del Portico d'Ottavia. Although Rome's Jewish inhabitants are now scattered all over the city, this district is still home to many traditional shops, such as haberdasheries, fabric shops and groceries specialising in kosher food, as well as to the impressive synagogue. It is also a pleasant, lively area to explore at night, with a good choice of bars, restaurants and trattorias. From the Jewish district, the walk continues to Largo di Torre Argentina, where the incessant noise of cars, buses and trams provides an anachronistic backdrop to one of the oldest archaeological sites in the city.

Location

Michelin map no 38 or Michelin spiral atlas of Rome: p 56 (L 11, M 11, N 11). Tour: 1hr 30min. This walk runs from Isola Tiberina to the old Jewish district on the east bank of the Tiber.

Neighbouring sights are described in the following chapters: BOCCA DELLA VERITÀ; CAMPIDOGLIO-CAPITOLINO; CAMPO DEI FIORI; PANTHEON; TRASTEVERE.

Walking About

ISOLA TIBERINA★

This peaceful spot was the subject of many legends connected with the origins of Rome. The island is said to have been created by silt piling up on the crops of the Tarquins thrown into the Tiber when the last king of this line, Tarquin the Proud, was driven out of Rome in the 6C BC. It is also said that the island's shape is that of the boat which brought Aesculapius, the god of medicine, from Epidauros in Greece. To stress the resemblance the southern point of the island has been paved with slabs of travertine round an obelisk, set up like a mast. Aesculapius is said

Directory

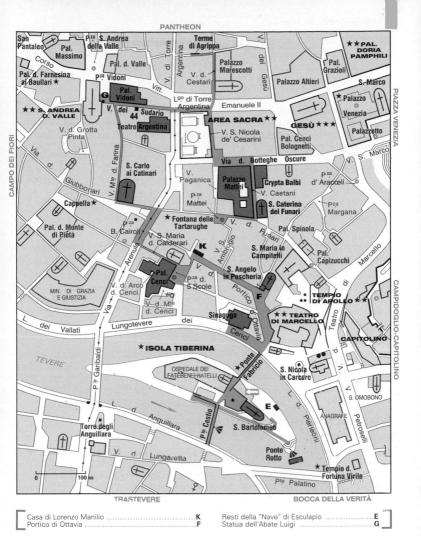

to have arrived in Rome in 293 BC in the form of a serpent. The boat had scarcely come alongside when the serpent disembarked and hid on the island; the Romans interpreted this as the serpent's desire to have a temple built on that spot. The sanctuary was built on the site now occupied by St Bartholomew's Church. The hospital of the Brothers of St John of God (*Fatebenefratelli* – literally do-good-brothers) continues the island's medical tradition.

San Bartolomeo (St Bartholomew's Church)

Its Baroque façade and the Romanesque bell-tower (12C) rise from the centre of the island. Inside the building, at the centre of the great staircase, is a cylindrical well-head (c 12m/39ft deep) surmounted by an ancient column carved with 12C saintly figures. One of the cannon balls fired during the French siege in 1849 is lodged in the wall (*left*) of the Lady Chapel at the back of the church. South of Ponte Fabricio, near the church, are the remains of travertine which faced the bow of the **"ship"** of Aesculapius (*see above*).

According to tradition it was in the hospital attached to this church that Rahere, courtier to Henry I of England, recovered from an attack of malaria, usually fatal in those days. He had vowed, if he was spared, to found a priory and a hospital, and on his return Henry granted land in Smithfield in London, where the church and the hospital still stand (*see The Green Guide London*).

Return to the square and take the steps opposite the church which lead to the bank of the Tiber. Downstream of the island, in the middle of the river, are the remains of Ponte Rotto.

Ponte Rotto

In origin this bridge (the Broken Bridge) goes back to the **Pons Aemilius**, which was built here towards the middle of the 2C BC. It had already collapsed twice when Pope Gregory XII rebuilt it in about 1575. It collapsed again in 1598 and only one arch now remains.

HORATIUS COCLES AND THE PONS SUBLICIUS

Downstream from Ponte Rotto and its modern neighbour, the Palatine Bridge, was the Pons Sublicius. This was the first bridge to span the Tiber, and was built to foster relations between the Latins on the Palatine and the Etruscans on the right bank.

Each year on 14 May human figures made of willow were offered to the river to appease it. The bridge was made of wood and the law forbade any iron to be used in its repair: it had to be easy to dismantle in the event of relations between the two peoples deteriorating. This happened when the last Etruscan king, Tarquin the Proud, was driven out of Rome in the 6C BC. Livy gives a good description; the Etruscans marched on Rome under the banner of Lars Porsenna; Horatius Cocles was guarding the bridge. While his men were dismantling the bridge, Horatius held back the enemy single-handed: "withering the Etruscan leaders with his look, he challenged them one by one or taunted them". Finally the bridge was breached. Horatius jumped into the Tiber and rejoined his men. He was treated as a hero: he was granted land, his statue was put up in the Comitium and "every citizen set aside part of his own income to be given to Horatius".

The incident is also well known through Lord Macaulay's stirring ballad *Horatius* from his *Lays of Ancient Rome*.

The channel of the **Cloaca Maxima**, dug in the 6C BC and still in use today, can be seen through Ponte Rotto and Ponte Palatino.

Ponte Cestio (Pons Cestius)

It links Tiber Island to the Trastevere district. Its origins go back to the 1C BC; it was partially rebuilt in the 19C. To the left there is a view of the bell-tower of Santa Maria in Cosmedin and to the right the Janiculum Hill with its lighthouse. *Cross to the north side of the island.*

Ponte Fabricio★ (Pons Fabricius)

It is sometimes also known as the Bridge of Four Heads because of the Hermes with four heads set at the far end. It is the only Roman bridge to survive intact from the Classical period. Above the arches is an inscription stating that the bridge was built in 62 BC by the consul Fabricius. It links the left bank with Tiber Island. *Cross the bridge.*

FROM ISOLA TIBERINA TO TORRE ARGENTINA

Ghetto

The presence of Jews living in Rome has been recorded since early Ancient times, but their number increased after the capture of Jerusalem by Pompey (1C BC) and again after the destruction of the Temple of Jerusalem and the campaigns of Vespasian and Titus in Palestine (1C AD). A new wave of Jewish immigrants to the city arrived after the expulsion of the Jews from Spain in 1492.

The Jews, who formerly lived in Trastevere, moved to the left bank of the Tiber in the 13C. In 1556 Pope Paul IV had the area enclosed within a wall which ran from Ponte Fabricio, along Via del Portico di Ottavia and around Piazza delle Cinque Scole. This crowded, disease-ridden ghetto was home to some 4 000 people and its gates were opened at dawn and closed at dusk. Jews were prohibited from any commercial activities, with the exception of money-lending and selling fabrics, which explains the large number of haberdasheries and fabric shops in this area. In 1848, the walls were taken down, in 1870 the new Italian State abolished all restrictions, and in 1885 this insalubrious district was completely demolished, with

Isola Tiberina

the exception of the houses on Via della Reginella. In 1943, during the German occupation, more than 2 000 residents of the ghetto were deported; very few of them were to return. Since the Second World War, the district has gradually been repopulated and today it has a pleasant, lively atmosphere.

Sinagoga (Synagogue)

The synagogue, inaugurated in 1904, occupies part of the old ghetto. It was designed by Costa and Armanni and is dominated by its large dome, visible from all over Rome.

The Museo della Comunità Ebraica (Hebrew Museum) inside the synagogue houses a display of souvenirs of the Jewish community in Rome, together with an exhibition of liturgical articles.

Open Jun-Aug, Mon to Thu 9am-7.30pm, Fri 9am-1.30pm, Sun 9am-noon; Sep-May, Mon to Thu 9am-4.30pm, Fri 9am-1.30pm, Sun 9am-noon. Closed Sat and Jewish holidays. Guided tours available (1hr) in various languages. €6. ☎ 06 68 40 06 61; Fax 06 68 40 06 84.

Take Via Portico di Ottavia.

Portico di Ottavia (Portico of Octavia)

This was one of the richest monuments in Rome. It was vast, extending back as far as the present Piazza di Campitelli and the church of Santa Caterina dei Funari. All that now remains is part of the entrance porch *(propylaea)* which faces the Tiber. The remaining Corinthian columns supporting sections of the entablature belonged to a portico built by Septimius Severus (193-211).

The original portico had been built in the 2C BC by Cecilius Metellus, who defeated the Macedonians, as an enclosure for two temples dedicated to Juno and Jupiter respectively. Augustus rebuilt the portico, which he dedicated to his sister Octavia, and included two public libraries, one Latin and one Greek, as well as an assembly hall where the Senate sometimes met.

Sant'Angelo in Pescheria

Nowadays the *propylaea* of the Portico of Octavia serves only as a monumental entrance to the little church of Sant'Angelo in Pescheria (founded in the 8C).

The name, like those of the neighbouring streets, recalls the **fish market** which occupied the Antique ruins in the 12C. The activity surrounding the stalls set out on the huge paving stones in front of the church and in Via di Sant'Angelo in Pescheria made this one of the most picturesque corners of Rome.

On the right of the portico is a stone bearing a Latin inscription which says that fish above a certain length went to the Conservators of Rome. This privilege was abolished in 1798.

Lorenzo Manili's house *(nos 1, 1b and 2, Via Portico d'Ottavia)* was built in 1468 with shops on the ground floor. It is decorated with low reliefs and has the proprietor's name written up in Latin and Greek. Above the name is an inscription praising the owner for contributing to making the city beautiful.

Turn left into Piazza delle Cinque Scole.

The name of this piazza, Square of the Five Schools, refers to the fact that the synagogues serving the Ghetto once stood here. The arch and two columns on the left are the remains of a 1C building.

Palazzo Cenci

The narrow streets which surround the palace repeat like variations on a theme the name of the great family involved in a scandal which hit the headlines in the 16C: Via dell'Arco de' Cenci, Vicolo de' Cenci, Piazza de' Cenci, Via Beatrice Cenci, Via del Monte de' Cenci. The palace itself stands on a slight rise (Monte Cenci) formed by the rubble from Ancient buildings (perhaps the Circus Flaminius).

> ### AN "ANGELIC PARRICIDE"
> The scandal broke on 9 September 1598. In those days a bold man could get away with almost anything. The head of the rich Cenci family was Francesco Cenci, whose father had been Pius V's treasurer. A cruel and perverted man, Francesco was eventually murdered at the instigation of his daughter Beatrice, with the support of her brother Giacomo and Francesco's wife Lucrezia. Pope Clement VIII sentenced them to death despite public opinion which supported the plea of self-defence. The scandal, in which incest, opium and crime were all involved, set Rome in a ferment. The guilty parties were beheaded on 11 September 1599 in Piazza di Ponte Sant'Angelo. Each year on 11 September a mass is celebrated in St Thomas' Church in Piazzetta di Monte Cenci for the soul of Beatrice Cenci.

Follow Via S. Maria de' Calderari. Turn right into Via Arenula and then left into Via dei Giubbonari.

San Carlo ai Catinari

The grandiose but rather heavy façade of this church was erected between 1635 and 1638. It is in the style of the Counter-Reformation.

The **interior★**, which is shaped like a Greek cross, is dominated by a handsome coffered dome. The artists who painted Sant'Andrea della Valle are to be found here too: **Domenichino** painted the Cardinal Virtues on the pendentives of the dome; in the apse **Lanfranco** accomplished his last work (1647), the Apotheosis of St Charles Borromeo; above the high altar is St Charles Borromeo leading a procession in Milan to ward off the plague by **Pietro da Cortona** (1650); the 17C St Cecilia's Chapel *(right of the chancel)* is verging on the rococo, with its strained perspective, its broken lines and animated stucco figures.

Take Via Monte della Farina, which runs alongside the west side of the church, as far as Piazza Vidoni.

Statua dell'Abate Luigi

This statue of a Roman in a toga is one of the famous "talking" statues which exchanged comments with Pasquino, Madam Lucrezia and Marforio.

Turn right into Via del Sudario.

Casa del Burcardo (Johannes Burckard's House)

Open Mon-Fri, 9am-1.30pm. Closed Sat-Sun and public holidays and during Aug. No charge. ☎ *06 68 80 67 55 or 06 68 80 19 71; Fax 06 68 19 47 27.*

There used to be a tower on the site where **Burckard**, the Papal Master of Ceremonies, built his house in 1503. He called it **Torre Argentina** after the Latin name *(Argentoratum)* for Strasbourg, his home town. The house, which has been restored, is in the Gothic and Renaissance style. It contains a library and a collection of masks, theatrical costumes and playbills connected with the theatre.

Palazzo Vidoni

Via del Sudario, 10-16. The decision to build a palace here was taken by the Caffarelli, a rich Roman family, in 1500 and Raphael was asked to design it. One of his pupils, Lorenzetto, supervised its construction in 1515. The robust elegance of the palace was altered in the 18C and 19C when the façade was enlarged and re-sited to face the Corso Vittorio Emanuele II and the top storey added.

Tradition has it that Charles V lodged here in 1536. In 1853 the Bishop of Perugia, the future Leo XIII, lived on the ground floor. Later the building became the offices of the Fascist Party.

Continue along Via del Sudario as far as Largo Torre Argentina.

Teatro Argentina (Argentina Theatre)

The first performance of the *Barber of Seville* took place here in 1816 and was one of the most resounding failures in the annals of opera. It is said that Pauline Borghese was behind it: she had wanted to help the tenor, who was a friend of hers, to avenge himself on Rossini, who had refused to alter the score.

Area Sacra del Largo Argentina★★ (Largo Argentina Sacred Precincts)

The best overall view is from the east side (Via S. Nicola de' Cesarini).

This is the name given to a group of ruins excavated between 1926 and 1929 in the Largo Argentina. The remains, which date from the days of the Ancient Roman Republic, are among the oldest found in Rome. This marshy ground on the banks of the Tiber near the Campus Martius was often flooded. The necessary work of draining and embanking meant raising the ground level and modifying the buildings on the site. Traces of five building levels from the 5C BC to the beginning of the Empire have been revealed by the archaeologists. In Antiquity this large precinct was at the heart of a busy district: to the southeast stood the theatre built by Balbus in Augustus's reign, to the west Pompey's Theatre and Curia (Teatro e Curia di Pompeo), to the north the rear façade of Agrippa's Baths (Terme di Agrippa) and the Saepta *(see map of Rome during the Empire, p 74).*

AREA SACRA DEL LARGO ARGENTINA

0 — 30 m

━━━ Remains of St Nicholas' Church

━━ Extant parts   ▬▬ Non-extant parts

The Sacred Precinct consists primarily of four temples, including a round one, all facing east onto a square paved in travertine in the Imperial period. As it is not known to which gods the temples were dedicated, they are known as temples A, B, C and D.

The tower and portico in the southeast corner of the site, which were preserved during the excavations in 1932, were originally part of a group of medieval houses, built in the 12C near the church of San Salvatore which stood in front of Temple C.

Temple C – This is the oldest temple, dating back to the 6C or 5C BC. The plan is that of the early Roman temples which followed the Etruscan model: a triple *cella* (containing three shrines) and a fairly high podium without columns at the rear. In the Imperial period the *cella* was rebuilt at a higher level, the columns and the podium were faced with stucco and the floor was covered with mosaics.

Temple A – The first building on this site dates from the 4C or 3C BC. The present remains of a temple surrounded by columns date from the 2C or 1C BC. Temple A was converted into a church dedicated to St Nicholas, with a nave and south aisle both ending in an apse.

Temple B – This circular building dates from the 2C BC and may have been dedicated to Juno (a statue which is probably a representation of this goddess was found in the temple). The podium of tufa was covered by one of peperine, which in turn was covered in stucco. The *cella* was enlarged and the surrounding columns were linked by tufa walls. The floor was raised and re-covered in mosaic.

Temple D – The greater part of this temple lies beneath the road (Via Florida). The north and east sides of the precinct were bounded by a portico **(1)**. The high wall **(2)** on the west side behind Temple A belonged to a public lavatory. The drainage trough is still visible. Further south several large blocks **(3)** have been identified as the remains of the podium of Pompey's Curia where, in 44 BC, Julius Caesar was assassinated during the Ides of March.

Take Via de' Cestari and turn left into Via Arco della Ciambella.

Wedged between n° 9 and n° 15 Via Arco della Ciambella, a small fragment of wall is all that remains of the **Terme di Agrippa**, the oldest baths in Rome. The baths, built in 19 BC, were supplied by an aqueduct constructed specifically for the purpose. Part of the channel still runs under Via dei Condotti and supplies water to a number of fountains in the city, including the Fontana di Trevi.

Return towards Largo di Torre Argentina and continue to Via delle Botteghe Oscure.

Via delle Botteghe Oscure was famous in the Middle Ages for its dimly lit basement shops (*oscura* means dark in Italian), which had been set up in the ruins of **Balbus' Theatre** (1C BC). The **Crypta Balbi** archaeological site, which houses part of the Museo Nazionale Romano (*see Worth a Visit below*), is situated here. The name of the street is also associated with the Italian Communist Party (now known as the Democratici di Sinistra), whose main office can be seen at no 4.

Turn right into Via Caetani.

A commemorative bronze plaque marks the spot where the body of the statesman **Aldo Moro** was found on 9 May 1978, 54 days after he had been kidnapped by Red Brigade terrorists.

Santa Caterina ai Funari

This church has a very graceful façade, built between 1560 and 1564; the shallow pilasters are typical of the Renaissance, but the many garlands indicate an attempt at the decorative effects typical of the Mannerist period. Note the unusual bell-tower.

Palazzo Mattei

Five palaces were built by the Mattei in the 16C and 17C; they occupy the confined space bordered by Piazza Mattei, Via dei Funari, Via Caetani, Via delle Botteghe Oscure and Via Paganica. Carlo Maderno (1598-1611) was the architect of the palace with two entrances (*Via dei Funari 31 or Via Caetani 32*). The decoration of the courtyards (statues, busts and low reliefs) shows the taste for Antiquities which was then the fashion.

Follow Via dei Funari as far as Piazza Mattei.

Fontana delle Tartarughe★ (Turtle Fountain)

This is a late Renaissance work (1581-84), full of grace and charm, by Taddeo Landini, probably from a design by **Giacomo della Porta**. Local legend tells how Duke Mattei, the owner of the neighbouring palace and an inveterate gambler, lost his fortune in one night. His prospective father-in-law advised him to look for another fiancée. To prove that a Mattei, even when ruined, could achieve wonders, he had the fountain built in one night.

Worth a Visit

Crypta Balbi

♿ *Open 9am-7.45pm (last admission 6.45pm). Closed Mon, 1 Jan and Christmas. €4, €20 for a "Roma archeologica" card, valid for nine archaeological sites.* ☎ *06 39 08 071; Fax 06 39 75 09 50; pierreci@pierreci.it*

This museum is part of the Museo Nazionale Romano and is housed in a number of medieval buildings on the site of Balbus's Crypt, a portico added to the theatre by Lucius Cornelius Balbus in 13 BC.

The different levels of the museum, which include the basement crypt, house displays which explain the history of the site through archaeological finds, reconstructions, ceramics and excavations. Over the centuries, the site has been home to Balbus's Theatre, the late-medieval monastery of Santa Maria Domine Rose, merchants' shops and houses, and the 16C complex of Santa Caterina dei Funari, built on the orders of St Ignatius of Loyola to house the daughters of Roman prostitutes. An exhibition on the first and second floors of the museum examines the evolution of Rome from Ancient times to the Middle Ages.

Montecitorio★★

The best way to discover this district is on foot, heading out from bustling Piazza di Montecitorio, fronted by banks, newspaper offices, department stores, restaurants and cafés. Also home to the Italian Chamber of Deputies, the piazza is surrounded by narrow Renaissance-style streets lined with elegant, luxury shops. Plunge further away from the square, and the atmosphere changes: the charming, quiet streets of the quarter beyond Via della Scrofa are dotted with 16C buildings and arts and crafts workshops.

Location

Michelin map 38 or Michelin spiral atlas of Rome: pp 96-97 K 10-11. Metro line A: Spagna (approximately 700m/770yd from Piazza di Montecitorio). Tour: 1hr. This district lies between the Tiber and Via del Corso, which marks the boundary with the Fontana di Trevi and Quirinale quarter. Piazza Navona and the Pantheon lie a few hundred metres to the south.

Neighbouring sights are described in the following chapters: FONTANA DI TREVI-QUIRINALE; PANTHEON; PIAZZA NAVONA; PIAZZA DI SPAGNA.

Background

This district corresponds to the northern part of the **Campus Martius**, which was mostly reserved for the colossal tombs belonging to the Imperial families and the funeral pyres *(ustrina)* where the bodies were burnt.

Like the other districts of the city through which the pilgrims passed on their way to the Vatican, this one was raised out of its medieval misery under Sixtus IV (1471-84). In his 13 years on the Papal throne he changed the face of Rome, using the money from the sale of indulgences to pay for his projects. Early in the 16C Leo X cleared the way for Via Leonina (now Via di Ripetta) to run straight from the Porta del Popolo, through which foreigners from the north entered the city, to the Mausoleum of Augustus.

In the second half of the 19C the old river port of the **Ripetta** was destroyed. It had been built in 1706, a set of curving riverside steps, of which Piranesi has left some attractive engravings. It was one of the most famous views in Rome.

Walking About

Piazza di Montecitorio

In the square stands a 6C BC **Egyptian obelisk**, re-erected in 1792 by Pius VI and surmounted by a bronze ball bearing his coat of arms. The obelisk, which was brought back from Heliopolis by Augustus in the 10C BC, served as the pointer for a gigantic solar clock marked out on the ground, more or less on the site of the church of San Lorenzo in Lucina.

Directory

Where to Eat
See "Where to Eat" in the Practical Points section at the beginning of the guide.

Taking a Break
Giolitti – *Via Uffici del Vicario 40* – ☎ 06 67 98 147 – *Open 7am-2am.* Despite having no outdoor tables, this pleasant gelateria is an excellent meeting point in the heart of the city and serves a wide range of ice creams and milk shakes.

La Caffettiera – *Piazza di Pietra 65 –* ☎ *06 67 98 147 – Open 7am-9pm.* In this elegant and attractive café, coffee is served in a typical Neapolitan cafetière. Food choices include savoury snacks, as well as Neapolitan cakes and pastries.

Shopping
Maria Favilli – *Via della Scrofa 93.* This shop sells jewellery; the delicate designs take their inspiration from Ancient Rome.

Palazzo di Montecitorio

& *Guided tour (30min) of the Chamber of Deputies on the first Sun of the month, 10am-5.30pm (groups limited to 50). Times may change as a result of political events taking place. For up-to-date information, consult the Chamber of Deputies' website at www.Camera.it, section "servizi ai cittadini". Closed during Aug and Sept. No charge.*
The palace stands on the site of the funeral pyres belonging to the Antonine family for the cremation of their dead. It was begun by **Bernini** in 1650, taken over by one of his pupils and completed in 1697 by Carlo Fontana. Little remains of Bernini's Baroque fantasies: the rustic effect is reminiscent of rockeries, with the rough-hewn stones framing some of the windows, and the impression of enhanced size is conveyed by the slightly convex façade, which is surmounted by a clock tower. Since 1870 the palace has housed the Chamber of Deputies, which contributes to the bustling atmosphere of Piazza Montecitorio, often the scene of demonstrations and protest meetings.
To the rear (Piazza del Parlamento) the building was extended and provided with a majestic new façade (1903-25).

Piazza Colonna★

This square is one of the most crowded places in Rome, being at the junction of the two main shopping streets (Via del Corso and Via del Tritone). The **column★** at the centre of the square was probably erected between 176 and 193 in honour of **Marcus Aurelius** (161-80), who preferred philosophy to war but was forced to campaign on the banks of the Danube. He died at the front, of the plague. His victories were short-lived and did not contain the barbarian thrust. Just as Trajan's Column illustrated that Emperor's exploits against the Dacians, so Marcus Aurelius's Column depicts the significant episodes in his wars, with low-relief carvings arranged in a spiral. The carving was done by a group of sculptors and even the designs were probably the work of several artists. To make the work more visible the scenes are larger and in higher relief than those on Trajan's Column, but the quality of the craftsmanship has suffered.
The overall appearance is spoiled by the lack of entasis two-thirds of the way up the shaft, which would have avoided the impression of concavity.
In 1589 Pope Sixtus V had the statue of the Emperor on the top of the column replaced with a statue of St Paul. He also restored the base and added an inscription wrongly attributing the column to Antoninus Pius, Marcus Aurelius's predecessor.

Palazzo Chigi

The building was begun in 1562 to designs by **Giacomo della Porta**. It was continued by Carlo Maderno according to the severe concepts of the Counter-Reformation and completed in 1630 in the Baroque era. In 1659 it was bought by Pope Alexander VII for his family, after whom it is named. Since 1917, when it was acquired by the State, the Palazzo Chigi has been associated with politics: it housed the Ministry of Foreign Affairs after the First World War, the Head of the Government in the Fascist period and now it belongs to the Presidency of the Council of Ministers.

Take the street between Palazzo di Montecitorio and Palazzo Chigi; turn left into Piazza del Parlamento and left again into Via di Campo Marzio.

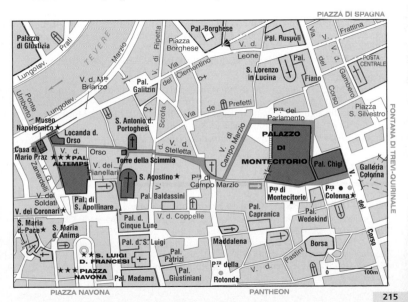

In the reign of Octavius Augustus a vast area of the Campus Martius was occupied by an enormous **solar clock** (160m/525ft by 60m/197ft). Some pieces of travertine paving, marked with bronze insets representing the signs of the zodiac, are still to be found beneath Via di Campo Marzio.

Bear right into Via di Stelletta, right into Via della Scrofa and immediately left into Via dei Portoghesi.

Torre della Scimmia (Monkey Tower)

The building on the corner of Via dei Portoghesi and Via dei Pianellari incorporates a 15C tower. It has been immortalised by the American novelist, Nathaniel Hawthorne (1804-64), with the following story:

The family living in the house owned a very facetious monkey. One day it climbed to the top of the tower carrying the new-born baby of the family. The father was terrified, not knowing what to do and fearful that the animal would let its precious burden fall. After praying to the Virgin for her to intercede, he decided to whistle to the monkey to bring it back. The monkey came down by the drainpipe holding the child in its arms and they both returned safe and sound. Since then, at the top of the tower, a little light burns continuously before an image of the Virgin.

Sant'Antonio dei Portoghesi

Open Mon-Fri, 8.30am-1pm and 3-6pm; Sat, 8.30am-noon and 3-6pm; Sun and public holidays, 9am-noon and 3.30-7pm. No charge. ☎ 06 68 80 24 96; Fax 06 68 65 234.
The Portuguese national church, which was built in the 17C, has an attractive Rococo façade; the interior is gorgeously decorated with gold, stucco, marble and paintings. The first chapel on the right contains a funeral monument by Canova (1806-08). In the first chapel on the left above the altar is a fine painting by Antoniazzo Romano (15C) depicting the Virgin between St Francis and St Anthony.
Take Via dei Panellari.

Sant'Agostino★

The church, which is dedicated to St Augustine of Hippo, was built between 1479 and 1483.

The broad travertine façade, with its rose windows, was one of the first to be built in Rome according to the concepts of the Renaissance. The two orders are linked by large loose scrolls; the powerful moulding adds character to their ornamental effect.

The interior, which was decorated according to contemporary taste by Luigi Vanvitelli in 1760, has been cluttered by 19C additions which rob it of its soaring elegance, now only faintly perceptible in the nave.

The surviving features of the Renaissance building are the Latin cross plan, with apsidal chapels in the transept and side aisles, and the dome, one of the earliest of its type in Rome, which rises directly above the transept crossing without a drum. The church contains several fine works of art: near the main door is the **Madonna del Parto★** (1521) by **Jacopo Sansovino**; he took great interest in Antique sculpture (filmy draperies and proud bearing) during his visits to Rome and was also influenced by the vigour of Michelangelo's work. The third pillar on the left in the nave bears a fresco painting by **Raphael** (1512) of the **Prophet Isaiah★**, which owes much to Michelangelo's work in the Sistine Chapel.

The first chapel on the left contains the **Madonna of the Pilgrims★★★** (1605) by **Caravaggio**, a work which was much criticised by the artist's contemporaries for its rugged pilgrims, inspired by ordinary people, and for the ugliness of the man's feet. Even the Virgin, for all her gentleness, is nursing her bonny baby in a very realistic manner.

Return to San Antonio dei Portoghesi and continue west along Via dell'Orso.

Locanda dell'Orso (Bear Inn)

From the Middle Ages to the Renaissance, this district consisted almost entirely of inns, which provided lodgings for pilgrims making their way to St Peter's. The hostelry at the sign of the bear was set up in a fine 15C building. Montaigne stayed here for a few days during his visit to Rome in 1580.

The tour finishes with the three museums described below.

Worth a Visit

PALAZZO ALTEMPS★★★ (Museo Nazionale Romano)

This palace, along with Palazzo Massimo alle Terme, the Terme di Diocleziano (see PORTA PIA-TERMINI) and the Crypta Balbi (see ISOLA TIBERINA-TORRE ARGENTINA), houses the Museo Nazionale Romano. ♿ Open daily (except Mon) 9am-7.45pm (last admission 6.45pm). Closed 1 Jan, 1 May and Christmas. €5.16. Guided tours and audioguides available (1hr 30min) in various languages. ☎ 06 68 33 759; Fax 06 68 97 091.

PALAZZO ALTEMPS

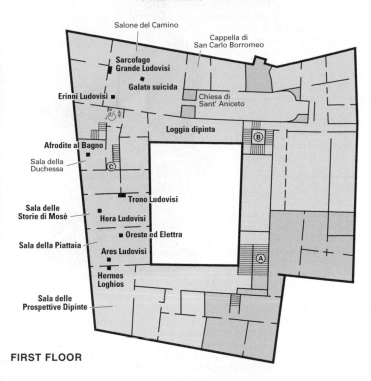

Salone del Camino

Cappella di
San Carlo Borromeo

**Sarcofago
Grande Ludovisi**

Galata suicida

Erinni Ludovisi

Chiesa di
Sant' Aniceto

Loggia dipinta

Ⓑ

Afrodite al Bagno

Sala della
Duchessa

Ⓒ

Trono Ludovisi

**Sala delle
Storie di Mosè**

Hera Ludovisi

Oreste ed Elettra

Sala della Piattaia

Ares Ludovisi

Ⓐ

**Hermes
Loghios**

**Sala delle
Prospettive Dipinte**

FIRST FLOOR

0   50 m

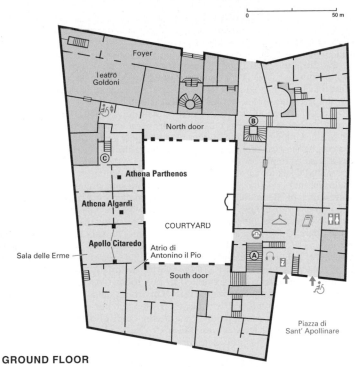

Foyer

Teatro
Goldoni

North door

Ⓑ

Ⓒ

Athena Parthenos

Athena Algardi

COURTYARD

Apollo Citaredo

Sala delle Erme

Atrio di
Antonino il Pio

South door

Ⓐ

Piazza di
Sant' Apollinare

GROUND FLOOR

🛈 Tourist information	↨ Lift	🚻 Toilets	
🎧 Audio guide	Ⓐ Stairs	📖 Bookshop	
♿ Wheelchair access	⌂ Cloakroom	☎ Telephone	

The palace was begun in about 1480 by Girolamo Riario, Sixtus IV's nephew. In 1568 it was acquired by Cardinal Marco Sittico Altemps who had it rebuilt by Martino Longhi the Elder. In 1725 it became the residence of Cardinal de Polignac, the French Ambassador. Recently restored and reopened to the public, the museum now houses the Ludovisi-Boncompagni collection. In the first half of the 17C Cardinal Ludovico decided to decorate his villa with a substantial number of Ancient statues, some of which had been found during construction of the villa itself (in the area known in Antiquity as the Sallustian Gardens), and others which had been purchased by the Cardinal (some probably from the Altemps family). The statues were restored very much according to the ideas and criteria of the 17C. Some of the greatest artists of the time, including Algardi and Bernini, were called upon to work on the statues; they not only restored them but replaced any missing parts. One of the more unusual aspects of this collection is the strange (and nowadays unthinkable) combination of the Ancient original and the Baroque restoration.

Ludovisi Ares

Museo Nazionale Romano

Of equal interest is the recently restored palace itself, with its frescoed drawing rooms, old 15C and 16C structures and beautiful ceilings.

Tour

A beautiful harmonious 16C courtyard designed by Antonio da Sangallo the Elder, Baldassarre Peruzzi and Martino Longhi the Elder greets the visitor upon entering the palace. Rectangular in shape, the courtyard is closed on its two shorter sides by a loggia-topped portico; the arcades on the longer sides serve as decoration only. On the third and final floor square windows surrounded by cornices complete the harmonious whole. Four Roman statues can be seen under the northern portico (copies of Greek originals), arranged in their original location. The loggia above the statues is decorated with a beautiful fresco *(see below)*.

Cross the Atrium of Antoninus Pius (Atrio di Antonino il Pio), who is depicted wearing only a cloak, his left arm raised to address the crowd, and enter the room dedicated to the Ludovico marble statues. Two heavily restored statues of *Apollo with his Lyre (Apollo Citaredo)* can be seen in the Sala delle Erme. The **Athena Algardi** is a good example of 17C restoration work, carried out by the artist from whom the statue takes its name. It is thought that the statue originally portrayed Hygeia. The helmet and the aegis (chest decoration with a gorgon's head in its centre), attributes of the goddess of war, were modelled by Algardi. In the next room is the **Athena Parthenos**, a 1C Greek copy thought to have been inspired by the imposing statue (12m/39ft high) sculpted by Phidias for the Parthenon.

A large monumental staircase leads to the first floor. The **Sala delle Prospettive Dipinte** contains frescoes painted in the second half of the 16C with a false colonnade. A series of painted "tapestries" between the two groups of columns depicts landscaped scenes. A Roman copy (1C-2C BC) of an original statue by Phidias (5C BC), **Hermes Loghios**, is also exhibited in this room. The 15C **fresco★** in the **Sala della Piattaia** is of outstanding beauty. This room takes its name from the array of kitchenware painted on the walls; the plates, pitchers and bowls depicted are wedding gifts and are accompanied by greeting cards displayed on both sides of the table. The group of **Orestes and Electra★** *(Oreste ed Elettra)* is the work of the Greek sculptor Menelaos and dates from the 1C AD. The **Ares Ludovisi★★**, more recently identified as Apollo, depicts the god (or hero) in a sitting position, his hands around his knees holding his sword, with his shield resting by his side, and a cupid peeping out from between his legs. This is a Roman copy of a statue from the Hellenistic period.

The **Sala delle Storie di Mosè** (named the Room of the Stories of Moses, from the frieze depicting episodes from the Exodus which runs along the upper part of the walls) houses the most famous exhibit of the collection, the **Ludovisi Throne★★★** *(Trono Ludovisi)*. This strange monument suggests a throne for a cult statue (although it is probably part of a ritual ornament from a place of worship) and was found in the Villa Ludovisi in 1887. It is an original Greek sculpture from the early Classical period (5C BC). The high quality of the decorative low-relief carving makes it a masterpiece of Antique art.

The main panel shows a young woman being assisted by two attendant young women who shield her body with a veil. Archaeologists have interpreted this scene as the birth of Aphrodite (Venus), goddess of love, who emerged from the sea foam, accompanied by the Seasons, whose feet brush the pebbles of the shore. The very light, delicate mantle gently envelops the lower half of the goddess's body, its rippling folds echoing the curves of the tunic about her neck. The artist has endowed the face of Aphrodite with joyful serenity. The side panels are ornamented with scenes associated with the cult of Aphrodite: a naked woman plays the flute while another, fully clothed, burns incense – these figures are often regarded as embodiments of sensuality (the courtesan) and modesty (the wife). In the same room is the monumental head known as the *Hera Ludovisi*, which is, in fact, a portrait of Antonia, wife of the Emperor Drusus and mother of Claudius. Decoration from various periods can be seen in the Cardinal's bedroom, which later became his audience chamber: the ceiling and upper part of the walls date from the 15C, the battle scenes were painted in the 17C. In the middle of the next room is a base with a fine, delicate relief depicting slender-winged dancing figures. Decoration of the **Loggia dipinta**★★ was commissioned at the end of the 16C by Marco Sittico Altemps. The fresco attempts to create the illusion of an arboured garden, in which vegetal, animal and cupid motifs are richly interwoven. The portraits of the Caesars from the Ludovisi collection are displayed here.

Three of the most interesting exhibits from the collection can be seen in the Salone del Camino. The *Gaul taking his own life*★★★ (*Galata suicida*), a Roman copy of an original Greek bronze, dominates the centre of the room. Note the strength and movement of the barbarian, with the dramatic twist of the bust, and the forlorn stance of the wife, supported only by her husband's hand. This is a magnificent example of Hellenistic art, copied for Julius Caesar to commemorate his victory over the Gauls. The *Dying Gaul (Galata morente)* in the Capitoline Museum is part of the same group *(see CAMPIDOGLIO-CAPITOLINO)*. At the end of the room, the **Grande Ludovisi**★★ sarcophagus *(sarcofago Grande Ludovisi)*, (3C AD), depicts scenes from battles between the Romans and the barbarians. Three levels are arranged horizontally: the victorious Romans can be seen in the top level, with Hostilian, son of the Emperor Decius, in the centre; in the middle section the soldiers attack the barbarians, who are depicted on the bottom panel. Note the different characteristics of the two peoples: the Romans appear proud and courageous; the barbarians seem to wince in pain. The fine, delicate face of the **Ludovisi Erinyes**★ *(Erinni Ludovisi)* is emphasised by the dark base on which it stands.

In the Sala della Duchessa, decorated with mythological scenes in the 17C by Romanelli, is *Aphrodite bathing (Afrodite al Bagno)*, a work by the sculptor Doidalsas.

Museo Napoleonico★ (Napoleon Museum)

Open Tue-Sat, 9am-7pm; Sun, 9am-2pm. Closed 1 Jan, 1 May and Christmas. €2.58. ☎ *06 68 80 62 86; Fax 06 68 80 91 14.* The museum was founded in 1927 by Giuseppe Primoli, a descendant of Lucien Bonaparte, and contains many souvenirs of the Napoleonic presence in Rome. Lucien lived in Via dei Condotti, Pauline had her villa near to the Porta Pia, and Napoleon's mother died in her palace in Via del Corso.

The museum displays a collection of portraits of the Emperor and his family, as well as mementoes, furnishings and personal effects. Two rooms are devoted to Napoleon's son, who was declared king of Rome at his birth in 1811. Room VI, which is devoted to Pauline, Napoleon's sister, contains a couch similar to that featured in her portrait by Canova.

Casa di Mario Praz

Entrance in Via Zanardelli. Open Tue-Sun, 8.30am-7.30pm; Mon, 2-7.30pm. Guided tours only (45min). Closed 1 Jan and Christmas. No charge. ☎ *06 32 29 83 02; Fax 06 32 21 579; comunicazione.gnam@arti.beniculturali.it* This is the house of Mario Praz (d 1982), a renowned Anglicist and essayist who earned great recognition for his study of English 19C literature. A passionate collector, he accumulated a huge number of knick-knacks, pictures, sculpture, neo-Classical furniture and *objets d'art*, which he crammed into every corner of his house. Of particular note is the rare collection of 17C-19C wax models (effigies, portraits, busts, religious and mythological compositions). In the study is a fine early-19C maple bookcase inlaid with mahogany intarsia.

Monte Mario

The green slopes of Monte Mario form an attractive backdrop to this district, the sporting hub of the city. Major national and international events are held here, either in the austere and impressive Stadio dei Marmi, so typical of the Fascist period, or in the more modern Palazzetto dello Sport, situated on the other side of the river. Football fans may wish to experience the excitement of a local derby between Roma and Lazio at the Stadio Olimpico, at which supporters exchange colourful insults in the local Roman dialect.

Location

Michelin map 38 or Michelin spiral atlas of Rome: pp 6-8 and 22-23 C 8-12, D 7-12, E 7-8, F 7-10, G 9- 10. Tour: 2hr, excluding travel. Sights are described in alphabetical order. The monuments described below are spread over a large area to the north and northwest of the city, and extend across both banks of the river. The district is bordered to the north by Viale del Foro Italico, to the west by the residential Balduina district, to the south by the Prati quarter, and to the east, on the opposite bank of the Tiber, by the Flaminio district.

Neighbouring sights are described in the following chapters: PIAZZA DEL POPOLO; VATICANO-SAN PIETRO.

Directory

TAKING A BREAK

Antonini – *Via Sabotino 21/29* – ☎ *06 37 51 78 45* – *Open 7am-9pm*. This *pasticceria* is considered to be one of the best in the city and is particularly well known for its cream and berry tarts and Mont Blanc chestnut purées. Excellent aperitifs and canapés can be sampled at the bar.

Lo Zodiaco – *Viale Parco Mellini 90* – ☎ *06 35 49 66 40* – *Open 9am-2am; closed Tue morning*. Sample some excellent ice cream on the romantic terrace or covered verandah of this *gelateria*, which enjoys a magnificent view of the city.

Vanni – *Via Col di Lana 10* – ☎ *06 32 23 642* – *Open 7am-midnight*. A traditional meeting place for television personalities, situated a few steps from the Italian state television studios. The bar gets very busy at lunchtime and has a wide selection of aperitifs and cakes.

Worth a Visit

Foro Italico

The huge sports centre was created by the Fascist Government, and construction was started on 5 February 1928. Once the seat of the Academy of Physical Education, it is now occupied by the Italian National Olympic Committee (CONI). There are tennis courts, a fencing school and a swimming pool, but the most important facilities are the Olympic Stadium and the Marble Stadium (Stadio dei Marmi). The opening ceremony of the 1960 Olympic Games was held in the former (capacity: 100 000 spectators); the latter (capacity: approximately 15 000 spectators) is decorated with 60 statues of athletes and groups of wrestlers in bronze (on the podium).

The road from the Piazza L. de Bosis, with its great **obelisk** to the Piazzale del Foro Italico, is paved with mosaics bearing inscriptions to the glory of "Il Duce".

Monte Mario

The natural beauty of this little hill makes it a popular place among Romans for taking a walk. It offers a fairly extensive **view**★ of the Tiber and Rome which is particularly interesting at night when the city monuments are floodlit.

Monumento a Matteotti

This elegant monument in bronze gilt was designed by Iorio Vivarelli and erected by the Tiber in 1974. Its symbol – a young shoot bursting from the earth – commemorates the Socialist MP Giacomo Matteotti who was assassinated in June 1924 for denouncing the illegality of the Fascist regime.

Palazzetto dello Sport

This concave structure was designed by Annibale Vitellozzi and Pier Luigi Nervi for the 1960 Olympics. It is composed of prefabricated concrete sections supported on a ring of distinctive piers, which gives the impression of a lightweight construction.

Parco di Villa Glori

The steep slopes of this pleasant public park are dedicated to the memory of those who died for their country: one of the Cairoli brothers fell in combat here.

Ponte Milvio (Milvian Bridge)

There has been a bridge here since the 2C BC; it has frequently been restored and rebuilt, particularly in the 15C, and 19C when it was enlarged and a fortified gate was added.

It was near here that the famous battle took place on 28 October 312 between **Constantine** and **Maxentius**, rival pretenders to the Imperial throne. On the eve of the battle, Constantine had a vision which resulted in

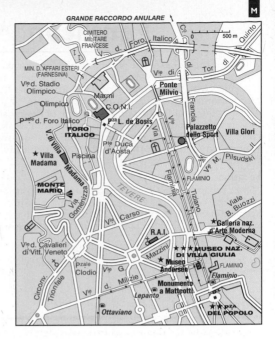

his victory: Christ appeared to him and told him to mark his soldiers' shields with a Christian symbol. The alternative legend that a cross appeared in the sky with the words "You will conquer in this sign" is less reliable. Certain historians consider this to be the date of Constantine's conversion to Christianity.

RAI (Palazzo della Radio e della Televisione)

The Radio and TV Centre is one of the many successful modern constructions in Rome. It is distinguished by a magnificent bronze statue of a rearing horse by Francesco Messina and is situated in the new district which has grown up around the **Piazza Mazzini**.

Villa Madama★

Walk up Via di Villa Madama. Open daily (except Sun and public holidays) 9am-noon. Guided tours only (1hr) by appointment. Write at least 10 days in advance to the Ministero degli Affari Esteri – Cerimoniale diplomatico della Repubblica, Servizio Segreteria. ☎ 06 36 91 42 84; Fax 06 36 91 34 01. This Renaissance villa, which has an enchanting **position★** on the slopes of Monte Mario, was restored in 1925 to be used by the government for the entertainment of foreign visitors. It was built in 1515 by Cardinal Giulio de' Medici, the future Clement VII, to plans by Raphael and completed by Sangallo the Younger. Like the Palazzo Madama, it passed to Madam Margaret of Austria and was named after her. The main entrance is set in the centre of the semicircular south front. The north front contains a magnificent deep loggia decorated with stucco work and grotesques by Giovanni da Udine and Giulio Romano, Raphael's pupils, which overlooks a beautiful formal garden (9ha/22 acres).

Pantheon★★★

Although this square is a popular sight for tourists, as witnessed by the tour groups, crowded cafés and souvenir stalls here, the attractive Piazza della Rotonda, with the magnificent Pantheon at its heart, still exercises a fascination that little can dispel; the harmony of the piazza and its Classical and Baroque architecure make this one of the most appealing squares in the city. It is worth returning to the piazza after dusk, when the artificial light casts shadows on the monuments and the square is lively with locals and visitors enjoying a coffee or a meal, or simply taking a leisurely stroll through the area.

Location

Michelin map 38 or Michelin spiral atlas of Rome: pp 96-97 L 11-12. The Pantheon stands in the heart of the Ancient Campus Martius, nowadays surrounded by splendid Baroque architecture. The Tiber runs to the west of the district and the straight Via del Corso separates the area from the rest of the city to the east. *Tour: 1hr 30min.*
Neighbouring sights are described in the following chapters: FONTANA DI TREVI-QUIRINALE; ISOLA TIBERINA-TORRE ARGENTINA; MONTECITORIO; PIAZZA NAVONA; PIAZZA VENEZIA.

Background

For many years the **Campus Martius** was merely a marshy plain used for drilling the soldiery or conducting a census of the citizenry. In the 2C BC, however, under the influence of the urban planning they observed in their new provinces in Greece, Macedonia and Pergamum, the Romans began to divide up the area into lots. In the eastern half, between the Pantheon and the present Corso, Caesar erected the *Saepta*, an enclosure for the assemblies which elected the tribunes of the people *(comitia tributa)*. In about 43 BC two Egyptian temples dedicated to Isis and Serapis were built beside the *Saepta (see Insights and Images, map of Rome during the Empire, p 74)*.
Each Imperial dynasty felt honour-bound to leave its mark on the Campus Martius. Augustus' son-in-law, Agrippa, built the Pantheon and, between 25 and 19 BC, the first public baths in Rome (Terme di Agrippa). Domitian was responsible for a

Directory

WHERE TO EAT
See "Where to Eat" in the Practical Points section at the beginning of the guide.

TAKING A BREAK
Sant'Eustachio – *Piazza S. Eustachio 82* – ☎ *06 68 61 309 – Open 8.30am-1am.* This café is famous for its delicious, creamy coffee known as a *gran caffè speciale*; the secret recipe is jealously guarded by its creator. Let the waiter know if you like your coffee unsweetened, as coffee is usually served with the sugar already added.

Tazza d'Oro – *Via degli Orfani 84* – ☎ *06 67 89 792 – Open Mon-Sat, 7am-8pm.* This specialist coffee bar serves strong and aromatic coffee and has a wide selection of coffee to take away. In the summer, don't miss the coffee *granita* with double helpings of cream.

BARS
Trinity College – *Via del Collegio Romano 6* – ☎ *06 67 86 472 – Open noon-3am.* This pub is situated on two floors of a splendid old *palazzo*. Furnished and decorated in an authentic Irish style, it serves a range of Irish and English beers. Popular with Italian and overseas youngsters.

SHOPPING
Ditta G. Poggi – *Via del Gesù 74/75* – ☎ *06 67 93 674 – poggi@getnet.it – Open Mon-Wed, Fri and Sat, 9am-1pm and 4-7.30pm; Thur 9am-7.30pm.* This art shop, opened in 1825, provides students of the nearby Fine Arts School with all the materials they need, from water-colours to drawing tables.

La Procure – *Piazza S. Luigi dei Francesi 23* – ☎ *06 68 30 75 98 – Open Tue-Sat, 9.30am-7.30pm; Mon, 3.30-7.30pm.* A wide range of books and guides, including texts on theology and law, for those who want to improve their knowledge of the French language and culture.

Libreria Antiquaria Rappaport – *Via Sistina 23* – ☎ *06 48 38 26 – Open Mon-Fri, 9.30am-12.30pm and 3.15-7pm.* The perfect bookshop for collectors of old books, prints and old maps, some of which are particularly valuable and can fetch considerable prices.

Barbiconi – *Via di S. Caterina da Siena 59 (junction with Via dei Cestari)* – ☎ *06 67 94 985. Open Mon-Fri, 9am-1pm and 3.30-7.30pm; Sat, 9am-1pm.* This is the most famous of the shops along Via dei Cestari selling religious garments, vestments and church ornaments.

temple to Minerva and a portico to the deified Flavians. Under the Antonines a temple to the deified Hadrian was built. Alexander Severus, the last of the Severans, rebuilt Nero's Baths (Terme di Nerone).

In the 4C the Christians held sway. The Bishop of Rome, henceforward in control of the Caesars' capital, constructed Christian buildings often on the ruins of pagan monuments.

During the medieval struggle between the Ghibelline (Empire) and the Guelf (Papacy), Rome was peppered with towers. In the 16C and 17C, the higher clerics and the wealthy citizens bought up whole blocks of hovels and replaced them with unostentatious but luxurious palaces.

Special Features

Piazza della rotonda

This square, surrounding the Pantheon, is typically Roman. At the centre is a fountain designed in 1578 by Giacomo Della Porta; in 1711 it was surmounted by an obelisk by Clement XI. Like the one in the Piazza della Minerva, the obelisk came from the Temple of Isis and rests on a base decorated with dolphins and the Papal coat of arms.

The **Albergo del Sole** (Sun Inn) at n° 63 dates from the 15C. It is one of the oldest inns in the city; its guests have included Ludovico Ariosto, the poet (1474-1533), and Pietro Mascagni, the musician (1863-1945).

PANTHEON★★★

Note: The building is a church and should be treated as such. ⑤ *Open Mon-Sat, 8.30am-7.30pm; Sun, 9am-6pm (1pm on weekday public holidays). Closed 1 Jan, 1 May and Christmas. No charge.*

Originally the Pantheon was a temple, built by Agrippa, the great town planner, in 27 BC; it was dedicated to all the gods and faced south. In AD 80 it was damaged by fire and restored by Domitian. Then Hadrian (117-38) rebuilt it and gave it its present orientation to the north. It was closed in the 4C by the first Christian Emperors together with all other places of pagan worship, sacked by the barbarians in 410, but saved from destruction by Pope Boniface IV, who received it as a gift in 608 from Phocas, the Emperor in Byzantium *(see FORO ROMANO)*. It was then converted into a church dedicated to St Mary *ad martyres*.

Until 756, when the **Papal States** came into being, Rome was subject to Byzantium. The only Eastern Emperor to visit the Christian capital was **Constantinus II** in 356, when the Pantheon was despoiled of its bronze tiles for the embellishment of Constantinople. It was restored early in the Renaissance and then Urban VIII removed the nails and bronze plates which covered the beams of the porch roof and had them made into the magnificent baldaquin now in St Peter's. Pasquino responded with a neat pun on the Pope's family name: *Quod non fecerunt Barbari, fecerunt Barberini* (what the barbarians did not do, the Barberini have done).

Piazza della Rotonda, with the columns of the Pantheon in the foreground

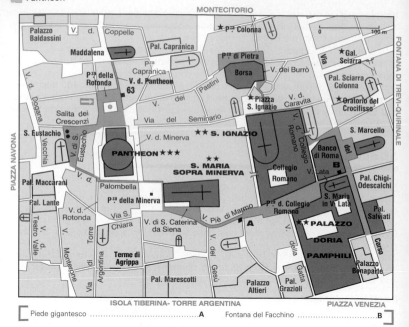

Exterior – The Pantheon is a compact building comprising the main circular chamber and a pillared porch *(pronaos)* beneath a pediment. The porch cornice bears two inscriptions: one concerns the original building by Agrippa and the other inscription below, scarcely visible, mentions restorations carried out by Septimius Severus and Caracalla.

From the side street, Via della Rotonda, the powerful relieving arches are visibly set into the massive walls (6.20m/over 20ft thick). At the rear of the building are an apse, some hollow niches and sculpted fragments; they belonged to the Neptune Basilica which stood between the Pantheon and Agrippa's Baths *(see map of Rome during the Empire, p 74)*.

Interior★★★ – The entrance is under the porch, which is supported on 16 monolithic granite columns, all original except for the three on the left which were replaced because of weakness under Urban VIII and Alexander VII; the Papal emblems (the Barberini bees and the Chigi stars) can be seen on the capitals.

The bronze doors, which date from the Empire, were restored under Pius IV (16C). Once inside the building, the harmony and grandeur of the interior have an immediate impact. The proportions are striking; the diameter of the building is equal to its overall height (43.30m/142ft). The **antique dome★★★** is an incredibly bold feature; its weight is distributed via relieving arches incorporated in the walls onto the eight piers of masonry which alternate with the deep recesses. At the centre of the coffered ceiling is an enormous round opening (oculus), through which the interior is lit.

A series of superb monolithic columns punctuate alternate round and rectangular recesses. The piers between the recesses are decorated with shrines with alternating triangular or rounded pediments; later Renaissance architects turned to these for inspiration in designing palazzo windows.

The upper stage between the cornice and the base of the dome was redesigned in the 18C with the present series of panels and blind windows. A section above the third chapel on the west side has been returned to the original decor.

The recesses have been converted into chapels: in the first to the west of the entrance is an attractive Annunciation attributed to Melozzo da Forlì. The next chapel contains the **tomb of Victor Emmanuel II** (1820-78), the first king of unified Italy.

Between the fifth and sixth chapels is the **tomb of Raphael**, composed of a fine Antique sarcophagus. He died, aged 37, in 1520. On the upper edge is an inscription by Cardinal Pietro Bembo, poet and Humanist (1470-1547), which Alexander Pope translated without acknowledgement for another epitaph:

"Living, great nature feared he might outvie
Her works; and dying fears herself to die".

Walking About

North of Piazza della Rotonda, Via del Pantheon leads to Piazza della Maddalena.

Santa Maria Maddalena

Open Mon-Fri, 8am-noon and 5-8pm; Sat-Sun and public holidays, 9.30am-noon and 5-8pm. ☏ *06 67 97 796.* The church, which is dedicated to St Mary Magdalene, stands on the site of a 15C oratory and hospice which were occupied in 1586 by St Camillus of Lellis, the founder of the Ministers of the Sick, a nursing order. The church was rebuilt in the 17C by Carlo Fontana, who was succeeded by followers of Bernini. The façade was erected in 1735; its contorted lines and abundant decoration are an exaggeration of Borromini's style.

The **interior★** is a rare example of the Rococo in Rome. The elaborate plan, also suggesting Borromini's influence, gives the church a majestic appearance despite its small size: an elliptical nave with recesses for altars set at an angle and a short transept covered by a dome. The rich decoration in stucco, gold and marble and the frescoes on the dome and in the apse, which is bathed in a clear light, lend the church the charm of an old-fashioned drawing-room.

The relics of St Camillus are venerated at the altar in the south transept beneath the *Glory of St Camillus,* painted by Sebastian Conca. In the passage south of the chancel is a 15C wooden statue of Mary Magdalene. The sumptuous organ dates from the 18C as do the attractive furnishings in the sacristy.

Return to Piazza della Rotonda.

On the west side of the Pantheon *(Via Salita dei Crescenzi and Via di S. Eustachio)* is the site where the Crescenzi fortress stood in the Middle Ages. Nearby a tower was erected by the Sinibaldi family. Two Ancient columns, once part of the baths of Alexander Severus, have been re-erected at the junction of the two streets.

The famous Sant'Eustachio café is located in Piazza di S. Eustachio *(see Directory).*

Go southeast along Via della Palombella to Piazza della Minerva.

Piazza della Minerva

It was **Bernini**'s idea to embellish this charming square with an obelisk supported on an elephant's back. The obelisk is Egyptian and dates from the 6C BC; it was once part of the nearby Temple of Isis. The fantastic marble elephant, affectionately called the "chick of Minerva", was sculpted by one of Bernini's pupils, Ercole Ferrata (1667).

Santa Maria sopra Minerva★★

The church was founded in the 8C near the ruins of a temple to Minerva built by Domitian and has undergone many alterations. In 1280 it was rebuilt in the Gothic style and then modified towards the middle of the 15C. The façade was constructed in the 17C; it is rectangular and very plain, with the original 15C doorways. Six plaques *(right)* mark the heights reached by the flood waters of the Tiber between 1598 and 1870. The church has long been the headquarters of the Dominicans, historical rivals of the Jesuits in the defence of Roman Catholic orthodoxy against the Reformation.

Interior – The construction of the side chapels began in the 15C and the chancel was rebuilt in the 17C. The broad nave and aisles, with heavy intersecting 19C vaulting, can give the illusion of a Gothic church. The **works of art★** conserved here rank the church as one of the first "museum churches" of Rome.

South aisle – In the fifth chapel **(1)** the painting by Antoniazzo Romano recalls the beneficence of Cardinal Juan de Torquemada (uncle of the infamous inquisitor) who provided poor girls with dowries. This work, against a gold background, is typical of the style of this late-15C painter, which is marked with a certain religious conventionality.

The sixth chapel **(2)** was designed late in the 16C by Giacomo della Porta and Carlo Maderno. In the spirit of the Counter-Reformation the extravagance of the marble is tempered with a certain severity. The tombs of Clement VIII's parents are by Giacomo della Porta and the French sculptor Nicolas Cordier.

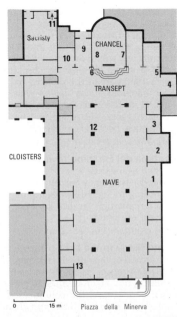

Piazza della Minerva

The next chapel **(3)** contains one of **Andrea Bregno**'s most famous works *(right)*: the restrained and delicate decoration on the tomb of Cardinal Coca, who died in 1477.

South transept – The Carafa Chapel **(4)**, which has a finely carved marble altar rail, was built and decorated between 1489 and 1493 with **frescoes★** by **Filippino Lippi**: above the altar, in a typical late-Renaissance frame, is an Annunciation in which Thomas Aquinas presents Cardinal Oliviero Carafa to the Virgin. The expressive faces, the slender figures and the deeply pleated garments are characteristic of Filippino Lippi's art. The rest of the wall is taken up with an Assumption in fine colours. The right-hand wall shows scenes from the life of Thomas Aquinas. On the left of the Carafa Chapel is the 13C tomb of Guillaume Durand **(5)**, Bishop of Mende in France, who died in 1296, by Giovanni Cosma.

Presbytery – The statue of Christ **(6)** was commissioned by a Roman nobleman from Michelangelo. The artist, having returned to Florence in 1520, started on the statue but then sent it to Rome, where it was finished by his pupils. The gilded bronze drapery was added later. The tomb of **St Catherine of Siena**, patron saint of Italy, lies under the main altar.

The funeral monuments of the Medici Popes, **Clement VII (7)** and Leo V **(8)**, modelled on commemorative arches, are the work of Antonio da Sangallo (1483-1546); contemporary taste preferred architectural to decorative features in funerary art.

North transept – The first chapel **(9)** contains many fine **tombs★**; the tomb with the dead man resting on his elbow *(left)* is by Giacomo della Porta (late 16C). Set into the floor is the tomb of Fra (the Blessed) Angelico, Giovanni da Fiesole, the Dominican painter who died in 1455. In the next chapel **(10)** is a 15C tomb composed of an Antique sarcophagus *(Hercules and the lion)*.

St Catherine of Siena's Chapel (11) – This chapel was built in the 17C using the walls of the room in which the saint died (1380) in the neighbouring Dominican convent.

North aisle – Monument to Venerable Sister Maria Raggi **(12)**: flowing garments, an ecstatic expression and lively cherubs exemplify the art of Bernini (1643). The Renaissance tomb of Francesco Tornabuoni **(13)**, who died in 1480, is one of Mino da Fiesole's most successful works because of its fine decorative carving.

Walk westwards along Via Piè di Marmo.

The street is named after the enormous stone **foot** which probably belonged to a Roman statue, although no one knows how it came to be in its present position. The **Roman College** (Collegio Romano), formerly the **Jesuit College**, was founded in 1583 by Gregory XIII, who strove to re-establish the primacy of Rome after the Council of Trent. At the corner of Via della Gatta beneath a canopy there is a charming Madonna, so typical of Rome.

Palazzo Doria Pamphili★

This palace, one of the largest in Rome, was begun in the 15C and gradually enlarged by the succession of noble families who owned it. It is home to the gallery of the same name, which houses a fine collection of paintings and sculpture *(see Worth a Visit below)*. First acquired by the Della Rovere family, it then passed to Pope Julius II's nephew, the Duke of Urbino. Clement VIII, a member of the Aldobrandini family, then bought it for his nephew. Finally Donna Olimpia, Clement VIII's niece and heir, married Camillo Pamphili, whose family was later allied with that of the Dorias.

The façade facing the Corso is an imposing 18C construction in the Baroque style, whereas the front looking into Via del Plebiscito dates from 1643. The palazzo extends the whole length of Via della Gatta behind a 19C façade and round two sides of Piazza del Collegio Romano.

Since 1966 part of the palazzo has housed the Anglican Centre in Rome, a tangible outcome of the formal visit paid by Archbishop Michael Ramsey to Pope Paul VI in that year. Students of any age, particularly Roman Catholics, who wish to learn about the Anglican Communion, can consult the library of Anglican authorities, books of reference and history.

Take Via Lata between Santa Maria in Via Lata and Palazzo del Banco di Roma.

Fontana del Facchino (Porter's Fountain)

Tucked against the wall *(right)* is an amusing little fountain composed of a porter *(facchino)* holding a barrel with water issuing from the bung hole into a basin. According to legend, the sculptor took as his model a Renaissance water-carrier with a reputation for drunkenness, who is thus obliged to make do with water for the rest of time.

Turn right into Via del Corso.

Santa Maria in Via Lata (Church of St Mary in Via Lata)

The façade of the church is of particular interest. Built between 1658 and 1662 by Pietro Cortona, it marks the transition in Baroque art to the period when detached columns, no longer an integral part of the walls, took on an essential role. Set out along two storeys, the columns seem to support the whole building and create remarkable effects of light and shade.

Palazzo Salviati

It was built in the 17C by the Duke of Nevers, Cardinal Mazarin's nephew, to house the French Academy.

Retrace your steps along Via del Corso.

San Marcello

The **church of St Marcellus** was founded in the 4C on the site of a *titulus*, a private house used as a place of Christian worship.

The church was burned down in 1519 and completely rebuilt in the 16C and 17C. In 1683 Carlo Fontana designed the slightly concave Baroque façade. The palms linking the two storeys are typical of the Baroque style, which delighted in the unusual. The empty frame above the entrance has never received its intended sculpture.

The single nave with side chapels, typical of the Renaissance, was designed by **Jacopo Sansovino** (1486-1570) in the 16C. The late-16C coffered ceiling is richly decorated in gold, blue and red.

Works of art from the Renaissance to the Baroque period are to be found here. To the left of the entrance is the tomb of Cardinal Giovanni Michiel, who was poisoned on Alexander VI's orders in 1503. Below it is the tomb of his nephew, Bishop Antonio Orso, who died in 1511. The work was begun in 1520 by **Andrea Sansovino** and finished in 1527 by his pupil **Jacopo Sansovino**.

In the fourth chapel on the right is a fine 15C wooden crucifix. The realistic figure of Christ in agony gave rise to a lugubrious legend: the sculptor was so obsessed with the desire to depict the suffering as realistically as possible that he killed a poor fellow who happened to be passing that way and studied the death throes to inspire his own carving. When the church burned down in 1519 it is said that the crucifix was recovered intact in the ruins. The frescoes in the vault are by Perin del Vaga, one of Raphael's pupils. In the base of the altar is a 3C Roman stele which was decorated with incrustations of marble in the 12C to serve as a reliquary.

The fourth chapel on the left contains busts of the noble family of the Frangipani; the three on the right were carved by Algardi in 1625.

Palazzo del Banco di Roma (Bank of Rome)

The palazzo was built between 1714 and 1722 for the Carolis, and converted early in the 20C. At the end of the 18C it was the home of the French Ambassador, who gave a number of splendid receptions here for guests including the French writer, Chateaubriand.

Turn left and right into Via del Collegio Romano and left into Via del Caravita to reach Piazza Sant'Ignazio.

Piazza Sant'Ignazio★

The square is best observed from the steps of the church. It was designed in imitation of a theatre set, in ochre and stone, and has an unusual charm, with curved façades on the street corners, where people make their entrances and exits like actors on a stage.

Sant'Ignazio★★

The church, which is dedicated to the founder of the **Jesuit** Order and of the Roman College, the first free school, is typical of the Counter-Reformation and was begun in 1626 to the plans of a Jesuit, Orazio Grassi. It stands within the precincts of the Roman College and served for many years as the college chapel. Orazio Grassi also designed the high façade; the two superimposed orders linked by scrolls produce a solemn and austere ensemble.

Central ceiling fresco★★ – For the best view of the stunning fresco painted on the central vault and the *trompe l'oeil* cupola, stand on the disc in the centre of the nave. The fresco is the work of **Andrea Pozzo** (1684). A Jesuit, he chose a subject dear to the Counter-Reformation, which exalted the saints in the face of Protestantism. Here St Ignatius is bathed by a divine light which is reflected on the four corners of the world, shown allegorically. Pozzo used his knowledge of three-dimensional perspective (between 1696 and 1702 he wrote a treatise entitled *Perspectiva pictorum et architectorum* which had considerable influence on painters and architects in the 18C) to create the *trompe-l'oeil* effect. Against an architectural background he has arranged an animated crowd of figures.

The apsidal fresco, also the work of Andrea Pozzo, glorifies the miracles worked by St Ignatius's intercession.

The altar at the end of the right transept is dedicated to St Luigi Gonzaga. Above the lapis lazuli urn containing the saint's relics and between the beautiful green marble columns wreathed in fronds of bronze is an admirable *Glory to St Luigi Gonzaga*, a "marble picture" carved by **Pierre Legros**, a French student at the French Academy (1629-1714).

In the left transept opposite is a corresponding altar in honour of St John Berchmans. The high-relief sculpture of the Annunciation is the work of Filippo Valle. Both altars boast bold interpretations by Andrea Pozzo of the pediments so dear to Borromini.

Take Via dei Burrò.

Via dei Burrò owes its name to the administrative offices established in the area by Napoleon Bonaparte (*bureau* is the French word for office).

Piazza di Pietra

The south side of this colourful square is occupied by a building which now houses the Stock Exchange. In the 18C it was the Customs House, where any visitor to Rome was obliged to present themself.

Incorporated in the present building are 11 beautiful marble columns of the Corinthian order belonging to a **temple** which stood here in Antiquity. It was erected in honour of the deified **Hadrian** by his adopted son Antoninus Pius and consecrated in AD 145. The Ancient columns give the square a feeling of grandeur.

Worth a Visit

Galleria Doria Pamphili★★

In Palazzo Doria Pamphili, Piazza Collegio Romano, 2. ⚲ Open daily (except Thu) 10am-5pm. Closed 1 Jan, Easter, 1 May, 15 Aug and Christmas. €7.30. ☎ 06 67 97 323; Fax 06 67 80 939.

The first rooms in the gallery are the **Sale di Rappresentanza** (Reception Rooms) including the **Sala dei Velluti** (Velvet Room), which retains its original 17C floor. The decorations include an eagle, symbol of the Doria family, of Ligurian origin, and a fleur-de-lis, symbol of the Pamphili. Exhibited in the corner of the **Sala da Ballo** (Ballroom) reserved for the musicians is a 17C harp made from ivory and wood. The walls of the Rococo-style **Saletta Gialla** (Yellow Drawing Room) to the right display tapestry panels depicting Allegories of the Twelve Months, made at the Gobelins factory in Paris during the reign of Louis XV.

The **gallery** itself is quadrilateral in shape. It was once the loggia over the internal 16C courtyard and was closed during the time of Camillo Pamphili (18C) to house the collection of paintings and sculpture. The discovery of a manuscript dating from 1767 has allowed the paintings to be displayed according to their original layout. Some of the more outstanding works are mentioned below. The numbers used in the text correspond with those in the gallery.

First gallery – This gallery houses paintings by **Annibale Carracci**, including the series of lunettes depicting the Stories of the Virgin Mary (i5, i9, i14, i27, i29 and i33). In the *Flight into Egypt★★* (i5), the religious scene seems to have a marginal role and it is the gentle but realistic landscape that takes up almost all the picture, presaging a taste which was to develop throughout the 17C. In *Erminia finding Tancred wounded* (i28), by **Guercino**, the drama of the scene is intensified by the contrasts between light and dark. *The Usurers★* (i47) by **Quentin Metsys** is an important painting by this Flemish master, in which the characters depicted (especially the two userers on the left) have exaggerated features.

Detail of Rest after the flight into Egypt *by Caravaggio*

At the end of the gallery, a small studio houses the **Portrait of Innocent X★★★**, a masterpiece by **Velázquez**, painted in 1650 during his second visit to Rome; the painter has succeeded in painting an official portrait which is realistic and quite lacking in idealisation (note the stern expression). Here, also, is a bust of Innocent X by **Bernini**, a very expressive interpretation of the Pope's authoritative personality.

Galleria degli Specchi – This Hall of Mirrors makes up the second part of the gallery. The decor dates from the 18C and the **ceiling** is painted with frescoes by Aurelio Milani, depicting the Labours of Hercules.

Four **small rooms** lead off the gallery, dedicated to the 15C, 16C, 17C and 18C respectively. In the second room, dedicated to the 17C, the visitor's attention is immediately drawn to the magnificent **Rest after the flight into Egypt★★★** by **Caravaggio**. The scene is one of natural beauty: the tired Virgin sleeps with her head gently bent over her child, her hand lying in her lap; Joseph seems entranced by the music of the angel, a young man with large dark wings who stands in front of him (the position is unusual). Just visible behind Joseph's shoulder is the donkey, who also seems enchanted by the music. Caravaggio has used the same model for his *Mary Magdalene,* cleverly positioned next to the painting of the Virgin. Even the pose is the same, but whereas the Virgin, through fatigue, has given herself up to sleep, Mary Magdalene is depicted as a despairing young woman with reference only to earthly pleasures; note the bottle of perfume and jewellery at her side.

St Sebastian by Ludovico Carracci and **Endymion** by Guercino are exhibited in the same room. The main focus in the room dedicated to the 16C is the beautiful **Salome★★** by **Titian**. Notice the play of expressions: the servant looks at Salome with a pious and reprimanding expression; Salome is only able to glance quickly, almost with horror, at the head of John the Baptist as she runs away; the hair of the Baptist almost seems to caress the hand of the man who killed him. In the same room the *Portrait of a Young Man* by Tintoretto, the *Portrait of Two People* by Raphael and a delicate *Winter Landscape* by Peter Bruegel the Elder can also be admired. A masterpiece by Hans Memling, **Mourning the Death of Christ★★**, in which the drama of the composition is highlighted by the harsh traits and angular position of Christ, is exhibited in the 15C room.

Third Gallery – An unusual painting by Bruegel the Elder, *Battle in the Bay of Naples* (q21), can be seen in this gallery. The **Sala Aldobrandini,** a room to the left at the bottom of the gallery, houses statues from both the Archaic and late Imperial eras.

Fourth Gallery – At the entrance to this gallery is a **bust of Olimpia Maidalchini Pamphili★★** by **Algardi.** She is said to have pestered and hounded her brother-in-law, Giovanni Battista Pamphili, until he attained the Papal throne as Innocent X. Algardi, who was an accomplished portraitist, knew precisely how to express the energy and ambition of Donna Olimpia, as she was called by the Romans; she is shown in the distinctive headdress which she alone wore. Paintings in this gallery include a 17C copy of *John the Baptist as a Child* (s57) by Caravaggio, which hangs in the Palazzo dei Conservatori, and the *Madonna and Child* (s71) by **Parmigiano.** Two further reception rooms open off the gallery. A richly gilded cradle dating from 1761 can be seen in the Red Room.

Appartamenti privati★ (Private Apartments) – These are the rooms inhabited from the 16C to 18C by the families who owned the palace. In the Wintergarden are a small sleigh used in the 18C and a fine sedan chair, painted and gilded (18C). The Andrea Doria Room bears the name of the most famous member of the Genoese Doria family; a mercenary *(condottiere),* he commanded the French fleet for François I before being employed by Charles V.

The smoking room is decorated in 19C English style.

The frieze in the dining room depicts the various properties belonging to the Doria Pamphili family (19C).

In the Green Drawing Room one of the many paintings is a graceful *Annunciation* by the Florentine Filippo Lippi (1406-69), Botticelli's master. A large 15C Tournai tapestry illustrates the medieval legend of Alexander the Great.

Piazza Navona★★★

Piazza Navona has always been a popular setting for festivals, celebrations and public meetings. Today the piazza is busy day and night with crowds of tourists and locals who come here to enjoy the relaxed atmosphere and watch the street artists, mimics, musicians and portrait painters. The square is surrounded by a network of picturesque medieval streets, lined with pizzerias, restaurants and shops, a reminder of the district's traditional role of providing services for pilgrims on their way to St Peter's. This delightful quarter is dotted with magnificent Renaissance and Baroque *palazzi*, interesting churches and a number of attractive small squares, one of which is home to Pasquino, one of the famous "talking statues" of Rome.

Location

Michelin map 38 or Michelin spiral atlas of Rome: p 96 K 10, L 10-11. Tour: 1hr 30min. This district, situated on a loop in the Tiber, is bordered by Corso Vittorio Emanuele II, Corso del Rinascimento and Via Zanardelli (opened in the late 19C and early 20C) and was once part of the **Campus Martius** *(see PANTHEON) (the area on the bank of the river is described in CASTEL SANT'ANGELO).*
Neighbouring sights are described in the following chapters: CAMPO DEI FIORI; CASTEL SANT'ANGELO; MONTECITORIO; PANTHEON.

Background

Except for the outline of Domitian's Stadium, which is preserved in the shape of the Piazza Navona *(see below)*, no traces of ancient Rome have survived here. The square is now adorned with fine Renaissance and Baroque buildings designed by the most famous architects of the 16C and 17C.
Churches and palaces were built in the area as early as the beginning of the 16C, as the Popes attempted to smarten up the narrow, medieval streets around the piazza and cardinals, ambassadors, Papal officials, wealthy bankers and distinguished courtesans took up residence here. Around them intellectual life flourished: booksellers, engravers and miniaturists settled around Piazza Navona and Piazza Pasquino and to this day there are still numerous craftsmen to be found in the area.

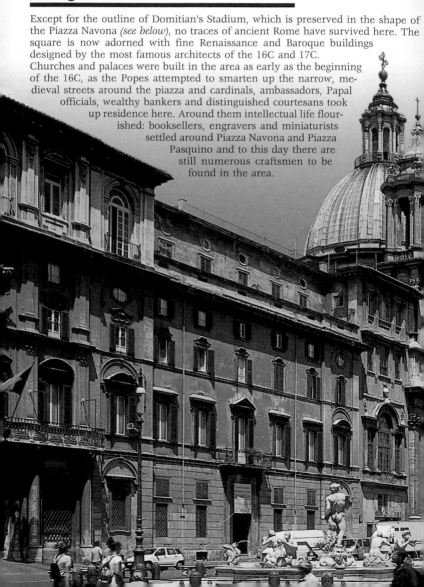

Special Features

PIAZZA NAVONA★★★

This is perhaps the place which most effectively characterises the true spirit of the Eternal City, where tourists can gain a unique image of the contrasting facets of Rome. Set apart from the noise and smell of the traffic, Piazza Navona seems to be permanently on holiday: the balloon-seller has his pitch beside a caricaturist who sketches his customer with a few deft strokes of charcoal; an old woman lovingly feeds the pigeons next to a trade unionist exhorting his comrades; tourists and locals come to savour a *tartufo* on the terrace of the Tre Scalini.

The long and narrow shape of the square is due to **Domitian**: in AD 86 he had a **stadium** built on this site (Stadio di Domiziano) and immediately instituted a series of games in the Greek style. Unlike the games in the amphitheatre, where the gladiators confronted one another with violence, these games were contests of wit and physical fitness; the speaking, poetry and musical competitions were held in the Odeon, situated roughly where Palazzo Massimo and Piazza S. Pantaleo now stand, with running, wrestling, and discus and javelin throwing taking place in the stadium.

Domitian's Stadium was stripped of its marble in 356 by Constantinus II on a visit to Rome and by the 5C it was in ruins.

It came to life again during the Renaissance, when it developed into one of the most beautiful sights in Rome under the Popes. In 1477 the market from the foot of the Capitol was moved here and other attractions were added to bring in the crowds, such as the *cuccagna*, a greased pole which strong men tried to climb, or puppet shows. In the mid-17C the square was partially flooded to accommodate summer weekend water games. Since 1869 it is only at Christmas and Epiphany that market stalls appear in Piazza Navona.

The Fountains

There are three fountains in the square.

Fontana dei Fiumi★★★ – The **Fountain of the Rivers**, which occupies the centre of the square, was created by **Bernini** for Pope Innocent X, who wanted to provide worthy surroundings for his residence, the Palazzo Pamphili, which stood on the piazza. The brilliant Baroque architect contrived a pile of rockwork hollowed out into grottoes on top of which he erected an obelisk; the rigidity and symmetry of the latter contrasts strikingly with the fluid lines of the base; the wind seems to tear at the trees and the marble statues seem to gesticulate. They were carved from the master's designs by some of his pupils and represent four rivers, symbolising the four quarters of the world: the Danube for Europe, the Nile for Africa (the veiled head indicated that the source was unknown), the Ganges for Asia and the Plate for America. The obelisk, a Roman work dating from Domitian's reign, was recovered by Innocent X from the Via Appia where it lay. The fountain was completed in 1651.

Fontana del Moro – The **Fountain of the Moor** was built at the end of the 16C. In 1653, at Innocent X's request, it was renovated by **Bernini**, who designed the central figure of the Moor; one of his pupils was responsible for the vigorous way in which it was interpreted. The statues on the tritons and the edge of the basin date from the 19C.

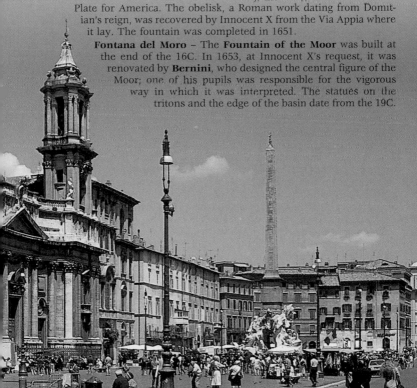

WHERE TO EAT

See "Where to Eat" in the Practical Points section at the beginning of the guide.

TAKING A BREAK

Tre Scalini – *Piazza Navona 28* – ☎ *06 68 80 19 96* – *Open Thu-Tue, 9am-1am.* Situated on one of the most beautiful squares in Rome, this café is renowned for its excellent truffle ice cream.

Antico Caffè della Pace – *Piazza della Pace 4* – ☎ *06 68 61 216* – *Open 10am-2am.* Situated in a lovely little square near the main piazza, this café attracts a number of personalities from the theatre, especially in the evening when they can be seen sitting at the outdoor tables. The two rooms inside the café have a Central European feel, with padded sofas, soft lights and tinted mirrors.

Bar del Fico – *Piazza del Fico 26/27* – ☎ *06 68 65 205* – *Open 8am-2am.* This bar, one the of busiest in the district, has tables set out in the shade of the fig tree which gives both the bar and the piazza their name. Temporary exhibitions of paintings and photography can be admired inside the bar. It serves delicious canapés and snacks at aperitif time and plays a good selection of music.

I Paladini – *Via del Governo Vecchio 29* – *Usual pizzeria opening times, but closed 2.30-5pm* – 🗷. This pizzeria serves excellent freshly-baked *pizza bianca* (pizza without a tomato base), topped with artichokes, cheese, different types of ham, or nutella.

Bar Piccolino – *Via del Teatro Valle 54/a* – ☎ *06 68 72 279* – *Open 7am-11pm.* This tiny bar is known for its delicious hazelnut-flavoured coffee.

SHOPPING

Antonella Marani – *Via di Monte Giordano 27* – ☎ *06 68 30 78 66* – *Open Mon-Fri, 10.30am-6pm.* Miniature façades of Roman churches made from plaster casts are on sale here, as well as stuccoes, friezes, low reliefs and busts, all in Roman style.

Galleria di Orditi e Trame – *Via del Teatro Valle 54/b* – ☎ *06 68 93 372.* Two innovative artists create beautiful and original cotton hats for this boutique.

Jaracandà – *Via del Teatro Pace 2/a.* This workshop repairs and restores traditional Italian and foreign musical instruments.

Orsantico – *Via dell'Orso 60/61/63* – ☎ *06 68 77 759* – *Open Tue-Sat, 10am-1pm and 4-7.30pm; Mon, 4-7.30pm.* This shop specialises in furniture and Italian and French antiques and is housed in the Palazzo della Scimmia (Monkey's Palace – the name refers to a miracle said to have taken place here in the past).

Set – *Piazza del Fico 23.* This little shop, situated opposite the famous Bar del Fico, has a selection of splendid furniture and articles dating from 1900-50.

CHRISTMAS MARKET

Piazza Navona is particularly atmospheric around Christmas and the New Year, when the square is decorated with brightly coloured market stalls.

Fontana del Nettuno – The **Fountain of Neptune** was moved to Piazza Navona at the end of the 16C. The statue of Neptune at the centre and those around it date from the 19C.

Sant'Agnese in Agone★★

Open Tue, Wed and Fri, 2-6.30pm; Thu and Sat, 4-7pm; Sun and public holidays, 10am-1pm. Closed Mon. ☎ *06 32 92 326; Fax 06 67 92 903.*
According to tradition, a small oratory was built in the 8C on the site where St Agnes was thought to have been martyred. In 1652 Pope Innocent X commissioned Girolamo Rainaldi and his son Carlo to rebuild the church as a family chapel attached to his palace. From 1653-57 **Borromini** took charge of the work.

> **ARTISTIC RIVALRY**
> A number of stories illustrate the rivalry that was said to exist between Bernini and **Borromini**, who designed the façade of St Agnes's Church. One such Roman legend explains that the statues of the Nile and the Plate, their arms raised in a defensive gesture, are trying to protect themselves from the façade, which is about to collapse. In fact, the façade was built several years after the fountain.

The church was completed at the end of the century by a group of architects. Borromini was responsible for part of the dome and for the façade, which demonstrates his taste for contrasting convex and concave lines, particularly in the campaniles. The **interior★** is captivating: the deep recesses in the pillars supporting the dome transform the Greek cross plan into an octagon. The altars are adorned with beautiful "marble pictures" by Bernini's pupils. The decorations in stucco, gilt and painting are far from the spirit of Borromini's sober interiors and were added at the end of the 17C.

Palazzo Pamphili

This was the Pamphili residence; it was enlarged between 1644 and 1650 by Girolamo Rainaldi when Giovanni Battista Pamphili became Pope Innocent X.

Walking About

At the north end of the Piazza take Via Agonale.

The remains of **Domitian's Stadium** can be seen in Via di Tor Sanguigna, adjacent to the piazza.

Santa Maria dell'Anima

As the main entrance is usually closed, enter by the side door in Via della Pace and start with the interior. This is the church of German-speaking Roman Catholics. There had been a pilgrim hostel on the site since 1386 when the present building was begun in 1500. It was restored in the 19C.

Interior – Designed as a "hall church", where the nave and aisles are all of the same height, the plan is rather unusual for Rome, which has almost no Gothic architecture. The decoration dates from the 19C.

There are several works by pupils or lesser artists imitating the styles of the great masters. Above the high altar is a *Holy Family with Saints* by Giulio Romano, one of Raphael's assistants.

The **façade** in Via dell'Anima was designed by Giuliano da Sangallo and built in 1511. Its flatness, which gives it the appearance of a screen, belongs to the Renaissance period. The pediment above the central door contains a sculpture of the Virgin between two figures, each representing a soul (*anima* in Italian), which is a copy of a painting which gave the church its name. The original is kept in the sacristy *(apply to the sacristan)*. To the right of the façade there is a view of the bell-tower which is capped by a slim cone faced with multicoloured ceramics (1516-18).

Santa Maria della Pace★

Open Mon-Fri, 10am-6pm; Sat, 10am-10pm; Sun and public holidays, 10am-1pm. Donation welcome. ☎ 06 68 61 156.

There was already a small church on this site in the 12C. Sixtus IV had it rebuilt in 1480. In the Baroque era it changed in appearance when Alexander VII (1655-67) invited Pietro da Cortona to design a new **façade**. He created a pleasing combination of contrasting effects: a semicircular porch flanked by two concave wings. To provide a suitable setting for his work the architect designed a charming square lined with elegant *palazzi*.

Interior – The 15C plan is very unusual; it comprises a short rectangular nave and an octagonal domed section. The arch of the first chapel on the right in the nave was decorated by **Raphael** in 1514; he painted the four **Sibyls★** inspired by the angels, no doubt after seeing Michelangelo's Sibyls in the Sistine Chapel. His

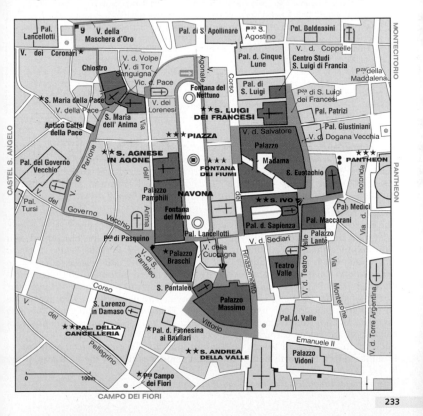

skill in turning an awkward surface to good account is to be admired. The Prophets were painted by one of his pupils. The first chapel on the left is decorated with elegant frescoes by **Baldassarre Peruzzi** (1481-1536), who also worked on the Farnesina. The very rich decoration on the arch leading into the second chapel on the right is typical of the high Renaissance.

In the octagonal section over the high altar is an image of the Virgin, which is supposed to have bled when struck by a stone in 1480; Sixtus IV had the church rebuilt to house the miraculous image.

Cloisters – *Entrance at Vicolo Arco della Pace 5.* They were built in 1504 and were one of **Bramante**'s earliest Roman works. The handsome proportions give an air of great simplicity. The columns on the ground floor are complemented by those on the first floor, which alternate with smaller columns placed centrally over the lower arches.

Between the chuches turn into Vicolo Arco della Pace which leads into Via della Pace. Follow this street to Via dei Coronari; turn left into Piazza Lancellotti to find Via della Maschera d'Oro.

Via della Maschera d'Oro

N° 9, on the corner of Vicolo di San Simeone, is a small palace which shows how secular architecture developed in the 16C as a result of Sixtus IV's essays in town planning.

At this period the streets of Rome were lined by charming façades engraved and painted with monochrome frescoes. **Polidoro da Caravaggio** and **Maturino da Firenze** were the masters of this technique. The wall was first given a rough rendering blackened with smoke and then covered with a coat of plaster. The artist then engraved mythological scenes or motifs taken from Antique art to reveal the dark undercoat. These decorations were extremely fragile and almost all have disappeared.

Return to Via della Pace.

The **Antico Caffè della Pace** has stood in the picturesque Via della Pace since the beginning of the 19C *(see Directory)*.

Continue south along Via di Parione; turn left into Via del Governo Vecchio to reach Piazza di Pasquino.

PASQUINO

The statue of **Pasquino**, which was probably part of a 3C BC group, was found in Piazza Navona in the 15C. It was in such a pitiable state that no collector wanted it, and so it was placed on the corner against the building which occupied that site before the Palazzo Braschi, and there it stayed. People called it Pasquino after a local tailor with a very caustic tongue and used it as their mouthpiece. During the night satirical or even libellous comments, criticising morals and politics and expressing popular claims, sometimes in Roman dialect, were secretly hung on Pasquino. The following day the "Pasquinades" spread through Rome as far as the doors of the Papal officials; some were even carried to the ears of foreign sovereigns and started more than one diplomatic incident. The draconian laws sentencing the perpetrators of these libels to death were rarely applied; or if they were, the prisoner was immediately pardoned. Pasquino was the most famous and most loquacious of the Roman "talking statues", which included Madama Lucrezia *(see p 250)*, Marforio *(see p 134)* and the Abate Luigi *(see p 212)*.

Palazzo Braschi★

It is named after the family of Pope Pius VI who had it built in the late 18C for his nephews. It was the last Papal family palace to be built in Rome. The neo-Classical style then in vogue was used for the ponderous façades which dominate the surrounding streets: Via della Cuccagna, Via di Pasquino and Via di San Pantaleo. The *palazzo* houses the Museo di Roma *(see Worth a Visit below)*.

Palazzo Massimo

The palace, which belongs to the Massimo, one of the oldest families in Rome, comprises three separate buildings. The one on the right of the **church of San Pantaleo** (designed by Valadier in 1806) is known as the Pyrrhus Palace, because of a statue which was kept there. The Palazzo Massimo *alle colonne (facing on to Corso Vittorio Emanuele II)* is screened by a fine curved portico of Doric columns, designed (1532-36) by **Baldassarre Peruzzi**. The original windows of the upper storeys of the façade herald the Mannerist style. The oldest part of the palazzo is on the north side *(access from Corso Vittorio Emanuele II via a narrow lane into Piazza de' Massimi)* and is known as the "illustrated palace" because of the grisailles painted on the façade c 1523 by some of Daniele da Volterra's pupils.

The column standing in Piazza de'Massimi may have been part of the **Odeon** of Domitian. From the north end of the piazza there is a view of the Fountain of the Rivers in Piazza Navona.

Turn right and then left into Corso del Rinascimento.

Palazzo della Sapienza

Until 1935 this *palazzo* was occupied by Rome University. Now it houses, among other things, the archives of the **Papal States** from the 9C to the 19C. The simple façade, begun in 1575 to a design by Giacomo della Porta and coloured burnt umber, gives no hint of the elegance of the inner courtyard, which is surrounded on three sides by a two-storey portico.

Sant'Ivo alla Sapienza★★ – Equally unexpected is the audacity of Borromini's façade for St Ivo's Church, which closes the fourth side of the courtyard. Just as **Bernini** aimed at extensiveness, so Borromini tried to confine his ideas within a restricted space, using such exaggeratedly curved lines that his architecture was termed perverse and contrary. An amazing variety of curves is used in this building: in the many-faceted drum, in the convex line of the dome and the concave buttresses, in the spiral surmounting the lantern.

The interior, very high and light, is a constant interplay of concave and convex surfaces, a foretaste of the Rococo style; it incorporates the bee from the Barberini coat of arms. *Open Sun and public holidays, 9am-noon. Donation welcome.* ☎ *06 69 88 61 64; Fax 06 69 88 64 35.*

Exit by the side door (under the arcade on the right) into Via del Teatro Valle.

In this street, where basket-makers still work at their craft, stands the **Teatro Valle**, with its 19C decor.

Return up the street to Piazza S. Eustachio.

From the piazza there is a splendid **view★★** of the spiral dome of St Ivo's Church. On the south side stands the **Palazzo Maccarani** (1521), an austere building in the Renaissance style by Jules Romain; it incorporates one of the most popular cafés in Rome, the Caffè Sant'Eustachio (*see Directory, PANTHEON*).

The early-18C façade of the **church of Sant'Eustachio** is screened by a portico; the head of a deer bearing a cross between its antlers recalls the vision which St Eustace experienced in the hunting field while he was still a Roman general and which led to his conversion.

Take Via della Dogana Vecchia to Piazza S. Luigi dei Francesi.

San Luigi dei Francesi★★

Open 7am-12.30pm and 3.30-7pm (6.30pm Sat). Closed Thu afternoons. No charge. ☎ *06 68 82 71; Fax 06 68 82 72 28.*
The first stone of this building was laid in 1518 by Cardinal Giulio de' Medici, the future Pope **Clement VII**. After very slow progress between 1524 and 1580, the church was completed in 1589 partly with the aid of subsidies from France given by Henri II, Henri III and Catherine de' Medici, and was consecrated as the national church of the French in Rome and dedicated to St Louis.

The façade, which bears the salamander of François I of France, was probably designed by Giacomo della Porta between 1580 and 1584. Its elegant lines accord well with Piazza di San Luigi dei Francesi. The prominent columns hint at the flamboyance of the Baroque style.

Piazza di San Luigi dei Francesi

The interior, consisting of a nave, side aisles and lateral chapels, was embellished in the Baroque period and in the 18C with marble, paintings, gilding and stucco work. The church houses tombs of famous Frenchmen, the beautiful chapel of St Cecilia and the chapel of St Matthew with its magnificent frescoes by Caravaggio, as well as numerous works whose themes recall the French status of the building.

Frescoes by Domenichino★ – *In the chapel of St Cecilia (second chapel in the north aisle).* The frescoes, which were executed in 1614, tell the story of St Cecilia. Domenichino, who had arrived in Rome in 1602, resisted the exuberance of the Baroque and strove after balance and clarity of texture in his art. On the right, *St Cecilia distributing her own wealth;* on the left, *The Death of St Cecilia;* on the ceiling, *An Angel crowns the saint and her husband Valeriano; Cecilia refuses to carry out sacrifices to pagan gods; St Cecilia in Glory.*

The altarpiece on the high altar is by Bassano and depicts the *Assumption.*

Caravaggio's paintings★★★ – In St Matthew's Chapel (*fifth chapel in the south aisle*) are three works depicting St Matthew's life, painted between 1599 and 1600. The vault is by **Cavaliere d'Arpino**, in whose studio Caravaggio worked.

Above the altar: *St Matthew and the Angel:* the artist's delight in contradiction is expressed here in the unusual posture of the old man, who has one knee balanced on a footstool and his face turned towards the angel, who is absorbed in the act of dictation.

On the left: *The Calling of St Matthew:* in a dark room five men, seated at a table, are distracted from their occupation by the entrance of Christ accompanied by St Peter. His pointing finger singles out Matthew seated beside an old man who is counting out the money. The shaft of light striking the wall and illuminating the faces is typical of Caravaggio and here symbolises the calling of the future disciple; the young man with a feather in his cap watching with a slightly scornful air is a familiar figure in Caravaggio's paintings.

On the right: *The Martyrdom of St Matthew*: in the middle of the picture lies the saint, wearing only a band of cloth around his hips, towered over by his persecutor, a soldier sent by the Ethiopian king. To the right of the picture an altar boy can be seen running away in terror. The most innovative element of the painting is the angel who emerges from a cloud to offer the saint the palm of martyrdom, thus immediately drawing the visitor into the action of the painting, which is both violent and dramatic in tone. To the left a face can be seen in the dark background: this is a self-portrait of the artist who observes the scene with a contrite expression.

Detail of The Martyrdom of St Matthew *by Caravaggio*

Take Via Salvatore; turn left into Corso del Rinascimento.

Palazzo Madama

Not open to the public. It was built by the Medici in the 16C. In the days of Cardinal Giovanni de' Medici, the future Leo X, banquets and literary gatherings were held here. Later Pope **Clement VII** made it the residence of his great niece, Catherine de' Medici. When she became the queen of France she renounced her Medici possessions and the palace passed to Alessandro de' Medici, whose wife, Madama Margherita d'Austria (1522-86), gave the palace its name. Since 1870, when Rome became the capital of Italy, the Senate has occupied the building.

The Baroque façade in the Corso del Rinascimento was built c 1642.

At the southern end of the street rises the façade of Sant'Andrea delle Valle *(see CAMPO DEI FIORI, p 138).*

Worth a Visit

Museo di Roma★

In Palazzo Braschi. & *Open daily (except Mon) 9am-7pm. Closed 1 Jan, 1 May and Christmas.* €6.20. ☎ *06 69 78 05 32 or 06 71 08 303 (Dottoressa Tittoni); Fax 06 67 10 31 18.*

The paintings and frescoes exhibited in the Museum of Rome trace the history of the city from the Middle Ages to the present day. The colossal staircase leading to the first floor is by Cosimo Morelli, who designed the palace.

A number of anonymous paintings depict the jousts held in the 16C and 17C in the Belvedere courtyard in the Vatican, Piazza Navona and on the Testaccio; these are followed by **frescoes★** taken from demolished buildings. The museum also houses various anonymous paintings illustrating the bustle of the old market near the Capitoline in the 17C and the pageantry of the Corpus Christi processions in St Peter's Square, as well as an attractive room hung with 18C Gobelins tapestries. In the first room on the second floor hang three huge canvases on Greek mythological themes by **Gavin Hamilton** (1723-98), a Scottish painter who settled in Rome in 1755 and spent most of his working life in Italy. Also on the second floor are the famous **watercolours★** in the series "Lost Rome" *(Roma sparita) and* fragments of mosaic from the old St Peter's Basilica (late 12C-early 13C).

On the ground floor *(entrance in northeast corner of the courtyard)* is the Papal train built for Pius IX in 1858. One of the coaches is fitted out as a small chapel.

Piazza del Popolo★★

In the days of the Grand Tour, travellers approaching Rome from the north along the Via Flaminia would arrive in Rome through the Porta del Popolo. Piazza del Popolo is one of the largest and most grandiose squares in the city, with its famous trio of streets running south from the piazza: the quiet Via di Ripetta, popular for its attractive boutiques; the bustling Via del Corso, the main commercial artery of the city, with shops to suit all tastes and budgets; and the elegant Via del Babuino, home to a number of fine antique shops. The highlight of a walk through the monumental and commercial heart of Rome is, however, without a doubt, the climb up to the Pincian Hill, where a shady, leafy park offers splendid views of the city.

Location

Michelin map 38 or Michelin spiral atlas of Rome: p 40 H 11-12, J 11-12. Metro line A: Flaminio or Spagna. Tour: 2hr. The area described below extends between the Tiber and the Pincian Hill, backed by the magnificent Villa Borghese gardens. Three main streets run south towards Augustus's Mausoleum and Piazza di Spagna from Piazza del Popolo, which is dominated by its twin churches and by Porta del Popolo, a gate in the Aurelian walls.

Neighbouring sights are described in the following chapters: PIAZZA DI SPAGNA; VILLA BORGHESE-VILLA GIULIA.

Walking About

PIAZZA DEL POPOLO★★

The square was laid out by **Giuseppe Valadier** (1762-1839), the favourite architect and town planner of Pius VI and Pius VII. In an effort to open up Rome, he made Piazza del Popolo one of the largest squares in the city. He retained the Porta del Popolo, the central obelisk and the twin churches flanking Via del Corso, and opened out the space into two semicircles adorned with fountains and allegorical neo-Classical statues. The east side of the square was linked to the Pincio Gardens above by a series of monumental arcaded terraces screened by trees and shrubs

On 18 December 1813 a guillotine was set up in the square by the French Government to deter the gangs of thugs who roamed the streets.

Directory

WHERE TO EAT

See "Where to Eat" in the Practical Points section at the beginning of the guide.

TAKING A BREAK

Rosati – *Piazza del Popolo 4 – ☎ 06 32 25 859 – Open 7.30am-midnight.* This traditional, elegant café/restaurant and terrace is situated right on the piazza and is a pleasant meeting place.

SHOPPING

Piazza del Popolo is in the heart of one of Rome's busiest shopping districts. **Via del Corso** is home to a huge variety of boutiques and shops; antiques enthusiasts should make for **Via del Babuino,** and art collectors for **Via Margutta**.

Fattoria la Parrina – *Largo Toniolo 3 – ☎ 06 68 30 01 11 – Open Tue-Sat, 8.30am-1.30pm and 4.30-7.30pm; Mon, 8.30am-1.30pm.* The Tuscan producer La Parrina has opened a couple of shops in Rome selling cheese, vegetables, fruit and traditionally made oil and wine.

Bomba – *Via dell'Oca 39 – ☎ 06 36 12 881 – Open Tue-Sat, 11am-7.30pm; closed Mon morning.* This established boutique specialises in women's clothes and has a reputation for simple, elegant and sought-after designs.

David Saddler – *Via del Corso 103 – ☎ 06 80 01 59 54.* This shop has a number of outlets in the city for those who like classical styles and sells a range of English-style jackets, trousers, gloves and shirts at reasonable prices.

Il Discount dell'Alta Moda – *Via di Gesù e Maria 14/16.* Menswear and women's outfits from the previous season can be purchased here at a 40% or 50% discount.

ART EXHIBITION

Via Margutta – This normally quiet street attracts crowds of visitors in June and October, when artists exhibit examples of their work as part of the Via Margutta art exhibition (*Fiera di Via Margutta*).

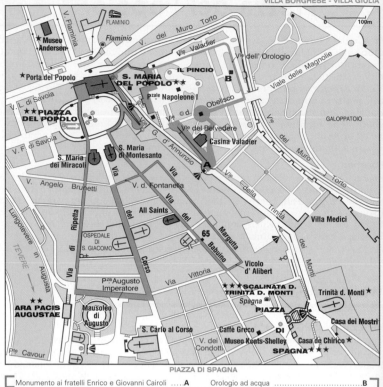

VILLA BORGHESE - VILLA GIULIA

PIAZZA DI SPAGNA

⌐ Monumento ai fratelli Enrico e Giovanni Cairoli .....**A**   Orologio ad acqua ....**B** ⌐

Porta del Popolo★

This gateway in the 3C **Aurelian Wall** stands more or less on the site of the Ancient *Porta Flaminia*. The exterior façade was built between 1562 and 1565 by Pius IV, who wanted to impress visitors arriving from the north with an entrance worthy of the splendour of his capital. The Medici arms are the dominant feature. When Queen **Christina of Sweden**, newly converted to Roman Catholicism, arrived in 1655 the internal façade was decorated by **Bernini** with two scrolls supporting a garland beneath the star of the Chigi coat of arms, which belonged to the then Pope, Alexander VII. On 24 May 1814 Pius VII, liberated by Napoleon, was given a delirious welcome.

Obelisk

It was brought from Heliopolis in Lower Egypt in the reign of Augustus and set up in the Circus Maximus. It was Sixtus V and his architect, **Domenico Fontana**, who raised it in the centre of Piazza del Popolo in 1589. The basins and marble lions at the base were added by Valadier at Leo XII's request in 1823.

Twin churches

From the obelisk one can appreciate the impact of good town planning on the south side of the square; **Carlo Rainaldi** designed the two churches to provide a background to the obelisk and a theatrical entrance to Via del Corso. Their apparent similarity is created by the fact that the sides of the drums facing the square have the same dimensions. In fact, the church on the left is eliptical in plan beneath a 12-sided dome and the church on the right is circular in plan with an octagonal dome and occupies a broader site. The domes were covered with slates by Leo XII in 1825.

Santa Maria di Montesanto was the first of the twin churches to be built: from 1662-67 by Carlo Rainaldi and from 1671-75 by Bernini. **Santa Maria dei Miracoli** was begun by Carlo Rainaldi and completed (1677-79) by Carlo Fontana.

Santa Maria del Popolo★★

Despite its simple exterior, the church contains **art treasures★** worthy of a museum.

The building, which was commissioned by Sixtus IV in 1472 and finished in 1477, is one of the first examples of the Renaissance style in Rome. Its façade rises, almost devoid of ornament, to a triangular pediment; the plainness is relieved by typical Renaissance features: shallow pilasters and simple scrolls linking the lower and upper stages of the façade (the elaborate curves are Baroque additions).

The **interior** abounds in Renaissance features. The Latin cross plan is used in preference to a basilical one. The nave, which has groined vaulting, is flanked by two aisles lined by side chapels. The usual columns and walls of a basilical church have been replaced by massive square pillars composed of engaged columns.

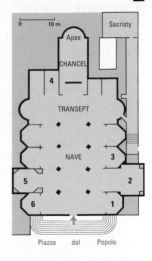

During the Baroque period stucco statues were added above the arches of the nave by Bernini.

Chapels – The chapel rail in the **Cappella della Rovere (1)** shows the coat of arms of the Della Rovere family to which Pope Sixtus IV belonged. Above the altar is the **fresco★** depicting the *Adoration of the Child* by the Umbrian painter **Pinturicchio** (1454-1513). The face of the Virgin is a typical expression of serene gentleness, and the scene is animated with incidental detail: a grazing goat, a lamb suckling its mother and a watchful ox. On the left is the tomb of two members of the Della Rovere family; the decorative motifs were carved by Andrea Bregno late in the 15C; the oval medallion of the Virgin, its simple lines expressing a harmony of strength and gentleness, is by **Mino da Fiesole**, who worked at the Papal court from 1473-80.

The **Cappella Cybo (2)** is a Baroque chapel designed by Carlo Fontana (1682-87) on a Greek cross plan beneath a dome.

On the right-hand wall of the **Cappella Basso della Rovere (3)** lies the tomb of Giovanni Basso della Rovere (15C) by a pupil of Andrea Bregno; the frescoes above the altar and on the left-hand wall are by the Pinturicchio School.

Transept – The chapels opening off the east side of the transept and the apses at either end are characteristic of the Renaissance. The Baroque style is represented by the cherubs supporting the picture frames above the transept altars.

The dome above the crossing was probably the first Renaissance dome to be produced in Rome.

The chancel arch is decorated with gilded stucco low reliefs, one *(right)* showing Pope Paschal II (1099-1118) chopping down a walnut tree. According to legend, the church was built on the site of the tomb of the terrible Nero, which was marked by a walnut tree; the tree was said to have been inhabited by demons, which took the form of black crows. The population, who went in fear and trembling of Nero's ghost, appealed to Paschal II who felled the tree, threw Nero's remains into the Tiber and erected a chapel, which under Sixtus IV became Santa Maria del Popolo.

Apse and Chancel – *Go round behind the high altar.* The apse was extended by **Bramante** for Julius II (1503-13). The ceiling fresco is by Pinturicchio. The stained glass in predominantly neutral tones picked out with flashes of brilliant colour is the work of a Frenchman, Guillaume de Marcillat (16C). The two **tombs★**, carved in about 1505 by **Andrea Sansovino**, are elegant works of art in which the influence of Classical architecture (commemorative arches) mingles with the decorative style of 15C Florence.

Caravaggio's Paintings★★★ – The Cerasi Chapel **(4)** houses two magnificent pictures painted in 1601, which illustrate two scenes from Holy Scripture.

In the *Conversion of St Paul (right)*, as in all Caravaggio's works, light is the dominant feature. The effect of the divine light illuminating St Paul on the road to Damascus should have been sublime but it falls first of all on the horse, which is out of proportion, before touching the foreshortened figure of the saint.

The *Crucifixion of St Peter (left)* illustrates Caravaggio's taste for creating a diagonal axis. The treatment of the subject avoids all reference to the sublime: three brawny men, whose faces are hidden, are raising a cross bearing a man of rugged but noble mien. Above the altar is *The Assumption of the Virgin* by **Annibale Carracci**.

Cappella Chigi★ (5) – The design of this chapel was entrusted to **Raphael** in 1513 by his champion, Agostino Chigi, banker, patron and consort of princes and Popes. The dome mosaic, from a drawing by Raphael, dates from the Renaissance, as do the figures of Jonah (after Raphael) and the Prophet Elijah in their niches, and the altarpiece, a Nativity in muted tones by Sebastiano del Piombo.

In the Baroque period **Bernini** was commissioned by Fabio Chigi, the future Alexander VII; he faced the base of the pyramid-shaped tomb of Agostino and Sigismondo Chigi with green marble, carved the figures of Daniel, the lion, Habakkuk and the angel, which seem to burst from their niches, and inserted in the floor a winged skeleton with the Chigi coat of arms.

IL TRIDENTE (THE TRIDENT)

To Romans this name means the three streets which diverge from Piazza del Popolo like the three prongs of a trident: Via di Ripetta, Via del Corso and Via del Babuino.

Via di Ripetta

This street follows the course of an Ancient Roman street which ran beside the Tiber. Originally it was called Via Leonina, as it was remodelled in 1515 by Leo X; some sources state that the cost of the work was financed by a brothel tax. Via di Ripetta, which is quite unlike the other two prongs of the trident, contains a multitude of shops and boutiques.

Via del Corso

Following the route of the Ancient Via Flaminia, the modern street runs in a straight line (1 500m/1 640yd) from Piazza del Popolo to Piazza Venezia. Its medieval name was Via Lata but now it is called after the famous horse races organised by Pope Paul II in the 15C. It is lined by handsome Renaissance palaces. Nowadays the "Corso" is the main shopping street of central Rome, with shops and cafés to suit all budgets and tastes.

AT THE HEART OF THE FESTIVITIES

Throughout the years, the Corso has been the place where fashionable Romans made their appearance. In the 18C it was good form for a lady to be seen there with her *sigisbeo*, a faithful admirer. The *sigisbeo* became so firmly fixed in local custom that the Church tolerated the practice, and clauses permitting a wife to have one or more admirers were included in marriage contracts.

During the **Carnival** in February processions and mascarades proceeded along the Corso. The high point of the festivities was reached when the horse racing began. Each evening in the week leading up to Ash Wednesday the grooms led the horses round the course. On the last evening of the Carnival the *Moccoli* (wax tapers) appeared; everyone carried a lighted candle in his hand and tried to put out his neighbour's flame. Only in 1809 did the Romans boycott the Carnival in protest against the French Government. Pasquino, the famous talking statue which presides over his own square west of Piazza Navona *(see PIAZZA NAVONA)*, observed mockingly: "The bear may dance under the rod but not men".

This area is where people from overseas traditionally gather. Indeed, before the railways extended to Rome, most travellers arrived in Rome southwards down the Via Cassia, crossing the Tiber over the Ponte Molle (now called the Ponte Milvio) to enter the city through the Porta del Popolo.

Via del Babuino

The street was opened by Clement VII for Jubilee Year in 1525. Its present name came from popular usage; the statue of a silenus was discovered in such a hideous state that the Romans compared it to a baboon. The statue is now next to the fountain on the corner by St Athanasius' Church (S. Atanasio) *(opposite no 65)*.

Today the street is known for its antique shops, often situated in the 17C and 18C palazzi.

Chiesa Anglicana (All Saints Anglican Church) – The church, which is now a protected building, was designed by **GE Street** in the early 1880s, shortly before his death. It is built in the English Gothic style of specially made bricks, with a distinctive white travertine spire erected in 1937. The spacious interior is enriched by a variety of coloured marble from different parts of Italy: white and green Carrara, red Perugia, black Verona, yellow Siena and white Como. The pulpit designed in 1891 by AE Street, the architect's son, is reminiscent of the early Christian basilicas. Above the high altar hang seven lamps bought in Venice by a former Honourable Assistant Chaplain from money given him by the congregation "to be spent on himself". The stained glass, depicting various saints and commemorating people connected with the church, is English, as is the organ, a large and complex instrument, originally made in Huddersfield and presented in 1894, which has been used by famous guest organists for recitals and masterclasses.

The first Anglican services, for which Papal permission was sought and granted, were held in Rome in 1816. After several years in hired rooms, the congregation found a more permanent base in 1824 in the granary chapel outside the Porta del Popolo, until the building was demolished in a road-widening scheme in 1882.

Via Margutta

This street in the artistic heart of Rome is named after a famous little 15C theatre where parodies of chivalrous epic poems, such as Luigi Pulci's comedy *Morgante* with its two heroes, Morgante and Margutta, were performed.

The houses in Via Margutta, often decorated with balconies and courtyard gardens, are occupied on the ground floor by art galleries.

Via Margutta leads into **Vicolo d'Alibert**, which in the 18C contained the *Teatro delle dame*; here, for the first time, women sang on stage in the Papal States. Formerly the female roles in opera had been sung by *castrati*.

IL PINCIO (PINCIAN HILL)

Take the flight of steps leading to Piazzale Napoleone I, on the Pincian Hill.

The Pinci family, who had a garden here in the 4C, have left their name to this little hill, which is still covered by a garden, one of the pleasantest in Rome. The Pincio was laid out in its present style during the Napoleonic occupation (1809-14) according to the designs of **Giuseppe Valadier**. The avenues are shaded by magnificent umbrella pines, palm trees and evergreen oaks. The statues of Italian patriots were added by Giuseppe Mazzini (1805-72).

From the terrace of Piazzale Napoleone I there is a magnificent **view***★★★**, particularly at dusk, when the golden glow so typical of Rome is at its best. Below the terrace is Piazza del Popolo with the domes of the twin churches marking the beginning of the Corso. Opposite are the buildings of the Vatican grouped round the dome of St Peter's next to the green slopes of the Janiculum; just in front stand Castel Sant'Angelo and the white bulk of the Law Courts. The line of the Corso is marked by the domes of San Carlo, San Giovanni dei Fiorentini, Sant'Andrea delle Valle, the Pantheon (shallow) and the Gesù Church, ending with the monument to Victor Emmanuel II.

The water clock in Viale dell'Orologio was built in 1867 by a Dominican monk, Giovan Battista Embriago and presented to the Universal Exhibition in Paris (1889).

Halfway along Viale dell'Obelisco, which leads to the gardens of the Villa Borghese, stands an obelisk which was set up here in 1822 by Pius VII after being found near the Porta Maggiore in the 16C; it was originally erected by the Emperor Hadrian in memory of his young friend Antinoüs.

From the Casina Valadier in Viale del Belvedere there is a magnificent **view** of the roofs of the city.

The **Cairoli Monument** commemorates two brothers, Enrico and Giovanni, Italian patriots who fought beside Garibaldi against the Papal troops and died in 1867 in the bloody struggles which marked the long road to Italian unity.

From the monument there is an extensive view of the city of Rome.

The unusual water clock on the Pincian Hill

Worth a Visit

Museo di Hendrik Christian Andersen★

Via Mancini 20. ♿ Open daily (except Mon) 9am-8pm (last admission 7.20pm). Closed 1 Jan and Christmas. No charge. ☎ 06 32 19 089.

Villa Helene was built by the Norwegian sculptor and painter Hendrik Christian Andersen at the beginning of the 20C as his residence and art studio. The building is now home to a museum dedicated to the painter and houses around 700 works of art, including sculptures, paintings and graphic art. Most of the work exhibited here was designed and produced by the artist for his World City futurist project, in which art, philosophy and science all played a major role. Andersen's studio, adorned with plastercast sculptures and works of art, and an exhibition room decorated with paintings, sculptures and designs relating to the artist's futurist project, once used by Andersen to display his most recent works, are all located on the ground floor. Note the finely decorated ceilings in the magnificent first-floor apartments, now used for temporary exhibitions.

Piazza di Spagna★★★

This district was once popular with artists and writers such as Goethe, Keats, De Chirico and Stendhal, and later became a favourite meeting place for actors and film stars. It is now one of the main tourist sights in Rome, with crowds milling around Piazza di Spagna day and night, stopping to sit and chat on the famous Spanish Steps, or wandering up and down the narrow streets leading off the square. Despite the invasion of fast-food outlets in the area, these elegant streets are still home to some of the most prestigious names in the world of fashion, jewellery and design. A stroll along Via del Condotti or Via Frattina for some leisurely window-shopping is an essential part of any visit to Rome.

Location

Michelin map 38 or Michelin spiral atlas of Rome: pp 40-41 J 11-12, K 11-12. Metro line A: Spagna. Tour: 2hr. This walk covers the district south of the Piazza del Popolo, between Villa Borghese and the Tiber, and follows on naturally from the tour described in the previous chapter. The area falls within the "Trident", the three

Directory

WHERE TO EAT
See "Where to Eat" in the Practical Points section at the beginning of the guide.

TAKING A BREAK
Caffè Greco – *Via dei Condotti 86 –* ☎ *06 67 91 700 – Open 8am-8.30pm.* A period atmosphere in one of the oldest literary cafés in Rome, situated near the Spanish square. The café was founded by a Greek in 1760 and frequented by writers and artists such as Goethe, Berlioz, Leopardi, D'Annunzio, Andersen (who lived in the same building) and Stendhal, whose last Roman residence was at n° 48. On 24 March 1824, Pope Leo XII forbade his citizens to enter the café, subject to a term of three months' imprisonment. This decision proved so unpopular that the café owner continued to serve customers through an opening in the window. The long, narrow, inner room known as the "omnibus" contains portraits of famous people.

Caffè Greco

Ciampini – *Viale della Trinità dei Monti 1 –* ☎ *06 67 85 678 – Open 8am-8pm.* Although this café is not as elegant as the café of the same name in Piazza San Lorenzo (Lucina 29), it has an unforgettable view of Rome, from the top of the famous Spanish Steps. Outside tables only.

Babington's – *Piazza di Spagna 23 –* ☎ *06 67 86 027 – Open Wed-Mon, 9am-8.15pm.* Opened in 1893, these old tearooms are decorated in typically English style; the waitresses even wear a uniform. A good address for tea and cakes, including English favourites such as scones, muffins and apple pie.

SHOPPING
De Clercq & De Clercq – *Via delle Carrozze 50 –* ☎ *06 67 90 988 – Open Tue-Sat, 10am-7pm; Mon, 2-7pm.* All the exquisite jumpers and tops on display are made from natural fibres, including cashmere and silk.

Fratelli Alinari – *Via Alibert 16/a –* ☎ *06 69 94 19.98.* An excellent introduction to the work of these great photographers, depicting views and landscapes of Ancient Rome.

Hausmann & C. – *Via del Corso 406 –* ☎ *06 68 71 501 – info@hausmann-co.com – Open Tue-Fri, 9.30am-1pm and 3.30-7.30pm; Mon, 3.30-7.30pm; Sat, 9.30am-1.30pm.* This shop was founded in 1794 and continues to mend and sell magnificent old clocks. Visitors will admire the red velvet decor and the old clock by the door, which has told the correct time for many years.

Myricae – *Via Frattina 36.* This shop specialises in hand-painted ceramics, especially from Puglia, Tuscany and Great Britain.

Sergio di Cori – *Piazza di Spagna 53 –* ☎ *06 67 84 439.* This tiny, long-established shop has a wide selection of all kinds of gloves.

Siragusa – *Via delle Carrozze 64 –* ☎ *06 67 97 085 – Open Mon-Fri, 10am-noon and 1.30-7.30pm.* Inspired by the jewels of Antiquity, the works of art made by this shop are produced using pieces of archaeological interest.

The Lion Bookshop – *Via dei Greci 33/36 –* ☎ *06 32 65 04 37 – Open Tue-Sat, 10am-7.30pm; Mon, 3.30-7.30pm.* As well as a wide selection of books in English, this bookshop also has a small café for those who want to enjoy a cup of tea or coffee.

streets leading south from Piazza del Popolo: Via del Babuino, which emerges into Piazza di Spagna; Via del Corso, which cuts the district in two; and Via di Ripetta, near the River Tiber.

Neighbouring sights are described in the following chapters: FONTANA DI TREVI-QUIRINALE; MONTECITORIO; PIAZZA DEL POPOLO; VILLA BORGHESE-VILLA GIULIA.

Special Features

PIAZZA DI SPAGNA*** (SPANISH SQUARE)

The square is famous throughout the world and the steps are a favourite meeting place for young Romans, as well as a popular backdrop for fashion shoots and publicity events.

Shaped like two triangles joined at their points, **Spanish Square** got its name in the 17C when the Spanish ambassador to the Holy See took up residence in the **Palazzo di Spagna**. After that, the area bounded by Via dei Condotti, Via del Corso and Via della Mercede became Spanish territory and any non-Spaniard crossing the boundaries at night often disappeared, having been pressed into the Spanish army. The French, however, who owned the land around the convent of the Trinità dei Monti, claimed the right to pass through the square. They named part of it "French Square" and set out to rival the Spanish by giving ever more sumptuous entertainments. In 1681 the Spanish celebrated the birthday of their queen, Marie-Louise, by transforming the square with a variety of paste-board decorations. In 1685 it was the turn of the French; to celebrate the Revocation of the Edict of Nantes they covered the whole hillside with candelabra and decorated the church to look like a wayside altar; from here they set off fireworks which lit up the whole town.

In the 18C it became very popular among the English on the Grand Tour. In 1820 Henry Matthews set down his first impressions in his diary:

"We were soon in the Piazza di Spagna, the focus of fashion and the general resort of the English. Some travellers have compared it to Grosvenor Square but the Piazza di Spagna is little more than an irregular open space, a little less nasty than the other piazzas in Rome because the habits of the people are in some measure restrained by the presence of the English ... The English swarm everywhere. We found all the inns full. It seemed like a country town in England at an assizes".

The Museo Keats-Shelley and the Casa-Museo di De Chirico can be seen on the piazza (see Worth a Visit below).

Fontana della Barcaccia* (Boat Fountain)

At the foot of the steps. It was designed by Bernini's father, Pietro (1627-29) for Pope Urban VIII. The boat, which is decorated at either end with the suns and bees of the Barberini coat of arms, seems to be letting in water. The sculptor is supposed to have conceived the idea from seeing a boat stranded in Piazza di Spagna by the flood waters of the Tiber.

Fontana della Barcaccia and the Spanish Steps

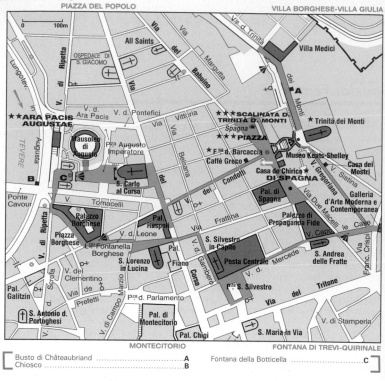

Busto di Châteaubriand ....A   Fontana della Botticella C
Chiosco ....B

Scalinata della Trinità dei Monti*** (Spanish Steps)

Built between 1723 and 1726, the steps show the Baroque taste for perspective and *trompe l'oeil*. At certain times of the year they are completely covered in flowers – azaleas in April – and offer a feast for the eye.

The idea of a flight of steps linking Piazza di Spagna with the church of the Trinità dei Monti had first been proposed in the 17C. Cardinal Mazarin proposed to make the steps a symbol of the greatness of the French monarchy in Rome. A grandiose design was prepared, dominated by an equestrian statue of Louis XIV. The idea of a king's statue in the Papal City! Alexander VII objected. Neither the cardinal's death in 1661 nor the Pope's in 1669 ended the quarrel. It was not finally settled until Innocent XIII (1721-24) agreed to the French architect and the French abandoned the statue of Louis XIV. De Sanctis, in accordance with designs by De Specchi (a pupil of Carlo Fontana), built three successive flights of steps, some broader, some narrower, some divided, exaggerating the effect of height and creating a graceful and majestic decor.

From the upper terrace there is an excellent view of the city. In the square in front of the church of the Trinità dei Monti stands an imitation Egyptian obelisk transported from the Gardens of Sallust (Giardini di Sallusto) near the Salaria Gate by Pius VI.

Trinità dei Monti*

The church of Holy Trinity on the Hill was founded in 1495 by Charles VIII at the request of St Francis of Paola for the Minims who lived in the neighbouring convent. The building rose slowly during the 16C. It was severely damaged by French revolutionaries and completely rebuilt in 1816. It is now French property and the convent is occupied by the Ladies of the Sacred Heart.

An elegant stairway, built in 1587 by Domenico Fontana, leads up to the **façade** which is surmounted by two belfries, erected in 1588 and modelled on those designed by Giacomo della Porta for St Athanasius in Via del Babuino. In 1613 a clock was added to tell the time in the "French manner".

Interior – The single nave flanked by intercommunicating chapels is reminiscent of the Gothic churches in the south of France. The decorative latticework in the transept vaults, the oldest part of the church, is typical of late-Gothic art. The side chapels are decorated with Mannerist paintings. The third on the right contains a fresco of the *Assumption* by Daniele da Volterra. The figure in red on the right of the picture is a portrait of Michelangelo, which was much admired by the artist. The much-restored **Deposition from the Cross*** (1541) in the second chapel on the left is a masterpiece by **Daniele da Volterra**, who was a great admirer of Michelangelo. See how skilfully he has arranged his composition around the pale body of Jesus.

Walking About

From the Spanish Steps, turn left into Viale della Trinità dei Monti.
On the right is a **bust of Chateaubriand**, better known as a writer, who was the French ambassador in Rome from 1828 to 1829.

Villa Medici

The Villa Medici now houses the French Academy (Accademia di Francia) and is used for temporary exhibitions. The villa was built c 1570 for Cardinal Ricci di Montepulciano and passed to Cardinal Ferdinando de' Medici in 1576. In the 1C BC the site was covered by the Gardens of Lucullus (Giardini di Lucullo). There is a fine view of Rome from the terrace opposite the entrance.

The famous fountain, which was installed in 1587 by Cardinal Ferdinando de' Medici, is the subject of several 19C paintings and engravings, including *The Fountain at the Villa Medici* by Corot. Legend has it that the ball in the centre of the basin is a cannon ball fired at the Villa from Castel Sant'Angelo by Queen Christina of Sweden, who adored practical jokes. She wanted to wake up the master of the house to invite him to join a hunting party. The main façade of the building contrasts sharply with the richly decorated **inner façade★**; the latter faces the luxuriant gardens and was decorated by Bartolomeo Ammannati at the end of the 16C with statues, reliefs, and fragments of Ancient marble, including garlands taken from the Ara Pacis.

Return to Trinità dei Monti and continue along Via Gregoriana.
In the 17C and 18C **Via Gregoriana** provided lodgings for the wealthier visitors to Rome. N° 30, the **Casa dei Mostri**, built by Federico Zuccari, has a door and windows framed by carved monsters with gaping mouths.
Continue along Via Gregoriana. At the end of the street, turn left into Via Crispi, where the Galleria Comunale d'Arte Moderna e Contemporanea can be seen (see Worth a Visit below). Take Via Capo le Case and cross Via Due Macelli.

Palazzo di Propaganda Fide

This imposing building, the property of the Holy See, houses the Congregation for the Evangelisation of Peoples, which originated in the institution of the Congregation for the Propagation of the Faith by Gregory XV in 1622. It was

The 16C inner façade of the Villa Medici

Urban VIII (1623-44) who began construction of the building by inviting his protégé, Bernini, to design the façade overlooking Piazza di Spagna. The result is unexpectedly sober for this brilliant Baroque architect. On Innocent X's accession, Bernini fell into disgrace. The new Pope wished to give his reign a new look and he turned to Borromini – the only architect able to compete with Bernini – whom he commissioned to design the façade overlooking Via di Propaganda. With Borromini a touch of fantasy was introduced, in the cornices and in the elaborate pediments over the windows.

Within the palazzo *(on the left of the door in Via di Propaganda 1/c)* is another building (1666) by Borromini, the tiny **church of the Re Magi** (Three Wise Men). *Open by appointment only. Contact the Congregazione di Propaganda Fide, Via Propaganda 1/C, 00187 ROMA; Fax 06 69 88 02 46, at least one week in advance.*

Sant'Andrea delle Fratte

St Andrew's Church, which originated in the 12C, stands in Via di Capo Le Case (end of the houses), which in the Middle Ages was the northeastern limit of the city. Its name recalls the thickets *(fratte)* which used to abound in the vicinity. Early in the 17C the rebuilding of the church was begun; the work was completed by Borromini. From higher up the street there is a view of the **campanile★** and the **dome★**, which he treated as precious objects, abandoning the traditional form and giving full expression to the eccentric products of his fertile imagination: the dome, which would normally soar into the sky, is imprisoned in a space circumscribed by convex and concave surfaces. The façade is 19C.

Inside, at the entrance to the chancel, are two statues of **angels★** presenting the Instruments of the Passion. When **Bernini** sculpted them in 1669, his art was very close to the extreme delicacy characteristic of the Rococo period. They were designed to accompany the other statues commissioned by Clement IX for the Ponte Sant'Angelo, but the Pope found them too beautiful to be exposed to the elements. They remained with Bernini's family until 1729, when they were placed in the church.

Take Via della Mercede.

Piazza San Silvestro is dominated by the façade of the Central Post Office, which was established in the 19C in the monastery of the church of San Silvestro in Capite. Every bus route and taxi fare seems to end in this square which, with its church and the post office, its café and its newspaper stall, is an excellent place for observing the Roman way of life.

Turn right into Via del Gambero and left into Via Frattina to reach Piazza S. Lorenzo in Lucina.

San Lorenzo in Lucina

The **church of St Lawrence** was built in the 12C on the site of a 4C *titulus*, the house of a woman called Lucina. The bell-tower, the porch and the two lions flanking the door date from the medieval period. The fourth chapel on the right contains a bust *(back left-hand corner)* of Dr Gabriele Fonseca by Bernini, a late and rather theatrical work (1668).

Take Via del Leone which leads into Largo Fontanella Borghese.

From the piazza there is an interesting view of the church of Trinità dei Monti.

Palazzo Borghese (Borghese Palace)

The palace was built at the end of the 16C and the façade overlooking Piazza Borghese demonstrates the dignity and austerity of the Counter-Reformation. The palace was acquired by Cardinal Camillo Borghese, who became Pope Paul V in 1605. The courtyard *(entrance in Largo della Fontanella di Borghese)*, with its loggias, statues, fountains and rockeries, is a beautiful evocation of the luxurious life of the noble families in the 17C.

Paul V gave the palace to his brothers, who commissioned the architect Flaminio Ponzio (1560-1613) to extend it towards the Tiber. It was he who designed the picturesque front in Via di Ripetta which used to overlook the Ripetta riverside port.

> **LOCAL SPECIALITY**
> Beside Ponte Cavour (Cavour Bridge) stands a small kiosk selling the famous *grattachecche* fruit syrup poured over crushed ice.

Take Via di Ripetta north as far as Piazza Augusto Imperatore.

Botticella Fountain

It was built in 1774 at the expense of the Ripetta watermen's association. There is a fine view of the apse and dome of San Carlo al Corso.

Mausoleo di Augusto

The ruins of the **Mausoleum of Augustus** are now surrounded by the modern buildings of Piazza Augusto Imperatore, which was laid out in 1940.

This mausoleum was one of the most sacred monuments in Antiquity. It was built between 28 and 23 BC and, like Hadrian's Mausoleum or Castel Sant'Angelo, it took the form of an Etruscan tumulus tomb. It consisted of a cylindrical base surmounted by a conical hillock of earth *(tumulus)* planted with cypress trees. A bronze statue of the Emperor stood in the middle of the monument, at its highest point. On the south side, flanking the entrance, stood two obelisks, Roman imitations of Egyptian models, which now stand in Piazza dell' Esquilino and Piazza del Quirinale. The funeral chamber in the middle of the mausoleum was reserved for the Emperor; round it was a series of chambers for the other members of the Julio-Claudian family.

In the Middle Ages the mausoleum was converted into a fortress by the Colonna family; Gregory IX (1227-41) dismantled it and stripped it of its blocks of travertine. In 1936 the concert hall which it then contained was closed and the remains were restored.

The Ara Pacis (see Worth a Visit below) is housed in a modern building between the Mausoleum of Augustus and Lungotevere in Augusta. Follow Via dell'Ara Pacis and Via dei Pontefici, then turn right into Via del Corso.

San Carlo al Corso

In 1471 the Lombard community in Rome was given a small church in the Corso by Sixtus IV. They rebuilt it and dedicated it to **St Ambrose**, who was Bishop of Milan in the 4C. In 1610 they wanted to enlarge the building in honour of Charles Borromeo, Archbishop of Milan, who had just been canonised. The full name of the church is therefore Sant'Ambrogio e San Carlo al Corso. Construction began in 1612. The majestic interior is in the shape of a Latin cross with an ambulatory, a rarity in Rome, more usually found in northern churches. The heart of St Charles Borromeo now rests in the chapel behind the high altar. The **dome★** is the work of **Pietro da Cortona** (1668). The *Apotheosis of St Ambrose and St Charles* on the high altar is one of the best works of Carlo Maratta (1685-90), restored in the 19C. The handsomely carved 15C tabernacle on the pillar to the left probably comes from St Ambrose's sanctuary.

Palazzo Ruspoli

This 16C palace is now a bank. After the downfall of Napoleon in 1825 it became the refuge of Hortense de Beauharnais, ex-Queen of Holland, under the name of the Duchess of St Leu. Her salon became the centre of attraction for every pleasure-loving member of society. Her son, Prince Charles Louis Napoleon, the future Napoleon III, brought this sumptuous life to an end when he was implicated in a scheme to declare a republic in Rome and, with his mother, was expelled from the Papal States.

Throughout the year temporary exhibitions are held in the palazzo *(Via del Corso 418/A).*

Go back to Via dei Condotti.

Via dei Condotti

The street is named after the conduits *(condotti)* which brought water to Agrippa's Baths (Terme di Agrippa) in 19 BC. Via dei Condotti is one of the most famous streets in Rome and is lined with small boutiques and elegant *palazzi* housing some of the most prestigious names in fashion. It is worth walking down the street for the splendid view back up towards Piazza di Spagna and the Spanish Steps. The famous **Caffè Greco** can be seen at n° 86 *(see Directory).*

Worth a Visit

Ara Pacis Augustae★★ (Altar of Augustus)

For information contact ☎/Fax 06 68 80 68 48.

The monumental altar was erected by the Senate and inaugurated in 9 BC in honour of the peace which Augustus established throughout the Roman world and in the capital, where the concentration of power in one person put an end to 20 years of civil war. The Ara Pacis originally stood in the Campus Martius, beside the Via Flaminia (now Via del Corso), about where the Palazzo Fiano stands today. In 1970, to celebrate Rome's centenary as the capital of modern Italy, the monument was opened to the public. It had been reconstructed from excavated fragments assembled from various museums and modern reproductions of the pieces which were missing. The altar was the major work of the Augustan "golden age" and marks the apogee of Roman art. It consists of the altar itself standing within a marble enclosure decorated with low-relief carvings. There were two entrances to the enclosure in opposite walls: the entrance facing the Campus Martius was the main one used by the Pontifex Maximus and his suite of priests and Vestals; the rear entrance was used by the *camilli*, the priests' young assistants, by the men who performed the sacrifice and by the animals to be sacrificed.

External decoration of the enclosure – On the outside of the enclosure the lower part is decorated with scrolls of acanthus leaves and swans, a faithful representation carved with great skill and variety. Two panels flank the main entrance: Aeneas making a sacrifice *(right)* and Faustulus the shepherd finding Romulus and Remus *(left – a few fragments)*. These two scenes illustrate the legendary founding of Rome and glorify Augustus, who claimed to be descended from Aeneas.

The east side, facing Via di Ripetta, shows a procession of people including the Emperor and his family, some of whom have been identified: at the head Augustus (incomplete figure); Agrippa, his son-in-law, is probably the tall figure following the four priests (*flamines*) and a sacrificer (the symbolic axe on his shoulder); Antonia has turned to speak to her husband Drusus, Augustus's grandson. The human touch is not omitted: the young couple is cautioned to be quiet by an old woman standing between them with a finger to her lips. The two children behind Drusus are shown with natural simplicity.

The rear entrance is flanked by two panels: the personification of Rome Triumphant (*right* – mostly missing) seated on a pile of weapons, dominating the world; the personification of the Fruitful Earth (*left*), accompanied by two figures symbolising wind and water. The latter scene is full of the realism characteristic of Roman art: a sheep is grazing at the goddess's feet while the two children play on her lap. Both scenes reflect the glory of Augustus, author of the Roman peace and personification of the earth's fertility. The side facing the river shows a procession composed of members of the various priestly colleges.

The procession shown on the Ara Pacis represents the procession which took place on inauguration day.

Internal decoration – The lower half is decorated with broad vertical flutes representing the temporary wooden palisade which surrounded the altar on the day of its consecration; the upper half is covered with garlands of fruit and flowers and the heads of the cattle which were sacrificed on that day; the vessels between the garlands were used for pouring a liquid onto the altar. The altar itself, which is flanked by winged lions, is decorated with a frieze of clear-cut small figures. On the outside of the modern building facing Via di Ripetta is a reproduction of the *Res Gestae*, the text drawn up by Augustus of the acts accomplished in his reign; it also contained his will. The original, which has been lost, was engraved on bronze plaques at the entrance to his mausoleum, but a copy of it was found in the Temple of Augustus in Ankara (formerly Ancyra in Asia Minor).

Casa-Museo di Giorgio de Chirico★

Piazza di Spagna 31. Open Tue-Sat and the first Sun of the month, 10am-1pm. By appointment only. €5. ☎ 06 80 88 664.

The house in which this artist lived from 1947 to 1978 (the year in which he died) occupies the top three floors of a 16C *palazzo*. The visit starts in a small entrance hall which houses two oval works, inspired by the great masters, and the **Thinker** who appears to be weighed down by his thoughts. A collection of self-portraits, depicting the artist in a range of costumes, but always with the same expression, is exhibited in the drawing room, which overlooks Piazza di Spagna. This room also contains portaits of the artist's wife and a few pieces of sculpture. De Chirico's armchair can be seen in his favourite corner, from where he used to watch the television with the sound turned down. The dining room is decorated with a number of still-life paintings. The second drawing room, added around 1970, is very different from the rest of the house, both in its furnishings and in the works on display here. These are known as the "neo-metaphysical works", produced towards the end of the artist's life, and include *Piazza d'Italia* and **Hector and Andromache★**. De Chirico's tiny bedroom can be visited on the top floor, as well as the more luxurious room which belonged to his wife, which has a magnificent view of Trinità dei Monti. The artist's studio, lit by a skylight, houses the paintings on which the artist was working at the time of his death: the fine outline of a woman bathing (the artist's wife, Isabella Far) and an unfinished copy of the *Tondo Doni*. The visitor's gaze is attracted by the artist's tools and plaster casts, the many books and, in particular, the numerous amulets.

Casa di Keats (Keats' House)

Piazza di Spagna 26. Open daily (except Sun) 9am-1pm (Sat 11am-1pm) and 3-6pm. Closed Christmas. €2.58. ☎ 06 67 84 235; Fax 06 67 84 167; www.keats-shelley-house.org

The house on the right at the foot of the Spanish Steps, where Keats died of tuberculosis in February 1821, was purchased in 1903 by the Keats-Shelley Memorial Association. The rooms which Keats occupied on the first floor now contain a collection of manuscripts, letters, mementoes and documents on the lives not only of Keats but also of Shelley, **Byron** and Leigh Hunt, together with a library of 10 000 volumes. In the entrance hall on the ground floor hang portraits of Keats and his contemporaries by English artists of the period.

Galleria Comunale d'Arte Moderna e Contemporanea

Via Crispi 24. Open Tue-Sat, 9am-7pm; Sun and public holidays, 9am-2pm. Last admission 30min before closing time. Closed 1 Jan, 1 May and Christmas. Guided tours available (1hr 30min). €2.58. ☎ 06 47 42 848 or 06 47 42 909; Fax 06 47 42 912; galleria.moderna@comune.roma.it The **Gallery of Modern and Contemporary Art** accommodates a collection of paintings and sculptures from the early half of the 20C. Of particular note are Rodin's *Bust of a woman* and Balla's allegory of **Doubt**, a beautiful portrait of his wife. On the second floor is Amedeo Bocchi's huge canvas entitled *In the Park* painted in vivid, almost violent colours. There are also works by Sartorio, Trombadori, Casorati, Morandi, Guttoso (*Self-portrait*).

Piazza Veneziaa

Piazza Venezia was transformed at the end of the 19C and is now dominated by the overwhelming and controversial monument to Victor Emmanuel II, which obscures the view of Capitol Hill from Via del Corso. Not far from the piazza, close to one of the centres of political power in the city, stands the magnificent Baroque Chiesa del Gesù.

Location

Michelin map 38 or Michelin spiral atlas of Rome: p 97 L11-12, M12. Tour: 1hr. Because of its position and its imposing 19C monuments to the glory of Victor Emmanuel, Piazza Venezia is a convenient meeting point for those new to the city. Today, Rome's principal thoroughfares all converge on the square, resulting in all-too-frequent gridlock here.

Neighbouring sights are described in the following chapters: CAMPIDOGLIO-CAPITOLINO; FONTANA DI TREVI-QUIRINALE; FORI IMPERIALI; PANTHEON.

> **WHERE TO EAT**
> See "Where to Eat" in the Practical Points section at the beginning of the guide.

Walking About

PIAZZA VENEZIA★

Formerly the square was much more compact than today. The south side – going towards the Victor Emmanuel II monument (Monumento a Vittorio Emanuele II, *below*) – was closed by the smaller Palazzetto Venezia, a building in harmony with the tower of the more famous Palazzo Venezia. In 1911, however, while work on the Victor Emmanuel II monument was in progress, the palazzetto was "moved" to its present position at the far end of Piazza San Marco. Although this change allows a better view of the monument, it has undoubtedly spoiled the balance of a Renaissance square.

Behind the Palazzo Venezia stands the beautiful Gesù Church, the main Jesuit church in Rome.

Walk to the Victor Emmanuel II monument.

From here there is a typical Roman view, including the domes of the churches of Santa Maria di Loreto and Santissimo Nome di Maria, as well as a group of umbrella pine trees around Trajan's Column.

Monumento a Vittorio Emanuele II (Vittoriano)

This huge monument by **Giuseppe Sacconi**, which was begun in 1885 and inaugurated in 1911, was erected in honour of **King Victor Emmanuel II**, who achieved the unification of Italy in 1870 with Rome as the capital city. The dazzling white marble clashes with the warm tones of the Roman townscape and the grandiloquent style strikes a jarring note. The monument has been given several nicknames, including the "wedding cake" and the "typewriter".

A very broad flight of steps, flanked by two allegorical groups in bronze gilt representing *Thought* and *Action*, leads up to the *Altar to the Nation*; the steps divide before meeting at an equestrian statue of Victor Emmanuel; they then divide again and lead up to the concave portico, which is surmounted by two bronze *quadrigas* bearing statues of winged victory. The foot of the stairway is flanked by two fountains representing the *Tyrrhenian Sea (right)* and the *Adriatic (left)*.

Victor Emmanuel II monument

Tomba di Caio Publicio Bibulo (Tomb of C Publicius Bibulus) – The travertine and brick remains of the tomb of Bibulus, who died 2 000 years ago, are of major archaeological interest. As burials were forbidden within the precincts of the city, the position of this tomb shows that in the 1C BC the city boundary skirted the Capitoline Hill, and the Via Flaminia, the trunk road to the north, began at this point.

Altare della Patria (National Shrine) – At the foot of the statue of Rome is the tomb of the Unknown Soldier constantly guarded by two sentries. Since 1921 the tomb has contained the remains of a soldier who died in the First World War.

Statue equestre di Vittorio Emanuele II – The **equestrian statue of Victor Emmanuel II** by **Enrico Chiaradia** was unveiled on 4 June 1911 in the presence of the king and some veteran Garibaldi troops before a crowd gathered in Piazza Venezia. A contemporary chronicler recorded that 50t of bronze had been used to cast the monument in a foundry in Trastevere and that His Majesty's moustaches were 1m/3ft long.

View★★ from the Portico – From the west terrace in the foreground are Santa Maria d'Aracoeli and the Capitol. Beyond the Tiber rise the Janiculum, the dome of St Peter's, the Vatican and Castel Sant'Angelo. On this side of the river are the domes for which Rome is famous: Sant'Andrea della Valle, the Gesù Church and the shallow curve of the Pantheon.

From the centre of the terrace: immediately below is Piazza Venezia linked to Piazza del Popolo by the straight line of Via del Corso. At the beginning of this street on the left is **Palazzo Bonaparte** *(see below)*. From the east terrace: the whole extent of the Imperial Fora (built by Caesar, Augustus, Trajan etc). In the distance, slightly to the left of the Colosseum, are the statues on the pediment of St John Lateran. To the right of the Colosseum is the Basilica of Maxentius and the bell-tower and façade of Santa Francesca Romana; in the foreground is the dome of the church of St Luke and St Martina.

Palazzo Venezia★

With this building, which extends from Piazza Venezia to Via del Plebiscito and Via degli Astalli, the Renaissance made a timid debut into civil architecture.

Historical Notes – Construction of the palace was begun in 1455 by Pietro Barbo, who required a palace worthy of his rank as cardinal; when he became Pope in 1464 as **Paul II** he continued his project on a larger scale. In 1471, the Pope died before his house was finished, and the palace was completed by his nephew. It was later altered several times: under Sixtus IV (1471-84) a smaller palace *(palazzetto)* was added opening onto a garden surrounded by a portico.

It was Pius IV, in 1564, who gave the palace its present name, when he allowed the ambassadors of the Republic of Venice to lodge in part of the building. Following the Treaty of Campoformio between Austria and Napoleon in 1797, the Republic of Venice ceased to exist and almost all its property (including Palazzo Venezia) reverted to Austria.

By order of Napoleon in 1806 the palace became the seat of the French administration, and was again at the forefront of Roman history in 1910 when the Italian Government decided to lay out a huge square in front of the monument to King Victor Emmanuel II; the *palazzetto* which stood at the foot of the tower in the southeast angle was pulled down and put up again where it stands today on the corner of Piazza di San Marco and Via degli Astalli. At the same time the **Palazzo delle Assicurazioni Generali di Venezia** was built on the other side of the square, in imitation of Palazzo Venezia.

During the Fascist era, Mussolini set up the Grand Council of Fascism and his office in the palace; he used to address the crowds gathered in the piazza from the palace balcony. Now Palazzo Venezia is one of the most prestigious buildings in the capital, housing a museum and the library of the Institute of Art and Archaeology.

Exterior

The crenellations on the façade overlooking Piazza Venezia and the huge tower in the southeast corner show how the severe style of the fortified houses of the Middle Ages persisted. The mullion windows, the doors onto the square and in Via del Plebiscito and above all the attractive façade of St Mark's Basilica are pleasing manifestations of the Renaissance.

Statue of Madama Lucrezia – The statue stands in Piazza di San Marco in the angle where Palazzo Venezia and the *palazzetto* join and may have belonged to the Temple of Isis, which stood on the Campus Martius.

It was one of the four "talking statues" of Rome, the others being Pasquino, Marforio and the Abate Luigi – Madama Lucrezia's favourite.

Interior

Access from Piazza di San Marco; entrance beside the statue of Madama Lucrezia. The unsophisticated outward appearance of Roman Renaissance palaces gives no hint of the elegant decor often to be found within.

Map labels:

ISOLA TIBERINA - TORRE ARGENTINA

FORI IMPERIALI

0 ——— 100m

★★ PAL. DORIA PAMPHILI

Palazzo Bonaparte

★ Palazzo Colonna

Museo d. Cere

Via del Corso

Via Cesare Battisti

PREFETTURA

Pal. Gatta

Palazzo Altieri

Pal. Grazioli

del Plebiscito

S. Marco

★ PIAZZA

Pal. delle Ass. Gen. di Venezia

SANTISSIMO NOME DI MARIA

V. del Gesù

Via del

★ Palazzo Venezia

VENEZIA

S. Maria di Loreto

★★★ COLONNA TRAIANA

Piazza del Gesù

GESÙ ★★★

V. d. Astalli

Palazzetto

C

Pª S. Marco

V. S. Marco

★★ FORO TRAIANO

Pal. Cenci Bolognetti

V. dell'Aracoeli

V. d. Botteghe Oscure

V. Margana

Delfini

Tomba di Bibulo

VITTORIANO

A

B

Portico

Piazza d'Aracœli

Pª Margana

Marcello

S. Caterina dei Funari

V. del

Scalinata d'Aracœli

★★★ S. MARIA D'ARACŒLI

★★ FORO DI CESARE

Cordonata

PAL. NUOVO ★★★

Carcere Mamertino

Pal. Spinola

V. d. Teatro di Marcello

★★★ Pª DEL CAMPIDOGLIO

Pal. Capizucchi

★★★ PAL. DEI CONSERVATORI

★★★ PAL. SENATORIO

★★★ FORO ROMANO

S. Maria in Campitelli

CAMPIDOGLIO-CAPITOLINO

Altare della Patria .... **A**
Statua di Madama Lucrezia .... **C**

Statua equestre di Vittorio Emanuele II .... **B**

The **courtyard** has a flourishing garden, partially flanked on two sides by an elegant but incomplete portico by Giuliano da Maiano (1432-90). The east side is formed by St Mark's Basilica, which stands within the palace, beneath its medieval belfry. The attractive fountain dates from the 18C: Venice, the lion of St Mark at its feet, is throwing a ring into the sea, a symbol of the marriage between the Serenissima and the sea.

The Museo di Palazzo Venezia is housed on the first floor of the palace *(see "Worth a Visit" below)*.

Basilica di San Marco (St Mark's Basilica)

Founded in 336 and dedicated to St Mark the Evangelist, this basilica was rebuilt by Gregory IV in the 9C. Excavations beneath it have uncovered traces of an earlier building and of the 9C crypt where Gregory IV had the relics of Abdon and Sennen, Persian martyrs, deposited.

In the 12C a belfry was added and in 1455 the church was rebuilt and incorporated into the Palazzo Venezia by Cardinal Pietro Barbo. In the 17C and 18C further restoration and alterations took place.

The **façade★** overlooking Piazza San Marco is attributed to Giuliano da Maiano or Leon-Battista Alberti: the double row of arches, in which the upper ones are carried on slimmer supports, lends elegance to this charming Renaissance composition.

In the porch, among the various fragments, is the tombstone *(right)* of Vanozza Caetani, mother of Pope Alexander VI's children, Caesar and Lucrezia Borgia *(see CAMPO DEI FIORI)*.

The sumptuous **interior★** is a typical Roman example of the overlapping of styles down the centuries. The medieval basilica plan of a nave and two aisles remains. In the 15C the elegant coffered ceiling was added with the arms of Paul II, and clerestories were inserted in the nave above the alternate panels of stucco and 18C paintings which illustrate the legend of Abdon and Sennen.

The mosaic in the apse was commissioned in the 9C by Gregory IV. To the right of Christ among a group of saints is the Pope offering his church; on his head is a square nimbus, indicating that he was still alive.

Below are 12 sheep, representing the Apostles, advancing towards the Lamb, symbol of Christ, over a flowered meadow.

The chancel arch shows a bust of the Saviour, the Evangelists and St Peter and St Paul.

In the sacristy is a charming 15C tabernacle carved by **Mino da Fiesole** in collaboration with Giovanni Dalmata; it originally stood on the high altar, but was moved in the 18C.

Head to the beginning of Via del Corso.

Palazzo Bonaparte

This 17C palazzo of modest appearance was once the property of Napoleon's mother, who lived here from the fall of the Empire until her death in 1836. It is said that she spent much of her time sitting in the first-floor loggia, watching the busy street below from behind the shutters, hidden from the glances of passers-by.

Take Via del Plebiscito to Piazza del Gesù.

Chiesa del Gesù★★★ (Gesù church)

Open 4-6pm. Donation welcome. ☎ 06 69 70 01.

The Chiesa del Gesù is the main **Jesuit** church in Rome and stands in Piazza del Gesù, once home to the Christian Democrat Party and now the headquarters of the Partito Popolare. The Society of Jesus was founded in 1540 by Ignatius of Loyola (1491-1556), a Spaniard. After the Council of Trent the society became the prime mover in the Counter-Reformation, which sought to rebut the ideas put forward by **Martin Luther** and Calvin. In 1568 the decision was taken to build a church in the centre of Rome. Cardinal Alexander Farnese undertook to provide the funds and insisted on his choice of architect: Vignola. The Vicar General of the Society engaged his own Jesuit architect, Father Giovanni Tristano, to see that the demands of the Jesuit rule were met.

Façade

The design chosen in 1575 was by **Giacomo della Porta.** Very solemn and severe, it became a model for a transitional style, halfway between Renaissance and Baroque art, known as the "Jesuit style", which was often copied by Italian and foreign architects.

The façade consists of two superimposed orders linked by powerful volutes and has a double pediment, one curved and one triangular. These are the features which later became characteristic of Baroque architecture: several engaged columns are used instead of the flat pilasters of the Renaissance; projecting features and effects of light and shade are more pronounced. The height and width of the façade to some extent mask the dome, which is seen to best advantage from above.

Interior

Compared with the purity of Gothic or the austerity of Romanesque, the richness of the decor is astonishing. A distinction must be made between the architecture of the building, a fairly plain product of the Counter-Reformation, and the ornate decoration, which was added a century later in the Baroque period when the Papacy was triumphant.

The majestic Latin cross **plan** was ideal for the Society's main purpose, preaching, which enabled the congregation to understand the ceremonies which they attended. In the single broad nave, unobstructed and well lit, the worshippers could concentrate on the celebrant and read the prayers with him. Special attention was paid to the acoustics to give resonance to the canticles, which were essential to the worship of God.

The **decoration** inspired by the Counter-Reformation was intended to celebrate the

The magnificent altar in the chapel of Sant'Ignazio di Loyola is adorned with semi-precious stones and gilded bronze

victory of the Roman Catholic Church and reinforce the conclusions of the Council of Trent: for example, the third chapel on the right which is decorated with angels and the Virgin interceding for the souls in Purgatory, illustrates ideas which were contested by the Reformers.

The abundance of polychrome marble, paintings, sculptures, bronzes, stuccowork and gilding which covers every inch of space is overwhelming.

Baciccia Frescoes★★ – In 1672, through the good offices of Bernini, Giovanni Battista Gaulli, called "Il Baciccia", was commissioned to do the paintings in the Gesù Church. *The Triumph of the Name of Jesus*, which he painted on the nave ceiling, was certainly his masterpiece and entitled him to be considered as the main exponent of Baroque decoration. The work, which was completed in 1679, combines the technique of composition with the exuberance of *trompe l'oeil*; the eye moves without check from the painted surface to the sculptures by Antonio Raggi. The Damned, who spill over the edge in a tumult of plunging bodies, do not break the unity of the composition imparted by the rays of divine light. He also painted the *Adoration of the Lamb* in the apse and the *Assumption* on the dome.

Chapel of Sant'Ignazio di Loyola★★★ – This chapel *(left of the transept)*, where the remains of St Ignatius rest in a beautiful urn, was built by **Andrea Pozzo**, a Jesuit, between 1696 and 1700. Behind a bronze rail embellished with cherubs bearing torches stands the altar, bearing a statue of the saint in marble and silver. The original statue, which was the work of Pierre Legros, a Frenchman, was of solid silver, but was melted down by Pius VI to pay the taxes imposed by Napoleon under the Treaty of Tolentino (1797).

Andrea Pozzo used precious stones and metals with which he achieved impressive colour combinations: four columns faced with lapis lazuli rest on green marble bases adorned with low reliefs in bronze gilt. Above, among the figures of the Trinity, is a child supporting a terrestrial globe in lapis lazuli.

On the sides of the altar, two groups of allegorical statues illustrate the work carried on by the Jesuits. On the left *Faith triumphing over Idolatry* by Giovanni Théodon and on the right *Religion vanquishing Heresy* by Pierre Legros, a pupil of Andrea Pozzo.

In the building to the right of the church are the rooms where St Ignatius lived and died *(access Piazza del Gesù 45)*. The ceiling and walls of the flanking passage are decorated all over in *trompe l'oeil* paintings by Andrea Pozzo (17C). *Open Mon-Sat, 4-6pm; Sun and public holidays, 10am-noon. Guided tours available (30min). No charge.* ☎ *06 67 95 131; Fax 06 67 80 780.*

Worth a Visit

Museo di Palazzo Venezia (Palazzo Venezia Museum)

On the first floor of Palazzo Venezia. (&) Open daily (except Mon) 8.30am-7.30pm. Closed 1 Jan, 1 May and Christmas. €4. ☎ *06 69 99 43 19; Fax 06 69 99 42 21.*

The first few rooms, devoted to medieval art, contain some particularly interesting antique ceramics, which include several 14C pieces from Orvieto. In the subsequent rooms, note the fine Byzantine enamel **Christ Pantocrator★★** from the second half of the 13C, a very finely carved ivory **Byzantine Triptych★★** from the 10C and a small bronze head sculpted by Nicola Pisano in 1248. The museum also contains paintings on wood by primitive artists from Florence and Siena belonging to the **Sterbini Collection★★**, as well as the 14C "Orsini" cross, made of embossed silver. In the last room, note the painted ceiling taken from Palazzo Altoviti (1533) with its central figure, Ceres, framed by medallions depicting the agricultural labours of the year. The wings of the museum display ceramics, porcelain and a large collection of small bronzes from the 15C to the 17C. Next comes a collection of terracotta objects.

Paul II's suite of rooms (overlooking Piazza Venezia and Via del Plebiscito) comprises the Royal Room where ambassadors waited to be received by the Pope; the Battle Room (from the battles of the First World War), which is the former Consistory Room where the Pope brought the cardinals together in assembly; and the Map Room, which owes its name to the map of the world displayed there in the 15C. The architectural features painted on the walls by Mantegna have been extensively restored in the 20C.

Piramide Cestia-Testaccio★

This district is further proof that Rome is a city of contrasts. Admire the mausoleum of Caius Cestius, an impressive white marble pyramid built into the old Aurelian walls surrounding parts of the city, and the Centrale Montemartini, a rare example of industrial architecture, which is now home to some of the collections from the Capitoline Museums. End your visit to the area with a stroll through the Testaccio, a working-class district of grid-system streets, known for their excellent trattorias serving a range of local dishes, such as "rigatoni co' la pajata".

Location

Michelin map 38 or Michelin spiral atlas of Rome: pp 70-71 R 11-12, S 11-12. Metro line B: Piramide (Centrale Montemartini is approximately 800m/880yd from the Metro station). Tour: 1hr 30min. The Testaccio district lies between the Tiber and Piazzale di Porta S. Paolo, the latter a busy intersection of major roads such as Viale della Piramide Cestia from the Aventine Hill to the north and Via Ostiense to the south. The Centrale Montemartini stands on Via Ostiense opposite the General Market. *Neighbouring sights are described in the following chapters: AVENTINO; SAN PAOLO FUORI LE MURA.*

Directory

Where to Eat
See "Where to Eat" in the Practical Points section at the beginning of the guide.

Taking a Break
Café du Parc – *Piazza di Porta S. Paolo. The* café's shady tables are the perfect setting for a fruit *cremolato*, a creamier and more delicate version of the crushed-ice *granita*. The milk shakes and ice creams are also excellent.

Chiosco Testaccio – *Via Giovanni Branca 100 – ☎ 06 57 46 585 – Open Mon-Sat, 8am-12.30pm and 3-11pm.* A number of original varieties of *grattachecca*, including tamarind and the very popular lemon and coconut.

Dolce Notte – *Via dei Magazzini Generali 15 – Open Mon-Wed, 8pm-3am (4am Thu, 6am Fri and Sat).* As its name suggests, the Dolce Notte has late opening hours and is ideal for those in need of a bite to eat after a night out at one of the many nightclubs in this district.

L'Oasi della Birra – *Piazza Testaccio 38/41 – ☎ 06 57 46 122 – Open 7.30am-midnight (1.30am Fri and Sat).* This beerhouse is one of the oldest in Rome. More than 500 beers to choose from, served with cheeses, soups, *bruschette* and German salamis.

Shopping
Art & Music – *Via Ignazio Persico 78 – ☎ 06 51 35 389 – Open Tue-Sat, 9am-1pm and 4-8pm; Mon, 4-8pm.* For South America enthusiasts. Sells CDs, prints and tickets for concerts.

Tendenza – *Via Giovanni Battista Bodoni 55/d.* This shop receives new imported titles weekly, especially house and underground music.

Le Bambole – *Via Luca della Robbia 11 – ☎ 06 57 56 895 – Open Tue-Fri, 9am-1pm and 4-7.30pm; Mon and Sat, 9am-1pm.* Two artists skilfully repair antique dolls in this unusual shop, which is overflowing with knick-knacks, such as toys and costume jewellery.

Walking About

Piramide di Caio Cestio★ (Mausoleum of Caius Cestius)
Caius Cestius, praetor and tribune of the people, who died in 12 BC, devised the most original mausoleum in Rome. The marble-covered pyramid testifies to the grandeur of the Augustan era, when a simple citizen could erect a tomb worthy of a Pharaoh. Nowadays the white silhouette is one of the most famous sights in Rome.

Porta San Paolo★ (St Paul's Gate)
This gate is an interesting example of the alterations that have been made to the **Aurelian Wall** (Mura Aureliane) (270-75); in Aurelian's day the gate consisted of two arches flanked by two semicircular towers on the outside. Maxentius (306-12) raised the towers, extended them towards the inside and linked them to an inner gate also consisting of two arches. Honorius, Emperor in the west (395-423), replaced the two outer arches with the present single arch and added the crenellations to the towers. The gate has been restored on subsequent occasions, particularly in the 15C and 18C.

Known in Antiquity as the Porta Ostiensis, the gate opened into Via Ostiense which led to St Paul's Basilica from which the gate took its present name in the Middle Ages.

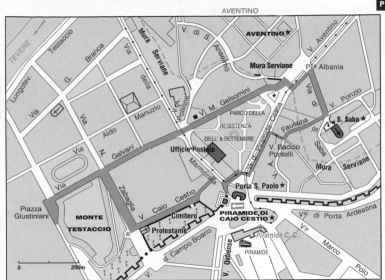

Via Ostiensis

The road dates from the 4C BC; it was one of the most important commercial arteries in Antiquity. Starting in the Forum Boarium, it followed the line of Lungotevere Aventino and Via della Marmorata, passed through the wall by a gate situated slightly to the west of the Porta Ostiensis and then more or less followed the route of the present Via Ostiense as far as Ostia, thus linking the salt marshes of the Tiber estuary to Rome.

The road continued to be used in the Christian era since it led to the site of St Paul's martyrdom (Tre Fontane) and to his tomb in St Paul's Basilica.

Take Viale della Piramide Cestia, turn right up the steps in Via Baccio Pontelli and then left into Via Annia Faustina.

The San Saba district occupies one of the peaks of the Aventine; its elegant mansions, interspersed with open spaces, dating from early this century, have made it a model of town planning for many years.

San Saba★

The church is dedicated to St Sabas, who founded a monastery called the Great Lavra in Palestine in the 5C. Two hundred years later its monks were dispersed by the Persians and then by the Arabs; many took refuge in Rome in a building inhabited a century earlier by St Sylvia, the mother of St Gregory the Great. Towards the end of the 10C the monks from the East constructed the present church on top of their smaller 7C oratory. Over the centuries the building was subject to various alterations, but was restored from 1911. Excavations below floor level have revealed traces of the early oratory and of a building from the Imperial era which may have been the headquarters of a fire brigade formed by Augustus. A flight of steps and a porch lead into a courtyard.

Piramide Cestia

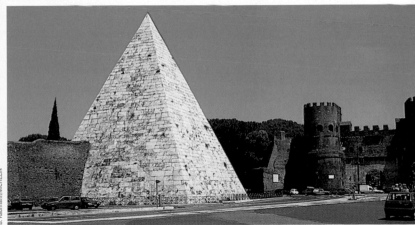

Façade – The portico is contemporary with the church but the columns have been replaced with thick pillars. In the 15C a single storey surmounted by a loggia was built on top of the portico by Cardinal Piccolomini, nephew of Pius II; later the floor of the loggia was lowered and the original windows filled in and replaced by the five existing openings. The bell-tower on the left dates from the 11C.

The main door was attractively decorated in 1205 by one of the Cosmati at the invitation of the Cluniac monks who had succeeded the original community.

Interior – The basilica plan, with a nave and two aisles each ending in an apse, has been conserved. The lack of uniformity between the pillars (bases, shafts and capitals) is typical of medieval buildings, in which material from a variety of sources was used. An unusual feature is the additional aisle on the east side of the church; it probably linked the church to the monastery of the Eastern monks. It was the Cluniac monks who rebuilt the convent in a new position in the 13C, thus exposing the additional aisle on the exterior of the church; it contains vestiges of 13C paintings.

The paving was part of the refurbishment carried out by the Cosmati, as is a section of the chancel screen, now placed against the wall in the west (right) aisle. In the frieze at the top of the right-hand central pillar is a small sculpted head with black stones for eyes; both it and its inscription are an enigma.

During the Counter-Reformation (16C) the paintings in the apse were executed for Gregory XIII; the paintings above the episcopal throne date from the 14C. The Annunciation above the apse dates from the 15C.

Take Via di S. Saba down into Piazza Albania.

In Piazza Albania, at the beginning of Via Sant'Anselmo, are the remains of the **Servian Wall** (Mura Serviane), which was built round Rome by Servius Tullius from the 6C BC; this stretch of the wall was probably rebuilt in the 1C BC.

Take Via M. Gelsomini and Via Galvani as far as Piazza Giustiniani.

TESTACCIO

This district, with its more down-to-earth atmosphere, grew out of an area which had been abandoned for 1 500 years and was then included in the development plans of 1873 and 1883 as a district for working-class people, organised according to the general town-planning principles current in Roman times.

The main attraction is the **Monte Testaccio** (some 35m/115ft high). It takes its name from the amphorae (*testae* in Latin) which, either unusable or broken in the food shops in the immediate vicinity or in the port of Ripa Grande (very little evidence remains of any of these), were reduced to potsherds (*cocci* in Italian) and piled up here. It is, therefore, also called "Monte dei Cocci". Excavations have uncovered several "grottoes", some of which revealed what appeared to be Roman restaurants and night spots.

Return to the previous crossroads; turn right into Via N. Zabaglia and left into Via Caio Cestio.

Cimitero Protestante

It is also known locally as the **Testaccio Cemetery**, a better name as it is, in fact, a cemetery for non-Roman Catholics, both Italian and non-Italian, and includes the graves of members of the Orthodox Church. Between the neat box hedges in the shade of pines and cypress trees many famous people are buried: at the eastern end of the gravel path – John **Keats** and his faithful friend Joseph Severn, Axel Munthe, the author of *San Michele*; at the foot of the last tower in the Aurelian Wall – **Shelley**'s tombstone on which Byron had some verses of Shakespeare engraved; halfway down the slope in the main cemetery between two tall cypress trees – a tombstone bearing a bronze medallion which marks the grave of **Goethe**'s son, who died in Rome in 1830 (the son's name is not given).

Continue along Via Caio Cestio; turn left into Via della Marmorata.

On the left is the **Post Office** (Ufficio Postale) of the Aventine district, a good example of Italian rationalist architecture, designed by the architects A Libera and M de Renzi, who adhered to the rules of the Modern Movement which formed the debate on architecture between the two World Wars.

Worth a Visit

Centrale Montemartini★★

Close to the General Market on Via Ostiense, not far from the Pyramid. ⅚ Open daily (except Mon) 9.30am-7pm. Closed 1 Jan, 1 May and Christmas. €4.13, €9.81 combined ticket with the Capitoline Museums. ☎ 06 57 48 030; Fax 06 69 92 05 63.

This centre, opened in 1912, was the first public thermoelectric power station in Italy. The steam turbines and diesel engines which powered the station are still an impressive sight. The power station remained in operation until the 1950s, when it was forced to close as a result of the development of more technologically advanced stations. Restoration work started at the beginning of the 1990s when the power station, which has retained its original structure and machinery (in particular two engines and a boiler), became a multi-media centre hosting exhibitions, conventions and shows. Since 1997, the museum has housed a collection of sculptures from the Capitoline Museums, which provides an interesting contrast between Ancient art and industrial archaeology. The exhibits will continue to include the Antique collections from the Capitol Hill.

Industrial architecture and Classical sculpture in the Centrale Montemartini

The Capitoline Museum Collection – The collection is housed in three rooms. The first room is the Sala Colonne on the ground floor displaying the oldest exhibits from the Archaic period to the late Republican era. Among the most interesting artefacts is the group of Heracles and Athena (6C BC), which once adorned the acroter of the Temple of Fortune and Mater Matuta in the sacred precinct of Sant'Omobono, and two funerary monuments (1C BC), one decorated with bronze leaf finely inlaid with silver and copper, the other covered with bone. The decoration of both monuments was inspired by the cult of Dionysus. On the walls, a fragment of mosaic depicting fish, thought to be part of the atrium of a house, bears witness to the expressive delicacy and realism achieved in naturalistic reproductions. At the end of the gallery, housing portraits from the late Roman Republic, the **Togato Barberini** and statues of his ancestors are particularly worthy of note (the head is a 17C restoration). The rich drapery of the toga and the transversal folds, showing how the toga would actually have been folded, are good examples of the desire for realism and fine sculpting. On the first floor, the Sala Macchine (Machinery Room) houses a sculpture gallery, with its two powerful diesel engines as a backdrop. Two images of Athena face each other at the ends of the room; one is a huge Roman copy of an original Greek statue dating from the 5C BC, the other was part of the **decoration** of the pediment of the **Temple of Apollo Sosianus**. The subject is an Amazon and is thought to refer to one of the labours of Hercules (the hero's mission was to steal the girdle of Hippolita, queen of the Amazons). The sculptures are Greek originals, dating from the second half of the 5C BC, and once stood in a place of worship; they were brought to Rome during the reign of Augustus. The *cella* of the temple has been partially reconstructed on the back of the pediment. Before entering the third room, note the beautiful basanite **statue of Agrippina praying**: the head is a copy of the original on display in Copenhagen. The Sala Caldaie (Steam Room) houses exhibits from the *Horti*, residential areas of villas and gardens on the outskirts of the city which were surrounded by greenery and richly decorated with statues, fountains, vases and mosaics. The splendid *Winged Victory*, an original Greek statue (5C BC), comes from the Gardens of Sallust (now in the Ludovisi district); the beautiful **Esquiline Venus★★**, a Roman copy from the Imperial period, was found in an underground room in the Gardens of Lamia (Giardini di Lamia e Maia), and the gracious **Seated Girl★★** and the two stern magistrates, captured in the act of opening the circus games, come from the Gardens of Licinius (Giardini di Licinio). The magnificent **Polyhymnia Muse** has a surprisingly natural rapt expression. In the centre of the room a large mosaic portrays the hunting of wild animals, probably for use in the circus; the mosaic is reminiscent of the one from Villa del Casale near Piazza Armerina in Sicily.

Porta Pia-Termini★

Stazione Termini is often the first introduction visitors will have to Rome. Sadly, the majority of those arriving here head elsewhere in the city, overlooking the many sights of interest around this busy station, such as the magnificent Baths of Diocletian and the collections of the Museo Nazionale Romano. The area is typical of many station districts, with its large urban spaces, noisy traffic, fast-food outlets, small hotels and travel agents. It is also characterised by a somewhat grandiose and anonymous architecture of wide avenues and grand ministerial palazzi built after 1870 to give Rome the appearance of a modern capital city.

Location
Michelin map 38 or Michelin spiral atlas of Rome: pp 42-43 H 15-16, J 14-15, K 14-15. Metro line A: Termini or Repubblica. Tour: 1hr. The tour described below starts in the area around Stazione Termini, Rome's main railway station, and then heads northwest through Porta Pia in the old Aurelian walls to the Nomentano district. *Neighbouring sights are described in the following chapters: SAN LORENZO FUORI LE MURA; SANTA MARIA MAGGIORE-ESQUILINO; VIA VENETO.*

Directory

WHERE TO EAT
See "Where to Eat" in the Practical Points section at the beginning of the guide.

TAKING A BREAK
Quelli di Via Nizza – *Via Nizza 16 –* ✉ For those who may prefer a slice of pizza to the traditional croissant after their evening's entertainment, this pizzeria stays open until 3-4am. Specialities include original toppings such as turkey, porcini mushrooms and rocket salad, prawns or apple purée and nutella.

Pasticceria Antonio Lambiase – *Via Cernaia 49/a –* ☎ *06 49 41 363 – Open Mon-Fri, midnight-2pm; Sat, midnight-8am.* This *pasticceria* is particularly well known for its croissants with cream and nutella and is easily identifiable by the crowds waiting outside in the middle of the night. Note the imaginative names of the specialities created by Antonio, the owner, on the signs inside the bakery. Hungarian and Austrian cakes are available by prior order.

SHOPPING
Latticini Micocci – *Via Collina 14 –* ☎ *06 47 41 784 – Open Mon-Sat, 8am-1.30pm and 5-7.30pm.* Known throughout the city as "Micocci on Via Collina", this friendly shop is paradise for cheese lovers, with its excellent buffalo mozzarella and a wide selection of French and Piedmontese cheeses. Make sure you sample the sheep's ricotta and the creamy yoghurt!

Special Features

TERME DI DIOCLEZIANO AND THE MUSEO NAZIONALE ROMANO
(BATHS OF DIOCLETIAN AND THE ROMAN NATIONAL MUSEUM)
Historical notes – The few extant rooms and the bold vaulting are evidence of the original splendour of the building, part of which now houses the church of St Mary of the Angels.

In the 4C there were some 900 bath-houses in Rome but the largest (13ha/32 acres) and most beautiful were the baths of the Emperor **Diocletian**. Building took 10 years, from 295 to 305, under the direction of Maximian, acting for Diocletian, who lived in Nicomedia in Asia Minor until he moved to Split after his abdication in 305; he never visited Rome. As well as the suite of rooms, each at a different temperature, in the bath-house itself, which could accommodate up to 3 000 people simultaneously, there were libraries, concert halls, gardens with fountains playing, galleries for the exhibition of sculpture and paintings, and exercise rooms.

MUSEO NAZIONALE ROMANO
(Roman National Museum)
The Museo Nazionale Romano was inaugurated in 1889 and evokes the history and culture of the city of Rome. The museum's collections are divided into different themes and housed in various locations, of which the **Palazzo Massimo alle Terme**, which exhibits the figurative arts from the late Republican and Imperial eras, is the most important. The **Baths of Diocletian** present an introduction to the prehistory of Rome, with a large epigraphical section illustrating the birth of Latin. **Palazzo Altemps** (*see MONTECITORIO*) houses the Ludovisi collection of Antique sculpture, while the **Crypta Balbi** (*see ISOLA TIBERINA-TORRE ARGENTINA*) recounts the development of an area from the Roman era to the Middle Ages, as well as exhibiting objects from the little-known medieval period.

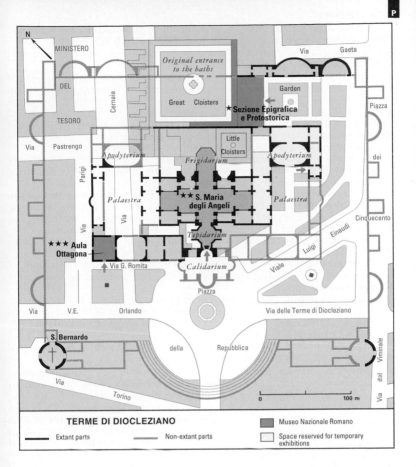

The baths were abandoned in 538 when the aqueducts were destroyed by the Ostrogoths under Witigis. Michelangelo was commissioned by Pius IV (1559-65) to convert the ruins into a church and Sixtus V (1585-90) removed a great deal of material from the site for his many building projects.

Santa Maria degli Angeli**

Entrance in Piazza della Repubblica. According to tradition, the Baths of Diocletian were built by 40 000 Christians condemned to forced labour; in 1561 Pius IV decided to convert the ruined baths into a church and a charterhouse.

Michelangelo, by then 86 years old, was put in charge. His design, which closely followed the architecture of the original baths, was continually altered after he and the Pope had died within a year of one another (1564 and 1565 respectively), so that by 1749 the church was a jumble of dissociated features and **Vanvitelli**, the Neapolitan, was commissioned to reintroduce a degree of uniformity.

The outer façade which he designed was demolished in the early 20C, revealing the unusual unadorned curved wall of the *calidarium* of the original baths.

Interior

The interior, which is designed to the Greek cross plan, was extensively remodelled by Vanvitelli.

Vestibule – This was the *tepidarium* of the baths. On the left is the tomb **(1)** of the Neapolitan poet and painter **Salvatore Rosa**, who died in 1673; on the right the tomb **(2)** of **Carlo Maratta** (1625-1713), who designed it himself.

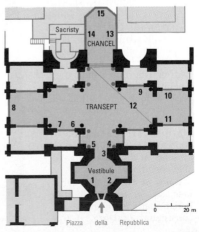

S. MARIA DEGLI ANGELI

Between the vestibule and the transept the statue of **St Bruno** (**3** – *right*), founder of the Carthusian order, is by the French sculptor Houdon (1741-1827).

On either side of the entrance to the transept are two **stoops**; the one on the right is 18C Baroque **(4)**, the other a modern copy **(5)**.

Transept★ – This part of the church gives the best idea of the solemn magnitude of the Ancient building. It occupies the central hall of the baths, with its eight monolithic granite columns. To create a uniform effect, Vanvitelli copied the columns in painted masonry, adding four more in the two recesses leading to the vestibule and the chancel. In addition to the present entrance, Michelangelo had intended two more, one at each end of the transept, but eventually two chapels were created instead and painted in *trompe l'oeil* with architectural effects.

The transept is a virtual picture gallery, particularly of 18C works. The majority come from St Peter's, where they were replaced by mosaics. Here in St Mary's, Vanvitelli arranged them to cover the wall spaces between the pillars.

Of particular significance is the painting depicting *St Basil celebrating Mass before Emperor Valens* **(6)** by the French painter Subleyras (1699-1749), who settled in Rome in 1728; the Emperor, overwhelmed by the dignity of the ceremony, has fainted; his uniform and background are treated in the Classical manner.

The Fall of Simon Magus **(7)** by **Pompeo Batoni** (1708-86) is typical of this artist's work, with its fine colours and effects of contrasting light and shade.

The Virgin with St Bruno and other saints **(8)** is a gentle and luminous work by Giovanni Odazzi (1663-1731), a pupil of Baciccia; he continued to work in the Baroque Mannerist style.

The south transept contains the **tombs** of three First World War heroes: Marshal Armando Diaz **(9)**, who won the Battle of Vittorio Veneto in 1918; Admiral Paolo Thaon di Revel **(10)**, commander-in-chief of the Allied forces in the Adriatic 1917-18; Vittorio Emanuele Orlando **(11)**, Minister of State.

Running across the floor from the south transept to the chancel is a meridian **(12)**. Between 1702 and 1846 the clocks of Rome were regulated by it.

Presbytery – Like the transept, the presbytery is generously decorated with paintings, the most notable being *The Martyrdom of St Sebastian* **(13)** by **Domenichino** (1581-1641), and *The Baptism of Jesus* **(14)** by Carlo Maratta.

Behind the high altar is a much-venerated picture **(15)** showing the Virgin surrounded by adoring angels. It was commissioned from a Venetian artist in 1543 by Antonio del Duca, a Sicilian priest, who had a vision in which he saw a cloud of angels rising from the Baths of Diocletian. From then on he never stopped demanding the construction of a church on the site of the baths; eventually Pius IV acceded to his request.

Aula Ottagona★★★ (or Baths of Diocletian Planetarium)

Entrance on Via Romita. Open daily 9am-7.45pm (last admission 6.45pm). Guided tours with an archaeologist available by appointment Sat-Sun, 10am, noon, 3.30pm and 6pm. Closed 1 Jan and Christmas. €5, €20 for a "Roma archeologica" card valid for nine archaeological sites. ☎ 06 39 08 071; Fax 06 39 75 09 50; pierreci@pierreci.it

Painted in the 1920s to resemble a planetarium, this wonderful domed octagonal room houses bronze and marble sculptures taken from Roman baths dating from the Imperial era (2-4C BC). The **works of art★★★** exhibited include:

– *Pugilist resting*: this superb figure cast in bronze is an original from the Hellenistic period. Typical is the realism which characterises Greek works of the 3C BC: this fighter is no longer the ideally handsome hero represented by the Classical artists, but a man overwhelmed with fatigue. The figure was found in 1884 at the same time as the *Youth leaning on his spear*. Not only are these statues rare examples of supreme craftsmanship, they are also in the most remarkable condition.

– *Venus of Cyrene*: this fabulous statue is made from Parian marble, which has the consistency of ivory. It was

Pugilist resting

Museo Nazionale Romano

discovered during the excavations of the baths at Cyrene in Libya. Venus is tying up her hair while still rising from the sea. The figure is a copy of a Greek original typical of the female divinities produced by Praxiteles. In order to stabilise the statue, the sculptor has devised a draped garment falling over a dolphin which has a fish in its mouth.

– *Venus Anadyomene*: Venus emerging from the waves, tying up her hair.
– *Hercules*: fine example of an athletic figure in motion.
– *Lycean Apollo* and head of *Aesculapius* (who was invoked against pestilence). Set into the central part of the floor is a glass panel revealing the excavated foundations of the building.

Epigraphical and Prehistoric Museum★

Entrances on Piazza della Repubblica, Viale Einaudi and Viale de Nicola. Audioguides recommended. ♿ Open daily (except Mon) 9am-7.45pm (last admission 7pm). Closed 1 Jan, 1 May and Christmas. €5. ☎ 06 48 90 35 01.

16C garden – This garden, which acts as an entrance to the museum in Diocletian's Baths, houses a collection of archaeological fragments, most discovered in Rome and the surrounding area. The huge vase in the centre, which has stood here since the early 20C, once adorned the villa of a rich Roman citizen.

Museum – This 1920s building has been completely rearranged to house the rich epigraphical collection of the Museo Nazionale Romano, which is displayed on three floors. An introductory section on the ground floor provides information on the different materials used and on writing techniques. This is followed by an exhibition of objects from the Archaic era to the late Republican period (8C-1C BC). The two upper levels are dedicated to inscriptions dating from the Imperial era (1C BC-4C AD), which give information on the Emperor and his entourage, social structure, political and economic activity, and private and public religion in Roman society.

The raised floor around Michelangelo's cloisters *(access from the second floor of the Epigraphical Museum)* houses a section dedicated to the prehistory of the Latins between the 9C and 7C BC, divided into two parts. The first section describes the culture of Latium and the relationship of the Latin people with neighbouring populations; the second provides information on the major settlements in the Rome area, investigated from 1960 onwards.

Chiostro Michelangiolesco – The Great Cloisters of Santa Maria degli Angeli are sometimes attributed to Michelangelo, although he died in 1564, aged 89, and the cloisters were completed in 1565, if the date inscribed on the corner pillar near the entrance is to be believed. Recent restoration work has revealed the original plaster. The sculptures on display, most of which come from excavation sites in and around the city, have been reorganised.

PALAZZO MASSIMO ALLE TERME★★★

Entrance on Largo Villa Peretti, at the end of Viale Einaudi. ♿ Open daily (except Mon) 9am-7.45pm (last admission 6.45pm). Closed 1 Jan and Christmas. €6, €20 for a "Roma archeologica" card valid for nine archaeological sites. ☎ 06 39 08 071; Fax 06 39 75 09 50; pierreci@.pierreci.it

The largest part of the **National Roman Museum**'s collection is now permanently housed in the former Collegio Massimo, founded by the Jesuit Massimiliano Massimo in 1883 and used as a college until 1960. The collections are displayed on four floors in a few rooms arranged around the inner courtyard and divided into bays, using glass. Greek and Roman statues are exhibited on the ground and first floors, frescoes and mosaics on the second, and gold and numismatics in the basement.

Ground floor

The entrance to the museum is dominated by a statue of Minerva (seated) **(1)**, which dates from the 1C BC and is made of pink alabaster, basalt and Luni marble; the face is a plaster cast of another statue of the goddess.

Gallery I houses a series of portraits from the Republican era, arranged according to physical similarities to highlight family relationships.

Room I: The two fragments on display in this room **(2)** represent a typical calendar and a list of consuls and censors who held office between 173 and 67 BC. The explanatory panel shows the columns which indicated the months and the days subdivided into *dies fasti* (marked by the letter F), which were the days when civil activity could take place, *dies nefasti* (letter N), the days when civil activity could not take place, *dies endotercisi* (letter EN), considered auspicious only in the middle of the day, and *dies comitiales* (letter C), when meetings were held.

The **Tivoli General (3)** is an excellent example of the union of the ideal of beauty, typical of Greek art, and that of the portrait, which is typically Italian in its adherence to reality. The general is portrayed as a hero and wears only a cloak, allowing his powerful physique to be emphasised; the Classical beauty of the body contrasts with the realistic features of the face, which clearly shows signs of age.

PALAZZO MASSIMO ALLE TERME

SECOND FLOOR

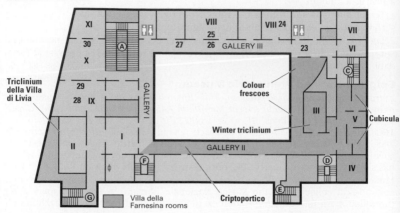

Triclinium della Villa di Livia

Colour frescoes

Winter triclinium

III

Cubicula

GALLERY I

GALLERY II

GALLERY III

Criptoportico

Villa della Farnesina rooms

FIRST FLOOR

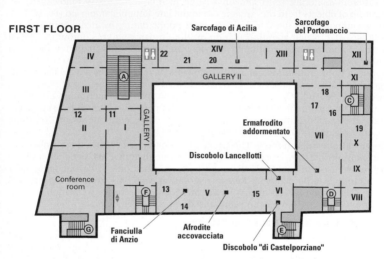

Sarcofago di Acilia

Sarcofago del Portonaccio

GALLERY II

Ermafrodito addormentato

Discobolo Lancellotti

Conference room

GALLERY I

Fanciulla di Anzio

Afrodite accovacciata

Discobolo "di Castelporziano"

GROUND FLOOR

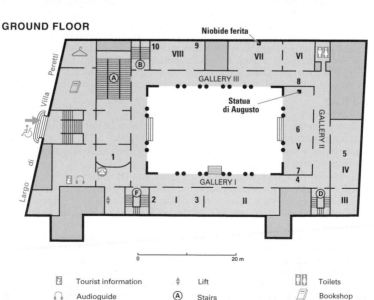

Niobide ferita

Peretti

Villa

Largo di

GALLERY III

Statua di Augusto

GALLERY II

GALLERY I

0   20 m

📖 Tourist information   ⇕ Lift   🚻 Toilets
🎧 Audioguide   Ⓐ Stairs   📄 Bookshop
♿ Wheelchair access   △ Cloakroom   ☎ Telephone

THE CALENDAR

The first recorded Roman calendar is traditionally attributed to Romulus and consisted of 304 days divided into 10 months (March was the first month). The months of January and February were then added by Numa Pompilius, bringing the total number of days to 355, to which an extra day (23 February) was added every three years so that the course of the sun and moon would coincide. It was Julius Caesar who radically reformed the calendar by increasing the number of days to 365 and adding an extra day in February every four years. The names of the months were taken either from gods and goddesses (March from Mars, May from Maia, June from Juno), from Emperors (August from Augustus and July from Julius Caesar) or from their position in the calendar (September was the seventh month and October the eighth). The name February is an exception; it derived from the verb *februare*, meaning to purify, as this was the month dedicated to ceremonies of purification.

A beautiful **floor mosaic (4)** (end 2C-beginning 1C BC) can be seen at the end of Gallery I; the emblem panel in the centre shows the abduction of Hylas (depicted with his cloak billowing in the wind) by water nymphs. This myth tells how the young man, a companion of Hercules on the expedition of the Argonauts, wandered off on his own to look for water and was abducted by a nymph, close to a spring. The youth cried out and Hercules ran to his aid, but found no trace of his companion.

In the middle of Room IV is a **young girl (5)**, similar to Artemis, depicted wearing a richly draped chiton. Attention to detail is shown in the footwear, which has been carved with panthers' heads.

Room with three arches – Room V is the only one to give directly on to the inner courtyard and is therefore one of the best lit. It encloses the **statue of Augustus★★★** *(statua di Augusto)*. The Emperor is shown at about the age of 50, dressed in the High Priest's toga, with his head covered as was the custom for priests about to offer a sacrifice. The face is treated with simple realism, and perhaps a little flattery. The hair is arranged in two "swallow-tail" locks, in a style typical of portraits of the Emperors. Age does not seem to have wrought any change since the Emperor was portrayed at the time of the Battle of Actium when he was 32 years old; the earlier statue preserved in the Capitoline Museums, together with the later one displayed here, convey the solemn majesty and authority of Augustus. No better psychological study could be made of the Emperor.

On the back of the **Altar to Mars and Venus (6)** can be seen the *Lupercale*, which tells the legend of Romulus and Remus, brought up by a she-wolf. The personification of the Palatine can be seen at the top to the left, with, beneath it, the eagle, symbol of Jupiter, and to the side the two shepherds, Faustulus and Numitor, the former the adoptive father of the twins. The personification of the Tiber can be seen at the bottom.

The theme of the legendary founding of Rome is also taken up in the **frescoes from a Columbarium on the Esquiline (7)**. Shown from right to left are the foundation of the city, the struggle between the Rutules and the Trojans, the meeting between Mars and Rhea Silvia, the father and mother of Romulus and Remus, and the she-wolf who nursed the twins.

A colourful and realistic mosaic **(8)** of a cat and ducks can be admired in **Gallery III**; note the ruffled fur of the cat, captured in the act of catching a bird, and the lifelike representation of the ducks.

Gli Horti Sallustiani (Gardens of Sallust) – The exhibits in Room VII include some original Greek statues from this residential

Museo Nazionale Romano

Statue of Augustus dressed as Pontefix Maximus

district of the city, including the noteworthy **Wounded Niobe★★★** *(Niobide ferita)*, dating from 440 BC *(see also Palazzo Altemps and Centrale Montemartini)*. The statue represents an episode in Greek mythology: Niobe was mother of 14 children, and was scornful of Leto, who had borne only two. The angry goddess asked her children, Artemis and Apollo, to avenge her by killing all of Niobe's children. The sculptor has captured the moment in which Niobe is wounded by an arrow; the goddess looks up to the skies and attempts to withdraw the arrow with both hands behind her back. This statue was one of the first representations of the naked female figure in Greek art after the cycladic statues from the third millenium BC.

Neo-Attic period – *Room VIII*. Among the works dating from this period, inspired and modelled upon Hellenistic figurative art, note the statue of the **Melpomene Muse (9)**, dating from the 1C BC, and the various ornamental garden pieces, including a base of dancing maenads **(10)**.

First floor

The works exhibited on the first floor date from the Imperial era and are good examples of the propagandist use of portraits during this period.

Portraits – Among the portraits from the Flavian dynasty *(Room I)*, that of **Vespasian (11)** is particularly worthy of note. This realistic work depicts an old man with a wide and solid face, small eyes and a furrowed brow. The portrait of **Sabina (12)** *(Room II)*, Trajan's wife, shows a woman of quite advanced years but is fairly idealised in tone.

Villas and gymnasia – *Rooms V-VI*. This large double room, once the theatre of the college, houses works from three of the large Imperial villas: Nero's villas at Subiaco and Anzio and Hadrian's villa at Tivoli *(see page 367)*.

The **Ephebe of Subiaco (13)** is thought to represent one of Niobe's children, hit by Apollo's arrow *(see Room VII)*. Admire the beautiful drapery of the chiton of the **Young girl from Anzio★★** *(Fanciulla di Anzio)*, shown with the upper half of her body twisting slightly, looking down at a tray of offerings, among which a priest's fillets and olive or laurel branch can be seen, identifying her as a priestess. The statue was made from two different blocks of marble; the finer-grained marble was used for the unclothed upper half of the body. The statue of **Apollo (14)** is also from the villa at Anzio and is a Roman copy (1C AD) of a Hellenistic work; typical features from the Hellenistic period (4C BC) include the gentle, swaying pose, the shoulders at different heights and the slightly bowed head. These features contrast with those of the **Apollo of the Tiber (15)**, which is typical of the Classical period in its statutory pose, level shoulders, strong body and idealised beauty, and is thought to be a copy of a statue by Phidias. The **Aphrodite crouching★★★** *(Afrodite accovacciata)* is one of the most beautiful copies of an original Greek work of the 3C BC; the goddess is shown bathing, a theme often reproduced by the Romans.

At the end of the room are two Roman copies (2C AD) of the original Greek bronze statue of the *Discobolus by Myron* (5C BC). The **Lancellotti Discobolus★★★** *(Discobolo Lancellotti)*, named after its former owner, is considered to be an excellent copy. The artist has chosen to represent the moment where the athlete has already grasped the discus in his right hand and is flexing the muscles of his whole body prior to the throw. The impassive expression, devoid of any sign of physical effort, is characteristic of Greek works from the Classical period. The hair and the veins in the arms are sculpted in great detail. The two small protuberances on the head are what remains of the two reference points used by the artist when reproducing the original.

The other replica is the **Castelporziano Discobolus★** *(Discobolo "di Castelporziano")*, named after the estate on which it was found in 1906; it is less complete and less well executed.

Portraits of gods – *Room VII*. The **Sleeping Hermaphroditus★★** *(Ermafrodito addormentato)* is a beautiful copy of a Greek original thought to date from the 4C BC. The graceful, pure lines of the statue and the gently twisting body emphasise the ambiguity (the sexual organs are not visible from one side of the statue).

Detail of fresco in Cubiculum C of the Villa Farnesina

According to mythology, Hermaphroditus (son of Hermes and Aphrodite, hence the name) was sitting by a lake one day when he was spotted by Salmacis, a water nymph who fell in love with him; rejected by the youth, the nymph requested to be joined to Hermaphroditus for ever. Her wish was granted and a new being of both genders emerged from the lake. The headless statue of **Apollo with his lyre (16)** is wearing a full chiton, which emphasises the movement of the body. Also exhibited in this room are two very different statues of Dionysus. The first, in bronze, shows **Young Dionysus (17)** with his traditional attributes, the thyrsus in his left hand and the taenia (headband) with vine leaves in his hair; note the copper inserts (nipples and lips) and the glass paste eyes. The second, a marble copy of an original probably by Praxiteles, portrays an older **Dionysus (18)**, with a long beard and dressed in a long chiton covered with a himation thrown over the left shoulder. It presents a different iconographical representation of the god, and is known as **Sardanapalo**, from the name which has been carved by the owner on the back of the statue, possibly to associate the god with the wealthy Assyrian king Sardanapalos, who was famous for his dissolute nature and his habit of wearing women's clothes (the chiton).

Room X houses a collection of **bronzes** from the ships in Lake Nemi. Note the balustrade decorated with herms **(19)**.

Historical events – *Room XII*. The large **Portonaccio Sarcophagus★** *(sarcofago del Portonaccio)* is decorated with a rich battle scene between the Romans and barbarians. The figures are crowded together and overlap to highlight the fighting. Two defeated figures to one side show their unbound hands to symbolise Roman *Pietàs*. The commander, who can be seen in the middle of the composition, is faceless, probably because he would have been among the last of the figures to be completed. At the top of the scene, slightly to the left, a snake symbolises evil. The top strip depicts childhood and adulthood scenes from the life of the commander.

Iconography and celebrations from Severus to Constantine – *Room XIV*. The 3C AD oval-shaped **Acilia Sarcophagus★★** *(sarcofago di Acilia)* is finely and elegantly decorated with beautiful high-relief carvings, illustrating a consular procession. The youngest figure wears the consular ring and is possibly the consul's son (on his shoulders to the right); the character wearing the toga and diadem is the personification of the Roman Senate. From a later period are the **Sarcophagus with Muses (20)**, fitted with internal recesses, and the **Annona Sarcophagus (21)**, with a wedding scene shown in the middle of the sarcophagus; this depicts the ceremony of the *dextrarum iunctio,* the union of hands which corresponds to the modern-day exchanging of rings. The **Sarcophagus of Marcus Claudianus (22)** was made after the edict of Constantine and is carved with scenes from the Old and New Testaments. The commander in the centre is portrayed as Christ praying.

Second floor

This floor is dedicated to mosaic art and frescoes. Most of the floor mosaics are shown in Galleries I and III.

Triclinium della Villa di Livia★★★ – *Room II*. This is the reconstruction of a semi-underground room, probably a summer triclinium (dining room) from a villa where Livia, wife of Augustus, lived at Prima Porta (north of Rome). The fine decoration, dating from 20-10 BC, runs along the four walls and depicts a garden in full bloom. An incredible variety of plants (firs, cypresses, oaks, pines, pomegranates, oleanders and palm trees) and birds can be seen. The garden is demarcated by a double enclosure, the first made of reeds and the second of marble. Perspective is heightened by the skilful use of chiaroscuro and the varying heights of the plants, and the muted fresco colours are used to suggest depth and relief, making this cycle of frescoes a masterpiece of Roman painting.

Museo Nazionale Romano

Villa della Farnesina*** – The stuccoes and paintings in this part of the museum come from a surburban villa dating from the Augustan era, built on the banks of the Tiber, with a large semicircular porch facing the river. The stuccoes, which decorated the ceilings, are marvellously delicate. The paintings are typical of the second and third styles *(see Insights and Images: Roman art: Painting, p 87)* and were probably executed for the marriage of Giulia, the daughter of Augustus and Agrippa. The frescoes which decorated the cryptoporticus *(criptoportico)*, an underground corridor lit by narrow slits, can be admired in Gallery II. The decoration shows a fine colonnade with panels of Bacchic and Dionysiac scenes painted on a white background between the columns. At the end of the corridor is a reconstruction of the **winter triclinium** *(triclinium invernale, Room III)*. Slender columns hung with vegetal festoons are painted on a black background. The panels have an Egyptian theme and contain illustrations of sphinxes and trial scenes. Panels showing scenes from everyday life and tragic and comic masks can be admired on the other side of the corridor. The magnificent frescoes from the three cubicola (bedrooms) of the villa *(Room V)*, two with a Pompeian red background (the colour of passion) and one with a light background, are very well preserved. The ceilings still retain some of the beautifully executed stuccoes.

Gallery III – The mosaic of a Nike *(centre)* surrounded by Dionysiac masks **(23)** dates from the end of the 1C BC. Small openings run off the gallery *(Room VIII)* which house the **Water nymph from Anzio (24)** with, in the middle recess, a portrait of Hercules resting (the hero is easily recognisable by his club) and **frescoes (25)** of underwater fauna (2C AD) found near a river port on the Tiber. At the end of the gallery is a beautiful **mosaic with a Satyr's head and Pan (26)** and a large **mosaic of Nile landscape (27)** from the 2C AD, characterised by the presence of crocodiles and hippotami, which can be compared with the fresco on display at the Museo Archeologico Prenestino *(see p 366)*.

Villa di Baccano – *Room IX.* This room houses floor mosaics from Villa di Baccano (on Via Cassia), which date from the 3C AD. The large **marine mosaic (28)** with the personification of Neptune, god of the sea, in the centre would have decorated the bathing area. The four panels depicting the charioteers **(29)** (the colours of their tunics correspond with the four factions competing) would have decorated a bedroom.

Megalographs – *Room X.* Dedicated to a collection of megalographs (large paintings), this room contains a fresco **(30)** portraying a goddess understood in the 17C to be Roma (helmet) but since identified as Venus.

Basement

The basement houses a large display from the numismatic and antique gold collections.

Numismatic Collection** – This large room displays coins used in Italy from the 4C BC onwards, including models for the euro. Equipment, measures and weights used for minting coins are exhibited in the display cases along the walls.

Prices and wealth in Rome – In AD 301 Diocletian promulgated an edict to fix prices and measures. In the first display case is a collection of calculus equipment, including an abacus (n) 14). The second contains an unusual statuette of a skeleton. This was known as the "convivial skeleton", and was placed in the middle of the table during banquets as a *memento mori* (eat, but remember that you must die). The other cases exhibit collections of Roman goldwork. A reliquary in the centre of the room contains the perfectly preserved mummy of a child of about eight years old, thought to date from the 2C AD.

Walking About

Piazza dei Cinquecento – This vast, open space is the terminus for all public transport services in the city and home to the main **railway station**, Stazione Termini. The present building was begun before the Second World War to replace the old station, which had been built when the railway first arrived in Rome during the reign of Pope Pius IX (1846-78). Interrupted during the war, work on the new station began again in 1947 and was completed to mark the Holy Year in 1950. The roof, with its undulating lines, is considered one of the most significant examples of architecture of this period. In the station forecourt are imposing remains of a wall built round the city after the Gauls invaded in the 4C BC.

On the south side of Viale Luigi Einaudi stands a monument to the memory of 500 Italians (after whom the piazza is named) who died at Dogali in Eritrea in 1887; this was an incident in the wars of Italy's colonial expansion. The obelisk surmounting the monument comes from the Temple of Isis in Campus.

In Piazza Beniamino Gigli, south of Piazza della Repubblica, is the **Teatro dell'Opera**, a theatre begun by A Sfondrini and completed in 1880. The façade is the work of M Piacentini, who restored and enlarged part of the building in 1926.

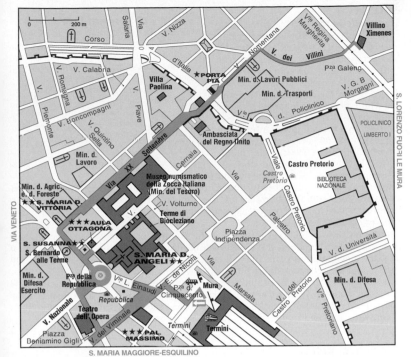

S. MARIA MAGGIORE-ESQUILINO

Follow Via Torino alongside the theatre, then turn right into Via Nazionale.

Via Nazionale – This long, busy street links **Stazione Termini** with Piazza Venezia in the city centre. It is one of the city's most important commercial centres, and is lined with a variety of shops which attract both tourists and Romans. Halfway down is the **Palazzo delle Esposizioni**, which houses art exhibitions of international reputation. Near the south end is the **Teatro Eliseo.**

Piazza della Repubblica (Piazza dell'Esedra)

Despite the heavy traffic the circus is one of the better post-1870 examples of town planning.

It is sometimes called Piazza dell'Esedra because of the semicircle formed by the two palaces which flank the southwest side. They were designed in 1896 by Gaetano Koch to trace the line of the exedra in the southwest wall of the Baths of Diocletian. The porticoed buildings are reminiscent of the architecture of Turin; the unified Kingdom of Italy, with Rome as its capital, had as its king Victor Emmanuel II, head of the House of Savoy, who lived in Turin.

The attractive Naiad Fountain at the centre of the circus is adorned with bronze water nymphs and sea monsters, and was sculpted by the Sicilian artist Mario Rutelli (1901).

Follow Via V.E. Orlando as far as Via XX Settembre.

Via XX Settembre

The street is named after the date – 20 September 1870 – when Italian troops entered the Papal capital. It replaced the old Strada Pia and was the first street to be developed in the post-1870 town planning. It was designed to link the ministries and to reflect the grandeur of the city's new status. It was therefore lined with pompous buildings in imitation of the Renaissance and Baroque styles. The Ministery of Finance, to the right, is home to the Museo della Zecca italiana (*see Worth a Visit below*). At the end of the street *(right)* is a very modern building by Sir Basil Spence which houses the **British Embassy** (Ambasciata del Regno Unito).

Villa Paolina

Seat of the French ambassador to the Holy See. Open by appointment to groups only. Contact M. l'Ambassadeur, Via Piave 23, 00187 Roma, at least two weeks in advance.
The villa is named after Napoleon's sister Pauline, who in 1803 married Prince Camillo Borghese, great-nephew of Pope Paul V. She took up residence after the fall of the Empire since her husband, whom she had abandoned a few years earlier, had banished her from the family property. She spent long periods in the house until her death in 1825.

Porta Pia

The **inner façade★** of the gate, facing down Via XX Settembre, is spectacular, the last architectural design by Michelangelo. It was erected between 1561 and 1564 at the request of Pope Pius IV. At the centre are six balls, the device of the Medici family. The curious white motif, which appears several times, is said to be a barber's basin wrapped in a fringed towel, a reminder to Pius IV that one of his ancestors was a barber. The outside façade, facing down Via Nomentana, is the work of Benedetto Vespignani (1808-82), who, with Giuseppe Valadier, was very active during the 19C.

> **20 SEPTEMBER 1870**
>
> That day was the culmination of the Risorgimento. The united kingdom of Italy had been in existence since 1861. Cavour had declared in Parliament: "I assert that Rome, and Rome only, ought to be the capital of Italy". On 20 September 1870 Italian troops entered Rome through a breach in the Aurelian wall.
>
> The site of the breach, in Corso d'Italia on leaving the Porta Pia, is marked by a column surmounted by a representation of Victory.

The government of the newly unified Italy installed its soldiers in the **Castro Pretorio**, formerly the barracks of the Emperor's personal bodyguard – the Pretorian Guard founded by Augustus. *Continue along Via Nomentana and turn right into Via dei Villini.*

Via dei Villini – This road is an excellent example of early-20C town planning. It is worth strolling along the road to admire the two types of dwellings defined in a new development plan: the *palazzino*, a four- or five-storey block of flats for letting, and the *villino*, a smart little house with its own garden.

Beneath this district lie the catacombs of St Nicomedes.

The road ends in Piazza Galeno, opposite **Villino Ximenes**, an unusual little house, built for himself by Ettore Ximenes (1855-1926), sculptor, painter and illustrator, who designed many official buildings in Rome and abroad.

Worth a Visit

Museo Numismatico della Zecca italiana (Currency Museum)

On the ground floor of the Treasury building. Open Tue-Sat, 9am-12.30pm. Closed Aug and public holidays. No charge. ☎ 06 47 61 33 17.

The Treasury building dates from 1877. The Numismatic Museum displays the currencies of every country in the world including coins issued by the Popes from the 15C. There is also a fine collection of wax impressions (about 400) by Benedetto Pistrucci (1784-1855), who was chief engraver to the Bank of England for 40 years: heads of George IV, Victoria, Duke of Wellington, Napoleon, Pauline Borghese.

San Giovanni in Laterano★★★

As in so many parts of the capital, pagan remains stand side by side here with some of the most important churches of Christian Rome: the basilica of St John Lateran – the official seat of the Pope in his capacity as Bishop of Rome – and Santa Croce in Gerusalemme, one of the seven churches visited by all pilgrims making their way to the city. Today, there is a marked contrast between the noisy square, Piazza di Porta San Giovanni, which is a busy road junction, and the calm solemnity diffused by the east front of the basilica. Also worth a visit in this area is the small, busy clothing market that runs along Via Sannio, on the other side of Porta San Giovanni.

Location

Michelin map 38 or Michelin spiral atlas of Rome: pp 58-59 and 72-73 P 15-16, N 16-17, M 16. Metro line A: San Giovanni or Manzoni. Tour: 3hr. This district stretches from the southeast of the city to the Caelian Hill and is almost wedged inside the Aurelian walls. The *Tangenziale* provides a fast road link with the districts of San Lorenzo and Nomentano.

Neighbouring sights are described in the following chapters: COLOSSEO-CELIO; SAN LORENZO FUORI LE MURA; SANTA MARIA MAGGIORE-ESQUILINO.

Background

The name is taken from the wealthy Laterani family who owned a property confiscated by Nero and restored by Septimius Severus. Excavations in Via dell'Amba Aradam (beneath the INPS building) have revealed traces of a house identified as belonging to the **Laterani**. It was combined with a neighbouring property in the 4C and may have been the residence of Fausta, who was Maxentius's sister and Constantine's wife. In 313, she lent her house to Pope Melchiades so that he could hold a council of bishops, one of the first official manifestations of Christianity. Beneath the St John Lateran Hospital (Ospedale di San Giovanni in Laterano) are traces of a building which has been identified as the house of the Annii, Marcus Aurelius's family. The remains of the base of a statue were found in a peristyle; it may have carried the statue of the Emperor which now stands in the Capitoline Museum.

St John's Gate (Porta San Giovanni) was erected in the 16C in the **Aurelian Wall** (Mura Aureliane), which was built around Rome in the 3C and is very well preserved.

The **monument to St Francis of Assisi** is a reminder that the saint and his companions came to the Lateran one day in 1210 to have their rule approved by Innocent III.

Directory

WHERE TO EAT

See "Where to Eat" in the Practical Points section at the beginning of the guide.

TAKING A BREAK

Il Gelato di S. Crispino – *Via Acaia 55/56* – ☎ *06 70 45 04 12 – Open Wed-Mon, 11am-midnight.* The owners of this *gelateria*, considered to be one of the best in Rome, only make flavours which they like themselves. Try the honey with ginger and cinnamon, cream with Armagnac, liquorice, meringue with hazelnut or chocolate and cream with Pantelleria raisin wine.

Nabel Art Café – *Via di S. Giovanni in Laterano 244* – ☎ *328 26 62 426 (mobile) – Open Tue-Sun, 9pm-3am.* Admire the photography and painting exhibitions displayed in this café while enjoying a plate of charcuterie or one of the many salads on the menu. Poetry classes are occasionally held here in the evening, and every Sunday musicians come to the café to perform impromptu concerts.

SHOPPING

All American Comics – *Via Tarquinio Prisco 89* – ☎ *06 78 48 292 – Open Mon-Sat, 9.30am-1pm and 3.30-8pm.* Specialises in Japanese and American comic books, available in both Italian and the original language, and has a large science fiction section.

BASILICA DI SAN GIOVANNI IN LATERANO★★★ (ST JOHN LATERAN)

Open 7am-6.30pm. ☎ *06 77 20 79 91.*

This basilica was the first church to be dedicated to the Holy Redeemer; it symbolised the triumph of Christianity over paganism and thus deserved its title of "Mother and Head of all the churches in the city and the world". It is the cathedral of Rome. The dedication to St John came later.

Constantine's Basilica – On 28 October 312, after defeating Maxentius in battle, Constantine made a triumphal entry into Rome and immediately forbade the persecution of the Christians. In 314 Pope Sylvester I took up residence in the Lateran (a group of buildings comprising a palace, a basilica and a baptistry); the palace became the official Papal residence from the 5C until the Papacy departed to Avignon in France.

Before starting St Peter's in the Vatican, Constantine built the Lateran basilica on the site of Maxentius's bodyguards' barracks. He thus asserted his victory by destroying one of the signs of his enemy's greatness and by stressing his intention of giving the Christians his approval.

After being laid waste by the barbarians in the 5C, damaged by an earth tremor in 896 and destroyed by fire in 1308, the basilica was rebuilt in the Baroque era and in the 18C. In all, over 20 Popes contributed to its rebuilding, restoration and embellishment, from Leo the Great (440-61) to Leo XIII (1878-1903).

> **A STRANGE TRIAL**
>
> The trial took place in 896 in the Lateran. The accused was the corpse of Pope Formosus, dressed in his Papal vestments; his enemies had not forgiven him for having bestowed the Emperor's crown on the "barbarian" Arnoul, last of the Carolingians.
>
> He was set up opposite his judge, Pope Stephen VI, declared unworthy and a perjuror, and finally thrown into the Tiber.
>
> Stephen VI was, in his turn, punished and strangled in prison.

Lateran Councils – Some of the most decisive councils in the history of the Church took place in the Lateran. In **1123** the Diet of Worms was confirmed, putting an end to the Investiture Controversy. The council of **1139** condemned **Arnold of Brescia**, a canon, who challenged episcopal authority and preached in favour of a return to the poverty of the early Church. He founded a free commune in Rome and drove out Eugenius III.

In **1179** Alexander III called for a crusade against the Albigensian (Cathar) heresy. Following the Council in **1215**, which was attended by 400 bishops and 800 abbots and at which every court in Europe was represented, it was laid down that the

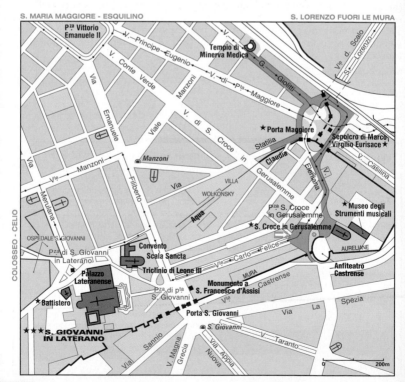

Pediment of St John Lateran

faithful must go to confession once a year and take Communion at Easter. Innocent III decided to put an end to the Albigensian heresy and launched a crusade in the Languedoc. In **1512** Julius II opened the fifth Lateran Council by asserting the supremacy of the Church of Rome.

Exterior

The well-balanced 18C **façade** is the major work of Alessandro Galilei (1691-1736), one of the architects who built in the Baroque style in Rome. He had a masterly touch in contrasting the clear lines of the columns with the dark cavities behind them. On the roof, the gigantic figures of the saints surrounding Christ, St John the Baptist and St John the Evangelist seem to be preaching to the heavens. The **huge statue of Constantine**, the first Christian Emperor **(1)**, in the porch comes from the Imperial baths on the Quirinal. Since 1656 the **central entrance (2)** has been fitted with the doors from the Curia in the Roman Forum; in 1660 they were enlarged by the addition of a border decorated with the stars on the arms of the reigning Pope, Alexander VII.

Interior

It is hard to envisage the basilical plan of Constantine's building. The central nave and four aisles of today are those of a Baroque church, sometimes considered cold and severe because of its grandiose dimensions and pale stuccoes. In fact, it is a very old building dressed in 17C taste.

Nave and aisles – This part of the church was designed by the great Baroque architect **Borromini**; his plan included a dome. Just as Urban VIII had commissioned **Bernini** to complete St Peter's, so his successor **Innocent X**, in his desire to mark his reign in a prestigious manner, invited Borromini in about 1650 to refurbish St John Lateran. Whereas Bernini knew exactly how to adapt Baroque art to earlier styles of construction, Borromini was unable to give free rein to his genius as Innocent III asked him to retain the existing ceiling. The ceiling seems to crush the pillars in the nave which replace the ancient columns and were designed to support a dome; the prominent niches faced with dark marble spoil the effect of the low-relief sculptures and the oval medallions above them.

Ceiling★★ – It was begun by Pius IV in 1562; his arms are in the centre. It was completed in 1567 by Pius V, whose arms are near the chancel. In the 18C it was restored by Pius VI who added his arms near the main door. The original design was by a group of Michelangelo's pupils.

Statues of the Apostles★ (3) – They are in the late Baroque style by some of Bernini's followers. Borromini created 12 huge recesses in the pillars of the nave to receive them. The columns of green flecked marble, which Borromini shortened and re-employed, originally separated the nave and aisles in the Ancient basilica. Above each recess he placed the dove from the arms of Innocent X.

The low-relief sculptures *(above)*, executed under the direction of Algardi, depict stories from the Old and New Testaments. The Prophets in the oval medallions *(top)* were painted in the 18C. This decoration replaced the 15C frescoes painted by Pisanello and Gentile da Fabriano for **Martin V** and Eugenius IV.

Corsini Chapel★ (4) – Alessandro Galilei, who designed the east front, was also responsible for this chapel, which is built on the Greek cross plan beneath a dome. The red porphyry coffer *(left)* beneath Clement XII's tomb came from the Pantheon.

The allegorical statues are fine 18C work. The fragment of heavily restored **fresco (5)**, attributed to **Giotto**, shows Boniface VIII announcing the Jubilee Year in 1300.

Transept – The nave is as bare of ornament as the transept is adorned with frescoes, marble and gilding. It was renovated in about 1595 by Clement VIII, with **Giacomo della Porta** as architect. It is a good example of Mannerist decoration: the great wall frescoes resemble a theatrical decor and were painted principally by Cesare Nebbia, Pomarancio and Cavaliere d'Arpino who, in the *Ascension (end of left transept)*, imitated the *Transfiguration* by Raphael (Vatican Gallery).

The elaborate marble decoration includes high-relief angels, placed in small niches, which do not show the liberty of movement which characterises Baroque art. The ostentatious **ceiling★★** bearing the arms of Clement VIII is rich in colour and gilding and was designed by Taddeo Landini (late 16C).

The pediment in the **chapel of the Holy Sacrament (6)** is supported by four beautiful Antique **columns★** in gilded bronze, the only ones of this kind in Rome. Legend has it that in the 1C BC they belonged to the Temple of Jupiter on the Capitol.

The 14C **baldaquin (7)** was repainted during the Renaissance. At the top some relics of the heads of St Peter and St Paul placed in silver reliquaries are kept, partly paid for by Charles V of France (repaired in the 18C). In the 19C Pius IX had the high altar faced in marble. During this work it became apparent that the wooden altar contained some much older planks, one of which very probably belonged to the altar at which Pope Sylvester I officiated (314-35).

The *confessio* **(8)**, created in the 9C, contains the tomb of Martin V, the first Pope to reign after the Great Schism. His tomb is the work of Donatello's brother.

Apse – The apse of Constantine's Basilica was rebuilt in the 5C and again in the 13C but was not substantially altered until the 19C, when Leo XIII moved it back in order to extend the chancel. The ogival windows and particularly the **mosaic** in the top of the apse were retained. This mosaic had already been restored in the 13C by **Jacopo Torriti**, who took several features from the original model: the representation of the Cross, celestial Jerusalem with the palm and the phoenix, symbols of the Resurrection *(beneath the cross)* and the Jordan full of fishes, birds and boats, which forms the base of his composition. To these he added the Virgin and Nicholas IV kneeling, St Peter and St Paul *(left)*, St Andrew and the two St Johns, the Baptist and the Evangelist *(right)*. He also included two smaller figures: St Francis of Assisi *(left)* – Torriti was a Franciscan monk – and St Anthony of Padua *(right)*. The mosaic is dominated by the figure of Christ; the first representation of Christ in the apse dates from the 4C. Not long before, paganism was still the state religion so that, when Pope Sylvester consecrated the basilica, the appearance of such an image was considered miraculous by the faithful. In his desire to perpetuate the "miracle", Jacopo Torriti managed to transfer the Ancient figure to his own composition. During the 19C alterations this original figure was broken and replaced by a copy.

Museo della Basilica – *Right of the chancel. For information on admission times and charges call* ☎ *06 77 20 79 91.* The Basilica Museum displays the treasures of the basilica – gold chalices and reliquaries. The **station cross** (Cabinet V) is in silver gilt (12C).

Chiostro★ – *Open 9am-6pm. €2.* ☎ *06 77 20 79 91.* These charming 13C cloisters are one of the most remarkable by the Vassalletti (father and son). Their art, like that of the Cosmati, consisted of cutting and assembling fragments of Antique marble. The twisted columns with varied capitals, the mosaic frieze and the delicate carving of the cornice make this a poetic place where one would like to linger. A fine 9C well has been placed in the middle of the garden.

Leave the basilica by the right transept.

In the **porch** is a bronze statue of Henri IV of France **(9)** by Nicolas Cordier (1567-1612) in recognition of the king's gift to the Lateran Chapter of the Abbey of Clairac in Agenais. In memory of France's beneficence to the Lateran, the President of the French Republic belongs as of right to the Lateran Chapter (a mass is said for France on 13 December).

The **façade of the north transept** is so majestic it could be the main front; it was built by Domenico Fontana in 1586.

BATTISTERO* (BAPTISTERY)

Like the basilica, the baptistery was built by Constantine. In the 4C every Christian was baptised there; nowadays it is used for the ceremonies of Holy Saturday. It was rebuilt in the 5C by Sixtus III who set up the eight porphyry columns in the centre and had verses appropriate to baptism inscribed on the octagonal entablature. The upper colonnade and the lantern are 16C additions. Various Popes built the adjoining chapels and Urban VIII gave it its present appearance when he added the wall frescoes in the 17C.

Chapels – *Ask the keeper to open the doors.* The **chapels of St John the Baptist (10)** and **St John the Evangelist (11)** were built by Pope Hilary (461-68). While legate to Pope Leo the Great, Hilary was sent to the Council of Ephesus to argue against a heresy. During the hearing there was a disturbance and Hilary took refuge on the tomb of St John the Evangelist, where he made a vow to build a chapel to the Baptist and the Evangelist.

The chapel of St John the Baptist has kept its original door, which is made of an alloy of silver, bronze and gold and is very heavy; it makes a very special sound when it swings on its hinges.

The chapel of St John the Evangelist was given a new bronze door in the 12C. The ceiling is covered with a beautiful 5C mosaic (delicate colours on a gold ground).

Chapel of St Rufina and St Secunda (12) – In the 12C the original narthex, which was the entrance to the baptistry, was converted into a chapel. It is rectangular in shape with an apse at either end, one of which is decorated with a fine 5C mosaic.

Chapel of St Venantius (13) – Built in the 7C by John IV, it is decorated with mosaics in the Byzantine style (slim, slightly stiff figures) and has a fine cedar ceiling.

PIAZZA DI SAN GIOVANNI IN LATERANO

In the piazza stands a fine **Egyptian obelisk** made of granite, the tallest in Rome. It dates from the 15C BC and was brought to Rome in the 4C by Constantinus II to adorn the Circus Maximus at the foot of the Palatine, where it was found in 1587. It was repaired and re-erected in its present position by Domenico Fontana, at Sixtus V's behest.

Palazzo Lateranense (Lateran Palace)

When Gregory XI returned to Rome in 1377 after the Popes' period in Avignon, he found that the palace had been gutted by fire and was obliged to install his household in the Vatican.

The present building was constructed in 1586 by **Domenico Fontana**, during the reign of Sixtus V. The **Lateran Treaty** *(see VATICANO – SAN PIETRO, p 301)* was signed here. The palace is now the headquarters of the Diocese of Rome (Vicariate), with the Pope at its head, in his capacity as Bishop of Rome, and of the Vatican Historical Museum.

Museo Storico Vaticano (Vatican Historical Museum) – *Entrance by the main portico. For information on admission times and charges call ☎ 06 69 88 16 62; Fax 06 69 88 50 61.*

The museum comprises two parts – the **Papal Apartment** and the **Historical Museum**. The apartment contains 10 rooms, each decorated with frescoes by late-16C artists. It was in the last salon, called the Conciliation Room, that the Lateran Treaty was signed in 1929 by Cardinal P Gaspari and Mussolini. The Historical Museum consists of three sections devoted to the history of the Papacy, to Papal ceremony and to the Papal guard respectively.

Traces of the medieval palace – In the Middle Ages the Papal palace extended from its present site as far as Via Domenico Fontana. Two features from this building, the *triclinium* of Leo III and the Scala sancta, have been reconstructed on the east side of the square.

Triclinium of Leo III – This Pope (795-816) built two rooms in the palace. All that remains of the *triclinium* (dining room) is an apse decorated with a mosaic, repaired in the 18C. It celebrates the alliance of Leo III with Charlemagne: the Emperor reinstated the Pope on his throne and the Pope crowned the Emperor in St Peter's in the Vatican.

Scala Sancta – *Open 6.15am-noon and 3.30-6.30pm; Sancta Sanctorum: open Apr-Sep, Tue, Thu and Sat, 10.30-11.30am and 3.30-5pm; rest of the year, Tue, Thu and Sat, 10.30-11.30am and 3-4pm. €2.58.* ☎ *06 70 47 62 40.*

Sixtus V (1585-90) demolished what remained of the medieval palace with two exceptions: the stairs, which according to tradition came from Pontius Pilate's palace and had been used by Christ, and the private chapel of the Popes, which was re-sited not far from its original position in a building specially designed by Domenico Fontana to incorporate the famous steps, which are climbed by the faithful on their knees. There are other stairs on either side for those who prefer to go up on foot.

At the top is the Popes' chapel, known as the **Holy of Holies**** (*Sancta Sanctorum*), by analogy with the temple in Jerusalem, because of the precious relics it contained. The interior is decorated with fine Cosmati work. The paintings in the chapel, damaged by rainwater over the centuries, were carefully restored in 1995; as a result of the restoration it is now possible to see the 11C frescoes, considered by medieval experts to be one of the most important discoveries of the century. Above the altar is the famous icon of Christ called the *Acheiropoeton*, which means it was not made by human hand: St Luke began it and it was completed by an angel; it arrived in Rome miraculously from Constantinople in the 8C. The Ancient bronze door with its impressive locks, which gives access to the Popes' chapel, can be seen from St Lawrence's Chapel *(right)*.

Walking About

PORTA MAGGIORE DISTRICT

Start from Piazza S. Croce in Gerusalemme.

In Antiquity the district to the east of the Esquiline was a suburb of Rome, well wooded and covered with tombs which stretched for miles along the Praenestina Way and the Labicana Way (now Via Casilina). From Augustus's reign (31 BC to AD 14) onwards, the cemeteries gradually gave way to huge gardens laid out by rich Romans. Under the Empire these sumptuous properties, designed by skilful landscape gardeners, with temples and avenues lined with works of art, were absorbed into the Imperial estates either by confiscation or by legacy (members of the patrician class often willed their property to the Emperor). This practice restricted development to the east and aggravated the problem of lack of space in the city centre, which was becoming overcrowded with huge, prestigious buildings. In the 3C the district was enclosed by the Aurelian Wall (Mura Aureliane). It remained untouched by the building projects of the Popes in the Renaissance and Baroque periods and was not developed until the 19C, when Rome had become the capital of Italy.

Santa Croce in Gerusalemme*

Open 7am-7pm. ☎ *06 70 14 769 or 06 70 29 272; www.santacroce.it*

In this church, originally known simply as Jerusalem, the legend of the Holy Cross is closely linked with history. Here stood the **Sessorium** where Constantine's mother, Helen, lived; it was built in the 3C and remained an Imperial palace until the 6C. In the 4C Helen went on a pilgrimage to Jerusalem, as was the custom at that time. She returned in 329 bearing a fragment of the True Cross, which she kept in the palace. The same year she died. A legend then developed according to which she herself had found the True Cross. The cult of the Holy Cross was not introduced to Rome until the 7C.

History of the church – In memory of his mother, the Emperor Constantine (or perhaps his sons) converted part of the Sessorian Palace into a church to house the precious relic. It consisted of one large chamber with an apse where the services were held and a smaller room (the present St Helen's Chapel) where the relic was kept. In the 12C Pope Lucius II (1144-45) divided the larger chamber into three and built a campanile without altering the outside walls. He raised the level of the floor in the church but not in the chapel, perhaps because according to tradition the floor of the chapel was composed of soil brought back from Calvary. The chapel was isolated from the church and had a separate entrance until the Renaissance, when it was linked to the church by two stairways, one on each side of the apse. The church acquired its present appearance in thc 18C.

Tour – The 12C campanile is flanked by a lively façade and oval vestibule in the 18C style, consistent with the principles dear to Borromini.

The nave vault was refashioned in the 18C; the impressive baldaquin over the altar is of the same period. The apse has conserved the mark of the Renaissance; it is decorated with an attractive fresco by Antoniazzo Romano (late 15C), illustrating the legend of the Discovery of the Cross by St Helen.

Cappella di Sant'Elena (Chapel of St Helen) – *Access by one of the sets of steps beside the chancel).* The chapel is decorated with beautiful **mosaics★**, designed by Baldassarre Peruzzi and, perhaps, by Melozzo da Forlì. The statue above the altar is a Roman work originally representing Juno but converted into St Helen.

Cappelle della Croce e delle Reliquie (Chapel of the Holy Cross and Relics Chapel) – *Access by steps to the right of the left aisle.* The relics of the Passion kept in the chapel of the Holy Cross attract large numbers of pilgrims. In the first chapel they venerate the arm of the cross of the good robber crucified next to Christ *(at the beginning of the flight of steps opposite the entrance).* In the Relics Chapel a glass case behind the altar displays fragments of the True Cross; the "heading" on the Cross, ie the inscription it bore; two thorns from the Crown; St Thomas's finger; some fragments from the Flagellation stake, from the grotto in Bethlehem and the Holy Sepulchre; a nail from the Cross.

On leaving the church, bear left through the opening in the Aurelian Wall.

Anfiteatro Castrense

Its name comes from the Latin word *castrum*, which in the 4C meant an Imperial residence. This amphitheatre, like the Sessorian Palace *(see above)*, was probably part of the imperial properties in this district. It seems to have been of great importance since there is a detour in the Aurelian Wall to enclose it. It was built entirely of red brick and dated from the end of the Severan dynasty (3C); it originally consisted of three storeys, of which only the first is well preserved.

Take Via Eleniana to Porta Maggiore.

Porta Maggiore★

The gate was built in the 1C AD to carry the Claudian Aqueduct across the Praenestina Way and the Labicana Way where it entered the city. The use of huge, roughly hewn blocks of travertine (even for the supports) is an innovation typical of the Claudian era. The upper section which carried the water channels is inscribed with details of the work ordered by Claudius and the restoration work ordered by Vespasian (AD 71) and Titus (AD 81).

In the 3C the gate was incorporated into the Aurelian Wall. When Honorius (395-423) restored the fortifications a bastion was added on the outside; its demolition in the 19C revealed the tomb of Marcus Vergilius Eurysaces.

Sepolcro di Eurisace★ (Tomb of Marcus Vergilius Eurysaces)

Eurysaces was a baker who lived in Rome at the end of the Republic. As supplier to the army he probably grew rich during the civil wars of this period and built an enormous tomb in travertine (dating from c 30 BC), designed to commemorate his trade.

The cylindrical motifs, some vertical and some horizontal, recall the receptacles in which the flour was kept. The inscription identifies the owner of the tomb. The low-relief frieze round the top illustrates the different steps in breadmaking.

Go west along Via Statilia.

On the left among the trees are the elegant arches of the Claudian Aqueduct.

Porta Maggiore, an example of innovative architecture from the 1C AD.

Aqua Claudia (Claudian Aqueduct)

Aqueducts are without doubt the most remarkable public works in Roman architecture. This one, which was begun by Caligula in AD 38 and completed by Claudius in AD 52, is the most impressive. Starting in the mountains near Subiaco, it reached Rome after 68km/42mi of which 15km/9mi were above ground. From Porta Maggiore, Nero (AD 54-68) built a branch channel, traces of which remain in the gardens of Villa Wolkonsky, in Piazza della Navicella and in the Arch of Dolabella, at the eastern end of Via di San Paolo della Croce. This aqueduct was extended by Domitian as far as the Palatine, to supply his palace with water.

Turn left into Via G. Giolitti.

Tempio di Minerva Medica

The beautiful circular temple (4C) was originally covered by a dome and was probably a *nymphaeum* in one of the patrician gardens.

Worth a Visit

Museo degli Strumenti Musicali★

Open daily (except Mon) 9am-7pm. Closed 1 Jan, 1 May and Christmas. €2.07. ☎ 06 70 14 796; Fax 06 70 29 862.

The charming **Museum of Musical Instruments** displays a variety of instruments dating from Antiquity to the 19C. Antique whistles, horns and handbells are succeeded by exotic instruments such as beautiful inlaid mandolins; tambourines and ocarinas evoke provincial folk dances. Every sort of instrument is here: mechanical, portable, military, religious and domestic, adorned with fine paintings or inlaid with mother-of-pearl and ivory.

The sumptuous exhibits of the museum include the 17C Barberini harp, which bears the name of the famous Roman family to which it belonged and is decorated with magnificent gilt carvings, and a rare example of a vertical harpsichord (17C) with a pretty painted lid.

San Lorenzo Fuori le Mura★

The major point of interest in this part of the city is the Basilica of San Lorenzo Fuori le Mura, situated in the heart of the university district. Although this area lacks the attractive appearance of an old European university town, it still has a lively atmosphere with its crowds of students, the constant noise of mopeds and trams and the many specialised bookshops and other small outlets catering for the student population. This vibrant atmosphere is intensified by the fact that some of the university departments have moved off campus and are now dotted around the quarter.

Location

Michelin map 38 or Michelin spiral atlas of Rome: p 44 K 17-18. Metro line B: Policlinico (500m/550yd from the university campus). Tour: 1hr. This district is located to the east of the city and is bordered by the inner by-pass (the *tangenziale*) that leads to San Giovanni. From here, the suburbs of Rome stretch as far as the eye can see.

Neighbouring sights are described in the following chapters: CATACOMBE DI PRISCILLA; PORTA PIA-TERMINI; SAN GIOVANNI IN LATERANO.

Worth a Visit

SAN LORENZO FUORI LE MURA★★
(ST LAWRENCE WITHOUT THE WALLS)

The church is also known as San Lorenzo al Verano since it is built on land that belonged to a certain Lucius Verus in Antiquity. To the north ran the Via Tiburtina, lined, like other roads on the outskirts of Rome, with pagan tombs and then with underground Christian cemeteries, the catacombs. One of them contains the grave of St Lawrence, who was martyred in 258 under the Emperor Valerian soon after Pope Sixtus II was put to death. According to legend, Lawrence was roasted on a grill; he was highly venerated in the Middle Ages.

As pilgrims to the tomb of St Lawrence became more and more numerous the Emperor Constantine had a sanctuary built (330). By the 6C it was in such a poor state of repair that Pope **Pelagius II** (579-90) had it rebuilt.

Directory

WHERE TO EAT
See "Where to Eat" in the Practical Points section at the beginning of the guide.

TAKING A BREAK
Antico Forno – *Via dei Rieti 61* – ✉. *This bakery* attracts local residents, with its reasonably priced *pizza bianca* and biscuits.
Superpizza – *Largo Osci* – ✉. In the heart of San Lorenzo, opposite the market stalls along Largo degli Osci, **Superpizza** bakes delicious pizzas for students from the nearby university.

BARS
Internet Café – *Via dei Marrucini 12* – ☎ 06 44 54 953 – www.internetcafe.it – Open Mon-Fri, 9am-2am; Sat-Sun, 5pm-2am. There are 22 computer screens for Internet enthusiasts to surf the web, while they enjoy a drink and a snack.
Lancelot – *Via dei Volsci 77/a* – ☎ 06 44 54 675 – Open 8pm-2.30am. This bar is particularly popular with students and has over 300 board games available to customers. The bar has a good beer and cocktail list, in addition to a reasonable selection of rolls and salads.
Squinternet – *Via dei Luceri 13* – ☎ 06 44 70 28 34 – Open 4pm-2am. Surf the Internet for little more than €4 an hour, using one of the nine screens of this small café. The tea is imported directly from Ceylon.

SHOPPING
Claudio Sanò – *Largo Osci 67/a* – ☎ 06 44 69 284. Original leather bags in the most unusual shapes – cubes, triangles, trapezia, and even some in the shape of buttons.
Disfunzioni Musicali – Disfunzioni Musicali Usato e Rarità – *Via degli Etruschi 4* – ☎ 06 44 61 984 – disfunzionimusicali@tiscalinet.it – Open Tue-Sat, 10.30am-7.30pm; Mon, 3.30-7.30pm. The first shop sells mainly imported, avant-garde and rare records, as well as second-hand CDs. The second, (Via dei Marrucini 1; closed Sat afternoons) opened just a few years ago and specialises in avant-garde and rock singles and LPs.

It was probably enlarged in the 8C but underwent major alterations in the 13C under Pope **Honorius III** (1216-27): the apse of Pelagius's church was demolished, the church was extended westwards and its orientation reversed. The original nave was raised and became the chancel of the new church.
Later Baroque additions were removed by Pius IX in 1855; he also revealed the original nave but retained Honorius's chancel.
On 19 July 1943 a bomb fell on the church; the roof, the upper part of the walls and the porch were destroyed. Repair work was put in hand immediately with the aim of restoring the church to its 13C appearance.

Façade
The very elegant porch, which dates from the time of Honorius III, was reconstructed after the 1943 bomb damage using some of the original material. Above the architrave which is supported by simple columns, is a beautiful mosaic frieze in vivid colours. Above this is a cornice delicately carved with flowers, fruit and acanthus leaves punctuated with lion-head gargoyles. This fine example of medieval decorative sculpture is attributed to the Vassalletti, a family who worked in marble with the Cosmati from early in the 12C to late in the 13C.
The bell-tower (*right*) was erected in the 12C, probably at the same time as the cloisters. Its restoration in the 14C may have been due to damage caused by an earthquake or a fire.
Under the portico there is a rare example of a sarcophagus **(1)** with a sloping canopy, which probably stood over a tomb in the floor of a church. The work is probably 11C.
Next to it is a 4C sarcophagus **(2)** with a likeness of the occupant in a medallion. The concise decoration depicts scenes from the Old and New Testaments.
The **"harvest" sarcophagus★** (**3** – *left*) is quite remarkable. It is shaped like a funeral bier and decorated with vine leaves, bunches of grapes gathered by Cupids, birds and animals, very varied and lively. It was carved in the 5C or 6C; the clear-cut relief and the large smooth surfaces are characteristic of the Middle Ages.
Two modern works honour Pope Pius XII **(4)** and Alcide de Gasperi **(5)**, President of the Council from 1945-1953, in recognition of their assistance in the work of restoration following the bomb damage.
The two lions **(6)** on either side of the main door are Romanesque.

Interior
The two distinct parts of the church are immediately apparent, divided by the triumphal arch and built on two different axes: one for the church built by Honorius III (13C) and one for the church built by Pelagius II (6C).

Church built by Honorius III
The funerary monument (**7** – *right of entrance*) of Guglielmo Fischi (1256), nephew of Pope Innocent IV, was reconstructed in 1943. Beneath a small temple resembling a 13C baldaquin is a 3C sarcophagus decorated with a marriage scene.

Honorius's church comprises a nave and two aisles separated by beautiful Antique granite columns of varying diameters. The Ionic capitals, like those in the porch, date from the Middle Ages and are attributed to the Vassalletti. They show with what happy results the medieval marble workers adapted their technique to Ancient columns.

The lighting of the nave has hardly changed since the 13C. After 1943 the ceiling was rebuilt exactly as it had been in the 19C when Vespignani, who was working for Pius IX, had inserted a wooden coffered ceiling beneath the open roof frame.

The floor, which was damaged by the bomb, is bright with the colours of the 13C **Cosmati** work.

The two **ambones★** are not identical. They are Cosmati work: a combination of white marble, porphyry and serpentine, encrusted with multicoloured insets gleaming with touches of gold. The one on the right **(8)** was used for reading the Gospel and was more sumptuously decorated (early 13C) than the one on the left **(9)**, which was used for reading the Epistle and has the simple elegance of late-13C Cosmati work.

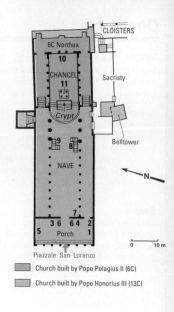

Church built by Pope Pelagius II (6C)

Church built by Pope Honorius III (13C)

Church built by Pelagius II

The central section containing the high altar has been raised and is approached by two sets of steps. Its original orientation with the apse projecting west of the present chancel arch was reversed so that it could serve as the chancel of Honorius' church, as it does today. Pelagius's church comprised a nave and two aisles. From the raised nave only the tops of the Ancient fluted columns are visible, supporting a magnificent sculpted architrave composed of disparate fragments which once belonged to a frieze or a door lintel. Over the aisles are galleries (*matrones*) for the women; the arcades rest on fine slim columns, their capitals decorated with leaves (6C).

The chancel arch which opened into the apse of Pelagius's church is decorated with a late 6C mosaic. At the centre is Christ, his hand raised in blessing. On his right are St Peter and St Lawrence and Pope Pelagius II offering his church to the Saviour. On his left are St Paul, St Stephen and St Hippolytus.

The bishop's **throne★ (10)** at the east end of the chancel is by the Cosmati (1254). The whiteness of the marble contrasts with the vivid colours and the gold inlays to create a fine decorative effect. The elegance of the throne is enhanced by the fine craftsmanship of the screen which closes off the choir.

The **baldaquin (11)** over the high altar is supported by four porphyry columns. The last two sections of the columns were repaired in 1862. This is Cosmati work (1148) and is signed by the four sons of Paolo, the oldest of the group. It is one of the earliest examples of this sort of miniature temple with columns supporting an architrave.

Beneath the high altar in the **crypt** are the remains of St Lawrence, St Stephen and St Justin.

It was during some work commissioned by Pope Pius IX in the 19C that the lower part of the 6C church and the narthex were discovered. There are two sets of steps leading down, one on each side of the chancel (*if the gates are closed, enquire in the sacristy*).

The narthex is decorated with modern mosaics by craftsmen of the Venice School and contains the **tomb of Pius IX** (1846-78).

Cloisters

Entrance through the sacristy in the south aisle or from the outside on the right of the bell-tower. The 12C cloisters with their archaic charm formed part of the fortified convent which was like a citadel in the Middle Ages. St Lawrence's Basilica, being outside the walls of Rome, was easy prey for thieves and looters. The cloister walk contains many inscriptions from the neighbouring catacombs.

CITTÀ UNIVERSITARIA (UNIVERSITY CAMPUS)

In 1935 the University of Rome, which had suffered cramped conditions in the Palazzo della Sapienza (Palace of Wisdom), was transferred to the new university campus near the Municipal Clinic (*Policlinico Umberto I*) built in 1890. The campus includes many buildings designed by the leading architects of Rome at that time, who worked on developing a collection of buildings reflecting the various thematic possibilities of modern architecture.

The overall design was awarded to **Marcello Piacentini** who, having become the major exponent of large-scale building projects (he had also overseen the plans for Rome's EUR), was inclined to apply the rules so dear to the "Twenties", as can be seen in the Rectorate and the vast entrance area. The overall impression is, however, one of balance and shows no excess of grandeur for its own sake. The final effect was the work of various architects, some of whom were members of the Rationalist movement, whose inclinations differed somewhat from those of the academics. One of the most important of the Rationalists was Giuseppe Pagano, whose style can clearly be seen in the Institute of Physics.

The architects who collaborated on the project were: Pietro Aschieri – Institute of Chemistry; Giò Ponti – Institute of Mathematics; Giovanni Michelucci – Institute of Mineralogy and Institute of Physiology; Giuseppe Capponi – Institute of Botany. All the faculties are not, however, located on the university campus itself but are spread all over Rome. In recent years, in fact, another faculty, the University II, was set up at Tor Vergata.

San Paolo Fuori le Mura★★

This area contains two sites situated outside the Aurelian Wall which are linked by the history of St Paul: the basilica of St Paul Without the Walls, built over the saint's tomb, and the demesne of Tre Fontane, a few kilometres away, the site of his martyrdom. Although these religious monuments are of major significance to Christian pilgrims, they also hold a certain fascination for those visitors with an interest in the history of Christianity.

Location

Michelin map no 38 or Michelin spiral atlas of Rome: p 84 (W 11) and p 95 (T 5). Metro line B: Basilica S. Paolo (Metro station 300m/330yd from the basilica) and Laurentina (approximately 1.5km/1mi from the Abbazia delle Tre Fontane). For access by bus, consult a public transport directory. Tour: 1hr for San Paolo Fuori le Mura and 45min for the Abbazia delle Tre Fontane, excluding travelling time. This district is situated to the south of the capital on Via Ostiense, which joins with the Via del Mare to link Rome to Ostia. The Abbazia delle Tre Fontane is situated on Via Laurentina further to the south.

Background

Saint Paul – Paul was a Jew called Saul, who was born early in the 1C AD at Tarsus in Cilicia in Asia Minor (southeast Turkey, not far from Adana). At first he persecuted Christ's disciples; then on his way from Jerusalem to Damascus one day, he was blinded by a light, fell from his horse and heard Jesus's voice saying: "Saul, Saul, why persecutest thou me?" This event precipitated his conversion: he changed his name from Saul to Paul and became the chief agent in preaching Christianity to the Gentiles. His very active life as an Apostle included long missionary journeys throughout Syria, Cyprus, Asia Minor, Macedonia and Greece. Accused by the Jewish community of Caesarea in Palestine, he demanded to be brought before the Emperor Nero (Paul was a Roman citizen). This is why he set out for Rome in about AD 60. Two years later he appeared before the Imperial court and was acquitted.

The date of Paul's martyrdom is not known for certain. Like Peter, he may have been a victim of the persecution of the Christians organised by Nero after the terrible fire in AD 64 which destroyed the greater part of Rome. When the rumour began to spread that Nero himself had started the fire to clear the land for his Golden House, he quickly found someone to take the blame. Innumerable Christians died a variety of deaths.

As a Roman citizen, St Paul was sentenced to be beheaded.

Special Features

BASILICA DI SAN PAOLO FUORI LE MURA★★
(BASILICA OF ST PAUL WITHOUT THE WALLS)

Open 7am-6.30pm (6pm in winter). ☎ *06 54 09 374.*

Together with St Peter's in the Vatican, St John Lateran and Santa Maria Maggiore, St Paul Without the Walls is one of the major basilicas in Rome. Its historical significance attracts visitors and pilgrims from all over the world.

St Paul's body was buried beside the Via Ostiensis, which was lined with tombs, as were all the major roads leading out of Rome. A small shrine *(memoria)* was erected over his grave. In the 4C the Emperor Constantine undertook to build a basilica over the tomb, as he had done for St Peter's tomb. This first basilica was consecrated by Pope Sylvester I in 324. It was smaller than St Peter's Basilica and faced the Via Ostiensis. The Apostle's tomb was enclosed by the apse on the spot where the high altar now stands. By 386 it had become such a popular place of pilgrimage that three Emperors – Valentinian II, Theodosius I and his son Arcadius – decided to enlarge the building. It could not be extended across the road (because of the rising ground), and since the Apostle's tomb could not be moved, the orientation was reversed, with the apse on the Via Ostiensis and the façade facing the Tiber so that the tomb occupied a central position at the head of the nave.

The new basilica was magnificent; it was larger than the contemporary basilica of St Peter in the Vatican. The huge project was not completed until 395, in the reign of the Emperor Honorius. For the next 14 centuries the basilica was maintained with great care and attention.

When the building was sacked by the Lombards in the 8C and by the Saracens in the 9C, the damage was immediately repaired. John VIII (872-82) had a defensive wall built enclosing both the basilica and the community which had grown up around it; this came to be known as "Johannipolis", after the Pope.

The greatest artists were employed to embellish the basilica: from Pietro Cavallini and Arnolfo di Cambio to Carlo Maderno.

When, therefore, on the night of 15 July 1823 fire broke out in the roof and almost totally destroyed the basilica, it was a great catastrophe.

Reconstruction began immediately and it was decided not to preserve the undamaged parts which had survived. Thus the nave and aisles were rebuilt in their entirety, although the south side of the basilica had not been touched by the flames; the apse and transepts were extensively restored.

Although St Paul's Basilica is now adorned with gleaming marble and vivid colours, it still follows the original plan and manifests the grandeur of the early Christian basilicas in Rome.

Tour

To appreciate the vast size of the building, enter by the main door from Viale di S. Paolo.
The west front is preceded by a huge courtyard surrounded by covered arcades *(quadriporticus)* built early in the 20C.

The statues of St Paul **(1)** and St Luke **(2)** are 19C. The mosaics now on the pediment replaced those done in the 14C by Pietro Cavallini.

The central portal **(3)**, which replaced the 11C original, is flanked by statues of St Peter and St Paul and has two magnificent bronze and silver doors depicting scenes from the lives of the two saints.

Interior★★★ – No visitor can fail to be impressed by the multitude of columns – 80 granite monoliths – which divide the nave and four aisles.

The gold and white coffered **ceiling** bears the arms of Pope Pius IX (1846-78), who consecrated the new basilica. At the west end of the inner south aisle is the **Holy Door**, an 11C bronze door, made in Constantinople for Gregory VII (1073-85).

During the reconstruction every alternate window in the **nave** was removed; the daylight is filtered by a screen of alabaster.

The medallion portraits of the Popes painted in the 5C have been replaced by mosaic roundels showing the long line of succession from St Peter to John Paul II.

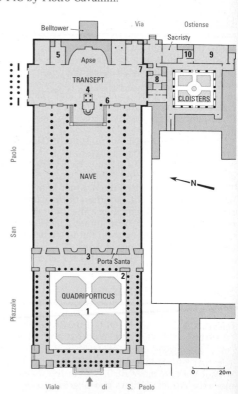

In the long **side walls** windows and recesses alternate. The recesses contain statues of the Apostles sculpted by various 19C and 20C artists.

Two gigantic granite columns support the **chancel arch**, above which are two inscriptions recalling the construction of the basilica by Theodosius and Honorius and its embellishment by Galla Placidia, Theodosius's daughter. She was responsible for the 5C mosaic, which was reconstructed after being badly damaged in the fire. It shows Christ flanked by two angels and the 24 elders of the Apocalypse; above are the symbols of the Evangelists; below are St Peter and St Paul.

The **Ciborium★★★ (4)** is a Gothic work by **Arnolfo di Cambio** (1285). It is supported on four fine porphyry columns with gilded capitals.

Detail and proportion are delicately blended: the many decorative figures are executed with great skill, from the pairs of angels supporting the pierced rose-window on each of the four pediments to the animals on the vault.

Beneath the baldaquin is the high altar; the table is 1.37m/4.5ft above a 4C marble plaque engraved with the name of Paul, Apostle and Martyr. The plaque marks the position of Paul's grave and has never been moved.

The mosaic in the **apse** dates from the 13C and is the work of Venetian artists commissioned by Pope Honorius III. It is in the characteristic style of the Venetians, who, even at that time, still followed Byzantine models: the little figure at Christ's feet represents Pope Honorius in all humility. The whole work was restored in the 19C.

The ceiling of the broad **transept** is richly decorated with the arms of St Paul (an arm and a sword) and the arms of successive Popes from 1800-46. The altars which face one another from the far ends of the transept are symmetrical and decorated with lapis lazuli and malachite.

To the left of the apse is the **chapel of the Holy Sacrament★ (5)**, the work of Carlo Maderno (1629), which contains a 14C wooden crucifix, a statue of St Bridget kneeling by Stefano Maderno (c 1576-1636) and a wooden statue of St Paul dating from the 14C.

The Paschal **candlestick★★ (6)** by Nicolà di Angelo and Pietro Vassalletto (12C) is a remarkable piece of Romanesque art. The base is decorated with monsters and on the shaft are decorative motifs, scenes from the life of Jesus (note the expressions of the squat figures), tendrils and more monsters supporting the candle socket.

The **stoop (7)** is a charming piece of sculpture by Pietro Galli (1804-77), showing a child threatening a terrified demon with holy water.

The **baptistry (8)**, rebuilt in 1930, is an elegant chamber in the shape of a Greek cross, incorporating four Ancient columns.

B. Kaufmann/MICHELIN

The elegant, slim columns in the cloisters of St Paul's

Cloisters★ – These probably formed part of the work done by a member of the Vassalletto family (13C) who, like the Cosmati, was skilled in marble incrustation work. The north gallery (backing on to the church) is particularly fine. The great variety among the columns, their marble incrustation picked out in gold and the exquisite workmanship of the mosaic frieze above the arcades make the cloisters a charming composition.

Picture gallery (9) – The gallery displays not only 13C-19C pictures but also a series of engravings showing the basilica; the *St Paul Bible*, a 9C illustrated manuscript; and a reproduction of the slab over St Paul's tomb.

Chapel of Relics (10) – Among the precious articles housed here is a beautiful 15C reliquary cross in silver gilt.

ABBAZIA DELLE TRE FONTANE★ (THREE FOUNTAINS ABBEY)

From Via Laurentina a drive leads to Three Fountains Abbey.

The place known in Antiquity as *Ad Aquas Salvias* is where St Paul was beheaded. Legend has added an epilogue: the Apostle's head bounced three times and three fountains sprouted from the ground.

Pilgrims have been coming here since the Middle Ages. Many oratories were built; one of them, still decorated with traces of 9C painting, is now the entrance gateway. Surrounded by green hillsides and the scent of eucalyptus trees is a group of buildings: a Trappist monastery, a convent of the Little Sisters of Jesus and three churches.

Santa Maria Scala Coeli

Cistercian monks settled here in 1140. The history of the church is connected with one of St Bernard's ecstatic visions: while celebrating mass in the crypt he had a vision of the souls in purgatory ascending into Heaven, released by his intercession. The present church, which was restored in 1925, was built in 1583 by Giacomo della Porta to an octagonal plan beneath a shallow dome.

Behind the altar in the crypt is a room supposed to be where St Paul waited before his execution.

Santi Vincenzo e Anastasio alle Tre Fontane

The church, which is dedicated to **St Vincent** and **St Anastasius**, is the abbey church of the Trappist monks who have occupied the neighbouring monastery since 1868. The origins of the church go back to the 7C, when Pope Honorius I (625-38) built a convent to house some Oriental monks (as at St Sabas).

The church, which was rebuilt in the 13C, is austere in appearance and still retains traces of paintings of the Apostles executed by some of Raphael's pupils.

San Paolo alle Tre Fontane

The church of **St Paul at the Three Fountains** was designed in the 16C by Giacomo della Porta to replace two chapels built on the spot where, according to legend, the fountains had spouted from the earth. A small building commemorating the saint's martyrdom stood here as early as the 7C.

The statues of St Peter and St Paul on the façade are by Nicolas Cordier. The Ancient mosaics set into the floor come from Ostia. The sites of the three fountains are marked by three shrines set at different levels.

Santa Maria Maggiore-Esquilino★★★

This lively, bustling quarter, with its myriad shops, offices and crowded streets, has a distinct ethnic flavour, largely concentrated around the busy market in Piazza Vittorio, which sells mainly clothes and shoes. Oriental shops and supermarkets line the streets surrounding the square.

Location

Michelin map 38 or Michelin spiral atlas of Rome: pp 58-59 L 14, M 14-16). Metro line A: Vittorio Emanuele. Tour: 1hr. Piazza Vittorio is the hub of this district, which extends from the northern slopes of the Esquiline Hill (the Domus Aurea once stood on the southern side, overlooking the Colosseum) and Termini Railway Station.

Neighbouring sights are described in the following chapters: COLOSSEO-CELIO; FORI IMPERIALI; PORTA PIA; SAN GIOVANNI IN LATERANO.

Background

The **Esquiline**, one of the seven hills of Rome, has been inhabited since the 8C BC. It is an uneven plateau with three peaks which the Romans named the **Oppius**, now covered by the Parco Oppio, the **Fagutalis**, which overlooks the Imperial Fora, and the **Cispius**, now crowned by Santa Maria Maggiore.

Long used as a burial ground for poor people, the Esquiline was one of the most sinister parts of Rome. Augustus gave it a new face. He divided the city into 14 districts, one of which was the Esquiline; he arranged for part of it to be given to his friend Maecenas, who built a magnificent villa surrounded by gardens. In the course of time the district came to be coveted by the Emperors themselves and after a series of confiscations it was added to the Imperial domain. After the fire in AD 64 had cleared the ground, Nero built his Golden House on the Oppius *(see COLOSSEO-CELIO).*

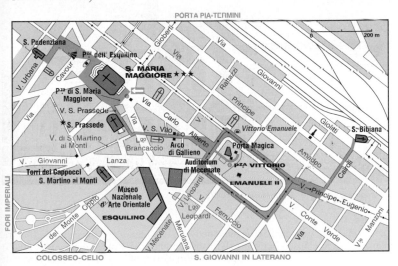

Directory

Special Features

Piazza di Santa Maria Maggiore
The fluted column which stands at the centre is the sole survivor of the eight columns which graced the basilica of Maxentius in the Forum. It was brought here in 1614 on the initiative of Pope Paul V, set up on its base by the architect Carlo Maderno and crowned with a statue of the Virgin.

BASILICA DI SANTA MARIA MAGGIORE★★★ (ST MARY MAJOR)
For information and reservations for the basilica and the loggia call ☎ 06 488 10 94; Fax 06 48 90 43 92.

This church is one of the four Roman basilicas which bear the title "major" (the others are St John Lateran, St Paul Without the Walls and St Peter's in the Vatican) and enjoys the privilege of extraterritoriality conferred by the Lateran Treaty in 1929.

The basilica was built by Sixtus III (432-40) in honour of Mary a year after the Council of Ephesus, at which Nestorius, the Patriarch of Constantinople, had claimed that Mary was not the Mother of God.

Subsequent Popes have left their mark; in their desire to contribute to the glory of the Virgin, they made numerous alterations. The campanile, the highest in Rome, was added in 1377 by Gregory XI. In the 17C and 18C the apse was remodelled. The main façade was given its present appearance in the 18C under Benedict XIV by Ferdinando Fuga (1743-50).

The imposing basilica of Santa Maria Maggiore

Façade
The porch and loggia are sandwiched between two identical wings, although more than a century elapsed between the construction of the one on the right (1605) and the one on the left (1721-43). Like the majority of architects in the first half of the 18C, **Ferdinando Fuga** had a taste for Classical forms, but also adopted certain elements from the Baroque art of Borromini. The façade is enlivened by sculptures, the broken lines of the pediments and the interplay of the openings in the porch and the arcade of the loggia.

In the porch stands a statue of Philip IV of Spain **(1)**, a benefactor of the basilica; it is by a pupil of Algardi (1692). The loggia from which the Pope used to give his blessing *Urbi et Orbi* was added to the original façade, which still retains its early-14C mosaic decoration, restored in the 19C.

Loggia Mosaic★
Access by the steps on the left of the porch.

The upper part – Christ, angels, the evangelistic symbols, the Virgin and the saints – is the work of **Filippo Rusuti** (late 13C), who took over from Pietro Cavallini.

Below are four scenes illustrating the **legend of the basilica,** which was built here late in the 4C by Pope Liberius; the Virgin appeared in a dream to a Giovanni Patrizio, a rich man, and to Pope Liberius, inviting them to build a church in her honour; the site for the sanctuary was to be marked by a fall of snow on the morrow. When the Pope and Patrizio consulted one another they were astonished to find that, in spite of the time of year (5 August 356), there had been a snow-fall on the Esquiline. The Pope drew up a plan of the church; Patrizio financed the construction. The graceful lines, richly apparelled figures and fine, deep per-spectives link these scenes with the Florentine style of Cimabue and Giotto.

Interior★★★

The interior has also undergone many alterations: at the end of the 13C Nicholas IV (1288-92) extended the chancel and, in the middle of the 15C, Cardinal Guillaume d'Estouteville, archpriest of the basilica, covered the aisles with vaulting in keeping with Renaissance taste. Despite that, the interior of this basilica, with its almost perfect proportions and two rows of Ionic columns, is a remarkable example of early Christian architecture; brilliant with colour, it is at its most spectacular on Sundays and feast days.

Mosaics★★★

Those in the nave, on the chancel arch and in the apse are beyond compare.

Nave – Dating from the 5C, they consist of a series of panels above the entabla-ture, which is decorated with a fine frieze of interlacing. They are some of the oldest Christian mosaics in Rome, together with those in Santa Pudenziana, Santa Costanza and the Lateran Baptistry. They are examples of an art which had redis-covered a taste for vivid narrative, after accepting the rigidity of the late Empire. The scenes are taken from the Old Testament with Abraham, Jacob, Moses and Joshua in the leading roles. On the left-hand side of the nave, beginning at the chancel end, are incidents from Genesis:

(2) Melchizedek comes to meet Abraham.

(3) Abraham's dream near the Mamré oak.

(4) The separation of Abraham and Lot.

Next comes the arch opened up in the 17C during the construction of the Pauline Chapel which entailed the destruction of the mosaics at this point. Then:

(5) Isaac blesses Jacob. Esau returns from hunting.

The next panel is a painting.

(6) Rachel tells Laban of the arrival of Jacob, his nephew. Laban and Jacob embrace.

(7) Jacob agrees to serve Laban for seven years and to receive Rachel as his wife.

(8) Jacob reproaches Laban for giving him Leah, his elder daugh-ter, in marriage. Jacob marries Rachel.

(9) Jacob asks Laban for the speckled and spotted sheep. The division of the flock.

(10) God tells Jacob to leave. Jacob announces his departure to the women.

Next between two painted panels:

(11) The meeting of the two brothers, Jacob and Esau.

(12) Hamor and his son Shechem ask Jacob for the hand of his daughter Dinah, whose brothers are angry.

(13) Dinah's brothers insist that the men among Hamor's people be circumcised. Hamor and Shechem explain the situation to their people.

The last three panels on this side are painted.

On the right-hand side of the nave, starting at the chancel end, there is first a painted panel and then:

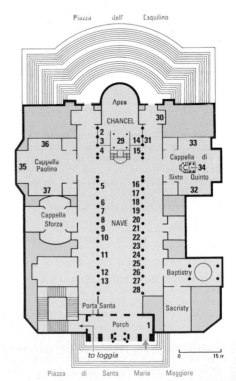

285

(14) Pharaoh's daughter receives Moses. He speaks with the Egyptian doctors.

(15) Moses marries Zipporah. God appears in the burning bush.

Then comes the arch opened up during the construction of Sixtus V's Chapel, which takes the place of the mosaics (1741-50).

(16) The passage of the Red Sea.

(17) Moses and the people of Israel. The miracle of quails.

(18) The salt sea of Mara. The people of Israel reproach Moses who, after praying to God, touches the water with a rod sent by God and makes it fresh. The meeting of Moses and Amalek.

(19) The battle against the people of Amalek and Moses praying on the hillside.

(20) The return of the chiefs of the tribes who had gone to explore the Promised Land. The stoning of Moses, Joshua and Caleb.

(21) The tablets of Law are handed down. The death of Moses. The transport of the Ark.

(22) The passage of the Jordan. Joshua sends spies to Jericho.

(23) The angel of God (the captain of the Lord's host) appears to Joshua. The harlot Rahab helps the spies to scale the walls of Jericho. The return of the spies.

(24) The besieging of Jericho. The procession of the Ark to the sound of trumpets.

(25) The taking of Ai. Joshua before God and among the soldiers.

(26) Joshua fights the Amorites. Hail of stones on Israel's enemies.

(27) The sun and moon stand still upon Gibeon.

(28) Joshua punishes the rebel kings.

The last three panels are paintings.

Chancel arch – The arch dates from the 5C and has the liveliness of the first Christian mosaics. It is divided into four horizontal bands. Probably later than the mosaics in the nave, it shows Byzantine influence:

– In the Annunciation scene *(top row left)*, where Mary is dressed like an Oriental empress;

– In the Epiphany scene *(second row left)*, presented as a sumptuous court reception, where the Child Jesus is sitting on a throne decorated with precious stones. The cities of Jerusalem and Bethlehem, with sheep representing the Apostles, can be seen in the two lower rows.

Apse – This dazzling composition comprises elements taken from a 5C mosaic, which was transformed at the end of the 13C by **Jacopo Torriti** when Nicolas IV rebuilt the apse. All the figures are the work of Torriti, since the earlier mosaic consisted only of birds, foliage and scrolls. The main subject of the composition is the *Crowning of the Virgin*, surrounded by groups of angels and a procession of saints. Kneeling before them are Nicolas IV and Cardinal Colonna.

The four 15C sculptured panels lower down come from the altar of Sixtus IV.

Baldaquin (29)

It was designed by Fuga and is supported on porphyry columns wreathed in fronds of bronze. Unfortunately, it hides some of the mosaic.

Beneath the baldaquin is the **Confessio**, where Pope Pius IX (1846-78) is shown at prayer, resplendent in bronze gilt, marble and frescoes (19C). Fragments thought to belong to Jesus's crib are kept in the silver urn.

Ceiling*

The coffers were decorated with the first gold to come from Peru, which was offered to Pope **Alexander VI**, a Spaniard (1492-1503), by Ferdinand and Isabella of Spain. The Pope continued the work begun by Calixtus III (1455-58) in constructing this ceiling, which is decorated with the arms of the Borgia family to which the two Popes belonged. The roses at the centre of the coffers are 1m/3.75ft in diameter. Vasari, a 16C art historian and author of *Lives of the Artists*, attributes this work to Giuliano da Sangallo (1445-1516).

Floor

The 12C Cosmati work was radically restored by Ferdinando Fuga in the 18C.

Right aisle

The tomb of Cardinal Consalvo Rodriguez **(30)** (late 13C) is typically Gothic (a recumbent figure under a trilobed arch, flanked by angels beneath a mosaic of the Virgin). In the floor is the tombstone **(31)** of the family of Bernini *(qv)*.

Cappella di Sisto Quinto (Sixtus V's Chapel)

The chapel is named after Sixtus V, who, during his five year reign (1585-90), turned Rome into a huge building site with his restorations, conversions and new constructions. His favourite architect was **Domenico Fontana**, to whom he entrusted the design of this chapel. It is almost a church in itself. Designed on the Greek cross plan beneath a dome painted with frescoes, it is resplendent with gilding, stucco and marble. In the right and left arms of the cross are the monumental tombs of Popes Sixtus V **(32)** and Pius V **(33)**, decorated with low-relief sculptures illustrating the great events of their reigns.

Beneath the high altar **(34)** in 1590 Domenico Fontana set up the Oratory of the Crib, which had held the relics of the grotto in Bethlehem since the 7C.

Baptistry

The baptistry is the work of the Baroque architect Flaminio Ponzio. The beautiful porphyry font was decorated in the 19C by Giuseppe Valadier. The high relief of the Assumption on the altar is by Pietro **Bernini**, father of Gian Lorenzo.

Left aisle

It contains, in particular, two beautiful chapels.

Cappella Sforza (Sforza Chapel) – Its highly original architectural style is by Giacomo della Porta, probably from designs by Michelangelo.

Cappella Paolina (Pauline Chapel) – It is also called the **Borghese Chapel**, after the family name of Pope Paul V, who commissioned it in 1611 from Flaminio Ponzio. It is identical in plan to Sixtus V's Chapel but with even more sumptuous decoration. In 1612 Cigoli painted the dome without first subdividing it with ribs; he was the first to follow this course and the result was not perfect. When, some 10 years later, Lanfranco (who also worked on the Pauline Chapel), painted the dome of Sant'Andrea della Valle using the same process, he achieved a masterpiece. The main altar **(35)** is incomparably rich, like a jewel, set with jasper, lapis lazuli, agate and amethyst.

The altarpiece is of a Virgin and Child in the Byzantine style. She may have been painted in the 12C after a 9C Byzantine original. She is greatly venerated among the faithful and has even been attributed to St Luke. She is surrounded by a "glory" of angels in gilded bronze, a feature very popular with Baroque artists. Above the altarpiece is a sculpted panel by Stefano Maderno illustrating the legend of the tracing of the basilica's plan *(see above)*. As in Sixtus V's Chapel, the right and left arms of the cross contain Papal tombs: Clement VIII **(36)** and Paul V **(37)**.

Leave the church by the door at the end of the aisle to the right of the choir.

Walking About

Piazza dell' Esquilino

From here there is a fine **view**★★ of the apse of Santa Maria Maggiore. When the Pauline and Sistine Chapels were added beneath their domes they looked like two separate buildings. Clement IX (1667-69) therefore commissioned Bernini to integrate them with the basilica by altering the apsidal end of the church. **Bernini** conceived a grandiose design, but the excessive cost prevented it from being carried out. The following Pope, Clement X, therefore gave the work to Carlo Rainaldi.

The **Egyptian obelisk** at the centre of the square comes from the Mausoleum of Augustus. Sixtus V ordered it to be moved and set up by Domenico Fontana, a specialist in such matters.

Turn left into Via Urbana.

Santa Pudenziana

The church, dedicated to St Pudens or the Roman virgin St Potentiana, is one of the oldest in Rome and is now very popular with the local Filipino community, who have their own chaplain here. Legend tells how Senator Pudens, who lived in a house on this site, welcomed Peter under his roof. In the 2C a bathhouse stood on the site. Late in the 4C a church *(ecclesia pudentiana)* was established in the baths. The similarity between the girl's name Pudentiana and the adjective derived from Pudens turned Pudentiana into the daughter of Pudens. Pudentiana, like her sister Praxedes, was not martyred, but both are shown with the martyrs whose bodies they prepared for burial.

The façade was repaired in the 19C. The bell-tower dates from the 12C, as does the elegant doorway, with its fluted columns and its sculpted frieze inset with five medallions. The interior shows the signs of many changes: in 1589 the dome was built and the chancel altered so that several figures in the fine 4C **mosaic**★ were lost. It is one of the oldest examples of a Christian mosaic in Rome. The way in which Christ is represented, the brilliant colours and the lively figures show the persistence of Roman qualities in Christian mosaic art before it was influenced by Byzantium and its stylised forms.

Excavations – *For information on opening hours, call* ☎ *06 48 14 622.*
Excavations carried out under the church have uncovered the remains of Pudens' house, mosaics and baths which partly covered it at the end of the 2C, as well as the Roman road built in the 3C. A 6C fresco depicts St Peter with the sisters St Pudentiana and St Praxedes.

Return to Piazza di Santa Maria Maggiore and beyond the church bear right into Via Santa Prassede.

Santa Prassede★

Entrance in the right aisle. The brick façade with the main doors giving on to a small courtyard can be seen through the entrance arch *(closed)*, which opens into Via di San Martino ai Monti beneath a loggia supported on two columns.

The church is an old *titulus*, ie a private house where Christian services were held in Antiquity. The present building was put up by Paschal I in 822.

It was built to the basilical plan, the nave and aisles separated by two rows of columns directly supporting the architrave. It was later altered by the addition of three transverse arches in the nave, and a coffered ceiling in the 19C. The frescoes date from the 16C-17C.

Chancel mosaics★ – They date from the 9C and show the influence of both Byzantine traditionalism and Carolingian art. Colour is paramount and no longer used in half-tones. Against a background of sky quite lacking in depth, the figure of Christ is flanked by St Peter and St Paul presenting Praxedes and Pudentiana. The other two figures are St Zenon and Pope Paschal I offering his church (his square halo an indication that he was alive at the time). The two palms represent the Old and New Testaments and the phoenix on the one on the left symbolises the Resurrection.

The chancel arch shows *(upper part)* the arrival of the Elect in the Celestial City of Jerusalem with groups of the Blessed *(lower part)* (spoiled in the 16C by the balconies).

Cappella di San Zenone★★ – *Right aisle.* St Zenon's Chapel was built between 817 and 824 by Pope Paschal I. The doorway is made up of various elements taken from earlier buildings. Above this are several portrait medallions arranged in two arcs, one centred on Christ surrounded by the Apostles and the other on the Virgin and Child surrounded by various saints. The two portraits in the rectangular panels at the bottom of the arrangement are much later than the 9C.

The interior is covered in mosaics with a gold background *(time switch)*: on the central vault Christ, in strict Byzantine style, is supported by four angels; above the opening to the left of the altar is the Virgin accompanied by two saints and the mother of Paschal I, Theodora Episcopa, with a blue halo; the mosaic above the opening to the right of the altar was spoiled in the 13C when an oratory was built to house a fragment of the scourging column. This relic is greatly venerated by pilgrims, especially during Holy Week.

Take Via S. Vito.

Arco di Gallieno

The **Arch of Gallienus** was erected in 262 in honour of the Emperor Gallienus (253-68), who was assassinated by some Illyrian officers. It stands on the site of the Esquiline Gate (Porta Esquilina) in the Servian Wall *(see plan of Rome during the Empire)*. Traces of this wall, which was probably started in the 6C BC and several times repaired, can be seen in Via Carlo Alberto (next to the church of St Vito e Modesto).

Piazza Vittorio

The square is usually thronged with people attending the large ethnic market here. It was laid out in the late 19C by Gaetano Koch and other architects, with arcades at street level, as in Turin.

In the north corner of the square are the ruins of a huge 3C fountain, which was adorned with the "Trophies of Marius". The adjacent **Magic Gate** (Porta Magica) continues to excite speculation; the signs inscribed round the doorway (bricked up) have never been deciphered.

Take Via Principe Eugenio, then turn left into Via Cairoli.

Santa Bibiana

The church was rebuilt in the 17C and was one of Bernini's first architectural projects. His **statue★** of St Bibiana (or Viviana) *(inside above the altar)* is also one of his early works; note the pictorial effect of the left hand gathering up the folds of the garment.

Worth a Visit

San Martino ai Monti

Open Mon-Sat, 9am-noon and 3-5.30pm. Book at least 10 days in advance by writing to Ufficio parrocchiale di S. Martino ai Monti, Via Monte Oppio 28, 00184 Roma, or by calling ☎ 06 48 73 166 or 06 48 73 126.

This venerable church, dedicated to St Martin, was founded in the 5C next to a *titulus* existing in the 3C in the house of Equitius *(the underground remains can be visited: ask in the sacristy)*.

The church was completely transformed in the 17C. The interior was divided into a nave and two aisles by two rows of Ancient marble columns with 5C capitals (the bases date from the 17C). The aisles are decorated with frescoes of Roman landscapes and the story of the Prophet Elijah. At either end of the left aisle are views of the interiors of the old basilicas of St Peter in the Vatican and of St John Lateran (before the intervention of Borromini) by Filippo Gagliardi (17C).

Leave the church and walk around to the apse.

The apse of the church of San Martino ai Monti dates from the 9C.

In the square, the two **Cappocci towers**, despite extensive restoration, still evoke the power of the noble families in the Middle Ages.

Museo Nazionale d'Arte Orientale

Open Tue, Thu, Sun and public holidays, 8.30am-7pm; Mon, Wed, Fri and Sat, 8.30am-2pm. Closed first and third Mon in the month, 1 Jan, 1 May and Christmas. Guided tours available (1hr 30min). €4. ☎ 06 48 74 415 or 06 48 75 077; Fax 06 48 70 624.

On the *piano nobile* of **Palazzo Brancaccio** is the National Collection of Oriental Art. On the right before going upstairs, is the nymphaeum designed by Francesco Gai, who was also charged with the interior decoration of the palace.

The museum charts the history of the Orient starting with the Near and Middle East, particularly Iran. The first section of the exhibition is particularly interesting, it illustrates through artefacts from Shahr-i-Sokta daily life in the third to the second millennia BC: social organisation, pottery, tools, the working of semi-precious stones. The neighbouring rooms are dedicated to areas of western Iran: note the intricate zoomorphic figures in bronze from Luristan.

Two further sections are given over to exhibits from the Far East, notably Tibet and Nepal, Gandhara and finally China.

Auditorium di Mecenate

Open Apr-Sep, 9am-7pm; rest of the year, 9am-5pm; Sun, 9am-1.30pm. Closed Mon and public holidays. €2.58. ☎ 06 67 10 32 38; Fax 06 67 10 31 18.

The **Auditorium of Maecenas**, part of the luxurious Villa of Maecenas (early 1C), which was surrounded by large gardens, was discovered in 1874. Steps lead down to a vestibule and a large hall with a tiered exedra. The underground structure, with its drainage system and fresco decoration of gardens and landscapes, was probably a nymphaeum originally, but Maecenas used it as an auditorium where he entertained his learned friends.

Terme di Caracalla★★

This pleasant district of shady trees and abundant greenery is home to Ancient Roman ruins and small medieval churches. From the impressive FAO building, follow the original Appia Antica, now a busy thoroughfare leading south to the EUR district, and step back in history at the Baths of Caracalla. Once frequented by the Ancient Romans, the baths offered facilities for exercise and bathing, as well as providing a setting where scholars could meet and enjoy conversation. An enjoyable end to a stroll is along one of the most evocative sections of the old Aurelian Wall.

Location

Michelin map 38 or Michelin spiral atlas of Rome: pp 71-72 P 13, R 13 14, S 14-15. Metro line B: Circo Massimo. Tour: 2.5km/1.5mi – about 3hr including the baths (1hr). The area surrounding the Baths of Caracalla is situated inside the Aurelian Walls, to the south of the Colosseum and Circus Maximus. The district of San Giovanni lies to the northeast, beyond the Caelian Hill. *Those visitors travelling here by Metro should refer to the Walking About section below.*

Neighbouring sights are described in the following chapters: APPIA ANTICA; AVENTINO; COLOSSEO-CELIO.

> **WHERE TO EAT**
> See "Where to Eat" in the Practical Points section at the beginning of the guide.

Special Features

TERME DI CARACALLA★★★ (BATHS OF CARACALLA)

Open summer, 9am-1hr before dusk; winter, 9am-5.30pm (last admission 1hr before closing time). Closed Mon afternoon, 1 Jan and Christmas. €5, €20 for a "Roma archeologica" card, valid for nine archaeological sites. ☎ 06 39 08 071; Fax 06 39 75 09 50; pierreci@pierreci.it

Four sets of baths had already been built – by Agrippa, by Nero on the Campus Martius, by Titus near the Golden House and by Trajan on the Aventine – when the Emperor Antoninus Caracalla began the largest baths Rome had ever seen

(11ha/25 acres); only Diocletian's Baths were to be more extensive. Work started on the baths in AD 212 and they were opened in AD 216. They were finished by Elagabalus (AD 218-22) and Alexander Severus (AD 222-35), the last two Emperors of the Severan dynasty.

The sober exterior concealed a contrastingly rich interior: floors paved with marble and mosaic, walls covered with mosaic and gilded stucco work; the white marble capitals and cornices contrasting with the multicoloured marble, porphyry and granite of the columns. The huge building, with its massive walls and bold vaulting (30m/98ft high), was much admired; it offered facilities for 1 600 bathers at one time and was able to cater for 6 000 people a day. The Romans used the baths daily, around noon at the end of a day's work. The poorest people were not excluded, although they had fewer slaves than the rich to assist them with their ablutions. Baths were an important element in Roman life; they offered facilities for keeping fit through bathing and physical exercise, as well as libraries for the cultivation of the mind. They were also, however, places of assignation, and by Caracalla's time the Romans were already denouncing the notorious manners of such establishments.

The Baths of Caracalla were in use until 537, when the Goths under Witigis damaged the aqueducts which supplied water to Rome. **Shelley**'s poem *Prometheus Unbound* "was chiefly written upon the mountainous ruins of the Baths of Caracalla".

Excavations carried out in the 16C (by Cardinal Farnese for the construction of his magnificent *palazzo* in the square of the same name), and later in the 19C and 20C, have uncovered magnificent statues, vases and mosaics, in addition to a **mithraeum** (temple of Mithras) in the northeast corner, and a network of underground tunnels. These tunnels were used by horse-drawn carts transporting wood to the 50 ovens that once heated the baths and saunas.

Plan

See above. The baths consisted of a central block enclosed by a wall with gateways opening into Via Nova; this runs at the foot of the Aventine, parallel with the Appian Way. The southwest side of the enclosure was almost entirely taken up with water tanks screened by an amphitheatre, on either side of which were two pavilions containing the libraries. The bays in the southeast and northwest sides housed meeting rooms known as *diaetae*.

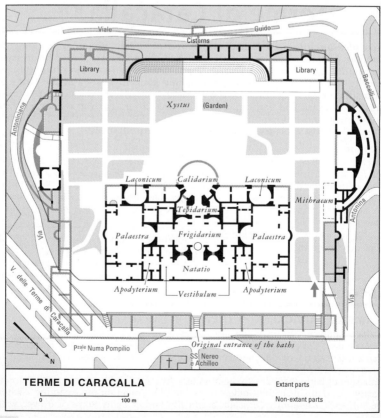

Baths of Caracalla

The principal rooms *(calidarium, tepidarium, frigidarium)* were at the heart of the central block; symmetrically arranged on either side were the secondary rooms (changing rooms, gymnasiums, steam baths). On entering the building the bathers separated, some to one side, some to the other, to meet again in the main rooms.

Tour

After passing the chambers *(right)*, which were perhaps used for meetings, one enters *(left)* the central block. Immediately on the right is an oval room *(laconicum)*, where the temperature was kept constantly high for use as a Turkish bath. This leads to the gymnasium *(palaestra)*, where some coloured mosaic fragments can still be seen on the floor; note also the black and white mosaics adorned with marine motifs which have fallen from the terraces of the upper floors and now stand against the walls. In the changing room *(apodyterium)*, a fair amount of the mosaic floor is still intact. Next comes the swimming pool *(natatio)*; the fresco *(right)* has a religious theme and was probably added in the 17C, when the baths housed the oratory of St Philip Neri. The tour returns to the startingpoint symmetrically via the second changing room and the second gymnasium, which has fine mosaics. The Romans followed the routine prescribed by their doctors. From the changing rooms (traces of fine mosaics on the floor) they went into the gymnasiums, where they indulged in various forms of exercise; it is such a setting that Petronius described in his *Satyricon*, when Encolpius and his friends meet the rich Trimalchio, a "bald old man ... who played ball with his long-haired slaves ...".

A typical day at the baths – Perspiring after the exercise, the bather went on into an oval room heated to a very high temperature *(laconicum)*; the heat induced greater perspiration. The heating system was very efficient; hot air from huge stoves in the basement circulated beneath the floors, which were supported on sturdy brick pillars, and spread into ducts in the walls.

Next the bather passed into the *calidarium* for a very hot bath, after which he scraped his skin to remove all impurities. The *calidarium* was a huge circular room (34m/112ft in diameter), covered by a dome; some of the supporting pillars can still be seen. Bathers from both sides of the building met in the *calidarium*. From here they went on into the *tepidarium* for a cooler bath, before plunging into the bracing water of the cold bath *(frigidarium)*. They could then take a swim in the open-air swimming pool *(natatio)*.

After bathing, Trimalchio, who followed the latest fashion, went off in his litter to carouse. Less wealthy or more serious Romans stayed to talk to their friends, to walk in the gardens or to read in the libraries until the baths closed. The following day they would all be back again.

Walking About

Visitors can either begin this tour from the Circo Massimo metro station or directly from the Baths of Caracalla. In the case of the latter, see the church of Santi Nereo e Achilleo below.

The **Porta Capena** is a gate in the defensive wall built by **Servius Tullius** in the 6C BC. It was rebuilt at the end of the 4C BC, after its weakness had been made apparent by the invading Gauls. It was here, according to Livy, that in the reign of Tullus Hostilius (672-640 BC) the last of the **Horatii**, who had defeated the **Curiatii** of Alba, slew his sister with his sword because she had dared to weep for her fiancé, one of the Curiatii; "Let that be the fate of any Roman who mourns the enemy".

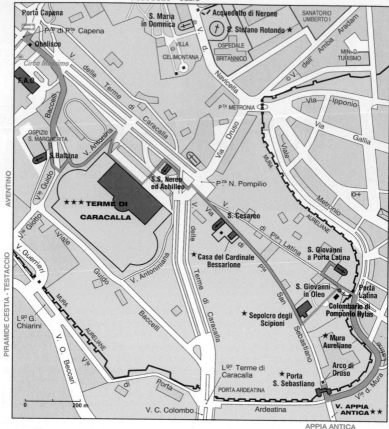

An **obelisk** (obelisco), brought back from Axum, a religious town in Ethiopia, in 1937 and soon to be returned to its country of origin, marks the beginning of Viale delle Terme di Caracalla, which is flanked by umbrella pines and flowering laurels.
Take Viale delle Terme di Caracalla and bear right into Via Guido Baccelli.
On the right stands the building of the **FAO** (Food and Agriculture Organisation), an agency of the United Nations, which employs over 3 000 people of all nationalities. It studies food production, control of plant and animal diseases and experimentation with new strains.

Santa Balbina

Entrance is usually permitted from the courtyard of Santa Margherita rest home (casa di riposo), to the right of the church. Open 8.30-11.30am. No charge. ☎ 06 57 80 207.
In 1927 the church underwent a thorough restoration, which returned it to its medieval simplicity. It was probably a 4C house converted into a place of worship. A pitched roof covers a single nave punctuated by recessed chapels and lit by high barred windows.
On the right of the entrance is Cardinal Surdi's **tomb★**, bearing a recumbent Gothic figure and decorated with multicoloured marble inlay in the Cosmati style (1295). In the fourth chapel on the right the low relief showing Mary and John the Baptist standing by the Cross is a fine sculpture by Mino del Reame (15C); it came from the medieval church of St Peter in the Vatican.
The third chapel contains the remains of some 13C frescoes.
The *Schola Cantorum*, where the choristers stood, has been reconstructed in front of the high altar.
Behind the high altar is the **episcopal chair★**, a fine piece of Cosmati work (13C). The frescoes in the apse are 17C.
Beyond the church turn left into Via Antonina and then sharp right. Turn left in front of the Baths of Caracalla.

Santi Nereo e Achilleo

Open from the first week after Easter to Oct, daily (except Tue), 4.30-6.30pm. ☎ 06 57 57 996.
There was a little church here in the 4C called *Titulus Fasciolae*. Its presence on this site is explained by the legend of the bandage (fasciola) which had been bound round St Peter's leg to cover the sores caused by the chains which had held him

in the Mamertine Prison; when Peter fled from Rome in fear of the fate which awaited him there, the bandage fell from his leg on this spot, which was venerated as a place of worship. A little further on along the Appian Way came St Peter's meeting with Christ and his question *"Domine, quo vadis?" (see APPIA ANTICA)*. The church was completely rebuilt by Leo III (795-816) and later restored by Sixtus IV (1471-84). In 1596 the incumbent appointed to the church was Clement VIII's confessor, Cardinal Baronius, who had a great devotion to St Nereus and St Achilleus. He had their relics transferred from Domitilla's Catacombs and converted the church into a handsome sanctuary for them. He retained the basilical plan, with its pitched roof and the octagonal pillars dating from the 15C restoration which divided the nave and aisles. He transferred the high altar from the crypt of St Paul Without the Walls, decorated it with Cosmati work and crowned it with an attractive baldaquin.

The left-hand reading desk *(ambo)* stands on a porphyry base which came from the Baths of Caracalla. Baronius commissioned Pomarancio to paint the walls, but the mosaic on the chancel arch dates from the reign of Leo III and shows Byzantine influence. The mosaic has been much restored and is eclipsed by the painting in the apse. On the back of the bishop's throne, which is adorned with beautiful medieval lions, Baronius had engraved a passage from the sermon given by St Gregory over the two martyrs' tomb.

From Piazzale Numa Pompilio take Via di Porta San Sebastiano.

Via di Porta San Sebastiano is bordered by buildings of historical and architectural interest set in attractive rural surroundings.

San Cesareo

To visit the church contact the custodian at Via di Porta San Sebastiano 4. Donation welcome.

Little is known of the church's history before 1600, when Clement VIII entrusted its restoration to Cardinal Baronius. The latter followed contemporary taste in the coffered ceiling bearing the arms of Clement VIII and in the paintings by **Cavaliere d'Arpino** on the upper walls of the nave. Elsewhere he tried to reproduce the decoration of a medieval church: the marble facing on the chancel screen, the pulpit, the altar and the bishop's throne were composed of rich Cosmati fragments; the apse and chancel arch are decorated with mosaics from drawings by Cavaliere d'Arpino. There is some Renaissance work: the two angels drawing back the curtains before the *confessio (below the altar)* and the pretty little fresco of the Madonna and Child *(above the throne)*.

Beneath the church is the floor of a 2C bathhouse *(apply to the custodian)*, paved with a marine mosaic in black and white.

Continue along Via S. Sebastiano to the Casa del Cardinale Bessarione and the Sepolcro degli Scipioni (see Worth a Visit below). Turn left immediately after the Sepolcro degli Scipioni to reach the temple of San Giovanni in Oleo.

San Giovanni in Oleo

Key available from the rector of S. Giovanni a Porta Latina. This small octagonal temple was built in the Renaissance style in 1509 by Benoit Adam, a Frenchman and member of the Rota (Roman Catholic ecclesiastical court); over the door he placed his arms and his motto *"Au plaisir de Dieu"* (at God's pleasure). The oratory commemorates an event in the martyrdom of St John the Evangelist, which took place during the reign of Domitian; St John was supposed to have emerged unscathed from a cauldron of boiling oil.

Turn left into Via di Porta Latina, then right into Via di S. Giovanni a Porta Latina.

San Giovanni a Porta Latina

The church of **St John at the Latin Gate** occupies a charming **site★**; the peaceful forecourt, flanked by the campanile, is decorated by a medieval well and shaded by a cedar tree.

The beautifully simple interior is decorated with 12C frescoes; although much damaged, they are a fine example of Romanesque painting.

Return to Via di Porta Latina.

Porta Latina (Latin Gate)

This gate in the Aurelian Wall (Mura Aureliane) was restored by Honorius (5C) and again by Belisarius (6C). The keystone bears a Greek cross on the town side and the chi-rho on the outside.

Turn right outside the gate into Viale delle Mura Latine, which skirts the city wall.

Mura Aureliane★

Work on the wall was initiated under the Emperor Aurelian in the 3C as the existing walls could no longer contain the expanding city. Punctuated by a series of towers, remains of which are still in evidence today, this wall is a compelling piece of Roman civil engineering, notably between the Porta Latina and Porta San Sebastiano *(the section in the opposite direction to Porta Metronia is nonetheless interesting, and may be seen from bus n° 218)*.

Access up onto the wall itself is from Porta San Sebastiano *(see Worth a Visit below)*.

Porta San Sebastiano* (St Sebastian Gate)

The gate is without doubt the most spectacular of the gates of Rome, with its base of tall marble blocks supporting crenellated towers. Known as the Porta Appia in Ancient times, it was constructed by Aurelian (AD 271-75) when he built his defensive wall; it has been strengthened several times, particularly by the Emperor Honorius, who carried out fortifying work along the full length of the wall between 401 and 402, in the face of invasion by the Goths. The gate now houses the **Museo delle Mura** *(see Worth a Visit below)*. **Arco di Druso** (Arch of Drusus)

The arch dates from the 2C AD and was not therefore raised in honour of Drusus (39-38 BC), the younger brother of the Emperor Tiberius. It was used by Caracalla (AD 211-17) to support the aqueduct which supplied water to his baths.

Worth a Visit

Casa del Cardinale Bessarione* (Cardinal Bessarion's House)

Open by appointment only. €2.07. ☎ 06 67 10 32 38; Fax 06 67 10 31 18.

This handsome house, surrounded by gardens and furnished with fine Renaissance pieces, belonged to Cardinal John Bessarion, the Humanist scholar (c 1402-72). In 1439 he attended the Council of Florence and was one of the authors of the union between the Greek and Roman Churches. Pope Nicholas V, who started the Vatican library, invited him to translate Aristotle.

Sepolcro degli Scipioni* (Scipio Family Tomb)

Via di Porta S. Sebastiano 9. Closed for restoration at the time of going to press. For further information, call ☎ 06 67 10 20 70 or 06 67 10 38 19; Fax 06 68 92 115.

Before the construction of the Aurelian Wall this site was beyond the town boundary and could, therefore, according to Roman custom, be used as a burial ground.

The Scipios belonged to one of the greatest patrician families, which died out at the end of the Republic. As members of the Cornelia clan *(gens)*, the men all bore the name Cornelius Scipio, preceded by their own individual name (often abbreviated to an initial letter), and sometimes followed by a nickname.

The Scipio family tomb was discovered in 1614 and restored in 1926. The funeral inscriptions constitute a remarkable document of the Republican period and of the infancy of Latin literature. Their concentration on the dead man's public spiritedness and his moral rectitude reveal the mentality of those days, when Roman civilisation was being forged.

Tour – The tomb is hollowed out of a low hill. It consists of passages roughly arranged in a square. The sarcophagi, carved from a single block of stone or composed of separate panels assembled together, are placed in the passages or in recesses made in the walls. The tomb was probably full by the middle of the 2C BC, so an annexe *(to the right of the original square)* was excavated. It was at this period that the entrance façade was constructed in the northwest corner.

The first person to be buried here was L Cornelius Scipio Barbatus; consul in 298 BC, he

SEPOLCRO DEGLI SCIPIONI

3C BC   c 150 BC

fought against the Etruscans. His sarcophagus **(1)** – the original is in the Pius-Clementine Museum in the Vatican – bears a description of his exploits.

Of his son's sarcophagus **(2)**, only a few fragments and the inscription remain.

Opposite is a fine inscription **(3)** dedicated to a young man of the Scipio family who died at the age of 20; his courage made up for his lack of years.

In the next passage lay Scipio Africanus's son, P Cornelius Scipio **(4)**; as Augur, in 190 BC, he interpreted the auspices; he was also a priest of Jupiter *(Flamen Dialis)*, one of the highest religious offices. In all, about 30 people were buried in the tomb.

The inscription **(5)** to be found in a small recess in the later part of the tomb refers to the burial of a member of the Cornelius Lentulus family, which inherited the tomb during the Empire and buried some of its dead there.

In the northwest corner of the tomb a lime kiln was constructed in the Middle Ages for converting marble fragments into chalk.

Columbarium

Below ground in front of the Scipio tomb. The *columbarium* was a type of communal tomb which became popular at the beginning of the Empire. It consisted of a chamber fitted with rows of recesses in which the cinerary urns were placed. The wealthy families built them for the ashes of their slaves and freedmen.

Nearby are the remains of a three-storey house, built in the 3C on top of the Scipio tomb, without regard for the site's venerable connections.

Columbarium of Pomponius Hylas

Next to the small temple of San Giovanni in Oleo. Open by appointment only ☎ 06 67 10 20 70 or 06 67 10 38 19; Fax 06 68 92 115.

Part way down the Ancient stair which leads into the chamber is a recess decorated with a mosaic which contained the urns of one C Pomponius Hylas and his wife. The *columbarium* itself is decorated with stucco work and fine paintings and probably dates from the Julio-Claudian period (AD 31-68).

Museo delle Mura (Wall Museum)

In Porta San Sebastiano. Open Apr-Oct, 9am-7pm; rest of the year, 9am-5pm. Closed Mon, 1 Jan, 1 May and Christmas. €2.58. ☎ 06 70 47 52 84; Fax 06 68 92 115.

The museum, which is housed within the gate, consists of five rooms displaying documents and models which show how the wall has changed from Antiquity to the present day. It is possible to walk along part of the wall westwards as far as Via Christoforo Colombo.

Trastevere★★

Trastevere, on the right bank of the Tiber, was for centuries a popular district inhabited by artisans and small traders, known for the proud, independent nature of its residents. Today, this independence and the unique personality of Trastevere is celebrated every July during the traditional "Festa de Noantri". Trastevere is now highly fashionable, attracting wealthy Italian residents and those from abroad, who are drawn here by the vibrant atmosphere of the district, with its picturesque, narrow streets and small piazzas, excellent bakeries and traditional trattorias. The pace of life here tends to be slow during the day, but the quarter comes alive in the evening, especially in its northern section, where most of the nightclubs and restaurants are situated.

The famous Porta Portese market is held in Trastevere every Sunday. This vast flea market is one of the largest in the city and is well worth a visit for its colourful local atmosphere.

Location

Michelin map 38 or Michelin spiral atlas of Rome: pp 55-56 M 10, N 10-11. Tour: 2hr. This district, which is divided into two by Viale Trastevere, is situated on the opposite bank of the Tiber to the historic centre of Rome, facing Isola Tiberina. The Janiculum Hill and the vast green area of Villa Pamphili lie to the west.

Neighbouring sights are described in the following chapters: BOCCA DELLA VERITÀ; GIANICOLO; ISOLA TIBERINA-TORRE ARGENTINA.

Background

Trastevere (from *trans Tiberim* meaning "over the Tiber") was not originally part of Rome; it was the beginning of Etruscan territory.

From the time of the Republic it was inhabited mainly by Jews and Syrians and was incorporated into Rome by Augustus as the 14th administrative district. Not far from the present San Cosimato Hospital, Augustus created a *naumachia*, a vast pool where naval warfare spectacles were mounted. As a result of the proximity of the Mediterranean port of Ostia and the river port of Ripa Grande, trade flourished in the district, especially in food produce. This continues to this day in the number of small groceries and trattorias in the area and contrasted with the artisanal trades concentrated on the other side of the river.

Few public buildings were situated here; rather utilitarian services, such as a 2C fire station near Via dei Genovesi, of which traces were discovered in the 19C. Among the religious buildings is a Syrian sanctuary, traces of which were found under the Villa Sciarra near Via Emilio Dandolo.

In the 3C the whole of Trastevere was enclosed by the **Aurelian Wall** (Mura Aureliane) pierced by three gateways: the Porta Settimiana to the north, the Porta Aurelia (now Porta S. Pancrazio) (*see plan under GIANICOLO*) to the west and to the south the Porta Portuensis (further south than the present Porta Portese).

In the Middle Ages, however, some powerful Roman families had palaces in Trastevere. The tradition persisted under the Renaissance and into the 18C (*see GIANICOLO*).

Trastevere has never lost its popular character. Throughout the centuries the inhabitants have kept their reputation of stout fellows ready to lend their strength and courage to a revolutionary cause. The district has sometimes been decried, but Stendhal thought it superb; it was, he said, "full of energy".

Poets who celebrated Rome in the local dialect have always found a response there. The exploits of the Trasteverians, who defied the inhabitants of the Santa Maria Maggiore district with catapults, have been the subject of several sonnets in Roman folklore. Even nowadays the cafés of Trastevere re-enact the comic efforts of Meo Patacca in his dogged defence of his district against Marco Pepe.

Walking About

Torre degli Anguillara (Anguillara Tower)

The 13C tower, attached to a small palace of the same name, recalls one of the most powerful Roman families. Whether as warriors, magistrates, outlaws, forgers or clerics, the Anguillara were at the forefront of events from the Middle Ages to the Renaissance.

The palace, built in the 15C, underwent major restoration in the 19C and now houses the Institute for Dante Studies.

Directory

WHERE TO EAT

See "Where to Eat" in the Practical Points section at the beginning of the guide.

TAKING A BREAK

Sisini – *Via S. Francesco a Ripa 137* – ☎ 06 58 97 110 – *Closed Sun.* – 🖵. As well as pizzas, this pizzeria serves some first courses, such as cannelloni or lasagne, as well as excellent *crostini con fiori di zucca* (a type of toast with courgette flowers).

Frontoni – *Viale Trastevere 52* – ☎ 06 58 12 436 – *Closed Sun morning*. This pizzeria also operates as a snack bar until late in the evening. Serves traditional Roman deep-fried antipasti, as well as pizza, washed down with a selection of 120 draught or bottled beers.

Latteria Ugolini – *Via della Lungaretta 161* – ☎ 06 58 16 440 – *Open Mon-Sat, 8am-1.30pm and 5-8.15pm*. This old dairy is one of the few in Rome to have retained its old marble counter. Here customers can sit and taste traditional Gentilini biscuits, once produced in the biscuit factory of the same name.

Sora Mirella – *Lungotevere degli Anguillara*. Enjoy traditional Roman *grattachecce* with a wonderful view of the Isola Tiberina. The "superfrutta" with kiwi, strawberries and melon is available on request and is slightly more expensive.

Fonte d'Oro – *Lungotevere Sanzio*. This kiosk is always very crowded on warm summer evenings. The excellent mixed fruit and tropical fruit *grattachecca* are full of flavour but not too sweet.

Laboratorio a Trastevere – *Vicolo del Cinque 40*. After a night out at one of Trastevere's many nightclubs, enjoy a freshly baked croissant or pastry at this excellent *pasticceria*.

SHOPPING

Al Tempo Ritrovato – *Via dei Fienaroli 31d/32* – ☎ 06 58 17 724 – libreriadelledonne@libero.it – *Open Tue-Sat, 10.30am-1.30pm and 4-8pm; Mon, 4-8pm*. Completely dedicated to work by women writers, this bookshop also acts as a research and documentation centre for women's studies.

Bibli – *Via dei Fienaroli 27/28* – ☎ 06 58 84 097 – *Open Tue-Sun, 11am-midnight; Mon, 5pm-midnight*. This bookshop is divided into different sections and has a number of Internet terminals, as well as a tearoom and restaurant which serves brunch on Sunday mornings.

Biscottificio Artigiano Innocenti – *Viale della Luce 21*. This is the ideal spot to buy a souvenir of Rome. Savoury and sweet snacks include fried puff-pastry cakes, *castagnola* cake, almond biscuits, teacakes and small pizzas.

Lattonieri – *Piazza de Renzi 22*. The old trade of the tinsmith is still practised here today. Objects made from tin include traditional Italian coffee pots, lanterns and oil cruets.

Porta Portese Flea Market – See "Shopping" in the Practical Points section at the beginning of the guide.

TRASTEVERE IN FESTA

Trastevere takes on a festive air from 15-30 July, when its streets are lined with stalls and crowds of people flock to the district for the popular Festa de Noantri.

San Crisogono

The church of **St Chryso-gonus**, which dates from the 5C, bears witness to the many and various changes which have taken place in it over the centuries.

The **belfry**, which was erected in the 12C when the church was almost entirely rebuilt, was altered in the 16C by the addition of a spire.

The **façade** is the work of **Giovanni Battista Soria**, who was put in charge of the refurbishment of the building in the 17C by Cardinal

The faint outline of a fresco adds to the attraction of this picturesque, crumbling façade

Scipione Borghese, a nephew of the Pope and incumbent of the church at the time.

Interior★ – Only the basilical plan of a nave and two aisles has survived from the 12C; the floor is 13C work by Roman marble masons. The overall effect – half-Mannerist, half-Baroque – was created in the 17C by GB Soria, who retained the Ancient pillars, refashioned their capitals in stucco, opened up great windows in the nave to let in more light and installed a fine coffered ceiling of complex design, showing the arms of Cardinal Borghese. Two monolithic porphyry columns support the chancel arch. The baldaquin is also the work of Soria. The fine wood carving in the chancel dates from 1863. The mosaic in the apse, showing the Virgin and Child with St James and St Chrysogonus, comes from the Cavallini School (late 13C).

Palaeo-Christian church – *Access from the sacristy by an awkward iron stair. Open Mon-Sat, 7-11am and 4-7pm; Sun and public holidays, 8am-1pm and 4-7pm. Closed for visits during church services. €2.* ☎ *06 58 18 225; Fax 06 58 10 076.*

At a depth of 6m/20ft below floor level archaeologists have discovered traces of the 5C building which was altered in the 8C and abandoned in the 12C, when the present church was built.

Here is the lower part of the apse (probably partially 5C) below which Gregory III hollowed out a *confessio* in the 8C; it follows the curve of the apse before drawing in on each side into a horseshoe shape, thus creating a semicircular corridor; it is

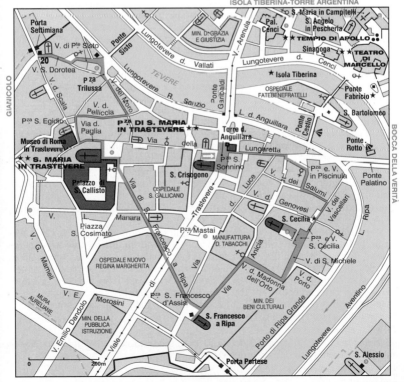

divided in two by a straight passage, at the end of which (towards the nave) is a relic chamber. This passage and the apse still bear traces of 8C painting. There are 10C paintings on the walls of the semicircular corridor.

The baptistry (left), now divided into two by a wall, was used for the baptism of early Christians.

From Piazza Sonnino take Via della Lungaretta, Piazza in Piscinula, Via dei Salumi and Via dei Vascellari to reach Piazza Santa Cecilia.

Santa Cecilia★

Open 9.30am-12.30pm and 4.30-6.30pm. Crypt: €2.50. ☎ 06 58 99 289.

A sanctuary dedicated to St Cecilia existed in a private house on this site in the 5C. Pope Paschal I (817-24) replaced it with a church, which was much altered in the 16C, 18C and 19C.

The church is preceded by a courtyard planted with flower beds around a large Antique vase. A fine 12C campanile flanks the façade; this was remodelled in the 18C, but the 12C porch, with its Ancient columns and mosaic frieze, was preserved.

Interior – The interior has lost its overall medieval appearance, although it still retains the **mosaic** with which the apse was adorned by Paschal I in the 9C. The influence that Byzantine art exerted on Roman mosaic workers in earlier centuries is evident in the way the figures are presented: on Christ's right – St Paul, St Agatha and Pascal I, with a square halo since he was still alive; on the left – St Peter, St Valerian and St Cecilia; the lively postures and the beautiful colours are also typically Roman.

The **baldaquin** over the high altar is by **Arnolfo di Cambio** (1293); it is eight years later than a similar work by the same artist for St Paul Without the Walls and shows a growing heaviness of style and the influence of Classical works; in the left back corner is an equestrian statue of a saint, reminiscent of the statue of Marcus Aurelius now in the Capitoline Museum.

The statue of **St Cecilia★** *(below the altar)*, a fine sculpture by Stefano Maderno (1599), recalls the history and legend of St Cecilia. Paschal I (817-24) who was desperately searching all the Christian cemeteries for the remains of St Cecilia, was guided by a dream. He found the saint's corpse lying beside her husband, St Valerian, in a catacomb on the Old Appian Way. He had them transferred immediately to a place beneath the altar. Seven centuries later, during the reign of Clement VIII, Cardinal Sfondrati undertook alterations to the chancel. During the work the sarcophagi came to light and St Cecilia's body was discovered in the posture in which Maderno has represented it.

The cardinal also wanted to restore the little room venerated as the site of St Cecilia's martyrdom. This work disclosed several pipes against the wall, which are thought to have served to raise the temperature in the room in which Cecilia was condemned to suffocate; she was saved by a miraculous dew, only to be beheaded so inefficiently that she lingered in agony for three days. The cardinal commissioned Guido Reni to paint the *Decapitation of the Saint*; the picture stands on the altar.

The tomb of Cardinal Rampolla is a dramatic exercise in perspective (1929) and commemorates the cardinal whose generosity made it possible to open up the crypt.

The **crypt** was created from 1899-1901 in the Byzantine style. The excavations uncovered the remains of several Ancient houses, among which was the first sanctuary dedicated to St Cecilia. Also visible is a room containing seven grain silos and another in which are exhibited sarcophagi and inscriptions: a low relief representing Minerva (2C BC) in a little recess and a column also from the Republican period.

Behind the grating in the *confessio (beneath the apse)* are several sarcophagi, including those of St Cecilia and St Valerian.

The Last Judgement by Pietro Cavallini★★★ – *In the convent. Open Tue and Thu, 10-11.30am; Sun, 11.15am-noon. ☎ 06 58 99 289.*

This masterpiece of Roman medieval painting by Pietro Cavallini (c 1293) was formerly on the inside wall of the façade of the church and is now kept in the monks' chancel. A magnificent work of art, the painting was badly damaged in the 16C. All that remains is the figure of Christ in Judgement surrounded by angels with magnificent outspread wings, flanked by Mary and John the Baptist, hands raised beseechingly; below are the Apostles, and angels blowing trumpets.

Note the perfect distribution of light and shade, the individual expression on each face and the subtle harmony of the colours.

Take Via di San Michele.

After turning into Via Madonna dell'Orto, note the impressive 19C tobacco factory behind the church of Madonna dell'Orto.

Turn left into Via Anicia.

San Francesco a Ripa

The church of St Francis was rebuilt in 1682 to replace the earlier church of the Franciscan order. The fourth chapel in the left-hand aisle contains a **statue of Blessed Ludovica Albertoni★★** by **Bernini**; she was a member of the Franciscan Tertiaries (1474-1533) and is buried beneath the altar. Bernini shows her suffering and in this, one of his later works (1674), the marble perfectly expresses the final agony of a saintly life.

Take Via di S. Francesco a Ripa to reach Piazza Santa Maria in Trastevere.

Piazza Santa Maria in Trastevere★★, the heart of the district, is probably the most charming corner of Trastevere and is full of local colour. The fountain at the centre was remodelled by Bernini in 1659.

On the left is the fine 17C façade of the **Palazzo di San Callisto**.

Basilica di Santa Maria in Trastevere★★
(Basilica of St Mary in Trastevere)

It was on this spot in 38 BC that a fountain of oil *(fons olei)* flowed for a whole day. Christians later interpreted this as a sign of the grace which Christ would spread throughout the world.

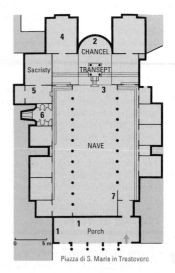

Piazza di S. Maria in Trastevere

Pope Calixtus (217-22) is said to have built the first sanctuary, but it was the energetic Pope Julius I (337-52), a keen builder, who constructed a proper basilica. The building was altered in the 9C by Gregory V, to provide a crypt in which he laid the saintly remains of Calixtus, Pope Cornelius and Calepodius.

The present basilica dates from the 12C; it was built about 1140 during a brief period of calm in the troubled reign of Innocent II, who was beset by the anti-Popes, Anacletus II and Victor IV. Despite St Bernard's assistance, when Innocent II died, Rome was in the hands of revolutionaries, who proclaimed a Republic. His successors restored and embellished the church on many occasions right up to the 19C.

Façade

The belfry is 12C; a small recess at the top is decorated with a mosaic of the Virgin and Child, to whom the basilica is dedicated. The Virgin and Child are also celebrated in the mosaic on the façade (12C-13C), which shows a procession of women approaching from both sides.

The statues of the saints on the balustrade over the porch were erected from the 17C to the 18C. The porch, which was restored early in the 18C, shelters several fragments, some from the buildings which preceded the present one. Two 15C frescoes **(1)**, (one rather damaged), depict the Annunciation. The door frames are made of friezes dating from the time of the Empire.

Interior

The basilical plan of Pope Innocent II's 12C church is still visible. As in all medieval Roman buildings, the columns dividing the nave from the aisles were taken from Ancient monuments; all are crowned with their Classical capitals in either the Ionic or the Corinthian orders; the figures of some Egyptian divinities were removed in the 19C by Pope Pius IX.

The cornice is composed of an assortment of Ancient fragments.

Chancel mosaics★★★ – The mosaics on the chancel arch (the Prophets Isaiah and Jeremiah and the symbols of the Evangelists) date from the 12C; so do those in the half-dome of the apse: to the right of Christ and the Virgin are St Callixtus, St Lawrence and Pope Innocent II offering his church to Mary; on the left are St Peter, St Cornelius, St Julius and St Calepodius. During the Romanesque period mosaic art was still influenced by the Byzantine style: the Virgin is adorned with gold like an empress, the group of figures betrays a certain Oriental rigidity and loses some of its expressive force in the multitude of detail (the Virgin's dress). At the top is a representation of Paradise, with the hand of God placing a crown on Christ's head; at the bottom are lambs, symbols of the Apostles, coming from the cities of Jerusalem and Bethlehem and facing the Lamb of God.

The mosaics between the windows and at the base of the chancel arch are a masterpiece by **Pietro Cavallini** (late 13C), representing scenes from the life of the Virgin. The medallion above the throne shows the Virgin and Child between St Peter and St Paul, with Cardinal Stefaneschi, who commissioned the work, on a smaller scale.

The bishop's throne **(2)** standing in the apse is made of marble (12C).

An inscription **(3)** before the chancel marks the site of the oil fountain.

Altemps Chapel (4) – The stucco and frescoes of this chapel are in the style of the Counter-Reformation, which developed after the Council of Trent (late 16C).

Transept – The fine coffered ceiling is late-16C work. The central low relief in gilded and painted wood illustrates the Assumption.

The **Sacristy** lobby contains two very fine old mosaics **(5)**.

The **Avila Chapel (6)** with its dome is the exuberant creation of Antonio Gherardi (late 17C); the *trompe l'oeil* has been used to create a Baroque effect.

Among the treasures of this church is the charming tabernacle **(7)** by Mino da Fiesole (late 15C).

A warren of narrow, picturesque streets lead to the square, making this an ideal spot for a leisurely stroll.

Take Via della Paglia, then turn right into Piazza S. Egidio, home to the Museo di Roma in Trastevere (see Worth a Visit below).

Take Via Pelliccia and Vicolo di Moro to reach Piazza Trilussa.

The Piazza Trilussa commemorates Carlo Alberto Salustri, who wrote poetry in the Roman dialect under the pseudonym **Trilussa** (1871-1950). In his racy and mildly satirical style he highlights the popular spirit of the Roman people, describing their lives in a long and colourful story. A monument was set up in his honour in 1954.

Nearby is a colossal fountain installed by Paul V in 1612 at the beginning of Via Giulia and transferred here in the 19C, when the Tiber embankments were built. Opposite is the **Sistine Bridge** (Ponte Sisto), named after Sixtus IV (1471-84), who had it built (modernised in the 19C).

Take Via di Ponte Sisto and then Via S. Dorotea.

According to local tradition, the house before the corner (n° 20), with the charmingly decorated window on the second floor, was the home of **La Fornarina**, Raphael's mistress, whom he immortalised in his famous painting now in the National Museum of Antique Art in Palazzo Barberini.

Worth a Visit

Museo di Roma in Trastevere

(&) *Open daily (except Mon) 10am-8pm (last admission 7.30pm); weekday public holidays, 9am-1.30pm. Closed 1 Jan, 1 May and Christmas. €2.58. ☎ 06 58 99 359; Fax 06 58 99 844.*

The museum occupies what was once the Convent of St Egidius in Trastevere. There are many artefacts (watercolours, prints and ceramics) which tell the story of life and popular dress in 18C and 19C Rome. As well as the various display cases showing scenes from everyday life, there is a reconstruction of the room where the poet Trilussa worked.

Vaticano-San Pietro★★★

The Vatican City is home to the largest basilica in the world and to a museum containing some of the greatest art treasures known to man. Situated in the centre of Rome and surrounded by fortifications, it covers just a tiny area of Italy's capital and yet, as the heart of the Roman Catholic Church, its influence extends to all four corners of the globe. For Catholics and non-Catholics alike, this unique state within a state is one of the highlights of a visit to Rome, with its grandiose architecture and magnificent works of art, such as Bernini's colonnade surrounding St Peter's Square, Michelangelo's frescoes on the ceiling of the Sistine Chapel, and the splendid dome of the basilica, which provides visitors with breathtaking views of the capital.

Location

Michelin map 38 or Michelin spiral atlas of Rome: pp 37-39 J 7-8, K 7-9. Metro line A: Ottaviano-San Pietro (500m/550yd from the entrance to the Vatican Museums and 800m/880yd from Piazza San Pietro) or Cipro-Musei Vaticani (600m/660yd from the entrance to the Vatican Museums). Tour: 1 full day. The Vatican City is situated on the right bank of the Tiber, north of the Janiculum Hill, level with Castel Sant'Angelo, to which it is linked by Via della Conciliazione. The Prati district lies to the north. *Neighbouring sights are described in the following chapters: CASTEL SANT'ANGELO; GIANICOLO.*

Background

VATICAN STATE

The decision to create **Via della Conciliazione** was taken in 1936 and this wide thoroughfare was opened in 1950, Jubilee Year. The façades of the buildings flanking the southern end bear the arms of Pius XII *(right)* and of Rome *(left)*. Two rows of street lamps in the shape of obelisks line the broad road which leads directly to St Peter's Basilica.

Once in St Peter's Square the visitor has left Italy and is in the Vatican State. The Vatican City, which lies to the north of the Janiculum Hill and is bounded on three sides by the wall overlooking Viale Vaticano and on the east by the curved colonnade in St Peter's Square, is the largest part of the Papal State. It comprises St Peter's Basilica, the Vatican Palaces and the beautiful gardens surrounding the various administrative offices of the Papal State.

Although the **Ager Vaticanus** lay outside the boundary of Ancient Rome, it was nonetheless well known in Antiquity. In the days of the Empire Caligula chose it as the site of a circus, which was embellished by Nero and used by him for the massacre of the first Roman martyrs; their number may have included St Peter. Hadrian built his mausoleum, the present Castel Sant'Angelo, in the gardens belonging to the Domitii. The history of the Vatican took on a new significance when the Emperor **Constantine** built a basilica there over St Peter's tomb, which is now St Peter's Basilica

Bishop of Rome – From the first days of Christianity, the bishop was Christ's representative on earth. The Bishop of Rome maintained that his See, in the traditional capital of the Empire, had been founded by the Apostles, Peter and Paul, and therefore claimed first place in the ecclesiastical hierarchy. The expression "the Apostolic See" appeared for the first time in the 4C, during the reign of Pope Damasus. Gradually the name "Pope", derived from the Greek *pápas*, meaning "father", which had originally been used for patriarchs and bishops from the Orient, was reserved for the Bishop of Rome alone.

Gift of Quiersy-sur-Oise – In 752, the Lombards occupied Ravenna and the Imperial territory between the River Po, the Apennines and the Adriatic. In Rome the king of the Lombards, Astolphe, demanded a tribute of one gold piece per head. When the intervention of the Emperor in Byzantium, Constantine V (to whom Rome was, in principle, subject) proved useless, Pope Stephen II approached the Carolingian dynasty. In 756, at Quiersy-sur-Oise, Pepin the Short, king of the Franks, undertook to restore the occupied territory not to the Emperor in Byzantium but to the "Republic of the Holy Church of God", that is, to the Pope. This led to the creation of the Papal States and to the temporal power of the Pope.

"Leonine City" – On 23 August 846 the Saracens invaded Rome, pillaging the basilicas of St Peter and St Paul. In the following year, therefore, Leo IV energetically set to work to raise a defensive wall round the Vatican district, which was known as the Borgo. The wall was restored in the 15C by Nicholas V, reinforced with bastions by Sangallo the Younger under Paul III in the 16C, and extended by Pius IV in 1564 to Porta Santo Spirito.

Directory

SAN PIETRO

Basilica – Open 7am-7pm (6pm in winter). Closed during Pontifical services. For information, call ☎ 06 69 88 16 62; Fax 06 69 88 50 61.

Visitors who are deemed to be inappropriately dressed may be refused access to the basilica: this restriction applies to shorts, mini-skirts, sleeveless shirts and bare shoulders.

Museo Storico e Tesoro – ♿ Open Apr-Sep, 9am-7pm (last admission 6.30pm); rest of the year, 9am-6pm (last admission 5.30pm). Closed Easter and Christmas. €4.13. ☎ 06 69 88 18 40.

Grotte Vaticane – Open 7am-6pm (5pm in winter). Closed during Pontifical services. No charge. For further information, call ☎ 06 69 88 16 62; Fax 06 69 88 50 61.

Necropoli Vaticana – Guided tours only (1hr), 9am-5pm. Closed Sun and during Catholic holidays. Apply well in advance to the Delegato della Fabbrica di San Pietro, Ufficio Scavi, Città del Vaticano, 00120 Rome (offices open to the public Mon-Sat, 9am–5pm). €7.75. No children under the age of 15. ☎ 06 69 88 16 62; Fax 06 69 88 50 61; uff.scavi@fabricsp.va

Ascent to the Dome – Open Apr-Sep, 8am-6pm; rest of the year, 8am-5pm. €4.13 (lift), €3.62 (stairs). For information, call ☎ 06 69 88 16 62; Fax 06 69 88 50 61.

PAPAL AUDIENCES

When in residence at the Vatican, the Holy Father gives a **public audience** on a Wednesday (10am in summer and 10.30am in winter), usually in Piazza San Pietro, and celebrates the **Angelus** on Sundays and public holidays in Piazza San Pietro at noon. Access to both is free of charge, but tickets are required for the Wednesday audience. These may be obtained by writing one to two weeks beforehand to the Prefettura della Casa Pontificata, Città del Vaticano, 00120 Rome. ☎ 06 69 88 32 73. To arrange group attendances, numbers of attendees and place of residence should be provided. Tickets should be collected between 3-8pm on the afternoon before the audience, or on the morning itself, from the Prefettura in Piazza San Pietro (large bronze door). Places are sometimes available at short notice, including on the day of the audience itself.

VATICAN MUSEUMS

Entrance: Viale Vaticano.

Admission times and charges – ♿ Two tours of the museum's main exhibits have been designed for disabled visitors. Tour A is dedicated to Classical Antiquity and the Etruscans, Tour B concentrates on the Vatican Palaces and the Picture Gallery (a plan of these tours is available at the information desk).

Open Mar-Oct, Mon-Fri, 8.45am-3.45pm (last admission 2.20pm); Sat, last Sun of the month and the rest of the year, 8.45am-1.45pm (last admission 12.20pm). Closed Sun (except the last in the month), 1 and 6 Jan, 11 Feb, 19 Mar, Easter Sun and Easter Mon, 1 May, Ascension Day, Corpus Domini, 29 June and public holidays. Audioguides available in English, Italian, French, German, Spanish and Japanese. €10.00; no charge 27 Sept and last Sun of the month. Bar, café and self-service cafeteria. ☎ 06 69 88 16 62; Fax 06 69 88 50 61.

Loggia di Raffaello – Open to specialists only by prior written request to the museum. Access is through the Hall of Constantine. The loggia occupies the second floor of the building, which consists of three loggias, one above another. This monumental addition to the façade of Palazzo Apostolico, which looked out over Rome, was commissioned by Julius II.

Museo delle Carrozze – Closed for restoration at the time of going to press. ☎ 06 69 88 30 41.

MAKING THE MOST OF YOUR VISIT

Allow at least one full day for an in-depth visit to all the galleries. However, if you are planning on visiting the ★★★ highly recommended sections only, allow approximately 3hr.

A plan detailing a "short tour" and a "detailed tour" of the museum is available from the information desk.

Some galleries in the Vatican Museums are open in rotation, and not all galleries have the same opening times. Visitors are advised to call the museum on ☎ 06 69 88 33 33 for up-to-date information.

Visitors must follow the official one-way tour, which has options at various points and is liable to variation. For more precise information, you are advised to consult a plan of the museum.

VATICAN CITY AND GARDENS

Tours by prior application to the Musei Vaticani. €9.00. ☎ 06 69 88 16 62; Fax 06 69 88 50 61.

WHERE TO EAT

See "Where to Eat" in the Practical Points section at the beginning of the guide.

TAKING A BREAK

Ottaviani – *Via Paolo Emilio 9/11* – ☎*06 32 43 302 – Closed Mon.* – ✉. This small shop will satisfy the most demanding customers with its *"pizza pazza"*, topped with as many ingredients as you want.

Non solo Pizza – *Via degli Scipioni 95/97* – ☎*06 37 25 820 – Closed Wed.* – ✉. A popular place for a bite to eat after a visit to St Peter's or the Vatican Museums. Specialities include pizza with cep mushrooms *(funghi porcini)*, broccoli and sausage *(salsiccia)*.

BARS

Morrison's – *Via Ennio Quirino Visconti 88* – ☎ *06 32 22 265 – Open Tue-Sun, noon-5pm and 7pm-2am.* This elegant pub has a wide range of beers, including the Guinness group, as well as a good selection of international whiskies.

Quelli della Notte – *Via Leone IV 48 – Open Tue-Sun, 6pm-5am.* This crowded bar is popular for its excellent *cornetti alla crema* (croissant filled with confectioner's cream), washed down with a cappuccino or espresso. The perfect end to a night out!

Shopping

Italia Garipoli – *Borgo Vittorio 91/a –* ☎ *06 68 80 21 96 – Open Mon-Fri, 10am-1pm and 4-7pm; Sat, 10am-1pm.* As well as producing and selling precious lace and embroidery using traditional techniques, this shop also restores valuable clothes and fabrics.

Souvenirs for modern-day pilgrims

Shops selling religious articles are mostly located in Via della Conciliazione, along with general souvenir shops *(also see PANTHEON)*.
Savelli – *Via Paolo VI 27-29 (on the corner of Piazza del Sant'Uffizio)* – ☎ *06 68 30 70 17 – Open Mon-Sat, 9am-6.30pm.* This large shop is known for its religious mosaics.

Lateran Treaty – The unification of Italy (1820-70) would have been incomplete without the inclusion of the Papal States in the new kingdom. On 20 September 1870 the troops of King **Victor Emmanuel II** entered Rome and proclaimed the city the capital of the kingdom. On 2 May 1871 the Italian Parliament passed the **Law of the Guarantees** to show that it did not wish to subjugate the Papacy. The Pope was to retain the Vatican City and to receive an annual allowance. Pius IX excommunicated the authors of the Act and shut himself up in the Vatican, declaring that he was a prisoner. His successors maintained this stance and the Roman Question was not resolved until 1929, when the **Lateran Treaty** was signed on 11 February by Cardinal Gaspari, representing the Holy See, and Mussolini, the head of the Italian Government.

The terms included a political agreement recognising the Pope as sovereign of the Vatican State, which comprised the Vatican City itself and a number of other properties which enjoy the privilege of extraterritoriality: the four major basilicas (St John Lateran, St Peter's in the Vatican, St Paul Without the Walls, Santa Maria Maggiore), the Roman Curia, colleges and seminaries and the villa at Castel Gandolfo; in all 44ha/109 acres and just under 1 000 inhabitants. The treaty also included a financial indemnity and a religious settlement granting the Church a privileged position in Italy in respect of schooling and marriage. The Republican constitution of 1947 established a new relationship between the Roman Church and the Italian State on the basis of the Lateran Treaty. Another agreement modifying the 1929 Lateran Treaty was signed on 18 February 1984 by the President of the Council and the Vatican Secretary of State.

Although the smallest state in physical size, the Vatican spreads the spiritual influence of the Roman Church throughout the world through the person of the Pope.

The Pope, supreme head of the Roman Church

The Pope is also called the Roman Pontiff, the Sovereign Pontiff, the Vicar of Christ, Holy Father and His Holiness. Sometimes he calls himself *Servus Servorum Dei*, the Servant of the Servants of God. In his mission as Pastor to the Church founded by Jesus Christ, he is assisted by the Sacred College of Cardinals and by the Roman Curia.

College of Cardinals – In 1586 Sixtus V fixed their number at 70; it was increased to 85 by John XXIII in 1960. In 1970 there were 145 cardinals; 128 in 1984. A cardinal's dress consists of a scarlet cape (a short hooded cloak) worn over a linen rochet (a surplice with narrow sleeves). The cardinals are the Pope's closest advisers; it is they, assembled in "conclave", who elect the Pope.

Conclave – This is the name of the secret meeting at which a new Pope is elected. This method of election was established by **Gregory X** (1271-76), whose own election lasted nearly three years. He imposed very strict regulations involving confinement and secrecy and required the election to be held within 10 days of the death of the previous Pope, in a palace from which the cardinals would not be released until the new Pope had been elected. He added that if after three days no vote had been held the cardinals would be reduced to one meal a day for five days and then to bread and water. Nowadays the cardinals meet in conclave in the Sistine Chapel and absolute secrecy is maintained. A vote is held twice a day and after each inconclusive vote the papers are burned so as to produce dark smoke. A majority of two-thirds plus one is required for an election to be valid; then a plume of clear smoke appears above the Vatican. The senior cardinal appears at the window in the façade of St Peter's from which Papal blessings are given and announces the election in the Latin formula: *Annuntio vobis gaudium magnum: habemus papam* (I announce to you with great joy: we have a Pope ...). The new Pope then gives his first blessing to the world.

Roman Curia – The Curia consists of a group of bodies, the dicasteries, which, together with the Pope, administer the Holy See. Each dicastery has a cardinal at its head. Since the reform instituted in 1967 by Paul VI, the Curia has consisted of two supreme bodies presided over by the Cardinal Secretary of State. One is the **Secretariat of State**, which carries into effect the decisions taken by the Pope; in the Pope's immediate entourage the Secretary of State periodically assembles the cardinals, who are heads of dicasteries, into a sort of cabinet under his presidency. The other is the **Council for the Public Affairs of the Church**, which deals with diplomatic relations with overseas governments.

Questions of doctrine, the organisation of the churches and the administration of the Papal household are dealt with by congregations (the equivalent of civil ministries), secretariats, councils, commissions, committees and offices.

There are also three courts contained in the Curia. The Tribunal of the Apostolic Signatura is a final court of appeal for ecclesiastical disputes and an administrative tribunal concerned with protecting the law. The Roman Rota is a court of appeal and of first instance, which deals, in particular, with the annulment of marriages. The Apostolic Penitentiary judges matters of conscience.

Councils – Within the Roman Church there are two rites (Oriental and Latin); all the constituent churches belong to one or the other and are grouped into dioceses under the direction of **bishops.** The spiritual authority of a bishop is symbolised by his crozier, his pectoral cross, his ring and his mitre. His dress is no different from that of a cardinal, except that it is purple. The Episcopal College, consisting of about 4 000 bishops spread throughout the world, is presided over by the Pope, who calls them together in an **Ecumenical Council** to discuss the life of the Church. There have been 21 Councils in 20 centuries, the last being the Second Vatican Council (the first ever council was held at St Peter's Basilica in 1869-70). The Second assembled in 1962 under John XXIII and was disbanded three years later by Paul VI.

Papal Audiences – The audiences are held in St Peter's Square in summer and in winter either in St Peter's Basilica or in the huge modern hall designed by Pier Luigi Nervi under Paul VI. During the ceremony the Pope gives his blessing and preaches on the great questions of the Church and humanity. His homily is delivered in Italian and then translated into English, French, German, Spanish and Polish. Official groups of pilgrims are greeted by name in the appropriate language.

The Pope, Head of State

The Pope is the Sovereign of the Vatican State and in this capacity wields the full range of legislative, executive and judicial power. He is assisted in the internal administration of the Vatican by a **Pontifical Commission**, composed of cardinals and a lay member. Beneath the commission is the **Administration (Governatorato)**, which, since 1969, has been assisted by a **Council of State**, and is composed of offices and directorates employing lay staff.

The Vatican State has a yellow flag, bearing the tiara and the crossed keys, and a hymn, the "Pontifical March" composed by Gounod.

The armed regiments were disbanded by Paul VI in 1970; only the **Swiss Guards** have been retained, dressed in their picturesque yellow, red and blue uniforms, which are supposed to have been designed by Michelangelo.

The Vatican issues its own stamps and, like Italy, started using euro notes and coins at the beginning of 2002; the coins show Pope John Paul II facing right. The Vatican also operates a post office and has a railway station linked to the national rail network.

Cultural, scientific and artistic activity – The **Apostolic Vatican Library** ranks very high; it was founded by Papal Bull in 1475 and contains over 60 000 volumes of manuscripts, 100 000 autographs, 800 000 prints, 100 000 engravings and maps and a collection of coins, including an important section consisting of Roman money from the Republican era.

The **Secret Archives**, composed of documents dating from the 13C, have been open to the public for consultation since 1881 and are of worldwide importance in historical research.

The **Pontifical Academy of Science** was founded in 1936 by Pius XI and consists of 70 Academicians chosen by the Pope from among scholars throughout the world.

The **Fabric of St Peter** is the body of architects and specialists in charge of the conservation of St Peter's Basilica. The mosaic workshop is annexed to it.

The Vatican has a printing works which produces texts in almost all languages; there is also a daily newspaper, the *Osservatore Romano*, and a weekly paper, the *Osservatore della Domenica*, which is published in several languages. The Vatican Radio transmits programmes in 40 different languages. Press conferences take place in the press room of the Holy See.

JUBILEE

> *Do not leave us in the atrium*
> *of our existence, before*
> *the closed Door, wandering*
> *like vain words;*
> *waiting for the last*
> *dark and icy dawn*
> *to close the main door to the sun*
> *on people once again:*
> *when the black Earth*
> *turns empty, and what was*
> *the Earth, is remembered no more.*
>> from *The Holy Door* by G Pascoli.

Origins – The origins of the Jubilee are buried deep in the Jewish religion. When Moses received the Ten Commandments from God on Mount Sinai, he was also given a set of laws to guide the behaviour of the people of Israel. In one of these laws God said to Moses "you shall send abroad the loud trumpet on the tenth day of the seventh month (of the forty-ninth year) ... you shall hallow the fiftieth year, and proclaim liberty throughout the land to all its inhabitants; it shall be a jubilee for you." This is known as the *Yôbél* in Hebrew, from the name given to the trumpet mentioned in the Bible and used for the horn sounded on special occasions (the term literally means "billy goat", but is used by extension to mean both the goat's horn and the instrument made from this horn). In the year of the Jubilee, "each man shall return to his property and his family ... in [this year] you shall neither sow, nor reap what grows of itself." The year was to represent an act of peace and reconciliation with God. This idea was later adopted by the Christian tradition, in which the Jubilee signifies a remission of sins.

The first Christian Jubilee took place in 1300, during the Pontificate of Boniface VIII. A huge number of pilgrims made their way to Rome in this year, in the belief that a full remission of sins would be granted in the centenary of the birth of Christ. This amazing influx of people led the Pope to issue a·Bull, sanctioning the "rules" for receiving indulgences: each pilgrim was required to pay 15 visits to the two basilicas of St Peter's and St Paul Without the Walls, which housed the relics of the two saints (30 visits if they were from Rome). Hereafter, Jubilee years were celebrated regularly every 50 years, as decreed by Clement VI (1342-52), with just a few omissions, and subsequently every 25 years, as established by Paul II (1464-71). Exceptional Jubilee years were also occasionally declared, such as the Jubilee of 1983.

In 1750 Benedict XIV established the conditions for obtaining full indulgence, which included visiting all four major basilicas (St Peter's, St Paul Without the Walls, Santa Maria Maggiore and St John Lateran), confession, communion and prayer.

Ceremonies and visits – The Jubilee year traditionally starts with the special Christmas Eve ceremony of the opening of the Holy Door, which is closed at all other times. The door of St Peter's is opened by the Pope. With a gold and silver mallet, he knocks symbolically three times on the wall behind which the door is hidden. Workers then physically knock down the wall. Until 1983 the doors of Santa Maria Maggiore, St Paul Without the Walls and St John Lateran were opened by the three cardinals of these churches. However, this tradition was changed for the Jubilee of 2000, when the Pope opened all four doors himself.

G. Giuliani/CPP-CIRIC

The door at St Peter's is closed again on 6 January of the following year (5 January for the other three basilicas). The Pope blesses the materials used to rebuild the wall and lays the first three bricks.

The pilgrims, who came to Rome from all over the world, were known as *Romei*. They came to the city not only to visit the major churches, but also the catacombs, each of which held saints' relics. Signs of their visits are still visible today in the form of graffiti: invocations to the saints, prayers, or sometimes simply names carved in the stone (similar to the "signs" left today by less respectful visitors). These signs are often used to identify sites where relics would once have been kept.

Then, as today, pilgrims and visitors wished to take home a memento of their visit. Various objects, such as medals, pectoral crosses, ampullae and relics, either genuine relics or articles which had been in contact with the relic, were sold to pilgrims. Scenes relating to the place of worship, or holy scenes, were often illustrated on the objects.

Accommodation – Suitable accommodation had to be found for this huge influx of people, many of whom were very poor. The hospices provided for pilgrims were originally known as *xenodochi*; they often included a hospital, school, other provisions for the poor, and a cemetery, in addition to the actual hospice itself. These establishments later came to be known as *scholae peregrinorum*. There were often different *scholae* for different nationalities; these were built and run by the authorities of the relevant country. One of the most important of these hospices was almost certainly the French Scholae, in the district of St Peter's, thought to have been founded during the reign of Pepin the Short and Pope Stephen II in the 8C.

PILGRIM ROUTES

Via Francigena (or Romea) was one of the most famous pilgrim routes of the Middle Ages. It followed the Ancient Via Cassia and linked Rome (or more precisely, St Peter's, with northern Europe.

Special Features

BASILICA DI SAN PIETRO (ST PETER'S BASILICA)

For practical information and admission times and charges, see Directory above. The basilica, which is the largest of all Christian places of worship, reflects many centuries of Christian history.

The building of St Peter's Basilica is linked to the martyrdom of **Peter** (c AD 64). After a huge fire, which destroyed the greater part of Rome and for which the Emperor Nero held the Christians responsible, he ordered many of them to be executed. Simon, called Peter by Jesus, was probably among the condemned. According to the law, he was simply a Jewish fisherman, a native of Capernaum in Galilee, sentenced therefore to the appalling punishment of crucifixion in Nero's Circus at the foot of the Vatican Hill. So as to distinguish his own death from Jesus's, Peter humbly begged to be crucified upside down.

Constantine's basilica – Following his conversion to Christianity, Constantine built a sanctuary in 324 over the tomb of St Peter, who had been chosen by Christ as his chief Apostle. In 326 Pope Sylvester I consecrated the building, which was completed some 25 years later. The basilica had a nave, four aisles and a narrow transept; the apsidal wall stood just behind the present Papal altar. The entrance was through an *atrium* graced with a fountain decorated with the beautiful pine cone *(la Pigna)* which can now be seen in a courtyard of the Vatican Palace. The façade gleamed with mosaics. The *confessio* (a crypt containing the tomb of a martyr) was not completely underground; an opening at floor level gave access to the tomb. At the end of the 6C Pope Gregory the Great raised the chancel; beneath it the *confessio* took the form of a corridor following the curve of the apse and contained a chapel called *ad caput*.

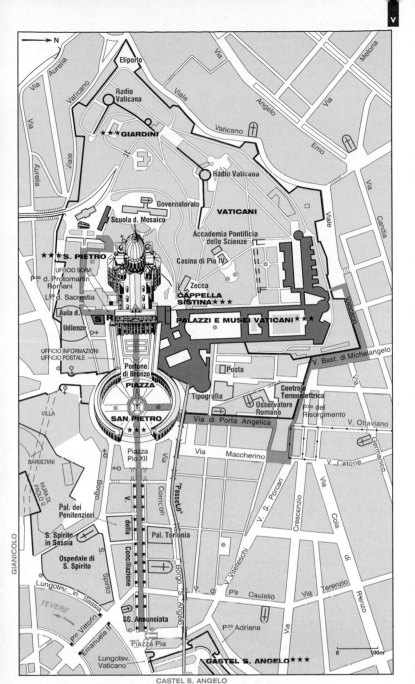

Arco delle Campane .... **R**   Camposanto teutonico .... **S**

For more than a century the basilica was pillaged by barbarians: Alaric in 410 and Totila in 546. In 846 it was raided by the Saracens. Its prestige, however, remained intact. Imperial coronations were held there in solemn state. On Christmas Day AD 800 Leo III crowned Charlemagne king of the Romans; 75 years later it was the turn of his grandson, Charles the Bald, during the Pontificate of John VIII, the first soldier Pope and the first to be assassinated. Arnoul, the last of the Carolingians, became Pope Formosus in 891. John XII, who lived like a Muhammedan prince, surrounded by slaves and eunuchs, crowned Otho I the first Emperor of Germany on 2 February 962 and then conspired against him. His intrigues brought the Papacy under the control of the German Emperor for over a century.

After 1 000 years, despite frequent restoration and embellishment, St Peter's Basilica was in a parlous state.

1452, Nicholas V intervenes – Bernardo Rossellino was appointed by the Pope to restore the basilica. He retained the dimensions of Contantine's building, but proposed a cruciform plan with a dome and a new choir. The Pope died in 1455 and the project was abandoned. For the next 50 years his successors were content to shore up the existing building.

1503, Julius II, an energetic Pope – His plan for renovation was radical. His architects were **Bramante**, who had arrived in Rome in 1499, and **Giuliano da Sangallo**. The chosen design was Bramante's: a Greek cruciform plan with jutting apses beneath cupolas and over the crossing a central dome similar to the Pantheon dome. On 18 April 1506 the first stone was laid at the base of a pillar; a temporary chancel had been provided and a large part of the apse and transept demolished, causing Bramante to be nicknamed the "Destructive Maestro". Sometimes a young man came to watch the work. His name was Michelangelo. Julius II had commissioned him to design his tomb, which was to be placed at the heart of the new basilica. Michelangelo admired Bramante's plan but disapproved of his administration. Having at first been regarded as an intruder, he came to be hated by Bramante. Believing himself to be in danger, Michelangelo retreated to Florence, but returned to Rome after violently denouncing the Pope and Rome where, so he wrote, "they turn chalices into swords and helmets".

Julius II died in 1513 and Bramante in 1514. For the next 30 years the design of the building was the subject of interminable discussion. Raphael and Giuliano da Sangallo suggested going back to a Latin cruciform plan. Baldassarre Peruzzi drew up another plan based on Bramante's design. Antonio da Sangallo, Giuliano's nephew, wanted to keep the Greek cross plan but add a bay in the form of a porch, with two towers flanking the façade, and alter the dome; he died in 1546.

From Michelangelo to Bernini – In 1547 **Paul III** appointed **Michelangelo**, then 72 and chief architect to the Vatican, to put an end to all the discussion. "To deviate from Bramante's design is to deviate from the truth", declared the Master. He therefore returned to the Greek cruciform plan, simplified to accentuate its circular base – the circle, the sign of infinity, glorifying the Resurrection. The dome was no longer the shallow dome of the Pantheon, but reached high into the sky. His intransigence in carrying out his ideas exasperated his detractors. He worked on St Peter's, surrounded by intrigues, refusing any payment, doing all for the

St Peter's Square – view of the basilica

glory of God and the honour of St Peter. When he died in 1564, the apse and transepts were complete and the dome had risen as far as the top of the drum. It was completed in 1593 by **Giacomo della Porta**, assisted by Domenico Fontana, who may have been inspired to raise the dome even higher by one of the Master's alternative designs.

In 1606 **Paul V** (1605-21) finally settled for the Latin cruciform plan; it was more suitable for high ceremony and preaching, and thus more in accordance with the preoccupations of the Counter-Reformation. The new basilica was to cover all the area occupied by the original church, whereas Michelangelo's plan had not extended so far east. The façade was entrusted to Carlo Maderno. The new basilica was consecrated by Urban VIII.

The final phase in St Peter's architectural history was directed by **Bernini**, who took over on Maderno's death in 1629. He turned what would have been a fine example of Renaissance architecture into a sumptuous Baroque monument.

In all, from Bramante to Bernini, the building of St Peter's encompassed 120 years, the reigns of 20 Popes and the work of 10 architects.

Piazza San Pietro★★★ (St Peter's Square)

The square, which was intended to isolate the basilica without creating a barrier in front of it, acts, in fact, as a sort of vestibule. The gentle curves of the colonnades, like two arcs of a circle framing the rectangular space, are a gesture of welcome extended to the pilgrims of the world.

The square was begun by **Bernini** in 1656 under Pope Alexander VII and completed in 1667. By flanking the façade with a broader and lower colonnade, the architect aimed to minimise the width and accentuate the height of the basilica. To create the effect of surprise so dear to Baroque artists, the colonnade was designed to enclose the square and mask the façade so the basilica was hidden from view until the visitor stood in the entrance between the arms of the colonnade. Bernini's intention was not fully realised: the triumphal arch planned to link the two arms was not built and Via della Conciliazione gives a distant view of the basilica. Two belfries were planned, but the foundations proved too weak to carry the additional weight. At its widest point the square measures 196m/643ft across. The **colonnade** is formed by rows of columns, four deep, surmounted by statues and the arms of Alexander VII: a remarkably sober and solemn composition.

At the centre of the square stands an **obelisk**, a granite monolith, carved in the 1C BC in Heliopolis for Caius Cornelius Gallus, the Roman Prefect in Egypt. It was brought to Rome in AD 37 by Caligula, who had it set up in his circus (left of the basilica). It was still there when **Sixtus V** decided to erect it in St Peter's Square. It was the first obelisk to be moved by this Pope, who was responsible for re-siting several others. His official architect was **Domenico Fontana**. The work took four months and gave birth to an appropriate legend. The obelisk was to be re-erected on 10 September 1585; 800 men and 75 horses were required to raise the 350t of granite to its full height (25.5m/84ft). After giving his blessing, the Pope enjoined absolute silence on pain of death; to make sure his order was clearly understood he set up a gallows in the square. The work began, but the ropes chafed on the granite and threatened to give way under the friction. Then one of the workers cried out *"Acqua alle funi"* ("water for the ropes") and the Pope congratulated him for disobeying the order. A relic of the True Cross is preserved at the top of the obelisk.

The two fountains are attributed to Carlo Maderno *(right)* and **Bernini** *(left)*. Between them and the obelisk are two discs set into the paving to mark the focal points of the two ellipses enclosing the square; from these points the colonnades appear to consist of only one row of columns. This perspective is achieved by increasing the diameter of the columns from the inner to the outer row and placing them an equal distance from one another.

East front

A majestic flight of steps, designed by Bernini, leads up to the east front. On either side stand statues of St Peter and St Paul (19C). The east front, which was begun by **Carlo Maderno** in 1607 and completed in 1614, was the object of spirited comment; owing to its dimensions (45m/147ft high and 115m/377ft wide), it masks the dome. It is from the balcony beneath the pediment that the Pope gives his blessing *Urbi et Orbi* (to the city and to the world). The entablature carried Paul V's dedication. The horizontal pediment above it is crowned by statues of Christ, John the Baptist and 11 Apostles (excluding Peter). The clocks at either end are the work of Giuseppe Valadier (19C).

Porch

It was designed by **Carlo Maderno**. On the left behind a grill stands an equestrian statue of Charlemagne **(1)** (18C). The Door of Death **(2)**, with sober sculptures on its bronze panels, is by **Giacomo Manzù** (1964); low down on the right in the left-hand section is a low-relief figure of John XXIII. The bronze door **(3)** was sculpted in 1445 by Antonio Averulino, known as **Il Filarete**. The true artistic spirit of the Renaissance is seen in the juxtaposition of religious scenes (in the six panels), episodes from the life of Eugenius IV (in the spaces below the panels) and mythological figures, animals and portraits of contemporary personalities (in the frieze surrounding the panels). In the two central panels strange inscriptions in Arab characters appear around the figures of St Peter and St Paul and in their haloes. To the right is the **Holy Door**: only the Pope may open and close this door to mark the beginning and end of a Holy Year.

The "Navicella" mosaic **(4)** by **Giotto** dates from 1300. It originally adorned the *atrium* of Constantine's Basilica but has been restored and re-sited many times since.

At the north end of the porch, in the vestibule of the Scala Regia *(closed to the public)*, stands a statue of Constantine **(5)**, the first Christian Emperor, by Bernini (1670).

Interior

Here everything is so well proportioned that the scale, though large, is not overwhelming. The seemingly life-size angels supporting the holy water stoops **(6)** are, in fact, enormous. St Peter's Basilica, with its 450 statues, 500 columns and 50 altars, and its reputed capacity to hold 60 000 people, is a record of the history of Christianity and art in Rome.

Nave – The overall length of the church, including the porch, is about 211m/692ft. Comparisons can be made with the length of other world-famous churches by means of marks set in the floor. When **Charlemagne** received the Emperor's crown from the Pope on Christmas Day AD 800 he knelt on the porphyry disc **(7)**, now let into the pavement of the nave, although in the original church it was placed before the high altar.

Michelangelo's Pietà★★★ – This masterpiece, sculpted in 1499-1500 by Michelangelo at the age of 25, can be seen in the Cappella della Pietà **(8)**. The execution of the profoundly human figures is perfect, revealing an amazing creative power. The group was commissioned by a French cardinal in 1498 and immediately hailed as the work of a genius. Even so, Michelangelo already had enemies, who started a rumour that the work was not his. He therefore added his signature across the Virgin's sash – the only piece of his work to be so marked.

BASILICA DI SAN PIETRO

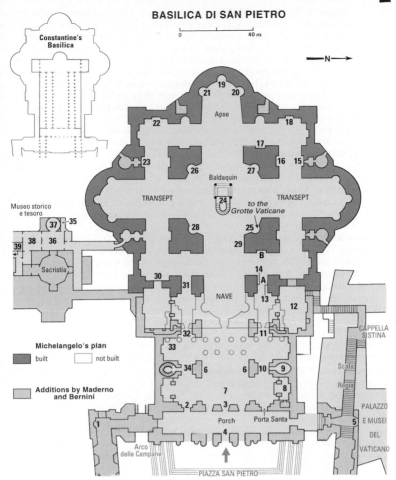

0 ——————— 40 m

—N→

Constantine's Basilica

19
21 20
Apse
22 18
17
23 16 15
26 27
Baldaquin
24
to the *Grotte Vaticane*
TRANSEPT TRANSEPT
Museo storico e tesoro
37 35
38 36
39
Sacristia
28 25
29
B
30 14
31 A
13
NAVE 12

Michelangelo's plan
██ built ☐ not built

██ **Additions by Maderno and Bernini**

32 11
33
34 6 6 10 9
7 8
2 3
1 Porch Porta Santa
4
Arco delle Campane
PIAZZA SAN PIETRO

CAPPELLA SISTINA
Scala
Regia
PALAZZO
E MUSEI
DEL
VATICANO

Cappella del Crocifisso o delle reliquie (Crucifix Chapel or Chapel of Relics) **(9)** – **Bernini** designed the elliptical chapel, which contains a fine wooden crucifix attributed to Pietro Cavallini (early 14C).

Queen Christina of Sweden's Monument (10) – In 1654 **Queen Christina** abdicated her throne; she was converted to Roman Catholicism and came to live in Rome the following year. She is buried in the "grottoes" *(see p 314).* Her monument was executed by Jean-Baptiste Theodon from designs by Carlo Fontana (18C).

Countess Mathilda of Tuscany's Monument (11) – She was the first woman to be buried in the basilica. At the time of the Investiture Controversy it was she who received the Emperor Henry IV, when he submitted to Gregory VII at Canossa (1077). This incident is represented in the low-relief carving on the sarcophagus. The monument was designed by Bernini, assisted by several of his pupils (1635).

Cappella del Santissimo Sacramento (Chapel of the Blessed Sacrament) **(12)** – The wrought-iron screen at the entrance is by Borromini. The high altarpiece representing the Trinity is one of the few paintings of St Peter by Pietro da Cortona (most pictures are mosaics). On the altar, the tabernacle, which is similar to the *tempietto* of San Pietro in Montorio, and the kneeling angels are by Bernini (1675); the angel on the right is by a pupil.

B. Kaufmann/MICHELIN

Pietà

Bernini brings unity to the Basilica – The passage **(A)** marks the line between Maderno's later and Michelangelo's earlier work. Bernini's task was to create a harmonised whole. The first problem was the junction of the nave with the eastern wall of Michelangelo's square plan. As this wall supports the oblique thrust of the weight of the dome, it could not be pierced to create a wide monumental doorway similar to the entrance doors in the nave. Bernini's solution was to erect two columns, like those flanking the doorways in the nave, and to fill the space below the arch and the pediment with a shield supported by two angels. The second problem was the pier **(B)**, which could not be pierced as it supports the dome. He erected two columns and an arch of identical size to those in the passage. The visitor approaching along the north aisle of the church receives an impression of depth, accentuated by the two narrow arches.

Gregory XIII's Monument★ (13) – The low-relief carving on the white marble sarcophagus (1723) illustrates the reform of the calendar which the Pope instituted in 1582. The Gregorian calendar has now been adopted worldwide.

Gregory XIV's Monument (14) – According to legend, the monument was despoiled to meet the expense of the Pope's illness which had to be treated with a mixture of gold and precious stones. The plaster sarcophagus was not faced with marble until 1842.

Clement XIII's Monument★★★ (15) – The fine neo-Classical design by Canova dates from 1792. The lack of emotion for which Canova's art is often criticised here contributes to the purity of line; the balance of the whole is, however, upset by the statue on the left, which represents the Triumph of Religion.

Pictures in mosaic – It was in the 16C that famous pictures began to be copied in mosaic. In the spirit of the Counter-Reformation, the Church hoped thus to make its glories more intelligible to the faithful. This practice was further developed when Benedict XIII founded a mosaic school in 1727. These mosaics therefore have immense religious significance. They illustrate the power of St Peter; his walking on the water **(16)** and his raising of Tabitha **(17)**; they celebrate the martyrs, Popes, saints and angels challenged by the Reformation.

Cappella di San Michele o di Santa Petronilla (St Michael's or St Petronilla's Chapel) **(18)** – The mosaic illustrates St Petronilla's martyrdom after a painting by Guercino. St Petronilla, whose relics lie beneath the altar, was venerated in St Peter's from 8C. Pepin the Short built a chapel to her, in which Michelangelo's *Pietà* was to have stood.

Apse – The dominant feature is **"St Peter's Chair"★★★ (19)**, an extraordinary work designed by **Bernini** to contain the remains of an ancient episcopal chair said to have been used by St Peter; these remains, which date from the 4C, are encased in a throne, decorated with ivory, which was given to John VIII by Charles the Bold at his coronation in 875. Bernini's throne is made of sculpted bronze, apparently supported by the four great Doctors of the Church (measuring between 4.50m/15ft and 5.50m/18ft). Above is a gilded stucco "gloria", veiled in clouds and a host of cherubs. Silhouetted against a sun-like central opening, which lets in the light, is the dove of the Holy Ghost (its wing span is 1.75m/just under 6ft). This work, completed in 1666 when Bernini was in his 70s, is a crowning example of his astounding art, full of movement and light.

Urban VIII's Monument★★★ (20), commissioned from **Bernini** in 1628 and finished in 1647, is considered to be the masterpiece of 17C funerary art. His hand raised majestically in blessing, the Pope sits enthroned above the sarcophagus, surrounded by statues of Justice and Charity, while Death inscribes his name.

For Paul III's Monument★★★ (21), **Guglielmo della Porta** (?1500-77), a follower of Michelangelo, conceived a grandiose project: the monument was to be surrounded by eight allegorical statues and placed in the centre of the chancel. Michelangelo objected and asked for the number of statues to be reduced to four. When Bernini altered the apse in 1628 he reduced the number to two; the other two statues are in the Farnese Palace.

St Leo the Great's Altar (22) – The **altarpiece★** is a "picture in marble" by **Algardi** of the Pope halting Attila at the gates of Rome. This type of sculpture, which resembles a picture because of the vivid effects it creates, is characteristic of Baroque art.

Alexander VII's Monument★★ (23) – **Bernini** completed this monument in 1678, two years before his death. He was anxious that he himself should sculpt the head of the Pope, who was his protector.

The Pope kneels among allegorical statues, the work of pupils who, in their effort to imitate their master, have somewhat exaggerated the effect of movement. Even Bernini's own art gives way to excess here (Death is represented by a skeleton draped in mottled marble beckoning the Pope).

Baldaquin★★★ – **Bernini**'s canopy, begun in 1624, was unveiled by Urban VIII in 1633. Despite the weight of the bronze and its great height (29m/95ft – the height of the Farnese Palace), it has captured the lightweight effect of an original baldaquin, usually made of wood and cloth, to be carried in processions. As the eye is caught by the wreathed columns, the valance seems to stir. The bees (on the columns and valance) are from the arms of the Barberini family, to which Urban VIII belonged.

The work attracted much criticism, because the bronze had been taken from the Pantheon and because it was thought to be too theatrical and in bad taste.

The high altar below the baldaquin, where only the Pope may celebrate Mass, stands over the *confessio* **(24)**, designed by Maderno, which contains St Peter's tomb.

Piers of the Crossing – They were begun by **Bramante** and completed by Michelangelo; they stand at the crossing of the transepts. Their austerity did not please Baroque taste; in 1629 Bernini faced them in marble and created recesses at the base, in which he placed four statues (5m/16ft high). Above them he designed balcony chapels for the exhibition of relics and re-used the wreathed columns from the baldaquin of the 4C church which had inspired his own canopy. Each statue represents the relics deposited in the basilica: a fragment of the spear (St Longinus – **25** – by Bernini commemorates the soldier who pierced Jesus's side with his spear, which has become a symbol of Pity); the napkin bearing the Holy Image (St Veronica – **26** – wiped Jesus's face on the road to Calvary); a fragment of the True Cross (St Helena – **27** – brought the remains of the Cross to Rome); St Andrew's head (St Andrew – **28**). The last three statues are by Bernini's collaborators: Francesco Mochi, Andrea Bolgi and François Duquesnoy.

Dome★★★ – Bramante's design was for a dome resembling the one on the Pantheon, but **Michelangelo** made it larger and raised it higher. He himself carried out the work up to the lantern; it was finished in 1593 by **Giacomo della Porta** and **Domenico Fontana**. It is the largest dome in Rome; the whole building seems to have been designed to support it, a symbol of God's perfection.

The pendentives carry four mosaic medallions (8m/26ft across) representing the Evangelists. Above in Latin are Christ's words to Peter: "Thou art Peter and upon this rock I will build my church; and I will give unto thee the keys of the Kingdom of Heaven". The interior of the dome is decorated with figures of the Popes and the Doctors of the Church; seated are Christ, Mary, Joseph, John the Baptist and the Apostles; above them are angels. The figure on the ceiling of the lantern is God the Father.

Statue of St Peter★★ (29) – This 13C bronze by **Arnolfo di Cambio** is greatly venerated. Countless pilgrims have kissed its foot. It is said to have been made out of the bronze statue of Jupiter on the Capitol.

Pius VII's Tomb (30)   Pius VII died in 1823, after bearing the brunt of the Napoleonic storm. His tomb was designed by **Thorwaldsen**, a Dane.

Leo XI's Monument (31) – **Algardi** was responsible for the white marble monument (1642-44). The low-relief sculpture on the sarcophagus illustrates Henri IV's conversion to Roman Catholicism; the king is being received by the future Pope, who was then Clement VIII's legate.

Innocent VIII's Monument★★★ (32) – This is a Renaissance work by Antonio del Pollaiolo (1431-98), one of the few monuments to be preserved from the earlier church. The tomb is designed in typical 15C style against a wall.

When the monument was re-erected in 1621 the two figures were reversed; originally the recumbent figure was above the Pope, signifying the supreme power of death. An error has crept into the epitaph which says that the Pope "lived" *(vixit)* rather than reigned for eight years, 10 months and 25 days.

John XXIII's Monument (33) – The low-relief sculpture on the right of the chapel of the Presentation is by a contemporary artist, Emilio Greco.

Stuart Monument (34) – **Canova** designed this work (1817-19) to the glory of the last members of the Scottish Royal family: James Edward, Charles Edward and Henry Benedict, who are buried in the crypt *(see below)*. The monument was commissioned by the Prince Regent and paid for by George III. The **angels★** in low relief were much admired by **Stendhal**, who also remarked that "George IV, in keeping with his reputation as the most accomplished gentleman in the three kingdoms, wished to honour the ashes of the unhappy princes, whom he would have sent to the scaffold had they fallen into his hands alive".

Museo Storico e Tesoro★

The Treasury has been pillaged on many occasions – by the Saracens in 846, during the sack of Rome in 1527, by Bonaparte under the Treaty of Tolentino in 1797 – but it has always been built up again, and today contains gifts from many countries.

In **Room I (35)** are two mementoes of the 4C basilica: the "Holy Column", which is identical to those reused by Bernini in the balcony chapels in the piers supporting the dome, and the gilded metal cockerel (9C), which Leo IV had placed on top of the basilica.

Room II (36) displays a fine dalmatic said to have belonged to Charlemagne; it is, in fact, a Byzantine-style liturgical vestment dating from the 10C at the earliest. This room also contains a copy of the wooden and ivory chair contained in Bernini's throne, and a 6C Papal cross.

The beautiful tabernacle in the **Benefactors' Chapel (37)** is attributed to Donatello, the Renaissance master artist from Florence. The plaster mould of Michelangelo's *Pietà* proved valuable when the original was damaged in 1972 and had to be repaired. **Room III (38)** contains the **tomb of Sixtus IV★★★** (1493) by Antonio del Pollaiolo. The accuracy of the portraiture and the delicacy of its execution make it a true masterpiece of bronze sculpture portraiture and delicate craftsmanship. Several rooms, glittering with gold and silverware and liturgical objects, including a terracotta version of Bernini's angel before it was cast in bronze for the chapel of the Blessed Sacrament, lead into the **gallery (39)** displaying the tiara of silver and gold and precious stones with which St Peter's statue is crowned on ceremonial occasions. **Junius Bassus's sarcophagus★★★** (4C) was found beneath the basilica and is a remarkable example of Christian funerary sculpture, richly decorated with biblical scenes; on the sides are children gathering the harvest, a symbol of the souls saved by the Eucharist.

Grotte Vaticane

Access in the northeast pier supporting the dome. The grottoes embrace the area beneath the basilica containing the Papal tombs and parts of the earlier basilica. They consist of a semicircular section which follows the line of Constantine's apse, with the Ad Caput Chapel *(see below)* on the eastern side, and three aisles projecting eastwards.

In the centre of the apsidal passage are Pius XII's tomb *(west)* and the Ad Caput Chapel *(east)*.

The low-relief sculptures by Antonio del Pollaiolo (15C) on the inner wall of the passage illustrate the lives of St Peter and St Paul.

Among the tombs in the aisles are those of Pope John XXIII, Christina of Sweden, Benedict XV and Hadrian IV, born Nicholas Breakspear, the only English Pope.

Salita alla cupola★ (Ascent to the Dome)

Access from the exterior to the right of the basilica. From an internal gallery at the base of the dome, visitors can best appreciate the vast dimensions of the basilica, the prodigious height of the dome as well as its decorations. As a result of the special acoustics, two people, diametrically opposite one another and facing the wall, can hold a conversation in low voices. A stairway inside the dome climbs up to a terrace surrounding the lantern at 120m/394ft above St Peter's Square. The **view★★★** is magnificent: the geometric precision of the square, a model of architectural town planning; the Vatican City, including an interesting aspect of the gardens, the palaces, the museums, and the fortress-like Sistine Chapel; and the whole city of Rome from the Janiculum to Monte Mario.

On the way down a broad terrace at the foot of the dome affords a **view** of the domes of the transept and aisles. There is also an extensive view of the city from the east balustrade, which is surmounted by huge statues of Christ, St John the Baptist and the Apostles (excluding St Peter).

Necropoli Vaticana★★ (Vatican Necropolis)

The excavations, carried out between 1939 and 1950 on the orders of Pope Pius XII, revealed a pagan necropolis completely infilled with earth by Constantine to form a foundation for the original ancient basilica in which the tomb of St Peter was found. After crossing one of the foundation walls in Constantine's basilica, the necropolis is reached. Two rows of tombs (dating from the 1C to early 4C), separated by a path, are arranged on a slope parallel with the axis of the main nave, and run from east to west. The entrance to one of the tombs bears an inscription recording the occupant's wish to be buried *"in Vaticano ad circum"*, alluding to Nero's circus, where St Peter may have perished. In another tomb, that of the Julian family, are the oldest known Christian mosaics. These show "Christ as the Sun", on a horse-drawn chariot, and the two stories of Jonah and the fisherman.

Return in the direction of the apse of the present basilica.

Set in the east side of the so-called "Red Wall" (Muro Rosso) is the recess (2C) known as the "Trophy of Gaius" (Trofeo di Gaio); beneath is the **tomb of St Peter**. It was the presence of the trophy in that location, apparently marking the site of the Apostle's tomb, that made Constantine decide to build the basilica on top of the necropolis, with the floor on the same level as the trophy. The Emperor then enclosed the tomb and trophy in marble and the whole structure was given the name of the "Constantine Memorial".

The position of St Peter's tomb has aroused lively controversy among historians, archaeologists and theologians. Until the Vatican excavations were made, his tomb was thought to be in St Sebastian's Catacombs. According to the historian Jerome Carcopino, the saint's relics have had a hazardous existence. In 258, fearing desecration during the Valerian persecution, the Christians may have moved them to St Sebastian's Catacombs, which did not then belong to the Church and were therefore unlikely to attract attention from the authorities. Not until 336, when Christians were again entitled to practise their religion, would the relics have been returned to their original resting place in the Vatican.

Cappella Clementina★ (Clementine Chapel) – This is the **Ad Caput Chapel** (at the head of St Peter). It stands behind the shrine very close to the Apostle's tomb. Some bones, found in one of the walls which in the 3C bordered the shrine to the north, are displayed by the guide; they may be the bones of St Peter.

MUSEI VATICANI (VATICAN MUSEUMS)

Entrance in Viale Vaticano; from Piazza Risorgimento take Via Bastioni di Michelangelo and turn left. For practical information on the museum (including admission times and charges), see Directory at the beginning of the chapter. The official tour starts with the Egyptian and Chiaromonti Museums (see below). The visit of the Pius-Clementine Museum begins from near Bramante's Staircase (see plan on p 316). The number of masterpieces in the Vatican is so great that a rigorous selection of the outstanding items has had to be made. For a more detailed description of the exhibits consult the "Guide to the Vatican City" and the "Guide to the Vatican Museums" published by Monumenti, Musei e Gallerie Pontificie.

The museums are housed in part of the palaces built by the Popes from the 13C onwards. The old entrance hall, opened in 1932, will now be used solely an an exit and a new bronze door, situated to the left of the old entrance, leads visitors into a spacious, modern area capable of handling 2 000 people at a time. From here a spiral ramp and an escalator lead up to the Cortile delle Corazze (Cuirasses), the Atrio dei Quattro Cancelli (Atrium of the Four Gates) and Simonetti's 18C staircases (**A** on the plan), where visitors start their actual visit to the museums.

Palaces

It was probably during the reign of Pope Symmachus (498-514) that some buildings were erected to the north of St Peter's Basilica. Nicholas III (1277-80) intended to replace them with a fortress and towers but his project was only partially realised. When they returned from Avignon in 1377 the Popes gave up living in the Lateran Palace, which had been destroyed by fire, and settled in the Vatican. **Nicholas V** (1447-55) decided to enlarge the accommodation. Around the Parrot Court (Cortile del Pappagallo) he constructed a palace incorporating the 13C buildings. He kept the fortress-like exterior, but the interior was sumptuously decorated. The chapel by Fra Angelico can still be seen. Almost all the Popes have altered or enlarged Nicholas V's palace.

Sixtus IV (1471-84) established a library on the ground floor of the north wing (now a conference room used by the Pope) and built the Sistine Chapel to the west. About 300m/984ft north of Nicholas V's palace, **Innocent VIII** (1484-92) built a summer residence, the Belvedere Palace. From 1493-94 **Alexander VI** added the Borgia Tower (Torre Borgia) to Nicholas V's palace and created his own apartments above Sixtus IV's library.

Pope **Julius II** (1503-13) commissioned Bramante to link Nicholas V's and Innocent VIII's palaces with two long narrow galleries, thus creating the Belvedere Court (Cortile del Belvedere). A huge rectangular courtyard, it provided a setting for grandiose spectacles and was later divided into the present Library and Pine Cone Courts (Cortile della Biblioteca e Cortile della Pigna). He lived above Alexander VI's apartments in the rooms which Nicholas V had had painted by Piero della Francesca, Benedetto Bonfigli and Andrea del Castagno, and had them redecorated by Raphael. The façade of the palace was too austere for his taste, so he had another built, consisting of three loggias, one above another. The second floor loggia was decorated by Raphael.

Paul III (1534-49) strengthened the foundations and restored the southwest wing of the early palace.

Pius IV (1559-65) commissioned Pirro Ligorio to alter the Belvedere Court. To the north (on the Belvedere Palace side) the architect constructed a large semicircular niche before which was erected the *pigna*, a huge pine cone, which had adorned the fountain in the *atrium* of Constantine's Basilica. The design is based on Classical architecture, particularly Domitian's Stadium on the Palatine Hill. To the south, backing on to Nicholas V's palace, he created a semicircular façade one storey high with a central niche. Later the Belvedere Court was divided by two transverse galleries: between 1587 and 1588, during the reign of Sixtus V, Domenico Fontana built the Papal Library (Sistine Rooms); later, between 1806 and 1823, **Pius VII** built the New Wing (Braccio Nuovo).

The Belvedere Court was thus divided into three separate courts: the Belvedere Court (Cortile del Belvedere), the Library Court (della Biblioteca), the Pine Cone Court (della Pigna).

During the Baroque period, the only addition to the Vatican Palace was the Scala Regia (Royal Stairway – *not open*), a monumental stairway constructed by **Bernini** between 1633 and 1666. From the Great Bronze Door (Portone di bronzo), which is the main entrance to the palace a long corridor along the north side of St Peter's Square leads to the foot of the Scala Regia.

MUSEI VATICANI

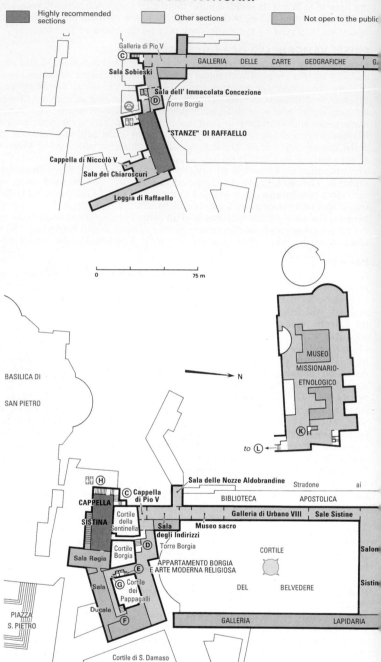

Papal Court

By providing his nephews with ecclesiastical titles and benefices and surrounding himself with rich cardinals, artists and men of letters, Sixtus IV (1471-84) created a virtual court like that of a secular prince.

Pope's Apartments

The 16C buildings surrounding Sixtus V's Court (Cortile di Sisto V) contain the present Papal apartments. Heads of State, diplomats and other important people enter the Vatican City by the Bell Arch (Arco delle Campane). Papal receptions are held in the Pope's private library, a large room between Sixtus V's Court and Majordomo Court (Cortile del Maggiordomo).

In the summer the Pope moves to Castel Gandolfo, a property 120km/75mi south-east of Rome.

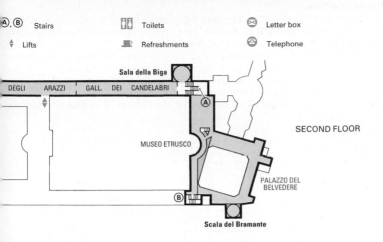

A, B Stairs
Lifts

Toilets
Refreshments

Letter box
Telephone

DEGLI   ARAZZI   GALL. DEI   CANDELABRI
Sala della Biga

Ⓐ

MUSEO ETRUSCO

SECOND FLOOR

PALAZZO DEL
BELVEDERE

Ⓑ

Scala del Bramante

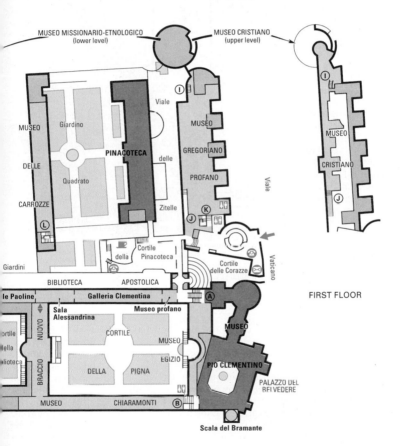

MUSEO MISSIONARIO-ETNOLOGICO
(lower level)

MUSEO CRISTIANO
(upper level)

Viale

MUSEO
DELLE
CARROZZE

Giardino

PINACOTECA
Quadrato
delle
Zitelle

MUSEO
GREGORIANO
PROFANO

Viale

MUSEO
CRISTIANO

Giardini

Cortile
della Pinacoteca

Ⓙ Ⓚ

Cortile
delle Corazze

Viale Vaticano

FIRST FLOOR

BIBLIOTECA   APOSTOLICA

le Paoline

Galleria Clementina

Ⓐ

Sala
Alessandrina

Museo profano

NUOVO

CORTILE

MUSEO
EGIZIO

MUSEO

BRACCIO

DELLA   PIGNA

PIO CLEMENTINO

MUSEO   CHIARAMONTI

Ⓑ

PALAZZO DEL
BELVEDERE

Scala del Bramante

MUSEUMS

Their origins go back to 1503, when Julius II displayed a few Classical works of art in the Belvedere Court. His successors continued to collect Greek and Roman, palaeo-Christian and Christian Antiquities. After acquiring a number of Antiques with the lottery revenues, Clement XIV created a new museum, which was enlarged by Pius VI and is called the Pio-Clementino after the two Popes. The rooms joining the Belvedere Palace to the West Gallery, now occupied by the Apostolic Library, were constructed by the architect Simonetti as an extension. Following the Treaty of Tolentino in 1797 many works of art were sent to Paris. Those that were left were arranged by Canova in a museum called the Chiaramonti Museum (after the Pope's family name). When the lost works were returned in 1816, Pius VII built the New Wing to house them.

In 1837 Gregory XVI opened an Etruscan Museum to house the results of private excavations of burial grounds in Etruria; an Egyptian Museum followed in 1839. The Art Gallery (Pinacoteca) was opened in 1932 by Pius XI.

The year 1970 saw the inauguration of a very modern building to house the Antique and Christian Art collections formerly in the Lateran Palace.

The Missionary collections were transferred from the Lateran in 1973, the same year as the creation of the History Museum and the Museum of Modern Religious Art. For the interest and diversity of their treasures, the Vatican Museums rank among the best in the world.

Museo Egizio
(Egyptian Museum)

Founded by Pope Gregory XVI, it was laid out in 1839 by Father Ungarelli, one of the first Italian Egyptologists to take an interest in Champollion's work. The collection includes antiquities acquired by the Popes in 18C and statues found in Rome and its environs; these were brought back from Egypt during the Empire or are Roman copies of 1C-2C works.

Room I contains inscriptions including documents from the Old Kingdom (c 2650 BC) to the 6C AD: throne of the bust-less statue of Pharaoh Ramses II (19th dynasty; c 1250 BC).

Room II is devoted to Ancient Egyptian funerary art: the mummy of a woman (c 1000 BC) with henna-dyed hair; sarcophagi in painted wood and stone; canopic vases (organs extracted from the body were mummified separately and kept in these vases) and various amulets.

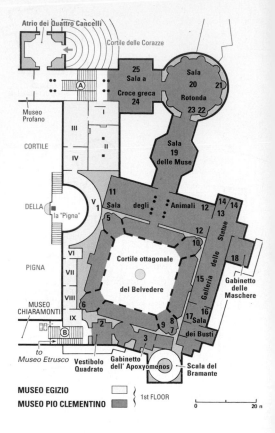

Room III displays reproductions of the sculptures which decorate the Canopus in Hadrian's Villa at Tivoli. The main theme is the reawakening, represented by twin busts on a lotus flower, of Osiris-Apis, also known as Serapis, a deity introduced in the 4C by Ptolemy. At the end of the passage stood a colossal bust of Isis-Sothis-Demeter, the goddess protecting the sources of the Nile; from it gushed a waterfall which symbolised the flooding of the Nile. Statues of Antinous, deified under the name of Osirantinoos, complete the decoration in the room.

In the **hemicycle (V)** are Egyptian statues discovered in Rome and its environs: the fine Pharaoh's head of the 11th dynasty (c 2100 BC) exemplifies the art of the Middle Kingdom. The colossal statue of Queen Thuya (**1**), Ramses II's mother (19th dynasty, c 1250 BC), illustrates the art of the New Kingdom. The pink granite statues are Egyptian-style representations of the Greek king of Egypt, Ptolemy Philadelphus (283-246 BC), his sisters Arsinoe and Philotera.

Museo Chiaramonti e Galleria Lapidaria (Chiaramonti Museum and Lapidary Gallery)

The **Chiaramonti Museum**, set up by Pius VII, whose family name was Chiaramonti, has generally kept the appearance given to it by Canova in 1807. It contains Roman copies of Greek works, portraits, funerary monuments: one low relief bearing a millstone, donkey, baskets etc obviously commemorates a miller *(on the right, Row X)*.

The **Lapidary Gallery** houses over 3 000 pagan and Christian inscriptions *(open to specialists on request)*.

From the Chiaramonti Museum the tour proceeds to the New Wing.

Braccio Nuovo (New Wing) (Roman antiquities)

The **"Doryphoros"** *(3rd recess on the left of the entrance)* depicts a spear-bearer. It is a copy of a bronze original by Polyclitus (440 BC). In all probability the original was the model (the Kanon), which demonstrated Polyclitus' theories about proportions in sculpture. The **statue of Augustus★★** *(4th recess on the right)*, known as "from the *Prima Porta*" because of where it was found, is a fine example of official Roman art. The decoration of the Emperor's breastplate is an extraordinarily precise illustration of the King of the Parthians returning the standards lost by Crassus in 53 BC. *The Nile (il Nilo) (in the central hemicycle)* is a 1C Roman work inspired perhaps by a Greek original from the Hellenistic period. It depicts the river god surrounded by 16 children, a symbol of the 16 cubits by which the river must rise in order to flood the plain and make it fertile. The gilded bronze peacocks may have come from Hadrian's Mausoleum. The **statue of Demosthenes** *(last recess on the left of the entrance)* is a Roman copy of a Greek bronze (3C BC). *Return to the entrance of the Chiaramonti Museum and go into the Pius-Clementine Museum (staircase (B))*.

Museo Pio-Clementino★★★
(Pius-Clementine Museum) (Greek and Roman antiquities)

The museum is housed in the Belvedere Palace and the rooms added by Simonetti in the 18C.

Vestibolo Quadrato (Square Vestibule) – This is the atrium of the former Clementino Museum. The sobriety of early Roman art shows in the **sarcophagus of Scipio Barbatus (2)**, carved in peperine (3C BC). Its shape is inspired by the Greek models which the Romans discovered after the capture of Rhegium in 270 BC.

Gabinetto dell'Apoxyomenos – The **Apoxyomenos★★★ (3)** is the name given to the statue of an athlete scraping his skin with a strigil after taking exercise. It is a 1C AD Roman copy of a Greek original by Lysippus (4C BC). In the weary body, the artist reveals the living human being rather than an idealistic image, as in the Classical period.

Scala del Bramante – Bramante's noble spiral stairway, which was used by men on horseback, was designed early in the 16C during the alterations ordered by Julius II.

Cortile ottagonale del Belvedere★ (Belvedere Octagonal Court) – The internal courtyard of the Belvedere Palace, originally on a square plan and planted with orange trees, acquired its octagonal outline when Simonetti added a portico in the 18C.

The extraordinary **Laocoön★★★ (5)** was unearthed in Nero's Golden House by a group of peasants. This sculpture was the work of a group of artists from Rhodes (1C BC), representing the death of Laocoön, priest of Apollo, who had incurred the god's anger and, with his two sons, was crushed to death by serpents. In this composition Hellenistic art attains an intense realism; in an attempt to show the extremes of suffering it achieved an exaggerated style which earned the description "Greek Baroque".

The expressive Laocoön is an excellent example of Hellenistic art

The statue of **Apollo★★★ (6)** was placed in the Belvedere Court by Julius II in 1503. It is probably copied from a 4C BC Greek original by a Roman sculptor, who has captured the serenity of the Greek gods. The figure may have held a bow in the left hand and an arrow in the right.

The three **neo-Classical statues by Canova** (1757-1822) were bought by Pope Pius VII to make up for the loss of certain works removed under the terms of the Treaty of Tolentino: **Perseus★★ (7)**, who conquered Medusa, and the boxers Kreugas **(8)** and Damozenos **(9)**, who met in fierce combat at Nemea in Argolis. **The Hermes★★★ (10)** is a 2C AD Roman work, inspired by an original Greek bronze, representing Zeus's son, the messenger of the gods.

Under the north portico sits the **Ara Casali**, a 3C altar presented by the Casali family to Pope Pius VI. On the front is carved a scene with Venus and Mars; the back shows Romulus and Remus.

Sala degli Animali (Room of the Animals) – Various animal sculptures, heavily restored in the 18C. The statue of **Meleager★ (11)** is a 2C Roman copy of a bronze sculpture by Skopas, a Greek artist (4C BC). Beside Meleager is the head of the boar which caused his death, at Diana's behest.

The fine mosaics of the pavement are Roman. A crab made of green porphyry, a rare stone, is displayed in a showcase **(12)**.

Galleria delle Statue (Statue Gallery) – This part of the Belvedere Palace was converted into a gallery in the 18C.

The Sleeping Ariadne★ (13) is a Roman copy of a Greek original, illustrating the characteristic taste for unusual poses and elaborate draperies of the Hellenistic period (2C BC). On waking, Ariadne will be married to Dionysius and carried away to Olympus.

The **Candelabra (14)** are fine examples of 2C Roman decorative work from Hadrian's Villa at Tivoli.

The statue of **Apollo Sauroktonos★ (15)**, showing the god about to kill a lizard, is a Roman copy of a work by Praxiteles, a Greek artist of the 4C BC. An expert in feminine models, he made the young god very graceful.

In the three rooms of the **Sala dei Busti** (Room of the Busts), divided by fine marble columns, note the **busts of Cato and Porti★ (16)**, a husband and wife group intended for a tomb (1C BC), which are in the typically austere style of the Republican era.

The numerous Imperial portraits include a particularly expressive bust of Julius Caesar **(17)**.

Gabinetto delle Maschere (Cabinet of the Masks) – This room owes its name to the mosaic of masks (2C) removed from Hadrian's Villa and let into the floor. The **Venus of Cnidos★★ (18)** is a Roman copy of Praxiteles's statue for the sanctuary at Cnidos in Asia Minor (4C BC), which was famous for its artistic merits and for being the first representation of a goddess in the nude. The Greeks, versed in the legend of Actaeon, who was killed for watching a goddess bathing, were shocked.

Return to the Room of the Animals.

Sala delle Muse (Room of the Muses) – It owes its name to the statues of the Muses which, together with statues of Greek philosophers, are arranged around the room.

Like the statue of the Pugilist *(in the Museo Nazionale Romano)*, the **Belvedere Torso★★★ (19)** is the masterly work of the Athenian Apollonius, Nestor's son, who lived in Rome in the 1C BC. The expressive torso, much admired by Michelangelo and originally thought to represent Hercules, has recently been identified as Ajax, a Greek hero and son of Telamon. According to mythology, having fought bravely during the Trojan War and saved the spoils of war of his friend Achilles, Ajax went mad and killed himself when the deceased hero's armour was given to Ulysses. The statue (of which only the torso remains) shows the hero overcome with shame.

Sala rotonda★ (Round Room) – This fine room by Simonetti (1780) was inspired by the Pantheon. The monolithic porphyry **basin (20)** may have come from Nero's Golden House. The **statue of Hercules (21)** in gilded bronze dates from the late 2C. **Antinoüs (22)**, the young favourite of the Emperor Hadrian, drowned in the Nile in 130. After his death, the Emperor raised him under the name Osirantinoos to the ranks of the gods. He bears the attributes of Dionysius and the Egyptian god Osiris (on his head is the uraeus, a serpent which formed part of the headdress of the Pharaohs). The **bust of Jupiter★ (23)** is a Roman copy of a Greek original, dating from the 4C BC.

Sala a Croce Greca (Greek Cross Room) – Two large porphyry **sarcophagi★** have pride of place. The one belonging to St Helena **(24)**, the Emperor Constantine's mother, dates from the early 4C and is heavily sculptured with conquering Roman cavalry and barbarian prisoners, an inappropriate theme for such a holy woman. This suggests that the sarcophagus was originally intended for her husband, Constantinus Chlorus, or her son Constantine, who may have had it made before moving his court to Constantinople. The other is the sarcophagus of Constantia **(25)**, Constantine's daughter, and dates from the middle of the 4C.

*Climb the Simonetti Stairs **(A)** to the second floor.*

Museo Etrusco★ (Etruscan Museum) *see plan p 316*

Founded in 1837 by Gregory XVI, this museum houses objects found in southern Etruria. In Room I are displayed the oldest artefacts (9C-8C BC cinerary urns in the form of a house). Room II accommodates the two-horse chariots used by high-born members of 8C BC society. A variety of exquisite Greek black- and red-figure vases found in several tombs provide some indication of the considerable wealth of the dead.

Items retrieved from the **Regolini-Galassi tomb** (named after the archbishop and the general who discovered it in 1836), south of Cerveteri are particularly fine. The items found in the tomb are displayed in the showcases along the wall on the right of the entrances: belonging to the woman were the bronze throne and jewellery; the incomparable golden **clasp★★**, decorated with lions and ducks in the round and dating from the 7C BC, shows the perfection attained by the Etruscans in such work; the incised pectoral medallion lay on the woman's breast surrounded by golden leaves (fragments) sewn onto her dress. The man lay on the bronze couch; the two-horse chariot *(biga)* would also have been his.

The little inkstand in *bucchero* is inscribed with an alphabet and a syllabary *(penultimate showcase facing the windows near the door to Room III)*. The **Bronze Room (III)** houses the **Mars★★** found at Todi, a rare example of a large bronze statue from the late 5C BC. The style of the work is akin to the rigour of Classical Greek works. The oval cist *(last case to the right of the Mars)*, a toilette receptacle, is attractively decorated with the Battle of the Amazons; fantastic figures adorn the handle.

The hemicycle and the adjoining rooms contain many Greek, Etruscan and Italiot vases from the 6C to the 3C BC.

In the hemicycle, note the striking large black-figure **amphora★★★** *(second middle glass case to the left of the entrance)*, painted by Exekias. In perfect condition, this object is a rare example of the master's artistry. It illustrates Achilles playing draughts with Ajax.

Sala Della Biga (Biga Room) *see plan p 316*

The **two-horse chariot★★** *(biga)*, after which the hall is named, is 1C Roman. It was reconstituted in the 18C, when the body of the chariot was recovered from St Mark's Basilica, where it had served as an episcopal throne.

Galleria degli Candelabri (Candelabra Gallery) *see plan p 316*

The loggia was transformed into a gallery in 1785 by Pius VI. It is subdivided by arches and pillars, flanked by 2C marble candelabra, and houses antiquities.

Galleria degli Arazzi (Tapestry Gallery) *see plan p 316*

The tapestries were hung by Gregory XVI in 1838. Facing the windows: the New School series, commissioned by Leo X in the early 16C, was woven by Pieter van Aelst's workshops in Brussels from cartoons by Raphael's pupils. On the window side: the life of Cardinal Maffeo Barberini, later Pope Urban VIII (Barberini workshop, Rome – 17C).

Galleria delle Carte Geografiche★ (Map Gallery) *see plan p 316*

The ceiling is richly decorated with stuccowork and paintings by a group of 18C Mannerists: 80 scenes from the lives of the saints closely associated with the maps below. The extraordinary maps on the walls were painted from 1580-83 from cartoons by Fr Ignazio Danzi, who explained that he had divided Italy in two down the line of the Apennines: the one side bathed by the Ligurian Sea and the Tyrrhenian Sea, the other bordered by the Alps and the Adriatic. The 40 maps are supplemented by town plans, a map of the region round Avignon (once a Papal possession) and two maps of Corfu and Malta. The 16C cartography is fantastically embellished with inscriptions, ships and turbulent seas.

Sala Sobieski e Sala dell'Immacolata Concezione (Sobieski Room and Room of the Immaculate Conception)

In the former hangs a 19C painting by Jan Mateiko of John III Sobieski, king of Poland, repulsing the Turks at the Siege of Vienna (1683). The 19C frescoes in the latter illustrate the dogma of the Immaculate Conception pronounced by Pius IX in 1854; an elaborate showcase displays richly decorated books on the same theme.

Stanze di Raffaello★★★ (Raphael Rooms)

During part of the year to avoid overcrowding, there is one-way access from the Room of the Immaculate Conception via an external terrace. The visit to the Raphael Rooms then starts in the Hall of Constantine. The rest of the year the tour is in the opposite direction. These rooms were built during the reign of Nicholas V (1447-55) and decorated with frescoes by Piero della Francesca among others, except the Hall of Constantine, which was part of the 13C wing of the Papal Palace. On becoming Pope in 1503, Julius II arranged to have the rooms redecorated for his own use by a group of artists which included Sodoma and Perugino. In 1508, on Bramante's recommendation, he sent for a young painter from Urbino. Charmed by Raphael's youthful grace, he entrusted the whole of the decoration to him; the other painters were dismissed and their work effaced. The frescoes in what came to be known as the "Raphael Rooms" are among the masterpieces of the Renaissance. They were damaged by the troops of Charles V during the sack of Rome in 1527, but have been restored.

Sala dell'Incendio del Borgo (Room of the Borgo Fire) (1514-17)

This was the last room to be painted by Raphael. The immediate success of his work and the large number of commissions that followed led him to speed up his work. From 1515 he worked with a group of assistants. In this room he only designed the frescoes and some of the cartoons, which were completed by his assistants. The ceiling frescoes are by Perugino.

To glorify the reign of Leo X, Julius II's successor, who had confirmed Raphael in his appointment, the artist painted the life of the Pope and of his predecessors Leo III and Leo IV. In the fresco of the *Coronation of Charlemagne* (1) the Emperor is portrayed as François I of France and Leo II as Leo X (who signed the Concordat of Bologna with François I in 1516).

The Borgo Fire (2) illustrates the account in the "Liber Pontificalis", according to which a fire which broke out in 847 in

Coronation of Charlemagne *(detail), Raphael Rooms*

the area near St Peter's (the Borgo) was quenched by Pope Leo IV with the sign of the cross. Inspired, like all Renaissance artists by Antiquity, Raphael painted the colonnade of the Temple of Mars Ultor on the left; the old man supported by a youth recalls Virgil (Aeneas fleeing from Troy, carrying his father Anchises, his son Ascanius at his side, as his wife Creusa follows behind).

In the background is the Loggia of Benedictions of Constantine's Basilica, as it was in Raphael's lifetime.

In the *Battle of Ostia* (3), Leo X is again represented in the guise of Leo IV, who defeated the Saracens at the battle of Ostia in 849.

A medieval legend is depicted in the *Oath of Leo III* (4). According to this account, when Leo III sought to clear himself of a libel in St Peter's itself, a voice rang out, declaring "It is for God not men to judge bishops" *(Latin inscription to the right of the window)*. Leo III is portrayed as Leo X.

Sala della Segnatura (Signature Room) (1508-11)

This room was used as a library, a study and for signing Papal Bulls. It was the first room painted by Raphael. The decorative theme, probably proposed by a court scholar versed in neo-Platonic philosophy, illustrates the three great principles of the human spirit: Truth, Goodness and Beauty.

The medallions on the ceiling and wall paintings illustrate closely linked subjects. Above the Triumph of Religion *(Dispute over the Blessed Sacrament)* is shown the allegory of Theology and, above that, Philosophy *(School of Athens)*. They represent the two aspects of Truth – the supernatural and the rational. Above the fresco representing canon and civil law and the cardinal virtues is the allegory of Justice. These represent Goodness. The allegory of Poetry, representing Beauty, crowns *Parnassus*. Smaller paintings in the corners underline the significance of the allegories: *Adam and Eve*, in which a woman imparts motion to the universe; the *Judgement of Solomon, Apollo and Marsyas*.

Part of the ceiling decoration is attributed to Sodoma and the octagonal area to Bramantino (c 1465-1530).

The name *Dispute over the Blessed Sacrament* (5) is wrongly attributed to the fresco illustrating the Glorification of Religion: at the top, surrounding the Trinity, appears the Church victorious with Mary, St John the Baptist, the Apostles, Prophets and Patriarchs, martyrs and angels.

On earth, grouped round the altar, stand the Doctors of the Church, the Popes and the faithful, including Dante *(right)*, crowned with laurel, Savonarola, Sixtus IV, Fra Angelico and Gregory the Great, with the features of Julius II. The lines converge on the Host, the incarnation of Christ, linking the Church on earth and the Church in heaven.

The *School of Athens* (6) depicts a crowd of philosophers standing beneath the vaults of a Classical building designed by Bramante. In the centre are the Greeks, Plato and Aristotle, representing the two main streams of Classical thought: idealism and materialism. Plato's raised finger indicates the realm of ideas, Aristotle's open hand indicates that without the material world ideas would have no existence. Raphael has given Plato the face of Leonardo da Vinci. On the left, Socrates, in a tunic, is speaking to his pupil Alcibiades. The cynic Diogenes is lounging contemptuously on the steps before a disapproving follower. Epicurus, in a laurel wreath, is giving a dissertation on pleasure, and Euclid, who resembles Bramante, is tracing geometric figures on a slate. In the right-hand corner Raphael has included himself in a black beret standing next to another painter, Sodoma, in a tunic and white beret. In the foreground is the solitary figure of Heraclitus, his head resting in his left hand; he has the facial features of Michelangelo, who was at that time decorating the Sistine Chapel. Raphael added this figure

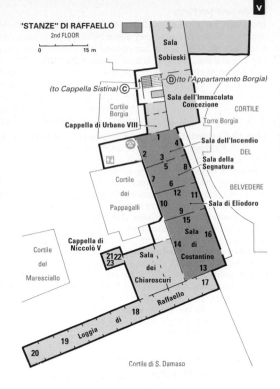

when the fresco was almost finished, in noble homage to this rival.

The Cardinal and Theological Virtues (7) – Above the window are Strength (oak branch, emblem of the Della Rovere family to which Julius II belonged), Prudence and Temperance, Faith, Hope and Charity (as cupids). On the right Raimond de Pennafort hands Gregory IX (1234) the body of rules which make up canon law (Decretals); on the left Justinian approves the "Pandects", a collection of Roman jurisprudence, comprising civil law. Gregory IX is a portrait of Julius II. Beside him stand Cardinal Giovanni de' Medici (future Leo X) and Alessandro Farnese (future Paul III).

Note the *"Parnassus"* **(8)** on the opposite wall. Around Apollo and the nine Muses are grouped the great poets, starting with Homer, Virgil and Dante.

Sala di Eliodoro (Heliodorus Room) (1512-1514)

This was the suite's private antechamber and was decorated by Raphael after the Signature Room. The theme is the divine protection of the Church.

The biblical subject of the *Expulsion of Heliodorus from the Temple* **(9)**, taken from the Book of Maccabees (Heliodorus, intent on stealing the temple treasure, is expelled by the angels), was probably chosen by Julius II himself, whose own policy was to expel usurpers from Papal property. He appears on the left in the Papal chair. It is an excellent portrait revealing the authority of the Pope, who fought alongside his own soldiers and one day broke his cane across Michelangelo's back. This fresco is exceptional for Raphael in the vigour and movement of the figures (Heliodorus, the three angels and a person flattening himself against a pillar).

The *Miracle of the Bolsena Mass* **(10)** commemorates the miracle which is celebrated today as the feast of Corpus Christi: in 1263 a priest, who doubted the doctrine of the real presence, saw blood on the host at the moment of consecration, while celebrating Mass in Bolsena. Julius II is kneeling before the priest. The Pope, his suite and the Swiss guards are among Raphael's masterpieces.

The composition is masterly. The problem of the round lunette with its off-centre window is accommodated by the asymmetric positioning of the stairs on either side of the altar and by the lively treatment of the crowd on the left where the painting is most restricted.

An episode described in the Acts of the Apostles is depicted in *St Peter delivered from prison* **(11)**. According to this account, Peter, while in prison in Rome, dreamt that an angel set him free and on waking found that he was free. One notable element in the composition is the use of various light sources: the moon, the guard's torch, the angel. This painting is a masterpiece in the painting of light, anticipating the work of Caravaggio and Rembrandt by more than a century.

In *St Leo the Great repulsing Attila* (12), Raphael shows Leo I meeting the Huns and repelling their advance, aided by the appearance of St Peter and St Paul armed with swords. The artist has moved the event to the gates of Rome, indicated by the Colosseum, a basilica and an aqueduct. The calm comportment of the Pope and his suite contrasts with the disorder of the barbarian hordes. The painting was not finished when Julius II died in 1513. Raphael therefore substituted a portrait of Leo X, although he already appeared in the picture as Cardinal Giovanni de Medici *(left)* wearing the *cappa magna* (a long hooded cloak).

A large part of the painting *(right)* was executed by Raphael's pupils.

Sala di Costantino (Hall of Constantine) (1517-1525)

In 1520 Raphael died. The painting of this room, intended for receptions, which had been begun during Leo X's reign, was finished in Clement VII's by a group of Raphael's followers led by Giulio Romano and Francesco Penni. This was the beginning of Mannerism; overwhelmed by the legacy of Raphael and Michelangelo, artists began to abandon national idealism in favour of exaggerated form and contorted movement.

The apparition of the Cross (13) and the *Battle of the Milvian Bridge* (14) are by Giulio Romano. Constantine's victory over Maxentius at the Milvian Bridge in 312 suffers from exaggeration.

The Baptism of Constantine (15) is by Francesco Penni. Pope Sylvester, who baptised Constantine, is shown with the features of Clement VII and in the baptistry of the basilica of St John Lateran.

Giulio Romano and Francesco Penni collaborated on *Constantine's Donation* (16), which is set inside the old St Peter's and shows the Emperor Constantine (306-37) giving Rome to the Pope, thus founding the temporal power of the Papacy. In his *Divine Comedy*, Dante spoke out vehemently against the gift: "Ah, Constantine, what evil was spawned not by your conversion but by that gift which the first rich Pope accepted from you."

The **vault** replaced the old beamed ceiling at the end of the 16C.

Loggia di Raffaello** (Raphael's Loggia) *see plan p 316*

Open to specialists only. Access via the Hall of Constantine. On the second floor of the galleried building.

At the beginning of the 16C, before the construction of St Damasus's Court (Cortile di San Damaso) and the buildings on its north, south and east sides, the façade of the 13C palace looked out over Rome. Julius II (1503-13) decided to give it a new look. He engaged Bramante to design three superimposed loggias. Work began in 1508 and when Bramante died in 1514 only the first tier had been built. Julius II's successor, Leo X, appointed Raphael to take over.

The loggia takes the form of a vaulted corridor, richly decorated (probably between 1517 and 1519). The walls and arches are adorned with stuccoes and "grotesques" inspired by Classical models Raphael and his friends had found in Nero's Golden House. Various artists collaborated with Raphael: Francesco Penni and Giulio Romano, Giovanni da Udine and Perin del Vaga. Their work abounds with fantastic invention: garlands of fruit and flowers, animals, reproductions of famous statues, people, scenes from contemporary life.

The loggia is divided into 13 bays; the vault of each is decorated with four paintings, representing scenes from the Old Testament, except in the first bay (17), which has scenes from the New Testament. The loggia is sometimes called "Raphael's Bible". These charmingly fresh paintings include *Moses in the Bullrushes* (18); *Building Noah's Ark* (19); *Creation of the Animals* (20).

Sala dei Chiaroscuri e Cappella di Niccolò V**

(Chiaroscuro Rooms and Nicholas V's Chapel) *see plan p 316*

The rooms owe their name to the monochrome paintings of saints and Apostles executed from Raphael's cartoons by his followers (1517). The paintings were restored in the late 16C.

Cappella di Niccolò V** (Nicholas V's Chapel)

The chapel is one of the oldest parts of the Vatican Palace. It probably formed part of a tower which was absorbed into the first Papal palace in the 13C. Nicholas V converted it into a chapel and had it decorated by **Fra Angelico** (1447-51), a Dominican monk and master of Florentine art. He was assisted by Benozzo Gozzoli, also from Florence.

In the angles are the Doctors of the Church; the Evangelists are on the ceiling. The two-tier wall paintings illustrate the lives of St Stephen and St Lawrence *(upper tier)* and were extensively restored in the 18C and 19C.

The Life of St Stephen is depicted in the upper level. On the right (21) are two legendary episodes in the saint's life: St Stephen being ordained deacon *(left)* by St Peter (whose figure shows great nobility); St Stephen distributing alms *(right)*. Above the entrance door (22): St Stephen preaching in a square in Florence *(left)* and St Stephen addressing the Council *(right)*. On the left (23): the stoning of St Stephen.

The **Life of St Lawrence** is represented in the *lower level*. Sixtus II, resembling Nicholas V, ordaining St Lawrence as deacon **(21)**, whose face shows that saintly expression which only Fra Angelico could impart. Above the door **(22)**: St Lawrence receiving the treasure of the Church from Sixtus II and distributing alms to the poor. The portrayal of a blind man *(right)* is exceptional in the idealised art of the Renaissance. On the left **(23)**: the Roman Emperor Decius pointing to the instruments of torture; the martyrdom of St Lawrence.

On leaving Nicholas V's Chapel, return to the first Raphael Room (Borgo Fire). Pass through Urban VIII's Chapel and turn right down the stairs to the Borgia Apartment.

Appartamento Borgia* (Borgia Apartment)

These rooms, which formed the suite of Alexander VI, the Borgia Pope from Spain, now house examples of modern art. They are decorated (end of 1492-94) with paintings by **Pinturicchio**, full of pleasant fantasy.

The first, known as the **Sybilline Room (I)**, is painted with figures of sybils and Prophets.

In the **Creed Room (III)** the Prophets and Apostles carry scrolls bearing the articles of the Creed.

Next is the **Liberal Arts Room (IV)**, probably used by Alexander VI as a study. It is decorated with allegories of the Liberal Arts, ie the seven subjects taught in the universities in the Middle Ages. On the ceiling are the arms of the Borgias.

The **Saints' Room (V)** was probably painted by Pinturicchio himself; in the other rooms he was assisted by many of his pupils. The legendary lives of the saints are combined with mythology, a common practice in the Renaissance period. Facing the window is one of Pinturicchio's best works, St Catherine of Alexandria arguing with the philosophers, against his usual landscape of delicate trees, rocks and hills. In the centre is the Arch of Constantine. Before the Emperor St Catherine expounds her arguments in defence of the Christian faith. The vault is painted with mythological scenes.

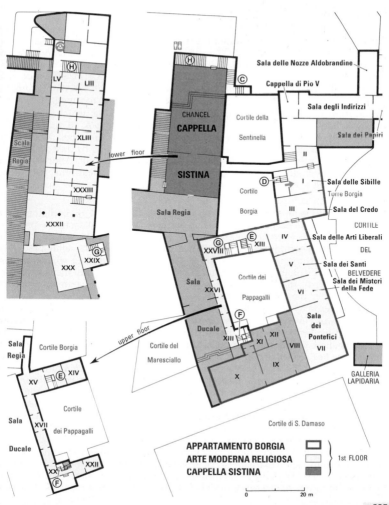

The **Mysteries of the Faith Room** (VI) depicts the principal mysteries in the lives of Jesus and his mother. On the wall framing the entrance: the Resurrection; on the left: a very fine portrait of Alexander VI, in rapt adoration.

The **Pontiffs' Room** (VII) was used for official meetings. The ceiling, which collapsed in 1500 narrowly missing Alexander VI, was reconstructed in the reign of Leo X and is decorated with stucco ornaments and "grotesques" by Perin del Vaga and Giovanni da Udine. At one time the room was hung with portraits of the Popes, hence its name. Nowadays only the dedications remain.

Collezione d'Arte Moderna Religiosa★★

This very rich collection of modern religious art brings together some 500 paintings and sculptures, given by artists and collectors. The greatest artists in the world are represented here. On the upper floor the Chapel of Peace by Giacomo Manzù (Room XIV) leads into a room devoted to Rouault (Room XV), followed by a series of smaller rooms revealing traces of the 13C palace and containing works by Chagall, Gauguin, Utrillo, Odilon Redon, Braque, Klee, Kandinsky, Moore, Morandi, De Pisis etc.

Downstairs in rooms partially beneath the Sistine Chapel gleams stained glass by Fernand Leger, Jacques Villon, George Meistermann. There are several canvases by Ben Shahn, Jack Levine, Bernard Buffet, Yugoslavian Naive paintings, sculptures by Marini, Lipchitz and Mirko, Picasso ceramics and Bazaine tapestries.

At the inauguration on 23 June 1973 Paul VI declared: "Even in our arid secularised world there is still a prodigious capacity for expressing beyond the truly human what is religious, divine, Christian."

Cappella Sistina★★★ (Sistine Chapel) *(Staircase H)*

It is named after Pope Sixtus IV for whom it was built from 1477-80. As well as being the Papal palace chapel, it seems to have served a defensive role, in view of the surviving external crenellations.

The long chamber has a barrel vault flattened by small lateral vaults and is lit by 12 windows. **Sixtus IV** sent for painters from Umbria and Florence to decorate the walls. His nephew **Julius II** (1503-13) commissioned Michelangelo to redecorate the ceiling (originally it depicted a starry sky). Twenty years later the artist was again engaged by **Clement VII** and **Paul III** to paint the wall behind the altar. The chapel is not only the setting for the most solemn ceremonies of the Holy See, where the cardinals meet in conclave, but also a masterpiece of Renaissance art. Its dimensions – 40.23m/132ft long, 13.41m/44ft wide and 20.70m/68ft high – are exactly the same as those given in the Bible for Solomon's Temple and the decorations, too, are charged with spiritual meaning.

Restoration of the Sistine Chapel – This vast undertaking, which was carried out by Italian experts and financed by Japanese patrons, took 18 years to complete, of which 12 (1980-92) were spent on Michelangelo's frescoes. Most of the restoration work consisted of cleaning the frescoes, darkened by dust and candle smoke, with a mixture of bicarbonate of soda and ammonium. After 500 years Michelangelo's original colours ranging from bright orange, clear pink, pale green to brilliant yellow and turquoise, sparkle gloriously.

Side walls

In the decoration of the walls (1481-83) Sixtus IV wanted to perpetuate the decorative tradition of the early Christian basilicas. The lowest section represents the curtains which were hung between the columns of the old basilicas. Between the windows are portraits of the early Popes from St Peter to Marcellus I (308-09). The figures of Christ and the first three Popes were obliterated when the Last Judgement was painted above the altar. The paintings halfway up the walls depict parallel scenes in the lives of Moses and Jesus, showing the human condition before and after the coming of the Messiah.

Life of Moses – *(South wall from the Last Judgement)*. The first fresco *(Moses in the Bullrushes)* was covered up by the *Last Judgement. Moses in Egypt* **(I)** by **Perugino** is followed by *Moses's Youth* **(II)** by **Botticelli**; the two female figures of Jethro's daughters show the more lyrical side of the artist's style. These are followed by *Crossing the Red Sea* **(III)** and *The Giving of the Tablets of the Law on Mount Sinai* **(IV)** by **Cosimo Rosselli**. In *The Punishment of Korah, Dathan and Abiram* **(V)**, for denying Moses's and Aaron's authority over the Jewish people, Botticelli set the scene against a background of Roman monuments: the Arch of Constantine and the Palatine Septizonium *(see FORO ROMANO-PALATINO)*. *The Testament and Death of Moses* **(VI)** is by **Luca Signorelli**.

Life of Christ – *(North wall from the Last Judgement)*. The first fresco, the *Nativity*, disappeared under **Michelangelo's Last Judgement**. The series begins with the *Baptism of Jesus* **(VII)** by **Perugino** and **Pinturicchio**, featuring many members of Sixtus IV's court. The next panel, *The Temptation of Christ* and *The Healing of the Leper* **(VIII)**, directly faces the Papal throne; here **Botticelli** has given greater weight to the healing scene in deference to Sixtus IV, who had written a theological treatise on the subject; he also painted the Temple in Jerusalem to look like the Santo Spirito Hospital, which the Pope had had reconstructed. The small scenes at the foot of the painting represent the *Temptation of Christ (left to right)* in a thicket, on a pinnacle of the temple and on a high mountain. The next painting is an illustration of *The calling of St Peter and St Andrew* **(IX)** by **Ghirlandaio**. In *The Sermon on the Mount* and *The Healing of the Leper* **(X)**, **Cosimo Rosselli**, assisted by **Piero di Cosimo**, made one of the first attempts to paint a sunset. The *Delivery of the Keys to St Peter* **(XI)** is a masterpiece by **Perugino**; the Arch of Constantine appears twice flanking the Temple in Jerusalem, which is drawn by the artist according to his imagination. The final panel is *The Last Supper* **(XII)** by Cosimo Rosselli in which Judas is shown face to face with Jesus, apart from the other Apostles.

Ceiling

When Julius II abandoned his project for a funerary sculpture, **Michelangelo** returned unhappily to Florence. In 1508 he was recalled to Rome by the Pope, who asked him to paint the Twelve Apostles on the ceiling of the Sistine Chapel. He had barely started, as he later recorded, when he realised the work was going badly; the Pope then gave him a free hand and instead of the blue star-spangled vault (some 520m²/660sq ft) he created a masterpiece filled with powerful movement. The animated figures compose an epic of the creation of the world and the history of the human race.

Julius II came regularly to ask Michelangelo when he would finish; from the top of the scaffolding came the regular reply "When I can."

On 14 August 1511, bursting with impatience, the Pope insisted on seeing the fresco; he was overwhelmed. About a year later it was finished.

From the Creation to the Flood – *Starting from the altar.*

(1) *God divides the light from the darkness.*

(2) *Creation of the sun, the moon and plant life.*

(3) *God divides the waters from the earth and creates living creatures in the seas.*

(4) *Creation of Adam.*

(5) *Creation of Eve.*

(6) *Original sin and expulsion from the Garden of Eden.*

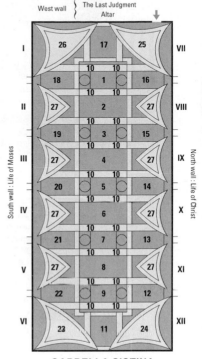

CAPPELLA SISTINA

(7) *Noah's sacrifice:* contrary to biblical chronology, this scene precedes the Flood. Michelangelo may have wanted to give more space to the Flood scene or to stress Noah's loyalty to God, thus justifying his being saved in the Ark.

(8) *The Flood:* this was the first scene to be painted. Some of the figures are too small in proportion to their surroundings.

(9) *Noah's Drunkenness:* the whole series could have terminated with the Flood; by including the last scene, where Noah is scorned by his son, Michelangelo pessimistically reminds us that life on earth began again under a bad omen.

The "Ignudi" (10) – These are the figures which Michelangelo painted at each corner of the central panels. These remarkable figures, which glorify the human body, are modelled on Classical sculptures and influenced many Renaissance and Mannerist artists.

Prophets and Sibyls – There is great variety in these 12 portraits: *Zacharias* **(11)**, the old man with a beard; *Joel* **(12)**, the critic; the *Erythraean sibyl* **(13)**, not knowing where to begin her study; *Ezekiel* **(14)**, in earnest debate; the *Persian sibyl* **(15)**, short-sighted and bowed with old age; *Jeremiah* **(16)** in his melancholy; *Jonah* **(17)**, symbol of Christ's Resurrection, ejected from the whale in a movement recalled by Baroque artists; the *Libyan sibyl* **(18)**, her study completed, descending from her throne with gracefulness; *Daniel* **(19)**, inspired by a new idea; the *Cumaean sibyl* **(20)**, a muscle-bound giant apparently puzzled by what she is reading; *Isaiah* **(21)**, troubled by an angel; the young *Delphic sibyl* **(22)**.

Bible Stories – At the centre of these four scenes are the heroes of the Jewish people – David, Judith, Esther, Moses – in whom Christ reaffirmed the promise of His coming foretold by the Prophets: *Judith and Holophernes* **(23)**, *David and Goliath* **(24)**, the *Punishment of Haman* **(25)**, the *Brazen Serpent* **(26)**.

ESAIAS

ERITHRAEA

Jesus's Forefathers (27) – Their names *(above the windows)* correspond to the scenes painted in the triangular sections. There the Jewish families wait for their deliverance.

The Last Judgement

Twenty years after painting the ceiling, in 1534, **Michelangelo** was sent for by Clement VII to complete the decoration of the chapel. The Pope, who had seen Rome sacked by Charles V's troops in 1527, wanted *The Last Judgement* to deliver its message boldly from above the altar as a warning to the unfaithful. Paul III took up his predecessor's idea and work began in 1535. The 15C frescoes were obliterated as well as two panels in the series depicting Jesus's ancestors. When the fresco was unveiled on 31 October 1541, people were amazed and dumb-founded. Stamped with the mark of violence and anger, this striking work, with its mass of naked bodies writhing in a baleful light, is an expression of misfortune: Rome had been sacked in 1527; Luther's doctrine was dividing the Western Church. In the 16C and 18C the fresco was touched up. The austerity of the Counter-Reformation moved Pius IV to have the naked figures clothed by Daniele da Volterra; in all about 30 figures were clothed.

This fresco introduced a new style in the history of art, which led to the Baroque. The composition follows a strict scheme: the elect are welcomed on high by the angels *(left)* as the damned tumble headlong into hell *(right)*.

At the bottom *(left)* the dead slowly awake; in vain the devils try to restrain them. Up above, the elect seem drawn by the movement of Christ's right hand. Beside the terrifying figure of Christ the Judge, the Virgin turns away from the horrific spectacle. Around them are the saints, bearing the instruments of their martyrdoms: St Andrew with his cross beside the Virgin, beneath them St Lawrence and his gridiron, St Bartholomew with his skin (in its folds appears the distorted face of Michelangelo).

In his boat Charon waits for the damned, whom he throws into the river of hell. Minos, the master of hell, his body wreathed by a snake *(in the corner)*, resembles Biagio da Cesena, the master of ceremonies at the Papal court. The latter was shocked that such a work could appear in so venerable a place and complained to the Pope, Paul III, who retorted that he did not have the power to rescue someone from hell. The fresco as a whole is dominated by angels bearing the Cross, the Crown of Thorns, the Column and the other instruments of the Passion.

Pavement and Choir Screen

The chapel was paved in the 15C in the Cosmati style. The delicate choir screen and the choristers' gallery are by **Mino da Fiesole** (15C).

Biblioteca Apostolica★ (Vatican Library) (Precious objects) *see plan p 316*

Cappella di San Pio V (Pius V's Chapel) – On display are the treasures of the Sancta Sanctorum, the private chapel of the Popes in the Lateran Palace.

Sala degli Indirizzi (Room of the Addresses) – Secular items from the Roman and early-Christian era are exhibited together with religious items from the Middle Ages to the present day.

Sala delle Nozze Aldobrandine (Aldobrandini Marriage Room) – A fresco from the Augustan period depicting wedding preparations *(centre wall)* is named after its first owner, Cardinal Pietro Aldobrandini.

Museo Sacro (Sacred Museum) – This museum was founded in 1756 by Benedict XIV for early-Christian antiquities.

Sale Sistine (Sistine Rooms) – Beyond the Gallery of Urban VIII, with its instruments of astronomy and *mappa mundi*, are the Sistine Rooms, created by Sixtus V (1585-90) to hold archives.

Salone Sistino★ (Sistine Salon) – *Used for temporary exhibitions.* The salon was built in 1587 by Sixtus V and was the reading room of the Vatican Library. The Mannerist decoration by Cesare Nebbia shows episodes of Sixtus V's Papacy, the history of books, the Councils of the Church and the inventors of the alphabet *(on the pillars)*. It contains 17C cupboards painted in the 19C.

The Vatican Library is followed by the Pauline Rooms, created by Paul V (1605-21). Next come the Alexandrine Room, created by Alexander VIII (1690), and the **Clementine Gallery**, commissioned by Clement XII. Next is the **Profane Museum**, which was founded in 1767 by Clement XIII (Etruscan, Roman and medieval artefacts).

Pinacoteca★★★ (Picture Gallery)

Italian Primitives – *Room I.* The **Last Judgement (1)**, painted on wood in the 12C, is an excellent painting of the Roman School and is very similar to Byzantine art.

Giotto and his School – *Room II.* The **Stefaneschi Triptych (2)** is named after the cardinal who commissioned it and was executed by **Giotto**, no doubt with the assistance of his pupils, in 1315. It was intended originally for the high altar of Constantine's Basilica.

Florentine School: Fra Angelico and his pupil Benozzo Gozzoli, Filippo Lippi – *Room III.* These artists are among the great 15C painters. Fra Angelico's (1400-55) slightly old-fashioned style, which links him to the Middle Ages, nonetheless expresses his deep religious feeling, as the small painting of the *Virgin and Child with saints and angels* (3) demonstrates; the two *scenes from the Life of St Nicholas of Bari* (4) come from an altarpiece predella. The *Coronation of the Virgin* (5) is by **Filippo Lippi** (1406-69) and *St Thomas receiving the Virgin's girdle* (6) by Benozzo Gozzoli (1420-97).

Melozzo da Forlì (1438-94) – *Room IV.* The graceful **Musical Angels** (7), with their bright colours, elegant curls and delicate features, are remarkable. They are fragments of a fresco depicting the Ascension of Christ painted on the apse ceiling of the basilica of the Holy Apostles (Santi Apostoli). The fresco (transferred to canvas) of *Sixtus IV and Platina the Librarian* (8) adorned the Pope's library. The cardinal is a portrait of Sixtus IV's nephew, Giuliano della Rovere, later Julius II.

Polyptychs – *Room VI.* The *Virgin and Child* (9) is by **Carlo Crivelli** (1430-93), a Venetian. While the Florentines were experimenting with line, the Venetians were taking an interest in colour. In addition, Crivelli had a marked taste for gold decoration (very beautiful painted fabrics).

15C Umbrian School – *Room VII.* The *Virgin and Child* (10) by **Perugino** and the *Coronation of the Virgin* (11) by **Pinturicchio** illustrate the clear and poetic style of the Umbrian artists.

Room VIII: Raphael★★★ **(1483-1520)** – The artistic development of the painter of the *Stanze* is illustrated by three works. The *Coronation of the Virgin* (12), painted in 1503 has a youthful freshness and shows the influence of Perugino. The *Madonna of Foligno* (13) was painted in 1511-12 while Raphael was in Rome at the height of his glory; the fine portrait of Sigismondo dei Conti, on his knees, which dominates the picture, the exquisite pose of the Virgin and the luminosity surrounding her are the work of a master. The beautiful *Transfiguration* (14), with its dramatic contrasts in chiaroscuro, was intended for Narbonne Cathedral in France and was completed by Raphael shortly before he died in 1520.

Room IX – With his *St Jerome*★★ (15) Leonardo da Vinci (1452-1519) shows his mastery of anatomy, expression and light. The picture was put together after being discovered in two pieces, one in an antique shop and the other at a shoemaker's. The *Pietà* (16) by the Venetian **Giovanni Bellini** (1429-c 1516) combines accurate drawing and deep inspiration with fine tonality.

Room X – In his *Madonna of San Nicola dei Frari* (17) Titian uses the marvellous colours of the Venetian painters. The *Coronation of the Virgin* (18), by Giulio Romano *(upper part)* and Francesco Penni *(lower part)*, two artists who often finished off Raphael's work, shows the Mannerist style. In Veronese's *Sant'Elena* (19) the saint is depicted in an unusual position, her hand supporting her head.

Mannerists – *Room XI.* The works include *Rest on the Flight into Egypt* (20) by **Frederico Barocci** (1528-1612), as delicate and luminous as a pastel.

Caravaggio and his followers – *Room XII.* The *Descent from the Cross*★★ (21) by **Caravaggio** (1573-1610) clearly expresses the painter's reaction to Mannerist sentimentality. His characters, even in the most religious scenes, are drawn from life. The firmness of his line and the way the light falls further emphasise his realism (note how Nicodemus and St John hold the body of the dead Christ). Mary Magdalen, her head bowed, is a truly remarkable figure. Caravaggio had a great influence on the French painter **Valentin** (1594-1632) – *Martyrdom of St Processus and St Martinian* (22). **Guido Reni** (1575-1642) was also inspired – *Crucifixion of St Peter* (23).

Rooms XIII-XIV – These rooms contain works from the 17C and 18C, particularly by **Pietro da Cortona**, the great Baroque artist. Note the portrait of Clement IX (24) by Carlo Maratta (1625-1713). There is also a model for St Peter's dome.

Room XV – Sir Thomas Lawrence's portrait of George IV of England was a gift from the king to Pius VII.

PINACOTECA

0   20 m

13 14 12
VIII
16 15   10
IX   VII
         11
18   17 9
   X   19 VI
20 XI   V
      22   8
      XII   IV
      21 7
      23
         5 6 III
         4 3 4
      XIII   2 II
              XIV
              24
      XV   1 I
XVII XVI
XVIII

Quadrato
Zitelle
Giardino
delle
Viale

Cortile della Pinacoteca

Musei Gregoriano Profano e Cristiano★

A fine modern building begun in 1963 houses the **Profane** and **Christian Museums**, which were opened to the public in 1970. They contain the collections comprising the Museum of Antique Art assembled by Gregory XVI (1831-46) and the Museum of Christian art founded in 1854 by Pius IX, formerly kept in the Lateran Palace.

Gregorian Profane Museum

It is divided into four sections: copies of sculpture from the Imperial period (1C BC to 3C AD); 1C and 2C Roman sculpture; sarcophagi; 2C and 3C Roman sculpture. The modern materials – metal, concrete and wood – provide an ideal setting for the exhibits, which can be viewed from all sides.

Imperial period copies – The **basalt head (1)** is a fine copy of a Greek original linked to the art of Polyclitus (5C BC). **Sophocles (2)**, the Athenian tragic poet, is represented by a large statue of noble mien with a headband to show he is a priest of Amynos, a healer. The beautiful **mosaic (3)** on the ground is decorated with fantastic designs. There are several **herms (4)**, their heads and shoulders springing from a pillar. The **relief of Medea and the daughters of Pelias (5)** is a 1C BC Roman copy of a late 5C BC Greek original; despite being damaged, it illustrates the story of the deception of Pelias's daughters by Medea with great elegance. There is a **headless statue (6)**, probably inspired by a 5C original, and the **"Chiaramonti" Niobe (7)**, a copy of a statue which was part of a group representing the death of Niobe and her daughters *(see p 263)*.

Roman sculpture (1C and early 2C) – The low relief of the **Vicomagistrates' altar (8)** is a particularly fine 1C sculpture, which probably decorated the lower part of an altar. It shows a procession of people leading animals to the temple for the sacrifice; following the four Vicomagistrates (street magistrates) are the assistants bearing statues of the Lares (the gods of the household and the highways). The narrative style of the sculpture and its naturalism make it a truly Roman work.

There is a fine collection of **urns and funerary altars (9)**, dating from the 1C, which come from the Via Appia in particular, and the **base of a column (10)** from the Basilica Julia in the Roman Forum, a fine example of Roman decorative art.

Among the major pieces in the section are the **Cancelleria Reliefs★**, so-called because they were discovered beneath the Palazzo Cancelleria in the Campus Martius. Classical in style, they illustrate two events in the life of the Emperor Vespasian and his son Domitian. One sculpture **(11)** shows Vespasian's arrival in Rome after his election to the Imperial throne; the Emperor, on the right, makes a noble figure in his toga. His son Domitian greets him. Between them is the genius of the Roman people, bearing the horn of plenty, with one foot resting on a milestone, showing that

MUSEO GREGORIANO PROFANO
FIRST FLOOR

MUSEO CRISTIANO
UPPER FLOOR

the meeting is taking place at the limit of the *pomerium* (the sacred boundary of Rome). The other sculpture **(12)** shows Domitian's departure on a campaign. When the Senate banned memorials of Domitian, his head was replaced by that of his successor, Nerva.

The **Haterii tomb sculptures** are the remains of a family tomb from the end of the 1C. They represent the popular taste in Roman art which developed parallel with the official style (realism and detailed precision to the detriment of the overall effect). The family concerned was probably that of Haterius Tychicus, constructor of public buildings; two low reliefs, in particular, allude to the building trade: one **(13)** represents the monuments of Ancient Rome (the unfinished Colosseum is easily recognisable); the other **(14)** shows a huge funerary monument in the form of a temple; appearing above the building are the scenes which took place inside the tomb; the detailed treatment lacks proportion: to the left of the scenes the sculptor has placed a crane. The portraits are particularly realistic: a woman in a recess with wavy hair **(15)** is executed with great skill; likewise the little pillar wreathed in finely modelled roses **(16)** is exquisite.

There are several fine **decorative sculptures**: two pillars ornamented with foliated scrolls **(17)** and fragments of 2C friezes **(18, 19, 20)**.

Sarcophagi – Many are illustrated with mythical subjects. The fragment of the "philosopher's" sarcophagus **(21)** shows a group of scholars: the faces are so realistic that they seem like portraits; they date from about AD 270.

Roman sculpture (2C and 3C) – The **porphyry torso (22)** probably belonged to an Imperial statue (2C). The statue of a **young woman arrayed like Omphale (23)**, (Queen of Lydia who assumed Hercules's attributes), is typical of the 3C style, which aimed at immortalising the subject in such a disguise.

Mosaics from the Baths of Caracalla★ – *Visible from the Christian Museum.* They **(24 and 25)** date from the 3C and show the figures of athletes, gladiators and their trainers; their brutality is evidence of the Roman taste for violent spectacles.

Christian Museum *(up Staircase I)*

Statue of the Good Shepherd (26) – It is heavily restored and probably dates from the 3C. The Christian artist has taken the pagan image of a shepherd offering his finest animal to the gods or of Hermes leading the dead into the next world, but here the figure is suffused with the meaning of the new religion and illustrates the parable of the lost sheep saved by the good shepherd: "When he hath found it, he layeth it on his shoulders, rejoicing."

Sarcophagi – The Christian sarcophagi are similar to the pagan ones in their decoration: figures in relief in a continuous band; the sides divided into panels separated by arcades; strigils and central medallions.

The first Christian artists decorated the sarcophagi with garlands, baskets and putti, using the pagan motifs to which they added the symbolic themes of sheep – Christ's flock, vine branches – symbol of union with God through the Eucharist, etc. From the middle of the 3C, scenes and figures were added to the symbols, as, for example, on the **side of a sarcophagus found in St Lawrence Without the Walls (27)**, which shows Christ and the Apostles as well as sheep representing the Christian flock.

In the 4C new subjects appear: on a **covered sarcophagus found in St Calixtus's Catacombs (28)** and on a **sarcophagus with two bands of decoration (29)** are two scenes often shown together: Peter's arrest and Moses striking water from the rock *(on the right-hand side of the former and in the lower section of the latter)*.

On a 4C **sarcophagus found in St Lawrence Without the Walls (30)** are various scenes including: Adam and Eve receiving a grain of wheat and a sheep from God *(upper section left of the central medallion)*, symbols of the labour to which they were condemned after their fall from grace.

On another 4C **sarcophagus from St Paul Without the Walls (31)** the cross is placed in the centre as a sign of triumph; the Christian monogram is surrounded with a crown of laurel.

Note also the **moulding of the sarcophagus of Junius Bassus (32)**.

Museo Missionario-Etnologico (Missionary-Ethnological Museum) *see plan p 316*

Take staircase K.

The museum was founded in 1927 by Pius XI and first housed in the Lateran Palace, but moved into ultra-modern premises in the Vatican during Paul VI's reign.

It comprises a large collection of articles illustrating the great world religions (Buddhism, Hinduism, Islam) and Christian artefacts designed in the ethnic style of the local artists from every continent except Europe.

Museo delle Carrozze (Carriage Museum) *see plan p 316*

Take staircase L.

The museum, which was opened in 1973 in the reign of Paul VI in an underground chamber, displays Popes' and cardinals' carriages and the first Papal motor vehicle.

VATICAN CITY AND GARDENS★

The Bell Arch (Arco delle Campane) leads into Piazza dei Protomartiri Romani, which is situated more or less in the centre of the Circus of Caligula and Nero, where many early Christians were martyred; a black stone with a white border set in the ground marks the former site of the obelisk, which is now in St Peter's Square. On the left is the German and Dutch burial ground which, according to a pious legend, consists of earth brought from Jerusalem. Next, on the left, comes the church dedicated to St Stephen, where Charlemagne spent the night before being crowned in 800. After the **Mosaic School** (Scuola del Mosaico) are the various buildings from which the Vatican State is administered. There are fine views of the Leonine City.

The tour finishes with a view of the dome of St Peter's, designed by Michelangelo, rising majestically above the magnificent **gardens★★★**; the fountains and statues are gifts from various countries. Pius IV's "Casina" is a charming 16C building decorated with paintings and stucco work.

The luxuriant, well-kept Vatican Gardens

J. Malburet/MICHELIN

Via Veneto★

During the 1950s and 1960s, this famous street was a popular and fashionable meeting place for Italian and overseas film stars. Although it has now lost some of its former glamour, the Via Veneto is still a favourite with wealthy tourists and is lined with some of the smartest hotels and restaurants in the city. This wide avenue is particularly lively at night, when the area is crowded with people enjoying a stroll past its famous cafés and magnificent *palazzi*.

Location

Michelin map 38 or Michelin spiral atlas of Rome: p 41 J 13, K 13. Metro line A: Barberini or Spagna (Via Veneto is easily reached from the latter via the underpass connecting Piazza di Spagna with the Villa Borghese underground car park). Tour: 1hr 30min. Situated near the Villa Borghese gardens, Via Veneto winds its way downhill from Porta Pinciana in the Aurelian Walls (now the Muro Torto), through the Ludovisi quarter to Piazza Barberini.

Neighbouring sights are described in the following chapters: FONTANA DI TREVI-QUIRINALE; PIAZZA DI SPAGNA; PORTA PIA; VILLA BORGHESE-VILLA GIULIA.

Directory

WHERE TO EAT
See "Where to Eat" in the Practical Points section at the beginning of the guide.

TAKING A BREAK
Café de Paris – *Via Vittorio Veneto 90 –* ☎ *06 48 85 284 – Open Wed-Mon, 8am-*

1am. A favourite meeting place during the *Dolce Vita* years, this bar is now mainly frequented by tourists.
Doney – *Via Vittorio Veneto 145 –* ☎ *06 48 21 790.* This elegant café has a legendary piano bar and a rather old-fashioned atmosphere.

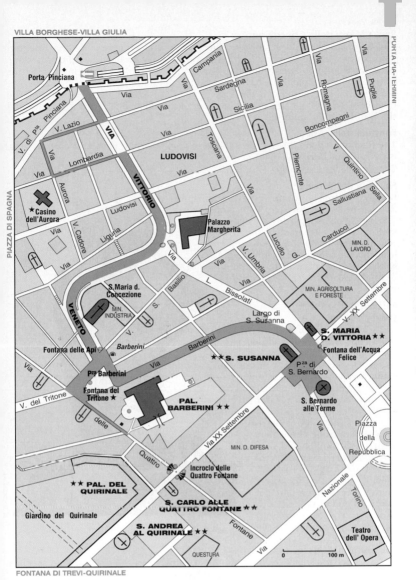

Walking About

Porta Pinciana

The gateway in the wall which Aurelian built around Rome in the 3C was fortified in the 6C by Belisarius, the Emperor Justinian's great general, who strove to regain the western territories of the Roman Empire. He captured Rome in 537 and expelled the Ostrogoths and Pope Silverius.

Via Vittorio Veneto

This street, which was created after 1879, bears the name of the commune of the Veneto, which, in 1866, adopted the name of King **Victor Emmanuel II** (Vittorio Emanuele) and in 1918 was the scene of the battle in which the Austro-Hungarian army was beaten by Italian troops. The Via Veneto, as it is often called, runs through the heart of the beautiful **Ludovisi district**, which was divided into building lots in 1883 when Prince Ludovisi sold up his magnificent 17C property. Its luxury hotels, boutiques and elegant cafés have made it a meeting place for the smart set: rich tourists and those who like the sophisticated life.

Palazzo Margherita

It was designed by Gaetano Koch in 1886 and was the residence of Margaret of Savoy, King Humbert I's wife; it is now the United States Embassy.

Santa Maria della Concezione

The church was built in 1624 in the austere style imposed by the Counter-Reformation. In the pavement at the entrance to the chancel lies the tombstone of Cardinal Antonio Barberini, who founded the church, with the inscription *Hic jacet pulvis, cinis et nihil* (Here lie dust, ashes and nothing).

Below the church *(access on the right of the front steps)* is the **cemetery of the Capuchin friars★**, an unusual gallery curiously "decorated" with the bones and skulls of the friars themselves.

Fontana delle Api

The fountain, which incorporates the **bees** *(api)* from the Barberini coat of arms, is the work of **Bernini** (1644).

Turn into Piazza Barberini.

Fontana del Tritone★

Bernini's **Triton Fountain** (c 1642) is a happy example of Roman Baroque. The composition – four dolphins supporting an open scallop shell in which a triton sits blowing into a conch – demonstrates the powerful and lively qualities of his art. The Barberini bees on the coat of arms recall that a Barberini, Urban VIII, was then Pope.

Palazzo Barberini★★
(Barberini Palace)

In 1623 Cardinal Maffeo Barberini be-came Pope Urban VIII and decided to build a Baroque palace to house his family. Work began in 1627 under Carlo **Maderno**; the palace was completed from 1629-33 by Borromini and Bernini.

The main façade, which is framed by two wings, in the style of a Roman country villa, is the work of **Bernini**.

By superimposing three tiers of attached columns and shallow pilasters to frame two floors of huge windows (slightly splayed on the upper storey) over an open porch at ground level, he created a sense of the dignity and solemnity appropriate to the Barberini family.

Triton Fountain – Piazza Barberini

B. Juge/MICHELIN

Borromini has left his mark in the two small curiously pedimented upper windows in the intermediate sections linking the wings to the central block of the palace.

The windows in the rear façade were decorated by Borromini, who also designed the couple-columned **oval spiral staircase★** at the right-hand *(south)* end of the front porch *(also visible at the end of the visit to the Galleria di Arte Antica, which is housed in the palazzo: see Worth a Visit below). Return to Piazza Barberini in order to turn down Via Barberini, which is lined with travel agencies and airline offices.*

Santa Susanna★★

Open 9-11.30am and 4-6pm (3.30-4.30pm Sun and public holidays). American church. Mass held in English. Donations welcome. ☎ 0335 72 25 253.

A Christian sanctuary was probably established here in the 4C in the house of Pope Caius, where St Susanna was thought to have been martyred. Rebuilt by Leo III in the 9C and restored at the end of the 15C by Sixtus IV, the church assumed its present appearance in the late 16C.

Façade★★ – This beautifully proportioned masterpiece was designed by Carlo Maderno and finished in 1603. It is derived from the Counter-Reformation style typified by the façade of the Gesù Church, but the use of semi-engaged columns and the effect of perspective, created by recesses and pediments which relieve the austerity, give it an individual distinction.

The two storeys are harmoniously linked by the repetition of the two superimposed pediments and the elegant lateral scrolls.

Interior – The decoration is typical of the Roman Mannerist style (late 15C): the walls of the nave are covered with paintings made to look like tapestries, which illustrate the biblical story of Susanna. The scenes in the chancel also depict the history of this saint. The wreathed columns framing the paintings in the nave were probably added in the 17C, after Bernini had designed the baldaquin in St Peter's (1624).

Santa Maria della Vittoria★★

Carlo Maderno was commissioned to design the church in 1608. Although the façade was built some 20 years after that of Santa Susanna, between 1624 and 1626, it is not so daring; with its flat pilasters in place of columns, it is closer to the Counter-Reformation style. It was designed by **Giovanni Battista Soria** for Cardinal Scipione Borghese.

Interior★★★ – Maderno's plan is based on the Gesù Church: a nave, a broad shallow transept and a dome over the crossing. The simple lines of the design enhance the elegant decoration of the cornice; during the 17C a very rich Baroque decor was applied throughout; the vault, originally white and coffered, and the dome, were painted with *trompe l'oeil* frescoes of the Virgin triumphing against heresy and entering into Heaven; the walls were faced with multicoloured marble, their warm tones mingling with the gilded stucco and the white cherubs.

The apse was entirely rebuilt after being destroyed in 1833 by a fire in which the sacred image of the Virgin also disappeared.

The Baroque decoration culminates in the **Cornaro Chapel** *(left transept)*, which was designed by **Bernini** in 1652 to resemble a theatre: eight members of the Cornaro family, as if in boxes at the theatre, gaze at the *Ecstasy of St Theresa of Avila*★★★. Marble has never been made to look so supple nor to express so accurately the texture of rough cloth (the Carmelite habit), the light veiling in the angel's garment and the delicacy of the flesh.

The chapel in the right transept was created late in the 17C to complement the Cornaro Chapel.

The paintings in the chapels include the *Life of St Francis* by Domenichino *(second chapel on the right)* and the *Trinity* by Guercino *(third chapel on the left)*.

Fontana dell'Acqua Felice

This huge fountain was designed in 1587 by Domenico Fontana. It is supplied by an aqueduct built by Sixtus V, which runs from near Colonna on the Via Casilina, and bears the Pope's Christian name: Felice Peretti.

It is dominated by the colossal statue of Moses; it was sculpted by Prospero Bresciano, who was, no doubt, inspired by Michelangelo's *Moses*; his disappointment was so great when he saw the finished work that he died.

San Bernardo alle Terme

St Bernard's Church was created late in the 16C in a rotunda, formerly the south-west corner of the Baths of Diocletian *(see PORTA PIA-TERMINI)*. The handsome coffered dome, similar to the one in the Pantheon, lends dignity to the interior.

Worth a Visit

Casino dell'Aurora★

For information on admission times and charges, call ☎ 06 48 39 42.

The Aurora Casino is the only extant building of the Ludovisi estate. Just as Cardinal Scipione Borghese, Paul V's nephew, had his casino decorated by Guido Reni, so Cardinal Ludovico Ludovisi, Gregory XV's nephew, invited Guercino to decorate his. Both artists, who were pupils of the Carracci, chose the subject of Aurora.

GALLERIA NAZIONALE D'ARTE ANTICA★★

Housed in Palazzo Barberini (see p 336). Entrance at Via delle Quattro Fontane 13 or Via Barberini 18. Open daily (except Mon), 9am-7.30pm (last admission 7pm). Closed 1 Jan and Christmas. €6.20. ☎ 06 48 14 591 or 06 48 24 184; Fax 06 48 80 560.

RESTORATION WORK

Palazzo Barberini is currently undergoing restoration work to rearrange the layout of the rooms and works of art. The museum's collections are described here according to their current layout, which follows a roughly chronological order. Plans for the new layout are as follows:

Ground floor (Via Barberini side): Visitor reception area, including a cloakroom, bookshop, educational rooms, audio-visual rooms, etc.

Ground floor North Wing: 12C to 15C paintings.

First floor North Wing: 17C works, the largest and most valuable part of the museum's collection.

First floor South Wing: This section of the palace has retained much of its original appearance. It will display what remains of the Barberini sculpture collection and the 17C collection of figurative arts.

Second floor: Paintings by non-Italian artists and the museum's 18C collection. Some of the rooms will contain minor works or works which have little relevance to the rest of the collection. The 18C apartment can be seen at the end of the rooms.

Third floor: The area originally occupied by Cardinal Francesco Barberini's library (17C) will house the cartoons by the School of Pietro da Cortona and tapestries made by the Barberini tapestry factory. The four cartoons depicting the life of Constantine by Pietro da Cortona and the cartoons showing scenes from the life of Christ by Ramonelli, his pupil, are worthy of note.

First floor

12C-16C Paintings – *The visit starts in the first room to the left of the entrance.* The **Virgin and Child** by the **master of the Palazzo Venezia** is an elegant drawing in which the influence of Simone Martini can be seen. The **Virgin and Child** and the **Annunciation** by **Filippo Lippi** (1406-1469) demonstrate some of the techniques typically used by this artist, such as the attention paid to perspective through the use of architectural elements (the windows and columns), a novelty in early Italian art, and the attention to detail due essentially to contact with Flemish artists. Also worthy of note are a fine **Mary Magdalene** by **Piero di Cosimo** and *San Nicolò da Tolentino* by **Perugino**. Three works by **Antoniazzo Romano**, chief exponent of the firm style being used in Latium at the end of the 15C, are also exhibited, among them the **Nativity with St Lawrence and St Andrew**.

Particularly worthy of note among the 16C works are **The Holy Family** by **Andrea del Sarto** and a fine **Virgin and Child with St John** by Domenico Beccafumi, which plays with contrasting light and uses the *sfumato* technique perfected by Leonardo da Vinci. Works by **Sodoma** (1477-1549), who was a great admirer of Raphael's flowing lines and was his friend and collaborator in Rome, include **The Mystical Marriage of St Catherine** and **The Rape of the Sabine Women**. The collection also boasts a masterpiece by **Raphael**, **La Fornarina★★★**, painted by the artist during the year he died. The authorship of this work was the subject of much argument for many years and was attributed to a pupil of Raphael, then to Sebastiano del Piombo. The painting is a portrait of Raphael's beautiful mistress, Margherita, known as La Fornarina because she was the daughter of a baker (*fornaio* in Italian). La Fornarina often features in Raphael's work *(see also the Madonna della Seggiola and the Veiled Lady in the Palazzo Pitti in Florence and Santa Cecilia in the Pinacoteca in Bologna)* and is depicted here with an unusual sensuality and a hint of cunning in her expression.

La Fornarina *by Raphael*

Raphaelesque influences are apparent in the *Ascension* by Tisi, a painter from Ferrara known as **Il Garofaio**, especially when compared with a work of the same name by Raphael exhibited at the Pinacoteca Vaticana in Rome. The **Portrait of Stefano Colonna** (1546) is by **Bronzino** and is typical of this refined artist and portrait painter, who endeavoured to present his subjects in a suitably noble pose rather than bring out their more ordinary characteristics. The gallery also houses works by Titian and Tintoretto, as well as the beautiful *Holy Conversation* by Lorenzo Lotto, a magnificent painting notable for the detailed portrayal of clothes and jewels, a typical characteristic of this artist.

Central Salon★★★ – The ceiling is the best work ever produced by **Pietro da Cortona**, who showed the true measure of his talent here. It was painted between 1633 and 1639 to celebrate the glory of the Barberini family, whose coat of arms (bees in a crown of laurel) is carried by allegorical figures representing the Virtues. On the left Divine Providence, holding a sceptre, reigns from the clouds. Note how skilfully the painter has used *grisaille* to separate the scenes.

Second floor

17C-18C Paintings – Works by **Guido Reni** (1575-1642) include the delicate **Portrait of Beatrice Cenci★** and a beautiful foreshortened fresco, the **Sleeping Putto★★**. The **Portrait of Bernini★** by **Baciccia** (1639-1709) is a rare portrait by this artist, who was famous mainly for his decorative skill. Two other Baroque masters are **Pietro da Cortona** with his **Guardian Angel** and **Bernini** with his two paintings **David with the Head of Goliath** and the **Portrait of Urban VIII**.

Two famous paintings can be seen among the works by non-Italian artists: the **Portrait of Henry VIII**★★★ (1540) by **Hans Holbein the Younger**, who became the official painter at the English court and produced portraits of members of the court with impartiality and psychological analysis, and the very expressive **Portrait of Erasmus**★★★ (1517) by **Quentin Metsys**, which also shows deep psychological insight into his subject. Note also the anamorphoses (distorted images to be viewed from a particular angle or in a curved mirror so as to regain their proper shape) by 17C French painters.

The gallery also houses two masterpieces by Caravaggio. The **Narcissus**★★ illustrates the novel style of **Caravaggio** (1573-1610), who was a contemporary of Guido Reni and Guercino. Dispensing with background, he portrays Narcissus bending over the water, lost in admiration for his own reflection, his hands almost brushing against their reflected image. As in all of Caravaggio's masterpieces, light plays a primordial role, highlighting the rapt face, immaculate corset and knee and hiding Narcissus's expression with shadow. Contrasting sharply with this painting is the atmosphere of **Judith and Holofernes**★. The cruelty and violence of the scene depicted here is conveyed in dramatic detail and is made even more striking by the troubled figure of the old woman. Only Judith, wearing a white corset and thrusting her sword into Holofernes's neck, appears to be in control of her emotions, frowning with the effort of her physical exertions.

18C apartments – These elegant, Rococo-style rooms were decorated between 1750 and 1770 for Cornelia Costanza Barberini, who married Giulio Cesare Colonna in 1728. Note the furniture placed at an angle in the dining room to hide the service passage used by the servants. The Sala delle Sete dipinte (Painted Silk Room) takes its name from the delightful tapestries illustrating the life of "savages" in America, recounted by the Jesuits on their return from the New World.

Villa Borghese-Villa Giulia★★

As well as being home to three of the most important museums in Rome, this district is also graced by one of the largest areas of greenery in the city, providing a welcome escape from the noise and chaos of central Rome. The park is a pleasant place for a stroll and is dotted with small lakes, temples and evocatively fragrant umbrella pines. A number of major international equestrian events are also held here.

Location

Michelin map 38 or Michelin spiral atlas of Rome: p 24-25 and 40-41 G-H 11-13. Metro line A: Flaminio. Tour: 1 day, including the museums. This walk explores Rome's largest public park, which borders on the elegant Parioli district and contains two museums, an art gallery and various national academies of art in a setting of lakes, lawns and groves of trees.

Neighbouring sights are described in the following chapters: PIAZZA DEL POPOLO; PIAZZA DI SPAGNA; VIA VENETO.

Background

When Cardinal Camillo Borghese acceded to the Papal throne in 1605 he made generous gifts to his family. To his nephew Scipione Caffarelli he gave his name. On becoming a cardinal Scipione Borghese started to build a private house, a little palace *(palazzina)* set in magnificent gardens. Two men were employed on the plans: the architect Vasanzio and the landscape gardener Domenico Savino da Montepulciano.

The section of the **Aurelian Wall** from the Porta del Popolo to the Porta Pinciana, which marks the southwest boundary of the Villa Borghese, follows such an irregular line that the

WHERE TO EAT
See "Where to Eat" in the Practical Points section at the beginning of the guide.

TAKING A BREAK
If you're looking for somewhere for a rest or a coffee during your walk in the gardens, why not try one of the museum cafés? There are two entrances to the restaurant-bar at the Villa Giuila: one from the museum, the other from the Villa Borghese gardens. The entrance to the Museo Nazionale d'Arte Moderna café is on Via Gramsci; that of the Galleria Borghese is found in the entrance hall to the museum. You do not need a ticket to the museum to use the museum cafés.

SHOPPING
Boutique Jaguar Collection – *Via Francesco Siacci 36* – ☏ *06 80 82 547* – *Open Mon-Fri, 9am-1pm and 3.30-7.30pm; Sat, 10am-1pm and 4.30-7.30pm.* Situated in the exclusive Parioli district, this shop sells luxury items such as bags, suitcases and accessories produced by this famous brand name.

Romans call it the crooked wall **(Muro Torto)** and tell many legends about it. When the Goths, led by Witigis, besieged Rome in the 6C, they failed to take advantage of a breach in the Muro Torto and the Romans concluded that the area must be protected by St Peter. Imagination ran riot in the Middle Ages when the vicinity was used as a cemetery where people denied a Christian burial were interred.

Walking About

BORGHESE GARDENS★★

This walk wanders through a romantic landscape of lakes, trees and flower gardens set with imitation Antique sculpture.

Take Viale di Valle Giulia and then the first path on the right which leads to Viale Pietro Canonica; turn left.

The little **castle** *(castello medievale)*, an imitation of a medieval fortress, used to be the house and studio of the sculptor Pietro Canonica (1869-1959).

The **Temple of Antoninus and Faustina** was built in the late 18C.

Continue along the path as far as Viale dell'Uccelliera; turn right.

The building topped by a wrought-iron cage is a 17C aviary. The Viale dell'Uccelliera (Aviary Avenue) leads to the Villa Borghese.

Villa Borghese★★★

This little palace *(palazzina)* was designed in 1613 by Flaminio Ponzio for Cardinal Scipione Borghese and is a delightful example of a rich prelate's house. Construction was continued after Ponzio's death by a Dutchman, Jan van Santen (called Vasanzio in Italian).

In the late 18C, during the restoration of the gardens organised by Prince Marcantonio, the southwest façade (the present front entrance) was considered too ornate; it was stripped of some of its decoration and the steps altered. Early

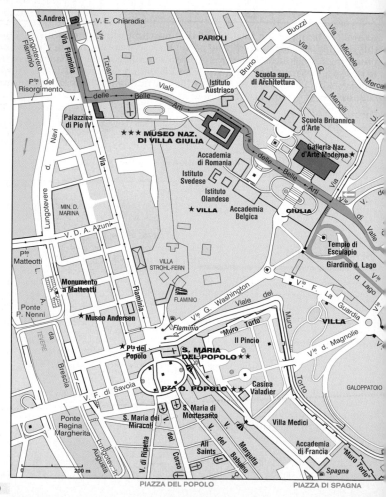

in the 20C, the balustrade bounding the forecourt (but not the statues, which were classed as works of art) was acquired by Lord Astor and removed to Cliveden.

Between 1801 and 1809 the Borghese collection was greatly depleted; Prince Camillo, Pauline Bonaparte's husband, sold over 200 sculptures, which went to swell the collection in the Louvre in Paris. In 1891 the paintings which had hung in the Borghese Palace were moved to the *palazzina*. Its silvan setting in the Borghese Gardens, its elegant late-18C decor and its outstanding collections make this gallery one of the most agreeable in Rome *(see Worth a Visit below for a description of the gallery)*.

The building – The massive square villa is divided into a number of sections, and is embellished by two avant-corps topped with towers and framed by a portico, which projects over a terrace. The front of the building is adorned with recesses and ovals decorated with statues. The double flight of steps leading to the building has been restored and repainted in its original colour: white with a slightly darker finish.

Take Viale dei Pupazzi to continue the walk in the gardens.

The **Sea-horse Fountain** was commissioned in 1791 by Prince Marcantonio Borghese, who renovated the gardens.

The **Piazza di Siena** further on is named after the native town of the Borghese. Set among umbrella pines, it is sometimes used for international equestrian events. On the northeast side stands the **Casina dell' Orologio**, built in the late 18C.

Viale dei Pupazzi leads to the **Temple of Diana**, modelled on an Ancient building. From there an avenue runs north to the **Lake Garden** (Giardino del Lago), one of the most popular corners of the park; it was created by the architect, Asprucci, who worked on the enlargement of the Borghese Gardens at the end of 18C. The waters of the lake reflect the columns of the little Temple of Aesculapius, another imitation of an Ancient building.

Return to Viale di Villa Giulia and turn left into Viale delle Belle Arti.

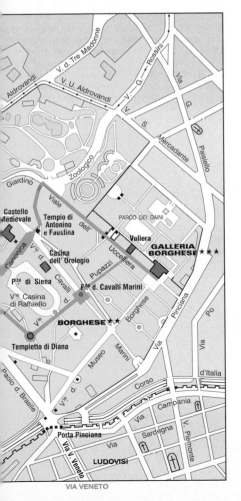

Various national academies of art can be seen on both sides of this avenue, between the Galleria Nazionale d'Arte Moderna and the Museo Nazionale di Villa Giulia *(see Worth a Visit below for a description of the two museums)*. One of these is the **British Academy** (Scuola Britannica d'Arte), which offers courses in history, the arts and classics for students from British universities and colleges.

Follow Via delle Belle Arti to the intersection with Via Flaminia.

Via Flaminia

This modern artery follows the line of the Ancient Flaminian Way, which was constructed in 220 BC by the Consul Flaminius, who died in the Battle of Lake Trasimene against Hannibal. The road ran almost straight from the city centre along Via del Corso to Rimini on the Adriatic (314km/195mi). The **Stadio Flaminio**, which stands on the northern section of Via Flaminia *(off the map)*, was designed by Pier Luigi Nervi and built in 1959 for the 1960 Olympic Games.

Palazzina di Pio IV

The little palace was built by Pius IV (1559-65), who offered it to his nephew Cardinal Charles Borromeo. The slightly concave façade exhibits the mannered style typical of late-Renaissance works. Since 1929 the building has housed the Italian Government Embassy to the Holy See.

Turn right into Via Flaminia.

Sant'Andrea

St Andrew's Church was built in the 16C by Vignola for Julius III. It is an unusual little building, with a clear-cut silhouette, stressed by heavy dentilated cornices, an elliptical dome resting on a solid base and plain brick walls.

Worth a Visit

GALLERIA BORGHESE★★★ (BORGHESE GALLERY)

(&) *Open 9am-7.30pm. Visit by appointment only.* ☎ *06 85 48 577.*

The collection – Cardinal Scipione was an avid collector of Ancient, Renaissance and neo-Classical art, although he showed little interest in work from the medieval period. He accumulated a substantial art collection and also commissioned work from some of the best-known sculptors of his time, such as Bernini and Cordier, both for the restoration of Antique statues and for the creation of new works. Unfortunately, the cardinal sold part of his collection to Napoleon and these works are now exhibited in the Louvre Museum in Paris. The cardinal was interested in painting as well as sculpture and bought and commissioned paintings from the greatest artists of his time, including Caravaggio, Rubens, Reni and Guercino.

The works were originally exhibited in no particular order, although they were occasionally arranged according to theme, to allow comparisons between paintings to be made. The works of art were separated in the 18C, with the sculptures exhibited on the ground floor and the paintings on the first floor. Some of the paintings have now been moved to the ground floor, partly because the first floor cannot accommodate large numbers of visitors. Those paintings exhibited on the ground floor have been carefully chosen to follow the same themes as the sculptures on display. The paintings on the first floor are arranged in mainly chronological order.

Ground floor

Cross the portico to enter the **main hall**, which is decorated with Antique statues (originals and copies), paintings and reliefs, and provides a good idea of neo-Classical taste. The pieces of 4C mosaic, set into the floor, were discovered on a property belonging to the Borghese family near Tusculum and depict scenes of hunting and wrestling between gladiators and wild animals. On the ceiling a fresco by Mariano Rossi, painted between 1775 and 1778, illustrates the deification of Romulus, who is welcomed to Olympus by Jupiter *(centre)*. Also exhibited in the main hall is an unfinished sculpture by **Bernini**, *Truth being unveiled by Time* (the figure of Time is missing); the figure of Truth is personified by a woman who holds the sun in her right hand. This rather grandiloquent work was started by **Bernini** in 1645.

Canova – *Room I.* The **statue of Pauline Bonaparte★★★** as Venus is a neo-Classical masterpiece by Canova. The polished, translucent statue is half naked, and reclines in a languid pose, holding the "apple of discord" in her left hand. According to mythology, Paris was asked to choose the most beautiful goddess among Venus, Juno and Minerva; Venus persuaded Paris to choose her by promising him his beloved, Helen, in return. Enthusiasm for the artist, together with the celebrity of the model, the "idol of high society", meant that the sculpture was immediately accepted as a masterpiece. The theme is repeated in the fresco on the ceiling by Domenico de Angelis. The small hooded marble statues in the corners of the room are the Roman precursors of gnomes, who were said to bring fortune or disaster.

Opere del Bernini★★★ (Bernini Rooms) – The artist was 21 when he sculpted **David** (Room II). Whereas Michelangelo, working during the Renaissance, chose to present the calm and victorious hero, Bernini has captured the moment of most intense effort, emphasised by the twisting body and the frown on the face, with the lips pursed in concentration, making this statue a masterpiece of Baroque sculpture.

In his **Apollo and Daphne** (Room III), Bernini shows the metamorphosis of Daphne from nymph to laurel bush coinciding with Apollo's attempt to seize her, thus embodying the intentions of Baroque art in an incomparably graceful composition: note the movement of the hair, which is almost indistinguishable from the laurel branches. Behind this sculpture a painting by **Dosso Dossi** (c 1489-1542) treats the same theme in a different way. Apollo can be seen in the centre of the painting, mourning his lost love, who is portrayed as a tiny figure to the left of the composition. Metamorphosis is also the theme of a second masterpiece by this artist from Ferrara, **Circe the Sorceress**.

The **Rape of Proserpina** (Room IV) is one of **Bernini**'s youthful works, probably carried out in collaboration with his father, Pietro Bernini. Although the statue of Pluto, god of the Underworld, shows traces of the Academic style, the supple modelling of Proserpina foreshadows Bernini's works of genius. The sumptuous room in which the sculpture is displayed is called the Emperors' Room because of the 18 busts sculpted in porphyry and alabaster in the 17C.

The group of **Aeneas carrying Anchises** (Room VI), in which the figures are rather stiff with set expressions, was for a long time attributed to Bernini alone, but his father's collaboration is now recognised.

Room V – The focus of this room is the **Sleeping Hermaphroditus★**, a beautiful Roman copy of an original Greek statue dating from the 2C BC: note the feminine shape of the back of the body and the way the head rests, turned to one side, on the arm. The subject very popular with the Romans, shown by the presence of a second copy of the statue at the Museo Nazionale Romano.

Caravaggio room★★★ – *(Room VIII)*. This room houses six masterpieces by **Caravaggio** (1573-1610). The artist led an adventurous and occasionally unlawful life and brought about a revolution in painting, drawing his inspiration from nature. His figures sprang out from the canvas with dazzling effects of light and were extremely realistic in tone, which often resulted in the work being refused by the person who had commissioned the painting.

This was the case with the altarpiece of the **Madonna dei Palafrenieri**, which had been intended for an altar in St Peter's Basilica, where it remained for only two days. It was then moved to the Chiesa di Santa Maria dei Palafrenieri and was eventually bought by Cardinal Borghese. The three characters are depicted with extreme realism, with St Anne depicted as a wrinkled old woman. The traditional iconography of the characters is distorted: St Anne is standing to one side, her hands clasped on her stomach, watching the scene, which is dominated by the Virgin, who supports Jesus and is helped by the child to crush the serpent's head. The scene is thought to refer to the theological debate of the time, in which the Protestants denied the Immaculate Conception (and therefore the Virgin's power to overcome evil). The Rosario Bull of Pius V (1569) could well be reflected in the painting: the Virgin may overcome evil if helped by Christ.

The **Boy with a basket of fruit** is an admirable still life, in which the fruit is carefully and accurately painted. The portrait of a rather weak and sickly looking Bacchus is known as the **Ailing Bacchus**. Caravaggio has used his own features for the god and appears frail and wan, possibly having just come out of hospital after an accident in which he injured a leg. The painting is infused with an atmosphere of death, suggested not only by the choice of colours used, but also by the yellowed leaves and the bare grey slab which evokes a tombstone. The same sorrowful atmosphere can be sensed in **David showing Goliath's head**. The boy who holds the vanquished giant's head is hardly portrayed as a triumphant victor. He wears an expression that is a mixture of sadness, compassion and horror; the expression of one who has carried out a just act, but is aware of the grave consequences of his action. An event in the artist's life may throw some light on the significance of the painting. Caravaggio was in exile in Naples when he painted this work, having killed a companion in a brawl. As a result he lived under the constant threat of death: in fact, anyone who came across his path had the right to sever his head from his body. It is not surprising that he has represented himself as Goliath, and perhaps also as David, who vaguely resembles the ailing Bacchus. The painting was almost a plea for intervention, sent to Cardinal Scipione asking him to plead his cause and enable him to return to Rome.

St Jerome was painted by Caravaggio for the cardinal. The saint is portrayed as a thin and muscular figure, absorbed in his task of translating the holy texts. The last work by the artist is a sorrowful **St John the Baptist**.

First floor

Access from the ground floor or through Room I.

The **entrance hall** houses two superb mosaics made with tiny tesserae by Marcello Provenzale **(1)** (1577-1639) portraying *Orpheus*, with references to Scipione Borghese (the eagle and the dragon on the left), and *Paul V Borghese*.

Room IX – The *Crucifixion with St Jerome and St Christopher* **(2)** by **Pinturicchio** (1454-1513) reflects the artist's liking for miniatures, which characterised the art of the 15C Primitives. In the *Virgin and Child with St John the Baptist* **(3)** by **Lorenzo di Credi** (1459-1537) and the *Adoration of the Child* **(4)** by **Fra Bartolomeo** (1475-1527), the influence of **Leonardo da Vinci** and the Renaissance is clearly evident. This influence can be seen in the delicacy of the Virgin's expression in the first painting and in the indistinct outline of the

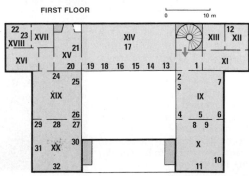

FIRST FLOOR   0   10 m

background landscape in the second. The room also houses three remarkable **works★★★** by **Raphael** (1483-1520). The *Deposition* **(5)** was commissioned by Atalanta Baglioni, who had just lost her son (identified as the character on the right) in the power struggle for the Signoria of Perugia, hence the importance of the group on the right around the Virgin, who is overcome with grief at the loss of her son. This painting shows both the influence of Michelangelo (the face of Christ recalls that of the *Pietà* in St Peter's) and of Leonardo da Vinci (the landscape scene in the background). The portrait of a *Lady with a Unicorn* **(6)**, spoiled by being changed into a St Catherine but restored in 1935, is a fine example of the nobility of Raphael's art: note the delicacy of the necklace and pendant. The presence of the unicorn is probably a reference to the chastity of the young woman; according to tradition, this impulsive animal could only be tamed by a virgin. The *Portrait of a Man* **(7)**, a work of admirable vigour, still shows signs of 15C art with a full-face presentation and an indistinguishable background.

Room X – Arranged in their original positions near one another in this room are *Venus* **(8)** by **Lucas Cranach** (1472-1553), one of the rare works by a Northern artist in Cardinal Borghese's collection, and the more sensual *Venus* **(9)** by **Brescianino.** In his painting of the *Virgin and Child with St John the Baptist* **(10)**, **Andrea del Sarto** (1486-1531) was influenced by Michelangelo's drawing and by Leonardo da Vinci's *sfumato* technique. The outstanding painting in the back of the room is *Danaë★★★* **(11)** by **Correggio** (c 1489-1534), which illustrates the myth of Zeus visiting Danaë as a shower of gold. The use of oils has produced very subtle colour tones.

Room XII – This room is dedicated to works from the Lombardy-Veneto and Sienese regions (Sodoma). The *Portrait of a Man* **(12)** by the Venetian **Lorenzo Lotto** (c 1480-1556) is thought to represent the widower Mercurio Bua.

Room XIV – This room contains sculptures and paintings by **Bernini**. The three paintings depict a young man **(14)**, possibly the artist's cousin, and two self-portraits, one of Bernini as a youth **(16)** and one as an old man **(15)**. Of the two fine **busts** of Cardinal Scipione Borghese, the second **(13)** was executed because there was a vein in the marble in the first one **(18)** on the cardinal's forehead. *Young Jupiter with the goat Amalthea* **(19)** was probably the artist's first work (c 1615). A small bronze statue, *Sleep* **(17)** by Algardi, can be seen in the middle of the room.

Room XV – Works by Dosso Dossi and **Jacopo Bassano** (1516-1592) are exhibited in this room. Bassano was a Venetian who used exceptional colour effects and enjoyed painting country scenes and interiors, which he used even in his religious works, as demonstrated in his *Last Supper* **(20)**. This lively colourful scene represents a gathering of ordinary people, such as peasants and fishermen, crowded around a table; some are deep in discussion, others gesture wildly, others still are lost in their thoughts and appear to be on the point of falling asleep. Only the figure of Christ in the centre of the picture remains calm and composed.

Tobias and the Angel **(21)** by **Girolamo Savoldo** (1480-1548) presages Baroque painting in the powerful figures and the bold effects of light.

Room XVIII – The *Mourning the Death of Christ* **(22)** by **Rubens** was painted early in the 17C during the artist's visit to Rome. The *Portrait of Monsignor Merlini* **(23)** by **Andrea Sacchi** (1559-1661) shows a restraint quite unusual in the Baroque period.

Room XIX – After the insipid Mannerist style, two currents brought about the transition to Baroque painting. In Bologna a style based on tradition developed around the Carracci, which **Domenichino** (1581-1641) helped to propagate; his painting of *Diana the huntress★★★* **(24)** demonstrates the Bologna expertise very well (the detail of the trees and the bird hit by arrows). The beautifully coloured *Sibyl★* **(25)** is by the same painter. Annibale Carracci succeeds in capturing his model's fresh expression in just a few strokes in his *Laughing Boy* **(26)**.

Domenichino's Sybil

Room XX – The *Portrait of a man*★★★ (27) by **Antonello de Messina** (1430-79), with its powerfully expressive look, its precision (garment folds) and the delicate modelling of the face, is a masterpiece. The *Holy Conversation* (28) by **Palma the Elder** (1480-1528) is remarkable for its colours and for the keenly observed portrait of the pious woman *(left side of the painting)*. In the *Virgin and Child* (29) by the Venetian **Giovanni Bellini** (c 1429-1516) the firm line of the figures is bathed in a beautiful luminosity.

Sacred and Profane Love★★★ (30) by **Titian** (c 1490-1576) shows the young artist's search for an ideal of beauty. When he painted *Venus tending Love* (31) at 75, his art had been utterly renewed. As well as Titian in 16C Venice there was **Veronese**; *St John the Baptist preaching* (32) demonstrates Veronese's attraction to the narrative picture.

MUSEO NAZIONALE DI VILLA GIULIA★★★ (VILLA GIULIA NATIONAL MUSEUM)

(&) *Open daily (except Mon), 8.30am-7.30pm. Closed 1 Jan and Christmas. €4. ☎ 06 36 11 434; Fax 06 32 02 010.*

The museum is devoted to **Etruscan civilisation**. The exceptional interest of the collection is enhanced by its charming situation in Julius III's country villa.

Etruscan Art

In addition to the works exhibited in this museum, Etruscan art can also be admired in the Vatican Museums *(see VATICANO-SAN PIETRO)*.

Pottery – The impasto technique used for rudimentary clay pots was succeeded in the 7C BC by bucchero (black terracotta). At first the vases were simply decorated with a stippled design, but the shapes grew ever more ornate up to the 5C, when they were fashioned in the form of human beings or fantastic animals. Many vases were imported from Greece: fine pieces are displayed in the Vatican Museum and at the Villa Giulia.

Ornamentation – The work is exquisitely rich: engraved on bronze, in gold filigree or granulation, in finely carved ivory.

Sculpture – The Etruscans never used marble; they worked in bronze and clay. Their statues are distinguished by an enigmatic smile and large staring eyes.

Architecture – An Etruscan temple was approached by a flight of steps at the front which led up to a columned portico. The sanctuary itself was a rectangular building, standing on a high podium and containing three shrines *(cellae)* at the rear.

> **THE ETRUSCANS**
>
> No one knows exactly where the Etruscans originated. Around the year 1000 BC peoples of Indo-European origin from the north are known to have settled in central Italy. These new arrivals were skilled in the use of iron and they also cremated their dead. This civilisation, which seems to have spread northwards from central Italy, is known as the **Villanovan** culture. The Etruscan culture seems to have grown up and developed out of this civilisation.
>
> More advanced than their neighbours, the Etruscans governed Rome from the end of the 7C BC. They established an "empire" stretching from Corsica to the shores of the Adriatic and from Capua to Bologna. Decline set in at the end of the 6C BC and Rome, now free of their domination, began to expand and attacked their cities; in the 1C BC the Etruscans became Roman citizens.
>
> Traces of Etruscan civilisation have mostly disappeared; some, however, have survived in their tombs, which contained objects, once the property of the dead person, from which it is possible to deduce the character of their society. Until the 18C Etruscan art was thought to be a derivative of Greek art, without any aesthetic value. The re-evaluation of the canons of Greek art, the elegant stylisation of Etruscan works and their expressive quality have aroused a very lively interest in Etruscan art, which has an unusual affinity with modern forms.

Villa Giulia★

Although Julius III's reign (1550-55) was contemporary with the Council of Trent, the Pope did not lose his taste for the cultivated life of a Renaissance prince. In 1551 he invited Vignola to design a summer villa for him. The plain and sober façade is typical of Vignola, who also studied and wrote about architectural theory. The first courtyard is framed by a semicircular portico with **frescoed vaulting★**, decorated with trellises of vines, climbing roses and jasmine.

In the main courtyard beyond is a charming Mannerist construction designed by Bartolomeo Ammanati, who collaborated on the Villa Giulia from 1552: a little loggia, perfectly proportioned, opens onto horseshoe steps descending to a *nymphaeum* adorned with caryatids, rockeries and false grottoes. Several pieces of Roman sculpture are on display.

In the past the public was permitted to enjoy the tranquillity of this villa and to gather the fruit and flowers. When the poet Joachim du Bellay was visiting Rome as secretary to his cousin, the French ambassador, Jean du Bellay, he disapproved severely of the Pope for leading a life of pleasure to the detriment of affairs of State. When Julius III raised a young man of 17, who led a troop of performing monkeys, to be a cardinal, Du Bellay did not omit to poke fun at the new Jupiter and his Ganymede.

The courtyard is laid out in pleasant gardens bordered by the wings built at the beginning of the 20C to house the museum. To the right of the *nymphaeum* the Etruscan temple of Alatri has been reconstructed.

Ground Floor *(see map)*

Vulci – *Rooms 1-4*. This major centre of Etruscan civilisation occupied the area corresponding to the present-day Maremma and excelled in bronzework. Particularly worthy of note is the laminated bronze cinerary urn shaped like a hut *(Room 2)*.

Maroie Tomb – *Beneath Room 5*. This is a reconstruction of a tomb dating from the 6C BC, with two funeral chambers, found in the Banditaccia necropolis at Cerveteri to the northwest of Rome.

Bisenzio Tombs – *Room 6*. Among the objects found in the tombs in this city are two remarkable **pieces of bronze★**, typical examples of early Etruscan art (late 8C to early 7C BC): a **miniature chariot** adorned with figures in the round depicting various aspects of everyday life (such as ploughing, hunting, and a duel), and a covered **vessel** decorated with warriors (also in the round), who are taking part in a ritual dance around an animal, on top of the vessel.

Veii (Veio) Sculptures★★★ – *Room 7*. The statue of **Apollo and Heracles** represents a dispute between the god and the hero over possession of the Ceryneian Hind, which lies at Heracles' feet; the sculpture dates from the end of the 6C BC when Etruscan art was at its zenith. Set up as they were originally on the roof ridge of a temple, they give an idea of how they would have looked silhouetted against the sky. They are made of terracotta and are strikingly realistic and animated.

The other sculptures include a statue of a goddess with a child, which probably represents Apollo and his mother Leto, a fine head of Hermes and several *antefixae* in the shape of Gorgon, Maenad, Silenus and Achelous heads, which masked the ends of the roof beams and the painted pediments. These sculptures all come from the same temple and may be the work of Vulca, the only Etruscan sculptor known by name; his reputation was such that it is said that the king of Rome sent for him in 509 BC to sculpt the statues for the Temple of Jupiter on the Capitol *(see CAMPIDOGLIO – CAPITOLINO)*.

Terracotta sarcophagus★★★ – *Room 9*. This is one of the masterpieces of Etruscan terracotta sculpture. It dates from the end of the 6C and comes from Cerveteri. It expresses the Etruscan belief in the afterlife. The husband and wife, reclining as if at a banquet, seem to be pursuing their life in the beyond. In contrast to the stylised lower bodies, the torsos are realistic in tone, which serves to emphasise the bond between husband and wife; note the husband's loving stance, his head slightly turned towards his wife and his arm lying across her shoulders.

The Veio Apollo,
Museo Nazionale di Villa Giulia

DAGLI ORTI, Paris

First floor

The **Antiquarium** *(Rooms 11-17)* of the museum is chiefly devoted to small **bronze objects★**, both useful and decorative. Bronze was one of the main Etruscan exports which contributed largely to their wealth. They fashioned it with great creative skill: rudimentary **clasps** dating from the 8C to the 6C BC, **mirrors** very finely etched on the back with elegant scenes from family life or mythology, statuettes with astonishingly modern forms. The Etruscans' liking for bronze is explained by the rich copper deposits in Etruria and the island of Elba, which belonged to them. The tin may have been imported from Great Britain or the neighbouring islands.

One of the most famous exhibits in the collection is the **Chigi wine pitcher★★**, which was found at Veii (Veio); it is one of the most beautiful examples of Greek art from the middle of the 7C BC. This is the proto-Corinthian period when the ceramics produced in Corinth, an important port on the sea routes to the East, were decorated with subjects treated in miniature in bands of delicate silhouettes. On the upper part two groups of warriors marching into battle against one another can still be seen. The incision work shows each detail clearly. The lower part is covered with figures and hunting scenes.

The same display cabinet shows two *bucchero* **vases**★ dating from the 6C BC (*bucchero* is a sort of clay); the technique for producing this particular type of Etruscan ceramic, which is black, is not well understood.

One of the vases bears the Etruscan alphabet, the other a long inscription. The Etruscan alphabet has been deciphered, but the meaning of their language is still unknown.

Biga di Castro – *Room 18*. Of particular interest is the reconstruction of this chariot, with the skeletons of two horses sacrificed in the burial place.

Castellani Collection★ – *Semicircular corridor (Room 19)*. The collection traces the evolution of Greek and Etruscan ceramics from the 8C BC to the Roman era. The Etruscans imported a considerable amount of Greek pottery, so much, in fact, that it could be said that the finest Greek vases have been found in Etruscan tombs.

The following exhibits are particulary worthy of note:

– the elongated **vases**, which date from the 7C and 6C BC and come from eastern Greece. These are imitations of Egyptian alabaster vessels and were used by athletes for the perfumed oil with which they massaged their bodies; hence the flat lip. There are several *bucchero* vases dating from the 7C and 6C BC.

– the beautiful **wine bowl** made in Sparta in about 570 (*stile laconico*) and decorated with lotus flowers, an Eastern motif.

– the two **water pitchers,** dating from between 530 and 520, which belong to the Caere *hydriae*, so-called because this type of water pot was found in a necropolis in Cerveteri (ancient Caere). The decoration of picturesque mythological scenes includes the abduction of Europa by Zeus on one and on the other Hercules in his lion skin leading Cerbcrus against Eurystheus, who is hiding in a large jar in terror.

– the **red-figure Attic vases**. From 540-530 BC Attic ceramic art was transformed by the change from black- to red-figure technique. Henceforth artists signed their work, as can be seen on the two amphorae signed by Nicosthenes. Note the two vases by Cleophrades; one is decorated with a very realistic painting of Hercules and the Nemean lion.

Castellani Collection of Jewellery★ – *Room 20*. This stunning collection of over 2 500 pieces assembled by the Castellani family of jewellers

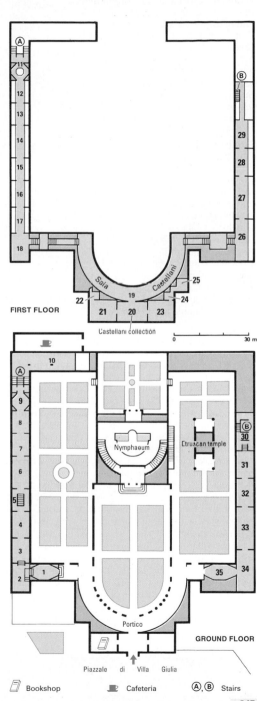

FIRST FLOOR

Castellani collection

0   30 m

Nymphaeum

Etruscan temple

Portico

GROUND FLOOR

Piazzale   di   Villa   Giulia

Bookshop   Cafeteria   Ⓐ,Ⓑ Stairs

consists of Antique jewellery dating from the 8C BC to the Roman and medieval periods, of 19C copies or of arrangements of Antique jewels. *(Reorganisation in progress)*.

Pyrgi Antiquities – *Rooms 21-22*. The old port of Cerveteri, where excavation work has uncovered the foundations of two temples, was mostly famous as a religious centre. The pediment of temple A (460 BC) can be admired in these rooms. The decoration on the back pediment (470-460 BC) recounts two of the most dramatic episodes of the legend of the Seven against Thebes. In the first, Zeus faces Capaneus, one of the seven rebels, and in the second, Tydeus lies mortally wounded on the ground, about to devour Melanippus's brain.

Return to the semicircular corridor. Take the two flights of steps on the right at the far end of the corridor that lead down to the first floor of the south wing of the museum.

Tombs from Capena and the Faliscan region – *Rooms 26-31*. The Capenans and Faliscans occupied neighbouring areas to the north of Rome, bordered to the east by the River Tiber. The two regions became known at the beginning of the 7C BC for their production of *impasto* ceramics. The black-varnished ceramic **plate** is a more recent example of their art and dates from the 3C BC. It was found at Capena and is decorated with an elephant accompanied by its calf and guided by an Indian; archers perch on the elephant's back. The decoration is thought to refer to a parade which took place after the Roman victory over Pyrrhus (275 BC) in Benevento, during which Pyrrhus lost eight of his elephants, four of which were brought to Rome. The beautiful gold trousseau (necklace with granulated decoration) comes from the Tomba degli Ori, in Narce, a Faliscan centre in southern Italy.

Among the exhibits from Falerii Veteres, the capital of the Faliscans, now occupied by Città Castellana, note the beautiful **Aurora wine bowl** which dates from the middle of the 4C BC; it shows Aurora and Cephalus in their chariot and Peleus abducting Thetis; round the neck a deer and a bull are being attacked by griffins.

Ground floor

Temples of Falerii Veteres★ – *Rooms 30-31*. The architecture of these buildings is known to us from plans left by Vitruvius, a Roman architect and theorist (1C BC). The room contains interesting partial reconstructions of pediments, examples of *antefixae* and *acroteria* (decorative elements, often in terracotta, which beginning in the 4C were placed on the peak and at either end of the pediments). The **bust of Apollo★** *(Room 30)* shows late-Greek Classical influence.

Praeneste: "Barberini" and "Bernardini" Tombs – *Room 34*. These rich tombs, situated near Palestrina (Ancient Praeneste) contained mid-7C BC articles, including carved **ivory pieces** – the result of trading relations between the Etruscans and Phoenicians.

The Etruscans were expert goldsmiths and worked in this metal from the 7C BC using the filigree technique; they perfected the granulation technique, splitting the gold into granules only a few tenths of a millimetre in diameter. The **jewellery★** on display includes some beautiful brooches and **rectangular plates★★** adorned with animal figures, such as chimera, lions, mermaids and horses, embellished with granulations; these were used as ornaments worn over the chest.

Ficoroni Cists★★★ – The cists were marriage coffers; they were also sometimes used for toilet or religious articles. Some magnificent examples were produced by the Etruscans between the 4C and 2C BC. Their manufacture was a speciality of Praeneste, where the largest known example, called the Ficoroni cist after its owner, was found in the 18C. It stands on feline feet which are attached to the body by carved plaques; it is decorated with fine engravings of the Argonauts arriving among the Bebryces, with Pollux tying King Amycos to a tree. On the lid are hunting scenes and three statues in the round – the central figure is Dionysius.

GALLERIA NAZIONALE D'ARTE MODERNA★ (NATIONAL GALLERY OF MODERN ART)

(&) *Open daily (except Mon), 8.30am-7.30pm. Closed 1 Jan and Christmas. Guided tours available (1hr) in various languages.* ☎ *06 32 29 83 02; Fax 06 32 21 579; comunicazione.gnam@arti.beniculturali.it*

The museum has recently been reorganised and as a result some of the works described below may no longer be exhibited in the order below.

The 1911 building houses the national collection of 19C and 20C painting and sculpture; it also accommodates temporary exhibitions and a good library.

After passing through the barrier in the entrance hall, bear left.

Entrance corridor and Spadini Room – These pieces by Galileo Chini, an exponent of the Italian Liberty style, explore the subject of spring.

In the room housing the **Giacomo Balla** (1871-1958) donation, three of the four panels that make up the *Polittico dei Viventi (Polyptych of the Living)* are particularly worthy of note: *The Beggar* and *The Sick* verge on the monochrome whereas *The Mad Woman* is a riot of colour.

Futurism – Light, colour, movement and speed were the principal concerns of Futurism. By 1910, a year after Filippo Marinetti (1876-1944) had published its manifesto, the group's cohesion was apparent in the works of such artists as Balla *(Dynamic demonstration + velocity)* and **Umberto Boccioni** (1882-1916) *(Horse + rider + building)*.

Giorgio de Chirico Room – The gallery houses some of the artist's early works *(The Mother)*, a number of paintings which demonstrate his return to Classicism in the 1920s, as well as examples of his metaphysical phase *(Hector and Andromache)*. Besides pieces by **Giorgio Morandi** (1890-1964), there is a Dada composition by Duchamp which characteristically desecrates the concept of Art.

Glass Room – Sculptures from the 1920s and 1930s, including works by Arturo Martini and Marino Marini.

Central Room – Dedicated to Italian painting from the 1920s and 1930s, the distinctive feature of which was a return to the Classical Italian tradition set by the early primitives and developed by masters before the Renaissance in the 15C. The principal protagonists are **Carrà** *(Horses)*, **De Chirico**, **Mario Sironi** *(Solitude)* – an artist associated with Fascism – **Guidi** *(Street Car)*, **Trombadori** *(Female Nude)*, **Felice Casorati** whose paintings *(Apples)* tend towards a palette of icy-cold colours, **Rosai** and **Morandi**, represented here by a selection of landscapes.

Filippo de Pisis Room – This artist used Impressionist techniques to infuse his perception of reality with magic and mystery: in his *Quai de Tournelles*, figures are reduced to patches of colour, which on occasion merge with their inanimate surroundings of houses, trees and street.

Abstract Art – Paintings displayed in this room include **Kandinsky's** *Angular Line* and works by the **Turin Six**; they aspired to a more European vision, looking to new movements emerging in France, notably at the hands of the Impressionists, Cézanne and Matisse.

Up the stairs.

Upper Room – This is dominated by the **Guttuso** gift *(Crucifixion)* and post-1945 Italian works, which seek to interpret new figurative experiences in reaction to international avant-garde ideas. By 1960 the break with tradition was complete: the artist **Fontana** was free to pierce, tear or split the canvas and use whatever materials he wished.

The section to the left of the main entrance is dedicated to painting from the 19C and early 20C.

After neo-Classical works by Canova *(Hercules and Lica)* come pieces from the Romantic Age and the likes of **Francesco Hayez** *(Sicilian Vespers)*. Paintings of the **Neapolitan School** by Toma *(Luisa Sanfelice in Prison)*, Mancini and Morelli show an uncanny sympathy with the French landscape painters of the Barbizon School. On the floor above are displayed the works from the late 19C and early 20C. Alongside works of Italian origin are works by overseas artists, which exemplify new international trends: *The Three Ages* by **Klimt**, the *Portrait* by **Boldini**, which bears a striking resemblance to Manet and Cézanne, **Monet's Waterlilies**, Van Gogh's *Portrait of the Gardener* and *l'Arlésienne*, or Rodin's *Age of Bronze*.

The Pointillists and later the Divisionists practised a special technique juxtaposing primary colours with their complementary colour to obtain a heightened, intense luminosity. The leading Italian exponent of this technique was **Giovanni Segantini** *(Mountain Huts in the Snow, Alla Stanga)*.

Rocca di Papa

Excursions from Rome

Lago di Bracciano★★

The rural setting and peaceful scenery surrounding Lake Bracciano make this a popular weekend and holiday destination for the inhabitants of nearby Rome. A boat service operates on the lake, allowing visitors to explore the attractive lakeside villages with their charming old houses and narrow alleyways. At nightfall, the tranquil sounds of rustling reeds and lapping water provide a welcome contrast to the noise and traffic of the capital.

Location
Michelin map 430, P 18. 39km/24mi NW of Rome. By bus (COTRAL): departure from Via Lepanto. By train (FS): departure from Ostiense, Termini or Tiburtina Stations. By car: take S 2 via Cassia, direction Viterbo; after crossing the Grande Raccordo Anulare (Rome ring road) and passing through Giustiniana, bear left towards Bracciano-Anguillare; after about 7.5km/5mi bear right in Osteria Nuova into Via Anguillarese to Anguillara-Sabazia. Tour: 1 day. Lake Bracciano occupies a series of craters in the Sabatini Mountains (Monti Sabatini), which lie to its northeast, and is situated in the north of the province of Rome, not far from the boundary with the province of Viterbo.

Background

Lake Bracciano is of volcanic origin, like the lakes at Castelli Romani. It is more or less circular and is the eighth largest lake in Italy ($57.5km^2/22sq$ mi; $160m/525ft$ at its deepest point; $164m/538ft$ above sea level). It produces a fairly rich variety of fish including pike, eel, carp and a local fish called *latterino*. The Ancient Romans called it *Lacus Sabatini* and it has always played an important part in supplying the city of Rome with water. In AD 109 Trajan built an aqueduct ($30km/19mi$ long) to carry water to the district of Trastevere; it terminated on the Janiculum. It was destroyed and restored several times. When Paul V restored it in 1609, he gave it his own name and also commissioned the Pauline Fountain (Fontana Paulina) on the Janiculum so that the water from Bracciano should emerge in Rome against a spectacular and dramatic background. In Ancient times Rome was connected to Bracciano by the Via Clodia (also Claudia), which then went on into Lower Etruria. Today the part of the Bracciano road near the lake ostensibly follows the route taken by the old road.

Directory

WHERE TO EAT
• *Moderate*

Il Grottino da Norina – *Via delle Scalette 1 – 00061 Anguillara Sabazia* – ☎ 06 99 68 181 – Closed 24 Dec-2 Jan, 20 Aug-10 Sep, Mon evening and Wed. – €23/31. A limestone tufa cave provides the setting for this attractive restaurant, which is furnished in simple, almost spartan style,in perfect keeping with its surroundings. A good choice of local dishes are on offer here.

La Grotta Azzurra – *Piazza Vittorio Emanuele 4 – 00069 Trevignano Romano* – ☎ 06 99 99 420 – Closed 24 Dec-4 Jan, Sep and Tue. – €28/41. This restaurant serves traditional, home-made dishes. In summer, meals are served in the restaurant's charming garden, overlooking the lake.

WHERE TO STAY
• *Moderate*

Relais I Due Laghi – *Le Cerque village, 3km/2mi NE of Anguillara Sabazia* – 00061 Anguillara Sabazia – ☎ 06 99 60 70 59 – Fax 06 99 60 70 68 – 🛏 – 25 rooms. €92.96/129.11 ⌂ – Restaurant. €34/52. This attractive hotel offers country house-style comfort and luxury in a rustic atmosphere, with the occasional hint of Etruscan influence in its architecture. The gentle hills and pastureland surrounding the hotel provide the backdrop for horseriding and drag hunting.

Tour

LAKE TOUR *36km/22mi*

Anguillara-Sabazia★
The village is set on a rocky promontory ($185m/607ft$ above sea level). Access to this charming medieval town is through an impressive 16C gate decorated with a clock. Opposite is Via Umberto I, which climbs to the top of the village. Immediately after the gate is a small belvedere *(left)* which has a fountain containing eels. Right

at the end of Via Umberto I is a flight of steps *(left)* leading to the 18C Collegiate Church of the Assumption (Collegiata dell'Assunta): from the small square there is a magnificent view across the lake. Narrow but enchanting streets lead down to the lake and there is a good view of the old town from the shore.

On leaving the town turn left immediately after the public garden into Via Trevignanese.

Trevignano Romano

This characteristic village has developed round an outcrop of basalt beside the lake. The medieval town, with its fishermen's cottages, extends along the lake shore like a fish bone and climbs up the hill, which is crowned by the ruins of the Orsini Rock (Rocca degli Orsini). From Via Umberto I *(right)* the road climbs to the church of the Assumption, where there are some interesting frescoes inspired by the School of Raphael. Beyond the clock tower in Piazza Vittorio Emanuele III is the town hall *(right)* with its 16C door.

Take Via IV Novembre to Bracciano.

Bracciano★

All the main streets converge on Piazza 1 Maggio. On the right is the town hall in Piazzetta IV Novembre. To the left Via Umberto I leads to Piazza Mazzini, where there is a splendid view of the cylindrical towers of the impressive **Orsini-Odescalchi Castle** (Castello Orsini-Odescalchi).

Castello Orsini-Odescalchi★★★ – *Visitors are advised to call the castle for information on admission times. Closed Mon, 1 Jan and Christmas.* €5. ☎ *06 99 80 43 49 or 0337 74 76 42.*

The castle was originally built around the medieval Rock of the Prefects of Vico, who governed till the 13C. It passed to the Orsini family in 1419, but it was not until 1470 that Napoleone Orsini added to the original, which then began to take on all the appearances and functions of a palace. In 1696 the palace was acquired by the Odescalchis, passed in 1803 to the Torlonia family, before reverting in 1848 to the Odescalchis, who are still the owners today.

Six impressive cylindrical but somewhat irregular towers mark the outer limits of the castle, which was built almost entirely of lava rock on top of volcanic tufa. There are two walls surrounding the monument and the old medieval township. Beyond the ticket office there is an open space; on the left can be seen the old armaments store; on the right there is a door decorated with roses, the Orsini family's coat of arms.

Interior★ – The tour passes through the second north tower to a lobby with a well and a stone arcade. A spiral staircase leads up to the first rooms on the main floor. **Room I** (library): this room is also called the Papal Room since Pope Sixtus V stayed there in 1481 when fleeing from the plague in Rome. The ceiling was painted by Taddeo Zuccari. As in all the rooms, the furnishings are of a later date. **Room II** *(closed)*: little study adjoining the library. **Room III**: interesting original coffered ceiling with beams painted in the 15C (all the ceilings on this floor are original). **Room IV**: large triptych from the Umbrian School (15C) depicting the *Annunciation* (the central panel is missing). **Room V**: numerous hunting trophies; the large painting *(left)*, previously in the porch leading to the central courtyard, is attributed to Antoniazzo Romano; a little balcony looks out over the lake.

Castello Orsini-Odescalchi – the Arms' Room

Room VII: a bust of *Paolo Giordano II Orsini* by **Bernini** and a bust of *Isabella de' Medici* by one of Bernini's pupils. **Room IX**: the last room on this floor leading via a spiral staircase to the second floor. **Room XIII**: also called the Arms' Room; display of arms and suits of armour from the 15C to the 17C. **Room XV**: a very beautiful 16C Sicilian wrought-iron bed. **Room XVII**: room leading to a loggia with a magnificent view of the old rock.

The tour continues with the **Sentry Walk** (Cammino di ronda), which connects the magnificent towers of the castle. From here there is a glorious view over the town and the lake. Steps then lead down to the charming **Central Courtyard★** (Cortile Centrale) with its double doors and fine external staircase made of lava rock. After a brief visit to the kitchens, the tour ends in the entrance hall.

Return to Piazza Mazzini and turn left into Via della Collegiata.

In the square beyond the archway is **St Stephen's Church**, which in Ancient times was actually inside the Rock of the Prefects. The walk continues along the narrow and picturesque streets of the old town.

Take Via Agostino Fausti and then Via Braccianese to return to Rome.

Castelli Romani★★

This attractive region of gently rolling hills, old villages and volcanic lakes is a popular weekend destination for many Romans. The charming landscape is dotted with fine 17C mansions owned by wealthy Roman families and graced with magnificent gardens, ponds and fountains; it is also home to a Greek-Orthodox abbey. Finish your day's touring with a meal in one of the region's many typical restaurants, sitting in the shade of a leafy arbour and enjoying a glass or two of the excellent local Castelli wine.

Location

Michelin map 430, fold 36. The best way to enjoy the tour described below is by car, although most of the villages mentioned are also accessible by train from Termini Station, or by bus (COTRAL) from Anagnina, the last station on Metro line A. Tour: at least 1 day. Castelli Romani is the name given in the Middle Ages to the area to the southeast of Rome, which is reached along the Via Appia Nuova or Via Tuscolana.

Background

Historical and geographical notes – The "Castelli" are situated in the **Alban Hills** (Colli Albani), which are volcanic in origin. They form a circle, whose circumference is the edge of an immense burnt-out crater, pockmarked with secondary craters which have now turned into lakes.

Meadows and sweet chestnut trees spread up the hillsides; the lower slopes are covered with olive groves and vineyards which produce the famous Castelli wine. In the valleys, the volcanic soil is particularly suited to the cultivation of early vegetables.

Directory

WHERE TO EAT

• *Budget*

Fraschette di Ariccia – *Via Borgo S. Rocco – 00040 Ariccia – ✍.* In this friendly restaurant meals are served at long, wooden tables, which are set outside during the summer months. Try the local charcuterie, cheeses and renowned roast suckling pig, washed down with a glass or two of Castelli white wine. A lively, friendly atmosphere, where the evening often ends in song!

Zarazà – *Viale Regina Margherita 45 – 00044 Frascati – ☎ 06 94 22 053 – Closed Aug, Sun evening (except May-Sep) and Mon. – Reservations recommended. – €21/28.* This spartanly furnished trattoria is centrally located, with places to park nearby. The restaurant offers simple cuisine, and although it has a written menu, the waiter will recommend additional local specialities when he takes your order.

• *Moderate*

Taverna dello Spuntino – *Via Cicerone 20 – 00046 Grottaferrata – ☎ 06 94 59 366 – Closed Wed and 10-31 Aug. – ▤ – €26/44.* This rustic taverna serves an excellent selection of salami, as well as traditional Italian and regional dishes. The walls and ceiling are decorated with hams and dried chilli peppers and tomatoes; the restaurant's wine cellar is carved directly into the limestone tufa rock.

The history of the Alban Hills is linked to that of Rome. Cicero, the Emperors Tiberius, Nero and Galba had country houses there and Cato the Censor was born near Tuscolo in 234 BC.

During the Middle Ages the region southeast of Rome became known as the Castelli Romani, or "Roman fortresses". While anarchy reigned in Rome, the noble families sought refuge in the outlying villages, building themselves castles. Thirteen villages were fortified in this way: Frascati, Grottaferrata, Marino, Castel Gandolfo, Albano, Ariccia, Genzano, Nemi, Rocca di Papa, Rocca Priora, Monte Compatri, Monte Porzio Catone and Colonna.

Tour

TOUR OF THE CASTELLI ROMANI★★

122km/76mi – 1day – local map below. From Rome take Via Tuscolana S 215 (exit 21 on Michelin map 430). After crossing the Grande Raccordo Anulare (Rome ring road) continue to Frascati.

On the outskirts of Rome the route passes **Cinecittà**, the Italian equivalent of Hollywood. *The studios at Cinecittà, which are open to the public at certain times of year, are closed for restoration at the time of going to press.*

Frascati★

This was the favourite resort of the affluent and insouciant youth of Ancient Rome. From the main square, Piazza G. Marconi, there is an extensive view downhill as far as Rome and uphill to the terraces of the Villa Aldobrandini.

Frascati has gained a reputation for its white wine and for its 16C and 17C villas, particularly the **Villa Aldobrandini★**, set high on the hillside above its terraces, clipped avenues, fountains and rockeries. *Gardens open in summer Mon-Fri, 9am–1pm and 3-6pm (5pm winter). Closed public holidays. By appointment only. Contact the Ufficio del Turismo, Piazza Marconi 1, ☎ 06 94 20 331; Fax 06 94 25 498. From Piazza G. Marconi take the road to the Ville Tuscolane and Monte Porzio Catone.*

The road offers a good view of **Monte Compatri** and **Monte Porzio Catone** as it climbs up to **Rocca Priora** which clings to the northern rim of the huge crater in the Alban Hills.

Continue downhill; turn right into Via Latina; after 4km/2.5mi turn right to Tuscolo (no sign) into a winding road leading to the ruins.

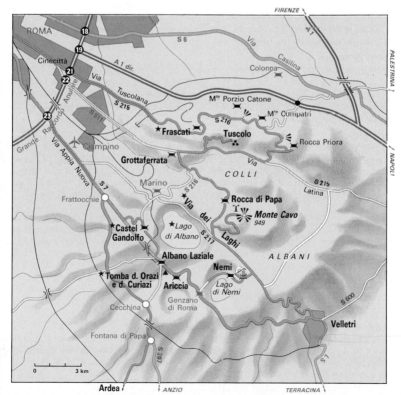

Tuscolo

It was in his villa in Ancient Tusculum that Cicero set his series of philosophical treatises known as the *Tusculanes*.

The city was once the fief of the counts of Tusculum; from the 10C to the 12C this powerful family owned most of the Castelli and extended its power as far as Rome, also providing several of the Popes. Tusculum was completely destroyed in 1191 in an engagement with the Romans and never rebuilt. A few traces survive: up the slope to the left near the large cross, which is now half hidden in the trees on what was once the citadel, are the ruins of a small theatre, with the remains of a water cistern at the back.

Return downhill; turn right into Via Latina. In Grottaferrata take Corso del Popolo (main street).

Grottaferrata

In 1004 a monastery was founded by Greek monks in the ruins of a Roman villa, which had perhaps been owned by Marcus Tullius Cicero himself.

Abbazia★ – The **abbey** is situated at the end of the main street. It looks like a fortress and is surrounded by ramparts and a moat which were added in the 15C by order of Cardinal Giuliano della Rovere, later to become Pope Julius II. The abbey is served by monks of the Eastern rite. In the courtyard of the castle there is a bronze statue of St Nilus and the entrance *(left)* to the monastery and the abbey museum.

Museo – *Closed for restoration at the time of going to press. For information, call ☎ 06 94 59 309; Fax 06 94 58 311.*

The large doorway opens onto a beautiful courtyard flanked by the church of St Mary of Grottaferrata *(see below)* and the Sangallo Doorway. The **museum** is housed in the rooms previously occupied by the commendatory cardinals. On display are Roman and Greek finds and paintings of scenes from the Old Testament which had been in the central nave in the church. One of the rooms is decorated with frescoes carried out by Francesco da Siena in 1547.

Santa Maria di Grottaferrata★ – *2nd castle terrace.* In the narthex *(on the left)* is an attractive marble font (10C). The doorway into the church is in the Byzantine style decorated with representations of animals and leaves; the carved wooden doors are 11C; above them is an 11C mosaic. The interior was remodelled in the 18C but the chancel arch is still decorated with a late-12C mosaic representing the Apostles at Whitsuntide. St Nilus's Chapel *(right)* has a 17C coffered ceiling and is adorned with frescoes (1608-10) painted by Domenichino. In the right aisle is the *cripta ferrata*, a room in the Roman villa which was converted into a place of Christian worship in the 5C, and which has given its name to the church and the village.

On leaving the church turn left into Viale San Nilo; after the traffic lights, turn right into Via Roma to Rocca di Papa.

Rocca di Papa

The village fans out on a picturesque **site★** on the slopes of Monte Cavo facing the Alban lakes and hills. It lies at the heart of hunting country and is a favourite spot among those who appreciate hare and rabbit dishes *(coniglio alla cacciatora)*.

Before reaching Via dei Laghi, turn left to Monte Cavo, which is surmounted by TV masts.

Monte Cavo

Alt 949m/3 114ft. *Road toll €0.52 per person.* On the way up there are glimpses of huge stones which paved the Ancient Sacred Way leading to the Temple of Jupiter on the top of Monte Cavo. Here, in the 5C BC, the representatives of the cities of the Latin League, including Rome, used to meet. In the 4C BC, however, Rome defeated the other cities in the League and embarked on her conquest of the peninsula.

The site of the Temple of Jupiter is now abandoned, but at one time it was occupied by a convent, which was later converted into a hotel. From the square there is a fine **view★** of the Apennines, the Castelli Romani, Lake Albano and Lake Nemi, Rome and the surrounding countryside.

Return downhill; turn left and left again into S 217, Via dei Laghi.

Via dei Laghi★

This is a beautiful road winding between oak and sweet chestnut woods.

After 3.5km/5.5mi turn right to Nemi.

Nemi

The village occupies a charming **site★★** in a natural amphitheatre on the steep slopes of a crater now filled by Lake Nemi. One tower of the Ruspoli Castle still stands, the only trace of the medieval *castello*. In June delicious wild strawberries are served in Nemi.

Drive through the town towards the lake.

Nemi

Lago di Nemi (Lake Nemi) – The road down to the lake passes through fields of daisies, poppies and strawberries. The lake is called Diana's Mirror, because the sacred wood next to the Temple of Diana is reflected in it. In 1929 the level of the water was lowered by 9m/30ft so that two boats from the reign of Caligula (AD 37-41) could be recovered. They were burned during the war and only a few charred remains are housed in the **museum**. *(&) Open Mon-Sat, 9am-6pm; Sun and public holidays, 9am-1pm. Closed 1 Jan, 1 May and Christmas. €2. ☎ 06 32 14 300. Continue on Via dei Laghi to Velletri.*

Velletri

The town has been prominently involved in Italian history: it resisted Joachim Murat, was captured by Fra Diavolo, the Calabrian brigand chief, was fought over by the troops of Garibaldi and Naples and damaged by bombardments during the Second World War. It is now a prosperous modern town on the south-facing slope of a crater in the Alban Hills, at the centre of a wine-producing region.

The imposing 14C **Torre del Trivio** rises from the main square, Piazza Cairoli.
From Velletri drive to Ariccia.

Ariccia

The main square, with its two fountains, was given its present appearance in 1664 by **Bernini**: the palace on the right *(north side)* of the road became the property of the Chigi banking family in the 17C; the **church of the Assumption** on the left *(south side)* is elegantly flanked by two porticoes (the circular interior, capped by a dome, is worth a visit).

In culinary matters Ariccia is known for its roast suckling pig *(porchetta)*.
Stop on the outskirts of Ariccia.

Tomba degli Orazi e dei Curiazi★ (Tomb of the Horatii and the Curiatii)

At the entrance to the Albano, on the left, over a wall and below the level of the road.
The tomb, which dates only from the last days of the Republic, is made of huge blocks of peperine, with truncated cones at the corners.

Albano Laziale

The town probably derives its name from Domitian's villa, Villa Albana. Monuments worthy of note include the church of **Santa Maria della Rotonda★** *(take Via Cavour, turn right into Via A. Saffi, then left into Via della Rotonda)*, a converted *nymphaeum* belonging to Domitian's villa. The church has been restored to its original brick appearance and has a bold Romanesque bell-tower (13C). The town has also preserved part of an old Roman gate, the **Porta Pretoria** *(return to Via Cavour, then turn into Via A. de Gasperi)*. These ruins were once the entrance gate to a fortress built by Septimius Severus (193-211).

The Villa Communale★ *(Piazza Mazzini)* is a huge public garden displaying vestiges of a villa which belonged to Pompey (106-48 BC).
Continue to Castel Gandolfo.

Castel Gandolfo★

On the edge of a crater now filled by Lake Albano stands Castel Gandolfo, famous worldwide as the summer residence of the Pope.

Alba Longa – The site of Ancient Alba Longa has been identified as that of Castel Gandolfo. It was the oldest town in Latium founded, according to legend, c 1150 BC. Its rivalry with Rome led to the famous battle between the Horatii and the Curiatii. Tired of fighting a costly war, the two cities decided to settle their differences by single combat between three Roman brothers, the Horatii, and three Alban brothers, the Curiatii. At the first encounter two of the Horatii were killed, the three Curiatii were wounded; the last of the Horatii pretended to take flight in order to separate his adversaries and then, turning, defeated them one by one. On returning to Rome, Horatius met his sister Camilla at the Capena Gate mourning her lover, one of the Curiatii, and cursing Rome, the "sole object of her resentment". He killed her, was put on trial but acquitted.

Papal Villa – *Not open to the public.* The entrance is in the main square. The Holy See acquired the "Castello" Gandolfo at the end of the 16C. In 1628 **Urban VIII** commissioned Maderno to design a villa on the site of Domitian's earlier villa (AD 81-96), which had extended as far as Albano Laziale. The Vatican Observatory (Specola Vaticana) was established here in Pius XI's reign.

Lake Albano★

There is a good **view**★ of its enclosed site from a terrace at the entrance to the village; there is a road down to the lakeside.

From Castel Gandolfo continue north; turn right into S 7, Via Appia Nuova.

In Frattochie EITHER continue north on S 7 to return to Rome OR make a detour south (30km/19mi) to visit the Manzù Collection in Ardea.

From Frattocchie take S 207 south (direction Anzio) via Pavona, south of Cecchina, then bear right into the road to Ardea.

Ardea

The town stands on land which once belonged to the Rutuli; it was their capital city. According to legend, the death of Turnus, king of the Rutuli, who was defeated by Aeneas, and the founding of Lavinium, in which Aeneas was involved, marked the decline of Ardea and the birth of the myth in Rome. The town stands on a tufa rock. At some spots the remains of the city walls, in the form of square blocks of tufa, can still be seen.

The museum is situated 100m/110yd after the junction with Via Laurentina, on the left going towards Rome.

Museo della Raccolta Manzù★★ (Manzù Collection) – ♿ *Open 9am-7pm (Mon, 2-7pm). Closed 1 Jan and Christmas. Guided tours available (1hr). No charge.* ☎ *06 32 29 83 02; Fax 06 32 21 579; comunicazione.gnam@arti.beniculturali.it*

The museum was the idea of the artist's wife and a group of his friends. It was inaugurated in 1969, given to the State in 1979, and opened to the public in 1981. Most of the work belongs to the artist's mature period (1950-1970), when he reworked some of the themes of his earlier years. Although there are only a few works from that earlier period, they are very important. Altogether there are 462 works in the collection, including sculpture, drawings, engravings and jewellery. The museum also puts on temporary exhibitions on other subjects.

Take Via Laurentina, S 148, to return to Rome.

Ostia Antica★★

Much of the charm of the old port of Ostia Antica lies in its attractive location near the coast, amid umbrella pines and cypress trees. Best seen in the soft early morning light, the extensive ruins provide an excellent introduction to the urban life of the early Romans. Step back in time as you wander through the ruined streets of this once busy commercial port, admiring the vast Piazzale delle Corporazioni and the now empty areas of the spacious baths. This pleasant archaeological site serves as a reminder that Roman architecture and influence extended far beyond the seven legendary hills of the capital.

Location

Michelin map 480 Q 18. 24km/15mi SW of Rome. Access – by car: along Via del Mare; by underground: (Metro Line B), direction Laurentina as far as Magliana and then by train to Ostia Antica; by waterbus: see Other Ways of Exploring the City in the Practical Points section at the beginning of the guide. As a result of the gradual silting up of the coast over the centuries, the ruins of the Ancient port of Rome are now situated on the banks of the Tiber some distance inland. The long grey sandy beach at **Ostia Lido**, the nearest to Rome and the most popular, lies to the south of the river mouth.

Background

Ostia, at the mouth of the Tiber, takes its name from the Latin word *ostium*, meaning mouth. According to Virgil, Aeneas disembarked here. Livy says it was Ancus Martius (640-616 BC), the fourth king of Rome after Romulus, who "extended his dominion to the sea, founded Ostia at the mouth of the Tiber and established salt pans all around". Archaeologists, however, place the founding of Ostia in the 4C BC, but also admit that an earlier village of salt extractors may have existed. Ostia's development has reflected that of Rome: it was a military port when Rome embarked on her conquest of the Mediterranean shores and a commercial port when the victorious city established an organised system of trade. There is nothing to see of the medieval village of Ostia except the 15C **castle** built by Cardinal Giuliano della Rovere (Julius II) to protect Rome from attack by sea.

From a military to a commercial port

Roman control of the mouth of the Tiber, set at c 335 BC, corresponds with her expansion in the Mediterranean; several years earlier (in 338 BC) the Romans had won their first naval victory at Antium. During the war against Pyrrhus (278 BC), the fleet sent by Carthage to assist the Romans docked in Ostia. During the Punic Wars (264-41 BC and 218-01 BC) Ostia served as an arsenal; Scipio's army embarked here for Spain (217 BC) to prevent reinforcements reaching Hannibal, who had already crossed the Alps and defeated Flaminius at Lake Trasimeno; two years later about 30 ships set sail from Ostia for Tarentum, which was planning an alliance with Hannibal; in 211 BC Publius Cornelius Scipio (known as Scipio Africanus Major) took ship for Spain to avenge the defeat of his ancestors; barely 25 years old and exceptionally invested with proconsular power, he covered himself with glory.

The commercial port – At first there was simply a castle *(castrum)* to protect the port from pirates, but by the 1C BC Ostia had become a real town. In 79 BC Sulla built a rampart round three sides, using the Tiber to protect the fourth side. The last bend in the river was then further east than it is now so the river flowed in a straight course along the north side of the town *(plan below)*. Rome imported food from her numerous overseas provinces. A cargo of wheat from Sardinia was unloaded in Ostia as early as 212 BC. It was essential that the cargoes should be protected. The efforts of Pompey in 67 BC and of Agrippa from 63-12 BC had rid the sea of pirates. Only the problem of entering port remained: frequent strong winds restricted access to the summer months and the adjacent coastline consisted of dunes, lagoons and shallows. As a result, the merchant ships usually docked in the Neapolitan ports and the goods had to be carried overland to the capital.

Claudian Harbour – In Antiquity the shoreline ran parallel to the west side of the excavated site *(plan above)*. Claudius's engineers avoided the mouth of the Tiber itself because of the presence of a sandbar created by the currents. Instead they sited the harbour on the right bank of the river, north of the town of Ostia and the Fiumicino branch of the river, (roughly corresponding to the site of Leonardo da Vinci Airport). The harbour covered about 70ha/173 acres and was protected by two incurving breakwaters, with an artificial island in the harbour entrance between the ends of the breakwaters. Since the entrance faced northwest, the harbour was sheltered from the strongest winds such as the *Libeccio* (from the southwest) and the *Scirocco* (from the southeast).

WHERE TO EAT
Monumento – *Piazza Umberto I 8 –* ☏ *06 56 50 021 – Closed Mon – €23/39.* This simply furnished restaurant in the centre of the village serves a variety of local fish and meat dishes.

Trajan's Harbour – When the Claudian Harbour became too small, Trajan (98-117) built a second harbour inland. It was hexagonal in shape, covered 30ha/74 acres and was lined with docks and warehouses. It was joined to the Claudian Harbour by a broad channel and to the Tiber by a canal *(Fossa Trajana)*.

Decline and excavation of Ostia Antica and the Isola Sacra

Like Rome, Ostia began to decline in the 4C. The harbours silted up, the alluvium deposited by the Tiber extended the shoreline seawards and malaria depopulated the town. Ostia suffered the fate of all Roman ruins and was pillaged for its materials. Regular excavations have been undertaken since 1909; the western sectors of the town were excavated from 1938-42.

Between the town and the harbour the **necropolis of Trajan's Harbour** was discovered on the Sacred Island (Isola Sacra), which had been created by digging the Fiumicino channel; since the days of Antiquity the land has advanced several miles towards the sea.

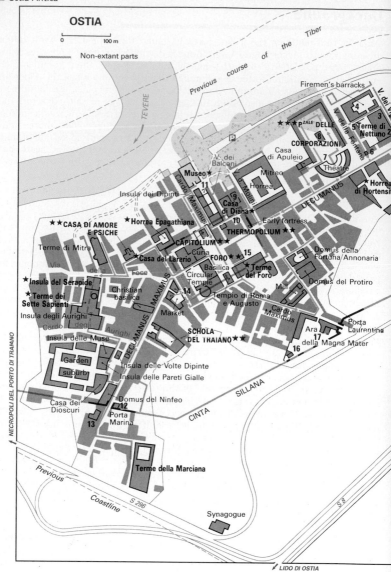

Life in Ostia

Ostia was a very busy commercial town and under the Empire its population rose to 100 000. Its main streets were lined with shops; administrative buildings clustered round the forum; warehouses and industrial premises were concentrated near the Tiber; the residential districts extended towards the seashore.

It was a cosmopolitan town, which welcomed a variety of overseas religions; several of their places of worship have been discovered: the oriental cults of the Great Mother (Cybele), of Isis and Serapis, of Jupiter Dolichenus and particularly of Mithras.

Christianity, too, had its adherents; Minucius Felix, a Christian writer, chose the sea baths at Ostia during the harvest holiday as the setting for his conversation with Octavius Januarius, another Christian, and Caecilius, a pagan whom they were trying to convert.

In 387 St Augustine's mother, Monica, died in Ostia on her way home to Africa.

Ostia dwelling houses – Their discovery has added to our knowledge of the houses of the lower-paid in the Ancient world.

The most common dwelling in this densely populated town was the **insula**, a block of flats to let, several storeys high; wealthier citizens lived in a **domus**, a detached house with a courtyard and garden.

All the buildings were of brick and probably unrendered. Some have elegant entrances framed by a triangular pediment resting on two pillars. Here and there a porch or a balcony adds interest to the street front. Sometimes the brickwork is finished with a decorative effect. **Opus reticulatum** is the technique most frequently

TIBER DELTA IN 2C AD AND TODAY

– – – – The coastline early in 2C AD

2 km

used: small squares of dark tufa and lighter limestone are laid on edge to form a diaper pattern; this technique was practised from the 1C BC to the 2C AD; after the 1C AD the corners were sometimes reinforced with courses of brick. Another technique used in Ostia, particularly in the 2C AD, is **opus testaceum**: pyramid-shaped bricks are laid very regularly on their sides – point inwards, flat bottom outwards; to strengthen the structure, courses of ordinary rectangular bricks were inserted every so often between the bands of triangular patterning.

EXCAVATIONS (SCAVI)

&. (with assistance, and only for the museum). Museum and excavations: open Apr-Oct, daily (except Mon), 8.30am-7.30pm (last admission 6pm); rest of the year, daily (except Mon), 8.30am-5.30pm (last admission 4pm). Closed 1 Jan, 1 May and Christmas. €4. ☎ 06 56 35 80 99; Fax 06 56 54 500.

On the left inside the entrance but outside the town limits is **Via delle Tombe**, reserved for burials of various types: sarcophagus, *columbarium* or chapel.

Porta Romana (Rome Gate) – This was the main entrance to the town and led into the **Decumanus Maximus**, the east-west axis of all Roman towns; in Ostia it was paved with large slabs and lined with porticoed buildings and warehouses *(horrea)*. From the outer side of the gate the broad and busy Via Ostiense carried traffic to Rome.

Piazzale della Vittoria – The small square took its name from a **statue of Minerva Victoria** (1C) **(1)**, a copy of an original Greek work. The statue probably adorned the town gate.

Terme di Nettuno (Baths of Neptune) – This 2C building has a terrace *(steps up from main street)* with a view of the fine **mosaics★★** which depict the marriage of Neptune and Amphitrite **(2)**.

Via dei Vigili – The construction of this street in the 2C meant the demolition of earlier buildings which contained a **mosaic★ (3)** showing the heads of figures symbolising the Winds and four Provinces (Sicily, Egypt, Africa, Spain). At the end of the street stand the **firemen's barracks** (caserna dei vigili) built in the 2C; on the far side of the courtyard is the *Augusteum* (for the cult of the Emperor) **(4)**; the floor mosaic shows a bull being sacrificed.

Turn left into Via della Palestra which leads into Via della Fontana.

Via della Fontana – This well-preserved street still contains its public fountain **(5)**. On the corner with the Decumanus Maximus stood Fortunatus's tavern; the mosaic floor bears the inscription: *"Dicit Fortunatus: Vinum cratera quot sitis bibe"* (Fortunatus says: Drink wine from the bowl to quench your thirst) **(6)**.

Horrea di Hortensius★ (Hortensius's Warehouses) – These grand 1C warehouses *(horrea)*, built round a pillared courtyard and lined with shops, are a striking example of *opus reticulatum*. On the right of the entrance is a small shrine dedicated to Hortensius (floor mosaic).

Teatro (Theatre) – Ostia was probably provided with a theatre under Augustus. It has been much restored. The three fine masks **(7)** come from the stage.

Piazzale delle Corporazioni★★★ – Under the portico in the square were the offices of the 70 trading corporations; set into the mosaic pavement are their emblems, showing in which commodity they traded and their country of origin: grain assessors, caulkers, rope-makers, shipbuilders and fitters, from Alexandria, Arles, Narbonne, Carthage etc.

The **temple (8)** in the centre of the square (only the podium and two columns remain) is sometimes attributed to Ceres and sometimes to the *Annona Augusta*, ie the Imperial corn supply which was worshipped like a god (Ostia was a centre for the *Annona*, the office responsible for organising the distribution of corn among the people of Rome).

Casa di Apuleio (Apuleius's House) – This house has a pillared *atrium* and mosaic floors.

Mitreo delle Sette Sfere (Seven Spheres Mithraeum) – This is one of the best preserved of the many temples dedicated to Mithras which have been found in Ostia. One can still see the two benches for the initiates and a relief showing the sacrifice of the bull.

Return to the Decumanus Maximus; turn right into Via dei Molini.

Via dei Molini – The street is named after some millstones which were found in one of the buildings **(9)**. Opposite are the ruins of several warehouses where goods were stored.

Return to the beginning of the street and turn right into Via di Diana.

Piazza dei Lari (10) – In the square *(left)* there is an altar dedicated to the Lares. Here also are traces of a primitive fortress *(castrum)* made of huge blocks of tufa.

Casa di Diana★ (Diana's House) – Facing onto the square is a striking example of an *insula* (block of flats), with rooms and passages arranged round an internal courtyard; note the fine corbel in the side street *(Via dei Balconi)*.

Thermopolium★★ – This was a bar, as is implied by its name, which is of Greek origin and means "sale of hot drinks". The building had a marble counter, shelving and paintings of the fruit and vegetables on sale within.

Turn right into Via dei Dipinti.

Insula dei Dipinti – Block containing several dwellings grouped round a garden; fine mosaics on the wall.

At the end of the Via dei Dipinti on the right an oil store **(11)** was found with huge jars half buried in the ground.

Museo★ – The museum displays the articles found at Ostia in a clear and well-lit presentation. **Rooms I** to **IV** are devoted to crafts, illustrated by low reliefs and to the Oriental religious cults which flourished in Ostia because of its overseas contacts. The Mithras group about to sacrifice the bull **(Room III)** is a clear indication of the strength of this cult, which had some 15 shrines in Ostia.

Room VIII contains a fine 1C BC statue of a Hercules by Cartilius Poplicola as well as a series of **portraits★**, especially of the Antonines; the quality of expression and the fine detail indicate the high standard of 2C Roman portraiture.

Room IX displays some sarcophagi (2C-3C) found in the city's burial ground.

Room X shows portraits of the last Emperors.

Room XI and **XII** contain examples of the rich interior decoration found in Ostia: walls covered with mosaics, paintings and frescoes from the 1C to 4C.

Take the Via del Capitolium which opens into Cardo Maximus.

Cardo Maximus – This important street, at right angles to the Decumanus, kinks left to skirt the temple known as the **Capitolium**.

Pass the Capitolium and enter the Forum.

Capitolium and Forum★★ – The **Capitolium** was the largest temple in Ostia, built in the 2C and dedicated to the Capitoline trio – Jupiter, Juno and Minerva. Although the marble facing is missing from the walls, the brick remains are impressive, as are the steps leading up to the *pronaos*; in front of the steps is a partial reconstruction of the altar.

The **forum** was enlarged in the 2C; the few pillars still standing belonged to the surrounding portico. At the far end stands the **Temple of Rome and Augustus** (1C), a grandiose building once faced with marble, which indicates the loyalty of Ostia, the first Roman colony, to the Government in Rome.

As in all Roman towns, the forum in Ostia had a **basilica**, a covered building where the citizens could meet, and a senate house **(Curia)**, where the municipal council met.

Return to Decumanus Maximus.

Tempio Rotondo (Circular Temple) – It was built beside the basilica and was probably dedicated to the cult of the Emperors in the 3C.

Casa del Larario★ (House with Lararium) – The building consists of shops ranged around an internal court. The recess, decorated in attractive red and ochre bricks, housed the statues of the Lares.

Continue along the Decumanus Maximus; turn right into Via Epagathiana.

Horrea Epagathiana★ (Epagathus's Warehouses) – This huge complex of warehouses built near the Tiber in the 2C has a fine doorway with columns and a pediment. It belonged to two rich freedmen: Epagathus and Epaphroditus.

Ruins of the once impressive Forum and Capitolium at Ostia Antica

Casa di Amore e Psiche★★ (House of Cupid and Psyche) – Like most of the buildings facing the seashore, this was a private house (4C); fine remains of mosaic and marble floors and of a *nymphaeum* decorated with niches, arcades and columns.

Turn left into Via del Tempio di Ercole, right into Via della Foce and right again into Via delle Terme di Mitra.

Terme di Mitra (Baths of Mithras) – An arcade leads into the 2C building. Inside is a flight of steps descending to the underground hypocaust (heating system) and traces of a *frigidarium* (pool and columns with Corinthian capitals). Traces of floor mosaics.

Return to Via della Foce and walk through the Insula del Serapide.

Insula del Serapide★ (Serapis Insula) – The two blocks of dwellings were built in the 2C with porticoes round a courtyard and a bathhouse in between. Traces of stucco work on a doorway.

Terme dei Sette Sapienti★ (Baths of the Seven Sages) – There is a mosaic floor in the large circular room and one room is roofed with a dome decorated with mosaics on a white ground.

Insula degli Aurighi (Charioteers' Insula) – At the centre of this block of dwellings is an attractive court with a portico; some rooms still have traces of paintings.

Turn left into Cardo degli Aurighi and right into Via delle Volte Dipinti.

Insula delle Volte Dipinte; Insula delle Muse; Insula delle Pareti Gialle – *Open only to specialists; apply to the Soprintendenzu di Ostia.* Residential houses from the 2C with traces of mosaics and paintings.

Città-Giardino (Garden Suburb) – *Right.* Example of a 2C residential complex with blocks of dwellings surrounded by gardens and fountains (remains of several fountains, one containing mosaic).

Casa dei Dioscuri (Dioscuri House) – It was built in the 4C in one of the garden suburb blocks. The rooms are paved with beautiful multicoloured mosaics, one of which shows the Dioscuri.

Domus del Ninfeo (House with Nymphaeum) – Incorporated in the 4C into a 2C building; one of the rooms is screened by three arches supported on slim columns with capitals.

Return to the Decumanus Maximus and turn right.

Porta Marina (Marine Gate) – This gate in Sulla's walls gave access to the seashore. A few huge blocks of tufa remain. Inside the gate *(left)* was the tavern of Alexander Helix **(12)** and outside *(right)* a tomb **(13)**.

The Decumanus came to an end outside the gate in a large colonnaded square.

Turn left into Via Cartilio Poplicola and walk to the end.

Terme della Marciana (Marciana Baths) – Behind the massive pilasters of the *frigidarium* apse, a beautiful **mosaic**★ shows athletes in the pose characteristic of the various sports, with trophies and equipment on a table in the centre.

From the baths there is a distant view of the columns and capitals of the synagogue built in the 1C.

Return to the Porta Marina and walk back along the Decumanus Maximus.

Schola del Traiano★★ – *Right.* This impressive 2C-3C building was the headquarters of a guild of merchants. On the left of the entrance is a plaster copy of a statue of Trajan which was found in the building, hence its name. Next comes a court with a rectangular central basin surrounded by brick columns. The basin was altered when more rooms were built on the far side of the court in the 3C. The central room, preceded by two columns, contains a fine mosaic floor. During excavations a 2C house was discovered on the east side of the court, furnished with a *nymphaeum* (paintings and mosaics) and a peristyle.

Basilica Cristiana (Christian Basilica) – *Left.* In this 4C Christian building, a row of columns separates the aisles which end in apses; an inscription on the architrave of a colonnade marks the entrance to what has been identified as the baptistry.

Mercato (Market) – There were two fishmongers' shops **(14)** on either side of an alley which led to a pillared podium standing on the west side of the market square. On the third pillar on the left it says in Latin: "Read and know that there is a lot of gossiping in the market."

Turn right into Via del Pomerio, then left into Via del Tempio Rotondo and continue past the Tempio di Roma e Augusto (left) and Cardo Maximus (right).

Terme del Foro★ (Forum Baths) – The largest baths in Ostia, showing the heating ducts in the walls. Adjacent to the north side of the baths is a public lavatory **(15)**.

Turn left into Cardo Maximus.

Mulino (Mill) – On the left of the Cardo Maximus are several millstones beneath a pergola.

Ara della Magna Mater (Altar of the Great Earth Mother) – This sacred enclosure contains the remains of a temple dedicated to Cybele (the Great Mother – *Magna Mater*) **(16)**. The Sanctuary of Attis **(17)** has a statue of the goddess in the apse and two fauns flanking the entrance.

The Cardo Maximus ends at the Laurentina Gate **(Porta Laurentina)** in Sulla's Wall **(Cinta Sillana)**.

Turn left into Via Semita dei Cippi.

The **Domus del Protiro** *(right; closed for restoration)* is an exception in Ostia because it has a marble pediment above the door.

Domus della Fortuna Annonaria – *Closed for restoration.* A 3C to 4C house with a well in the garden and mosaic floors; one of the rooms has three arches opening onto the garden.

Take Via del Mitreo dei Serpenti to return to the Decumanus Maximus.

Tour

Necropoli del Porto di Traiano★ (Trajan's Port Necropolis)

5km/3mi from the excavations. Access by car: by S 296 (direction Leonardo da Vinci Airport at Fiumicino); right turn into Via Cima Cristallo; entrance to the necropolis on the left of the access road.

Access by bus n° 02 (every 15min) from the bus stop on the panoramic road Guido Calza, in front of Ostia Antica Station, to the corner of Via Cima Cristallo; return journey in the direction Ostia Lido.

Open Apr-Oct, daily (except Mon), 8.30am-7.30pm (last admission 6pm); rest of the year, daily (except Mon), 8.30am-5.30pm (last admission 4pm). Closed 1 Jan, 1 May and Christmas. No charge. ☎ 06 56 35 80 99; Fax 06 56 51 500.

Isolated and silent, the necropolis is an impressive place, studded with umbrella pines, cypresses and laurels. The inhabitants of Trajan's Harbour buried their dead here from the 2C-4C. Ostia had its own graveyards outside the town.

There are tombs of every sort. The simplest are marked by an amphora buried in the ground or by several amphorae arranged in an oval or by a row of tiles set up to form a ridge. Other tombs built of brick comprise one or more chambers where the sarcophagi were placed. Sometimes there is a court in front of the chambers fitted out as a *columbarium* (with recesses for the cinerary urns), which the owner made available to his household.

The majority of the tombs have a low door beneath a lintel resting directly on the uprights; the inscription gave the name of the dead person, with sometimes a low-relief sculpture depicting their occupation in life.

Museo delle Navi (Ship Museum) *In Fiumicino*

Access: from Ostia Antica by bus n° 02 towards Fiumicino Paese; from Rome by underground (Metro) from Roma Ostiense Station to Leonardo da Vinci Airport and then by train.

For information and reservations, call ☎ 06 56 35 80 99; Fax 06 56 51 500.

The maritime museum, a modern building on the site of the Claudian Harbour *(see map on p 360)*, houses the Roman remains which were uncovered during the building of the airport in the late 1950s. On display are the hulls of five **vessels:** two large and one small shallow-draft cargo barges, drawn by oxen, for transporting goods from the port up the Tiber to Rome; a sea-going sailing boat; a fishing boat, propelled by oars, with a central wooden keep for live fish; and smaller articles: pottery, fishing floats, rope, nails, wooden pegs, needles, money. There are two electronic wall **panels** which show, at the touch of a button, the pattern of imports in the Roman Empire from the 1C-4C AD and the position of all the Roman boats which have been excavated. A low relief sculpture *(copy)* shows the boat which transported Caligula's Obelisk, now in St Peter's Square. The boat was sunk deliberately to provide a foundation for the lighthouse at the harbour mouth; the lighthouse stood 50m/164ft high and the light could be seen up to 30km/18mi out to sea.

Northwest of the museum are remains of the harbour quay where the lighthouse stood; northeast was the customs house; other related buildings have been excavated to the southeast *(across the road)*.

Palestrina*

According to legend, Ancient Praeneste was founded at the dawn of Roman history by Telegonus, the son of Ulysses and the enchantress Circe. Palestrina, now an attractive small medieval town, still occupies the same position, perched on the slopes of the Prenestini Hills, offering stunning views of the surrounding countryside. Highlights of a visit to the town include the ruined temple of the goddess Fortune and the famous Hellenistic Nile mosaic, further examples of the splendour of Ancient Rome.

Location
Michelin map no 430, fold 36 (Q 20). 42km/26mi SE of Rome. By car from Rome along Via Prenestina; by bus from Rebibbia (the last stop on Metro line B). Palestrina was built on the southern slopes of Monte Ginestro, an outcrop in the chain of Prenestini Hills overlooking the valley which separates them from the Albani Hills *(see CASTELLI ROMANI).*

Background

Praeneste rose to its full glory during the early days of its existence, in the 8C and 7C BC; it was besieged subsequently through the centuries because of its strategic position. Under the rule of Rome from the 4C BC, the town became a favourite country retreat in Imperial times for dignitaries and nobles. The cult of Fortune lasted well into the 4C AD, when the temple was abandoned and its site became encroached upon by the medieval city.

The superb 8C necropolis, together with the Barberini and Bernardini tombs, in which fabulous funerary ornaments were found (now displayed at the Museo Nazionale di Villa Giulia in Rome), are a lasting testament to Palestrina's illustrious past.

Directory

WHERE TO EAT
• *Moderate*
Il Piscarello – *Via del Piscarello 2* – ☎ *06 95 74 326* – ✗ 🍴 – €*26/50*. This country restaurant is decorated in a pleasant mix of rustic and classical styles and serves a range of traditional meat and fish dishes. In summer, meals can be enjoyed under the large wooden gazebo in the delightful garden.

WHERE TO STAY
• *Budget*
Stella – *Piazzale della Liberazione 3* – ☎ *06 95 38 172 – Fax 06 95 73 360 – 28 rooms. €41.32/56.81 –* 🍽 €*4.13 – Restaurant €15/26*. This simple family-run *pensione* is situated in the centre of the old town. The hotel has a friendly atmosphere and a good restaurant serving typical regional cuisine.

Worth a Visit

Tempio della Fortuna Primigenia★

This temple was once a grandiose sanctuary dedicated to the goddess Fortune. Built during the 2C-1C BC, it stands as one of the most important examples of Roman architecture based upon Hellenistic archetypes in Italy. The complex would have occupied most of the area now covered by the town; it comprised a series of terraces linked by a system of ramps and stairways aligned one above the other. A large basilica-shaped room, two lateral buildings, a natural cave and an apse paved with the famous *Nile Mosaic* (now in the local archaeological museum – Museo Archeologico Prenestino) survive from the lower sanctuary that was accommodated on the site of the old forum, on the second level of the temple. The upper sanctuary was located on the fourth terrace of the temple complex where Piazza della Cortina is now situated. On this platform, once graced with steps arranged in semicircles, was built the Palazzo Colonna (11C) – later known as the Palazzo Barberini (1640). Here, behind the elegant façade, ornamented with three Barberini bees (the family crest), is housed the local archaeological museum.

Park the car at the bottom of the steps. The ticket office is on the right of the building. The entrance to the museum is at the top of the stairs up to the Terrazza degli Emicicli.

Museo Archeologico Prenestino – (&) *Open 9am-7.30pm. €3. ☎/Fax 06 95 38 100.* The collection comprises important finds recovered from various necropoli excavated nearby and a series of artefacts relating to the Barberini family.

In the room to the right of the entrance are displayed cists (stone receptacles); bronze mirrors; wooden, ivory and clay toilet articles placed alongside the dead person in their sarcophagus or limestone urns. The room on the left houses sculpture: note the large marble Hellenistic head dating from the 2C BC – possibly a fragment of a larger statue of the divinity Fortune. Also on the ground floor is a collection of inscribed or carved stones.

The most interesting rooms are on the top floor: the **Nile Mosaic★★** depicts Egypt with the Nile in flood. This is the largest known mosaic from the Hellenistic era. Opposite is a detailed scale model of the Temple of Fortune complete with its superimposed Classical orders of columns rising from the Doric through the Ionic to the Corinthian.

On leaving the museum, cross the street and walk down the flights of steps to marvel at the succession of terraces, which still evoke the magnificent splendour and elaborate design of this ancient site.

Follow the one-way road system into town by means of the Via Anicia.

Town centre

Many buildings in the old town include stones from the former city walls. The main square, Piazza Regina Margherita, replaces the old forum.

The 11C duomo, flanked by a Romanesque bell-tower, was constructed among the ruins of a rectangular Roman temple (note the remains of the enclosure inside the church). It is dedicated to St Agapito, the patron saint of the town.

At the centre of the piazza is a statue of **Giovanni Pierluigi da Palestrina** (1524-94), the renowned composer of polyphonic religious music.

Nile Mosaic – *detail*

Tivoli★★★

One of the most impressive sites of Antiquity lies just outside the town of Tivoli to the east of Rome. The evocative setting and magnificent architecture of Hadrian's Villa has long fascinated visitors to Italy, despite the extensive plundering that has taken place here over the centuries. Once back in the centre of Tivoli, make sure you spend some time exploring the splendid Villa d'Este, a gracious country residence surrounded by elaborate gardens, once the property of Cardinal Ippolito II d'Este. Before returning to Rome at the end of the day, it is worth pausing for a moment in the town's main square to admire the views of the surrounding Roman countryside bathed in the soft evening light.

Location

Michelin map 430 (Q 20). 31km/19mi E of Rome. Access by coach from Rebibbia (last stop on Metro line B); by car from Rome along Via Tiburtina (see map on the inside back cover of the guide). This picturesque little town is situated on the lower slopes of the chalky Apennines (Monti Simbruini), where the River Aniene plunges in cascades into the Roman plain before joining the Tiber.

Background

A Greek seer and a Roman sibyl – Tivoli, Tibur in Antiquity, is said to have been founded earlier than Rome by Tiburtus, grandson of the Greek seer Amphiaraos, whom Zeus caused to be swallowed up in the earth outside Thebes. Tibur came under Roman control in the 4C BC and became a holiday resort under the Empire.

Several centuries later, according to a medieval legend, two great prophecies were made by a sibyl. When Augustus asked her whether there would be anyone greater than he, she sent him a vision of the Virgin and Child on the Capitol in Rome and added that on the Child's birthday a spring of oil would bubble up from the ground; this is supposed to have taken place in Trastevere.

The Tivoli Rebellion or the downfall of an Emperor and a Pope – In 1001 Tivoli rebelled against the German Emperor Otho III, who was in Italy with Pope Sylvester II. The Romans, who had no love for their neighbours in Tivoli, made common cause with the Emperor. The Pope intervened and the Emperor spared the town and the rebels but, when the Pope and the Emperor returned to Rome, the Romans reproached them for their leniency; both had to flee the mob. The following year Otho died and Sylvester the year after. Tivoli retained its independence until 1816, when it was attached to the Papal States.

> **WHERE TO EAT**
> **Sibilla** – *Via della Sibilla 50 – ☏ 0774 33 52 81 – Closed Mon – Reservations recommended – €26/46.* This unique restaurant serves traditional Italian dishes in a delightful setting amid the ruins of the temples of Vesta and Sybil.

Special Features

VILLA ADRIANA★★★ (HADRIAN'S VILLA.)

By coach: 4.5km/3mi before reaching Tivoli, get off the coach at the stop (fermata) called "Bivio Villa Adriana". 1.5km/1mi on foot from the turning to the excavations. By car: follow the signs.

Open May-Sep, 9am-8pm; Oct-Apr, 9am-5pm (last admission 1hr 30min before closing time). Closed 1 Jan, 1 May and Christmas. €6.20. ☏ 06 32 14 300; Fax 0774 53 02 03.

The perimeter (5km/3mi) enclosed an estate consisting of vast gardens adorned with works of art, an Imperial palace, baths, libraries and theatres. It was probably the richest building project in Antiquity and was designed entirely by Hadrian. He had visited every part of the Roman Empire and on his return from the Oriental provinces in AD 126 he began work on his villa. He was very knowledgeable about art and architecture and tried to recreate the works and sites he had visited during his travels. In 134 the villa was almost finished; Hadrian was 58. Ill and grief-stricken at the death of his young favourite Antinoüs, he died in Baiae in 138. His remains were buried in his huge mausoleum in Rome. The Emperors who succeeded him probably continued to come to Tivoli. It was here that Zenobia, Queen of Palmyra, ended her days as Aurelian's prisoner.

Then the villa fell into ruin. From the 15C to the 19C the site was explored; over 300 works were recovered, which now enrich museums and private collections in Rome, London, Berlin, Dresden, Stockholm and St Petersburg.

Since 1870 the site has belonged to the Italian Government, which has organised its excavation. The vegetation has been cleared from the ruins, revealing magnificent vaults, columns, stuccowork and mosaics.

The present entrance is probably not the one used in Hadrian's day. The design of the villa is so unusual that archaeologists have not been able to identify the buildings or their uses with any certainty. Before exploring the site it is advisable to study a model of the villa which is displayed in a room next to the bar.

Pecile★★

The **Poikile** was the name of a portico in Athens which Hadrian wished to reproduce. Only the north wall remains, through which the visitor enters the excavation site itself. Notice the lattice-work effect created by small blocks of tufa set on their edges to form a diaper pattern; Hadrian's Villa is one of the last examples of this technique, which fell into disuse in the 2C. The horizontal grooves in the wall were filled with bricks, which disappeared when the villa was plundered for its materials, in particular for the Villa d'Este in Tivoli.

The Poikile was built in the shape of a large rectangle with slightly curved ends and lined

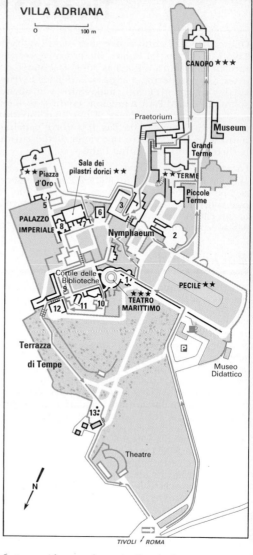

with a portico; it was sited so that one side was always in the shade.

The apsidal chamber called the **philosophers' room (1)** was perhaps a reading room.

Teatro Marittimo★★★

The **Maritime Theatre** is a circular construction consisting of a portico and a central building surrounded by a canal which was spanned by small swing bridges. It was obviously an ideal retreat for the misanthropic Hadrian.

Walk south towards the Ninfeo and climb the steps.

The ruins look down on a *nymphaeum*, which can be reached by part of the **cryptoporticus**, a network of underground passages which made it possible to walk from one end of the site to the other without returning above ground level.

Walk through the Cryptoporticus (right).

Ninfeo

The *nymphaeum*, the flat area enclosed between sections of high wall, was originally thought to be a stadium. The building *(west)* was composed of three semicircular rooms around a courtyard **(2)**.

Terme★★

The **baths** consist of the Small Baths (Piccole Terme) and the Great Baths (Grandi Terme). They both show the high architectural standards attained in the villa: rectangular rooms with concave walls, octagonal rooms with alternate concave and convex walls, circular rooms with recesses alternating with doors. The most impressive room is in the Great Baths; it has an apse and the remains of some superb vaulting.

The tall building, called the **Praetorium** (Pretorio), was probably a storehouse.

Canopus, Hadrian's Villa

Museo (Museum)

The **museum** contains the results of the most recent excavations: Roman copies of the Amazon by Phidias and Polyclitus; copies of the Caryatids from the Erechtheion on the Acropolis in Athens. These statues adorned the sides of the Canopus.

There are more ruins belonging to the villa to the west of the museum in a large olive grove, but it is private property.

Canopo★★★ (Canopus)

It was his visit to Egypt that gave Hadrian the idea of constructing a souvenir of the town of Canope with its famous Temple of Serapis. The route to Canope from Alexandria consisted of a canal lined with temples and gardens. Hadrian had part of his estate landscaped to look like the Egyptian site and completed the effect with a canal down the centre and a copy of the Temple of Serapis (Tempio di Serapis) at the southern end. He combined the cult of Serapis with the cult of Antinoüs, his young favourite who had been drowned in the Nile.

On leaving the Canopus bear right between the Grandi Terme and the Pretorio, climb to the upper level and continue towards the Ninfeo before bearing right.

The path goes round a large **fish pond** surrounded by a portico (Quadriportico con peschiera) **(3)**.

Return to the Pretorio and the Grandi Terme and walk as far as the ruins overlooking the Ninfeo and bear right.

Palazzo Imperiale

The **Imperial Palace** complex extended from the Piazza d'Oro to the libraries.

Piazza d'Oro★★ – The rectangular area was surrounded by a double portico; the Piazza was an aesthetic caprice serving no useful purpose. On the far side are traces of an octagonal chamber **(4)**: each of the eight sides, which are alternately concave and convex, was preceded by a small portico (one of these has been reconstructed). On the opposite side is a chamber **(5)** covered by a dome and flanked by two smaller chambers: the one on the left contains traces of a fine black and white mosaic pavement.

Sala dei pilastri dorici★★ – The **Doric Pillared Hall** takes its name from the surrounding portico, which was composed of pilasters with Doric bases and capitals supporting a Doric architrave (partial reconstruction in one corner). Opposite stood the **firemen's barracks** (caserma dei vigili) **(6)**.

Adjoining the Pillared Hall *(north side)* is a huge section of curved wall which may have been part of a summer **dining room** (triclinio estivo) **(7)**; the oval basins further east mark the site of a **nymphaeum** (ninfeo di palazzo) **(8)**. These buildings overlook a courtyard which is separated by a *cryptoporticus* from the **library court**; the east side of the latter court is composed of a complex of 10 rooms ranged down both sides of a corridor; this was an infirmary **(9)**; each of the rooms held three beds; the **floor★** is paved with fine mosaics. The library courtyard offers a pleasant **view★** over the countryside.

Biblioteche – The ruins of the **library buildings** are on the north side of the courtyard (Cortile delle Biblioteche); according to custom, there was a Greek library **(10)** and a Latin library **(11)**.

Next to the libraries *(east side)* is a group of rooms paved with mosaic which belonged to a **dining room** (triclinio imperiale) **(12)**.

Terrazza di Tempe

A grove of trees hangs on the slope above a valley which Hadrian called his **Vale of Tempe**, after the Greek beauty spot in Thessaly. The path runs through the trees past a **circular temple** (**13**) (reconstructed) which contained a statue of the goddess Venus and was thus attributed to her. Further along *(left)* is the site of a **theatre**.

Proceed to Tivoli (town plan in The Red Guide Italia).

Piazza Garibaldi is dominated by the **Rocca Pia**, a fortress built by Pius II (1458-64).

VILLA D'ESTE***

In 1550 Cardinal Ippolito II d'Este, who had been raised to great honours by François I of France but had fallen into disgrace when the king's son Henri II succeeded to the throne, decided to retire to Tivoli, where he immediately began to convert the former Benedictine convent into a pleasant country seat. The Neapolitan architect, Pirro Ligorio, was invited to prepare plans.

The simple architecture of the villa contrasts with the elaborate gardens (3ha/7.5 acres), which descend in a series of terraces on the western slope of the hill. The statues, pools and fountains enhance the natural beauty with all the grace of the Mannerist style. Many distinguished guests visited the villa, including Pius IV and Gregory XII, and after the cardinal's death, Paul IV, Paul V, Pius IX and writers and artists: Benvenuto Cellini, Titian, Tasso, and Liszt.

In 1759 when the avenues were overgrown with brambles and the fountains silent, Fragonard and Hubert Robert, who were staying at the French Academy in Rome, came to spend the summer in Tivoli with their patron the Abbé de Saint Non; there is scarcely a corner of the gardens where they did not set up their easels, nor a perspective that escaped their brushes.

Santa Maria Maggiore.

This is the old abbey church of St Mary Major belonging to the Benedictine convent. It has an attractive Gothic façade and a 17C bell-tower. The interior contains two 15C triptychs *(in the chancel)*. Above the one on the left is a painting of the Virgin by Jacopo Torriti, who also worked in mosaic at the end of the 13C.

Villa and Gardens***

Entrance from the old convent cloisters. Open daily (except Mon), 8.30am-1hr before dusk. Closed 1 Jan, 1 May and Christmas. €6.50.

The **Old Apartment** (Vecchio Appartamento) on the first floor of the villa now holds temporary exhibitions.

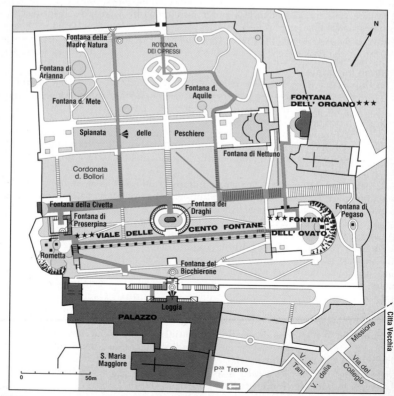

Descend to the floor below.

Sala grande – The **central Salon** is decorated in the Mannerist style by pupils of Girolamo Muziano and Federico Zuccari. The fountain, which is decorated with mosaics, faces a wall panel showing the gardens in the 16C. On the ceiling is a fresco of the *Banquet of the Gods*. From the Salon loggia is a lovely **view**★ over the gardens and Tivoli.

Leading out of this room is a series of four rooms in the west wing. The mythological paintings in the first room are attributed to Muziano and Luigi Karcher: the *Labours of Hercules* surround a fresco of the *Synod of the Gods (ceiling)*. Federico Zuccari and his school painted the allegorical frescoes in the next room, known as the Philosophers' Hall, and the frescoes called the *Glory of Este* in the third room. In the Hall of the Hunt, Tempesta's frescoes show hunting trophies and scenes of hunts in the country around Tivoli.

From the balcony of the Central Hall there is a pleasant **view** of the gardens and Tivoli itself.

Double flights of steps lead down to the upper garden walk.

Fontana del Bicchierone – The fountain, which is often attributed to Bernini, consists of a huge moss-covered **beaker** from which water overflows into a shell-shaped basin.

La "Rometta" – This fountain, known as **"mini Rome"** was an attempt by the cardinal to reproduce some of the most famous monuments of Classical Rome: a pool bearing a boat (representing Tiber Island) surmounted by an obelisk; higher up next to some artificial ruins an allegorical statue of Rome and the she-wolf.

Viale delle Cento Fontane★★★ – The **Avenue of a Hundred Fountains** is one of the most charming spots in the gardens. One side of the straight walk is lined by fountains of water spouting from small boats, obelisks, animal heads, eagles and lilies which recall the Este coat of arms.

Fontana dell'Ovato★★★ – The **Oval Fountain** is dominated by the statue of the sibyl, flanked by allegorical figures of rivers. Round the edge of the basin, half covered in moss, are statues of naiads pouring the water of the River Aniene from their water pots. An attractive ceramic decoration adorns the front rim of the oval basin.

Fontana dell'Organo★★★ – The **Organ Fountain** used to play music on a water-powered organ concealed in the upper part of the fountain. This ingenious mechanism was invented by a Frenchman, Claude Venard, in the 16C. After seeing and hearing the fountain, Montaigne, the French writer and philosopher, wrote in his journal that "the organ music is made by water falling into a cave with such power that the air is forced out through the organ pipes while another stream of water turns a toothed wheel which operates the keyboard; one can also hear the distorted sound of trumpets".

Spianata delle Peschiere – The three basins were **fishponds** which supplied the cardinal's table on fast days. There is a fine **view**★★ of the water spouts and the Organ Fountain.

Fontana della Madre Natura – The **Fountain of Mother Nature** is decorated with a statue of Diana of Ephesus, goddess of fertility.

The gate in the wall *(right)*, overlooking the valley below, is the main entrance to the villa.

Fontana dei Draghi – The **Dragon Fountain** was created in honour of Pope Gregory XIII, who visited the villa in September 1572 shortly before the cardinal's death; the dragons recall the coat of arms of the Buoncompagni family to which the Pope belonged.

Fontana della Civetta – The **Owl Fountain** is more commonly known as the **Bird Fountain** because of the hydraulic mechanism, originally concealed in a recess, which used to produce bird song; periodically an owl appeared and uttered a mournful screech. Several times restored, the fountain is now silent.

Fontana di Proserpina – *(left)*. The **Fountain of Proserpina** *(restored)* recalls the mythological figure who was abducted by Pluto.

It is possible to walk down to the Villa Gregoriana through the streets of the old town (città vecchia).

The town is agreeably lively and some traces of the past still remain.

The **cathedral**, rebuilt in the 17C and flanked by a 12C Romanesque campanile, contains a fine group of carved wooden figures depicting the **Deposition**★ (13C).

VILLA GREGORIANA,★

Closed for restoration at the time of going to press. ☎ *0774 33 45 22; Fax 0774 33 12 94.*
A tangle of paths winds down the steeply wooded slopes to where the River Aniene cascades through the ravine.

Take the path downhill from the entrance and bear right to the **Great Waterfall**★★ (Grande Cascata).

There is a terrace overlooking the waterfall from above. Take the path which zigzags down to a viewpoint near the foot of the waterfall *(Veduta inferiore della Cascata)*. Here the river plunges into the ravine, throwing up a fine spray.

Return to the last junction and take the path marked *Grotte di Nettuno e Sirena, cascata Bernine*. This starts with a short flight of steps and winds down into the valley bottom to the **Siren's Cave**, where, with a great roar, the Aniene plunges out of sight into a cavern.

Return to the sign marked *Grotto di Nettuno e Tempio di Vesta* and take the path leading up the opposite side of the valley. Ignoring the right-hand turning to *Tempio di Vesta e Sibilla*, bear left towards *Grotta di Nettuno*. After the tunnelled section bear left downhill. In **Neptune's Cave** the water bursts from the rock face, which has been eroded into eerie configurations.

Return to the beginning of the tunnelled section, but bear left up the path which climbs the slope overlooking the ravine and its many little waterfalls.

Next to the park gates which lead into the town stand the ruins of two temples.

Tempio della Sibilla

Access through to Sibilla Restaurant. The **Temple of the Sybil** is also known as the **Temple of Vesta**, as shrines dedicated to this goddess were usually round. This elegant Corinthian structure dates from the late Republic. Next to it stands a contemporary building in the Ionic style, also supposed by some to be dedicated to the sibyl. Both temples were built of travertine.

Index

Notes